INTERNATIONAL REGULATION OF INTERNAL RESOURCES

A Study of Law and Policy

VIRGINIA LEGAL STUDIES are sponsored by the School of Law of the University of Virginia for the publication of meritorious original works, symposia, and reprints in law and related fields. Titles previously published are listed below.

Studies Editors; Carl McFarland, 1967–73
Richard B. Lillich, 1973–

Central Power in the Australian Commonwealth, by the Rt. Hon. Sir Robert Menzies, former Prime Minister of Australia. 1967.

Administrative Procedure in Government Agencies—Report by Committee appointed by Attorney General at Request of President to Investigate Need for Procedural Reforms in Administrative Tribunals (1941), reprinted with preface and index 1968.

The Road from Runnymede: Magna Carta and Constitutionalism in America, by A. E. Dick Howard. 1968.

Non-Proliferation Treaty: Framework for Nuclear Arms Control, by Mason Willrich. 1969.

Mass Production Justice and the Constitutional Ideal—Papers and proceedings of a conference on problems associated with the misdemeanor, held in April 1969, under the sponsorship of the School of Law, edited by Charles H. Whitebread, II. 1970.

Education in the Professional Responsibilities of the Lawyer—Proceedings of the 1968 National Conference on Education in the Professional Responsibilities of the Lawyer, edited by Donald T. Weckstein. 1970.

The Valuation of Nationalized Property in International Law—Essays by experts on contemporary practice and suggested approaches, edited by Richard B. Lillich. v. I, 1972; v. II, 1973; v. III. 1975.

Legislative History: Research for the Interpretation of Laws, by Gwendolyn B. Folsom. 1972.

Criminal Appeals: English Practices and American Reforms, by Daniel J. Meador. 1973. Out of print.

Humanitarian Intervention and the United Nations—Proceedings of a conference held in March 1972, with appended papers, edited by Richard B. Lillich. 1973.

The United Nations, a Reassessment: Sanctions, Peacekeeping, and Humanitarian Assistance—Papers and proceedings of a symposium held in March 1972, edited by John M. Paxman and George T. Boggs. 1973.

Mr. Justice Black and His Books—Catalogue of the Justice's personal library, by Daniel J. Meador. 1974.

Legal Transplants, by Alan Watson. 1974.

Limits to National Jurisdiction over the Sea, edited by George T. Yates III and John Hardin Young. 1974.

Commentaries on the Constitution of Virginia (in two volumes), by A. E. Dick Howard. 1974.

The Future of the United States Multinational Corporation—Proceedings of a conference held in 1974, edited for the J. B. Moore Society of International Law by Lee D. Unterman and Christine W. Swent. 1975.

Dictionary of Sigla and Abbreviations to and in Law Books before 1607, edited by William Hamilton Bryson. 1975.

An International Rule of Law, by Eberhard Paul Deutsch. 1977. Out of print.

Mr. Justice Black: Absolutist on the Court, by James J. Magee. 1980.

INTERNATIONAL REGULATION OF INTERNAL RESOURCES

A Study of Law and Policy

Mahnoush H. Arsanjani

University Press of Virginia
Charlottesville

346
A781i

THE UNIVERSITY PRESS OF VIRGINIA
Copyright © 1981 by the Rector and Visitors
of the University of Virginia
First published 1981

Library of Congress Cataloging in Publication Data

Arsanjani, Mahnoush H
  International regulation of internal resources.

  Includes index.
  1. Natural resources—Law and legislation.
I. Title.   K3478.A8   346.04'4   80–21169   ISBN 0–8139–0879–5

Printed in the United States of America

85 – 7132

To Myres S. McDougal

Teacher and Friend

Contents

Acknowledgments

The basic research for this work was conducted at the Yale Law School, and many people on the faculty and library staff provided help and encouragement. My major debt of gratitude is to my teacher Myres S. McDougal. Like many others who came to study with him, I discovered that a great and creative scholar can also be a generous friend who guides his students toward their own independent vision. Michael Reisman was magnanimous and unstinting in constructive criticism and suggestions about both broad theme and detail. Quintin Johnstone, who chaired the Graduate Committee at Yale during most of my sojourn there, was consistently supportive and helpful in innumerable ways.

A version of one chapter was published in 3 *Yale Studies of World Public Order* 201–338 (1977).

I would like to express my appreciation for the support of the Organization for Social Services, a welfare organization active in Iran. When I conducted the basic research at the Yale Law School, the Organization generously granted me fellowships and has now provided indispensable financial support in making this study available to a wider audience.

The research and writing of the book were completed before I undertook my present post in the Legal Division of the Secretariat of the United Nations. I need hardly add that the views expressed here are my own and do not derive from anyone at the United Nations.

Introduction

The Problem: National Resources in Global Public Order

NATURAL RESOURCES—land, air, water, minerals, raw materials, and so on—are critical variables and potential values in global and other social processes. They are important base values for promoting community policies. The importance and potentialities of resources vary with changing technologies and other factors. In a technological and science-based civilization these resources can become especially vital. In a world in which the well-being of individuals and improvement in the conditions of life are of increasingly intense concern (in both public campaign and intellectual discussion) and in which the degrading condition of life of at least 800 million people in the world is considered to be an insult to "human dignity,"[1] the role of natural resources becomes ever more significant. The pattern of use and control of resources (management of resources) has come to comprise an important and increasingly controversial part of public order. The significance of the management of resources is further increased by such factors as interdependency, scarcity of resources, and international class-consciousness.

The interdependencies and interrelationships among natural resources and between such resources and the institutions by which they are exploited have been recognized and emphasized by both ecologists and policymakers.[2] The frequently proclaimed

---

[1] R. McNamara, *Preface* to WORLD BANK, THE ASSAULT ON WORLD POVERTY, at V (1975). It has been estimated that more than 300 million children are to suffer from retarded physical growth and development because of malnutrition and that some 70 percent of the world's population does not have access to dependable safe water. *See* RESHAPING THE WORLD ORDER 28–38 (J. Tinbergen ed. 1976) [hereinafter cited as TINBERGEN]; *see generally* L. BROWN, BY BREAD ALONE (1974); L. BROWN, WORLD WITHOUT BORDERS (1972).

[2] *See* J. McHALE, THE FUTURE OF THE FUTURE 65, 162–63, 253–54 (1968); *see also* M. McDOUGAL & M. ROTIVAL, THE CASE FOR REGIONAL PLANNING, WITH SPECIAL REFERENCE TO NEW ENGLAND (1947); E. MURPHY, GOVERNING NATURE (1967); B. WARD & R. DUBOS, ONLY

need for global cooperation in the application of a sound policy for the protection of the environment, for example, is expressive of the unity in the ecosystem. These interdependencies extend from local to regional and global scales. The interrelationship and unity in resources affects all value processes, though with different degrees of intensity. Disasters of unprecedented magnitude have demonstrated this fact. For example, the worldwide recession in recent years has affected a larger proportion of the globe than any since World War II; the industrial production in many industrialized countries for the first time since the war fell, and 17 million people were out of jobs in the most developed countries.[3] The shortage of raw materials has not only affected the productivity of industries but also in some cases threatened their very institutional basis.[4] The 1973–74 oil embargo and increase in the price of oil left no doubt about the intensity of interdependency of some of the more critical resources.

Technological development has made some of the natural resources that are its grist even more critical and has created a curious, reciprocating, two-step dependence that seems to be characteristic of twentieth-century international politics: technology and resources. Since high technology is a key characteristic of the present civilization, it is expected that the dependence of nation-states on technology as well as the dependence of technology on natural resources will increase until technology becomes responsive to some of its own basic needs for natural resources. The interdependency of nation-states on technology is already increasing.[5]

One author has observed that the more societies are modern-

ONE EARTH (1972); Mayda, *Conservation, "New Conservation," And Ecomanagement* 1969 WIS. L. REV. 788.

[3] TINBERGEN, *supra* note 1, at 15.

[4] *See* D. Novick, A WORLD OF SCARCITY: CRITICAL ISSUES IN PUBLIC POLICY 1–2 (1976).

[5] The new dwarf wheat, which has totally changed the cereal production of Asia, was bred in Mexico. Also, the creation of INTELS AT, which has enabled the entire world to benefit from solar-powered telecommunication satellite technology, was financed by the United States. *See* L. BROWN, WORLD WITHOUT BORDERS, *supra* note 1, at 190–92.

The capacity of national governments to improve their material well-being is not directly dependent on their access to skill and materials from abroad and access to foreign markets. *Id.* at 184.

ized, the more they become interdependent.[6] The increase of interdependence in wealth and economic activities is so significant
that it even affects nation-states that consciously seek to isolate
themselves from international economic waves by closing their
doors to the import or export of resources or at least to immunize
themselves by organizing in regional groups with a common protective economic policy. Thus, the recent increase of oil prices affected the countries of the Council of Mutual Economic Assistance
(CMEA) and left a number of these countries with serious balance-
of-payment problems.[7]

Sometimes economists and policymakers of developing states
have considered interdependency a potential instrument for en-
hancing national development.[8] They have assumed that the fact
that the underdevelopment of part of the world can paralyze the
continued growth in developed nations can make the latter more
concerned about the development in the former.[9] Ironically, in-

[6]Morse, *The Transformation of Foreign Policies, Modernization, Interdependence and External-
ization*, 22 WORLD POL. 371–92 (1970).

[7]Hungary, Czechoslovakia, the German Democratic Republic, and Bulgaria were particularly affected. Most Eastern European nations had balance-of-trade deficits in 1974 and
1975; most consequently recognize their interdependencies with the rest of the world market. As an editorial in a Hungarian newspaper noted: "Sometime ago we believed that we
are not affected by what is happening on the world capitalist market. Inflation could be
stopped, as an unwelcome quest, at our borders and here in our country we could live and
work under the same conditions as before. That 'hot house' atmosphere has cost us 20
billion foints." Magyar Nemzet, Budapest (1974) *quoted in* TINBERGEN, *supra* note 1, at 17.

[8]*See* THE UNITED STATES AND DEVELOPING ECONOMIES vii (rev. ed. G. Ranis ed. 1973);
S. BROWN, NEW FORCES IN WORLD POLITICS 36 (1974). Brown, however, warns that the
larger pattern of interdependence, where politically important groups may actively mo-
bilize to discredit and dismember the larger community, could have harsh economic
effects. *Id.*

[9]Developed nations, for example, have established national institutions concerned with
allocating resources to developing nations with which they may or may not have a direct
political tie. *See* G. OHLIN, FOREIGN AID POLICIES RECONSIDERED (1966). Similarly, the
awareness of developing nations of the effect of each other's economic activities on their
overall common interest has led to different forms of economic aid provided by developing
oil producers to some nonproducers. The establishment of international agencies, such as
IMF and IBRD, and of regional organizations designed to assist the developing nations,
are, in fact, a form of recognition of interdependencies and willingness to assist the poorer
nations. Such observation, of course, may be premature and open to interpretation, especially considering some of the past practices of these institutions. *See generally* Millikan, *An
Introductory Essay*, in THE GLOBAL PARTNERSHIP: INTERNATIONAL AGENCIES AND ECONOMIC
DEVELOPMENT 1–3 (R. Gardner & M. Millikan eds. 1968); Cooper, *Economic Interdependence
and Foreign Policy in the Seventies*, 24 WORLD POL. 159, 161–63 (1972); R. COOPER, THE

deed, the increase in interdependencies tends to incapacitate nation-states from harming others without simultaneously harming themselves.

A. INTERNATIONAL RESOURCE REGIMES

For the past several hundred years, natural resources widely distributed about the globe but of value to different political and economic units, have been sought, exploited, and redistributed in certain distinctive patterns. These patterns, though changing over time, have through long periods shown an extraordinary stability, characterized not only by certain patterns in investment and trade but also by a protective constellation of explicit and customary international norms and decisions. Intervals of stability and instability in exploitation have not been the result solely of market forces; they have been affected by complex international political and economic decision processes in which, to varying extents and with varying success, elites have employed power and authority to try to shape global or partially global arrangements for meeting their needs as they perceived them. In the past, jurisdictional regimes, or the allocation of competences that appeared to meet the needs of the elites and key states, generally involved virtually free access to resources outside nation-states (or shareable resources) and almost a complete exclusive jurisdiction over resources within nation-states (or internal resources).

Shareable resources, such as the oceans, the high seas, international rivers, space, and celestial bodies, are located outside nation-states in what is called a shared domain; activities for the productive use of these resources usually directly affect larger communities. Sometimes effective production and efficient use of shareable resources may require the cooperation of several communities, or sometimes the entire global community.

Historically, it has generally been accepted that actual shared use of these potentially shareable resources is in the common interest in terms of providing more values to larger communities. As

ECONOMICS OF INTERDEPENDENCE: ECONOMIC POLICY IN THE ATLANTIC COMMUNITY (1968). *See also* Friedmann, *The Relevance of International Law to the Process of Economic and Social Development*, in THE FUTURE OF INTERNATIONAL LEGAL ORDER: WEALTH AND RESOURCES 3, 4 (R. Falk & C. Black eds. 1970).

a corollary, it has been assumed that exclusive use of shareable resources is incompatible with the natural law, the law of nations, and the common interests of the global community. Grotius, for example, believed that nature created some things for the use of all mankind. He argued further that the exclusive use of shareable resources, such as the high seas, prevents the movements of goods and services across boundaries and limits beneficial contacts and interactions among the peoples of the world. He felt that the historical practices of exclusive uses of the high seas by Portugal and Spain were examples of such deprivations to others.

Another reason for shared and essentially unregulated use of shareable resources has been the notion of the inexhaustibility of this category of resources. This was first developed by Grotius with regard to ocean resources. The concept of abundant resources is now incompatible with present facts and theories about the limited potential of resources in relation to technology and socio-political systems. Nevertheless, many still contend that external resources should continue to be shareable because multiplier effects are still better achieved through their shared use.

The exclusive use of internal resources was never effectively questioned. Exclusive control of internal resources was generally accepted and honored through reciprocal behavior. Where the unequal distribution of resources among territorial communities stimulated or clashed with demands for equitable value distribution, appropriate conservation, and exploitation of resources, accommodations were achieved through customary practices of cooperative behavior, sometimes through deliberate and explicit agreement, sometimes through coercion.

Shared use of internal resources through cooperation and persuasion derives largely from the necessity of maintaining a productive and equitable world economy. A large segment of existing international agreements deals with the allocation of internal resources. The role of agreement in the use of such resources has long been significant as the best means of sharing internal resources with the fewest possibilities of violating minimum order. In other words, "agreement" has been employed to change and qualify the pattern of exclusive use of internal resources. The form of changes, however, and the pattern of qualification of such exclusive uses have remained controversial and have long concerned a substantial part of international law.

B. THE CONSTITUTIVE PROCESS

In response to the continuing claims made about the inclusive and exclusive competence over resources, certain patterns of explicit and customary international norms and decisions have been formulated by decisionmakers. Conventional legal analysis might describe the stable periods as having achieved a constitutional code. It is perhaps more useful to conceive of this achievement in dynamic terms as a constitutive process. The relevant legal framework is not a static code but rather a continuous flow of decisions that establishes and maintains a process of authoritative decision.[10]

From this perspective it is clear that for several hundred years there has been a global constitutive process which, among other things, has allocated and regulated the use of, and competence over, the resources regarded at any particular time as of economic importance. This process has allocated some resources (such as the land masses and immediately proximate air and water) to the relatively exclusive competence of the nation-state, and some resources I have referred to as "shareable" (such as the oceans, airspace over the oceans, outer space, and international rivers) to the inclusive competence of the larger community. Claims made to global constitutive process about the allocation of resources similar to other areas represent a continuing battle between proponents of domestic jurisdiction and exclusive competence and proponents of international concern and inclusive competence. This battle, historically, has been settled for shareable resources in favor of inclusive competence. For external resources international concern commonly prevails over domestic jurisdiction. With regard to internal resources, however, the battle continues. On the one hand, nation-states are still trying to eliminate any inclusive competence over their internal resources through the traditional concept of "domestic jurisdiction." On the other hand, claims have been made to limit or even exclude the exclusive competence of nation-states over the exploitation of some internal resources; such exploitation has extraterritorial impacts, and concerns the welfare and even security of the larger community. One of the most important tasks of the contemporary global constitutive pro-

---

[10] For definition and an analytical description of the concept of the constitutive process, *see* McDougal, Lasswell & Reisman, *The World Constitutive Process of Authoritative Decision*, 19 J. LEGAL EDUC. 253–300, 403–37 (1967).

cess is that of achieving an appropriate protection of both inclusive and exclusive interests and a necessary balancing of such competences in a great variety of problems.

Many laws have been made and applied with respect to resources. To the traditional processes of international law have been added the United Nations, the specialized agencies, regional organizations, intergovernmental, private, and private-governmental organizations. In the area of environmental protection, for example, the global decision process has begun to respond through more inclusive, organized, and official conventions, as the outcomes of the U.N. Conference on the Human Environment illustrate. The Conference, in addition to adopting more than 200 recommendations about specific environmental activities, passed a Resolution on Institutional and Financial Arrangements that formed the basis for creation by the General Assembly of the United Nations Environmental Program. Efforts have also been mounted by intergovernmental organizations, regional groups, and even some private organizations to formulate supportive measures to protect the human environment.

Regional and governmental organizations have been the major actors with regard to conservation. Thus, different regional fisheries commissions have regulated the enjoyment of fishery resources. Recently, however, the expansion of national economic and fishery zones has limited the geographical applicability of inclusive competence in favor of exclusive competence.

The World Food Conference of 1974 represents the major effort to date to expand inclusive competence over the planning and management of food resources. This Conference, similar to the conferences on the environmental problems, found international organizations to be more competent than national ones in the making and applying of policies to remedy the global shortage of food.

With respect to nonrenewable resources, however, the constitutive process has not been responsive. Decisions have been left to the exclusive competence of nation-states. Indeed, the very first recommendations about the conservation of nonrenewable resources have been made by OPEC to its member states with regard to oil resources; the specific formulation and implementation of policies has again been left to the individual nation-states.

The Third Law of the Sea Conference in Caracas, which raised the issue of management of seabed mineral resources, expressed the first global concern about the conservation of nonrenewable resources. This Conference recommended certain inclusive authorities as competent decisionmakers with respect to regulating the conservation of seabed minerals. There are doubts about the ultimate approval of such authority; among other problems, the regulation of conservation of stock resources may seriously affect the prices of internal resources and consequently the revenues of nation-states. Such an interrelation has substantially decreased the interest of potentially affected states in promoting an inclusive authority.

GATT and UNCTAD are distinct elements of the constitutive process peculiar to resource management, for they represent the contrasting interests of the developed and the developing countries. GATT performs a prescribing function for industrialized countries, and UNCTAD serves as a protector of the interest of the third world. The most recent development of the constitutive process concerning resources is in OPEC, which prescribes and implements decisions concerning pricing and distribution of the diverse values arising from oil resources. OPEC, with tremendous effective power deriving from control of oil supplies, has emerged (even if its existence proves to be only temporary) as an effective participant in making and applying law to some features of the process of resource management.

The global process of decision making with respect to shared use of internal resources through agreements may be the most important, yet the most open and unstable, of all. It is important because agreements represent the most significant persuasive strategies for shared use of internal resources. It is open because the participants in this process range from private parties to arbitral tribunals and nation-states, intergovernmental organizations, and the United Nations. Private organizations, such as the International Law Association, have been performing some prescribing functions with respect to agreements. Individual international arbitral tribunals as well as national courts have participated in making and applying laws with some degree of effectiveness, but nationstates are still the most effective decision makers. Some international organizations, such as the International Center for Investment Disputes, have established their own authority in this decision process. Finally, the United Nations, in adopting resolutions concerning agreements with respect to internal resources, has been changing expectations about the law in this area. Nevertheless, the process of decision making with respect to agreements remains uncertain because of the idiosyncratic distribution of effective power to different decision makers.

C. ABIDING PROBLEMS

The outcomes of the constitutive process have produced dramatic disparities between aspirations and achievements in world public order. There are serious and increasing problems concerning the deterioration of the environment and the continuing unplanned exhaustion of resources, with loss of potential gains. The present structures and processes of world order have produced an enormous maldistribution of resources as between the territorial communities of the world and of goods and services as between the peoples of the world. The breakdown of agreements and an uncertainty about the stability in expectation that is necessary for production and development of resources have affected the possibility of expansion of trade and exchange of goods and services across boundaries. The world's population increases at an alarming rate, with cumulative demands upon resources.

The scarcity of resources has created another complexity in the management of resources. The entire subject of "resource scarcity" is controversial. There are some who have much faith in technology and believe that, in a world of expanding technology, scarcity of resources does not stand; technology will provide new possibilities for resource development. The more pessimistic views, on the other hand, critically observe that the former fail to take into their calculation the changes of conditions under which the technological production is to operate as well as the interrelationship between resources. Richard Gardner's Report well summarizes the views of the more pessimistic:

> "[T]echnological fixes" and "market forces" failed to take adequate account of the limits inherent in the nature and of environmental, financial, and social costs. Global economic activity, they argue, was about one trillion dollars a year in 1950, will be about three trillion dollars a year in 1975, and would be nine trillion dollars in the year 2000 if this trend is maintained. In their view, this cannot happen—present population and economic trends

are not sustainable. Population growth combined with rising affluence is putting strains on nature and resources for which technology has no adequate answer. Shortages in one area (natural gas) trigger shortages in another (fertilizer). The capital need to expand food and energy supplies is also required for other social needs (*e.g.*, housing, education); the necessary private investment may not be forthcoming, particularly as the inflation resulting from scarcities deters long-term investment and stimulates the hoarding of natural resources. In theory there may be no shortage of resources, but there is "a shortage of the resources needed to produce the resources."[11]

Today many believe that there are limits to human expansion on earth; that even the magic power of technology can hardly cope with the present socio-political process of resource management; that that process is basically organized toward short-term, exclusive, and even sometimes special political interests—a system that does not incorporate a rational and systematic allocation of resources. Aurelio Peccei, the President of the Club of Rome, addressing the same issue, stated that there are further limitations caused by intangible but real boundaries. He believes that they are probably inherent in man, as an integral part of a biosphere governed by delicate equilibria, already dangerously upset by man's activities. They may also inhere in man's mental capacities, already overtaken by stresses and complexities.[12]

D. CLAIMS FOR CHANGE

The outcomes of this allocating process, including its incapacity to secure appropriate adjustments in new political contexts, have stimulated increasing dissatisfaction in large groups of nations and have increased demands for changes in both the constitutive process and the public order with regard to resource management.

---

[11]*See* a report prepared by R. Gardner, *The World Food and Energy Crisis: The Role of International Organizations* 55 (1974) [hereinafter cited as GARDNER REPORT].

[12]Peccei's remarks at the Conference on "The World Food and Energy Crisis: The Role of International Organizations." *See* GARDNER REPORT at 31. For a more moderate perspective on resource scarcity, which does not much rely on technology, *see* M. MESAROVIC & E. PESTEL, MANKIND AT THE TURNING POINT (1974), and Tinbergen, *Assigning World Priorities*, in ENVIRONMENT AND SOCIETY IN TRANSITION 25–31 (P. Albertson & M. Barnett ed. 1975).

The new demand for changing the public order and the constitutive process are fueled by what might be referred to as increases in "international class consciousness."[13] People and nations have become conscious of the different standards of living and have increasingly become aware of the unequal distribution of resources, not only within but also among nation-states. The expansion of information through different forms of communication and media reinforces these perceptions. Disparities in value possession between developed and developing nations have increased this international class-consciousness and have led to new demands about the management of resources—demands that challenge the older pattern of resource use and jurisdictional regime. The demands are about the use of, and competence over, both external (shareable) and internal resources. One paradoxical result is that the former notion of *res communis* is becoming "nationalized." Nation-states are extending their jurisdictions to some shareable resources, such as the oceans. Some of these practices include fisheries, economic, and pollution zones. Expansion of jurisdiction beyond territorial limits for self-help particularly in cases of pollution because of inadequate inclusive competence is also increasing. Disagreements and controversies among coastal developed and developing states and land-locked states about an adequate region for management of ocean resources also reflect the qualification of the concept of *res communis*.

Internal resources, the most exclusively controlled resources and formerly deemed quintessential matters of exclusive jurisdiction, are increasingly subjected to claims for inclusive or international competence. Such claims are constantly made about the shared use of internal resources through agreements and through the application of inclusive prescriptions to such agreements. National courts and arbitration tribunals have been asked to limit the authority of nation-states and expand the competency of inclusive bodies. Some inclusive organizations have also mandated compulsory inclusive jurisdiction over the exploitation of internal resources in case of disputes between their member states and investors having nationality of a member state. The International Center for the Settlement of Investment Disputes is an example of

[13] *See* E. Luard, Nationality and Wealth: A Study in World Government 343 (1964).

such an international organization. The European Economic Community also provides certain inclusive jurisdictions for disputes between its members.

Claims to inclusive competence over internal resources have also been made with respect to the regulation of injurious use of resources. The concept of state responsibility and application of preventive measures establishes some normative limits to the exclusive competence of states in the use of their internal resources with extraterritorial impacts.

Similarly, claims to an inclusive pricing process, a flow of supply, and an equal access to resources, as well as demands for changing the pattern of distributions of values arising from the exploitation of resources, limit the exclusive competence of nation-states. Bilateral and multilateral agreements concerning the moderation or elimination of the tariff barriers for free access to foreign markets limit the extent of exclusive competence of nation-states in their internal economic policies.

The principal features of the present constitutive process are inadequate to meet the urgent need for a functional management of resources. Officials of nation-states are still the most important effective decision makers. International organizations and regional and functional groups do not have adequate effective power. The decision makers have not yet sufficiently clarified the common interest of the larger community nor have they ranked priorities among policies. Their identifications are still largely with smaller communities, rather than with the whole globe. The important bases of power for enforcement of inclusive decision are still within nation-states. Consequently, the outcomes of the larger constitutive processes have been incapable of creating appropriate balance between stability in expectations and necessary changes.

E. A NEW DIRECTION

For a viable economic order, which serves the basic objectives of high productivity and of world development through fair and equitable distribution of values, the establishment and maintenance of a more effective global constitutive process to allocate and regulate the enjoyment of resources are indispensable. In a world characterized by finite resources and virtually infinite demands, a more rational allocation of resources is urgently required. An appropriate global process of decision making should formulate and reformulate common policies, establish priorities, and set up guidelines for the use of resources. It should also establish competent decision makers, appropriate structures of authority, ample bases of power, and economic procedures.

The focus of this study is on resources geographically located within particular territorial communities but of substantial importance to external political and economic entities. These "internal" resources are often a subject of controversy because of their location and the constant clash between organized communities for their shared or exclusive use. The aims of the study are to examine the outcomes of the past and the present constitutive processes in the allocation of resources and to generate recommendations for an improved global process for resource management. A major purpose is to clarify a decision process for maintaining appropriate levels of exclusive and inclusive competence, determined, of course, by reference to goals and context.

This study employs a policy-oriented approach to the problem of the international regulation of national resources.[14] In the

---

[14] A policy-oriented approach refers to the jurisprudential school of and about law, formulated by Professors Myres McDougal and Harold Lasswell and later joined by Professor Michael Reisman. This theory, which blends the traditions of American legal realism and some contemporary concerns of the social sciences, exhibits a common framework of inquiry, distinctively identifiable in its coherent and systematic approach to the study of law. For an inquiry about this theory of law and its application to some transnational problems, *see* H. LASSWELL & A. KAPLAN, POWER AND SOCIETY (1950); M. MCDOUGAL & ASSOC., STUDIES IN WORLD PUBLIC ORDER (1960); M. MCDOUGAL & F. FELICIANO, LAW AND MINIMUM WORLD PUBLIC ORDER: THE LEGAL REGULATION OF INTERNATIONAL COERCION (1961); M. MCDOUGAL & W. BURKE, THE PUBLIC ORDER OF THE OCEANS (1962); M. MCDOUGAL, H. LASSWELL & I. VLASIC, LAW AND PUBLIC ORDER IN SPACE (1963); M. MCDOUGAL, H. LASSWELL & J. MILLER, THE INTERPRETATION OF AGREEMENTS AND WORLD PUBLIC ORDER (1967); D. JOHNSON, THE INTERNATIONAL LAW OF FISHERIES: A FRAMEWORK FOR POLICY-ORIENTED INQUIRIES (1965); B. MURTY, THE IDEOLOGICAL INSTRUMENTS OF COERCION AND WORLD PUBLIC ORDER (1967); M. REISMAN, NULLITY AND REVISION: THE REVIEW OF ENFORCEMENT OF INTERNATIONAL JUDGMENTS AND AWARDS (1971). *See also* M. McDougal, H. Lasswell, & L. Chen, Human Rights and World Public Order: A Framework for Policy-Oriented Inquiry (1980). *See also* a forthcoming book on law, science, and policy by Lasswell & McDougal, from which the authors have published *Criteria for a Theory About Law*, 44 S. CAL. L. REV. 362 (1971); *Trends in Theories About Law: Comprehensiveness in Conceptions of Constitutive Process*, 41 GEO. WASH. L. REV. 1 (1972); *The Relation of Law to Social Process: Trends in Theories About Law*, 37 U. PITT. L. REV. 465 (1976); and *Trends in Theories About Law: Maintaining Observational Standpoint and Delimiting the Focus of Inquiry*, 8 U. TOL. L. REV. 1 (1976). *See also* a forthcoming book on the progress of the constitutive process by McDougal, Lasswell & Reisman, from which the authors have published *Theories About International Law: Prologue to a Configurative Jurisprudence*, 8 VA. J. INT'L L. 188 (1968); *World Constitutive Process of Authoritative Decision*, 19 J. LEGAL EDUC. 253, 403 (1967); and *The Intelligence Function and World Public Order*, 46 TEMP. L. Q. 365 (1973).

opening sections I clarify my observational standpoint and recommended policies, with specific emphasis upon policies about
resource distribution and pricrities in value shaping and sharing
in the larger community. In subsequent sections I study past
trends in a detailed examination of the flow of authoritative decisions establishing present allocation and use patterns and the distribution of benefits. This study includes claims concerning the
allocation of resources apart from agreement and through agreement, claims regarding conservation of resources, claims regarding the regulation of injurious use of resources, and, finally, claims
regarding the pricing of resources. The outcomes of each set of
decisions are appraised in terms of their effects on the aggregate
common interest and recommendations are made for achievement of preferred outcomes.

PART ONE

Clarification of Community Policies

CHAPTER I

Toward International Goals in an Interdependent World

A. PUBLIC ORDER GOALS

1. The Interdependent World

ACTIVITIES MAY appear to take place within a nation-state, but the negative or positive impact of any changes in processes by which resources are managed, from exploration and production to conservation and consumption, is reflected and felt in a large part of the entire world community. Thus, it has been said that business planning within the United States "must concern itself, not only with labor relations in an American city, but in the mines of Africa and Latin America from which some of its vital raw materials come, the maritime and transport unions of a number of states which participate in distribution, and national marketing unions at many different points of final consumption."[1] Like considerations apply to any important planning related to national or regional development, for these latter now demand consideration and understanding of many national, regional, and international factors. "A breakdown of any section of this global economy is felt everywhere else. The fearful memory of the world slump of the 1930's, which spawned economic misery for millions and, in its wake, fiendishly destructive political deviations, quickly stimulates wealth elites about the globe to aid the ailing sector."[2]

Involvement of nations in one another's affairs has become so pervasive and so deep that even partial changes in one society may be reflected in all.[3] The intensity of world interaction and inter-

---

[1] McDougal, Lasswell & Reisman, *Theories About International Law: Prologue to a Configurative Jurisprudence*, 8 VA. J. INT'L L. 191 (1968).

[2] *Id.*

[3] W. JENKS, LAW IN THE WORLD COMMUNITY 53 (1967).

dependence relates not only to wealth but to all values processes. Nation-states that attempted to achieve a greater economic self-sufficiency between the two world wars only injured themselves, for it became clear that in an interdependent world there were to be no private, national salvations.[4]

The appreciation of such interrelations and the demand that they be taken into account in the production and distribution of values find clear constitutive expression. Various provisions of the U.N. Charter express the demands of the majority of the people of the world for the fundamental rights of others as well as themselves to the minimum conditions of a "dignified human existence."[5] These growing demands are fortified further by the five major trends of global concern—industrialization, rapid population growth, widespread malnutrition, depletion of resources, and a deteriorating environment[6]—which make the whole process of interdependence ineluctable and more complex.

2. Community Perspectives

Many of the international decisions we will be examining have been taken unilaterally by nation-states, themselves acting within a recognized competence or jurisdiction. It is plain that the international lawyer cannot appraise these decisions unless he introduces broader perspectives and criteria. Hence, in approaching the policy problems of resources, we will take the standpoint of a citizen of the world who identifies with the whole of man's communities rather than with a single parochial group or community. Our overriding policies are toward creation and maintenance of a

[4] R. MacIver, The Web of Government 363 (1947).

[5] U.N. Charter art. 1, para. 2; art. 13, para 1(b); art. 55; art. 56. For other U.N. pronouncements on this subject, see Declaration on the Granting of Independence to Colonial Countries and Peoples, G.A. Res. 1514, 15 U.N. GAOR, Supp. (no. 16) 66, U.N. Doc. A/4684 (1960); Declaration on the Elimination of all Forms of Racial Discrimination, G.A. Res. 1904, 18 U.N. GAOR, Supp. (No. 15) 55, U.N. Doc. A/5515 (1964); International covenant on civil and Political Rights, G.A. Res. 2200, 21 U.N. GAOR, Supp. (No. 16) 49, U.N. Doc. A/6316, (1967). For a collection of important documents on human rights, see I. Brownlie, Basic Documents on Human Rights 178 (1971).

[6] For documentation, description, and analysis of these five major trends, *see* D. Meadows & Assoc., The Limits of Growth (1972); R. Falk, This Endangered Planet: Prospects and Proposals for Human Survival (1971); and M. Mesarovic & E. Pestael, Mankind at the Turning Point (1974).

public order of human dignity that establishes and promotes the conditions for individual freedom while maintaining a constitutive process to secure a high productivity and a wide and just distribution of all values. By "public order" we refer to the "value pattern and the basic institutions protected by legal order."[7] By "human dignity" we refer to a social process in which "values are widely and not narrowly distributed, and in which private choice, rather than coercion, is emphasized as the predominant modality of power."[8] The objective here is certainly not a world order of extreme centralization; for many sectors, even national development organizations, private choice must be retained. The idea of human dignity, as Harold Lasswell has observed, "is not a matter of giving a privileged few their freedom of choice, but of striking a balance among the claims of all."[9]

Generally our policies are to secure and facilitate the exploration, discovery, allocation, distribution, and development of resources in ways conducive to maintaining both minimum and optimum world order. The fullest production and more equitable distribution of values arising from the management of resources are, of course, long-term goals. The equitable distribution of resources refers to a form of value sharing that provides opportunities for the highest development of an individual's mental and physical capabilities within the farmework of general community policies without unduly upholding continued productivity. The well-being of the international community as a whole cannot be secured without the rapid improvement and development of value-shaping and value-sharing processes within the poorer nations. It is, however, a fact that actions taken now can alter only the future, not the past. Our recommendations must then clarify the patterns to be protected for the future, through the creation of necessary institutions and the establishment of appropriate legal orders.

The problems of resource exploration, production, distribution, and consumption are global in terms of their worldwide impact. The concerns for access to resources, employment in

---

[7] M. McDougal, H. Lasswell & I. Vlasic, Law and Public Order in Space 145 (1963) [hereinafter cited as McDougal-Space].

[8] M. McDougal & Assoc., Studies in World Public Order 16 (1960) [hereinafter cited as McDougal-Order].

[9] H. Lasswell, in Nomos IV 60 (1952) [hereinafter cited as Lasswell].

productive activities, pricing, and distribution are not issues of
interest to only one or a few states, even though a particular state
may sometimes have significant exclusive interests in the management of certain resources.

Collective and individual actions are needed for problem solving
regarding resources that were traditionally viewed as national.
There is a necessity for a global harmonization of particular and
larger-group policies regarding these resource uses for maximum
efficiency as well as for justice. Now international organizations,
nation-states, private interest groups, and individuals operating
on national, regional, and international levels participate in these
resource management processes.

The impact of a single state's resource policies or those of other
effective groups generally may have tremendous regional or
global impacts. A particular policy, or a combination of policies, of
one community, for example, may often have a major impact on
the interests of another country.[10] Changes resulting from different policies may have impacts on production, pricing, and consumption of resources and consequently on investment, trade
incentives, development process, and the general international
economy.[11] *Our purpose is not to create one policy and institutional practice for all major participants in the process of resource production and
distribution, but rather to formulate guidelines for major participants in
the social processes, and decision makers in the constitutive process, which
help to harmonize different individual and group approaches and minimize
the economic disturbance that is the result of conflicting interests and policies.* Our basic goal is unity of policy, not uniformity of institutional

[10] For a study of such impacts on industries, see Malmgrem, *Environmental Management
and the International Economy*, in Managing the Environment 53 (A. Kneese, S. Rolfe, &
J. Harned eds. 1971) [hereinafter cited as Kneese].

[11] Malmgren cites the example of differing international standards and regulations as
illustrative of the impact of policy differences on environmental protection. He notes that
"where one country's standards differ from another's imports may be substantially reduced
by technical restrictions, or the prices of such imports may have to be raised to cover the
costs of adopting these products to the differing national standard.

      " . . .

"Another type of problem, of potentially major international importance, is the cost
impact on industry arising from new environmental controls and pollution limits. If the
steel industry in the U.S. is forced to spend large sums on cleaning up and eliminating
effluence, its cost position will obviously alter vis-a-vis competitive imports from countries
where no such expenditures are required."

practice. To this end we seek to integrate different interests and to clarify the net advantages and common interests of all people and place such interests as the supreme and ultimate aim of all individual and group policies.

a. Common Interest

Common interest refers to shared demands for values whose achievement is affected by conditions of interdependence or inter-determination.[12] Special interests, on the contrary, are demands which are destructive of common interests, since such interests cannot be shared even in equivalences and their achievement is violative of the conditions of interdependence, imposing unnecessary harm upon others.[13] Interests compatible with human dignity are common; those incompatible with human dignity are special.[14]

Due to scarcity, many interests concerning resources in particular contexts are competitive. Therefore, formulating what the common interest will be in a particular instance and balancing the competitive interests requires consideration of all values arising from that interest in a larger context.

i. Inclusive Interest

Generally, the term *inclusive* refers to interests in activities with significant transnational effects. They affect more than one territorial community.[15] The demand for the protection of inclusive

[12] M. McDougal, H. Lasswell & M. Reisman, Public Order Materials (unpublished papers at Yale Law School).

By an *interest* we refer to "a pattern of demand together with its supporting expectations. This definition underlies the point that more than wishes are involved in interests." McDougal-Space, *supra* note 7, at 146.

The basic concepts and definitions used in this chapter were initiated and developed by Professors McDougal and Lasswell in their series of writings generally referred to as the Public Order Series. *See* note 14 in the Introduction.

[13] *Id.*

[14] "Human dignity" refers to a social process in which "values are widely and not narrowly shared, and in which private choice, rather than coercion, is emphasized as the predominant modality of power." McDougal-Order, *supra* note 8, at 16; *see also* McDougal-Space, *supra* note 7, at 148.

[15] McDougal-Space, *supra* note 7, at 151.

interests has increased because of the substantial value deprivation likely to be or actually suffered by a large segment of the world community as a result of the activities of a few participants.[16] Inclusive interest commonly entails an element of collectiveness in decision—decisions are made in organzied form or through calculations of reciprocity and retaliation, the outcomes are often widely distributed, and an inclusively authorized controlling process regulates and controls the process of formation and distribution of the outcomes. In other words, an interest is inclusive when its impact "use" is inclusive and the "competence" to make and apply law with regard to it is inclusive.[17] Inclusive use, as will be explained later, is a process in which the shaping and sharing of values are widely shared. Inclusive competence refers to the sharing of effective authority that influences and formulates community decisions.

Ideological considerations notwithstanding, the terms *collective interest*, *public interest*, and *inclusive interest* carry a common element of a large and widespread effect and shared concern. They may differ in their process of formation, their achievement, and the competence that controls the whole process, with regard to the "content" of the "inclusive interest" (in terms of formation and distribution) or the "procedural" aspect of formation and distribution of the interest. These differences are particularly apparent in claims for inclusive interests made by a "totalitarian society" and a "free society."

Many contemporary scholars have been concerned with the formation of common interests, but the conception proposed here is different from all of them, for it provides different intellectual tasks. James Buchanan and Gordon Tullock concluded that any action or change that secures unanimous support is desirable and is in the public interest.[18] Mancur Olson, in defining the "com-

---

[16]"In regard to oceans and rivers, the discovery of inclusive interest was encouraged by the prospect of avoiding value deprivation arising from piracy, capricious interference, burdensome tolls, multiple regulation, and kindred nuisances. The cost of special or even exclusive interests was conspicuous; and the benefits that justify cost were insufficiently general to win widespread support for the perpetuation of disorder. Inlanders who hoped to benefit from piracy, or villagers who hoped to profit by compelling a river boat to stop, were in such obvious pursuit of special interests that they obtained little outside support." *Id.* at 176–77.

[17]*Id.* at 151.

[18]J. Buchanan & G. Tullock, The Calculus of Consent 285 (1962).

mon," "collective," or "public" goods, emphasizes the "wealth" value and defines "public good" as "any good such that, if a person X_i in a group $X_1 \ldots, X_i \ldots, X_n$ consumes it, it cannot feasibly be withheld from the others in that group. In other words, those who do not purchase or pay for any of the public or collective good cannot be excluded or kept from sharing in the consumption of the good, as they can where noncollective goods are concerned."[19] Based on this distinction, he defines "exclusive" and "inclusive" groups in ways we will discuss later in this section.

In Buchanan's and Tullock's views, unanimous support is the only criterion for distinguishing the "public interest." But from the standpoint of an observer, unanimous support is *only one* component element of "public interest." Buchanan and Tullock fail to take into account the content of a public interest, not only in terms of *formation*, but, more importantly, in terms of *distribution* of values arising from that action. Olson, on the other hand, considers the sharing and distribution process. In the definition of the "public good," Olson gives tremendous emphasis to the "wealth" value and ignores other values. Olson is primarily concerned with the consumptive nature of certain goods, rather than with the aggregate impact a particular use may have on the entire community. As we intend to use "common interest," a resource may become common given new technology, new needs by other or even more general environmental changes.

We distinguish inclusive interest in terms of both important components: inclusive use and inclusive competence.[20]

(a) *Inclusive Use. Inclusive use* refers to a process in which all phases of an activity are or may be shared. One finds variety and pluralism both in types and in numbers of participants with public and private participants, organized, unorganized individuals, or different group associations. The participants seek equal opportunities for individuals to participate in choosing and maximizing their own values freely within the necessary limitation of public order, and they are free to deploy their power bases and to choose strategies which help them to reach their inclusive objectives in terms of geographical location and the degree of institutionaliza-

[19] M. OLSON, THE LOGIC OF COLLECTIVE ACTION 14–15 (1971).

[20] For an elaboration of these two components (inclusive use and inclusive competence), *see* McDOUGAL-SPACE, *supra* note 7, at 151–54.

tion. But a few participants cannot accumulate their base values and exercise them at the expense of others in some functional type of monopoly.

(b) *Inclusive Competence. Inclusive competence* refers to shared effective authority to participate in community decisions in an unorganized or organized way. Unorganized competence is based on unilateral decisions and community response to those decisions. Control mechanisms are comprised of reciprocity and retaliation. Organized competence refers to decisions made in formalized institutions, whether or not called governmental. Inclusive competence, whether organized or unorganized, may be constitutive, supervisory, regulative, corrective, or enterprisory. Decision makers with an inclusive competence include various types of participants who identify with expectations regarding the advantages of a collective action and are authorized to make collective decisions. The objective of an inclusive process is the establishment and implementation of the goals upon which the world public order is structured—protection of common interest versus special interest. This process will operate in relatively open, multiple, and flexible arenas. All decision makers who are in a similar situation should have equal, formal, and enough effective power to be able to assert their authority. Decision makers should have equal rights to employ available strategies with similar framework and restrictions. The outcome of such a process should include the general and formal participation in all phases of decisions.

ii. Exclusive Interest

Exclusive interests are interests in activities that predominantly affect only one territorial community; exclusive interests include both exclusive uses and exclusive competence.[21]

(a) *Exclusive Use.* Uses related only to one participant are exclusive; in an *exclusive use* choice is made by one participant. The objective that the participant pursues is maximization of his own values without harming others. That participant has unilateral control over the situation and the preponderance of base values are held only by that participant. The strategies employed to

---

[21] For an analysis, *see id.* at 154–56.

achieve the value outcomes are chosen by the participant. Therefore, the outcome is likely to the value formation and benefit for
that single participant.

(b) *Exclusive Competence.* *Exclusive competence* refers to authority
held by one single state to enable that state to act unilaterally, with
minimum control by others in protection of or access to resource
needs for securing minimal needs, regardless of differences in
ideologies. Such exclusive competence is necessary for the protection and maximization of community potentials. Of course, when
there are acts of violation of fundamental prescriptions, restoration, rehabilitation, and reconstruction strategies will be relevant
to reestablish the noncoercive situation.

The basic aspiration and practice in the international community should not only be in favor of minimizing unauthorized coercion, but also of promoting and maximizing the formation,
production, and just distribution of values of *optimum order.* Resources and values arising from resources are important bases for
development. One of the main public order goals should be the
establishment of access to resources and values arising from them
to maintain a desired living standard for every human being and
to allow individuals to develop themselves based on their own
natural capacity regardless of their race, age, ideology, and cultural differences.

Nation-states should have free access to shareable resources,
such as the oceans, international waterways, and space, under necessary inclusive control. States should have equitable access to resources within the territorial limits of states, based on respect for
the exclusive competence of the host state and necessary inclusive
competence for the protection of minimum order. Interests in
optimum order leave states free and encourage them to enter into
bilateral and multilateral agreements for the development of resources and substitute resources, and, generally, agreements for
the use of resources and values derived from them for development purposes. Every nation-state should have access to scientific
knowledge regarding resource exploration, management in production, consumption, and development of new resources.

The world community may exercise regulatory or enterprisory
functions to achieve the desired ends. The object of general regulation will be to provide a framework for resource exploitation in
which the essential interests of the larger community are protected

on a continuous basis and particularly in case of a conflict. Within this general regulation individual states make their own decision regarding the use of resources. Their objective is implementation of their own public order goals. Local arenas in which they operate are left to their own determination. Base values are held by only that state. Choice as to the employment of strategies is also left to that state, subject to minimum direct influence of other states. The outcome, then, is unilateral decisions about every phase.

b. *Minimum Order and Optimum Order*

As concern about resource management increases, the importance of clarification of common interest and distinguishing it from special interest becomes insistent. The common interests both in terms of inclusive and exclusive interest relate to minimum and optimum order. Inclusive *minimum order* refers to conduct of activities by the process of persuasion and agreement with a minimum of unauthorized coercion.

The protection of world security has often been threatened by violence and coercion. World Wars I and II led the peoples of the world to appreciation of the necessity for global security and their common interest in prevention of unauthorized coercion. The U.N. Charter, various bilateral and multilateral disarmament treaties, and agreements concerning the peaceful use of atomic energy express this realization.

Considering the turbulence of the international economy, on the one hand, and the national demand and need for more resources, on the other hand, the relation of world security and access to resources has become a major public order issue. One function of the concepts of universality and international law and institutions is the provision of a mandate for employment of strategies for the prevention of future coercion. These strategies are usually based on prescriptions. Such prescriptions should be concerned with establishment and protection of the preferred goals in terms of the defense of basic patterns of value protection and distribution compatible with such goals and the guiding of social interactions toward a better fulfillment of overriding goals.[22] The regulatory function should minimize the degree of permissible inequality in value positions derived from resources exploita-

----

[22] LASSWELL, *supra* note 9, at 74.

tion. It might seek "antimonopoly" policies designed "to forestall the possibility that creeping autocracy will transform free institutions before it is generally recognized that freedom is undermined."[23] An aim of the regulatory function might be to establish rules of competition. In the language of Harold Lasswell, "It is not compatible with the conception of human dignity to allow individuals to sink in the competitive struggle to the lowest depth of value deprivation."[24]

The enterprisory function is designed to serve those value effects whose achievement requires continuing and highly monopolistic administrative activity by inclusive organizations.[25] Such administration may be necessary for facilitating the fulfillment of regulative and other public order purposes.

The protection of internal order from external coercion and disruption is one of the most important exclusive interests of individual nation-states. The protection of national security is what we call the *minimum order* in terms of exclusive interest. In a contemporary world in which military power continues to be one of the most important elements of the game of politics and in which the possibility of unauthorized coercion is high and the expectations of protective reaction and subsequent aid for reconstruction of already imposed impermissible coercion from general community are substantially low, nation-states must be authorized to take necessary steps within the framework of the U.N. Charter and general community expectations for self-defense. States should, accordingly, be authorized to expand their exclusive competence over activities relating to resources that seriously threaten their internal security. With respect to such shareable resources as the oceans, space, and weather, only an occasional, not a comprehensive and continuing, exclusive competence should be authorized for the protection of an important national interest. Even this occasional competence should be designed only for security and other important internal purposes; these resources should be kept as free as possible from exclusive control.

Each state should also have the necessary competence for the maximization of its own internal value processes (*optimum exclusive*

[23] *Id.*

[24] *Id.*

[25] *Id.* at 75.

interest). Such competence could be exercised by imposing requirements upon foreigners conducting activities relating to resources
within the realm of state competence. It could also be achieved by
using internal bases of power to control production, processing,
and marketing. But such practices must not be permitted to become incompatible with the inclusive interest of the general community. We should emphasize that no act of exclusive use or
competence should be of "dubious" character in relation to purpose. By "dubious" character we refer to any activity whose basic
objective is discrimination on grounds of race, sex, group classification, or different ideologies rather than self-help, self-defense,
or the promotion of the healthy functions of an internal order
which operates for the benefit of all inhabitants.

c. Inclusive Interest v. Inclusive Interest—Partially Inclusive Interest

The major participants interacting in the management of resources are groups who claim to represent the inclusive interest of
their group members, or of a large number of human beings, not
directly associated with the group, who are somehow their beneficiaries. These groups are either governmental or private or jointly
governmental and private. In such situations it sometimes becomes difficult to identify the "inclusive interest," since any decision or activity will have a significant and differential effect upon
more than one group, including diverse groups. In other words,
in such a case we may face two or more "inclusive interests" and be
required to determine the more "inclusive" of the two.

The power bases of individuals are not usually strong enough to
achieve their desired outcomes. In simple contractarian terms one
might say that individuals form groups and, by accumulating individual bases of power, amass strong collective bases of power. It
is basically assumed that the aim of every organization is to further
the common interests of its members. Harold Laski states that
organizations exist to achieve interests that "a group of men have
in common."[26] R. M. MacIver also emphasizes that "every organization presupposes an interest which its members all share."[27] The

---

[26] H. LASKI, A GRAMMAR OF POLITICS 67 (4th ed. 1939).

[27] MacIver, *Interests*, in 7 ENCY. SOC. SCI. 147 (1932).

question arises, however, whether a group really always represents the common interests of its members. Ideologically, a group may represent the common interest of its members, but functionally its members may never receive their share of that common interest. The physical and psychological techniques operating within a group may skillfully be exploited to promote the special or exclusive interest of some individuals rather than interests shared by all the members.

Mancur Olson draws distinctions between groups as they behave inclusively or exclusively. He emphasizes that the difference between an exclusive and an inclusive group lies in the nature of the objective the group seeks, not in characteristics of the membership.[28] But a shared objective does not necessarily end with shared and just distribution of the benefits. To us an inclusive group is one whose participants demand and achieve shared value outcomes with respect to certain activities. The words *inclusive* and *exclusive* are not, however, terms of an absolute fixed reference. As Myres McDougal says, the terms refer to a continuum in degrees of shared participation in the features of a social process.[29] When we talk about inclusive groups, we do not mean that every single member of the group has an equal and direct share in all value outcomes, but that more than one member is substantially and directly affected.

In resource exploitation processes we sometimes face groups that, while precluding membership to some groups affected by their activities, claim to represent certain inclusive interests of their members. We refer to such groups whose activities affect more than one participant but exclude some as *partially inclusive*. It is sometimes necessary to distinguish even as between different inclusive interests in terms of differing degrees of comprehensiveness in interest. For the making of such determinations and the relation of all claims to aggregate common interest, we recommend detailed examination of the groups admitted to, and precluded from, membership, the value purposes for which membership is admitted or precluded, and the value outcomes achieved by such admission and preclusion; the internal processes of the different groups for the shaping and sharing of values

[28] *See* OLSON, *supra* note 19, at 8. Harold Laski makes a similar observation. *See* LASKI, *supra* note 26, at 39.

[29] McDOUGAL-ORDER, *supra* note 8, at 157 n.1.

among individual human beings; the degree to which the composition of the different groups affects the shaping and sharing of values on a global scale; the extent to which the different groups have previously shared in the benefits of a global society; and so on.

For our definitions of common interest, we begin, however, from a descriptive rather than a preferential standpoint. From such a perspective, common interests are divided into exclusive and inclusive interests, and inclusive interests are divided into "partially inclusive" and "inclusive." Exclusive interests relate to activities whose impact is predominantly upon one participant. Inclusive interests relate to activities which have substantial impact upon more than one participant. Partially inclusive interests relate to activities engaged in by more than one participant and affecting more than one participant but from whose control certain affected participants are excluded for functional or other reasons. Inclusive interests relate to activities affecting more than one in situations in which access to control is open to all who are affected.

d. The Accommodation of Interests

Thus far we have formulated a general theory about the processes of resource exploration; resources should be used for the establishment and maintenance of a public order of human dignity. We then gave certain definitions of human dignity and of common interests—exclusive, partially inclusive, and inclusive (special interests being defined as those destructive of common interests).

The difficult and important tasks for an observer or a decision maker are those of distinguishing common interests from special interests and of accommodating the three sets of common interests: inclusive, partially inclusive, and exclusive. As mentioned before, the content of these terms is not fixed, and different common interests require protection in different degree in different contexts. The fundamental task is to achieve and maintain a continuous balancing of inclusive, partially inclusive, and exclusive interests which will serve the long-term aggregate common interests. The decision maker should of course always reject claims of special interest.

The most appropriate assistance might take the form of a comprehensive set of principles of content and procedure designed to facilitate the disciplined contextual analysis of particular problems in their rich factual setting. The principles of content would, of course, relate to every feature of the processes of resource management, claims, and constitutive decision. The broad outlines of these features have already been suggested.

Something more, however, needs to be said about principles of procedures. These indicate how relevant content is to be examined and require employment of a variety of interrelated intellectual tasks, such as goal clarification, examination of trends in past decisions, analysis of conditioning factors, projection of the future probabilities, and invention and evaluation of alternatives. The importance of these procedures has been aptly emphasized: "The procedures employed in the group by which decision-makers are chosen are of enormous importance for the success of the group in transforming value aspirations into accomplishment. Similarly, the procedures of a decision-maker in examining and judging a specific controversy or set of controversies are of crucial significance for the discovery of the policies in concrete circumstances that give effective expression to the goals of the public order system."[30]

In examining a particular issue in resource management, an observer should remember that final judgment should be suspended until all relevant factors are examined. In performing the various intellectual tasks, all the features of the context should be examined. Approaches that take a larger context into account are preferable to those that fixate upon a few features. Time and facilities should be allocated in relation to the importance of decision, including the values at stake and community policies affected. The demands of parties in terms of facts, policies, and remedies should be clarified. Claims made by the parties about the protection of particular value processes should be studied in their factual relation to asserted authoritative prescriptions. Claims by states for exclusive competence in unilateral actions over shareable resources such as the high seas for the protection of internal security and safety should be compared in consequences, for example, with the claims for inclusive use of shareable resources. An observer, taking the standpoint of clarifying the aggregate interests of the larger community, should evaluate the facts, characterize them, and explore the whole range of relevant prescriptions and choices in decisions, independently of the claimant's perspec-

---

[30] McDougal-Space, *supra* note 7, at 166.

tive. The real beneficiaries of claims for exclusive, partially inclusive, and inclusive allocation of resources should be identified. The observer should focus on comparable problems in the past, studying decisions for their approximation to community policies. The observer should seek to identify the factors that have affected past application and estimate the probabilities of these and other factors affecting future decisions in resource management. The alternatives in decision should be compared for their possible impact upon the distribution of values. The relative costs and benefits for the general community in terms of the options available should be examined. And, finally, the decision that best promotes the basic goals of community policy should be made.[31]

e. Policies Related to Public Order Claims

A preliminary application of these principles of content and procedure to the public order problems with which we deal would suggest certain broad policies with regard to the following features.

i. Allocation of Resources

One function of the constitutive process is to allocate competences among the exclusive, partially inclusive, and inclusive use of resources among territorial communities. In general, *our preference is for an exercise of inclusive competence to protect an exclusive use and control of resources, unless the manner or impact of exclusive use is designed to detract from the fulfillment of common interest.*

"Territoriality" and "state sovereignty" are among the more traditional labels for exclusive competence of states over resources exclusively or inclusively enjoyed. Protection of exclusive interest led the states to effective occupation and enjoyment of some shareable resources, such as a contiguous zone, a territorial sea, and other special zones (fisheries, the 200-mile economic zone, air-defense zones over high seas, and space boundaries). *Our more detailed policies for allocation of competences between exclusive and inclusive are generally based on functional criteria. Rather than being the only criterion for division of competences, geographical criteria are only one important element.* The most relevant trends include demands for appropri-

---

[31] For an elaborate writing on principles of procedure, *see* McDougal, *Human Rights and World Public Order: Principles of Content and Procedure for Clarifying General Community Policy,* 14 VA. J. INT'L. L. 404–05 (1974).

ate change in the criteria hitherto employed, particularly in environmental policies.[32]

While promoting exclusive allocation of resources within territorial boundaries, we have always insisted that inclusive competence should be employed to protect and regulate such exclusive enjoyment in situations in which claims are made that contradict common interest. Keeping this policy in mind, we recommend further that states be left free choice to enter into agreements for sharing the values arising from the exploration of resources within their territorial competence. We have tried to balance inclusive and exclusive competence through regulation of activities both in cases of inconsistency with basic community policies and in the inevitable conflicts arising from or about the details of the processes of commitment, performance, and change.

ii. Conservation of Resources

Conservation policy requires a contextual approach. Such an approach, which relates conservation policy to the ultimate goal of resource management, has been better appreciated as scientific knowledge about the earth's reserve of resources, including both the possibility of future development of resources and the deterioration of resources, has increased. Our general policies, therefore, are aimed toward formulating guidelines that seek to optimize the rational use of resources through regulating the time, the rate, and the characteristics of the process of use to promote common interest. Our recommended policy promotes inclusive prescriptions and applying competence for conservation of shareable resources. With respect to resources exclusively enjoyed, exclusive policy prescriptions and competence are appropriate. The exclusive policies honored should, nevertheless, be within the structure of, and compatible with, more general (regional or universal) conservation policies.

iii. Regulation of Injurious Use of Resources

The increase in different forms of value deprivations caused by inappropriate employment of resources has made the control over injurious use of resources a matter of international concern. Such

---

[32] *See* McDougal & Schneider, *The Protection of the Environment and World Public Order: Some Recent Developments*, 45 Miss. L. Rev. 1092 (1972).

expectation has been supported by different community prescriptions that severely limit special interest. The doctrine of *sic utere tuo ut alienum non laedas*, "equitable utilization," and "the principle of good neighborliness" are some of the recognized labels which protect common interest and whose application balances the exclusive use of resources and the inclusive interest of the larger community in preventing or minimizing possible injuries.[33] Our recommended policies promote inclusive prescriptions to determine competent decision makers and relevant prescriptions to make judgments on claims regarding injurious use. Inclusive prescriptions, in some situations, have referred to national courts as competent decision makers. In such cases, however, national authorities have been obliged to apply inclusive prescriptions or in the absence of such prescriptions to refer to the general policy of protection of common interest.

We have promoted the policy of expanding exclusive competence regarding the regulation of injurious use of internal resources. However, this competence is limited by inclusive prescription in cases of extraterritorial impact. We have expanded some strategies, such as "prior consultation," as a way of countering exclusive regulation of internal resources to prevent extraterritorial damages. As to shareable resources, inclusive prescriptions have been accepted. The scope of inclusive competence, however, is limited to the expectation of the community with respect to effectiveness of inclusive authorities in protecting the common interest. Threat to internal safety and security will justify the unilateral actions of nation-states for an intermediate regulation until inclusive authority can alleviate the unjust deprivation or possible deprivation.

iv. The Pricing Process and Common Interest: Exclusive and Inclusive Competence in Contemporary Context

We regard the pricing process as an important strategy of optimum order. The main value involved in pricing is wealth, but

---

[33] Creation of such balance is the purpose of Principle 21 of the U.N. Declaration on the Human Environment, U.N. DOC.A/AC.138 (1972). For related doctrinal approaches, see International Regulations for the Prevention of Collisions at Sea, [1965] 16 U.S.T. 794, T.I.A.S. No. 5813; International Convention for the Safety of Life at Sea, [1965] 16 U.S.T. 185, T.I.A.S. No. 5780, 536 U.N.T.S. 27; Treaty on Principles Governing the Activities of States in the Exploration and Use of Outer Space, [1967] 18 U.S.T. 2410, T.I.A.S. No. 6347, *reprinted in* 6 INT'L LEGAL MATERIALS 336 (1967). *See also* INT'L LAW ASSOCIATION, REPORT OF THE FIFTY-SECOND CONFERENCE, HELSINKI 143–286, 447–533 (1967).

other values are important in and relevant to this process. Thus, the objective of the pricing process should be to secure an appropriate rate of exploitation and conservation of resources at any particular moment and through time. The immediate and long-term pricing policies on the distribution of resources and benefits arising from this process should be taken into account. The assessment of the cost of resource exploitation should be comprehensive and its distribution among different parties should be compatible with overall goals. Pricing policy should balance the stability in expectation with the possibility for necessary changes. The function of pricing may be expanded to include distribution of values not necessarily arising from particular exploitation of resources. Thus, such policies should be evaluated in terms of their aggregate value and public order effects.

We encourage wide participation in the pricing process not only of governmental organizations but also of private associations representing consumers and producers. As to primary products, primary producers may be given initial competence to set prices, but subject to review.

B. CONSTITUTIVE GOALS

Our policies for the constitutive process are the balancing of the inclusive competence of the larger community and the exclusive competences of nation-states to secure common interests. Such a balancing must be adequate for the production and fair distribution of resources and of the values produced in the continuous process of resource management. An appropriate balancing should represent

> a moving line of compromise varying with problems and contexts, between certain complementary, contraposed policies: all free peoples have a common interest in the establishment and maintenance of an inclusive competence adequate to secure common values and designed both to protect democratic access by peoples to participation in decisions which affect them and to achieve an assumption of responsibility adequate to ensure application of inclusive policies in arenas both external and internal to particular states; but such peoples have equally a common interest in the establishment and maintenance of an exclusive competence adequate to protect particular peoples from arbitrary external interference and oppression and to promote the

greatest possible freedom for initiative, experiment, and diversity in the effective adaptation of policies to local contexts.[34]

The constitutive process in a public order of human dignity hence encourages the formation and efficient operation of viable exclusive and regional communities but retains the competence to rearrange and reallocate competence over resources, people, and institutions to and between those communities so as to secure, through time and changing circumstances, the greatest approximation to individual and community goals. Each feature of the constitutive process should be established and maintained in such a way as to require a wide sharing of power in decision making regarding production and distribution of values.

At a high level of generality the constitutive goal is to increase the range of individual choices to available or potential services. *The policies are to maintain or possibly increase the autonomy of major regions in resource management. In other words, the policies are not so much to promote exclusive competence of nation-states as to give exclusive (or partially inclusive) competence to rationally organized regions; the regions themselves are delineated in ways which contribute to the optimum world affairs of other regions or the whole globe.* The function of these regions will be most productive in intelligence functions: to provide information about the process of resource management for the members. Such regions should also make special arrangements to handle coercion selectively to provide as much freedom of choice for the members as possible.

The introduction of an effective inclusive competence to the world constitutive process has never been an easy task. While in theory it was recognized, in application it faced a number of difficulties and severe oppositions. Noninterference with internal affairs of nation-states was predominantly recognized as a common interest during the nineteenth century. This perspective led to a carefully established regulation of some activities, such as the slave trade, maritime commerce, and war; their organized common practices were deemed essential to the minimum order through regimes of mutual respect for internally devised prescriptions. Since then the global constitutive process has been facing direct and indirect opposition and hesitations in formulating prescriptions which would promote inclusive competence. International treaties designed for automatic arbitration or general inclusive competence, for example, tend to be vague, with a wide range of

---

[34] McDougal-Order, *supra* note 8, at 233–34.

possibilities for escape. The pressure for formulating such vague inclusive prescriptions may be observed at all levels from the most inclusive to the least inclusive processes. The jurisdiction of the League of Nations was circumscribed in Article 15, Paragraph 8, for example, due to the concern for the traditional notion of sovereignty. It was a powerful factor in the political thinking in 1919 that hoped to make the League acceptable to the United States.[35] Similarly, in a number of bilateral agreements, particularly between states and private entities, the provisions regarding the extent of inclusive or exclusive competences with respect to the process of the shared activities are vague and open. This continuing tension between exclusive and inclusive competence, commonly described in terms of "domestic jurisdiction" and "international concern," becomes more critical with respect to management of resources, and particular internal resources.

The balancing of inclusive and exclusive competence is in fact only a specification of those more general human dignity principles that are the ultimate goals of public order and the constitutive process. A flexible and appropriate balancing must require the constitutive process constantly to reappraise and redetermine the allocation of exclusive and inclusive competence over any resource on earth in terms of the importance of the resource and the current needs of the entire world community. The policies relating to efficiencies in production, conservation, environmental protection, pricing processes, and improvement in production and distribution from a particular resource may all be made to contribute to this end.

1. Participants

The overriding policy is to permit and encourage participation of all who can affect or be affected by the making of such decisions.[36]

---

[35] C. FINCHAM, DOMESTIC JURISDICTION 20 (1948).

[36] The constitutive policies are structured of varying degrees of balance between official and unofficial organs, organized and unorganized participants. We observe that the world community is structured of many smaller arenas. In such circumstances the degree of organization in the worldwide decision-making process is not as visible as it might be in the internal organization of one community. For a description and analysis of participants in the world constitutive process, *see* McDougal, Lasswell & Reisman, *Trends in Constitutive Decisions* (unpublished paper in the Yale Law School). For a discussion of participation in airspace constitutive process, *see* McDOUGAL-SPACE, *supra* note 7, at 97–101.

The important complementary policies in participation are "representativeness" and "responsibility." Both producers and consumers should have adequate representation. The participants should be held responsible for carrying out decisions in accordance with their capabilities, but the relative size of resources held by participants may have some bearing on responsibility. Participants in the decision-making process may be official representatives or nonofficials, organized or unorganized, governmental or private associations. When the process of resource production and distribution threatens the minimum order of the larger community, the decision-making process should be as inclusive, as representative, and preferably as official and organized as possible. Many different private associations now represent basically the perspectives of individuals in environmental policies and, to a lesser degree, potential consumers of resources. Our recommended policies encourage the participation of private associations, which tend to represent a number of individuals who are primarily interested in the well-being rather than the wealth value in decision making. Thus, we encourage a balanced participation of individuals and organizations in this process.

The degree of inclusivity as well as official representation may change with respect to each type of decision. Participation in an intelligence function, for example, may be wholly inclusive. Unorganized and private associations as well as organized and official representatives may be active in this function. Participation in the promotion function may be equally open. The most controversial participation is in the prescription and application functions. As a general goal statement, we prefer more centralized, official, and organized participation in these two processes. Participants who have a vital interest in certain resources should actively be involved in formulating and applying prescriptions regarding those resources. In general, we encourage a more exclusive participation regarding resources exclusively enjoyed, while empowering inclusive decision makers with the competence to control constantly such participation and reallocate the exclusive competence if it detracts from the fulfillment of the common interest.

2. Perspectives

The constitutive process appropriate to a public order of human dignity should be directed toward the clarification, protection, and the promotion of common interests and rejection of special interests. Therefore, resources should be employed in a way to achieve maximization of the aggregate interest in all human dignity values. The perspectives of the participants should be oriented toward elimination, or at least minimization, of unilateral coercion in the processes of resource management.

In their identifications, participants should empathize broadly and recognize the global interdependencies that bind them. Changes in patterns of identification are critcally important, since such patterns are among the factors that prevent the exercise of inclusive competence[37] for the protection of minimum order and the maximization of many particular values.[38] Key factors are the jealousy of national elites of their own basis of power as well as the distrust among the effective national elites to submit to the control and regulation of an inclusive body. Changing the identifications of the decision makers from parochial to transnational may be a precondition to promoting inclusive competence. In making policies, decision makers should look beyond the interest of particular communities.[39]

Constitutive perspectives may be distinguished in terms of intensity in demand from those characterized as "ius cogens," or "fundamental," to the lesser prescriptions of customary international law. Similar gradations in intensity may mark demands for implementation or for the establishment of centralized, formal procedures for maintaining or changing certain policies.[40] Like all other human affairs, constitutive perspectives are in continuous change, "even to the point of partial disintegration during periods of conspicuous failure to sustain minimum public order."[41] Ideally, change should be toward clarification and implementation of more and more specific human dignity values.

3. Arenas

Every feature of the constitutive process should be responsive to the needs for creating a process of decision making appropriate to

---

[37] The exercise of inclusive competence for protection of minimum order is recognized in the U.N. Charter and in various Human Rights Treaties.

[38] *See* McDougal, Lasswell & Reisman, *supra* note 36, at 99.

[39] *Id.*

[40] *Id.* at 92.

[41] *Id.*

contemporary transnational interactions and preferred processes for the management of resources. The establishment of and access to constitutive arenas should be formulated in terms of the requirements of the various types of decision—whether diplomatic, parliamentary-diplomatic, parliamentary, adjudicative, or executive—to enable more participants, regardless of their formal relationship, to participate and collaborate in some decisions.[42] In the area of resource management there is a need for arenas specialized to different aspects of the processes of production to final consumption. In addition, the specialized arenas should be varied in structure to afford opportunity to all the different participants in world politics. Policies concerning constitutive arenas specialized to resource management will similarly change with changing considerations of minimum or optimum order.

a. Establishment

In general, our recommended policies promote more diplomatic and parliamentary arenas. The degree of formality of arenas, of course, depends upon the purpose and the function of the arena. Arenas specialized to gathering or distributing information may be less official or formal. We also encourage creation of special conferences to deal with particular resource problems.

i. Institutionalization

Our policies favor inclusive, institutionalized, official, and maybe specialized arenas with respect to matters of minimum order. The degree of institutionalization of resource management arenas may change, depending upon the function of the arena.

ii. Geographic Range

The geographic range of arenas becomes relevant as to the intensity of impacts of particular decisions within different arenas. Where resource problems threaten minimum order, we encourage more centralized and global arenas. Demands for global arenas have recently been made by developing countries in reorganizing the United Nations, the International Monetary Fund, and other U.N. organs to make them more responsive to their demands con-

[42] *Id.*

cerning the management of resources. Matters relating to optimum order and sometimes minimum order of less intensity and more limited impact may be taken through centralized or decentralized and universal or regional arenas.

iii. Temporality

Our policies prefer continuous arenas. Such arenas are more capable of dealing with resource problems in an appropriate time. Intermittent arenas may also be organized for a particular or unique problem that cannot be adequately resolved in an established continuous arena.

iv. Responsiveness to Crisis

Arenas should at least be made adequately responsive to major crises. These arenas should be established in ways that maintain their continuous and strong authority and control in approaching resource matters during crises.

b. Access

The access to constitutive arenas should be open and available to all participants with interests. Producers and consumers particularly should have approximately equal access to the arenas. The arenas should also be reasonably open to other interest groups. Decisions from these arenas should be compulsory for all who affect value distribution in resource management.

4. Bases of Power

The constitutive process must be provided with necessary bases of power: adequate authority to perform its functions and sufficient control to render its authority effective. Allocation of authority and effective control among participants in resource management should be made to promote the establishment and the maintenance of a public order of human dignity. The authority of the international community to perform basic constitutive functions is now widely recognized, but, because of the lack of effective control, the implementation of specific global policies within nation-states always faces severe resistance.[43] This lack of effective cen-

---

[43] Id. at 99.

tralized control is most clear and most damaging with respect to matters of minimum order.

a. *Allocation of Authority*

Authority should be allocated to protect common interest; no authority protecting special interest should be recognized. The allocation of competence with respect to each function of the constitutive process (intelligence, promotion, prescription, invocation, application, termination, and appraisal) among different participants in resource management should be effected to facilitate the production of both exclusive and inclusive interest. The inclusive competence of the general community should always determine the allocation between inclusive competence (international concern) and exclusive competence (domestic jurisdiction) regarding each function. Such determination with respect to particular resource problems should be made through a disciplined and systematic analysis of the features of the context that affect interest.

Inclusive decision makers should be accorded the competence necessary to protect inclusive interest. They should classify priorities in intensities of demands and more inclusive policies. The inclusive decision makers should also honor the exclusive competence of particular communities necessary to protect their exclusive interest. Such competence should also be expanded to major regions. These communities and regions should be allowed to formulate or choose their own prescriptions insofar as they are compatible with inclusive community prescriptions. In other words, the aim should be toward balancing exclusive and inclusive competences, which will preclude the monopolization, and promote an appropriate decentralization, of power in resource management that will sustain and not subvert public order.

b. *Allocation of Control*

The controlling bases of power should be allocated in ways that make authority effective. Distribution of effective control among different territorial communities and between functional and territorial groups is preferable to create a balancing control. Such allocation of effective power, however, should be made in ways that facilitate the economic performance of the seven functions. The wide dispersal of effective control in resource management is economical and almost mandated by the location of resources. When necessary we encourage the mobilization of these distributed effective controls for the application of inclusive decisions.

5. Strategies

Strategies are procedures for the performing of seven functions. Our policies regarding strategies always favor the persuasive over the coercive. Coercive strategies should be authorized only in response to severe deprivations of human rights. Nevertheless, their performance preferably should be inclusive. The U.N. Charter similarly provides for the use of force only by organized communities and solely for the maintenance of minimum order. When the organized community is incapable of taking appropriate coercive measures, the lawfulness of unilateral actions is determined by reference to community goals of minimum order.[44] In the process of resource management, strategies have usually been employed by unilateral actions, that is, actions taken by nation-states or effective private associations (multinational corporations) or regional powers (producers associations, a group of states interested in protection of living resources, and so forth).[45]

Our policies promote strategies that are open and not secret and are economical in the sense of making an efficient use of resources. We seek an appropriate balance between diplomatic, ideological, and economic strategies. We generally condemn any military strategy in resource management. Strategies should be fair, relevant, comprehensive, effective, dependable, and proportionate to the particular situation.

6. Outcomes

The outcomes of the constitutive process should be rationally designed to secure the common interest in an appropriate production and fair distribution of values. This requires comprehensive and effective procedures for taking into account both short-term

[44]*Id.*

[45]*Id.* at 100.

and long-term goals in all the different communities, from national to global. Such procedures must be calculated to achieve the
most economic (in terms of costs and benefits) employment of
resources. The outcomes must, of course, be inclusive in affecting
and applying equally to all participants, both producers and consumers, and with no discriminations irrelevant to merit. Such outcomes must also be comprehensive and appropriately integrative
in order to make all participants who affect the achievement of
public order goals responsible.

a. The Intelligence Function

The lack of appropriate intelligence is easily observed throughout
the constitutive process relating to resource management. The
great need is, therefore, to encourage establishment of governmental or private institutions for gathering, processing, and dis-
seminating information with respect to every phase of control,
production, and distribution. Access to this information should be
made as open and free as possible to all. Groups having particular
interests may be encouraged to provide specialized information
concerning their interests.

b. The Promotion Function

Decisions relating to promotion should be rational, integrative,
comprehensive and effective. In seeking a balance between the
promotional powers of consumers and producers, we would encourage the establishment of organizations of potential consumers. The consumers in one country might join with or be
represented by other promotional groups in other countries to
bring pressure on activities of different producers not compatible
with common interests. Promotional groups could also be organized as representatives of environmentalist and conservation interests. Such groups might be able to increase intelligence about
commodities and prices and recommend new methods for the
protection of the environment and conservation resources. Thus,
they might be able to provide secretarial and legal assistance or
other forms of services for their members. Promotional groups
could similarly be organized by potential producers to protect
their lawful exclusive interests.

c. *The Prescribing Function*

In general, the prescribing function should be designed to maintain a certain stability in expectations about authority and control regarding resource management, without impeding necessary change. It should be adapted to serve the common interest in an appropriate balance of inclusive and exclusive interests. The fullest use should be made of all modalities by which community expectations are created and changed, including all forms of agreement, customary behavior, and the procedures of the United Nations and other constitutive bodies, regional and functional. This prescribing function should be made sufficiently comprehensive and effective to prevail over inappropriate monopoly. By monopoly we refer to a relatively high degree of control over the terms of trade, through control of supply or demand. Such control limits the scope of competition. In some circumstances, monopoly may be acceptable; this is the case of *public* monopoly, when alternatives in the management of particular resources or a particular phase in production or distribution of resources are less attractive and advantageous to the larger community. We prefer representation in such organizations which give multiple voices rather than concentrate control. The test in any set of circumstances as to what monopoly control may be acceptable depends upon the consequences for the costs of producing goods and services and ultimate effects upon value distribution.

d. *The Invocation Function*

The invocation function should be made timely, open, and dependable. No matter how excellent the community's prescriptions about the management of resources, these prescriptions can scarcely serve common interest if community members are not afforded opportunity to invoke them. We also would encourage the establishment of specialized invokers concerning the management of resources, after the fashion of the Scandinavian Ombudsmen. Such specialized invokers might operate from both regional and global bases.

e. The Application Function

The ultimate test of a constitutive process is in the effectiveness with which general prescriptions are applied in particular instances. Such application should, of course, be uniform, unbiased, and independent of special interest. Historically, most international law has been applied by state officials. What is badly needed for the more rational management of resources is a more inclusive and a more organized mode of application and enforcement. Such a mode might take the form of new general or specialized agencies, regional and global.

The most effective application of community prescriptions could require new community assumption of enterprisors' activities, such as the establishment of new industries on a transnational scale.

f. The Termination Function

The function of terminating prescriptions and arrangements is performed in much the same way as the prescribing function, but adds the problem of ameliorating the costs of change. This function is especially important in relation to the management of resources, since rapidly changing conditions require continuous change in the arrangements about production and distribution. This function could be made effective in neutralizing all kinds of activities discouraging a productive management of resources. In order to minimize the effects of local activities counterproductive to the development of resources, global insurance companies may be organized to afford protection. The model of the insurance scheme proposed for the deep seabed might be adopted to broader purposes. The insurance principle could be employed to balance the necessary stability of expectation in the global economy with indispensable change.

The effective operation of this function will, of course, facilitate the continuous change of the community prescription. The maintenance of appropriate organizations specialized to termination might increase both substantive fairness and due process of procedures in termination.

g. *The Appraisal Function*

The appraisal function brings the intelligence function to bear upon the process of decision itself. The more dependable and realistic the appraisal function, the more effective is all reconstruction and improvement of the constitutive process. Since officials cannot always observe their own decisions without bias, much appraisal must, of course, come from the civic order. It is a principal function of universities and professional bodies to maintain a continuous review and assessment of the quality of decisions. This is as true of decisions relating to the management of resources as of other decisions.

PART TWO

Trends in Decision: Claims Relating to Public Order

CHAPTER II

Allocation of Resources

MYTH, PRESENTED in the guise of history, is a means of justifying the present and shaping the future. Historical theories that seek to explain the origins of individual or community control of resources seem in large part to justify and celebrate a prevailing authoritative distribution. Those writing from a socialist perspective conjure a prehistory of natural communism; those writing from a perspective of capitalism and the free market devoutly believe that before the Fall the world was happily peopled by independent and competitive yeomen. Neither position seems particularly complex or accurate.

A. THE DEVELOPMENT OF EXCLUSIVE COMPETENCE

Historical anthropology and detailed observation of the few primitive societies that still survive suggest that in most societies things of material or symbolic value have been subjected simultaneously to claims, on the one hand, of comparatively exclusive competence and, on the other, of more inclusive competence. In different settings and at different periods of time, we may encounter high degrees of exclusive control; for example, an individual family "owning" an oasis or high degrees of inclusive control, as, for example, the totally inclusive control of irrigation systems in ancient Babylon and Egypt. At the same time, other material or symbolic resources in these cultures or civilizations might be subjected to different forms of control. In the oasis case, we may discover that personal names belonged to the nation. In ancient Egypt we might discover some of the reserved personal spheres characteristic of every modern urban civilization.

Effective decisions about allocation are probably influenced by power distributions, the culturally attributed evaluations of the resources or symbols in question, special ecological considerations, available technology, and to indigenous conceptions of efficient resource exploitation. Changes over time in allocations of competence over resources can be attributed to changes in these key factors.

Property, a term of private law, commonly refers to an institution by which the exclusive rights of individuals and private or public associations are exercised. *Sovereignty* refers to the exclusive control of the state over a much wider range of resources. These labels appear to have been developed historically to justify and promote the exclusive control over enjoyment of resources. Both concepts have a number of equivalents that are recognized and employed almost universally. "Possession," "ownership," "title," "tenure," and "dominion" may refer to the same interests as property. A similar variety of equivalents can be observed in other languages and legal systems. "Domestic jurisdiction," "independence," and "nonintervention" are common equivalents of *sovereignty* in international legal terminology. Whatever labels are employed, *property* and *sovereignty* refer to the protection of comparatively exclusive interests in relation to resources.

Although their basic functions have remained the same through history, the conceptions of property and sovereignty have changed in their scope. The new limitations tend to modify the purposes of control, to "socialize" it, as it were, and to make it more compatible with the general community interest on many complex issues arising from resource exploitation, such as scarcity, environmental protection, and so forth. In the modern period these limitations have gradually increased the scope of inclusive competence over exclusive control. National prescriptions as well as different economic theories have been the main factors in modification of the domestic law of property. With respect to sovereignty, inclusive prescriptions and state practice have played dominant roles in effecting a new approach to this notion.

1. Property

Property, as we have said, refers to the notions and institutional practices through which the community protects the exclusive claims, or "ownership," of certain members over resources.[1] From

---

[1] The word *property* derives from the latin adverb *propter*, which meant "in accordance with custom." It comes more directly from the word *proprietas*, which at the time of the

the earliest times property has been an important, though changing, factor in basic community assumptions;[2] some authors believe
in a natural basis even among animals,[3] and some believe it is a
man-made artifact.[4] Even those who believe in the natural existence of property accept that, for human beings, "material objects
are in essence an extension and definition of personality."[5] Beaglehole in examining the psychoanalytical basis of property states that
"without being strictly necessary for personal or species survival,
many material objects are used by man to magnify his sense of self
and extend his influence by giving him power over other men or
over the spiritual forces of nature."[6]

"Ownership" has, indeed, always been a base value for acquiring
many values, such as respect and power. In Sanaye societies possession of valuable objects in the cultural context would enable the
possessor to acquire all kinds of values which a "nonowner" must

---

Norman Conquest came into English; under the influence of Christian doctrine it was
Anglicized and assumed such forms as *proprete, propriete, propirte* and *Proportie*. It was also
used to characterize a feudal privilege or relationship. *See* Hamilton & Till, *Property*, 12
ENCY. SOC. SCI. 528–35 (1931).

[2] For studies on definition, the nature, and the history of property from different per-
spectives, *see generally*, T. SKIDMORE, RIGHTS OF MAN TO PROPERTY (1829); P. LAFARQUE, THE
EVOLUTION OF PROPERTY FROM SAVAGERY TO CIVILIZATION (1890); C. LETOURENEU, PROP-
ERTY: ITS ORIGIN AND DEVELOPMENT (1892); G. O'BRIEN, AN ESSAY ON MEDIEVAL ECONOMIC
TEACHING (1920); A. EDDY, PROPERTY (1921); L. LIONBERGER, THE MEANING OF PROPERTY
(1919); J. COMMONS, LEGAL FOUNDATIONS OF CAPITALISM 11–21 (1932); H. BRAILSFORD,
PROPERTY OR PEACE (1934); C. NOYES, THE INSTITUTION OF PROPERTY (1936); A. JONES,
LIFE, LIBERTY AND PROPERTY: A STORY OF CONFLICT AND A MEASUREMENT OF CONFLICTING
RIGHTS (1941); R. SCHLATTER, PRIVATE PROPERTY: THE HISTORY OF AN IDEA (1951);
J. HOBSON, PROPERTY AND IMPROPERTY (1937); and R. BLODGETT, COMPARATIVE ECONOMIC
SYSTEM (1949).

[3] Ernest Beaglehole observes that a primitive property relationship is manifested among
animals by assertion of "exclusive" possession and active defense of objects against intervention and attempts at destruction by members of the same species or an entirely different
one. Beaglehole's studies conclude that, for animals, acquiring property means only acquiring "interests" over objects and possessing them, but not property "rights." Property concerned in terms of both possession and rights is a created institution for human beings only.
E. BEAGLEHOLE, PROPERTY: A STUDY OF SOCIAL PSYCHOLOGY 27 (1931). *See also* C. LETOUR-
NEAU, *id.* at 1–21; S. BARNETT, A STUDY IN BEHAVIOUR: PRINCIPLES OF ETHNOLOGY AND
BEHAVIORAL PHYSIOLOGY, DISPLAYED MAINLY IN THE RAT (1963), and H. THORPE, LEARN-
ING AND INSTINCT IN ANIMALS (2d ed. 1963).

[4] *See* BLODGETT, *supra* note 2, at 24–26.

[5] 12 ENCYC. SOC. SCI. 590 (1968).

[6] *Id.*

do without.[7] Thus, food accumulation was not only for consumption; possession of it was related to power and respect.[8] This was true with respect to some clothing and hunting equipment.[9] Sometimes even when cooperation among nomads was necessary for cultivation, the nature of property would still remain individual.[10] Thus, within a communistic society in which objects were shared by members of the community, some individual rights to property were recognized.[11] Significantly, the property right would be denied to aliens.[12]

There are, as indicated, some disagreements over the private or communal origin of property. Some argue that ownership in primitive societies started from private ownership and gradually passed to common ownership, particularly with respect to land. Scholars have speculated that the reason for the limitation of such exclusive use was the population growth and the increase of those without adequate land.[13] In some tribes private ownership over arable lands was limited to a number of years, after which the cultivator would lose his right. This in fact was a temporally limited exclusive use. The period in Siberia varied from three to twenty years.[14] Similar regulations existed in old German and Danish villages and the right of free occupation became restricted.[15] On the

[7] BEAGLEHOLE, *supra* note 3, at 167.

[8] *Id.* at 169.

[9] Possession of certain types of clothing and armaments was an index of social status as well as a method of protecting the body. In hunting, possessing trophies was a strong symbol of personal distinction. *Id.* at 178.

[10] J. LEWINSKI, THE ORIGIN OF PROPERTY 11 (1913).

[11] In the Kai of New Guinea, a communistic society, a thief caught in another man's field may be put to death. R. LOWIE, THE PRIMITIVE SOCIETY (1925).

[12] Tribes such as the Maidu of California and the Thompson River Indians of British Columbia regarded certain areas open to exploitation by any native but not by aliens. Maidu tribes safeguarded their territorial boundaries by an elaborate system of sentry service; trespassing led to serious bloodshed. *Id.* at 211–14.

[13] Lewinski distinguishes three stages in the process of the passage of private ownership to common ownership; "First stage—there existed no equalization, the community merely restricts the right of free occupation; Second stage—the community possesses the right to transfer property from one person to another; Third stage—the land is periodically divided." LEWINSKI, *supra* note 10, at 42.

[14] *Id.* at 43.

[15] M. MAURER, MARKENFERFASSUNG, at 171, *quoted in* LEWINSKI, *supra* note 10, at 43–44.

other hand, some argue that the institution of property started from common ownership and then moved to private property. The greater probability would appear to be with Beaglehole's view that property in primitive societies was neither extremely exclusive nor inclusive, in a form of collectivism:

> [F]or, on the one hand, the simpler peoples recognize rights over things in the same way as they recognize other rights—as claims which, if violated, give rise to approved methods of reaction by the sufferer or his group. Permanent rights in the exclusive use, enjoyment, and control of certain things are recognized within variable limits which are often set by customs of hospitality, kinship or good fellowship. On the other hand, common property and common rights in the production or distribution of goods— property or goods over which several or many individuals have rights but which, taken together, they hold collectively against the rest of the social group—this common property is no less a reality of the simpler peoples than individualism.[16]

Developments in the concept of property have been much influenced by economic factors. The doctrine of divided ownership, for example, distinguishing between general title and immediate enjoyment, was practiced through history. During medieval times this doctrine was apparently the result of economic conditions.[17] This doctrine today is manifested in forms of possession, tenure, uses, and estates. In Rome the development of the institution of property was influenced by its origin within the nearly self-sufficient social unit called the *familia*. Roman lawyers, the first creators of a near absolute concept of *dominium*, never themselves applied such a concept in practice. In theory, they made a distinction between varying kinds of *dominium* and lesser interests. Comprehensive *dominium* meant the exclusive right to a thing, "the right which had no right behind it."[18] The lesser interests reflected varying distinctions and policies in limitation on exclusive control over the use of resources.[19] In comparable limitation, an owner might not

---

[16]BEAGLEHOLE, *supra* note 3, at 131. *See also* R. LOWIE, PRIMITIVE SOCIETY 205–06, 214–15 (1920); A. GOLDENWEISER, EARLY CIVILIZATION: AN INTRODUCTION TO ANTHROPOLOGY 137 (1922).

[17]*See* F. MAITLAND, COLLECTED PAPERS 252 (1911).

[18]W. BUCKLAND, A TEXT BOOK OF ROMAN LAW 189 (1932).

[19]*Id.* at 189–99.

treat his slaves cruelly, or he might not use his house so as to make it a nuisance to his neighbors.[20] The law forbade the owner to build above a certain height, or within a certain distance of his boundary and did not permit him to pull down his house.[21] The right of the owner could be restricted by either the state or the owner, conferring rights on others, such as of servitude or right of way, without losing title.[22] Besides limitation on exclusive right of use of resources, in Roman law there were some resources that were considered inclusive for some or all purposes. A *res communis* was common property, open to the inclusive enjoyment of all, and the concept included air, running water, the sea, and later the seashore to the highest winter floods.

Feudalism offered a further step in the evolution of the conception of property. It arose from the dependent relation between families, called the *feod*. While the Roman law of property was, in theory, the result of a relationship between independent and equal units of *familia*, feudalism was the result of lineal relationship between dependent and ranked units. The feudal relation was based on the severance of use, *dominium utile*, from title or overlordship, *dominium directum*.[23] The economic importance of land was so significant that proprietary rights of *familia* in land became the basis for personal status in private and public law.[24] Feudalism thus represents a most extreme expression of private property. But as feudalism decayed the tenant began to behave as owner and to ignore the *dominium directum*; he then claimed that the direct and actual enjoyment cannot be separated from title. Therefore, tenants gradually came to consider themselves as owners.[25] In fact, the abolition of feudalism increased the possibility for individual ownership.

The felt necessities of a given time may create the expectation that the exclusive use of resources in forms of property is not unlimited, is not dependent upon the unilateral control of the

---

[20] *Id.* at 188.

[21] *Id.*

[22] *Id.* at 189.

[23] C. McIlwain, Growth of Political Thoughts in the West 707 (1932).

[24] R. Huebner, History of Germanic Private Law 230 (F. Philbrick trans. 1918); J. Brissaud, History of French Private Law (R. Howell trans. 1912).

[25] Philbrick, *Changing Conceptions of Property in Law*, 86 U. Pa. L. Rev. 691, 709 (1938).

owner. The contemporary view is that the extent of a property right may be understood to depend upon the ultimate consequences of its practice upon the interests of a larger number of people. Thus, the expansion of the role of the state for protection of the public interest has extended inclusive competence over certain theretofore private property rights. Whatever their origins, the concepts of "police power" and "eminent domain" function as basic doctrines that limit the exclusive control of individuals over their private property through regulation by the state.

The limitation on the exclusive rights of individuals over resources has been extended and exercised in accordance with different political-economic theories about property. The theory of property as a natural right was a defense for the early capitalist societies of the seventeenth, eighteenth, and nineteenth centuries. Private property was identified with liberty and singled out as a cause of prosperity.[26] Because of such reasoning, feudal privileges were opposed. Despite the present identification of the theory of economic freedom with natural law, this theory did not in the beginning argue for property as a natural right. To Adam Smith, the property which every man has in his own labor was the foundation of other property rights. Where, however, the institution of property applied to soil, land, and other natural resources and where people own many resources not acquired as a direct or indirect product of their labor, Smith's theory had little cogency.[27] Marx, in consequence, turned an exaggerated conception of exclusive property rights on its head and proposed communism as a cure for accumulated social maladjustments.

From time to time modern constitutionalists repeat the traditional conception of property as a natural right. But it is in no sense "inherent" in constitutional theory. The Weimar Constitution of the German Republic after World War I made no reference to the natural right of property and, indeed, empowered the state to confiscate property without compensation. In some territorial

---

[26] *See* Hamilton & Till, *supra* note 1, at 535; SCHLATTER, *supra* note 2, at 278; and F. BASTIAT, THE LAW 14 (1964).

[27] For a comparative study of the institution of property, see BLODGETT, *supra* note 2; *see also* H. DICKINSON, ECONOMICS OF SOCIALISM (1939); J. SCHUMPTER, CAPITALISM, SOCIALISM AND DEMOCRACY (2d ed. 1947); A. PIGOU, SOCIALISM AND CAPITALISM (1937); and H. LASSWELL, WORLD POLITICS FACES ECONOMICS (1945). For an interrelationship between the kind of government and the institution of property, see R. MacIVER, THE WEB OF GOVERNMENT ch. VI (1947) and C. MERRIAM, SYSTEMATIC POLITICS (1945).

communities, also, productive wealth, such as land and capital, are generally owned by society as a whole. As Frederic Harrison stated it, the contrasting theories move from diametrically opposed assumption, the "one looking to individualism to save society, the other to society to save the individual."[28] Soviet Russia in February 1918 became an example of a country with the largest expansion of inclusive use and competence over resources, through nationalization of land, capital goods in manufacturing, and other fields of activity. Such a limitation of the exclusive use of resources has been followed by a number of other countries in strictly confining the scope of private property rights. There are also, as mentioned earlier, some general conceptions developed in property law which for the benefit of others limit an owner's exclusive control of resources. The conception of servitude, for example, is one such conception. The customs of hospitality and the necessities of life may limit the exclusive right of property as *individual* property. Claims by other participants, such as family groups, neighbors, associations, and so forth, continue to be heard with respect to resources of "general social utility."[29]

The need for a new approach to the international conception of property in the contemporary world, a new approach to what and how much one can own and to what extent one may exercise exclusive manifest control over resources, is widely recognized. As we have seen, the traditional and less complex notion of property as a legally protected interest in resources has been changed to a complicated legal notion, related to the whole pattern of community expectations as well as the practices and decisions by which community forces are organized to respond to and protect, claims with respect to the use of resources. In order to clarify the present role and limits of property, an observer would have to examine the definitions and important supporting concepts and rules known as the law of property with reference to the responses of official decision makers to many varied claims made by people for control over enjoyment of resources.[30]

A realistic observer must examine precisely what individuals and groups make what claims for what use and control, in relation to

[28] F. HARRISON, ON SOCIETY 205 (1918).

[29] *See* note 24 *supra*.

[30] McDougal, *The Influence of the Metropolis on Concepts, Rules and Institutions Relating to Property*, 4 J. OF PUB. L. 94–97 (1955).

what resources, in pursuit of what values. The appropriate evaluation of all these claims must be made in terms of all basic community policies.[31] The continuing debates about the different concepts, doctrines, and practices labeled "property" find their more complete meaning in these fundamental policies. The most relevant inquiries are "with respect to what claims and practices, about what resources have decision-makers in fact applied to 'property' doctrine to achieve what effects."[32] In addition, what other doctrines have been applied in comparable contexts to achieve either equivalent or opposed effects.[33]

2. Sovereignty

Through long periods of history, the comparative simplicity of instruments of conflict probably hindered the development of a distinct warrior class. Since anyone could defend his space, proximity to a critical resource was probably a key base of power, the strength of which diminished the further an elite moved from the resource in question. Despite the subsequent development of specialists in violence, administrators who are distant from a social unit they seek to govern encounter greater difficulties in control. Hence, the practice, even in modern times, of recognizing domestic competence, internal affairs, personal matters, and so on, while retaining greater control over manifestly external activities.

From a long perspective it would appear that inclusive decision processes have generally tended to recognize a measure of exclusive competence over matters of intense local concern. "Sovereignty" became the symbol for the most exclusive claims for such competence by elites of territorial communities in relation to resources. Primitive and early practices of such competence were observed around the Mediterranean area about 700 B.C. While there was no single form of government, all the more progressive and militarily powerful states had some aristocracy: internally, the supreme authority was vested in a relatively small number of people with higher social and religious status. The head of these social organizations regulated the social, economic, religious, and

[31] For an elaborate discussion on policy questions, see M. McDougal & R. Haber, Land: Allocation, Planning and Development 28 (1948).

[32] *Id.*

[33] McDougal, *supra* note 30, at 97.

political life of the community internally and externally. The communities themselves, however, were still very much governed by a family and clan relationship. This was the characteristic state of the early Greek period of the seventh century B.C.[34] The internal process of control was changed during later developments, though their form of authority remained the same in their external relationship.

The development of the theory of sovereignty first began with respect to internal affairs. Human beings began associations in forms of family, then local groups, and then moved toward a self-sufficient union called a commonwealth, or state,[35] an entity Hegel characterized grandly as the highest expression of social purposes.[36] In the face of that majesty one can take a certain droll amusement in the fact that a scholar like Meyer believes in the existence of sovereignty among nomadic and hunting tribes and considers the state the equivalent of the herd among lower species.[37]

Franz Oppenheimer, influenced by Marx and Engels, in defining the state is more concerned with economic exploitation and domination. In his view the state is a political means for economic exploitation: "The moment when first the conqueror spared his victim in order permanently to exploit him in productive work, was of incomparable historical importance. It gave birth to nation and state, to right and the higher economics, with all the developments and ramifications which have grown and which will hereafter grow out of them. The root of everything human reaches down into the dark soil of the animal—love and art, no less than

---

[34] For the early history of state and sovereignty, see generally W. DUNNING, A HISTORY OF POLITICAL THEORIES, ANCIENT AND MEDIEVAL (1905); R. LOWIE, THE ORIGIN OF STATE (1927); H. LASKI, FOUNDATION OF SOVEREIGNTY (1921); P. VINOGRADOFF, HISTORICAL JURISPRUDENCE (1920); M. FRIED, THE EVOLUTION OF POLITICAL SOCIETY (1967).

[35] VINOGRADOFF, *id.* at 89.

[36] LASKI, *supra* note 34, at 12.

[37] Meyer thinks that that kind of state is a universal feature of human culture. He, however, talks about particular types of state; this is not acceptable in political science. *See* MEYER, KLEINE SCHRIFTEN ZUR GESCHICHTSTHEORIE UND ZUR WIRTSCHAFTLICHEN UND POLITISCHEN GESCHICHTE DES ALTERTUMS 10–12 (1910) *cited in* VINOGRADOFF, *supra* note 34, at 92.

Contrary to Meyer's view, Vinogradoff denies the existence of sovereignty in ancient civilizations. *See* VINOGRADOFF at 93.

state, justice and economics."[38] Oppenheimer thus defines the state as an organization of one class dominating other classes; such class organization, he believes, "can come about in one way only, namely, through conquest and the subjection of ethnic groups by the dominating group."[39]

The feudal unit was formed purely for protection of exclusive rights, with no sanction for the promotion and the safeguard of general interests.[40] Feudalism was a form of domination, the domination of a small minority, "interrelated and closely allied, over a definitely bounded territory and its cultivators."[41] One author goes so far as to claim that the relationships between commoner and feudal landlord were almost the same as the relations existing today between nation-states and their citizens.[42] In contrast, Oppen-

---

[38] F. OPPENHEIMER, THE STATE 68 (J. Gitterman trans. 1922). Lionel Curtis similarly believes that the state is the product of conquest. L. CURTIS, WORLD ORDER at 4–12 (1945).

[39] OPPENHEIMER, *id.* at 4.

[40] LASKI, *supra* note 34, at 5.

[41] OPPENHEIMER, *supra* note 38, at 82.

[42] Reeves argues that certain features of feudalism were identical to the present role of the nation-state; examples include: (1) The vassal-lord relationship. (2) Loyalty and mutual obligations, protection and services, binding together all the ranks of each separate feudal social unit. (3) Contractual relations of lord and tenant, determining all individual and collective rights, forming the foundation of all law. (4) Financial sovereignty of the feudal lord, with the power to tax his subjects and in some cases to coin money. (5) The juridical sovereignty of the feudal lord. His courts were the public courts, and revenue from all fines went to him. (6) The military sovereignty of the feudal lord. All subjects on the lands of the lord owed him military service, were obliged to take up arms whenever he called upon them. The feudal land lord was also commander of the troops composed of his subjects. (7) Each feudal baron had his symbol, emblem, flag, etc., to which all subjects living on his lands owed obedience and allegiance. E. REEVES, THE ANATOMY OF PEACE 107 (1945).

Oppenheimer observes that one part of the content of the feudal State was semicontractual. The duty of paying and working on the part of the peasants corresponds to the duty of protection on the part of the lords. The other content of the feudal State, he says, was economic exploitation, the political means for satisfaction of needs. The peasant surrenders a portion of the product of his labor, without any equivalent service in return. He argues that the same perspective exists even in the modern State: "The purpose [of the State,] in every case, is found to be political means for the satisfaction of needs. Its form, in every case, is that of dominion, where its exploitation is regarded as 'justice,' maintained as a 'constitution,' insisted on strictly, and in case of need enforced with cruelty." He calls this the type of earliest capitalist enterprise of modern times. *See* OPPENHEIMER, *supra* note 38, at 85. He also emphasizes that the essential role of the state has not changed, it is only been disposed in more grades; the form of the state is still domination and its content still remains exploitation, or, as economic theory puts it, "the distribution of wealth." *Id.* at 227, 258.

heimer contends that the development of the territorial state is due to the development of landed property.[43] Lowie challenges Oppenheimer's perspective of the state's origin in exploitation.[44] Yet common to all these views of sovereignty is the preoccupation with internal processes, a feature also characteristic of the writings and discussions of jurists of the period.

A new development in the theory of sovereignty with regard to these internal processes was made in the sixteenth century. Medieval political organization was different and the territorial conception of sovereignty unknown,[45] for the organizational structure of the period knew no geographical limits. Groups were constantly crossing each other's territory. Nevertheless, the middle ages had a clear conception of sovereignty, even if its territorial aspect failed to develop.[46] During feudalism sovereignty and property were almost indistinguishable; the feudal landlord was the sovereign power.[47] Gradually sovereignty separated from property because of changing political and economic circumstances,[48] and from their separation the modern conception of sovereignty evolved.[49]

The state emerged as the middle ages passed, but the medieval suspicion of pluralism as potentially anarchic has never deserted the modern world.[50] The idea of unity was being asserted as the new basis of all institutions. But until Bodin, jurists remained uncertain about how to formulate an appropriate notion of unity and

[43] OPPENHEIMER, *id.* at 118.

[44] Lowie notes the example of medieval Europe, in which the Blacksmiths—the unalloyed aboriginal class—are not exploited, but on the contrary receive horticultural produce from the Mandingo; and we are explicitly told that they are not so much disposed as freed." LOWIE, *supra* note 16, at 23.

[45] A. ZIMMERN, NATIONALITY AND GOVERNMENT 56 (1918).

[46] LASKI, *supra* note 34, at 3.

[47] R. HAWTERY, ECONOMIC ASPECTS OF SOVEREIGNTY 5 (1930).

[48] Hawtery explains the circumstances under which the separation of sovereignty and property took place in these terms: "[T]he survival of the Roman idea in the Church and the Holy Roman Empire kept alive the possibility of a single authority legislating for a wide area. Military exigencies promote combined action of allies and ultimately unification. Feudalism had originated in military tenure and from its military functions grew taxation. Taxation for war in due course became the foundation of national sovereignty." HAWTERY, *id.* at 5–6.

[49] *Id.*

[50] LASKI, *supra* note 34, at 13.

how to effect, at least in theory, a transfer of the exclusive competences of several sovereigns, feudal lords, and the church, to one
institution and thus render the nation a unit. Bodin was the jurist
who created the modern theory of sovereignty, and his theory
became the intellectual basis of the campaign against particularism
and antinationalism in France.[51] Bodin defined sovereignty as "the
absolute and perpetual power vested in a commonwealth which in
Latin is termed majesta. . . . [I]t is perpetual because one can give
absolute power to a person or group of persons for a period of
time, but that time expired they become subjects once more. . . .
[T]he true sovereign remains always seized of his power. Just as a
feudal lord who grants to another retains his eminent domain over
them."[52] With this definition Bodin proceeded to elaborate the
theoretical basis for seventeenth- and eighteenth-century absolutism. Sovereign power, he said, is not subject to any laws except the
"laws of God and nature."[53] This theory gave exclusive competence over the resources, human and otherwise, of a territory to
the supreme power of the state and justified the Princes' disobe-
dience to the power of church and other important external political powers.[54] In Bodin's political theory sovereignty becomes
the central fact and the vital element in commonwealth.[55]

Every theory has its own difficulty. Most scholars agree that part
of Bodin's infatuation with absolutism was an attempt to create a
solution to the manifold oppressions of France and many other
European countries. England under the Tudors faced the chaos
of civil war; the situation was similar in France and Spain.[56] In
Germany imperial centralization had broken down. Bodin was a
follower of the nationalist party in France, which gave priority to

---

[51] C. Merriam, Jr., The Theory of Sovereignty Since Rousseau, 16 (1900).

[52] J. Bodin, Six Books of the Commonwealth 25 (M. Tooley ed. 1949).

[53] *Id.* at 25–36.

[54] Bodin expands his definition of sovereignty by noting that "neither Roman Dictator,
the Harmost of Sparta, the Esymnete of Satanka, the Archus of Malta, nor the ancient Bolia
of Florence (who had the same sort of authority), nor regents of kingdoms, nor holders of
any sort of commission, nor magistrates whatsoever, who have absolute power to govern the
common-wealth for a certain term only, are possessed of sovereign authority." *Id.* at 25. He
went so far as to say that "an absolute sovereign is one who, under God holds by the sword
alone." *Id.* at 36.

[55] Merriam, *supra* note 51, at 14.

[56] Laski, *supra* note 34, at 13.

the interests of the state above religious or other special group considerations,[57] views reflected in his *Six Books of the Common-Wealth*.[58] His theory of sovereignty was the first systematic discussion of the power structure of exclusive competence over resources in the commonwealth.

Bodin's theory exceeded its plan. It did not stop with development of nationalism but promoted dictatorship by the Princes and stimulated a counterschool. Other philosophers, called the "Monarchomachs,"[59] stood against Bodin and advocated a theory of popular resistance.[60] The basic features of their doctrine were "the original and inalienable sovereignty of the people, the contractual origin of government, the fiduciary character of all political authority and the consequent right of the people to resist and destroy the existing rulers whenever found guilty of a breach of trust."[61] The ultimate goal of the Monarchomachs was to promote the sovereignty of the people.

Grotius defers to the Monarchomachs in holding that the supreme power always belongs to the people, excluding government. He defines sovereignty as the "power whose acts are not subject to the control of another, so that they may be made void by the act of any other human will."[62] Grotius, contrary to Bodin, believes that the duration of power does not change its nature. He compares sovereignty "to a field over which one may enjoy full ownership, the usufruct, or a temporary right only."[63] Grotius talks about sovereignty in terms of ownership of resources and treats the subject as a property right. He explains that sovereignty

----

[57] MERRIAM, *supra* note 51, at 13.

[58] *Id.*

[59] *Id.* at 17.

[60] R. TREUMANN, DIE MONARCHOMACHEN (1895); R. WEILL, LE POUVOIR ROYAL EN FRANCE PENDANT LES GUERRES DE RELIGION, cited in MERRIAM, *id.* at 17.

[61] MERRIAM, *id.* at 17.

Johanes Althusius was the most famous student of this school. In his opinion, "the bond of the primary political association is contract, tacit or express; the state is the final form in a series of contracts, and the authority of the government results from an agreement, tacit or express, between the ruler and the ruled. Sovereignty, he defines as 'The highest and most general power of administering the affairs which generally concern the safety and welfare of the soul and body of the members of the State.'" *Id.* at 18.

[62] *Id.* at 21.

[63] *Id.*

could be held with full property right (*jurepleno proprietas*), or with usufruct only (*jure usufructario*).[64] Where "the sovereignty is a full property right, it includes ownership of the land and the people, and the right to dispose of all at pleasure."[65]

The theory of absolutism found its strongest advocate in 1651, in Thomas Hobbes and his *Leviathan*. The historical situation under which Hobbes formed his argument was the conflict between the English throne and the people.[66] In Hobbes's opinion every man by nature is selfish and looks out only for his own preservation;[67] out of this uncivilized stage and disordered condition government arises.[68] To control and preserve the social order, Hobbes argued, all resources necessary for social peace should be surrendered to the sovereign authority.[69] The sovereign power then compensates and responds to individuals by balancing individual forces; to secure such a balance, the sovereign should have full exclusive competence over all pertinent resources, even opinion and religion.[70]

Hobbes's theory was developed further by Rousseau, also a contractualist, who tried to move Hobbes's theory from elitist absolutism to a sort of democratic absolutism.[71] Rousseau, like Hobbes, started with a postulated primitive state of nature, but "he saw nothing but good in man's original nature."[72] Instead of a state of war, Rousseau imagines a state of nature in which life evolved with peace and happiness.[73] Individuals were transformed to citizens

---

[64] *Id.* at 23.

[65] *Id.*

[66] *Id.* at 24.

[67] H. WARRENDER, THE POLITICAL PHILOSOPHY OF HOBBES 270 (1957); *see also* FRIED, *supra* note 34, at 47.

[68] J. MATTERN, STATE SOVEREIGNTY AND INTERNATIONAL LAW 14 (1928); *see also* MERRIAM, *supra* note 51, at 24–25. Machiavelli's doctrine, insofar as his method requires generalization or assumption as to motives by which men are guided in social and political life, is essentially identical with Hobbes' theory. DUNNING, *supra* note 34, at 303.

[69] WARRENDER, *supra* note 67, at 17.

[70] *Id.* at 18.

[71] A. OSGNIACH, THE PHILOSOPHIC ROOTS OF LAW AND ORDER 17 (1970).

[72] *Id.*, at 17–20.

[73] OSGNIACH, *supra* note 71, at 19. "Rousseau takes pains to repudiate at the outset the idea that man's life in the state of nature is regulated by reason. The truly natural man, *i.e.*,

because of "the state of affairs and the consequent necessity of self-defense . . . [w]hich led eventually to a contract."[74] Individuals entered into contract freely, he says, in which "each of us puts into a single mass his person and all his power under the supreme direction of the general will, and we receive as a body each member as an indivisible part of the whole."[75]

During the American Revolution, Locke's theory of sovereignty became popular. He started with the state of nature, "which is not however, as with Hobbes's, a state of war, but rather a condition where individual rights are imperfectly secured."[76] To obtain a guarantee for social order, there is established a civil or political society and a government.[77] To reach such an end, every man "surrenders irrevocably to the community his natural rights insofar as is necessary for the common good—and no farther."[78] Here the limitations upon property and sovereignty clearly appear.

Historically, trends appear to have favored the assertion, rather than the limitation, of sovereignty. The basic concept is considered to be an important element for the creation of independent and effective social units necessary for the promotion of production and distribution of values and essential for the protection of the common interest of its members. To a lesser extent, the limitation of sovereignty in cases of negative impacts has been recognized by some of the great supporters of absolute sovereignty. Bodin, the father of this notion, limited the absoluteness of sovereignty. He

----

the savage, acts on two principles that are anterior to reason, namely, the feeling of interest in his own welfare and preservation, and the feeling of repugnance toward the sight of death or suffering in any animate creature, especially a human being. These emotions rather than reason, determine the conduct of men throughout the various phases of the natural state and give way to reason only when degeneration has gone so far that civil society must be constituted from the operation of these primary sentiments—self-interest and pity." W. DUNNING, POLITICAL THEORIES FROM ROUSSEAU TO SPENCER 12 (1920).

[74] OSGNIACH, *id.* at 19.

[75] J. ROUSSEAU, THE SOCIAL CONTRACT 18 (ed. H. Tozer ed. 1920). The main feature of the Rousseau doctrine is that the government is vested not in a sovereign (as with Hobbes), but in the "'sovereign will,' which is one and indivisible, inerrant and omnicompetent." *Id.*, at 19.

[76] MERRIAM, *supra* note 51, at 30.

[77] *Id.*

[78] *Id.* Besides the external aspect of sovereignty, the exclusive competence of the state as a unit seeking survival among the community of states has also been recognized. *See* FRIED, *supra* note 34, at 237.

did not desire to free the sovereign power from obligations to any law. Although his limitations are ethical rather than political or legal in character, it is important that he accepted that the ruler is bound by the law of God and nature. The Monarchomachs denied absolute sovereignty. In a curious parallel to Bodin they found the power of the ruler subordinate to the laws of God and nature. Therefore, the ruler could not be absolute.[79]

To achieve limits upon sovereignty, Grotius goes farther than Bodin and the Monarchomachs. He believes that not only is the supreme power customarily limited by divine law and natural law but also by such agreements as are made between ruler and ruled.[80] An important contribution to the limitation of sovereignty is made also by Rousseau, who limits the power of the government by legal rather than by moral criteria.[81]

Resources are important components for the development of the state and the state's sovereignty. The historical trends show that sovereignty was created to protect the exclusive competence of a community over the resources within its boundaries. Some even relate the creation of state institutions to the importance of wealth. For example, Chodorov says that the "organized government does not make its appearance until property becomes a factor in social integrations, and its authority is called upon more and more as property becomes more important in the pursuit of happiness; hence the concept of Government and the concept of property are inter-related."[82] Chodorov explains the need for government in terms of an asserted relation between property and production: "[T]he indisputable right to the enjoyment of one's output of labor and some machinery for the safeguarding of this right is deemed necessary and this is the business of government."[83]

As the scope of sovereignty in its internal aspect has been limited, its external aspect appears to be undergoing the same process because of increasing needs for the exchange of values and, particularly, wealth, *between* different communities. Until recently the levels of interaction and technological development were at a stage

[79] MERRIAM, *supra* note 51, at 18.

[80] *Id.* at 22.

[81] MATTERN, *supra* note 68, at 18.

[82] F. CHODOROV, THE RISE AND FALL OF SOCIETY 68 (1959).

[83] *Id.* at 79.

at which many common interests could be adequately secured by exclusive allocations of competence. But changes in technology and general resource needs will increasingly require inclusive allocations in many formerly exclusive areas in order to secure common interests.

Some scholars have gone so far as to consider sovereignty the most dangerous conceivable enemy to peace and justice.[84] Some argue that the world should be looked at as a "single social organism all-inclusive and universal," which minimizes the sovereignty of states.[85] Richard Falk with respect to the world crisis of limited resources similarly argues that

> [a] world of sovereign states is unable to cope with endangered-planet problems. Each government is mainly concerned with the pursuit of national goals. These goals are defined in relation to economic growth, political stability, and international prestige. The political logic of nationalism generates a system of international relations that is dominated by conflict and competition. Such a system exhibits only a modest capacity for international cooperation and coordination. The distribution of power and authority, as well as the organization of human effort, is overwhelmingly guided by the selfish drives of nations.[86]

Global expectations expressed in contemporary international relations, based on the increasing demands being made upon limited resources, have already begun to restrict the sovereignty of states with regard to resources located *within* their territorial boundaries. The methods by which these restrictions are prescribed and applied vary greatly. The following chapters elaborate on and analyse these restrictions.[87]

---

[84] *See* THE STATE IN INTERNATIONAL RELATIONS 80–88, 89–92 (R. H. Cox ed. 1965); *see also* REEVES, note 42 *supra*.

[85] *See* Lansing, *Notes on World Sovereignty*, 15 AM. J. INT'L L. (1921), and G. NIEMEYER, LAW WITHOUT FORCE ch. XII (1941).

[86] R. FALK, THIS ENDANGERED PLANET 37–38 (1971).

[87] Comparable developments of the doctrines of sovereign immunity, acts of state, and state responsibility toward aliens and environmental problems are all expressive of limitations on the sovereignty of states. These limitations have increased the inclusive competence over some matters formerly under the exclusive competence. In other words, sovereignty should be regarded as a relative and flexible term, like other legal conceptions. It should always be defined in terms of aggregate common interests. The limits upon exclusive competence over resources should be directed toward the promotion of common interest.

B. THE DEVELOPMENT OF INCLUSIVE
COMPETENCE

The development of the inclusive competence of the larger community over global resources may be traced, first, through the historic allocation of such resources between those that must be held open for shared use, free of exclusive appropriation by particular states ("external" or "shareable" resources), and those that are held subject to the exclusive appropriation and continuing, comprehensive competence of particular states ("internal" resources) and, secondly, through the continuous making and application of law by the general community to govern the exploitation and enjoyment of both kinds of resources. Through several centuries of customary international law, many highly shareable resources, such as the oceans of the world, rivers that traverse more than one state, the airspace over the oceans, and outer space, have been held relatively free from exclusive appropriation and competence.[88] Other less shareable resources, such as the landmasses and their immediately proximate waters and airspace, have, in contrast, been made subject to highly exclusive appropriation and competence.[89] The distinction between external, or shareable resources, and internal resources is not, however, coextensive with that between inclusive and exclusive competence: the global constitutive process of decision honors in some measure both kinds of competences over both kinds of resources. The potentialities of different resources for differing degrees of cooperative exploitation and enjoyment in the shaping and sharing of values have required many varying degrees of inclusivity and exclusivity in both use and competence. It is our purpose here to outline the origins of these various distinctions and to indicate the degree of community recognition of the exigent necessity for a continuous balancing of both inclusive and exclusive competence with respect to all kinds of resources.

It was recognition of the immense potentialities of the shared use of shareable resources for the greater production and wider sharing of all values, and of the urgent need for a greater flow of goods and services between different communities, that led to the

---

[88] *See* M. McDougal, H. Lasswell & I. Vlasic, Law and Public Order in Space 749–50, 770–74, 776–77, 790–96, 803–05 (1963).

[89] *Id.*

emergence of a conception of some resources as open to all, free from exclusive appropriation. Grotius, for example, referred to the oceans as incapable of occupation and inexhaustible, and as created for the shared use of all mankind by employment of a few simple rules of the road. As interactions across state boundaries multiplied, the founding fathers of contemporary international law formulated new doctrines for new regimes governing the different shareable resources. Through the decades the struggles between the proponents of inclusivity and the proponents of exclusivity have, of course, been continuous and insistent, as they are today, but slowly the notion and policies of inclusivity have come to dominate the regimes for many important resources. Both customary international law, as exhibited in the reciprocal behavior of state officials, and a host of agreements, multilateral and bilateral, have, until very recently at least, reflected a realistic concern of the larger community to maintain a high degree of inclusive competence over all the more important shareable resources.

The inclusive competence established for shareable resources has not, as indicated, been regarded as absolute. The authority of nation-states over many activities involved in the exploitation and enjoyment of shareable resources has often been recognized. In part, this honoring of competence in individual states derives from the historic ineffectiveness of inclusive authorities in maintaining public order. The important doctrines of "self-help", "self-defense," or "self-preservation" have been the basis for the exercise of much exclusive competence. The recent developments in the law of the sea conferences are, further, expressive of trends in favor of a high degree of exclusivity in competence over the use of shareable resources. The expansion of the territorial sea and the adoption of fishery, pollution, and economic zones are dramatic examples of this same trend. The difficulties encountered in structuring a seabed authority governing the exploitation of mineral resources of the high seas but underline the policy problems inherent in balancing inclusive and exclusive competence over shareable resources.

Similarly, the global constitutive process has never honored a completely comprehensive competence in particular nation-states over their internal resources. The unequal geographical distribution of resources in relation to population and the necessity for interaction and exchange of goods and services among nation-states have long stirred the interest of the larger community with regard to the exploitation and enjoyment of internal resources. More recently several factors have intersected to increase this concern. Internal resources, mostly nonrenewable, are becoming scarce, hence more expensive. Industrial civilization is spreading about the globe and further increasing demand. The connection and interrelationship among states has become stronger and more intense; thus, the impact of events regarding internal resources is felt directly and more severely in other parts of the globe. One result is a growing demand for some degree of inclusive competence over internal resources. The doctrines of "state responsibility," broadly conceived, and the whole of "private international law" have long been employed as dominant principles against the unbridled unilateral competence of states in relation to internal resources. This assertion of counterposed principles has been made with respect to almost every phase of the management of internal resources, and particularly in relation to agreements, conservation, and regulation of injurious use. The difficulties in balancing inclusive and exclusive competences (as symbolized in state responsibility and state sovereignty) with respect to internal resources continue to pose major tasks for international conventions, international and national courts, and publicists.

In the pages immediately to follow, we review the development of inclusive competence in relation to shareable resources. In the later chapters constituting the bulk of this study, we examine in detail the balancing of inclusive and exclusive competences with respect to internal resources upon a series of important problems arising in a global context of diverse demands, scarcity of resources, and interdependency.

1. Oceans

The first great resources clearly held free from dominant exclusive competence were the oceans of the world. From the beginning the oceans have provided communities with natural resources and services, and freedom of the seas was among the early claims for shared enjoyment. The early absence of major conflicts among states for regulating the use of the oceans was due to the comparative abundance of the resource and minimum international contacts and competition.[90] The noncompetitive aspects of enjoyment and the absence of the threat to exclusive interests probably encouraged the Romans in the second century to develop the concept of the "common right of all men to a free use of the sea." In the sixth century the concept of the freedom of the seas was codified; the *Digest of Justinian* placed the seas in the category of common property for common enjoyment.[91] Practice, however, did not consistently approximate prescription. Although most ocean resources were not under the direct control of individual states, many sea activities were, to an extent, under the exclusive competence of individual states.[92]

Changes in the economic and technological conditions of medieval Europe modified the concept of freedom of the seas.[93] Furthermore, the development of feudal law at that time removed the prohibition against exclusive ownership and, while keeping the seas for common use, invested their *ownership* in the state.[94] But varied economic conditions in different geographical locations produced different regimes. England, because of a rate of internal consumption of fish which was higher than its production capacities, negotiated treaties recognizing some rights for foreign fishermen in her proximate waters, on the condition that they sell the fish to England;[95] Scots, on the other hand, discouraged foreign fishermen in their coastal fisheries.[96] By the fifteenth century the Scots claimed exclusive fishing rights within "land kenning;" almost twenty-eight miles from their shores.[97] In the sixteenth and early seventeenth centuries competition over fishing increased as

---

[90]Clarkson, *International Law, U.S. Seabeds Policy and Ocean Resource Development* 17 J. L. & ECON. 118–19 (1974).

[91] P. FENN, THE ORIGINS OF THE RIGHT OF FISHERY IN TERRITORIAL WATERS 119 (1926).

[92]*Id.*

[93]*Id.* at 6. Fenn observes that "[f]rom the beginning there seems to have been exercised extensive jurisdiction by the maritime powers over their seamen, over their seaborne commerce, over the ships flying the national flag, and over the relations, business and personal, between their merchants and seamen. The maritime laws of Rhodes are the earliest laws of this sort, record of which has been preserved."

[94]Clarkson, *supra* note 90, at 119.

[95]Some of the treaties that England entered into included the 1351 treaty between Edward III and the King of Castile and the 1403 treaty signed by Henry IV. *See id.* at 120.

[96]*Id.*

[97] I. FULTON, THE SOVEREIGNTY OF THE SEA 77 (1911).

fisheries became important components of national wealth and power. In addition to that, the military use of the oceans made the situation more competitive. The need for more food, development of international navigation and commerce, and demands by coastal states for exclusive competence over the territorial sea generated international conflict.[98]

These conflicts stimulated the formulation of new legal regimes for protection of the inclusive enjoyment of the oceans. Grotius, who revived and developed the concept of the freedom of the seas, based his argument mainly on what he thought were material characteristics of the oceans. He argued that the oceans were not capable of occupation and that their resources are inexhaustible. Today, the human pressure on the exploitation of ocean resources, coupled with available technology and economic considerations, has made these "inexhaustible" resources move rapidly toward exhaustion, and the oceans are now clearly in measure capable of occupation. The fundamental point made by Grotius remains, however, unchanged; because of their physical characteristics the oceans are shareable resources, and a multiplier effect, in terms of the production and distribution of values, can be achieved through their shared use.

Concern for the more general interests of the community of states expressed through both individual and group actions challenged the claims to exclusive enjoyment of the oceans and slowly freed a large part of the sea for shared use. Grotius, the first who made claims to a systematic form for freedom of the oceans, supported his claims by demonstrating community expectations as expressed in natural law, the customary law of nations, and past literature. He stated that there are some things which every man enjoys in common with other men, and "nature willed that some of the things which she has created for the use of mankind remains common to all. . . ."[99] The air and the sea were put in this category of common property.[100] "In the legal phraseology of the law of nations, the sea is called indifferently the property of no one (*res*

---

[98] *Id.* at 120–21.

[99] H. GROTIUS, THE FREEDOM OF THE SEAS 2 (R. Magoffin ed. & trans. 1916).

[100] Air belongs to the class of things which should be open for common enjoyment since "first it is not susceptible of occupation; and second its common use destined for all men. For the same reasons the sea is common to all, because it is so limitless that it cannot become a possession of anyone and because it is adopted for the use of all. . . ." *Id.* at 28.

nullius), or a common possession (*res communis*), or public property (*res publica*)."[101] Movement across the seas is an important means of communication. According to the law of nations, "[E]very nation is free to travel to every other nation and trade with it."[102] No nation has the right to prevent other nations from communicating with one another by exercising their exclusive control over the high seas.[103] In attacking the Pope's decision that admitted the exclusive control of Spain and Portugal over a large part of the high seas, Grotius averred that the Pope's real intention was to give to two nations one third of the whole world each. Furthermore, he questioned the competence of the Pope to make decisions with respect to matters of such global interest. Finally, even if the Pope was competent to make such a decision between the two nations, the binding power of his decision over other nations was dubious.[104] Grotius denied the lawfulness both of exclusive control over the oceans and of any activities by individual states prejudicial to common use.[105]

A principal opponent to the thesis of Grotius was John Selden. England then claimed exclusive competence over the high seas to its south and east and over other regions to the north and west. To forward that claim, Selden, an English lawyer, developed a theory that rejected the conception of inclusive use.[106] He conceded that in the beginning the seas were free from domination, but denied they were common property or incapable of private domination.[107]

---

[101] *Id.* at 22. In contemporary usage this difference in terminology is not, of course, indifferent. *Res communis* is used to refer to resources that are subject to exclusive appropriation. *Res nullius* is used to refer to resources which, though having no present owner, are subject to exclusive appropriation.

[102] *Id.* at 7.

[103] *Id.* at 4. Grotius observes that "neither a nation nor an individual can establish any right of private ownership over the sea itself. . . . The oceans, . . . can be neither seized nor enclosed. . . ." *Id.* at 37.

[104] When Portugal and Spain began to expand their influence over the new Continent, the conflict between these two conquerors was inevitable; it continued until the decision of Pope Alexander VI in 1495 to divide the new conquests into a Spanish and a Portuguese sphere of colonization. Spain claimed the Pacific Ocean and the Gulf of Mexico, and Portugal claimed the Atlantic south of Morocco and the Indian Ocean. N. GERHART, LAW WITHOUT FORCE, 33 (1941).

[105] *Id.* at 55.

[106] J. SELDEN, THE RIGHT AND DOMINION OF THE SEA (1635). Although Selden's book was not published until 1635, it was probably written in 1617 or 1618.

[107] *Id.* at 4.

During the seventeenth century there appeared many pamphlets and treatises similar to those of Grotius and Selden;[108] many merely consisted of thinly disguised defenses of specific national interests. A more detached attitude about the use of the oceans emerged only toward the end of the century.[109] In 1817, some two hundred years after Selden's book, Sir William Scott, a distinguished English jurist, rejected his country's claim for the exercise of jurisdiction over the ships of others on the high seas. In *The Le Louis*, he stated:

> [T]wo principles of public law are generally recognized as fundamental. One is the perfect quality and entire independence of all distinct States. Relative magnitude creates no distinction of right; relative imbecility, whether permanent or casual, gives no additional right to the powerful neighbour; and any advantage seized upon that ground is mere usurpation. This is the great function of public law, which mainly concerns the peace of mankind, both in their public and private capacities, to preserve inviolate. The second is, that, all nations being equal, all have an equal right to the uninterrupted use of the unappropriated parts of the ocean for their navigation. In places where no local authority exist, where the subjects of all states meet upon a footing of entire equality and independence, no one state, or any of its subjects has a right to assume or exercise authority over the subjects of another. I can find no authority that gives the right of interruption to the navigation of states on amity upon the high seas, excepting that which the rights of war give to both belligerents against neutrals.[110]

The principle of the shared use of the oceans won further support in the work of jurists such as Wolff and Vattel. Increasingly claims for the protection of the internal interests of coastal states were rejected when they appeared to be unreasonable.[111]

Attempts to balance the exclusive interests of coastal states and the inclusive interest of the larger community have produced a number of complementary technical concepts. The recognition of a three-mile territorial sea conferred certain exclusive jurisdiction

---

[108]*See* P. POTTER, THE FREEDOM OF THE SEAS 92 (1924).

[109]*Id.* at 93.

[110]The *Le Louis*, 2 Dods. 210, 165 Eng. Rep. 1464 (1817), *reprinted in* L. GREEN, INTERNATIONAL LAW THOUGH THE CASES 412 (1951).

[111]M. McDOUGAL & W. BURKE, THE PUBLIC ORDER OF THE OCEANS 585 (1962) (hereinafter cited as THE PUBLIC ORDER OF THE OCEANS).

upon the coastal state. This jurisdiction was recognized to be necessary for the protection of the particular state against any immediate danger from the sea. Demands for exclusive coastal competence have not, however, been limited to the territorial sea; concern for security, and particularly protection against hostile acts, have led coastal states to assertions of exclusive jurisdiction beyond their territorial waters.[112] The French,[113] the British,[114] and some Latin American countries were among the first to assert such a competence in the mid-nineteenth century.

The concept of the "contiguous zone" was formulated in response to the claims of coastal states for security and well-being. One of the earliest judicial decisions expressing the fundamental policies of this concept was *Church v. Hubbart,*[115] with an opinion by Chief Justice Marshall. A claim by Portugal to exercise authority on the high seas contiguous to its territorial waters for the protection of the commercial interests of its colonies was recognized. Comparable claims were also allowed in the nineteenth century.[116] Since 1935 the United States has extended its customs jurisdiction as far as sixty-two miles out to sea.[117] The law of quarantine in emergency situations has been applied beyond the territorial jurisdiction,[118] through British legislation of 1800[119] and United States practices.[120]

In addition to security and power, claims for a limited exclusive competence beyond the territorial sea have been recognized for

[112] *Id.* at 589.

[113] F. Wharton, Digest of International Law, 108–09 (2d ed. 1887). *See also* J. Moore, 1 Digest of International Law 723–24 (1906).

[114] The Public Order of the Oceans, *supra* note 111, at 591, footnote omitted. This Act declared: "Whereas the rightful jurisdiction of Her Majesty, her heirs and successors, extends and has always extended over the open seas adjacent to the coasts of the United Kingdom and of all other parts of Her Majesty's dominions to such a distance as is necessary for the defence and security of such dominions . . . "

[115] *Id.* at 587.

[116] *Id.* at 588–89.

[117] Canadian Embassy to the United States of America, *Canadian Reply to the U.S. Government,* 9 Int'l Legal Materials 607 (1970).

[118] Dickinson, *Jurisdiction at the Maritime Frontier,* 40 Harv. L. Rev. 1, 15 (1926).

[119] *Id.*

[120] R. Shinn, The International Politics of Marine Pollution Control 15–16 (1974).

such purposes as the protection of health, the conservation of living resources, and the prevention of pollution. These claims for a limited exclusive competence for the promotion of internal value processes have continuously been made and honored by most states. The objections occasionally offered relate to the reasonableness of the action in a particular context.[121]

The needs of economic reconstruction after World War II and the new potentialities for development of the seabed minerals as well as the increasing scarcity of resources have generated still another technical concept favoring the economic interests of coastal states. This concept asserts and honors exclusive rights in the coastal state to exploitation of the minerals and marine resources of the continental shelf.[122] President Truman's proclamation unilaterally extending United States jurisdiction over its offshore resources encouraged similar claims by states in other parts of the world.[123] Currently, countries claim rights to the continental shelf varying from a few miles to 100 miles or more.[124] Recent demands for the promotion of the coastal states' internal-wealth interest have created a widespread acceptance of the concept of an "economic zone" that extends to either 200 miles offshore or to the edge of the continental margin, whichever is further seaward.[125]

These changes in demands have led to problems in the accommodation of the interests of coastal states and those of the larger community. As we have seen, early advocates of the inclusive use

[121] THE PUBLIC ORDER OF THE OCEANS, *supra* note 111, at 594.

[122] E. WENK, THE POLITICS OF THE OCEAN 253 (1972).

[123] *Id.* It is reported that on September 28, 1945, President Harry S. Truman issued two surprising policy directives on ocean affairs. Intended to assist the domestic oil industry by clarifying federal versus state jurisdiction of offshore resources, they took the international community by surprise. Proclamation Number 2667 unilaterally extended American rights by stating that the "government of the U.S. regards the natural resources of the subsoil and the seabed of the continental shelf beneath the high seas but contiguous to the coasts of the U.S. as appertaining to the U.S., subject to its jurisdiction and control." The other proclamation, Number 2668, carefully differentiates jurisdiction over conservation zones in the water column from that over resources on the seabed beneath. *Id.* at 254.

[124] Fye, Maxwell, Emery & Ketchum, *Ocean Science and Marine Resources*, in USES OF THE SEA 66 (E. Gullion ed. 1968).

[125] STAFF OF SENATE COMMITTEE ON FOREIGN RELATIONS, 94TH. CONG. 1ST SESS., REPORT ON THIRD U.N. LAW OF THE SEA CONFERENCE 3 (Comm. Print 1975) (hereinafter cited as SENATE REPORT).

of the oceans contended that the peoples of the world have a basic natural right to communicate with one another and no one should bound or limit this right. Historically, demands by coastal states for the extension of their exclusive competence over high seas have been tolerated and honored by the community of states insofar as they did not interfere with the inclusive interest. The expansion of the territorial sea puts restraints upon transportation and communication, the most inclusive enjoyment of this shareable resource. A 12-mile territorial sea all around the globe would reduce the "high seas" by some 3 million square miles,[126] and it would "nationalize" approximately 112 international straits less than 24 miles wide.[127] Under the 1958 Geneva Convention on the Territorial Seas and Contiguous Zone and the existing customary international law, the passage of neither aircraft nor submerged submarines is ordinarily permitted in the territorial seas.[128] Consequently, the United States and the U.S.S.R. have put forward, as a condition to their acceptance of 12-mile territorial sea, a provision for a new right of "free transit or 'unimpeded passage.'"[129] "The United States' Delegation, particularly the Defense Department, considers this provision essential to the United States' national interests. They maintain that the current legal concept of 'innocent passage' is too ambiguous and would grant the coastal states a discretionary right to restrict the movement of vessels and planes through, over, and under international straits."[130]

The increase in ocean pollution has endangered interests of coastal states, both in terms of the health of the population and the exploitation of the living resources of the waters adjacent to the coast. To protect these interests, coastal states have sought to take protective measures against dangerous sources of pollution. Canada has been a leader in this matter, favoring the recognition of an exclusive competence on the part of the coastal states to establish environmental standards, pending an international agreement. Canada passed the Arctic Waters Pollution Prevention

[126] Uses of the Seas, *supra* note 124, at 6.

[127] Senate Report, *supra* note 125, at 2.

[128] *Id.*

[129] *Id.*

[130] *Id.*

Act, establishing an "antipollution zone" up to 100 nautical miles from the Arctic coast. The Act forbids pollution in that zone, imposes liability for violations, and authorizes comprehensive regulation and inspection of vessels to prevent pollution.[131] To justify its unilateral action, the Canadian Government explained that "a danger to the environment of a state constitutes a threat to its security";[132] the antipollution zone is based on the coastal state's right to self-defense. A similar claim has been made by the Iranian Government in an Act of 1974 extending the competence of the Government as far as 50 miles off the coast in the Gulf of Oman.[133]

Many coastal states now demand the establishment of "minimum ocean pollution standards."[134] The basic policy behind the demand is that if pollution standards are left to each coastal state, the array of different standards would impede the shipping industry and international trade and navigation. Each country would have to make choices between pollution control and availability of other goods and services necessary for the promotion of the internal value processes. The calculation would change from one country to another. Thus, some claim that they cannot apply high standard antipollution prescriptions because such application would increase the cost of the resources they need to import. Moreover, it could paralyze their young shipping industry since the price of antipollution devices would be too expensive for them. Hence, they demand that "the economic factors, including the stage of development of individual countries, be taken into ac-

---

[131]For example, "[A]ny deposit of waste must be reported (Sec. 5). The Governor in Council can require evidence of financial responsibility as a condition of passage (Sec. 8). He is authorized to prescribe shipping safety control zones, establish regulations for ships navigating in those zones and prohibit navigation and safety equipment, pilotage and ice-breaker escort (Sec. 11, 12). He may order the removal or destruction of ships or cargo which threaten pollution (Sec. 14–17). Many of the provisions apply as well to other activities which threaten pollution; *e.g.* the exploration and exploitation of natural resources." Henkin, *Arctic Anti-Pollution: Does Canada Make—or Break—International Law?* 65 Am. J. Int'l L. 131 (1971). For information about the Canadian Act, see Bilder, *The Canadian Arctic Waters Pollution Prevention Act: New Stresses on the Law of the Sea*, 69 Mich. L. Rev. 1 (1970); D. Pharand, The Law of the Sea of the Arctic, with Special Reference to Canada (1973).

[132]*Canadian Reply to the U.S. Government, supra* note 117, at 608.

[133]Principality of Iran, The Anti-Oil Pollution Act (1974).

[134]Stevenson & Oxman, *The Preparations of the Law of the Sea Conference*, 68 Am. J. Int'l L. 25 (1974).

count in both the formulation and implementation of all marine pollution control standards."[135] In rejecting such claims, developed countries are proposing a quasi compromise that would grant the competence to formulate antipollution standards to regional and global organizations.[136] Thus, it is argued that flexibility in control over pollution is extremely important "when one recognizes that specific controls would force many vessels toward inefficient production techniques and high costs."[137] This flexibility could be obtained through different liability acts.[138]

The need for scientific research in the sea has led to demands for free access for scientific purposes, not only to the high seas, but also to the territorial sea. These demands have been conditioned by many developing countries with regard to bona fide purposes and the disclosure of the outcomes, along with adequate interpretation and indication of the relevance of the information to the coastal state.

The most important part of the oceans in terms of resources is the continental shelf. All of the chemical and geological resources and about 90 percent of the biological resources have come from the shelf.[139] The world's continental shelves, with an area of 26.4 million Km^2, supplied $909 billion worth of resources during 1964.[140] The productivity of the shelves is only 5 to 17 percent that of the landmasses, but probable development of technology will increase the future productivity of the continental shelf, particularly with regard to chemical and geological resources.[141] The importance of the shelf has led to increasing claims for exclusive competence over the shelf as far into the sea as is exploitable.

Besides the mineral resources of the shelf, fishery resources in

[135]*Id.*

[136]Clarkson, *supra* note 90, at 134.

[137]Clarkson argues that "[i]f general liability rules, such as those illustrated in Table 1, are established, however, direct controls would not be necessary and would allow flexibility in meeting damage requirements." *Id.* at 134. See Table 1.

[138]R. Cooper, *An Economist's View of the Oceans* 48 (Nov. 1974) (Economic Growth Center, Yale University; Discussion Paper No. 219).

[139]SENATE REPORT, *supra* note 125, at 21.

[140]For example, countries such as Zaire, Chile, and Zambia derive a large share of their revenue from the export of the minerals contained in manganese nodules. *Id.*

[141]*Id.*

marginal seas have been claimed as subject to the jurisdiction of the coastal states. Conservation regulation has required the exercise of extraterritorial authority over extensive areas of the sea. Canada, in the Act of 1970 concerning exploitation and conservation of fisheries, claimed beyond a twelve-mile limit.[142] The United States has also proposed that coastal states extend their exclusive competence over the coastal species and salmon throughout their migratory range, subject to international standards of conservation.[143] Under this plan the coastal state could exercise its exclusive competence over minerals and living resources but the ocean would remain open for inclusive enjoyment of other values such as transportation and communication.[144]

The mineral resources of the deep seabed have also added a new dimension to controversy over inclusivity and exclusivity in relation to use and competence. In the nineteenth century it was discovered that what are called manganese nodules cover the deep ocean floor. These rocks contain small quantities of iron, copper, cobalt, nickel, and manganese. They are accumulating at a rate of 16 million tons a year.[145] Estimates of their abundance vary greatly; in the Pacific Ocean estimates have ranged from 100 billion tons to 1,600 billion tons.[146] In current international prescriptive efforts, the concept of a common enjoyment of deep seabed minerals has been accepted. The only disagreement is about the mode of regulation and management of these shareable resources. This disagreement relates to both the scope of competency of the Deep Seabed Authority, in terms of control of production and pricing, and the sharing of revenues resulting from these minerals. In addition, production of such minerals in any major degree could seriously upset trade patterns of various developing countries which produce the same minerals on their land masses.[147]

[142]Canada extends its jurisdiction over the Gulf of St. Lawrence, Hecate Strait, and Queen Charlotte Sound. *See* THE CHANGING LAW OF THE SEA; WESTERN HEMISPHERE PERSPECTIVES 24–26 (R. Zacklin ed. 1974).

[143]SENATE REPORT, *supra* note 125, at 3–4.

[144]McDougal & Schneider, *The Protection of the Environment and World Public Order: Some Recent Developments*, 45 MISS. L. J. 1085, 1093 (1974).

[145]*See* Cooper, note 138 *supra*.

[146]*Id.*

[147]Sweeney, Tollison & Willett, *Market Failure, the Common-Pool Problem, and Ocean Resource Exploitation*, 17 J. LAW & ECON. 182 (1974).

Table 1. Major provisions of treaties, statutes, and private schemes to increase liability for oil pollution damages

	Source of compensation	Coverage	Basis of liability	Exceptions
Limitation of liability(46 U.S.C. §183[1851])	Owner or charterer of vessel	Any vessel	Any damage from fault	Liability always obtains upon fault
Brussels Convention on Limitation of Liability(1957)	Owner of vessel	Seagoing vessels	Any damage from fault	Liability always obtains upon fault
Comité Maritime International (C.M.I.)	Registered owner of tanker	All ships carrying 2,000 T oil	Rebuttable presumption of fault for all damages	Liability always obtain upon fault
Intergovernmental Consultation Organization (I.M.C.O.)	Owner at time of incident	All ships carrying 2,000 T oil	Strict liability for all damages	1. War. 2. Phenomenal act of nature. 3. Act third party. 4. Negligen 5. Interference of plain
U.S. Public Law 91-224 (1970)	Owner or charterer of vessel	Vessel in U.S. territorial waters	Strict liability for clean-up expenses	1. Act of God. 2. Act war. 3. Act of negligen of U.S. government. 4. of a third party
Maine Public Laws, Chapter 572, 11-A §552	Coastal Protection Fund pays plaintiff and is reimbursed by oil terminal operations	State waters	Strict liability for all damages	1. Act of war. 2. Act government—feder state or municipal. 3. of God
Florida Statutes Annotated, Chapter 376, §12, et seq.	Coastal Protection Fund pays plaintiff and is reimbursed by oil terminal operators	State waters	Strict liability for all damages	1. Act of war. 2. Act government—feder state or municipal. 3. of God. 4. Act of thi party
Revised Code of Washington 90.48.315	Person having control over oil	State waters	Strict liability for all damages	1. Act of war or sabot. 2. Negligence of Uni States or Washington
TOVALOP	Owner of tanker	Damages to coastline	Rebuttable presumption of fault for clean-up cost	
CRISTAL	Oil Companies Institute for Marine Pollution Compensation, Ltd.	Same as I.M.C.O.	Same as I.M.C.O.	Same as I.M.C.O. p posed Convention on Liability

Limit of liability	Court with jurisdiction	Relationship with other laws	Instances of unlimited liability	Financial responsibility required	Statute of limitation
Value of vessel and freight pending for property damage $60 per net ton for personal injury or loss of life	U.S. district court with admiralty jurisdiction	Exclusive remedy in federal court except for "savings to suitor" cases	Privity or fault of owner or charterer	None	Laches
$67 per net ton for property damage, $207 per net ton for personal injury or loss of life	U.S. district court with admiralty jurisdiction	Exclusive remedy in federal court except for "savings to suitor" cases	Privity or fault of owner or charterer	None	Laches
$67 per not ton less clean-up expenditures of defendant	Any country where damage occurs	Exclusive remedy for oil-pollution damages	None	To extent of potential liability	2 years after incident
$134.40 per net ton or $14,112,000, whichever is lesser minus the defendant's clean-up expenditures	Any country where damage occurs	Exclusive remedy for oil-pollution damages	If fault or privity of owner	To extent of potential liability	3 years after damage discovered but not more than 6 years after the incident
$100 per net ton or $14,000,000, whichever is the lesser	U.S. district court with admiralty jurisdiction	Supplemental to other remedies	Willful negligence or willful misconduct of owner or in privity with the owner	For vessels larger than 300 gross tons	Laches
No limit	Maine state courts	Supplemental	Always	None	6 months
No limit	Florida state courts	Supplemental	Always	Depends on tonnage, etc.	3 years
No limit	Washington State courts	Supplemental	Always		
...00 per gross registered ton or $10,000,...o whichever is the lesser	Any country where damage occurs	Supplemental	None	None	
...umulated total to ...,000,000 for all expenses	Same as I.M.C.O. proposed Convention on Civil Liability	Supplemental	None	None	Same as C.L.C.

Source: John G. Gissberg, Civil Liability for Oil Pollution Damage from Tankers and Other Ocean Going Vessels 25 (1972) (unpublished Ph.D. dissertation in the University of Michigan Law Library)

These countries are demanding that the Seabed Authority be empowered with almost monopoly control over the exploration and exploitation of the seabed minerals.[148] Many feel that the developing countries should be the principal recipients of the revenues derived.

The United States position with regard to deep seabed mining has been to promote a licensing system designed to give U.S. corporations nondiscriminatory access to the resources under conditions that will protect the integrity of the firms' interest.[149] The American position has been supported by economists in free market societies. Their economic analysis suggests that access to the seabed should be as wide as possible;[150] hence, they are in favor of a licensing system and high competition in seabed mining.[151] The opposing argument contends that unregulated market activity will lead to too rapid a depletion of resources; the market system, this argument goes, is not able to lead to a correct investment-and-production decision because of a failure of the private investor to use a socially appropriate discount rate.[152] Unregulated competition would result in malexploitation, maldistribution, and international conflict.[153] U.S. firms believe that, without the creation of a system of property rights in specific deposits, continued investment in discovery effort and mining equipment will be discouraged.[154] They claim that private profit-motivated access to deepsea mining will not result in the overexploitation of ocean minerals. Hence, they argue there is no need, on economic grounds, to create an international regulatory authority to supervise ocean resource exploitation.[155]

[148]Eckert, *Exploitation of Deep Ocean Minerals: Regulatory Mechanisms and United States Policy*, 17 J. LAW & ECON. 143 (1974).

[149]Statements of T. S. Ary, Union Carbide Exploitation Corp.; C. H. Burgess, Kennecott Corp.; & John E. Flipse, Deepsea Ventures, Inc.; in *Development of Hard Mineral Resources of the Deep Seabed: Hearings on S. 2801 Before the Subcomm. on Minerals, Materials & Fuels of the Senate Comm. on Interior Affairs*, 92d Cong. 2d Sess., 25–44 (1972) *cited* in *id.* at 143–44.

[150]Eckert, *supra* note 148, at 192.

[151]USES OF THE SEAS, *supra* note 124, at 3.

[152]*Id.* at 4.

[153]THE PUBLIC ORDER OF THE OCEANS, *supra* note 111, at 11–12, footnote omitted.

[154]*Id.*

[155]ANGLO-NORWEGIAN FISHERIES CASE [1951] I.C.J. 3; H. STEINER & D. VAGTS, MATERIALS ON TRANSNATIONAL LEGAL PROBLEMS 197 (1968).

Because of their immense potentialities for the increased production and distribution of all values, and in the absence of alternative resources, ocean resources are critical to securing the common interest of the global community. Happily, the general recognition of such a common interest with respect to the management of the oceans can still be observed: "The delimitation of sea areas has always an international aspect; it cannot be dependent merely upon the will of the coastal states as expressed in its [*sic*] municipal law. Although it is true that the act of delimitation is necessarily a unilateral act, because only the coastal state is competent to undertake it, the validity of the delimitation with regard to other states depends upon international law."[156]

The balancing of inclusivity and exclusivity in relation to ocean resources is now undergoing considerable changes. Both multilateral conventions and unilateral state practices are molding a new international law in this area. The future law, it seems, will increase the jurisdiction of the coastal states substantially, though the form of exclusive practices may change and may be subjected to review by a more inclusive competence.

2. International Rivers

The ubiquity of international rivers and the interdependencies in their use have comparably required that such resources not be subjected to exclusive use. Because of their great potentials, the general community has expressed demands for inclusive use. The overriding community goal has been the widest possible sharing of river resources, for experience shows that the exclusive use of rivers running through more than one state is likely to result in increasing friction between the states, especially as modern technology makes the river more valuable and accessible. Such tensions may lead not merely to underutilization but also to serious disturbances of minimum order.[157]

The practices of the past century reflect an increasing shared use of these resources. Contemporary science and technology make such sharing even more urgent. The traditional uses of navi-

[156] H. Hajnal, The Danube: Its Historical, Political and Economic Importance 16 (1920).

[157] R. Nathan, International Rivers in Public Order (1966) (unpublished paper in the Yale Law School).

gation, domestic consumption, irrigation, and power production are now of vastly greater importance than before. The greater shared use of international rivers through participation of at least riparian states in regional development is necessary to maximize the values derived from such rivers. In allocating use and competence, all relevant factors, such as a nation's needs, the capacity to develop and use a river effectively, and the historical use of the river, have all been, and should be, taken into account. Thus, discrimination has not been permitted against participants who, because of a slow early development, did not achieve the technology and ability to exploit a river to the same extent as other riparians.

In the beginning the limited interdependence of states and the comparatively minor impact of exclusive uses of international rivers on the larger community led to a general tolerance of some exclusive competence of individual riparians over the part of a river within their territory. In the middle ages practices such as heavy legal charges for navigation of Zeeland on the Scheldt, of the towns along the banks of the Danube, and of Cologne and Mainz on the Rhine were widely accepted.[158] There were numerous river tolls and shipping duties.[159] Toward the end of the sixteenth century and the beginning of the seventeenth century, the rules governing international rivers changed due to new political and economic conditions. The creation of independent states in Europe and the increase in trade stimulated demands for changes in navigation regulation and heavy taxes.[160] States on the banks of such rivers as the Rhine, Meuse, and Scheldt tended to regard the rivers as their exclusive property and imposed high levies on those using the rivers. That aroused strong criticism in the early seventeenth century.[161]

Grotius was an early supporter of unrestricted freedom of trade on all rivers. His principle was the basis of the treaties of Westphalia, "the first of their kind, . . . based on the principle of the interdependence of all nations on each other."[162] Although the

[158] HAJNAL, *supra* note 156, at 9.

[159] *Id.*

[160] *Id.* at 15.

[161] *Id.* at 16.

[162] *Id.*

treaty of Westphalia was a failure in its application, it encouraged the including of provisions for free navigation in later peace treaties.[163] Later treaties, such as those for free navigation on the Po River[164] and the Danube,[165] abolished the medieval practices. Their scope was, however, limited to the contracting parties.[166]

Occasionally, claims for the exclusive use of rivers have been made. The most extreme expression of such a claim is the Harmon Doctrine. Harmon, the U.S. Attorney General in the controversy over the Rio Grande, in his response to a Mexican claim stated "[t]hat the rules of international law imposed upon the United States no duty to deny to its inhabitants the use of the water of that part of the Rio Grande lying wholly within the United States, although such use resulted in reducing the volume of water in the river below the point where it ceased to be entirely within the United States, the supposition of the existence of such a duty being inconsistent with the sovereign jurisdiction of the United States over the national domain."[167] The Harmon Doctrine, however, was a mere claim and did not become expressive of community expectations. Actions taken by one riparian in that part of an international river system within its own boundaries may affect co-riparians, as well as other more distant states. It is now regarded as impermissible for one state to take unilateral actions to promote its own interests without regard for the more inclusive interests and the interests of other particular states.

Even the Harmon Doctrine was some years later rejected by the officials of the United States. Deputy Assistant Secretary of State Frederick W. Jandrey, Jr., in the course of hearings on the question of the proposed diversions by Canada of waters from the upper Columbia River, stated: "Among other things our memorandum deals with this view and points out that international law, as it has developed in this field in recent years, has solidified the principle of the equitable apportionment of waters which cross international boundaries. The fundamental doctrine concerned is, of course,

---

[163] For such treaties, see *id.* at 20–23.

[164] *Id.* at 10.

[165] *Id.*

[166] *Id.* at 13–14.

[167] *See* MOORE, *supra* note 113, at 653.

that of not using one's own property rights to injure the property rights of others."[168]

In practice the shared use of, and competence over, international rivers has continuously been recognized and honored by states. The European practice of inclusive competence over international rivers has been summarized in several opinions of the Permanent Court of International Justice. In the *Jurisdiction of the European Commission of the Danube Case*, the Court observed:

> Prior to 1815, the right to navigate rivers which separated or traversed two or more States was not regulated by any general principle or general act, and formed a subject of constant dispute. For the most part, each State sought to monopolize the navigation of streams flowing through its own territory, and even the right to an upper riparian State to access to the sea was denied. As the existence of such conditions not only hampered the development of commerce but also tended to prevent the growth of international relations appropriate to a state of peace, the Parties to the general international conflict which covered the concluding years of the XVIIth century and the earlier parts of the XIXth, introduced into arrangements by which this long period of warfare was ended, provisions for the freedom of navigation of international streams.[169]

More inclusive policies on the use of international rivers have been formulated with respect to navigation. Free navigation for commercial shipping or riparian states was the basis for early treaties on the establishment of international river commissions,[170] though the scope of freedom of navigation was limited.[171] The Final Act of the Congress of Vienna, for example, was drafted in such a way as to restrict the right of navigation to the riparian states.[172] Article

---

[168] *See* Caylin & Bianchi, *The Role of Adjudication in International River Disputes*, 53 AM. J. INT'L L. 45 (1959).

[169] [1927] P.C.I.J., ser. B. No. 14 at 38.

[170] For some examples see R. BAXTER, THE LAW OF INTERNATIONAL WATERWAYS 110 n. 74 (1964).

[171] *Id.* In the convention between France and Germany on the Control of Navigation of the Rhine, signed at Paris, the Control Administration guaranteed free navigation on the Rhine only to the two signatories, France and Germany, and only on the part of river which they shared.

[172] Article 1 of the Articles concerning the Navigation of the Rhine, annexed to the Final Act of the Congress of Vienna, signed June 9, 1815, 2 Martens Nouveau Recueil 416 (1818);

I of the Mannheim Act of 1868 establishing free navigation on the Rhine for "the transport of merchandise and persons" was limited by the clause immediately following to the "condition of conforming to the stipulations contained in the present convention and the measures prescribed for the maintenance of the general security." [173]

Sometimes nonriparian states have claimed rights of common enjoyment of international rivers. When the Riparian Commission on the Danube reserved the right of navigation only to riparian states (with the exception of navigation between the high seas and river ports) the nonriparian states parties to the Treaty of Paris protested. [174] A similar view had been expressed in the Treaty of London of 1839 for the Scheldt. There, the mouth end of the lower part of the river was free to all vessels. [175] Similarly, from 1866 the River Pruth was opened to vessels of all nations. [176] There is no clear precedent for the right of navigation by landlocked states through rivers passing several states, but most jurists agree in principle that the privilege of innocent passage should not be totally refused when the passage is in the interest of the universal commerce. [177]

---

see the seventh meeting of the Committee, on the Freedom of Fluvial Navigation, March 3, 1815; 1 RHEINURKUNDEN 124 (1918); see also G. KAECKENBEECH, INTERNATIONAL RIVERS, 46–47 (1918).

[173] Article 1 of the revised convention for the Navigation of the Rhine, signed at Mannheim Oct. 17, 1868, 20 Martens Nouveau Recueil 355 (1875), 2 RHEINURKUNDEN 80 (1918) *quoted in id.* As the result of this clause, the treatment of riparians was different from the treatments of nonriparians.

[174] *See id.* at 112.

[175] *Id.*

[176] *Id.* There were some restrictions in the Treaty, but they were of minor significance.

[177] Among jurists who expressed this view are Grotius, Bluntschli, Calvo, Puffendorf, Vattel, and Wheaton. Grotius believed that "in the establishment of separate property, which he [Grotius] conceived grew by agreement out of an original community of goods, there were reserved for the public benefit certain of the pre-existing natural rights, and that one of these was the passage over territory, whether by land or by water, and whether in the form of navigation of rivers from commercial purposes, or of any army over neutral ground, which he held to be an innocent use, the concession of which it was not competent to a nation to refuse." *See* H. BRIGGS, THE LAW OF NATIONS 265 (2d ed. 1952). Bolivia, for example, is isolated from the coast, and it relies on the Amazon River for its access to the Atlantic Ocean through Brazil. And in application of article 5 of the Treaty of Delimitation between Bolivia and Brazil, signed at Petropolis (1903) 3 Martens N.R.G. 3rd ser. 62 (1910) and the Treaty of Commerce and Fluvial Navigation between these two countries, the Amazon became open for free navigation. 3 Martens N.R.G. 3rd ser. 62, 65 (1910).

Inclusive interests have also been recognized with regard to other river uses. The United States position in the settlement of the Columbia River with Canadians contradicted the Harmon Doctrine. This contradiction in the American view may be explained by the fact that the United States was the upper riparian on the Rio Grande and the lower riparian on the Columbia. Nevertheless, the Columbia River Treaty represents a trend toward a more inclusive use of international rivers. It adopts a more "flexible and individualistic case-by-case method of problem-solving"— the doctrine of equitable apportionment: "Equitable apportionment [has] emerged as the widely favoured principle. This concept embodying the notion of fair sharing, was extolled almost without exception by lawyers, scholars, and statesmen on both sides of the border."[178]

The doctrine of equitable apportionment has been recognized by Canada and the United States in other treaties[179] and affirmed in other international conventions. Article I of the 1923 Geneva Convention Relating to the Development of Hydraulic Power Affecting More than One State imposes limitations on exclusive use by the riparian state on the development of hydraulic power on common rivers.[180] In 1951 the Economic Commission for Asia and the Far East (ECAFE) suggested a study of the lower Mekong within Laos, Thailand, Cambodia, and Vietnam which was accepted by the governments. The four governments, "[c]onsidering that this study is of real usefulness for their economic development; [e]xpress the wish that such studies be continued jointly by the four countries concerned in order to determine with more detail in what measure the various projects concerning hydro-electric power, navigation, drainage and flood control can be of use to

---

[178] R. JOHNSON, THE LAW OF INTERNATIONAL DRAINAGE BASINS 235 (1967).

[179] For example, the 1967 Report of the International Joint Commission on the Cooperative Development of the Pembina River Basin complained in this connection that "[t]he Boundary Waters Treaty of 1909 provides no guidance in the matter of apportionment of waters in rivers which cross the international boundary. Article II states the principle that each country, along with its respective Provincial and State Governments, normally retains 'exclusive jurisdiction and control over the use and diversion' of all the upstream waters on its own side of the boundary. . . . [T]he basis for the apportionment required to bring about this cooperative development for the Pembina must be derived from sources outside the Treaty. 'Reports of the International Joint Commission on the Cooperative Development of the Pembina River Basin.'" Id. at 30–31.

[180] 105 L.N.T.S 223 (1923).

a number of countries."[181] This agreement among the above four countries itself represents application of the principle of inclusive enjoyment by cooperation in the development and the use of international rivers. The 1972 Report of the U.N. Conference on the Human Environment also reflects this doctrine.[182]

Many national courts have similarly upheld the principle of the inclusive enjoyment in the use of common rivers. In 1878 a Swiss Court held in *Aorgau v. Zurich* that riparians do not own the water, and because of sovereign equality of riparians, none may exercise sovereignty over common rivers to the detriment of other riparians.[183] An Italian Court in 1939 in *Societé Energie Electrique du Littoral Mediterranéen v. Compagnia Impreses Electtriche Liquri*, held:

> International law recognises the right on the part of every riparian State to enjoy as a participant of a kind of partnership created by the river, all the advantages deriving from it for the purpose of securing the welfare and the economic and civil progress of the nation. . . . [H]owever, although a State in the exercise of its rights of Sovereignty, may subject public rivers to whatever regime it seems best, it cannot disregard the international duty derived from that principle, not to impose or to destroy, as a result of this regime the opportunity of the other States to avail themselves of the flow of water for their own national needs.[184]

In 1922 a German Court in *Würtemberg and Prussia v. Baden* held that

> the exercise of sovereign rights by every State in regard to international rivers traversing its territory is limited by the duty not to injure the interest of other members of the international community. Due consideration must be given to one another by States through whose territories there flows an international river. No State may substantially impair the natural use of the flow of such a river by its neighbor. This principle has gained increased recognition in international relations, in particular in modern times when the increased exploitation of the natural

---

[181] Development of Water Resources in the Lower Mekong Basin U.N. Doc. E/CN. 11/457, ST/ECAFE/SER/12 (1951), *cited in* Griffin, *The Use of Waters of International Drainage Basins Under Customary International Law*, 53 Am. J. Int'l. L. 58 (1959).

[182] U.N. Doc. A/Conf. 48/14 (1972).

[183] H. Smith, The Economic Uses of International Rivers 104 (3d ed. 1972).

[184] Italian Court of Cassation, 1938–40 Annual Digest No. 47, at 120.

power of flowing water has led to a contractual regulation of the interests of States connected by international rivers. The application of this principle is governed by the circumstances of each particular case. The interests of the States in question must be weighed in an equitable manner against one another. One must consider not only the absolute injury caused to the neighboring State, but also the relation of the advantage gained by one to the injury caused to the other.[185]

The same principle has been recognized by U.S. courts in many cases.[186]

In the promotion of inclusive interests through the customary international law of common rivers, publicists have also played an important role. Oppenheim, rejecting the Harmon Doctrine, presents a rather unorthodox view: "Just like independence, territorial supremacy does not give a boundless liberty of action. . . . [A] state is, in spite of its territorial supremacy, not allowed to alter the natural conditions of the territory of a neighbouring state, for instance, to stop or divert the flow of a river which runs from its own into neighbouring territory."[187] Sauser-Hall, examining the domestic law of the United States, Switzerland, Italy, Germany, and France, expressed the opinion that no diversion of a stream which strongly prejudices the right of other riparians or communities whose territories are bordered or traversed by the same stream is lawful.[188] Lauterpacht in exploring the responsibility of states says: "The responsibility of a state may become involved as the result of an abuse of a right enjoyed by virtue of international law. This occurs when a State avails itself of its right in an arbitrary manner in such a way as to inflict upon another State an injury which cannot be justified by a legitimate consideration of its own advantage. . . . [T]he duty of the State not to interfere with the flow of a river to the detriment of other riparian States has its source in the same principle."[189] Professor McDougal classifies in-

---

[185] *See* SMITH, *supra* note 183, at 54, 117.

[186] Kansas v. Colorado, 206 U.S. 46 (1907).

[187] Oppenheim *quoted by* Barden, HOUSE OF COMMONS DEBATES III Sess. 11th Parliament 903–04 (1910–11).

[188] Sauser-Hall, *L'utilisation Industrielle des Fleunes Internationaux*, 83 RECUEIL DES COURS 517 (Academie de Droit International) (II–1952).

[189] 1 L. OPPENHEIM, INTERNATIONAL LAW, 345 (8th ed. H. Lauterpacht ed. 1955). Oppenheim observes: "The practice of states, as evidenced in the controversies which have arisen

ternational rivers as shareable resources like the oceans; both require shared use for the fullest production and widest distribution of common values.[190]

> [E]very particular river basin has its own peculiar unities and interdependences—unities and interdependences in the physical interrelation of land and water and different kind of waters, in the technology of necessary control, and in the reciprocal impact of different uses upon each other—and that the effective, conserving, and reproductive regulation of any particular basin requires that all these unities and interdependences be taken into account.
>
> . . . From this perspective, it follows that no single State should be accorded a permanent veto over development in the common river.[191]

Resolutions adopted by international private associations have also expressed preference for the protection of the inclusive interest. The Institut de Droit International at its Madrid Conference in 1911 supported the inclusive interest and rejected the complete exclusive competence of riparian states over the parts of rivers

---

about this matter, seems now to admit that each state concerned has a right to have a river system considered as a whole, and to have its own interests weighed in the balance against those of other states, and that no one state may claim to use the waters in such a way as to cause material injury to the interests of another, or to oppose their use by another state unless this causes material injury to itself." *Id.* at 347. Berber regards absolute territorial sovereignty as "based upon an individualistic, anarchical conception of international law, in which selfish interests are exclusively taken as the rule of conduct and no solution is offered regarding the opposite interests of upper and lower riparians." *See* Griffin, *supra* note 181, at 70.

H. R. Farnham holds the theory that "[a] river which flows through the territory of several states or nations is their common property. . . . It is a great natural highway conferring besides the facilities of navigation, certain incidental advantages, such as fishery and the right to use the water for power and irrigation. Neither nation can do any act which will deprive the other of the benefits of those rights and advantages. The inherent right of a nation to protect itself and its territory would justify the one lower down the stream in preventing by force the one further up from turning the river out its course or in consuming so much of the water for purposes of its own as to deprive the former of its benefits. . . . The gifts of nature are for the benefit of mankind, and no aggregation of man can assert and exercise such right and ownership of them as will deprive others having equal rights, and means of enjoyment. . . . [T]he common right to enjoy bountiful provisions of Providence must be preserved. . . ." H. FARNHAM, THE LAW OF WATERS AND WATER RIGHTS 33 (1904) *cited in* F. BERBER, RIVERS IN INTERNATIONAL LAW, at 22 (1955).

[190] INT'L L. ASSOC., REPORT OF THE 48TH CONFERENCE, NEW YORK CITY 46 (1958).

[191] *Id.* at 42–43.

flowing through their territories.[192] Several reports presented at the Seventh Inter-American Conference held at Montevideo in 1933 also underline the principle of equality of rights of co-riparians.[193] In 1956 the International Law Association Conference held in Dubrovnik recognized "the common interests of States in the great sharable resource of international rivers and began to clarify the appropriate principles and procedures for the development of that resource to common advantage."[194]

The Inter-American Bar Association at its Tenth Conference in Buenos Aires in November 1957 unanimously adopted a resolution in which the principle of equality of rights of co-riparians was considered the existing international law.[195] The International Law Association in later meetings in 1958 in New York resolved that "each co-riparian state is entitled to a reasonable equitable share in the beneficial uses of the waters of the drainage basin."[196]

---

[192] 24 Annuaire de L'Institut de Droit International 170 (1911).

[193] This principle became known as the Declaration of Montevideo. The text of the Declaration may be found in *Final Act of the Seventh International Conference of American States*, INTERNATIONAL CONFERENCES OF AMERICAN STATES, 88–89 (1933–1940) *cited in* Laylin & Bianchi, *supra* note 168, at 96.

[194] Article III of Dubrovnik Conf. Says: "[W]hile each state has sovereignty over the international rivers within its own boundaries, the State must exercise this control with due consideration for its effects upon other riparian states.

Article IV reads: "A state is responsible, under international law, for providing change in the existing regime of a river to the injury of another state, which it could have prevented by reasonable diligence." INT'L L. ASSOC., REPORT OF THE 47TH CONFERENCE, DUBROVNIK (1956); see also INT'L L. ASSOC., REPORT OF THE 48TH CONFERENCE, NEW YORK CITY 41 (1958) (Comment of M. McDougal).

[195] U.N. INTEGRATED RIVER BASIN DEVELOPMENT 33, U.N. Doc. E/3066, (1958).

[196] INT'L L. ASSOC., REPORT OF THE 52ND CONFERENCE, HELINSKI 486 (1966). In examining the equitable share, Article V reads:

"1. What is a reasonable and equitable share within the meaning of Article IV is to be determined in the light of all the relevant factors in each particular case.

"(2) Relevant factors which are to be considered include, but [are] not limited to

"(a) the geography of the basin, including in particular the extent of the drainage area in the territory each basin State;

"(b) the hydrology of the basin, including in particular the contribution of water by each basin State;

"(c) the climate affecting the basin;

Present community expectations about the use of international rivers were stated by the Fifty-second Report of the International Law Association, in Helsinki: "Each basin State is entitled, within its territory, to a reasonable and equitable shre in the beneficial uses of the waters of international drainage basin."[197]

It may, thus, be concluded that international rivers—in all their multiple uses relating to the movement of goods, the generation of electric power, the irrigation of land, industrial and domestic consumption, and so on—have come to be regarded as in high degree shareable resources, with priority being given to inclusive use and competence. At present the general community obviously gives a greater protection to the more inclusive interest in the use of international rivers. This trend is manifested in an increasing tendency of states to settle their conflicts about the use of common waters by means of agreements that protect their more inclusive interests. This trend is approved by many publicists and decision makers. The opinion in the famous *Lake Lanoux Case* was, for example, a clear rejection of the exclusive appropriation of international rivers. Creation of regional and multiregional bodies, often with the participation of the U.N. specialized agencies, was further encouraged for the promotion of inclusive interests.

"(d) the past utilization of the waters of the basin, including in particular existing utilization;

"(e) the economic and social needs of each basin State;

"(f) the population dependent on the wastes of the basin in each basin State;

"(g) the comparative costs of alternative means of satisfying the economic and social needs of each basin State;

"(h) the availability of other resources;

"(i) the avoidance of unnecessary waste in utilization of waters of the basin;

"(j) the practicability of compensation to one or none of the co-basin State as a means of adjusting conflicts among these; and

"(k) the degree to which the needs of a basin State may be satisfied without causing substantial injury to a co-basin State;

"(3) the weight to be given to each factor is to be determined by its importance in comparison with that of other relevant factors. In determining what is a reasonable and equitable share, all relevant factors are to be considered together and a conclusion reached on the basis of the whole." *Id.* at 488.

[197] *Id.* at 486.

3. Space, Including Outer Space

Among the important resources lately subjected to demands for shared use and competence is the space above nation-states, including outer space. As a vast "space-extension" resource enveloping the whole globe and extending indefinitely outward, this particular resource preeminently admits of shared use, with high promise of extraordinary riches in the shaping and sharing of values from such use.[198] In the present state of technology and relative lack of knowledge about the potentialities of space for stock and flow resources, the immediate utility of space relates largely to transportation and communication. With appropriate accommodation, one use made of space for such purposes need not interfere with other uses made for the same purposes; the production and distribution of values through employment of this resource can be made cumulative, not competitive or destructive. The exploitation of "airspace" in close proximity to the surface of the earth may of course be attended by special dangers to the society of particular communities on such surface.[199] Yet these special dangers may be taken into account in the allocation of inclusive and exclusive competence for the regulation of such activities. The allocation and accomodation of inclusive and exclusive competences with respect to the exploitation and enjoyment of space in general has been, as it should be, effected through a careful contextual analysis of all relevant factors.

The development of community policies with respect to space began with "airspace," when any idea of the use of outer space was still remote. The historic policy behind the assertion and honoring of exclusive competence of states in airspace has been for security. States sought to exercise sovereignty over airspace above their territories by vertical boundaries upward to a distance that would give adequate and reasonable protection. Today, however, with aircraft and rocket developments, protection of the minimum order of a state may not necessarily be secured by exclusive jurisdiction over superjacent space. Many observers note that the threat may come from space outside the state boundaries or from the

---

[198] *See* M. McDougal, H. Lasswell & I. Vlasic, Law and Public Order in Space 193, 770 (1963) (hereinafter cited as Law and Public Order in Space).

[199] *Id.* at 267.

distant reaches of outer space.[200] If every state could expand its sovereignty up to the point necessary for its protection, the result would be only "anarchy and endless strife."[201]

The early conception of state sovereignty over airspace was based on the general notion of property and the specific duty of the state to secure the private property rights of its citizens: "The State cannot give the landowner a right of property or of use over the airspace above his land, if that airspace is not submitted to its sovereignty. Consequently, by giving such a right to the landowner, the State says that it considers itself sovereign over the airspace."[202] It has been observed that the protection of rights in airspace above the land goes back as far as to the Romans, but there is no general opinion as to "whether such rights were rights of complete ownership or merely rights to so much of the airspace as needed for the enjoyment of the surface property below."[203] J. C. Cooper explains the asserted exclusive competence of the state over airspace above its territory as essential for the protection of the internal interests of the state.[204] Cooper assumes that the exclusive interests

[200]*Id.* at 322. *See also* Deresford, *The Future of National Sovereignty*, in Second Collo-QUIUM ON THE LAW OF OUTER SPACE (A. Haley & W. Heinrich eds. 1959). Deresford observes: "The inadequacy of sovereignty for purposes of national defense is shown by the 'hovering' of foreign ships or aircraft outside territorial limits. For example, submarines may lurk beyond the marginal sea but close enough to launch their missiles against cities and other targets on land. Intercontinental bombers may remain airborne, perhaps over international waters. Satellites already in orbit may be equipped to bomb strategic targets on radio command. Traditional national sovereignty could provide no protection against such threats unless extended to fantastic extremes. In addition, intercontinental missiles in their own homeland may be present for delivery against foreign targets." *Id.* at 5, 8. *See also* Johnson, *The Future of Manned Space Flight, and the "Freedom" of Outer Space*, NASA NEWS RELEASE, Aug. 4, 1962, at 4–5; L. LIPSON & N. KATZENBACH, REPORT OF THE NATIONAL AERONAUTICS AND SPACE ADMINISTRATION ON THE LAW OF OUTER SPACE 10–11 (1961).

[201]LAW AND PUBLIC ORDER IN SPACE, *supra* note 198, at 322.

[202]J. LYCKLAMA À NIJEHOLT, AIR SOVEREIGNTY, *quoted in* EXPLORATION IN AIR-SPACE LAW, 56 (I. Vlasic ed. 1968). The same principle has been mentioned in E. RICHARDS, SOVEREIGNTY OVER THE AIR 12 (1912), and in INTERNATIONAL L. ASSOC., REPORT OF THE COMMITTEE UPON AVIATION TO THE 28TH CONFERENCE, 1913. Protection of the owner of the air above his land has been recognized in a general term in many national laws. For example, the civil codes adopted in the nineteenth century in many states, including France, Austria, Germany, and Italy, and in the Province of Quebec (Canada), together with judicial decision of Great Britain and the United States, recognized this right. But none of them made clear the height above the surface which comes under the control of the owner, and also the nature and the scope of the right.

[203]EXPLORATION IN AIRSPACE LAW, *id.* at 59.

[204]Cooper, *Roman Law and Maxim "Cujus est Solum" in International Air Law*, in *id.* at 59.

of individual states could not be protected other than by assertions of absolute territorial sovereignty, an assumption that now seems too broad and rigid.[205]

In the early twentieth century, with the expansion of commercial flights, legal regulations began to emerge. The first diplomatic negotiation on flight regulation was the Paris Conference of May 10, 1910. The basic stimulus for this Conference was French concern over the flight of German balloons over French territory. This Conference, composed of only European countries, agreed upon the principle of state sovereignty over airspace by granting the right to the state to set up prohibited zones through which no international flight was lawful, recognized that internal transportation could be reserved for national aircraft, and provided that the establishment of internal airlanes could depend on the agreement of the interested states: "no general freedom of international transit [innocent passage] for aircraft of all states existed as a matter of international law in the usable space over sovereign States."[206] The Paris Conference of 1910 was the first diplomatic conference in which the principle of inclusive enjoyment of space was introduced. Paul Fauchille, a French Jurist, who remained the principal advocate of the freedom of space,[207] stated that, though air navigation is free "[n]evertheless subjacent States reserve rights necessary to their self-preservation, that is to their own security and that of the persons and goods of their inhabitants."[208]

The conclusion of the 1910 Paris Conference was the conferring of full sovereignty on each state in space over its national land,

---

Cooper observes: "Much of the confused thinking in dealing with air law problems in the past has stemmed from failure to realize that land and usable space above are legally indivisible and necessarily constitute a single social unit. Usable space is not an appurtenance to the land below but with such land forms the basic integrated sphere of human activity and has been for that reason treated by states as part of their territory. A state may not impose sanctions within the territory of another state. If a state is found to be protecting exclusive rights in a fixed area state cannot legally impose its will in any area to the exclusion of all other states if such area is outside its accepted and recognized territory.

[205] *Id.*

[206] *Id.*

[207] *See* Fauchille, *Le Domaine Aeriel et le Regime Juridique des Aerostats*, 8 REVUE GENERALE DE DROIT INTERNATIONAL PUBLIC 414 (1901).

[208] 23 ANNUAIRE DE L'INSTITUT DE DROIT INTERNATIONAL 297–311 (1910), *cited in* EXPLORATION IN AIRSPACE LAW, *supra* note 202, at 109.

rejection of any division of usable space into horizontal zones, and the rejection of the existence of any general right of international commerce for aircraft.[209] The conference was a political failure; the member states did not agree on the kinds of restrictions which could be applied by the subjacent state to aircraft of other contracting states without restraining future development of international flight.[210] But thereafter state practice tended toward more exclusive control of airspace. The 1911 British Aerial Navigation Act and its supplement of 1913 prescribed the principle of exclusive competence.[211] France, Germany, and Britain unilaterally granted themselves more control over airspace by the decrees of 1911 and the following years.[212] This practice of state control over usable space of national territories was acknowledged and restated during World War I and the Paris Convention of 1919.

The Paris Convention was an outgrowth of World War I. Some criticized the outcome of the Conference as a reflection of wartime philosophy. Albert Roper condemned "this brutal suppression of the freedom of the sky, so clear to eminent jurists in the early years of the century."[213] He strongly criticized the governments, who were concerned about the inclusive interest in the application of their rights of sovereignty over their space, none of whom made any attempt to change the general restricted policy.[214]

Eight years after the abortive Paris Convention, the countries of the Western Hemisphere concluded an agreement, known as the Havana Convention. According to it the contracting states in time of peace were to accord freedom of innocent passage to private aircraft of member states, subject to some conditions.[215]

The important role of aircraft during World War II reinforced the significance of the exclusive right of nations over their airspace. In 1939 the Government of the Netherlands claimed sov-

[209] J. Cooper, The Right to Fly, 19–20 (1947).

[210] Exploration in Airspace Law, *supra* note 202, at 118–20.

[211] Cooper, *State Sovereignty in Space: Developments from 1910 to 1914* at 127.

[212] *Id.* at 128–30.

[213] Roper, *Recent Development in International Aeronautical Law*, I. J. Airlaw & Com. 395, 405–06 (1930), *cited in* A. Haley, Space Law and Government 46 (1963).

[214] *Haley, id.* at 49.

[215] *Id.*

ereignty over the space above its territory up to a unlimited altitude.[216] This position was taken in response to the German claim to the right to overfly the Netherlands and Belgium at a height in excess of three miles. The German claim was based on the theory that national sovereignty over airspace is limited to a distance equal to the maritime territorial sea.[217]

Toward the end of World War II, in 1944, a Convention on International Civil Aviation was concluded in Chicago. This Convention, under the influence of the war and the vital role of aircraft, recognized the sovereignty of states over their space explicitly—"every state has complete and absolute sovereignty over the airspace above its territory."[218] The Chicago Convention is the most recent major international agreement concerning civil aviation. It has been ratified by sixty-seven states and is in force today.[219] Some have observed that with the principles adopted by the Chicago Convention, the doctrine of absolute sovereignty over airspace is now firmly placed in international law.[220]

During the 1950s, with the expansion of international scientific development in space activities, there were new attempts for international cooperation. The International Geophysical Year (IGY) was a major effort to this end. International cooperation in the study of the physical environment has not been a new phenomenon. International cooperation in gathering geophysical data began in 1882–83 with the first International Polar Year; a second Conference took place fifty years later, in 1932–33.[221] The IGY

[216]*Id.*, at 52.

[217]34 Am. J. Int'l L. 104 (1940.)

[218]61 Stat. 1180, T.I.A.S. No. 1591 (1947). The term *territory* under the convention is defined as "the land areas and territorial waters adjacent thereto under the sovereignty, seizerainty, protection of mandate of such state." Art. 2, *id.*

[219]The contracting states who have ratified the Convention are: Afghanistan, Argentina, Australia, Austria, Belgium, Bolivia, Brazil, Burma, Ceylon, Canada, Chile, China (Taiwan), Colombia, Cuba, Czechoslovakia, Denmark, Dominican Republic, Ecuador, El Salvador, Ethiopia, Finland, France, Greece, Guatemala, Haiti, Honduras, Iceland, India, Indonesia, Iran, Iraq, Italy, Ireland, Israel, Japan, Jordan, Korea, Laos, Lebanon, Libya, Liberia, Luxembourg, Mexico, Morocco, the Netherlands, New Zealand, Nicaragua, Norway, Pakistan, Paraguay, Peru, Philippines, Poland, Portugal, Spain, Sweden, Switzerland, Syria, Thailand, Turkey, Union of South Africa, United Arab Republic, United Kingdom, U.S.A., Uruguay, Venezuela, and Vietnam.

[220]Cooper, *Air Transport and World Organization*, 55 Yale L.J. 1190, 1195 (1946); Rhyne, *International Law and Air Transportation*, 47 Mich. L. Rev. 41, 43 (1948).

[221]A. Clarke, The Making of a Moon 20 (1958).

was a large intelligence organ. Its directing body, the Special Committee for the International Geophysical Year—known as CSAGI—had a membership composed of representatives of the International Council of Scientific Union, the International Union of Geodesy and Geophysics, the International Scientific Radio Union, the International Union of Pure and Applied Physics, the International Union of Geography, and the World Meteorological Organization.[222] The Joint Commission of the Ionosphere and the Joint Commission on Solar and Terrestrial Relationships were also represented.[223] At least 64 nations and 60,000 scientists undertook to assist in the IGY program.[224] No international cooperation in any scientific program has ever gained so much publicity. The IGY can be regarded as a successful demonstration of international cooperation in the promotion of the inclusive interest.[225] But the IGY program cannot be accounted a great success in international cooperation, for its procedures did not require state responsibility:

> The IGY involved governments almost exclusively on a purely domestic basis only. Its international relationships were conducted by committees of scientists representing not their governments but rather their own scientific institutions. These committees took care of the planning and loose coordination of scientific objectives. They achieved decisions only where unanimity was possible and they had no authority, as committees, to implement their programs. Instead, the scientists took the "agreements" they had reached back to their national scientific institutions at home which then sought government or other support for their work. An astonishing degree of such support was forthcoming, but it was essentially self-contained; there was no significant integration of national programs involving governmental agreement. For example, those nations which participated in the

[222] HALEY, *supra* note 213, at 63.

[223] *Id*; see also CLARKE, *supra* note 221, at 20.

[224] Nations participating in the program included: Argentina, Australia, Austria, Belgium, Bolivia, Brazil, Bulgaria, Burma, Canada, Ceylon, Chile, China (Taiwan), Colombia, Cuba, Czechoslovakia, Denmark, Dominican Rep., East Africa, Ecuador, Egypt, Ethiopia, Finland, France, Germany, Ghana, Greece, Guatemala, Hungary, Iceland, India, Indonesia, Iran, Ireland, Israel, Italy, Japan, Dem. Rep. Korea, Maylaya, Mexico, Mongolia People's Rep., the Netherlands, New Zealand, Norway, Pakistan, Panama, Peru, Philippines, Poland, Portugal, S. Rhodesia, Romania, Spain, Sweden, Switzerland, Tunisia, Union of S. Africa, U.S.S.R., United Kingdom, U.S., Uruguay, Venezuela, Vietnam, and Yugoslavia.

[225] *See* D. COX & M. STOIKO, SPACE POWER 102 (1958).

> Antarctic program of the IGY did so at their own bases. . . . [I]n short, the IGY consisted of a collection of national programs independently working toward purely scientific objectives loosely coordinated by a non-governmental mechanism.[226]

The difficulty in accommodation of inclusive and exclusive interests among the participants of the IGY program was aggravated by pressures from interest groups. One clear example was the conflict of interest of scientists and those of the officials responsible for U.S. security. Some of the controversies involved were:

> 1) The scientists wanted the IGY satellite program to be as open and unclassified as possible. Some military officials favored a secret non-IGY satellite program so that future military applications could not be given away to prospective enemies.
>
> 2) The scientists wanted the United States to contribute satellites to the IGY, using whatever means were available to launch instrumented payloads during the IGY. Some military officials opposed any diversion from the military missile research and development program just getting under way. Not until the first United States H-bomb tests, of Nov. 1, 1952, and March 1, 1954, had shown the possibility of constructing a high-yield warhead of low weight had the military embarked upon a sizeable missile program. Once it was established the thermonuclear warhead might be delivered by ballistic missiles, the Air Force did not look with favor upon a program that might cut into scarce resources of man power and skill. . . .[227]

With all the criticisms of the merits and procedural aspects of the program, IGY created the image of possible effective international cooperation in the use of resources. The most important achievement of the IGY was in affirming the free use of space for non-harmful purposes, characterizing that use as "a lawful activity

---

[226] For example, the IGY space program was not broad because Soviet Union scientific representatives restricted IGY agreements for exchange of information in this area. The Soviet Union was also attacked for providing virtually no advance information of a substantive character regarding either its satellite or sounding rocket programs, and the released information was the same as that normally appearing in conventional publications. *See* W. SULLIVAN, ASSAULT ON THE UNKNOWN, 403–07 (1961), *see also* Newell, *Igy Conference in Moscow Report on the Organizational Setup and on the Soviet Presentation of their Rocket and Satellite Work*, SCIENCE, Jan. 9, 1950 at 70; and L. BERKNER, ANNALS OF THE INTERNATIONAL GEOPHYSICAL YEAR, 453–73 (1972).

[227] J. GOLDSEN, OUTER SPACE IN WORLD POLITICS 7 (1963).

which does not infringe upon any protected interests of states or others."[228]

Following the IGY a number of official multilateral pronouncements affirmed the necessity for inclusive enjoyment of space. On December 12, 1958, the U.N. General Assembly adopted a resolution which recognized "the common interest of mankind in outerspace, and . . . the common aim that it should be used for peaceful purposes only."[229] This resolution created an Ad Hoc Committee and directed it to report on various questions, including "the nature of legal problems which may arise in the carrying out of programs to explore space."[230] The resulting report, in which thirteen countries concurred, assumed that the policies of the U.N. Charter and of the Statute of the International Court of Justice are not limited in their operation to the confines of the earth.[231] On the question of inclusive enjoyment of space, the report indicated that launchings during the IGY 1957–58 and later were "on the premise of the permissibility of the launching and the flight of the space vehicles which were launched regardless of what territory they passed over during the course of their flight through outerspace."[232] The Committee then concluded that, in principle, outer space is "on condition of 'equality,' freely available for exploration and use by all in accordance with existing or future international law or agreements."[233] This is a clear indication of rejection of unilateral control of flights in outer space.

In further developments in relation to space activities, the General Assembly, on December 13, 1963, adopted the Declaration of Legal Principles Governing the Activities of States in the Exploration and Use of Outer Space.[234] There have also been significant bilateral agreements. In March 1962 President Kennedy and Pre-

[228] Law and Public Order in Space, *supra* note 198, at 203.

[229] Exploration in Airspace Law, *supra* note 202, at 41.

[230] *Id.*

[231] *Id.* Those countries which concurred on the report were: Argentina, Australia, Belgium, Brazil, Canada, France, Iran, Italy, Japan, Mexico, Sweden, United Kingdom, and the United States.

[232] *Id.*

[233] *Id.*

[234] *See* New Frontier in Space Law 1 (E. McWhinney & M. Bradley eds. 1969).

mier Khrushchev agreed to negotiate on a U.S.–U.S.S.R. Joint Meteorological Satellite venture for the forecasting of world weather that "would inevitably be for the benefit of all mankind."[235] The most important development was, of course, the formulation under U.N. auspices of the 1967 Treaty on the Principles Governing the Activities of States in the Exploration and Use of Outer Space, including Moon and Other Celestial Bodies.[236] This resolution was followed by a Space Treaty and a General Assembly resolution of December 19, 1967, on the Rescue of Astronauts, the Return of Astronauts, and Return of Objects Launched into Outer Space.[237] Certain provisions of the International Telecommunications Convention prepared by the International Telecommunication Union deal with the common enjoyment of outer space.[238] Cooperation has been undertaken on the regional level, for example, the European Agreements Concerning ELDO and ESRO or Provisional Agreements on Telecommunications by Satellites and bilateral agreements on various subjects of astronautics.[239]

Technological advances in uses of space focused attention on the potential danger of space instruments. It is neither possible nor advisable to stop the development, but efforts have been mounted to regulate space activities in order to minimize the possible future danger. These attempts have basically been made through the United Nations. The U.N. Disarmament Commission to the General Assembly adopted at its Twelfth Session, on November 14, 1957, a resolution regarding disarmament which would provide for "the joint study of an inspection system designed to ensure that the sending of objects through outer space shall be exclusively for peaceful and scientific purposes."[240] Of course, there is always room for controversy as to what is a "peaceful" or "scientific" purpose. Thus, Soviet scholars objected to the U.S. Tiros weather satellite program, contending that the satellite took photographs of

---

[235]*See* HALEY, *supra* note 213, at 73.

[236]For the text of the Treaty, see I. WHITE, DECISION-MAKING FOR SPACE 213 (1970).

[237]NEW FRONTIER IN SPACE LAW, *supra* note 234, at 1.

[238]*Id.* at 2.

[239]*Id.*

[240]G.A. Res. 1148, 12 U.N. GAOR, Supp. (No. 18) 3–4, U.N. Doc. A/3805 (1957).

foreign territories and provided weather information that could be used for military purposes.[241]

The creation of the concepts of "airspace" and "outer space" is one aspect of the continuing attempt to balance exclusive and inclusive use and competence. Concern for creation of a boundary somewhere in space is not a new phenomenon; thus, "Grotius recognized freedom of space at an altitude beyond the range of a hunter's weapons."[242] Past practice and particularly recent developments in space activities show that accommodation of interests in forms of space boundaries is not easy. The issue is policy. No solution based solely on the physical or chemical character of the area or its instrumentalities is reasonable.

The term *airspace* has been used in many important international treaties. The first article of the Convention on the Regulation of Aerial Navigation, adopted in Paris in 1919, stated that "the High Contracting Parties recognize that every power has complete and exclusive sovereignty over the airspace above its territory. . . ." The Chicago Convention, the most important convention on airspace, could not produce an exact definition or scope of the term. Article 1 of the Convention states that "the contracting States recognize that every State has complete and exclusive sovereignty over the airspace above its territory." The Chicago Convention deals with the atmosphere, but does not define how far this zone extends. The implied assumption, however, is that national sovereignty extends as far as a state could exercise effective control from its own territory.[243] But with the development of new long-range rockets and satellites, this solution is no longer practical and invites abuse. Past and the present discussion suggests, however, that some states still seek accommodation of interests through fixed boundaries, between airspace and outer space. Many criteria have been essayed for such boundaries, based on:

(a) preexisting prescriptions in conventions relating to airspace;

(b) the varying physical characteristics of space;

(c) the varying natures of flight instrumentalities;

[241] *See* HALEY, *supra* note 213, at 124.

[242] *Id.* at 77.

[243] *See* Heinrich, *Problems in Establishing a Legal Boundary Between Air Space and Space*, in FIRST COLLOQUIUM ON THE LAW OF OUTER SPACE (A. Haley & W. Heinrich eds. 1958).

(d) the effective power of the claimant state;

(e) the limit of the earth's gravitational effect and;

(f) arbitrary altitudes.[244]

These criteria are, essentially, capricious, are not based on rational and meaningful policy basis, and cannot themselves provide principles for an appropriate accommodation.[245] The failure of these proposals drives us to a functional approach to the allocation of competence about space.

As past trends have demonstrated, with the enormous progress in the science of space and the design of space navigation instrumentalities, there are and will be new craft which can fly, with and without the use of oxygen, over different distances from the earth's surface. Satellites flying all over the globe, beyond the reach of any national jurisdiction, can take photographs and gather information that may be used for special interests. Therefore, no security purposes would be served by purporting to create fixed boundaries between airspace and outer space. In this new technological context, the only way of protecting the security of individual states is through differentiating kinds of lawful activities which may be performed in space. Distinctions should be taken through a contextual analysis in each case and the formulation and application of a set of principles as guidelines for decision making.[246]

The only possible rationale for creation of boundaries in space would be for commercial purposes to facilitate decisions in cases of accidents happening in or by air instrumentalities. For commercial purposes our recommended policy is exclusive control to the height at which conventional commercial aircraft fly. The same height may be used for solving problems relating to events happening in or by an aircraft based on customary private international law.

A comprehensive analysis requires clarification of the goals of space exploration besides the mere advancement of science:

> In making our choices we should remember the experiences of other civilizations. Those cultures which have devoted too much of their talent to monuments which had nothing to do with the

---

[244] LAW AND PUBLIC ORDER IN SPACE, *supra* note 198, at 324.

[245] For an elaborate appraisal of these categories, see *id.* at 323–49.

[246] Such contextual approach may be found in *id.* at 320–49.

real issues of human well-being have usually fallen upon bad days: history tells us that the French Revolution was the bitter fruit of Versailles, and that the Roman Colosseum helped not at all in staving off the barbarians. So it is for us to learn well these lessons of history: we must not allow ourselves, by short-sighted seeking after fragile monuments of big science, to be diverted from our real purpose, which is the enriching and broadening of human life.[247]

Space has much potential value, in terms of resources and services, though a great part of those resources is unknown yet. One space activity which may benefit the whole of mankind is the use of satellites. The earth-orbital satellites are extraordinary means of gathering data about the earth's mineral, fish, and other resources and providing warning information, such as the movement of ice in the oceans, flood predictions, and so forth. Indeed, the Carlin Mine, the second largest gold mine in the United States, was found through the use of radar and infrared sensors in an airplane.[248] The possible transportation of cargo and human beings by rockets has also been predicted.[249] Hope for the use of more distant resources of celestial bodies may make activities in space more important.

All nations have an interest in accurate weather forecasting. The field of meteorology is one in which space activities are already playing an important role.[250] Integrated satellite systems could predict and report on the weather conditions over the entire world and work the information into local forecasts. A better prediction of weather would save the world billions of dollars in direct costs of damage "to crops, in water resource conservation, in prevention of loss of life and property, and in shipping and aviation."[251] The kind of information that meteorology satellites gather could also be used for special interests of individual states. For example, weather information is essential to military as well as civil opera-

---

[247]Dr. A. M. Weinberg, Director, Oak Ridge National Laboratory, *quoted in* Skill, Values and Goals of Space Exploration, *reprinted in* H. TAUBENFELD, SPACE AND SOCIETY 45 (1964).

[248]*See* LAY & H. TAUBENFELD, THE LAW RELATING TO ACTIVITIES OF MAN IN SPACE 32 (1970).

[249]On possibilities of manufacturing in space, see N.Y. Times, Feb. 27, 1966, at 3, col. 1.

[250]*See* LIPSON & KATZENBACH, *supra* note 200, at 30.

[251]*See* LAY & TAUBENFELD, *supra* note 248, at 23.

tions. "it was the weather which gave the Allied Command pause before D-Day in 1944, and weather information continues to be essential for normal operations although presumably not for the use of ICBMs."[252] Claims that the United States used the weather information from its satellites to guide bombers in Vietnam seems to be supported by facts.[253] Another problem caused by the increasing development of satellites is the possible attempts by states to modify the weather, with adverse effects on the other states. Weather satellites may also take clear pictures of the earth's surface and gather information which could be considered "embarrassing." Because of such activities, these satellites have been referred to as "spies in the sky."[254] The U.S. Gemini V led the Russians in 1965 to claim that, "to a limited extent, some . . . military experimentation is being carried out in Gemini program. In the Gemini flight, for example, the two astronauts have made visual, photographic and infrared observations of a Minuteman ballistic missile being launched. They have also conducted relatively crude photographic reconnaissance of the earth and experimented with rendezvous radar."[255] There have been attempts to limit the military use of outer space, such as a U.N. Resolution prohibiting the placement of weapons of mass destruction in orbit and the 1967 Space Treaty.

The information gathered by satellites can be extremely useful for navigation and could "provide the basis for all-weather, long-term navigation systems to determine with accuracy geodetic position, speed, and direction of a surface vehicle or aircraft, north reference and vertical reference."[256] The U.N. Committee on the Peaceful Uses of Outer Space asked its Technical Subcommittee to study the possibility of establishing a civil, worldwide navigation satellite system on a nondiscriminatory basis.[257]

[252] N.Y. Times, April 15, 1967, at 1, col. 5.

[253] *Id.*

[254] Petrov, *Spy Satellites and International Law*, Cosmos and International Law (Russian) 171, 176, 177 (1963) *cited in* Lay & Taubenfeld, *supra* note 248, at 23.

[255] N.Y. Times, Aug. 26, 1965, at 14, col. 5.

[256] Lay & Taubenfeld, *supra* note 248, at 24.

[257] N.Y. Times, Nov. 8, 1964, at 12, col. 3. On the uses of navigation satellites by merchant ships, see N.Y. Times, July 30, 1967, at 1, col. 7. On Japanese plans to create a navigation system, see N.Y. Times, Sept. 1, 1966, at 59, col. 1. On the use of navigation satellites by

Satellite communication systems vastly extend man's ability to transmit knowledge and information over great distances. UNESCO has considered the use of space communication for the promotion of a "free flow of information, the rapid spread of education and greater cultural exchanges."[258] The satellite communication system includes television, telephone, data transmission, and cheaper long-range communications in general.[259] For the first time, once the system is established, cost is independent of distance:[260]

> The total band width of land lines, cables, and low frequency radio now in use is limited and short-wave radio bands tend to be crowded and unreliable due to atmospheric interference and ionospheric irregularity. Ultra-short-wave and microwave radio are usually limited to line-of-sight range. Satellites make possible round-the-world communications because the line-of-sight range at satellite altitudes is very great. . . . [I]t is predicted that satellite systems, together with advances in other areas such as radio and cable technology, will go far toward solving foreseeable international communications needs.[261]

This modern communication system offers a whole new approach to communication links for development purposes. Unhappily, not much cooperation has been achieved in this area.[262]

Communication is through the radio frequency spectrum, a limited natural resource in space vitally needed by all countries.[263]

---

commercial aircraft, see N.Y. Times, March 30, 1967, at 52, col. 1 *cited in* LAY & TAUBENFELD, *id.* at 24.

[258] NEW FRONTIER IN SPACE LAW, *supra* note 234, at 5.

[259] LAY & TAUBENFELD, *supra* note 248, at 19–20.

[260] *Id.*

[261] *Id.*

[262] *Id.* at 21.

[263] D. LEIVE, INTERNATIONAL TELECOMMUNICATIONS AND INTERNATIONAL LAW: THE REGULATION OF THE RADIO SPECTRUM 11 (1972). The problem of radio spectrum utilization and the nature of the natural resource is set forth in a recent study:

"It was less than a century ago that man found an entirely new natural resource that could be put to his use. In the early days of the use of the radio spectrum, the only limit to the resource was that imposed by man's inability to cope with the technical enormity of the task of spectrum utilization and by his lack of vision in finding more need for utilization. Over the past twenty years this situation has changed drastically. We have now surveyed the resource more thoroughly and know much about its technical characteristics. We know of

This natural resource has become increasingly important and scarce as worldwide communication expands: "[S]ince the available supply of the spectrum as presently used will not be adequate to meet anticipated worldwide demand, it must somehow be apportioned among contending users. An equitable apportionment of frequencies, however, presents the same difficulties as an equitable apportionment of any other natural resource. Moreover, one country's use of the spectrum affects its use by other countries."[264] The enjoyment of this scarce resource is governed partly through international agreements, such as the international Telecommunication Convention and Annexed Radio Regulations, and by internationally adopted technical recommendations.[265] These regulations are administered, interpreted, and enforced by the International Frequency Registration Board, a body of five independent members within the framework of the International Telecommunication Union (ITU), a specialized agency of the United Nations with a membership of more than 135 countries.[266]

With the increase in participation in space activities through international or regional organizations, the outcomes of these activities, through international organizations open to all participants,

---

its limitations and whether these are man made or result from natural physical laws. We have developed equipment capable of operating in further reaches of the spectrum. We have had our eyes opened to the tremendous potential of useful contribution that can arise from utilization of the resource. As a result, today we find ourselves faced more than ever before with the problem of how to use it efficiently and effectively for the greatest public good. . . .

"The radio spectrum is somewhat different from other resources or minerals, water, fossil fuels, etc. We must be concerned about the following characteristics: 1) this resource is used—not consumed; it is being wasted when it is not being used. 2) this resource has dimensions of space, time, and frequency, and all three are interrelated. . . . 3) It is an international resource—available to all. Any one nation cannot operate solely under its own scheme of allocation. Just as surely as it might unconcernedly interfere with the spectrum allocations of a neighbor, so it will be subject to return situations of interference—both of which actions will multiply waste of the spectrum throughout the world. Local plans and possibilities can be developed only within an overall framework of international agreement. 4) This resource is wasted when assigned to do tasks that can be done as easily in other ways. . . . 5) This resource is wasted when its parameters are not correctly applied to a task. . . . 6) This resource is subject to pollution. . . ." *Report prepared by Joint Technical Advisory Council (JTAC) of the Institute of Electrical and Electronics Engineers and Electronic Industries Association, quoted in* LEIVE, *id.*, at 15–16.

[264]*Id.* at 11.

[265]*Id.*

[266]*Id.*

will minimize the use of space for special interests. The common participation and cooperation will lead to a better production and development of this shareable resource.

4. Climate and Weather

Other resources subject to consistent demands for inclusive use and competence include climate and weather. So long as control and modification of the weather was fantasy, no one was concerned about the ownership of clouds, winds, ocean currents, or storm systems. Scientific experiments in weather modification began in the early nineteenth century.[267] The first successful attempt to produce rain by seeding clouds with dry ice was made in 1930.[268] Recent rapid technological advances have forced policymakers to spend enormous amounts of time on problems dealing with weather modification, including questions about competence over the resources involving that control.

The control of weather is a sensitive issue; "attempts to interfere drastically with the weather, which if successful would adversely affect another nation's way of life, even if inadvertently, might equally well serve as a *causus belli*."[269] Modification per se is not unlawful. Weather modification may be used for both common and special interests. Today, with the increased possibility of changing weather on an international scale, conflicts of interests are more likely to erupt.[270] The World Meteorological Organization (WMO) has observed:

> It is not unrealistic to expect that mankind will eventually have the power to influence weather, and even climate, on a large scale. However, the complexity of the atmospheric processes is such that a change in the weather induced artificially in one part

[267] SENATE COMM. ON COMMERCE, WEATHER MODIFICATIONS AND CONTROL, S. REP. No. 1139, 89th Cong. 2nd Sess. 12 (1966).

[268] *Id.* at 15.

[269] HALEY, *supra* note 213, at 24.

[270] Taubenfeld, *Weather Modification and Control: Some International Legal Implications*, 55 YALE L.J. 492 (1967). At least seven cases dealing with modification have been decided in American courts. *See* Taubenfeld, *Weather Modification, Law, Control Operations* (Report to the Special Commission on Weather Modification of the National Science Foundation) (1966), *cited in* Frenzen, *Weather Modification: Law and Policy*, 12 B. C. IND. & COMM. L.R. 513 (1971).

of the world will necessarily have repercussions elsewhere. This principle can be affirmed on the basis of present knowledge of the mechanism of the general circulation of the atmosphere. However, that knowledge is still far from sufficient to enable us to forecast with confidence the degree, nature or duration of the secondary effects to which a change in weather or climate in one part of the earth may give rise elsewhere, nor even in fact to predict whether these effects will be beneficial or detrimental. Before undertaking an experiment on large-scale weather modification, the possible and desirable consequences must be carefully evaluated, and satisfactory international agreements must be reached.[271]

The significance of weather modification was observed by the General Assembly in a 1962 resolution, specifically mentioning the need for more studies in this area.[272]

One special use of weather modification is its possible military application, and the control of atomic, bacterial, and chemical warfare. General Kenny, commander of the Strategic Air Force of the United States, asserted that "the nation which first learns to plot the path of air masses accurately and learns to control the time and place of precipitation will dominate the globe."[273] That was the sort of hyperbole one had come to expect from his organization. During the Vietnam War "the United States Central Intelligence Agency had tried rainmaking over the Ho Chi Minh trail of Southern Laos in an effort to hinder North Vietnamese truck movements."[274] Global domination eluded the rainmakers.

The development of weather modification in terms of its benefits to mankind could be as important as atomic energy, for weather modification, like other shareable resources, has great potential for the promotion of common interests. But only by inclusive use, through organized inclusive competence, will the general

---

[271] WORLD METEOROLOGICAL ORGANIZATION, SECOND REPORT ON THE ADVANCEMENT OF ATMOSPHERIC SCIENCES AND THEIR APPLICATION IN THE LIGHT OF DEVELOPMENT IN OUTER SPACE 19 (1963). *See also* Taubenfeld, *id.* at 493.

[272] G. A. Res. 1721, 16 UN GAOR Supp. (No. 17) 16, UN. Doc. A/500 (1962).

[273] In an address *quoted in* N.Y. Times, June 15, 1947, at 3, col. 1. *See also* Bliven, *Death in the Air*, THE NEW REPUBLIC, Feb. 2, 1948, at 17; Lapp, *Atomic Bomb Explosions—Effects on an American City*, 4 BULL. OF THE ATOMIC SCIENTISTS 49, 52, 53 (1948).

[274] Samuels, *International Control of Weather Modification Activities: Peril or Policy?* 13 NATURAL RESOURCES J. 327 (1973).

community be assured of the achievement of great production, fair distribution, and conservation of values produced by weather control. The potential benefits of weather control in terms of increased productivity and decreased property damages are great. The control of weather would save many lives and prevent millions of dollars of damages each year. For example, in the United States alone, during 1914 to 1916, 456 people were killed by nontornadic storms and tornadoes; and nearly $45 million in property damages during the same time and for the same reason were reported.[275] In the same period the annual hail damage was over $13 million.[276] In a lightning accident 700 to 800 were killed and twice as many were injured, plus fire damages of $12 million.[277] The Soviet Union claimed that it suffered losses of 10 million rubles in crops in 1964 through hail-suppression activities.[278] The amount of human and economic damages on an international scale that could be prevented is extremely high.

For the promotion of inclusive interest through weather modification, the principle of "state sovereignty" over territorial space is woefully anachronistic. Since much of the potential of weather modification will be lost without inclusive use, the goal of securing the greatest measure of common interest at a minimum cost will be best furthered by, for example, permitting one state to enter the territorial airspace of another for the purpose of seeding clouds that will precipitate rainfall on the former state.[279] An occasional exclusive competence should be allowed when it is necessary for the protection of some unique, vital national interest.

The world weather system is very much a part of the earth's general environment system; any alteration in environment will cause an alteration in weather. Given the uncertainty surrounding the present technology of weather modification, the interdependencies of the world weather system, and the possibility that major weather-control activities may prove to be "zero-sum games," we

[275]*Id.*

[276]*Id.*

[277]*Id.*

[278]S. Rep. No. 1139, *supra* note 267, at 45. In 1951 damage amounting to $15 million was caused by hailstorms on the State of Kansas alone. *Id.* at 24.

[279]Barry, *Weather Modification and World Public Order* (1968) (Unpublished paper in the Yale Law School Library).

recommend organized inclusive supervision over weather modification.[280] Moreover, competition for scarce weather modification resources is likely to increase in the future. Hence, we prefer an organized inclusive body, having official representatives with equal power from all nation-states, to formulate policies and control their enforcement. This international body could gather and distribute information both at the national and international level concerning any new developments or changes and effects in or resulting from weather modification. This organization could be authorized to give capital or technical assistance to nations who cannot afford the high cost of shipping fleets and rockets or trained personnel necessary for modification and control of their weather.

The rest of this study deals with the application of the concept of inclusivity to internal resources, resources historically subject to exclusive appropriation. It is an examination of increasing demands for some degree of "internationalization" of national resources, with accommodation of both inclusive and exclusive use and competence.

---

[280]"A zero-sum game" is a term used in game theory to describe situations where the parties' objectives are inversely related, so that any gain by *A* requires a corresponding loss by *B*. In a zero-sum game there is no logical basis for cooperation between the parties. *See* T. Schelling, The Strategy of Conflict, 83–87 (1960) *cited in* Taubenfeld, *supra* note 170 at 494.

CHAPTER III

The Inclusive Enjoyment of Resources Through Agreement

IN A world geographically divided by states whose boundaries conform but roughly with the physical, technological, and engineering unities and imperatives of resource use, states must inevitably seek accommodations in shared use for a more abundant, and appropriately conserving, exploitation of resources. Sometimes these necessary accommodations are sought implicitly through the customary practices of cooperative behavior, sometimes through deliberate and explicit agreement, and sometimes through outright coercion. The difficulties in achieving appropriate accommodations are today intensified both by the diversities in the conflicting social, economic, and political structures of states and by the increasing demands for a greater production and more equitable distribution of potential values among the different territorial communities. A public order aspiring toward human dignity will seek to promote the use of agreement as a fundamental strategy in effecting the necessary cooperation between states.

The problem of achieving an inclusive exploitation and enjoyment of resources, even in relation to those resources located physically within the boundaries of particular states, derives basically from the necessity for the maintenance of a productive and equitable world economy. This problem has long concerned a large part of international law and has been a subject of continued inquiry among scholars. Thus, Dunn once referred to the maintenance of a global economy and society as the most important problem in international affairs: "Since the middle of nineteenth century, by far the greater part of international relations has been concerned, not with high politics, alliances, armaments, and balance of power, but with the difficulties and clashes of interest arising out of the tremendous flow of people and goods across the borders of nations."[1] The contemporary interdependencies of the

---

[1] Dunn, *International Law and Private Property Rights*, 28 COLUM. L. REV. 170 (1928).

peoples of the world, whatever their social organizations and ideologies, in the production of goods and services and for achieving
high standards of living as well as other values have been many
times documented. The historically inherited and uneconomic political boundaries of contemporary states cannot be permitted, as
Hansen has observed, to defy the necessities of these interdependencies.[2]

The inclusive interest of all peoples lies, as most historic practice
indicates, in the establishment and protection of peaceful and persuasive channels in the cooperative sharing of resources. The most
important persuasive channel is that of voluntary agreement, a
device much honored in the decisions and policies of past practice.
Many existing international agreements are concerned with the
allocation of resources. These agreements may represent or create
shared expectations among the parties or others about the use of
resources located within the exclusive domains of states. The role
of agreement in the use of such resources has long been significant; agreement is commonly considered the best means of sharing this category of resource with the fewest possibilities of
violating minimum order. The recent demands to reconsider the
terms of many historic agreements because of changing circumstances (such as in the supply system, in the market system, in the
conservation system, and so forth) do not diminish the utility of
the device as such. These changes have not lessened the important
role of agreement, as an alternative to coercion, in the distributions of values arising from, or associated with, resources historically under exclusive competence. The future role of agreement
in this respect, though some modalities and legal consequences
may change, will remain essential for the shared use of resources.

It is axiomatic, from our perspective, that resources should be
employed to secure a production of goods and services that will
promote a public order of human dignity. Resources should be
allocated and reallocated in a way to create, distribute, and redis-
tribute all values among the peoples of the world toward the end
of continuous transnational development. Agreements concerning the allocation and use of the earth's resources should, accordingly, be fashioned and regulated toward the same goal. Agreements
do in fact constitute a large part of contemporary planning for
transnational development. When agreements are made to follow

[2] A. Hansen, Economic Policy and Full Employment 24–28 (1947).

appropriate policies, the inclusive interest of all countries is defined in terms of the promotion of transnational planning for development in an increased production and wider distribution of human dignity values. For the promotion of transnational development planning, it is necessary to encourage both a continuity and stability in agreements compatible with community policies and the possibility for authorized change, irrespective of the changing composition of controlling elites. The exclusive interest of the grantor state that agrees to share its resources is of course in maintaining enough control and authority over the resources physically within its boundaries to protect its internal value processes. This exclusive interest has been recently recognized in several U.N. Resolutions.[3]

For an observer interested in a just and economic allocation of the enjoyment of resources, the policies for guiding the regulation of international agreements should not be oriented only toward political factors, but also toward economic and other factors. In a context in which any group is dependent for most values on the cooperation of other groups, we agree with Greaves that "the political myths must be made to fit the economic realities."[4] It has been well said that

> the world must be organized not vertically in political areas, but horizontally as a series of services or functions whether for the production of raw materials like coal or rubber, the manufacture of products like cotton goods, or the supply of services like transport or defense. Each has its own peculiar problems and development, and each must be organized with as much regard for these and little regard for political irrelevancies as possible, and each must be subject in the last resort to general international supervision and coordination.[5]

The policies for guiding international agreements should, furthermore, go beyond mere economic efficiency to embrace economic growth, as well as the production and equitable distribution of other values. Such policies, while permitting creative change, should stabilize the expectations necessary for the richest development of international intercourse and cooperation.

---

[3]G.A. Res. 1830, 17 U.N. GAOR Supp. (No. 17) 55, U.N. Doc. A/5217 (1962). *See* Hyde, *Permanent Sovereignty over Natural Resources*, 50 Am. J. Int'l L. 854 (1956).

[4]W. Greaves, Raw Materials and International Control 4 (1936).

[5]*Id.*

It is our purpose here to study past trends in the making and regulation of agreements between states for the allocation and use of resources. We propose to review how and for what purposes allocating agreements have been made, whether past practices have promoted the inclusive and exclusive use of resources, what kinds of resources have been involved in the allocating agreements, and how effective these agreements have been for the promotion of basic community policies. Finally, we consider what the future of such practices may be and what role these agreements may play in future transnational development.

Most people of the world are affected in different ways and in varying degrees by agreements concerning resources. They may benefit or be damaged by changes in resource production, distribution, and marketing. They may gain or seriously get hurt by sharing resources; the whole process of formation and distribution of values may, in other words, be changed by agreements. In any event, though states and other entities may make the agreements, the ultimate beneficiaries or deprived parties are individual human beings.

The formal participants in an allocating agreement may be categorized into two groups.[6] The first group includes those subject to the burdens of an agreement, whom we will call grantors; the second group includes those entitled to the benefits of the agreement, or grantees. The grantors are always nation-states. The grantees can be nation-states, international organizations, or foreign private enterprises. A difference in grantee can make a difference in policies; hence, we will study trends in decision about allocating agreements based on these differences in participation.

Agreements about the shared use of resources, like other agreements, may project a common policy with respect to formation and distribution of many values. In such agreements the main objective of the participants is to achieve a common policy concerning resources physically located within the territory of the grantor. The more detailed objectives may relate to any value, such as power, wealth, enlightenment, respect, well-being, skill, affection, or rectitude, and to any particular resource. The objectives often relate to the more important uses for which resources are demanded: transit (power, wealth) strategy (power) production,

---

[6]For an elaborate description of this feature, *see* M. McDougal, H. Lasswell & J. Miller, The Interpretation of Agreements and World Public Order (1967).

consumption (wealth, power). These are the main values and modalities most frequently sought, but nuances are infinite. Demands for values and particular modalities in shared use vary both in the intensity with which they are asserted and in their compatibility or incompatibility with overriding community policies.

The geographical location of the pertinent resources within particular territorial communities is crucial. The significance of such location is even more important when it is within critical zones between the grantor and grantee. The location of particular resources not only increases the possibility of making or terminating agreements but also plays an important role in creating expectations concerning the details of the shared use of resources. Thus, the location of resources in a strategic area between potential belligerents, as on a river flowing through two or more communities, may play a vital role in shaping many expectations.

The time features of negotiation and performance are an important element that may change the expectations of the parties either during the negotiations or after commitment. The degree of institutionalization, in terms of stability and organization, may affect expectations about commitment, change, or termination. The intensity of external crisis may affect similarly both demand for resources and every aspect of the process of agreement by which resources are shared.

The participants in an agreement process may employ the whole range of values controlled by them to obtain their objectives. The potential base values at the disposal of the parties may affect the expectations of the parties as well as their subsequent performance. Because of the importance of differing value positions in the creation and changing of expectations, differences between participants in power, wealth, enlightenment, skill, affection, rectitude, and well-being must be taken into account in appropriate prescription and application of law.

The parties may mediate their subjectivities in negotiation and perform their commitments through a great variety of strategies: diplomatic, ideological, economic, and military.[7] These strategies may be employed in a broad continuum of differing degrees of persuasion and coercion. The communication between the parties

---

[7]"Strategies" refers to "the sequences of negotiations and other activities by which the parties mediate their subjectivities (demands, identifications, expectations) to achieve outcomes in shared commitment." *See id.* at 18.

may be in the form of both words and deeds. In whatever form the communications are expressed, they may exhibit infirmities in many varying degrees, such as complementarity, ambiguity, and incompleteness.[8]

The outcomes achieved by the parties in a projection of common policies about the shared enjoyment of resources differ greatly both in the content of the performance specified and in their degree of explicitness. The expectations created may require positive acts in performance or mere refraining from action about a great variety of resources. They may also vary in form, from oral or mere inference from behavior to highly complex written documents. The important question is in what degree expectations are created under the agreement that the projected policies between the parties will remain relatively stable, whether for a certain period of time, or until a certain event or conditions occur, or in perpetuity.[9]

We divide allocating agreements into three groups based on their participants: (a) agreements between states, (b) agreements between states and international organizations, and (c) agreements between states and foreign enterprises, or development agreements.

A. AGREEMENTS BETWEEN STATES

The rising demands for the shared use of resources located within the territorial boundaries of particular states have increased the number and variety of agreements purporting to confer rights to such resources. Agreements between states play a significant role in such shared use. These agreements purport to confer upon one territorial community rights to enjoyment of resources physically located within another territorial community which commits itself to bear the agreed burdens. Such agreements have generally been referred to as international servitudes. When a state, *i.e.*, a grantor, limits or restricts its rights to use resources located within its territory for the benefit of another country or community, it is referred to as negative servitude. When the commitment calls for more affirmative action or results in a sharing of the resources within exclusive zones, it is sometimes called a positive servitude.

[8]*Id.* at 19.

[9]*Id.*

1. The Factual Background

The concept of servitude derives from the Roman law concept of "ownership," which could be divided into several elements, such as the right of the user, the right of enjoyment, and the right of disposition.[10] Any of these could be detached and transferred to another person without destroying the superior right of the owner. The English common law offers an equivalent conception under many different labels.[11] The history of international servitudes is almost as old as the history of international relations. Arrangements of this kind can be found in the earliest interactions between organized communities, such as tribes, cities, and states.[12] Historically, the device of servitude has been used for shared use both of depletable resources and of spatial-extension resources.[13] This wide practice in the employment of servitudes with respect to many different kinds of resources is generally attributed by publicists to the exigencies of economic need. The mutual interests of the states have caused them to extend their activities beyond their territories in order to satisfy their various exclusive needs.[14] Thus, advances in transportation and communication since the turn of the century have resulted in vast networks of rail and air routes that have paid little attention to national boundaries. Similarly, the

[10] H. Reid, International Servitude in Law and Practice 3–4 (1932) [hereinafter cited as Reid].

[11] *See* M. McDougal & D. Haber, Property, Wealth, Land: Allocation Planning and Development 475 (1948).

[12] When the members of a nomadic tribe were allowed to use a well within the area under the control of another tribe, or to hunt or fish, there were, in fact, agreements and grantors to give rights to grantees with respect to resources physically located within the territory of another party. F. Vali, Servitudes of International Law 33 (2d ed. 1958) [hereinafter cited as Vali].

[13] Spatial-extension resources are those resources which are not depletable as stock resources, and their most distinctive characteristic is their utility as media of transportation and communication, such as land, ocean surfaces, airspace, and outerspace. For more detailed definition of stock and spatial extension resources see S. Ciracy-Wantrup, Resource Conservation: Economies and Policies 38–40 (1952).

[14] G. Turner, the American representative at the North Atlantic Fisheries Case [N.A. C.F. IX, at 566], has said that "[s]ervitudes in their essential characteristics have existed ever since men became sufficiently polished to understand their dependence upon each other. They have existed ever since nations began making treaties providing for the necessities of the one out of the superfluous abundance of the other." *See also* Reid, *supra* note 10, at 43, Vali, *supra* note 12, at 33.

scientific explorations of modern times have increased demands by territorial communities for rights to employ resources within the exclusive zones of others in aid of scientific observation. Political controversies, such as the Cold War, have resulted in demands for extraterritorial strategic rights; the requirements of security have increased global interdependencies and, hence, the scope of servitudes. In general, servitudes have come to be considered a most effective method of shared enjoyment of global resources.[15]

The beneficiaries of servitudes may include, of course, not merely the grantees or grantors but all the members of the large communities that the grantees and grantors affect. Servitudes may serve as a highly important means in the exploitation of resources and production of values; other features of the context may, however, importantly affect the distribution of the values so produced.[16] Servitudes may also serve as a means for conservation when one state restricts or modifies the modalities of exploitation of its own resources (in what are called negative servitudes) in favor of another state. These negative servitudes are often attacked upon the ground that "production, on the whole," must overshadow "conservation in the general estimation of the world."[17] International economic servitudes, it is sometimes asserted, must always be of a positive nature because one can "allege no legitimate interest sufficient to impose upon a state a mere reduction of its economic capacity."[18]

In the contemporary context of urgent needs and demands for conservation of many resources, it cannot be expected that these attitudes in rejection of negative servitudes will survive. A change in perspectives is quite clear with respect to the conservation of the living resources within the territorial seas of nation-states; here negative agreements relating to conservation are of the utmost importance for improving the total supply of maritime resources both in quality and quantity.[19] The Convention for the Protection of Migratory Birds signed in Washington in 1916 is an example of

---

[15] *See* Potter, *The Doctrine of Servitudes in International Law,* 9 Am. J. Int'l. L. 632 (1915).

[16] Reid, *supra* note 10, at 44.

[17] *Id.* at 47.

[18] Charles de Visscher, "La question de iles d'Aland," R.G.D.I. 3ᵉ Série 11 at 253, *quoted in* Reid, *supra* note 10, at 47.

[19] Reid, *supra* note 10, at 48.

a negative agreement by which the hunting rights of both contracting parties, United States and Canada, were limited for fifteen years.[20] The inclusive interests of both Canada and the United States in the protection of their natural resources have been served by this agreement. A number of fishing agreements between states also prohibit overexploitation of certain species.[21] The device of negative economic servitudes may, therefore, provide a useful means for preventing the overexploitation of important natural resources, particularly those resources whose exhaustion can be prevented by an appropriate rate of use and the prevention of pollution.[22] In such instances the application of negative agreements may constitute an important step toward international cooperation for the general welfare of the world.

The conception of an international servitude, as important as it has been in effecting a transnationally shared use of resources, has been the subject of great controversy. Questions and serious doubts about the nature and component elements of this servitude have been raised. A great variety of claims has been made by participants as to varying legal consequences of different features of the processes of commitment, performance, and change of servitude. In response to these controversies and claims, reliance has been placed by both decision makers and scholars mainly upon contradictory and ambiguous traditional doctrines.[23] Consequently, decision makers have not been able to offer guidance in the management of these claims that either protects the broad common interest or encourages transnational planning. In defining servitudes, words of high levels of abstractions, such as "real," "personal," "permanent," "succession of benefits," "succession of burdens," and so on, have been used. Such ambiguities have been increased by describing these terms in relation to their legal consequences rather than to their uniformities in the facts of interaction.[24] The ambiguities and complementarities in the legal doctrine

[20] T.S. No. 628, 39 Stat. 1702 (1916), *reprinted in* III U.S. Treaties & Conventions 2645 (1923).

[21] *See generally* Part III, chap. 3.

[22] *See generally* Part III, chap. 4.

[23] For a discussion of normative ambiguity see M. McDougal and Assocs., Studies in World Public Order 119–27 (1962).

[24] *See, e.g.*, the definition offered by Reid: "An international servitude is a *real* right, whereby the territory of one state is made *liable* to permanent use by another state, for some

have accordingly afforded decision makers both a broad discretion
and the means for concealing their discretion. Too much reliance
upon past decisions, without analysis of the differences in the present context and probable future consequences, has further
impeded rational decision about this important instrument for the
shared use of resources.

2. Basic Community Policies

The basic policy with respect to agreements between states is to
promote a shared cooperative use of resources that will facilitate
an abundant, appropriately conserving production and equitable
distribution of all values by persuasive and economic strategies.
This basic policy requires, therefore, that every feature of a process of agreement between states be appraised in terms of its compatibility with, and contribution to, the basic goal values of human
dignity. A recommended policy for promotion of persuasive
strategies for shared use of resources is the utmost respect for the
parties' expectations about the different features of the processes
of commitment, performance, and change insofar as these expectations are not incompatible with overriding community goals.
Only when the parties have conflicting demands and expectations
or when their objectives or strategies are inimical to common interest is community intervention necessary.

In broad statement the inclusive interest of the larger community is in an appropriate production form and distribution of the
benefits of resources, regardless of the formal allocation or physical location of such resources. Because of the inescapable interdependencies in the use of resources for achieving these goals,
agreements between states regarding transnational planning
should be promoted and protected. The exclusive interest of each
territorial community is, of course, in the maintenance and
healthy functioning of its own internal value processes. Thus, each
community has an interest in maintaining its internal security

---

specified purpose. The servitude may be *permissive* or *restrictive*, but does not invoke any
obligation upon either party to take *positive* action. It establishes permanent *legal relationship*
of territory to territory, unaffected by *change of sovereignty* in either of them, and terminable
only by mutual consent, by renunciation on the part of the dominant state, or by consoli-
dation of the territories affected." REID, *supra* note 10, at 25 (italics supplied). *See also*
L. McDougal, Transnational Resource Planning: International Servitudes in Policy Oriented Perspectives (1966) (unpublished paper in the Yale Law School Library).

against external threat. To this end, maintenance of authority and control over internal affairs is of the utmost importance to individual nation-states. The rational accommodation of both sets of these interests, inclusive and exclusive, is the task of authoritative decision making. Such accommodation requires of the decision maker a disciplined, contextual analysis of every particular controversy through the employment of appropriate principles of content and procedure.

One important factor affecting community policy is the kind of resources involved, whether depletable or spatial-extension. When the resource in question is exhaustible, the issues of conservation and the significant role of the resource in the local economy of the grantor must be considered. In other words, the exclusive interest of the grantor in a depletable resource may be more significant than that of the grantee, and the traditional conception of servitude as a permanent commitment with respect to these resources may not require full deference. This policy has been appropriately expressed in the flow of past decisions. As these trends will show, there has been serious reluctance by authoritative decision makers to regard agreements concerning depletable resources between states as anything more than an ordinary treaty subject to interpretation.

Spatial-extension resources, because of their inexhaustible nature, raise a different policy. A major use of spatial-extension resources is transit in order to achieve some other exclusive use. Under the traditional doctrines of national sovereignty, the grantor state has absolute control over transit. The conception of servitude was a beginning effort to secure a limited inclusive use of spatial-extension resources as between two or more states. Our broad policy recommendation about this right is the encouragement of transit rights, with continuity as between two or more states. Our broad policy recommendation about this right is the encouragement of transit rights, with continuity as between successor states and with suitable safeguards for the servient state.

3. Trends in Decision

The relevant past trends reveal that a variety of labels has been used to describe agreements between states for the shared use of resources within exclusive territories. Among the most common labels are "servitudes," "licenses," and "leases." It is not always recognized that these labels make inaccurate and confused references to facts, to authoritative responses, and to relevant policies, and efforts are sometimes made to draw legal consequences from the labels alone. The term *servitude* is the label most commonly used for these agreements by participants and in authoritative decisions. The common label does not, however, preclude a wide variety of descriptions and evaluations made by courts and the writers.[25] This great variety in doctrinal formulation about servitude comes mainly from two sources. One doctrine, taken from Roman Law, incorporated into the Civil Law, and introduced into International Law, employs the concept of servitude to define the rights and burdens of a somewhat permanent nature in the shared use of resources. The other doctrine regards servitude largely as a form of agreement, to be regulated mostly by a general law of agreement that emphasizes the expectations of the parties.

It would appear, by and large, that the authoritative prescriptions establishing the legal consequences of servitudes have been those of the law of treaties. The specific legal consequences on a particular claim, and any modifications of the general law, have related only to the facts and features of the particular agreement. Past decisions suggest that legal consequences are seldom drawn merely because of the label attached to an agreement. Important factors regarding an agreement—such as the differences in the nature of resources, whether depletable or spatial-extension; their importance to the grantor and the grantee in terms of internal value processes; and the interrelationship between the parties, such as between states and their former colonies, and so forth—are commonly regarded as relevant in determination of ultimate legal consequences. Agreements that permit the taking of depletable resources from one country have, based on the past experience, been faced with serious questions about conservation and environmental injuries. With respect to spatial-extension resources, the issue of the security of the grantor influences the long-term burdens imposed upon the grantor. Varying expectations about different resources and different problems have required different policies with respect to particular problems in the processes of commitment, performance, and change of a servitude.

[25] For collection of a variety of definitions of servitude, *see* J. Scott, North Atlantic Coast Fisheries Arbitration, International Servitude (1909) (Report compiled by James Brown Scott for use before the permanent Court of Arbitration at The Hague).

The automatic transfer of burdens to a successor government by mere reason of "servitude," whatever the controversial writings, has not been accepted in past decisions. In such a situation the claim for performance of the commitment is considered in the same way as is any other problem in state succession. The ultimate decision as to succession to the commitment is achieved by a balancing of interests in minimum and optimum order. The internal and external effects of the changes claimed in one of the parties and the interests of all parties in the continuation of the servitude are examined. This requires a careful identification of the particular problem or termination and a broad contextual analysis to ascertain what is reasonable in the particular situation.

The policies indicated have been reflected in the bulk of past decision and practice. The important question has been regarded as, not what label can be given to a particular agreement, rather but what protection should be afforded under the facts of a particular agreement whatever the label attached. The *North Atlantic Fisheries Arbitration*, decided in 1910, has remained the leading case.[26] This case involved a United States claim that Britain did not have the right to enforce certain regulations in the latter's coastal waters. The claim of the United States was based on the two nineteenth-century treaties granting to the United States extensive fishing rights in these waters. In support of its claim the United States insisted that the treaties created a servitude. By this label the United States was demanding permanent performance of the agreement, free of Canadian regulation, and therefore objecting to changes in prior practice. The U.S. counsel developed an extremely rigid definition of servitude along the lines that it entailed a surrender of authority by the servient state. The court, while accepting the concept of servitude in international law, did not apply the demanded conception in this case. Mentioning that even if the liberties of fishery for the United States constituted an international servitude, the Court continued:

> the servitude would derogate from the sovereignty of the servient State only insofar as the exercise of the rights of sovereignty by the servient State would be contrary to the exercise of the servitude right by the dominant State. Whereas it is evident that, though every regulation of the fishery is to some extent a

[26] The North Atlantic Coast Fisheries Arbitration, *reprinted in* S. Doc. No. 870, Vol. I, p. 64. 61st Cong. 2d Sess. (1910).

limitation, as it puts limits to the exercise of the fishery at will, yet such regulations as are reasonable and made for the purpose of securing and preserving the fishery and its exercise of the common benefits are clearly to be distinguished from those restrictions and "molestations," the annulment of which was the purpose of the American demands formulated by Mr. Adams in 1782, and such regulations consequently cannot be held to be inconsistent with a servitude.[27]

The Court considered the right and burdens between the parties as obligations created by agreement subject to the ordinary rules of interpretation. The Court found that the economic measures taken by Britain were reasonable. It agreed that the liberty of Britain to regulate the rights granted to the inhabitants of the United States was limited to "bona fide" measures and could not be in violation of the treaty, but stated:

> Regulations which are (1) appropriate or necessary for the protection and preservation of such fisheries, or (2) desirable or necessary on grounds of public order and morals without unnecessary interfering with the fishery itself, and in both cases equitable and fair as between local and American fishermen, and not so framed as to give unfairly an advantage to the former over the latter class, are not inconsistent with the obligation to execute the treaty in good faith, and are therefore reasonable and not in violation of the treaty. . . .[28]

The Court did, however, recommend the establishment of a Permanent Mixed Fishery Commission for prescribing reasonable measures. This recommendation was accepted by the parties.

Another example in which an authoritative decision maker rejected the mere deduction of legal consequences from the label "servitude" is in the *Wimbledon Case*.[29] This case was decided by the International Court of Justice by application of ordinary principles of interpretation, though the doctrine of servitude had been invoked by Germany. The British ship S.S. *Wimbledon*, loaded with arms for Poland, was refused access by Germany to the Kiel Canal upon the ground that permitting such access would violate her neutrality in the war between Russia and Poland. The issue was

[27] *Id.*

[28] *Id.*

[29] The S.S. Wimbledon, [1923] P.C.I.J. ser. A, No. 1.

the interpretation of Article 380 of the Treaty of Versailles by which Germany had agreed with the rest of the contracting parties that the Kiel Canal (located within German territory) should be maintained free and open to all the vessels of commerce and war of all nations at peace with Germany. The applicants (United Kingdom, Italy, France, and Japan) argued that they were entitled to free passage through the Kiel Canal under Article 380. Germany argued that Article 380 created a servitude and that, "like all restrictions or limitations upon the exercise of sovereignty, this servitude must be construed as restrictively as possible and confined within its narrowest limits, more especially in the sense that it should not be allowed to affect the rights consequent upon neutrality in an armed conflict."[30] The Court refused to take any stand on the question of "servitude." It found that, whether the German government was bound by virtue of servitude or by its contractual obligation, there was no potential violation of German neutrality and that the applicants had a right of passage by interpretation of the "plain terms of the article [Article 380]."

The most recent case in which the doctrine of servitude was invoked was the controversy between Portugal and India about certain rights of passage. The facts about the case, before the International Court of Justice, were that, by a treaty between Portugal and the Marathan ruler of India, Portugal had been given in 1779 extensive authority over certain sections of Indian territory that included two small areas completely surrounded by territory retained by India. After England took control of India, Portugal continued its exercise of control over these territories, and this right was recognized by England. Over the years and until 1954 Portugal continued, without challenge, the use of Indian territory for passage to the territories under its own control. The materials being transported by Portugal were not inspected. In official papers, however, the parties had agreed that in the case of arms, ammunition, and troops, Portugal should file, before dispatch, a request with local authorities. For some 125 years Portugal enjoyed this right without question. Shortly after India's independence, there occurred a series of rebellions within Portugal's controlled territories. Portugal alleged that these rebellions were inspired by the Indian government. India suddenly refused the Portuguese any passage through its territory.

---

[30] *Id.* at 24.

In this case the Court was faced with a problem in succession of burden characteristic of the doctrine of servitude. After reviewing the facts of the case in the light of the overall community policy of decolonization and emphasizing the independence of India and its need for having effective control over all parts of its territory that would be inconsistent with the authority of Portugal over a part of that territory completely surrounded by India, the Court recognized the right of Portugal to passage, but subject to control by India. In reply to the question whether India was responsible for suspending the right-of-way for Portugal for all purposes during a certain period of time, the Court observed that the security of India would justify its refusal of passage for ammunitions and troops. In other words, the Court recognized that security and the protection of minimum order within a servient state may justify changes in the content of a servitude. The end result was of course that Portugal shortly lost both effective control and authority within its claimed territories.

a. Rights in Depletable Resources

This right refers to any rights of the grantee state to enjoy depletable resources from the territory of the grantor, such as fish and minerals, or to use certain resources within the territory of grantor for production of certain values, such as use of water for hydroelectric power, or to use the territories of the grantor for strategic benefits. Agreement creating rights of this kind basically developed because of the irrational and unequal distribution of the world's resources and population among territorial communities; they have a great significance for the internal value processes of both grantee and grantor, particularly in terms of wealth and well-being. With the exception of strategic rights, rights to depletable resources within the exclusive areas of states derive mostly from the fact that the grantor has a greater supply of, than demand for, the resources for which the grantee state has a demand. The contemporary changes in supply and demand, because of natural, technological, economic, and political circumstances, have given a new dimension to expectations about the future performance of such commitments. Such new expectations are directly linked to the depletable nature of resources. The exploitation of these resources under certain conditions may become detrimental to the grantee state; the situation in the grantee state may change economically or otherwise to require its more effective control over the resources that significantly affect its internal needs and development. In such cases the important exclusive interests of the grantee become incompatible with its external commitment. The flow of past decisions reflects a sympathy with the grantee state in these circumstances. There is, further, a tendency among states to minimize the use of agreements between states concerning such resources and to increase the use of concession agreements or development agreements as a more appropriate persuasive strategy for sharing their internal depletable resources.

i. Flow and Stock Resources

One of the oldest rights to resources is that for animal resources, and particularly for fishing. Generally, the grant of fishing rights has been based on changes in political boundaries and a separation of fishing areas, or on an unequal distribution of population. The latter base, because it allows access to more fishing resources for the more populated areas, particularly reflects recognition of the need for a redistribution of resources in a more equitable way. The general policy promoted in these agreements has been the protection of the genuine expectation of the parties in shared use of fishing resources; this is the reason for the existence of fishing agreements between states for several hundred years. Changes in conditions, particularly in economic conditions, such as the over-exploitation of fishing resources, have, however, been recognized by authoritative decisions as grounds for the termination or modification of the original commitment. The doctrine of *rebus sic stantibus*, though not often directly invoked about agreements concerning this class of resources, has been indirectly applied.

Some of the early fishing rights were the Swedish rights on the seas and coasts of Great Britain granted by the Treaty of Westminster,[31] and the fishing rights claimed by Holland on the British sea through historical use and the declaration of the King of England.[32]

The French North Atlantic fisheries dispute is an example of challenging the exclusive right of the grantee in the enjoyment of fishing resources of the grantor. When France lost her possessions

---

[31] Reid, *supra* note 10, at 62.

[32] *Id.* at 63.

in Canada to Great Britain, Great Britain granted a fishing right based on the Treaty of Paris of 1793 to French subjects along the coast of Newfoundland.[33] Later France claimed exclusive fishing rights, which were rejected by Great Britain on the grounds that the right granted to France was not exclusive but rather inclusive: enjoyment of coastal fishing resources was to be for both British and French subjects. The dispute was never submitted for judicial review. France, however, in a Convention with the United Kingdom about issues relating to Newfoundland and West and Central Africa, signed in 1904, agreed to the equal rights of French and British subjects in fishing in the disputed areas.

The *North Atlantic Fisheries Arbitration*, discussed earlier, is a leading authoritative decision which recognizes that changes in conditions, such as overexploitation of fishing resources, may justify changes in a commitment. The changes in the substantive content of the agreement, the court said, result from the need for incorporating reasonable measures for conservation and protection of fisheries. The court, however, recognized the interest of the grantee state in recommending the establishment of a joint commission by the grantor and grantee for prescribing reasonable measures.

Changes other than in economic conditions, such as changes in political boundaries, do not always seem to be enough for change of the commitment. For example, the demands and needs for shared use of fishing resources of the eastern Adriatic by the neighboring states resulted, in spite of the political changes in that area, in several agreements for shared use. After the Second World War, Italy lost the island of Pelegosa in the mid-Adriatic to Yugoslavia by the Treaty of Peace signed in Paris in 1947.[34] But Article 10 of the Treaty provided a right for Italian fishermen to enjoy the fishing rights in Pelegosa and surrounding waters. Later on this right was confirmed by the agreement between Italy and Yugoslavia in 1949.[35] This treaty was replaced by other agreements between the two governments in 1951 and 1956. Thus the fishing rights for fishermen of Chioggia on the coast of Dalmatia was secured by 1878 agreement even after the Austro-Italian war of 1866, in spite of the intervening territorial changes.[36]

---

[33] VALI, *supra* note 12, at 88.

[34] 49 U.N.T.S. 507, 61 Stat. 1245, T.I.A.S. No. 1648 (1947).

[35] 171 U.N.T.S. 279 (1949).

[36] *See* VALI, *supra* note 12, at 99–100.

The Japanese fishing rights in Russian territorial seas offer an example of fishing rights based on unequal distribution of population. After the Russo-Japanese War there was a territorial change based on the Peace Treaty of Portsmouth of 1905.[37] The east coast of Siberia was occupied by Russians along the Japan, Okhotsk, and Behring seas but was relatively scarcely populated. In the south, however, in one of the Japanese islands with an overcrowded population, fishing played a vital role in the economy. The Japanese used these coasts as permanent fishing grounds before the Russian occupation. The Russo-Japanese War interrupted these fishing rights for the Japanese. But the Japanese claims did not arise from this change; rather, they arose from the importance of fishing resources to the crowded population as against the unpopulated neighboring ports in Russia. Based on such claims, Article XI of the Peace Treaty granted the fishing rights to Japanese fishermen in 1907.[38] The duration of this treaty was twelve years, but after the fall of the Tsarist regime, the new government denied all the treaties made under the former regime. Japanese fishermen continued to use these fishery resources unilaterally until a new agreement, signed in 1925, recognized the Japanese fishing rights under the 1907 treaty. The political problems between the Soviet Union and Japan ended this fishing right in 1945. This prohibition gave the Japanese fishing industry serious problems after World War II. The independence of Korea, a former territory of Japan, denied the right of Japanese fishermen in her territorial waters, thus increasing the Japanese economic and political difficulties. The Russian realization of the importance of fishing resources in the Russian territory for Japan led in 1956 to a new compromise through diplomatic channels between the two countries, granting a limited fishing right to Japanese fishermen.[39]

Authoritative decisions, as well as state practices, have promoted important exclusive interests of the grantee state in fishing resources. Changes in the economic situation of the grantee and the development of the resources involved have been predominant factors in justifying modification of commitments. The flow of past decisions and practices, while recognizing the need for protection of the interest of the grantee, does not encourage expectations about permanency in the commitment of such agreements.

[37] *Id.* at 101.

[38] *See* 2 Am. J. Int'l. L. 274–85 (1908 Supp.).

[39] *See* VALI, *supra* note 12, at 104.

ii. Economical Use of Waters

In their continuous interactions, nation-states make agreements with each other regarding the use of common waters, such as boundary rivers or lakes, or rivers that flow through several territorial communities. Some of these agreements are negative, restricting states in building dams or in drainage from the common water. Others may authorize the state to construct certain works in the territory of another state necessary for the economic use of the common water resource.

The rapid expansion of population in various territorial communities and increasing demands for food, as well as the development of industries and needs for manufactured goods, have resulted in a growing demand for large water supplies for both irrigation and hydroelectric power. These increasing demands for development have created the need for transnational and regional planning to secure the most efficient use of water sources.

Once neighboring states recognize the need for cooperation for inclusive use of the common water and make plans for development through shared use of the water, their common interest is in the continuity of such plans. The common body of water may have a greater or smaller importance according to the circumstances of the individual states, a factor that should be considered in development planning agreements. Sometimes states may agree to preserve certain natural or artificial conditions in the common body of water, such as the maintenance of the water level at a given height; this is illustrated in the Peace Treaty between Lithuania and Soviet Russia of 1921.[40] An example regarding the right to construct necessary work in another state for economic use of the common water is the agreement reached concerning the Kunene River. This river was, from its mouth on the Atlantic, the frontier between the Mandated Territory of South-West Africa and the Portuguese colony of Angola up to the point where on both sides it became Portuguese territory. On December 30, 1886, a treaty on frontier delimitation was reached between Germany, which at that time was exercising sovereignty over South-West Africa, and Portugal.[41] After the treaty was concluded, a new survey was made of

[40] Article 2 of this Treaty reads: "The artificial diversion of water from the frontier rivers and lakes, causing a lowering of the average level of the water of the same, is not permitted." 3 L.N.T.S. 106 (1921), *quoted in* VALI, *id.* at 153.

[41] VALI, *id.* at 154.

the region covered by the treaty and this proved the existence of two different waterfalls in the area mentioned in the treaty, the delimitation of which remained uncertain. One of these falls, the southern, known as the Rua Cana Fall, became the subject of dispute between Portugal and the Union of South Africa, the Mandatory power of South-West Africa. After a long negotiation a compromise was reached. The Rua Cana Fall was declared to be in the territory of Portugal, but because of the importance of the supply of water to the Mandated territory, Portugal agreed to the construction of works for the economic exploitation of the power on her territory by the Mandatory power of South-West Africa and the partial diversion of the water above the Rua Cana Fall, dependent only on findings made by an expert investigation.[42]

A good example of the protection of common interests in the economic use of common water through regional planning is the agreement of 1927 between Portugal and Spain concerning the River Douro.[43] Portugal and Spain have over sixty miles of shared boundaries along this river. The international section of the Douro is particularly suitable for hydroelectric exploitation. The unregulated exclusive use by both countries not only prevented a productive economic use of the international section but also created serious problems in the exclusive use by each country of their own individual sections.[44] The recognition of their inclusive interest led the two countries to cooperate and collaborate on a better use through the agreement of 1927. This agreement thus illustrates the protection of both inclusive and exclusive interests of neighboring states. Article 2 of the agreement incorporates inclusive and exclusive interests that

> [t]he power capable of being developed on the international section of the Douro should be distributed between Portugal and Spain as follows:
>
> (a) Portugal shall have *exclusive right* of utilizing the entire fall in level of the river in the zone included between the beginning of the said section and the confluence of the Tormes and the Douro.
>
> (b) Spain shall have the *exclusive right* of utilizing the entire fall in level of the river in the zone included between the con-

[42] This agreement was signed in 1926 at Cape Town, 70 L.N.T.S. 315–28 (1926).

[43] 28 L.N.T.S. 114 (1923).

[44] VALI, *supra* note 12, at 158–59.

fluence of the Tormes and Douro and the lower limit of the said international section.

. . . .

(d) Each state shall have the right to utilize for the production of electric power the entire volume of water which flows through the zone of development allotted to it in accordance with the provisions of paragraph (a) and (b) with the exception of whatever may be necessary for common needs.

Paragraph (e) limits the rights of both countries to reduce the volume of water in a way to damage the development planning of the international section. Article 4 provides rights to be exercised within the territory of the other state: "The off-lets, canals, buildings and, generally, all the works and installations necessary from the utilization of each zone shall be situated on the national territory of the state entitled to such utilization, with the exception of the dams and works for the discharge of water or other accessories which have to be built in the bed or on the bank of the river belonging to the other state." This treaty provides a basis for maximum economic use through the cooperation of the parties involved.

In general, states, in practice, have accepted their burdens under agreements with other riparian states concerning the shared use of waters passing through their territories. When there have been claims for change in original commitment, it has been because of a change of conditions, such as natural changes in the water or economic changes related to development and requiring greater use of the water. The only claim for change based on state succession was made by the Sudan, a British protectorate, after its independence, concerning a 1929 agreement for the shared use of the Nile River.[45] This unilateral termination was not subjected to judicial review. Instead, intermittent negotiations between Egypt and the Sudan occurred until finally agreement was reached in 1959. The unilateral action of the Sudanese government was based on the idea that the British had not properly protected their interests in the 1929 agreement. The unilateral termination of agreements concerning the economic use of waters based only on a governmental structure or body politic would appear incompatible with the community interest. A more desirable policy is the

---

[45] For a comprehensive coverage of the various Nile River agreements, *see* Hosni, *The Nile Region*, 17 EGYPTIAN REV. OF INT'L L. 70 (1961).

joint promotion of the interests of all parties to the agreement based upon facts reflecting the genuine needs of each party.

The number of agreements for inclusive economic use of common waters has been increasing. There are many examples of agreements for inclusive economic use of common waters. Such were the agreements between Turkey and the Soviet Union of 1927 for cooperation in construction of a dam on the Aras River (the common frontier of the two countries),[46] and between the Soviet Union and Iran on the construction of a dam on the same river in the 1960s. Another example is the 1953 agreement between the United Kingdom and Portugal on the so-called Shire Valley Project.[47] Similar agreements have been made between the United States and Canada[48] and among the countries on the European continent and in Latin America. Such agreements can be expected to become more frequent in the future; the outcomes of past practices have greatly benefited the parties involved, aiding their attempts for securing and expanding their internal value processes.

iii. Minerals and Plants

Agreements between states with respect to access to mineral resources located within the boundaries of a single state, never very frequent, have decreased in both number and scope. The decrease in such practice between states, however, has not been the result of a loss of interest by grantors or grantees in cooperation for a maximum economic use of the minerals. Changes in world politics and international relations have been the main reason for a decrease in agreements between states for the development of mineral resources. Progress in world technology intensifying internal demands for raw materials has also been important. The main concern of states has, however, been the potential negative impact on their interrelations of the direct involvement of one government in the use of mineral resources within the territory of another state; this has been thought to carry the possibility of direct

---

[46] VALI, *supra* note 12, at 165.

[47] 175 U.N.T.S. 13, [1953] Gr. Brit. T.S. No. 35 (Cmd. 8855). This agreement concerns the Shire River, which is fed by the waters of Lake Nyasa. This project provides for the construction of a dam and stabilization of the lake and river waters for the production of hydroelectric power.

[48] [1950] 1 U.S.T. 694, T.I.A.S. No. 2130.

intervention, or the threat of intervention, by the grantee in case of disputes over the agreement. Some consider these agreements susceptible to many abuses and issue warnings to states not to be "careless of their territorial integrity."[49] Clearly it is possible that direct state involvement in such development agreements may threaten the world minimum order. The cooperative or shared use of minerals has nevertheless been secured through the modality of agreements between states and foreign private enterprises considered later in this section.

There has been some state practice in the use of agreements about minerals and plant resources within the territory of another state. The 1897 agreement between Great Britain and Abyssinia provided for reciprocal grazing rights for the tribes on the Somali coast frontier.[50] The practice of customary pasturage rights on the Turko-Syrian frontier was recognized by the Ankara Accord of 1921 and the Convention of 1926.[51] These two agreements both involved underdeveloped regions; seminomadic tribes were the actual beneficiaries. Such pasturage agreements have been usually concerned with border rights and were designed basically for the benefit of those who lived close to the frontier.[52]

There are a few examples of agreements between states about mineral resources, such as Article IX of the Prusso-Dutch Boundary Treaty of 1816.[53] By this article the Dutch Government acquired mining rights in Prussian territory. Article 45 of the Treaty of Versailles granted exclusive rights to French coal miners in specific areas of German territory.[54]

Sometimes the special geographical location of particular minerals, as along common frontiers, has encouraged state agreements. The Treaty of 1950 between Belgium and the Netherlands fixed a new mining boundary between the two governments, solely

---

[49] *See* REID, *supra* note 10, at 56.

[50] *Id.* at 52.

[51] *Id.* at 53.

[52] *Id.*

[53] *See* 8 AM. J. INT'L L. 908–909 (1914).

[54] Article 45 of the Treaty says that "Germany cedes to France in full and absolute possession with exclusive rights of exploitation, uncumbered and free from all debts and charges of any kind, the coal mines situated in the Saar Basin." Treaty of Versailles, Part III, Sec. IV, art. 45, *cited in* REID, *supra* note 10, at 59.

for the purpose of facilitating coal mining exploitation in the two countries. The Treaty thus explains its goal: "Desirous of facilitating the mining of coal in the mines situated along the Meuse on both sides of the Netherlands-Belgium frontier and of thus reducing to a minimum the loss of extractable coal."[55] Article 1 of this agreement provides mining boundaries which are different from the political boundaries.[56]

Even mineral resources located within military bases have sometimes led to agreements between states for access to and use of such resources. Thus, mineral resources within the American military bases in the Philippines led to the 1957 agreement[57] by which the Philippine government's access to her mineral resources within the American military bases was limited: "the United States Government welcomes the fostering of economic development of the Philippines by proper utilization of its natural resources in the military bases if, and to the extent, that exploitation of natural resources is possible without prejudice to the military purposes for which the bases are being used." This agreement was supplemented by another treaty in 1967, whereby the access and permission for the Government of the Philippines to her natural resources located in American bases should be approved by the U.S. military authorities.[58] Article 2 of this treaty provides:

> Application for access to bases used by the United States for the purpose of evaluation or exploitation of natural resources located therein will be transmitted by the Philippine Department of Foreign Affairs to the Embassy of the United States for forwarding to the appropriate United States military authorities. Such application has the approval of the responsible Philippine authorities to evaluate or exploit the scientific natural resources, as set forth in the application for access, in accordance with Philippine Law.

Article 3 states: "Each such application for access to bases for evaluation or exploitation of natural resources shall be promptly

[55] 136 U.N.T.S. 31 (1950).

[56] Article I provides that "[a] new mining boundary for underground operations, independent of the frontier between the two States, is hereby agreed upon in respect of the mines of the 'Societe Anonyme des Charbonnaye de Limbourg-Heuse' in Belgium and the Maurits State Mine in the Netherlands."

[57] [1957] 9 U.S.T. 309, T.I.A.S. No. 4008.

[58] [1967] 18 U.S.T. 2340, T.I.A.S. No. 6335.

received by the Philippine–United States Mutual Defense Board which shall determine whether the evaluation or exploitation can be undertaken in a manner consistent with the security and operation of the base area." As already indicated, development agreements between states and private parties have largely supplanted agreements between states as an appropriate strategy for shared use of minerals within exclusive zones. States nevertheless sometimes make agreements for the development and exploitation of such resources, such as agreements between the United States and Brazil for exploration for oil in Brazil.[59] It is not, however, the purpose of these agreements to create a right for one contracting state to minerals of the other state.

iv. Strategic Rights over Resources

The world's science and technology of destructive instruments has developed along with other branches of inquiry. There are now weapons capable of shattering attack halfway around the globe. This emphasis on the development of destructive weapons comes from a view that has always considered military strategies to be an effective way for acquiring and maintaining power and other values. This perspective, in conjunction with the competition among the effective powers for establishing their own preferred policies of world order and by their own methods, has led to the making of treaties whereby some states are given the right to establish military bases in the territory of other states, whether for stationing of troops or for the testing of nonnuclear weapons or other defense systems. By *strategic agreements* we refer to agreements whereby one state has been granted the use of resources located within the territory of another state for such military purposes.

For a long time strategic rights in other territorial communities were considered, since such rights might create a desirable balancing of power, to be in the inclusive interest both of regions and of the larger community. During the Cold War period, the number of such agreements increased, until in more recent years the mere presence of foreign military bases abroad may of themselves create and promote expectations of violence on a regional or transnational scale. The exercise of strategic rights has come into increasing conflict with the exclusive interests of the grantor territorial

---

[59][1951] 2 U.S.T. 1554, T.I.A.S. No. 2296; [1952] 3 U.S.T. 5145, T.I.A.S. No. 2706; [1954] 5 U.S.T. 2918, T.I.A.S. No. 3149.

community. Due to the emergence of a new ideology among the developing areas of the world about independence—economic and other—many of these strategic agreements have begun to vex the developing countries. The growth of national pride, the encouragement of group unity among the developing and nonaligned countries, and the formation of new strategies to fulfill changing demands about world order have all become inconsistent with the granting of strategic rights to the effective powers among the developed nations. The granting of strategic rights never furthermore really stabilized the balance-of-power competition. On the contrary, it rather increased the competition among the effective powers for control over world order through all strategies, including the economic, diplomatic, and ideological. We do not recommend a blanket opposition to strategic rights and the willingness of grantors to respect such rights. Such rights should, however, be made dependent upon the continuing consent of the grantee.

Because of the realization of the potential dangers to internal processes from the exercise of strategic rights, particularly of the rights to military bases and testing areas, the majority of agreements for such rights are made of relatively short duration. Such agreements often contain a provision providing a right of unilateral denouncement for the grantor. In such situations, the question of succession, of course, does not arise because of the overriding authority of the grantor. Even if such a clause is not provided by the agreement, expectations about the future performance of such agreements are generally limited. It seems that in one instance only has a successor state recognized the burden of such an agreement. This instance involved an agreement between the United States and France in 1950, whereby the United States was authorized to establish five military bases within the French protectorate of Morocco.[60] Upon Morocco's emancipation in 1956, while it clearly opposed the location of these bases,[61] Morocco continued to recognize the American agreement until it was terminated by negotiation.[62]

A considerable number of strategic rights are given through

[60] *See* VALI, *supra* note 12, at 246–47.

[61] *See* O'Connell, *Independence and Succession to Treaties* 38 BRIT. Y. B. INT'L L. 84, 147–50 (1962).

[62] *Id.* at 155.

bilateral agreements. There are, however, some multilateral agreements, creating organizations, by which the maintenance of troops by members on the territory of other members has acquired a "confederate character,"[63] such as, the Brussels Treaty Organization,[64] The North Atlantic Treaty Organization (NATO),[65] and Western European Union.[66] Some strategic agreements give a right to the grantee to intervene in the territory of another state at times of crisis. This was the interpretation by the United States of the 1846 Treaty about transit routes in Central America.[67] Based on this interpretation, the United States intervened from time to time whenever war or domestic disturbance threatened to interrupt communication across the Isthmus. Another example of strategic agreement permitting intervention is the 1903 Panama Treaty.[68] This treaty explicitly granted strategic rights to the United States. Article XXII states: "If it should be necessary at any time to employ armed forces for the safety or protection of the Canal, or of the ships that make use of the same, or the railways and auxiliary works, the United States should have the right at any time and in its discretion, to use its police and its land and naval forces or to establish fortifications for these purposes." Articles II and XIV expand the right of the United States to use Panama resources by providing that the United States has the right to "*use, occupy*, and *control*" any *lands* or *waters*, "necessary and convenient for the . . . protection of the said canal," and a "*right to buy* or *lease land* for naval and coaling stations on both coasts." Article III states: "The Republic of Panama grants to the United States all the rights, power and authority within the zone mentioned . . . which the United States could *possess* and exercise *if it were the sovereign of the territory within which said lands and waters are located to the entire exclusion of exercise by the Republic of Panama of any such sovereign rights, power or authority* (emphasis added)." The United States has used these articles to claim practical sovereignty over the territories covered by the Treaty. The Government of Panama, in oppo-

---

[63] *See* VALI, *supra* note 12, at 208.

[64] *Id.*

[65] The NATO pact was signed in Washington, D.C., on April 4, 1949.

[66] *See* VALI, *supra* note 12, at 208.

[67] REID, *supra* note 10, at 190.

[68] *See* H. ARIAS, THE PANAMA CANAL 168–78 (1970).

sition, has asserted that the 1903 agreement conflicts with her internal security and her exclusive interests.

The 1864 agreement between the United States and Honduras was a strategic agreement for intervention.[69] According to this agreement, the United States was to protect the projected railway from "interruption, seizure, or unjust confiscation from any quarter."[70] The Nicaragua Treaty of 1867 accorded a limited intervention right to the United States, "with the consent or at the request of the government of Nicaragua," to employ forces "for the security and protection of persons and property passing over any of the routes."[71] "[In addition, in time of crisis,] . . . the United States was authorized to protect the life and property of her own citizens with or without specific prior consent."[72] This treaty was subsequently terminated by the government of Nicaragua, due to the conflict with her internal security and her exclusive interest. The 1903 agreement between the United States and Cuba, later terminated by Cuba, was in the category of strategic rights for intervention.[73]

Some strategic rights are negotiated through negative agreements whereby a state agrees to restrict its rights to use its resources for its own strategic purposes for the benefit of another state or states. There are a number of such treaties, many of them the result of postwar attempts at security through disarmament. Although we would recommend policies for general disarmament, in the sense of restriction on all nations or all parties to an agreement in the destructive use of resources, we would discourage policies that discriminate among the nation-states in this right. The most obvious example of such discrimination is in treaties, concluded usually after a major war, which impose disarmament upon the vanquished while leaving the victors fully armed.[74] Such agreements are not, as past experience has shown, in the inclusive interest of the world community. Any such discriminatory agree-

---

[69] REID, *supra* note 10, at 191.

[70] *Id.*

[71] *Id.*

[72] *Id.* For a detailed history of this agreement, *see* L. KEASBEY, THE NICARAGUA CANAL AND THE MONROE DOCTRINE (1896).

[73] REID, *supra* note 10, at 192–3.

[74] *Id.* at 197.

ments, as Reid says, "can be expected to last only until the opportunity comes to throw them off."[75] Thus, article 9 of the Treaty of
Utrecht of 1713, forbidding France to construct fortifications for
Dunkirk, was terminated by Article 17 of the Treaty of Versailles
in 1783;[76] and the demilitarization of the Black Sea imposed on
Russia in 1856 was abrogated in 1871.[77] Article 42 of the Treaty of
Versailles forbade Germany "to maintain or construct any fortifications either on the left bank of the Rhine or on the right bank to
the west of a line drawn 50 kilometres to the east of the Rhine."[78]

Negative strategic agreements may impose restrictions upon the
use of certain areas vitally important to the transnational community, such as international waterways, in order to secure transnational commerce and communications; these agreements are in
the inclusive interest and should be protected. Excepting the Panama Canal and in recent years the Suez Canal, almost all international waterways have been more or less under a demilitarized
regime. The 1881 Treaty between Chile and Argentina provides
that "no fortifications or military defenses shall be erected that
could interfere with the liberty and neutrality of the Straits of
Magellan."[79] In the Anglo-French Declaration of 1904, the parties
agreed not to permit the erection of any fortification or strategic
works in order to secure the free passage of the Strait of Gibral-
tar.[80] Sometimes this neutralization involved common boundaries,
such as the 1905 agreement between Sweden and Norway, the
Treaty of Portsmouth between Japan and Russia, and the Anglo-
Chinese treaty of 1894 concerning the boundaries between Burma
and Tibet.[81]

Some positive strategic agreements are concerned with the establishment and the maintenance of stations within the territory
of another country. Such agreements once were common practice

[75] *Id.*

[76] *Id.*

[77] *See* W. PHILLIMORE, THREE CENTURIES OF TREATIES OF PEACE (1918); E. HERTSLET, A
COMPLETE COLLECTION OF TREATIES OF GREAT BRITAIN (1895) [hereinafter cited as HERTS-
LET]; and REID, *supra* note 10, at 192.

[78] REID, *supra* note 10, at 197–8.

[79] *Id.* at 198.

[80] *Id.* at 198–199.

[81] *Id.*

among the major powers and their allies around the world. Recently, however, there are increasing demands for change in, or termination of, these agreements. The main reasons for such increasing demands, as explained above, are in the changes in perspectives and circumstances within the territorial countries as well as in their interactions with each other. Some of these positive strategic rights for establishment of military bases include: the right of Austria in Ferraro and Commechio under the Treaty of Vienna, Belgian rights under the Barrier Treaty of 1715 (now extinguished),[82] the British right in Iraq (terminated in 1955),[83] and the British right in Jordan (terminated in 1957).[84]

One of the oldest positive strategic agreements to survive up to the present time and recently the subject of controversy is the 1947 agreement between the Philippines and the United States.[85] This agreement was signed one year after the Philippines gained independence from Japanese occupation with the assistance of the United States. This agreement is one of the most extensive in its grant of the use of one country's resources by another for strategic rights. Article I of the agreement grants to the government of the United States "the right to retain the use of the bases in the Philippines [Listed Islands]." Moreover, the Philippines agree "to permit the United States, upon notice to the Philippines, to use such of those bases listed ... as the United States determines to be required by military necessities." Article III determines the extent of the rights to the United States: "the United States shall have the right, power and authority within the bases which are necessary for the establishment, use, operation and defence thereof or appropriate for the control thereof and the rights, power and authority within the limits of territorial waters and airspace adjacent to, or in the vicinity of, the bases which are necessary to provide access to them, or appropriate for this control."

Paragraph (1) of Article XXV limits the power of the Philippines to grant any rights about those bases to any third party. The 1947 agreement gave sovereignty over Crark and Subic Bases to the United States for 99 years, rent free. Some of the original rights

---

[82] *Id.* at 194.

[83] 132 L.N.T.S. 364 (1932).

[84] VALI, *supra* note 12, at 222–226.

[85] For the complete text of the treaty, *see* 43 U.N.T.S. 271 (1949).

have, however, been changed, for example, in reducing the time to 1991. Yet the hold by the United States of strategic rights over parts of the Philippines has since last year become a critical issue for a number of reasons.

According to the treaty, authority and control of the Philippines over its territory have been considerably restricted in many ways. With respect to internal matters the treaty restricts the Philippines' rights

1. In the economic use of natural resources in these bases in the 1957 treaty, as explained earlier;[86]

2. In the promotion of well-being of the people within these bases, including its own citizens. The 1955 agreement[87] stipulates that control and operation of the schools within the bases are to be given back to the Philippine Government on the condition that the schools will employ "only such persons as do not, in the opinion of the Naval authorities, constitute or become risks to the security of the Naval Base," that those admitted to these schools as students are to be "only those who are authorized and remain authorized by Naval authorities to reside on the Naval Reservation";

3. In competence over activities done within the bases, based on Article XIII of 1947 agreement.

With respect to the interactions of the Philippines with other people, the presence of American bases has created certain problems in the promotion of values. Thus, with reference to:

1. Respect; the American sovereignty in the Philippines has damaged the respect for this country as an independent nation among her neighbors and among other countries as well. The American strategic rights in the Philippines have created the image of the "Philippines as client of the United States."[88]

2. Wealth and Power; the presence of American bases has lessened the Philippines' ability to increase her power and wealth through participation in regional and transnational activities, such as those involving third world nations or nonaligned nations. For example, when the Philippines attended the Conference of nonaligned nations in Lima, her membership was questioned by For-

[86][1957] 9 U.S.T. 309, T.I.A.S. No. 4008.

[87][1955] 6 U.S.T. 3109.

[88]N.Y. Times, Sept. 7, 1975, at 2, col. 3.

eign Minister Nguyen Thi Bing of South Vietnam on the ground that American bases in the Philippines disqualified the Philippines' membership in the organization.[89] Such damage to external reputation will harm internal minimum order and well-being.

In an interview the President of the Philippines expressed his country's desire to obtain more control over the American bases. He explained that the objectives of the recent negotiations for such control are designed to place the bases under Philippine sovereignty and so turn them into "economically productive facilities as well as military installations."[90] He recognized the need for a balancing of power in the Pacific but expressed fear that the internal minimum order of the Philippines, as well as regional minimum order, could be in danger if the United States continued with its present rights. In the interview he remarked that "the Vietnam War has taught all of us, including the Americans, I suppose, that for people trying to fight for their independence it does not pay to appear to do the bidding of the United States."[91]

Because of the scarcity of authoritative decisions with regard to succession to strategic rights, it is impossible to state that there is a clear past trend of decision consistent or inconsistent with basic community policies. As to our policies favoring inclusive interest, we generally would not encourage the making of strategic agreements, since, as has been shown in the past, the enjoyment of such rights may itself be a major threat to world security. Such rights may also be obstacles to the protection of the internal value processes of the grantor. In a world where the expectation of violence is high, it could be in the inclusive interest to grant some strategic rights to United Nations' troops and to establish and maintain bases for protection of general security and human rights. It might also be in the inclusive interest to promote regional or transnational negative strategic agreements; these might provide for restriction or prohibition of certain destructive weapons and for the demilitarization of places that have vital importance in the world, such as international waterways. The improved organization of a region for security becomes inimical only when the accumulations

[89] *Id.*

[90] *Id.*

[91] *Id.*

of power threaten the minimum order or other common interests of the more general community.

b. *Rights in Spatial-Extension Resources (Transit and Scientific Rights)*

The need for cooperation in the shared enjoyment of spatial-extension resources for the movement of goods and services across political boundaries has always been an important component of international relations. Because of this, states' transit agreements, and more recently agreements for the shared use of spatial-extension resources for scientific purposes, constitute a major part of transnational development planning. By *state transit agreements* we refer to any agreement between states that promotes the movement of transportation or communication across or through territorial boundaries. Transit rights have in the past probably been the content of more international servitudes than any other rights. Transit rights are most significant to landlocked states, that is, those surrounded by other territorial communities. The main objectives underlying demands for such rights over land masses and water and through air are the promotion and facilitation of the use of other resources in research, exploitation, processing, marketing, and distributing activities; in other words, demands for more and better production and distribution of values. The significance of transit servitudes may vary from the indispensable to a mere convenience. The degree of utility may become a factor in the promotion of, or restraint upon, the future employment of transit servitudes. Where the right of transit is a mere convenience to the grantee, the claims of the grantor for security and important exclusive interests may seem more persuasive than in situations where the transit right is vital or indispensable to the grantee or grantees.

The transit servitudes may be for passage across land, water, or sea or through air, and they may serve the exclusive interests of one territorial community or of many. Because an important prerequisite to the attainment of an appropriately wide production and distribution of values is the ability to transport and communicate freely across national boundaries, transit rights become a vital component of optimum world public order. Therefore, the inclusive interest of the larger community is in the continuity and stability of such agreements for transnational development, particularly with respect to economic activities; it is necessary for decision makers to distinguish between political and economic and other considerations with respect to both the right of transit and the shared use of resources for increase of scientific knowledge. Political considerations should not be permitted to overshadow the economic, social, and scientific necessities involved in such rights. Thus, the inclusive interests of the larger community would seem to demand that transit rights not be terminated merely because of a change in the government or other features of the grantor.

i. Transit Through Landmasses

State agreements for transit through landmasses have long been looked upon as productive and worthy of protection[92] because they have usually involved construction of transportation and communication facilities, such as roads, railways, and telegraphs. The construction of transit facilities was either incorporated in the agreement or was implied from the necessities of implementing the agreement. There have been many state agreements for construction of transit facilities in which the largest benefit to the grantee was the right of transit through the grantor's territory. Often the desire to obtain transit privileges in foreign territory was an influential factor in inducing construction agreements. Most of the transit agreements relate to African territories. A main objective behind many of the earlier transit agreements in African countries was not so much that of developing the region itself as of increasing the control of the European powers in their colonies. Nevertheless, construction of transit facilities created the possibility for development by increasing opportunity for contact with the outside world. For example, in the treaty of 1902 between Ethiopia, the United Kingdom, and Sudan, the King of Ethiopia granted the other two goverments the right to construct a railway through Abyssinian territory to connect the Sudan with Uganda.[93] Ethiopia at that time was a landlocked country because her eastern port on the Red Sea, Eritrea, was under Italian domination; the railway, however, was connected with the Cairo railway and a line in British East Africa. The construction of the railway was, hence,

[92]*See* REID, *supra* note 10, at 105.

[93]*See* XXIII HERTSLET 1 (1902).

not only in the interest of the grantees but also in the interest of the grantor and many other countries of the region.

In the era of formal colonialism in Africa, Portugal and Great Britain, for the promotion of their influence over their respective spheres in Africa, agreed in 1891 that "each power shall have the right as far as may be reasonably required for purposes of communication between territories under the influence of the same power, to construct roads, railways, bridges, and telegraph lines across the district reserved to the other. . . . [A]ny railway so constructed by one Power on the territory of the other shall be subject to local regulations and laws agreed upon between the two Governments."[94] Prior to this agreement Portugal concluded another agreement with the South African Republic in which the Government of South Africa granted the Portuguese Government "all facilities in accordance with the laws of the Republic, for the construction and working of a railway."[95] The South African Republic in another agreement with Great Britain in 1890 recognized the validity of various construction rights acquired by South Africa in the British protectorate of Swaziland and consented to the acquisition of the ownership of a strip of land approximately three miles wide.[96]

Not all the transit agreements in Africa included construction of transit facilities. There were many agreements by which the native tribes of Africa accorded to various European nations a perpetual right to passage across their territories, with no obligation for construction.[97]

The situation in the European continent was rather different. The rights to transit and the construction of transit facilities were based more on the inclusive interests and the shared demands of

[94] *See* XIX HERTSLET 776, 780 (1891).

[95] REID, *supra* note 10, at 106.

[96] *Id.* at 107.

[97] For example, the agreement between the Colony of Good Hope and the Pondo Chief in 1886 states: "The said Umquikela for himself, his heirs, and successors, and on behalf of the Pondo nation, hereby concedes to the Colonial Government the right to enter in, make, construct, and maintain the road through Eastern Pondo land to the mouth of the St. John's River, following the existing line as far as practicable, granting unto them all such outspans and grazing rights as may be required, and the free and undistributed use of such road exempt of all tolls or other charges whatever." XVII HERTSLET 50, 51 (1886).

the parties than upon the benefits of the colonialism. Some transit rights in Europe have been given through peace treaties because of changes of the boundary lines and subsequent economic effects.

The changes in the boundaries between Germany on the eastern side and Poland on the western side in the Treaty of Versailles of 1919 created an undesirable situation;[98] first, a part of Germany, Eastern Prussia, became separated from the rest of the country; second, the changes in the boundaries caused re-routing of existing railways, with changes in the distances between the important economic centers in Germany, as well as for traveling from Polish cities across German territories. "Had the present frontier been in existence a hundred years ago, then 90 percent of the existing railway tracks would not lie where they were at the moment and probably more than half of the present economic centers [in the 1920s] would not be there, the whole railway system and the economic configuration of the country would in fact, have adopted another form."[99] Since it was impossible to draw boundary lines to conform with the economic necessities of the two countries, a compromise was recommended for granting transit rights to the state whose economic equilibrium and transportation were endangered in particular situations. Article 98 of the Treaty provided that

> Germany and Poland undertake within one year of the coming into force of this Treaty, to enter into Conventions of which the terms, in case of difference, shall be settled by the Council of the League of Nations, with the object of securing, on the one hand to Germany full and adequate railroad, telegraphic and telephonic facilities for communication between the rest of Germany and East Prussia over the intervening Polish territory, and on the other hand to Poland full and adequate railroad, telegraphic and telephonic facilities for communication between Poland and the Free City of Danzig over any German territory that may, on the right bank of the Vistula, intervene between Poland and the Free City of Danzig.[100]

To promote their common interest, Germany, Poland, and the Free City of Danzig entered into an agreement signed in Paris in

[98] VALI, *supra* note 12, at 108.

[99] *Id.*

[100] *Id.*

1921.[101] There was a similar agreement between Germany and Poland regarding the transit between Polish Upper Silesia and the remainder of Polish territory through German Upper Silesia, signed in 1922.[102] Although the Second World War changed the German and Polish boundaries, nevertheless the cooperation of the two countries in promotion of their inclusive interest is a hopeful trend for meeting expectations for the future.

Another example of transit problems resulting from shifting boundaries involved the consequences of independence for the State of Finland, which deprived Russia of her former common frontier with Norway and Sweden. A compromise between Finland and Russia was reached in 1922 by which the Russian authorities and Russian nationals had the right to free passage through Finnish territory from Russia to Norway and from Norway to Russia.[103]

World War II extended Polish territory along the Silesian side of the former German-Czechoslovakian frontier. This expansion brought some disadvantages to Czechoslovakia in the transit between the two parts of her territory. A Convention was signed in Warsaw in 1948 between Poland and Czechoslovakia by which Poland granted Czechoslovakia freedom of transit between the two Czechoslovak cities through the Polish territory by railway.[104]

In times of crisis, agreements may be concluded for transit in order to overcome exigencies. Such agreements are usually of a short-term nature. There was an arrangement between the United States and Canada during World War II (1942), which entitled the United States to construct a strategic road across Canada to Alaska.[105] After the war Canada agreed to make available to the United States certain communications facilities, particularly tele-

---

[101] 12 L.N.T.S. 61 (1921). Article 27 of the Treaty reads: "This recognition of common interest led to a significant cooperation between the three countries. Even Germany agreed to lend Poland a certain number of engines for a limited time, to enable her to carry out her obligations under treaty. There were also many provisions to minimize the problems and restrictions in this passage. For example, passengers on privileged transit need not even have identification cards when passing over the foreign territories."

[102] 26 L.N.T.S. 311 (1922).

[103] 19 L.N.T.S. 207, art. 1 (1922).

[104] 84 U.N.T.S. B47 (1951).

[105] 101 U.N.T.S. 205 (1951).

phone and telegraph lines located along that road.[106] In general, however, unless the grantor agrees, the continued enjoyment of such commitments after the crisis is not likely.

The decision of the Permanent Court of International Justice in *Free Zones of Upper Savoy and the District of Gex* cases reflects community expectations about the continuity of transit agreement in a case of succession.[107] It specifically recognizes that a successor body politic could not unilaterally deny responsibility for the burden of an international servitude granted by its predecessor. This case involved several claims about certain custom-free zones Switzerland enjoyed in France. One of the zones was established by Article 3 of the Treaty of Turin on March 18, 1816, by which Sardinia conferred upon Switzerland the right to a custom-free zone in and around the town of Saint-Gindolph. When the controversy concerning France's refusal to continue to respect this and other custom-free zones arose, the French claimed that these zones were abrogated upon its succession to the Sardinian territories. The court, however, expressly declared that France must respect the agreement of her predecessor.[108]

Today a right of transit in terms of innocent passage through land masses among territorial communities is a general practice because of the need for movement of people, goods, and services. This consensus has become clear in the operation of railways passing from one country to another. The earliest way of controlling such transit was for the passengers to leave their train at the frontier station or some place near the border and then walk over the border and take another train. Eventually the carriages were allowed to run from one country into the other, but staff, such as the train crew, customs officials, and frontier guards, except the engine drivers, did not cross the border. Still later the train was allowed to run to the first station in the foreign countries with all staff and passengers.

Because of a lack of authoritative decision concerning transit servitudes through land masses, it may appear that expectations

[106] VALI, *supra* note 12, at 123.

[107] [1929] P.C.I.J. ser. A, No. 22; [1930] P.C.I.J. ser. A, No. 24; [1923] P.C.I.J. ser A/B No. 46.

[108] [1930] P.C.I.J. ser. A, No. 24, at 17.

about the future performance of these agreements are unclear. However, the lack of conflict on this matter, and the easy cooperation among nation-states, indicates a recognition by all of the need for reciprocal accommodation and of the importance of compliance with expectations.

ii. Transit Through Water

The international agreements on the right of transit through water are those concerning the use of a nation's territorial waters as a connecting link for interoceanic traffic. Such territorial waters include international straits, canals, rivers, and territorial seas. States' agreements on transit through waters are either multilateral[109] or bilateral[110] or based on unilateral prescriptions.[111]

Historically, both international canals and international straits, as well as international rivers, have served as important highways of commerce and communication for various types of shipping. The general prescriptions and past practices regarding international rivers could be summarized thus: the rivers of international importance were to be kept open to navigation by ships of all states.[112] In spite of the continuous development of agreements for free navigation in international rivers,[113] transit through territorial seas has been a controversial issue in law of the sea conferences. Because of the difficult nature of the problem, particularly in the light of continuous demands for expansion of the territorial seas and economic zones, there has been a collective attempt to resolve this problem through international agreement. Since we have already dealt with international rivers and the territorial sea in a previous chapter, we here emphasize only international straits and canals.

---

[109]Cf. Treaty of Versailles; Convention of Constantinople, 1888.

[110]Cf. Anglo-French Agreement of 1954; Hay-Pauncefote Treaty, 1901.

[111]Cf. The Egyptian Nationalization Law of 1956; Egyptian Declaration of April, 1957.

[112]*See* C. Hyde, 1 International Law 563 (2d ed. 1945), L. Oppenheim, 1 International Law, 421 (7th ed. H. Lauterpacht ed. 1948), P. Ogilvie, International Waterways 150 (1920). Baxter, *Passage of Ships Through International Waterways in Time of War*, 29 Brit. Y.B. Int'l L. 188 (1954).

[113]*See e.g.,* Article 1, Revised Convention for the Navigation of the Rhine, signed at Mannheim, Oct. 1868.

International canals are artificial waterways, and straits are natural ones. Most straits and canals are located within the territorial sovereignty of one state, though some straits run between two or more territorial countries. Despite such differences they serve much the same functions as major highways which interrelate the high seas and accept vessels of many different types. While straits and canals have common characteristics in their importance with respect to right of passage, they each have their own particular problems. For example, international straits have problems with regard to the breadth of the territorial waters and exploitation of natural resources, and international canals have some problems which derive from their artificial character. Since they are prominent resources of revenue, the problems of ownership and nationalization have become important issues.

In formulating policies about international waterways it is necessary to distinguish between waterways essential for international commerce or intercourse and those not so essential, since world public order is vitally concerned with waterways necessary for international transportation and communication. When a waterway is sufficiently important to international commerce, policies regarding the continuous enjoyment of the waterway are more clearly formulated both by authoritative decisions and by the customary practices of states themselves.

Inclusive rights of passage through international transit routes may be enjoyed either by all territorial communities or smaller groups. These inclusive uses are granted by agreements or unilateral prescriptions or both. The transit routes whose inclusive use is granted to all nations on equal terms are exceptionally important because they are common highways which connect two oceans for commerce and intercourse among the peoples of the world. Because of their special commercial and strategic importance to the world community, these transit routes have acquired international status, not only through agreements and prescriptions, but also through a century of interactions and responses in cases of disputes concerning such rights.

A right of free passage through straits connecting two open seas has been recognized by multilateral and bilateral agreements and unilateral actions. The Straits of Magellan, for example, are entirely within the boundaries of Chile, but the universal right of passage was recognized in the 1881 agreement between Chile and Argentina, by which they declared that the "Straits of Magellan are neutralized forever, and their free navigation is guaranteed to the flags of all nations."[114] Sometimes use of a waterway becomes so vital to the inclusive interests of the larger community that nation-states do not recognize any exclusive control over the use of the waterway. The United States, for example, officially declared that it would not "tolerate exclusive claims by any nation whatsoever to the Straits of Magellan."[115] In 1916 the British Prize Court declared: "[The Strait of Magellan] connects the two vast free oceans of the Atlantic and the Pacific. As such, the Strait must be considered free for the commerce of all nations passing between the two oceans. . . ."[116]

The right of passage through the Dardanelles and the Bosphorus was first given to the great powers of the late eighteenth century through individual agreements.[117] Later, by the Treaty of 1923 between the United Kingdom, France, Italy, Japan, Bulgaria, Greece, Rumania, Russia, the Serb-Croat-Slovene and Turkey, the passage was open to universal use. Turkey "agreed to recognize and declare the principle of freedom of transit and navigation by sea and by air in the Strait of Dardanelles, the Sea of Marmara and the Bosphorus, hereinafter comprised under the general terms of the Strait."[118] Under this treaty Turkey "as a neutral Power cannot . . . take any measures liable [likely] to interfere with navigation through the Strait, the waters of which, and the air above which, must remain entirely free in time of war, Turkey being neutral, just as in time of peace."[119]

Because of the expansion of territorial seas which embrace many international straits, there has been a universal attempt to solve the problem of right of transit through these straits by international agreements. Though bilateral agreements can still be made for some individual ancillary rights, their validity must be

[114]3 AM. J. INT'L L. (Supp.) at 122, Part. V (1909).

[115]REID, *supra* note 10, at 141.

[116]*Id.*

[117]With Russia by the treaty of Katchuk-Kainordji, 1774, Austria in 1784, France in 1802, Purssia in 1806, Spain in 1827, Sardinia in 1824. For full texts of all these agreements, see the official Turkish Collection, P. NORADOUNGHIAN, RECEUIL D'ACTES INTERNATIONAUX DE L'EMPIRE OTTOMAN, Paris 1879–1913, Vols. I and II, *cited in* REID, *supra* note 10, at 142.

[118]Treaty of Peace with Turkey, [1923] Gr. Brit. T.S. No. 16 (Cmd. 1929) at 114.

[119]*Id.*, art. 2.

made to depend on their conformity with the general rules set up by the major international agreements. In the recent law of the sea conferences, the international arrangement for the shared use of international straits has been a complicated subject, particularly with the expansion of territorial seas to 12 miles and of the economic zone to 200 miles. A 12-mile territorial sea all over the world would affect approximately 112 international straits less than 24 miles wide.[120] At the Geneva session of the Law of the Sea Conference, the majority agreed on the subjection of international straits to "unimpeded transit."[121] In this session the United Kingdom and Fiji made a proposal of a regime that was accepted by the majority, with the exception of the United States, in Committee II.[122] This proposal would apply to the Straits "which are used for international navigation between one area of the high seas or an exclusive economic zone and another area of the high seas or an exclusive economic zone."[123] The proposal recognized the right of transit by all ships.[124] Article 41, while allowing control by the coastal state of the strait for regulating the use of the strait, forbids any discrimination in terms of prescription or application of such regulations as between states.[125] Article 42 emphasizes the cooperation of

[120] STAFF OF SENATE COMM. ON FOREIGN RELATIONS, 94TH CONG., 1ST SESS., REPORT ON THE THIRD U.N. LAW OF THE SEA CONFERENCE 2 (Comm. Print, Feb. 1975).

[121] STAFF OF SENATE COMM. ON FOREIGN RELATIONS, 94TH CONG., 1ST SESS., REPORT ON THE THIRD U.N. LAW OF THE SEA CONFERENCE 16 (Comm. Print Aug. 1975).

[122] *Id.*

[123] U.N. Doc. A/Conf.62/WP.8/Part II (1975), Article 37.

[124] Article 38, *Id.*

[125] Article 41, *Id.*

"1. Subject to the provisions of this section, the Strait State may make laws and regulations relating to transit passage through straits, in respect of all or any of the following:

"(a) The safety of navigation and the regulation of marine traffic provided in Art. 40;

"(b) The prevention of pollution, giving effect to applicable international regulations regarding the discharge of oil, oily waters, and other noxious substances in the strait,

"(c) With respect to fishing vessels, the prevention of fishing, including the stowage of fishing gear;

"(d) The taking on board or putting overboard of any commodity, currency, or person in contravention of the customs, fiscal, immigration, or sanitary regulations of the strait State.

"2. Such laws and regulations shall not discriminate in form or fact among foreign ships,

states through agreements for "establishment and maintenance in a strait of necessary navigation and safety aids or other improvements in and of international navigation. . . ."[126] And, finally, Article 43 declares that "[a] Strait State shall not hamper transit passage and shall give appropriate publicity to any danger to navigation or over flight within or over the Strait of which it has knowledge. There shall be no suspension of transit passage."[127] This proposal, while protecting the inclusive interest in shared use by transit passage through international straits, promotes the exclusive interest of the coastal state by recognizing the status of a strait as the exclusive economic zone of the coastal state[128] and empowering the state with the competences necessary for exploitation of the natural resources of the strait and protection of the environment.[129] The negotiations at the Law of the Sea Conference, despite conflicts about the details of regulation, reflect the expectations of the world community in recognition of inclusive use for transit through international straits.

The inclusive use of international canals was first secured by agreement between states. The inclusive use of the Panama Canal, for example, was protected by the Hay-Pauncefote Treaty of 1901 between the United States and the United Kingdom,[130] whereby the United States agreed that "the Canal shall be free and open to the vessels of commerce and of war of all nations observing these rules, on terms of entire equality."[131] However, this Treaty obligated only the two states; third parties have no rights or duties under the agreement. Yet the common practice of such rights and obligations in the course of time has created a worldwide expectation concerning free transit through the Canal as a part of customary international law. Furthermore, the agreement of 1903 between the United States and Panama provided that the Canal

---

nor in their application have the practical effect of denying, hampering, or imparting the right of transit passage as defined in this Section. . . ."

[126]*Id.* Article 42.

[127]*Id.* Article 43.

[128]*Id.* Article 35.

[129]*Id.* Article 41.

[130]32 Stat. 1903 T.S., No. 41 (1901).

[131]*Id.* Article III.

shall "be opened . . . in conformity with all the stipulations" of the Hay-Pauncefote Treaty and thus adopted by reference the language of the entire agreement. The expectation of inclusive use of the Canal has been promoted by the unilateral actions of the Government of Panama. The Republic of Panama because of her peculiar geographical situation considers the Canal an international waterway that should be open for the use of all nations. On September 10, 1927, Don Eusebio Morales, Minister for Foreign and Internal Affairs and the Chief of the delegation of Panama at the Eighth Assembly of the League of Nations, declared:

> Panama is a country favored by a unique geographical position to which she owes, in large measures, her existence as an independent nation, and to which she will doubtless owe, in the future an eminent place in the pacific concert of peoples; for a canal connecting the two oceans has been constructed within her frontiers, through which pass more than 4,000 merchant vessels every year. Her whole territory is like a public highway for the commerce of the world, and it is the international duty of her inhabitants to permit to all peoples the free and equal use of the Canal which the genius of mankind has constructed.[132]

The Suez Canal as well as the Panama Canal is subject to inclusive use in terms of universal utilization. In the case of the Suez Canal the inclusive use is based explicitly on provisions of the Convention of Constantinople of 1888. Article 1 of the Convention provides that "the Suez Maritime Canal shall always be free and open, in time of war as in time of peace, to every vessel of commerce or of war, without distinction of flag. . . ."[133] At that time there was pressure for internationalization of the Suez Canal by France, Germany, and Russia, but the United Kingdom, which then had forces in Egypt, was not willing to accept such a system.[134] A similar position was later taken by the United States and Panama on the internationalization of the Panama Canal.[135] The inclusive right of passage through the Suez Canal was violated by the British

---

[132] 8 LEAGUE OF NATIONS O. J. 95 (1927), cited in REID, *supra* note 10, at 137.

[133] For a good survey of the Suez Canal and the Convention of 1888, *see* J. MOORE, 3 DIGEST OF INTERNATIONAL LAW, 262–66 (1906); R. BOWIE, SUEZ 1956 (1974); C. HALLBERY & J. OBIETA, THE INTERNATIONAL STATUS OF THE SUEZ CANAL (1960).

[134] BOWIE, *id.* at 4.

[135] R. BAXTER, THE LAW OF INTERNATIONAL WATERWAYS 47 (1964).

government, which was the acting authority and control over the Canal for the fulfilment of the Convention during the First and Second World Wars. This universal right was again violated by Egypt in excluding the Israelis from using the Canal. The crisis over the Canal was intensified by the nationalization of the Canal in 1955, and international attention became focused on a way to solve the problem so as to protect the universal right of transit passage. The first proposal was for the establishment of an international authority whose purpose would be to take over the operation of the Canal, ensuring Egypt her equitable return, a proposal which was rejected by Egypt.[136] The failure of the first proposal led to the London Conference, which suggested the establishment of a Suez Canal Users Association, basically the same as internationalization of the Canal.[137] This association was "to assist the members in the exercise of their rights as users of the Suez Canal."[138] This proposal was also rejected by Egypt.

Great Britain and France, because of the Egyptian opposition to reconciliation with the Canal users, appealed to the United Nations on September 12, 1956. In a joint letter to the President of the Security Council they suggested that the refusal of the Government of Egypt to negotiate constitutes "an aggravation of the situation which, if allowed to continue, could constitute a manifest danger to peace and security."[139] After a series of negotiations between the Government of Egypt, the Council, Great Britain and France, the parties agreed to continue negotiations in Geneva on the 29 October.[140] These negotiations were never concluded because of the joint agreement between Great Britain and France to support Israel against Egypt.[141] The unwillingness of the Council in making decisions on the dispute may represent the confusion and difficulties that the Council had in accommodating the policies of self-determination and those of an optimum order in establish-

---

[136] U.S. Dept. State, Suez Canal Problem 1956, at 44. *See also* Bowie, *supra* note 133, at 36–42.

[137] Bowie, *id.* at 42–47.

[138] Suez Canal Problem, *supra* note 136, at 365.

[139] 11 U.N. SCOR, Supp. (July.-Sept. 1956) 28, U.N. Doc. S/3645 (1956).

[140] Bowie, *supra* note 133, at 50.

[141] *Id.*

ing an appropriate competence to secure the universal use of the Suez Canal.

The Egyptian Government, however, on 24 April 1957 declared that "the Government of Egypt are more particularly determined: (a) to afford and maintain free and uninterrupted navigation for all nations within the limits of and in accordance with the provisions of the Constantinople Convention of 1888."[142] Article 4 states that "the Government of Egypt are looking forward with confidence to continued cooperation with the nations of the world in advancing the usefulness of the Canal. To that end the Government of Egypt would welcome and encourage cooperation between the Suez Canal Authority and the representatives of the shipping and trade." Article 7 emphasizes the principle of equal treatment: "In pursuance of the principles laid down in the Constantinople Convention of 1888, the Suez Canal Authority by the terms of its Charter, can in no case grant any vessel, company or other party any advantage or favour awarded to other vessels, companies or parties on the same condition." Article 7 continues that in the case of violation of the Canal Code or discrimination the problem should be resolved by the Suez Canal Authority and later, if necessary, by an arbitration. The Canal was practically opened to all nations except Israel until 1967 when war broke out between Egypt and Israel. The Canal was closed until September 1975 when it opened to all ships, including those of Israel.[143]

The inclusive right of passage through international canals not only promotes the inclusive interests of the larger community in universal intercourse and commerce, but it also may increase the productivity of the internal value processes of the grantor. The Suez and Panama Canals are major sources of revenue for their respective countries. The importance of universal use of the Suez Canal for the internal development of Egypt has been appreciated by the Egyptian Government, and since the opening of the Canal in September 1975 there has been an extensive effort to encourage the use of the Canal by all nations and all kinds of vessels. Such efforts have included the reduction by almost one-third of insurance cost for war-risk imposed on the ships using the Canal.[144]

[142] HALLBERY & OBIETA, *supra* note 133, Appendix D, at 124–27.

[143] N.Y. Times Sept. 14, 1975, at 9, col. 1.

[144] *Id.*

There are plans to develop the operation of the Canal in order to accommodate supertankers.[145]

The Kiel Canal is another artificial waterway through which universal right of passage has been secured by a multilateral treaty. The Kiel Canal was constructed by Germany primarily for strategic purposes and entirely within domestic waters. By the Treaty of Versailles the internationalization of the Canal was imposed upon Germany. Article 380 of the Treaty provides that "the Kiel Canal and its approaches shall be maintained free and open to the vessels of commerce and of war of all nations at peace with Germany on terms of entire equality."[146] This prescription was applied by the Permanent Court of International Justice in the case, discussed above, of the *S.S. Wimbledon*:

> It follows that the Canal has ceased to be an internal and national navigation waterway, the use of such by the vessels of states other than the riparian states is left entirely to the discretion of that state, and that it has become an international waterway intended to provide under treaty guarantee easier access to the Baltic for the benefit of all nations of the world. Under its new regime, the Kiel Canal must be open, on a footing of equality to all vessels, without making any distinction between war vessels and vessels of commerce, but on one express condition, namely, these vessels belong to nations at peace with Germany.[147]

The Kiel Canal has thus been explicitly recognized for universal use by states at peace with Germany.

The inclusive right of passage through international waterways has, thus, been recognized by the world community, basically through multilateral state agreements. The common practice of states, built upon the necessity in the modern world (for facilitating the exchange of goods and information) of such shared use, has resulted in no major attempt to teminate any agreement regarding such practices. This fact in itself represents the recognition on the part of the territorial communities of their common interest in, and expectations of, the continuity and stability of such agreements.

The right of transit is a broad concept; it may include not only

---

[145] *Id.*

[146] Treaty of Versailles, Part XII, Sec. VI, Article 380.

[147] S.S. Wimbledon, [1923] P.C.I.J. ser. A, No. 1, at 22.

passage but certain ancillary rights, such as management and construction or security of passage. The ancillary rights have significant effects upon the shared use of waterways. The difficulties that these rights may create are that sometimes their scope becomes unclear so that the grantee's claim to exercise such rights may become inconsistent with the inclusive use of the waterway. The policies we recommend are that no ancillary right incompatible with the policies of inclusive use of waterways should be protected. Basically the main purpose of such rights is the better protection of the shared use of waterways; they should not, therefore, be made to include any rights contradictory of their basic purpose.

The conflicts between the United States and Panama over the Panama Canal offer an example of such problems. The United States claims that the Hay-Varilla Treaty of November 18, 1903, with Panama not only accorded the United States the right to construct the Canal, but also surrendered to the United States full competence over the territory known as the Panama Canal Zone.[148] Article 2 of the Treaty provided that

> [t]he Republic of Panama grants to the United States in perpetuity the use, occupation and control of a zone of land and land under water for the construction, maintenance, operation, sanitation and protection of the said Canal of the width of ten miles extending to the distance of five miles on each side of the center line of the route of the Canal to be constructed; the said zone beginning in the Caribbean Sea three marine miles from mean low water mark and extending to and across the Isthmus of Panama into the Pacific Ocean to a distance of three miles from mean low water mark.

The United States claims that Article 3 confers upon the United States a competence over the Canal Zone tantamount to sovereignty:

> The Republic of Panama grants to the United States all the rights, power and authority within the zone mentioned and described in Article 2 of this agreement and within the limits of all auxiliary lands and waters mentioned and described in the said Article 2 which the United States would possess and exercise it if were the sovereign of the territory within which the said lands

---

[148]*See* M. GERSTLE, THE LAND DIVIDED: A HISTORY OF THE PANAMA CANAL AND OTHER ISTHMIAN CANAL PROJECTS (1944); D. MINER, THE FIGHT FOR THE PANAMA ROUTE (1940); H. ARIAS, THE PANAMA CANAL (1970).

and waters are located to the entire exclusion of the exercise by
the Republic of Panama of any such sovereign rights, power or
authority.

Panama, on the other hand, claims that the competence demanded by the United States is incompatible with Panama's independence and sovereignty and that the 1903 agreement does not
grant the United States sovereignty over the Canal. This has been
the position of Panama since 1904. The controversy between the
United States and Panama concerning the extent of the right of
the United States over the Canal has been the result of the ambiguities in the language of the 1903 Treaty between the two countries. The interpretation of the Treaty therefore, in accordance
with its major purpose, must determine the rights and burdens to
which the parties committed themselves.

The relevant background, as mentioned earlier, is that the
United States as a country on the American continent of great
economic, military, scientific, and political power has significant
interests in developing the American continent under its own attention in a way that its own exclusive interests will not be endangered by interference from other powerful states. The United
States, accordingly, entered into the 1903 Treaty with Panama to
build and operate a canal that would be neutral and free and open
to commercial vessels of all nations. Article 2 states the major purposes of the Treaty to be "the construction, mainenance, operation, sanitation, and protection of said canal." These are ancillary
rights granted to the United States to put it in the position to utilize
a natural waterway for the inclusive use of the world community.
To facilitate construction of such a waterway, Article 3 ambigu-
ously referred to the right of the United States in this operation as
the right of a sovereign. One of the most important principles of
international law for the interpretation of treaties is that all ambiguities in a treaty must be interpreted in accordance with the major purposes of the treaty. The ambiguous language of Article 3
should be interpreted, as the rest of the entire Treaty presents,
that Panama granted to the United States those competences, and
only those competences, necessary for the construction, maintenance, operation, sanitation, and protection of the Canal which it
as territorial sovereign might otherwise have exercised. The purpose of the Treaty was not to confer sovereignty over the Canal to
the United States. What Panama granted to the United States

based on the Treaty was a right of transit to which all other rights were ancillary, a right in sum much less than sovereignty.

The United States from the beginning, however, expressed its intention through different means of communication to assert more than a servitude, and it unilaterally put its broad claims into practice. The trend of its unilateral practices suggests that they have been more for the protection of the special interests of the United States than for promotion of the inclusive use of the Canal. When the provisions of the 1903 Treaty were reaffirmed in 1955 in the preamble of the Eisenhower-Remon Treaty of Mutual Understanding and Cooperation, Secretary Holland, in response to one of the Senators emphasized that "we [do] not want to leave one grain of evidence that could a hundred years hence be interpreted as implying any admission by the United States that we possess and exercise anything less than 100 percent of the rights of sovereignty in this area [the Panama Canal Zone]." [149] Such a perspective was unhappily accepted in the Conference of the Suez Users Association in 1906, when Panama was excluded from the Conference because of the United States claims of sovereignty over the Canal, so that the United States allegedly represented the interests of Panama. [150] Such a position was vigorously opposed by Panama. [151]

The United States under the Hay-Pauncefote Treaty with Great Britain (1903) is, in addition, "obligated to maintain in perpetuity the neutrality of the Canal." This policy was unilaterally affirmed by the United States when in 1952 Secretary Dulles expressed that "if it means anything that the Canal is affected with an international use, it means that the Canal is open to all without discrimination." [152] In practice, however, this policy has not been respected. In 1950, for example, as was mentioned by Travis and Watkins,

> the Congress authorized the President to issue special security regulations for the Zone when he deemed it to be endangered by reason of subversive activity. By law the Zone authorities are

[149] *Hearings Before the Senate Committee on Foreign Relations on the Panama Canal Zone*, 84th Cong., 1st Sess. 164 (1955) (Statement of Secretary Holland).

[150] *See* N.Y. Times, August 29, 1956, at 8, col. 1. *See also* Travis & Watkins, Control of the Panama Canal: An Obsolete Shibboleth? 37 FOREIGN AFFAIRS 407, 415 (1959).

[151] Travis & Watkins, *id.* at 415.

[152] *Id.* at 414.

prohibited from selling petroleum products to ships flying the flags of the Soviet Union, Red China and the Soviet Satellites except under special permits issued by the Department of Commerce. In 1954 the French liner Wyoming was detained at Cristobal pending investigation of a hidden arms cargo suspected of being shipped from an Eastern European State to Guatemala . . . in 1957 [also] Moscow filed a formal complaint when the passage of a Soviet vessel was delayed by Zone officials.[153]

Such practices of the United States over the Canal would appear incompatible with the legitimate exclusive interest of Panama. Panama claims that the Canal is her primary natural resource and should be the basis for the country's own economic development.[154] Panama has asserted that, despite the American claim that the only goal in operating the Canal is to make it self-supporting rather than profitable to the United States, the Canal operation represents a greater benefit to the United States, in terms of both military and economic advantages, than to Panama. It urges that in fact Panama's benefit is minimal vis-à-vis that of the United States.[155] The exercise of sovereignty by the United States in the Canal Zone is, furthermore, regarded as incompatible with the independence of the State of Panama and the growing feeling of nationalism and national pride in the country. Panama makes clear her unhappiness about the United States' emphasis on not having any intention of sharing, or returning, the sovereignty of the Canal Zone to Panama.

The claims of Panama, which are supported by the sympathy of other nations, particularly newly independent states, and the evergrowing unrest in Panama, have forced the United States toward the gradual recognition of Panama's sovereignty over the Canal. In 1960 the American government announced that the Panamanian flag should be flown with the American flag at one point in the Zone in recognition of the "titular sovereignty residing in the Republic of Panama."[156] Further impetus toward change in the status of Panama with respect to the Canal has come from the

[153]*Id.*

[154]J. Morgan, The Panama Canal (unpublished paper in the Yale Law School Library) at 7.

[155]*Id.*

[156]42 DEP'T STATE BULL. 552–59 (1960).

successful nationalization of the Suez Canal by Egypt. In 1962, during the Kennedy administration, there was a further agreement on the establishment of the authority of Panama on the Canal.[157] This agreement was followed by a 1964 agreement, the result of a request by Panama and pressure from the Security Council and the Organization of American States.[158] This development in the relationship between the two countries with respect to the ancillary rights of the United States has been continued until recently when serious negotiations began on the basis of transferring complete authority and control over the Canal to the Government of Panama in fifty years, with the United States enjoying the shared participation in the security of the Canal with Panama after that time.[159]

The rights of the United Kingdom over the Suez Canal offer another example of ancillary rights. It is interesting to note that under the original agreement the Convention of Constantinople in 1888, involving the Suez Canal between the great powers, Great Britain had no other rights than rights of free passage through the Canal equal with the other signatory powers.[160] Under this Convention the Suez Canal was open to all nations with no discrimination. However, Great Britain played a crucial role through most of the history of the Canal. During the construction of the Canal, Great Britain moved its troops to Egypt on the excuse of guaranteeing the security of the Canal in 1882.[161] Once they occupied the country, the British began appropriate strategies for their new de facto protectorate.[162] In 1914 the United Kingdom unilaterally declared Egypt a protectorate; and in 1922, while granting independence to Egypt, it reserved exclusive control of the defense of Egypt and the protection of the Canal.[163] This unilateral action was supported by an agreement between Egypt and

[157] Morgan, *supra* note 154, at 120–22.

[158] *Id.* at 128–30.

[159] N.Y. Times Sept. 16, 1975, at 11, col 1.

[160] The signatory powers to the Convention of Constantinople were Great Britain, Germany, Austria-Hungary, Spain, France, Italy, the Netherlands, Russia, and Turkey. *See* THE SUEZ CANAL PROBLEM, *supra* note 136, at 16–20.

[161] HALLBERY & OBIETA, *supra* note 133, at 10.

[162] *Id.*

[163] BOWIE, *supra* note 133, at 4.

the United Kingdom in 1936 whereby the United Kingdom was to enjoy the right to keep troops in the Canal Zone for the protection of the Canal until Egypt was in a position to defend it.[164]

However, the United Kingdom, by virtue of the 1888 Convention, was obliged as was any other signatory power, to keep the Canal open "in war time as in the peace time to every vessel of commerce or of war, without distinction of flag."[165] On August 7, 1914, it formally closed the Canal to German shipping on the ground that there was a risk of blockage.[166] During the Second World War, furthermore, the Convention was totally suspended, and from the start the Canal was closed to hostile vessels and the passage of neutral vessels was severely limited by allied military vessels.[167] After the Second World War the situation was changed and Egypt acquired more control over the Canal, because of the internal demands for such control. Egypt used her control over the Canal by closing the Canal to Israeli ships and cargo after the 1948 Arab-Israeli War. Bowie observed that "Egypt's method was to impose search and seizure of war contraband at the ports at either end of the Canal. It justified this action by analogy to the Allied practices in the First and Second World Wars, and by Article 10 of the 1888 Convention."[168] This unilateral action by Egypt was objected to by the Security Council, and the Council called for a reopening of the Canal to Israel, which was rejected by Egypt. In 1954, however, Egypt agreed to allow transportation of goods for Israel through the Canal, on the condition that they were not carried in Israeli ships.[169]

The ancillary rights of the United Kingdom over the Canal were decreased by a 1954 agreement in which it agreed to withdraw all its troops by June 1956; however, it was entitled to return them only if a power other than Israel attacked a member of the Arab League or Turkey. The coup de grace to the decline of Great Britain's special status occurred in 1955, when the Canal was nationalized by the Egyptian Government.

[164] *Id.*

[165] XVIII HERTSLET 369 (1893).

[166] BOWIE, *supra* note 133, at 5.

[167] *Id.*

[168] *Id.*

[169] *Id.*

Agreement concerning ancillary rights could come within the scope of transnational development planning. Such rights could be made to serve security, construction, and management purposes. The expectations about the stability of such agreements, as long as they do not oppose the obligations of the grantor to the world community's demands for free passage, depend on the conflicting exclusive interests of the grantor and the grantee. To accommodate such interests, decision makers should interpret such agreements in accordance with their major purpose and a policy of protecting the inclusive interests of the larger community.

iii. Transit Through Air Space

The rapid development of technology and correspondingly increased use of air transportation have created great concern for air transit through foreign territories. In the past the use of foreign territories consisted only of wireless transmission; there was no particular concern about granting such rights to other states. When, however, the time came for the physical use of the air and the possible dangers resulting from such use, as well as the need and demands for air transit rights, cooperation and regulation through agreement were required. Facilitation of air transportation was the concern of almost all countries. Such common concern and inclusive need have led to collective action through multilateral agreements, such as the Convention for the Regulation of Aerial Navigation, signed in Paris in 1919–20.[170] In this Convention there was an explicit demand for innocent passage. However, it was stipulated that such right should be given through agreement and could not be extended to noncontracting states. This Convention was amended in 1922 so that it permitted agreements between member states and nonmembers under certain conditions.[171] The Convention of 1919–20 was a model for two other multilateral treaties. The first agreement was the Ibero-American Convention, signed in Madrid in 1926, which included Spain, Portugal, and all Latin American states except Haiti.[172] The second was the Pan American Convention on Commercial Aviation, signed at the Sixth Pan American Conference at Havana in

[170] 11 L.N.T.S. 190 (1920).

[171] REID, *supra* note 10, at 181.

[172] *Id.* at 183.

1928.[173] This was a regional agreement in which the members excluded any aircraft of non-American nationality.[174]

The only agreement which granted the use of air space of one nation to all nations for transit was the Convention of July 1923, which granted freedom of air navigation over the Dardanelles, the Sea of Marmara, and the Bosphorus.[175] This agreement was replaced by Montreux Agreement of 1936, by which the Convention of 1923 was amended. Article 23 of the later agreement provides that "in order to assume the passage of civil aircraft between the Mediterranean and the Black Sea, the Turkish government will indicate the air routes available for this purpose outside the forbidden zones which may be established in the Straits. Civil aircraft may use these routes provided that they give the Turkish government as regards occasional flights a notification of three days, and as regards regular service, a general notification of the dates of passage. . . ."[176] Recognition of the inclusive interest in the cooperation of territorial communities in facilitating air transportation and the exclusive interest in relation to political and economic factors resulted in an international convention in 1944 in Chicago, the Convention on International Civil Aviation. The preamble of the Convention expressed the members' realization of their common interest and their hope for accommodation of conflicting interests, in these words:

> Whereas the future development of international civil aviation can greatly help to create and preserve friendship and understanding among the nations of peoples of the world, yet its abuse can become a threat to the general security; and
>
> whereas it is desirable to avoid friction and to promote that cooperation between nations and peoples upon which the peace of the world depends;
>
> therefore, the undersigned governments having agreed on certain principles and arrangements in order that international civil

---

[173]*Id.*

[174]Pan-American Convention on Commercial Aviation (1928), art. 5.

[175]28 L.N.T.S. 116 (1923). The signatory powers were Great Britain, France, Italy, Japan, Bulgaria, Greece, Roumania, Russia, and Yugoslavia. For a detailed history of this Convention, see Hughes, *Airspaces, Sovereignty over International Waterways,* 19 J. Air L. & Comm. 149 (1951).

[176]18 Brit. Y.B. Int'l L. 187 (1937).

aviation may be developed in a safe and orderly manner and that international air transport services may be established on the basis of equality of opportunity and operated soundly and economically;

Have accordingly concluded this Convention to that end.[177]

Although accommodation of conflicting interest has been difficult from time to time, there is no doubt that the Convention and subsequent state practices have created expectations for shared use of the airspace of territorial communities for transit purposes. Such community expectations have resulted in the reinforcing of air transit agreements made by their colonial governments long before their independence by many newly independent states, such as Nigeria, Pakistan, Ghana, Sudan, the Ivory Coast, Congo (Zaire), and Libya.[178] Although many of these states began negotiations to modify or terminate the agreements some time after their independence, the fact that they honored the agreements rather than terminated them is evidence of their realization that the international need and their own interest lie in the continuation of the agreements. Besides multilateral agreements, there are bilateral agreements between states which provide for the use of special airports or air facilities within the territorial boundaries of another state.

The Berlin crisis of 1958 was an incident in which the issue of servitude in the form of transit through land masses, water, and air was raised.[179] After the Berlin occupation by allied forces, a number of agreements were concluded between the four occupant powers for the control over Berlin, its unification and demilitarization. The four-power agreements recognized the right of free access of Western forces to Berlin. This right was respected in practice with the exception of a 1948–49 blockade by the Soviet Union. After the establishment of the German Democratic Republic, the Soviet Union, on November 27, 1958, declared that the

[177]CONVENTION ON INTERNATIONAL CIVIL AVIATION, FINAL ACT AND RELATED DOCUMENTS, Dept. of State No. 2882, Conference Ser. 64 (1945).

[178]*See* O'Connell, *supra* note 61 at 147–50.

[179]For literature on the Berlin crisis see Bishop, *What Are Our Rights?* THE NEW REPUBLIC Oct. 2, 1961; R. BOWIE, THE ISSUES IN THE BERLIN-GERMAN CRISIS, (L. Tondel ed. 1962)(papers from the First Hammarskjold Forum); J. SMITH, THE DEFENSE OF BERLIN (1963) and H. SPEIER, DIVIDEND BERLIN (1961).

U.S.S.R. could no longer tolerate the continued occupation of West Berlin, and since the U.S.S.R. planned to turn over to the German Democratic Republic all its occupation functions in East Germany, including control over the West's access routes to West Berlin, the four-power agreements of 1944–45 were null and void. The Soviet Union declared that such nullification would arise from the right of the G.D,R., like any other independent state, fully to exercise its sovereignty on land, water, and air. In other words, the new state of G.D.R. would not be obligated to respect the burdens created by its predecessor, the Soviet Union, unless it consented to the burdens.

The West on the other hand argued that the right of transit to West Berlin for Western subjects was a servitude and could not be terminated because of the establishment of a new state. Furthermore, the West claimed that the right of transit not only included that for Western military and civilians but also for German civilian traffic. The West claimed that under the Hague Regulations a military occupier has a duty to "ensure public order and safety," which includes the physical well-being of the West Berlin population and the maintenance of its economy. The Soviet Union rejected this interpretation and stated that maintenance of public order and safety refers to such communication in fact necessary to the normal life of the population. This they claimed had been recognized by 1949 agreements, removing restrictions on "communications, transportation and trade" between Berlin and the rest of Germany.

Eventually the Soviet Union withdrew from its position and the West continued to enjoy its right as was originally anticipated. Though affected by many harsh political realities, of course, all the negotiations were in the context of the firm legal position of the West. The west was able to argue through the concept of servitude that not even the succession of state much less of government could change the right of the claimant state.

iv. Scientific Rights

With the expansion of scientific research, which promises to increase man's knowledge about the resources of the globe and their potential for the production of values, there are increasing demands to facilitate such research by giving access to such resources that is necessary to serve inquiry. These resources are spatial-extension resources, such as the surfaces of water and land and stock and flow resources.

Sometimes landmasses are needed for space tracking stations, meteorological stations, and other scientific observation posts. There are several series of agreements between the United States and other countries regarding the right of the United States to establish and maintain stations for "the advancement of scientific knowledge of man's spatial environment and its effects; the application of this knowlege to the direct benefit of man; and the development of space vehicles of advanced capacities, including manned space vehicles." [180] These agreements include: the 1967 agreement between the United Kingdom and the United States concerning the establishment of a tracking station in Antigua, British West Indies, [181] the United States and United Kingdom agreement of 1967, [182] the United States and Australia agreement of 1960, [183] the United States and Ecuador agreement of 1960, [184] and the United States and Japan agreement of 1960. [185]

There is a series of state agreements concerning the establishment of meteorological stations, such as the 1968 agreement between the United States and Brazil, [186] the 1961 agreement between the United States and Chile, [187] the 1968 agreement between the United States and Colombia, [188] the 1969 agreement between the United States and the Dominican Republic, [189] the 1969 agreement between the United States and Ecuador, [190] and the 1970 agreement between the United States and Mexico. [191]

[180] [1960] 11 U.S.T. 223–28, T.I.A.S. No. 4435.

[181] [1967] 18 U.S.T. 112–128, T.I.A.S. No. 6207.

[182] *Id.* at 129–37.

[183] [1960] 11 U.S.T. 223–30, T.I.A.S. No. 4435.

[184] *Id.* at 179–184.

[185] [1966] 17 U.S.T. 2281, T.I.A.S. No. 6170.

[186] [1968] 19 U.S.T. 4933, T.I.A.S. No. 6500.

[187] [1961] 12 U.S.T. 1233, T.I.A.S. No. 4842.

[188] [1968] 19 U.S.T. 7820, T.I.A.S. No. 6615.

[189] [1969] 20 U.S.T. 647, T.I.A.S. No. 6670.

[190] *Id.* at 4078.

[191] [1970] 21 U.S.T. 1978, T.I.A.S. No. 6941.

The scope of agreements on rights to resources for scientific purposes is expanding. There are some state agreements on the use of resources for research programs on aerospace disturbances, such as the 1964 agreement between Australia and the United States[192] and the 1963 agreement between the United States and New Zealand.[193] The main objectives of these treaties are "studying aerospace disturbances and their effect on radio communications."[194]

The rights in relation to landmasses are generally given through bilateral agreements, but the scientific rights in territorial seas are commonly negotiated through multilateral agreements. One of the issues at the Law of the Sea Conferences in Caracas (1974) and in Geneva (1975) was the inclusive right for scientific research in territorial seas. There was some closing of differences at the Geneva Conference; there are still serious difficulties in achieving a multilateral agreement. At the Geneva Conference,[195] three approaches to this problem were developed; the first proposal was from some of the states within the Group of 77, which provided that all scientific research in areas under coastal state jurisdiction shall be concluded only with the explicit consent of the coastal state. The second proposal is from many Western European countries, with amendments by a group of landlocked and geographically disadvantaged states, that marine scientific research can be conducted if a list of internationally agreed-upon obligations are fulfilled, subject to dispute settlement procedures. And the third proposal, by the Soviet Union, later drawn upon by Mexico and others, distinguishes between research concerning resources and non-resource-related research, requiring consent for resource-related research and compliance with internationally agreed-upon obligations for research not concerned with resources.

Today marine scientists are concerned with the use of water as a power system, with development in the exploration of seabed mineral resources, and, more importantly, with the development of farming systems in the seabeds. These are only a few of the demands from marine scientists for which states should make avail-

[192][1964] 15 U.S.T. 1–3, T.I.A.S. No. 5510.

[193][1963] 14 U.S.T. 524, T.I.A.S. No. 5350.

[194]*Id.*

[195]Report on *The Third U.N. Law of the Sea Conference.*

able the necessary access and use of their resources for conducting such research. It is in the inclusive interest of mankind to facilitate and promote scientific research into the aerospace environment. To promote such an inclusive interest, the territorial communities should cooperate in every manner, including the granting of rights to their resources for use by scientists of other territorial communities for peaceful purposes. The inclusive interest is in the continuity of such agreements.

The common interests of the larger community would appear to require encouragement of the share and use of spatial-extension resources. As past trends have indicated, the primary fear of territorial communities in allowing transit through landmasses, superadjacent air space, and internal waters has been the possibility of endangering national security. Once this fear is removed, the willingness of communities to enter into transit agreements will increase. In other words, "if minimum public order is accepted as a goal, the speed by which optimum order can be sought will greatly increase."[196] The world as a whole is vitally concerned not merely with maintaining minimum order or peace but with an optimum order in the greatest production and widest distribution of all values. The device of servitude is a useful strategy for achieving such broad goals. Past trends have shown that expectations about the performance of servitudes may differ with respect to depletable or spatial-extension resources. Concession or development agreements between states and private enterprises have become the predominant strategy in sharing depletable resources. With respect to spatial-extension resources, however, expectations of the future performances may perhaps be best promoted by agreements between states and an appropriate customary international law.

B. AGREEMENTS BETWEEN STATES AND INTERNATIONAL ORGANIZATIONS

International organizations are formed by nation-states to promote their inclusive interests. These international organizations acquire legal character and independent institutions. However, they have no independent resources to carry out their functions.

---

[196] L. McDougal, *supra* note 24, at 115.

These resources are provided by nation-states either in the pre-liminary agreements for the establishment of such organizations or later in agreements between the organizations and the nation-states. Many such agreements concern the use of resources physi-cally located within the territorial states, such as land for offices and research stations.

The most famous and perhaps most important of such agree-ments are those between the United Nations and the United States concerning the United Nations building in New York signed on June 26, 1947, and known as the "Headquarters Agreement."[197] This agreement granted the right to the United Nations to estab-lish and maintain a building necessary for its operation and au-thority and control over property necessary for its function as an international agency. Under this agreement the United Nations may establish and operate a broadcasting station, an aerodrome, and its own postal service. Although the United Nations has the right to exclusive use of the building, the authority and control are shared by both parties. Section 9 provides that "[t]he headquarters district shall be inviolable. Federal, state or local officers or officials of the United States, whether administrative, judicial, military or police, shall not enter the headquarters district to perform any official duties therein except with the consent of and under con-ditions agreed to by the Secretary-General." Under the agreement the United States shall have jurisdiction over acts done and trans-actions taking place in the headquarters district, but when dealing with such cases, the United States shall take into account the regu-lations enacted by the United Nations.

The United Nations concluded a similar agreement with the Swiss Confederation involving its stations in Geneva, in 1946.[198]

There are also similar agreements between international agen-cies and different territorial states for the establishment of offices or research stations, such as the agreement between the European Space Research Organization and the United States in 1966.[199] In this agreement the United States granted the right to ESRO to establish and operate a satellite telemetry/telecommand station

---

[197]11 U.N.T.S. 11–41 (1947). See C. JENKS, THE HEADQUARTERS OF INTERNATIONAL IN-STITUTIONS—A STUDY OF THEIR LOCATION AND THEIR STATUS 53–80 (1945).

[198]1 U.N.T.S. 163–81 (1946).

[199][1966] 17 U.S.T. 2219, T.I.A.S. No. 6160.

near Fairbanks, Alaska, in connection with peaceful space activities to be undertaken by ESRO.

Because of the vital role that these international organizations and agencies play in facilitating a better relationship between countries for the promotion of all values, it is in the inclusive interest to encourage the creation and stabilization of such agreements.

C. AGREEMENTS BETWEEN STATES AND FOREIGN CORPORATIONS (DEVELOPMENT AGREEMENTS)

The third type of agreement for promoting shared use of resources physically located within the territorial boundary of states is *development agreements.* These agreements have been referred to as "concessions," "international contracts," "investment agreements," and "development agreements." Though each of these names emphasizes a particular characteristic of these agreements, they all refer to an agreement between a nation-state and a private foreign entity about the development of resources and the production, processing, transportation, and marketing of goods from resources. The more comprehensive resources brought together by development agreements include natural resources, such as raw materials; human resources, such as skill and labor; or industrial resources, such as technology; and so forth. Such agreements facilitate the inclusive use of the potential values embodied in these resources. They distribute resources and their benefits from one country to another, either in their basic or their processed form.

Given the unequal distribution of resources in the world, the importance of modalities for redistributing essential resources for the world economy and international development is undisputed.[200] Consider, for example, the present production and con-

---

[200] A major share of the free world's present and potential sources of copper and cobalt lies in the Congo and in Northern Rhodesia. The Union of South Africa and Southern Rhodesia are the world's largest sources of bony-fiber asbestos. Furthermore, South Africa is the largest single source of chemical grade chrome and, with the Congo, British West Africa, French Equatorial Africa, and Angola, supplies much of the Western world's industrial diamonds. Africa also supplies the Western world with iron ore, tin, lead, zinc, manganese, chrome, columbite, tantabite, and cadmium. Latin America is also a major metallurgical source: copper in Chile and Peru, iron ore in Venezuela and Brazil, manganese in Brazil, lead and zinc in Mexico, tin in Bolivia, and bauxite in Surinam, British Guiana, Haiti, and Jamaica. South and South-East Asia are one of the world's largest producers of tin and natural rubber and a major source of other vital materials, including

sumption of natural resources in the world. Some countries produce more raw materials than they consume, while others consume more than they produce.[201] The United States, the United Kingdom, Belgium, and Luxembourg are the largest importers of iron ore.[202] Japan depends on Southeast Asia for its supply of iron ore.[203] Since 1940 a large part of the lead used in the United States has been imported, mainly from Canada, Peru, Australia, Bolivia, South-west Africa, and Yugoslavia.[204] Based on a 1956 report, the United States consumes 50% and Europe 40% of the world's tungsten production. Of this production, however, 54% comes from Asia, 14% from North America, 14% from South America, 13% from Europe, and 5% from other countries.[205] Almost all of Western Europe's and Japan's oil is imported from the Middle East.[206] These interdependences also exist in industrial goods. The main imports of Middle Eastern oil producers are from Japan, Western Europe, and the United States.[207] Furthermore, many of the highly industrialized countries, such as the EEC area and Japan, also depend on the outside world for exporting their products. A comparison between production and consumption in relation to

---

tungsten and manganese. 1 PRESIDENT'S MATERIAL POLICY COMMISSION, RESOURCES FOR FREEDOM 60 (1952), cited in Carlstan, *International Role of Concession Agreements*, 52 Nw. U. L. REV. 440 (1957).

[201] For U. N. statistics on production and consumption of some resources, see U.N. STATISTICAL Y.B., U.N. Doc. ST/ESA/STAT/Ser.S/5 (1978).

[202] RESOURCES FOR FREEDOM, *cited in* Carlston, *supra* note 200, at 441.

[203] *Survey of Iron Ore Resources*, U.N. Doc. No. E/26/55.ST/ECA/27 (1955), at 37.

[204] U.S. Bureau of Mines, DEP'T INTERIOR BULL. 434–35, 437, 440 (1956).

[205] *Id.* at 932.

[206] Eighty percent of Japan's energy consumption is oil, which is 100 percent imported. Of this, 76% is from the Middle East. Western Europe's oil is 98% imported. Out of this 98%, 84% is from the Middle East. The U.S. has an estimated 47% of energy consumption in oil, of which 38% is imported, and 19% is from the Middle East. STOCKHOLM INTERNATIONAL PEACE RESEARCH INSTITUTE, OIL AND SECURITY, 14 (1974).

[207] Fifteen percent of Bahrain's import is from Japan, 30% from Western Europe, and 13% from the U.S; 14% of Iran's import is from Japan, 44% from Western Europe, and 17% from the U.S; 4% of Iraq imports is from Japan, 37% from Western Europe, and 3% from the U.S; 16% of Kuwait's import is from Japan, 27% from Western Europe, and 13% from the U.S; 4% of Oman's import is from Japan, 78% from Western Europe, and 4% from the U.S; 12% of Qatar imports is from Japan, 42% from Western Europe, and 10% from the U.S; 19% of Saudi Arabia's import is from Japan, 34% from Europe, and 25% from the U.S; 19% of the Emirates' import is from Japan, 31% from Western Europe, and 14% from the U.S. *See id.* at 42.

all these different resources around the world indicates the need for, and importance of, the movement of goods across boundaries. Much of this movement is accomplished through development agreements.

One necessary element of economic development, achieved through production, employment of labor, and full utilization of natural resources, is capital.[208] Besides capital, enlightenment (education), skill (management), technology, and transportation facilities are all necessary elements for economic development. For development through production and distribution of resources, the Royal Commission on Canada's Economic Prospects has observed that there is a need, aside from capital, for "extensive industrial experience and market connections which must be associated with that capital before a large investment undertaking can go ahead." "This embraces such diverse requirements," the Commission added, "as an advanced technology, specialized entrepreneurial and managerial skills and, in many cases, an assured export market for a large part of the output. . . ."[209] The scarcity of many of these basic resources is the major problem for the economic development of many developing countries.[210] And the establishment of viable economic development planning in a country with little of these resources requires importation of key resources through either the public or private sector. The movement of key resources for development across boundaries is not a new phenomenon. During the nineteenth century the movement of these key resources was established through foreign investment,

[208]C. KINDLEBERGER, ECONOMIC DEVELOPMENT 34–55 (1958). A. FATOUROS, GOVERNMENT GUARANTEE OF FOREIGN INVESTMENT 11 (1962); ECONOMIC DEVELOPMENT FOR LATIN AMERICA 110 (R. ELLIS & H. WALLISH eds. 1961).

[209]ROYAL COMMISSION ON CANADA'S ECONOMIC PROSPECTS, PRELIMINARY REPORT (1956) at 86–87.

[210]U.N. DEPT. OF ECONOMIC AND SOCIAL AFFAIRS, PROCESSES AND PROBLEMS OF INDUSTRIALIZATION IN UNDER-DEVELOPED COUNTRIES (1955); Res. 33 (11) of UNCTAD, by 67 votes to 3 with 6 abstentions, recognized the necessity of providing foreign capital for the development of underdeveloped countries. They requested the Secretary-General of the U.N. to provide useful guidelines for both developing and developed countries. These guidelines, among others, include "[c]riteria and practices employed by developing countries for the acceptance and promotion of foreign investment." U.N. PANEL ON FOREIGN INVESTMENT IN DEVELOPING COUNTRIES, U.N. Doc. E/4654.ST/ECA/117 (1969) at 39–40; B. DATTA, THE ECONOMICS OF INDUSTRIALIZATION (1952); Galbraith, *Conditions for Economic Change in Under-Developed Countries*, 3 J. FARM. ECON. (1951); R. HURKSE, PROBLEMS OF CAPITAL FORMATION IN UNDER-DEVELOPED COUNTRIES (1953), and FATOUROS, note 208, *supra*.

which contributed to the economic development of countries in the "new continents," such as the United States.[211] In the nineteenth century, foreign investment came from the private sector, although the governments of the foreign investors played active leadership roles.[212] The direction of private capital and resources in the twentieth century has been toward either European countries or the United States, Canada, Argentina, New Zealand, and Australia, which have been called "regions of recent settlement."[213] Such a change in direction occurred because of the immigration of Europeans to these countries, a movement that carried the flow of key resources for economic development. There was, therefore, little or no attention given to African and Asian countries. Between the world wars, also, the major portion of foreign investment was concentrated in developed or semideveloped countries.[214] After the Second World War greater attention was paid to developing countries in terms of public capital for foreign investment. Large sums of public foreign capital have been supplied by newly established public and international institutions for development loans. These institutions include the Export-Import Bank of Washington and the Development Loan Fund in the United States, the International Bank for Reconstruction and Development, the International Finance Corporation, the International Development Association, and so forth. A large part of the movement of capital and personnel from the West is in the form of public capital. For example, between 1958 and 1961 about $20 billion of public aid went to developing countries,[215] but despite the tremendous increase in public foreign capital for development, the importance of private foreign capital cannot be ignored. The 1958 United Nations study on the flow of capital to developing countries through private foreign investment stated that "when considering together the flow of new funds and the profits which foreign enterprises reinvest in the underdeveloped countries where they

[211] *See* FATOUROS, *supra* note 208, at 16.

[212] *See* THE STATE AND ECONOMIC GROWTH (H. Aitken ed. 1959) at 35.

[213] FATOUROS, *supra* note 208, at 17.

[214] Between 1924–28 about 75% of the average annual U.S. portfolio investment went to developed or semideveloped countries. About 65% of Dutch and 60% of British portfolio investment went to the same countries. See FATOUROS, *id.* at 19.

[215] NEWSWEEK, Nov. 21, 1960, at 54.

operate, the total contribution of private investors is comparable to that of Governments."[216] Besides, the actual or potential capital-exporting countries today outside the communist bloc, such as the United States, the United Kingdom, and the Federal Republic of Germany are all committed in their domestic as well as foreign economy to supporting private enterprise, and the attitude of these governments will not change immediately.[217]

Private foreign capital[218] can be used for the promotion of economic development planning in heavy industries and in the exploitation, processing, and marketing of raw materials, as well as in the production of manufactured goods.[219] This view has been opposed by the United Nations Economic Commission for Africa.[220] Their recommendation as to the most desirable form of development assistance was for bilateral aid at a public level, and preferably through international organization. This recommendation, however, is in conflict with the views expressed by developing countries in the UNCTAD recommendation adopted in the General Assembly Resolution 2087 (XX) of December 12, 1965, and the General Assembly Resolution 2091 (XX) of December 20, 1965.[221] The positive role that private capital, through development agreements, could play in development planning programs has been recognized by the Group of 77 in the Charter of Algeria. This Charter was adopted by the Ministerial Meeting of the Group of 77 in October 1967,[222] and confirmed that "[p]rivate investments should be of permanent benefit to the host developing country. Subject to nationally-defined priorities and within the framework of national development plans, private investment may be encouraged by incentives and guarantees."[223] In the UNC-

---

[216]U.N. Secretariat Study, THE INTERNATIONAL FLOW OF PRIVATE CAPITAL (1956–1958) U.N. Doc. No. E/3249 (1959) at 9.

[217]*See* FATOUROS, *supra* note 208, at 61.

[218]"Capital" here refers to all necessary elements for economic development.

[219]*See* 10 INT'L & COMP. L. Q. 470 (1961).

[220]U.N. Docs. E/3452 Rev. 1 (1961) and reports of ECOSOC U.N. Doc. (A/4820) (1960) at 46 and U.N. Doc. A/6003 (1964) at 45, cited in A. AMERASINGHE, STATE RESPONSIBILITY FOR INJURIES TO ALIENS 8 (1967).

[221]*Cited in* U.N. Doc. E/4945.St/ECA/117 (1970).

[222]U.N. Doc. TD/38 (1967), art. 24.

[223]*Id.*

TAD meeting held in Amsterdam in 1968 to study foreign investment in developing countries, the panel recognized that the internal rate of capital formation in developing countries is far below that necessary to promote a reasonable rate of per capita economic growth.[224] The panel observed that, if a satisfactory rate is to be achieved, there must be a massive increase in the rate at which capital is flowing in to the developing nations from outside sources. "This can only be accomplished if all sources of capital, multinational agencies, individual industrial nations, capital exporting countries among the developing nations and private investors, step up their pace of investment."[225] The panel correctly observed that private foreign investment is a complement to and not a substitute for official aid and technical assistance needed by developing countries. The panel also recognized that private investment is playing an important role in the economic growth of developing countries by supplying them not only with much needed capital but also with managerial and technological expertise.[226]

Individual states have recognized the importance of private foreign investment in their development and have tried to attract foreign investment by unilateral prescriptions or by bilateral or multilateral agreements. It is interesting to observe that countries which have nationalized foreign properties continue to encourage foreign investment. For example, Indonesia's Petroleum Law states that "economic incentives should be introduced to enable Indonesia to attract foreign companies to operate under the conditions of the law and at the same time to safeguard the national interest."[227] A similar position has been taken by Fiji. In a 1971 law designed to encourage foreign investment in developing the resources of the country, the Government guarantees the "stability of concession terms over an adequate period, including guarantees as to stability of the overall incidence of tax and guarantees against unilateral action on the part of the Government to vary the

---

[224]*See* Panel on Foreign Investment in Developing Countries, note 210, *supra.*

[225]*Id.* at 4.

[226]*Id.* The Panel recognized that governments of host countries are the best judges of their development objectives and priorities and of the tools to achieve these objectives.

[227]Legislation No. 44 (1960). *See* Proceedings of the Seminar on Petroleum Legislation with Particular Reference to Offshore Operation, U.N. Mineral Resources Development No. 40 U.N. Doc. E/CN 11/1052 (1972) at 95.

terms of the concession agreement."[228] Egypt, known as a socialist country, wanting to attract investors from neighboring countries—particularly Kuwait, Libya, Saudi Arabia, and the Arab Emirates—has created the Arab International Bank for Foreign Trade and Development (AIB).[229] AIB finances Egypt's foreign trade and acts as an agent for foreign investors. This bank is exempt from all taxes and regulations and deals entirely in convertible currencies. In the investment laws of many other countries there are provisions for protection of foreign investment.[230]

There is an increasing number of bilateral agreements for the promotion and protection of foreign investment concluded between developing countries and the United States,[231] the United Kingdom,[232] Japan,[233] the Federal Republic of Germany,[234]

[228] *Id.* at 90 (emphasis supplied).

[229] Law No. 77, Oct. 10, 1971, concerning the establishment of the Egyptian International Bank for Foreign Trade and Development, *cited in* Mikdashi, *The Changing Framework of Concession Agreements and the Oil Industry Policy Issues in Primary Industries.* 7 Vand. J. Trans. L. 299 (1974).

[230] For the investment laws in Africa see U.N. Pub. Sales No. 11.K.3; Afghanistan investment Law Art. 12 (Afro-Asian Review, No. 26, 27 Nov. 1961); Argentina, Com'l Code 2511, 1324, of 1963 (Pan-Am U. 1963 at 258); Bolivia investment law of 1960, Article 3; Brazil, Constitution of 1946, Article 141, (3), (16); Burma Investment Act of 1959, Art. 6; Cameroon Investment Law 1960, Art. 16; Ceylon Investment Act of 1966 (V International L.M. 16, 1966 at 591): Chad Investment Act of 1963, Arts. 2, 3, Congo (Brazzaville) Investment Act of 1961, Art. 2; Dohomey Investment Code of 1961, Art. 2; Gabon Investment Code of 1961, Art 2; Guinea Investment Code; Ivory Coast Investment Code of 1959, Art. 10; Kenya Investment Code 1964, Art. 8 (IV International L.M. 1965 at 241); Korea, F.I.C. Art, 32; Senegal Investment Code of 1962; Togo Investment Code of 1965, Arts. 25, 28; Uganda F.I.C. 1964, Art. 2.

[231] Israel (1951), Ethiopia (1951), Iran (1955), Nicaragua (1956), Republic of Korea (1956), Muscat and Oman (1958), Pakistan (1959), Togo (1966), Thailand (1966), and a great number of agreements on investment guarantees (on convertibility, expropriation, war, revolution, and insurrection and extended risk). For these agreements see U.N. Dept. of Econ. and Social Affairs, *Foreign Investment in Developing Countries* U.N. Doc. E/4446 (1968) at 60–61.

[232] The U.K. has agreements with Iran (1959) and the Cameroons (1963). Cited in *id.*, at 60; *see also* U.N. Doc. TD/35/Rev. 1 (1968) at 102, 103.

[233] Japan with Cuba (1960); Malaysia (1960); Pakistan (1961); Philippines (1960); Indonesia (1961); India (1958); Haiti (1958); Peru (1961); El Salvador (1963). *Id.* at 24 and 59.

[234] Germany with Dominican Republic (1959), Pakistan (1959), Malaysia (1960), Greece (1961), Thailand (1961), Togo (1961), Guinea (1962), Turkey (1962), Cameroon (1962), Madagascar (1962), Sudan (1963), Ceylon (1963), Tunisia (1963), Senegal (1964), Republic of South Korea (1964), India (1964), Niger (1964), Sierra Leone (1965), Ecuador (1965). *Id.* at 59.

France,[235] the Netherlands,[236] Switzerland,[237] and Belgium.[238] Bilateral treaties for protection of foreign investment are not only between developed and developing countries but also between developing countries themselves, such as the treaties between India and Iran, India and Afghanistan, Kuwait and Iraq.[239] The developing countries have also attracted private foreign investment through regional organizations with programs guaranteeing private foreign investment. The Arab Establishment of Investment Insurance, based in Kuwait, with capital of 10 million Kuwaiti dinars, is one such regional organization. This organization was established by agreement among the countries of Egypt, Jordan, Kuwait, Sudan, and Syria in May 1971.[240] The main function of this organization is to protect losses sustained by Arab investors in member countries. This insurance is against noncommercial risks, such as expropriation, nationalization of property, or inability to transfer income or principal out of the host country as a result of unforeseen restrictions and losses resulting from wars, military operations, and civil disturbances.[241]

On the other hand, considering the number of noncommunist countries that have nationalized or negotiated purchases of foreign-owned assets since 1960 (34 countries:[242] 9 in Latin America, 15 in Africa, 5 in the Middle East and 5 in Asia), the reasons for the confusion and conflicting behavior of some developing countries become clearer. Such confusion could only be explained by the historical role of foreign investment, the general nature of the interaction between developed and developing countries, the con-

---

[235] France with the Federation of Mali (1960), Senegal (1960), Madagascar (1960), Togo (1963), Tunisia (1963). *Id.*

[236] The Netherlands with Tunisia (1963), Ivory Coast (1965), Senegal (1965), Cameroon (1965), *Id.* at 24.

[237] Switzerland with Tunisia (1961), United Republic of Tanzania (1965), Nigeria (1962), Guinea (1962), Ivory Coast (1962), Senegal (1962), Congo (1962), Cameroon (1963), Togo (1964), Madagascar (1964), Malta (1965), Dahomey (1966). *Id.* at 59.

[238] Belgium with Tunisia (1964), Morocco (1965). *Id.*

[239] *See* THE ROLE OF PRIVATE ENTERPRISE IN INVESTMENT AND PROMOTION OF EXPORTS IN DEVELOPING COUNTIRES 104 U.N. Doc. T/D/35/ Rev. 1 (1968).

[240] See Mikdashi, *supra* note 229, at 298.

[241] *Id.*

[242] U.S. DEPT. OF STATE RESEARCH STUDY, *Nationalization, Expropriation, and Other Takings of U.S. and Certain Foreign Property Since 1960*, 1971 (hereinafter cited as RESEARCH STUDY).

cern of developing governments for the betterment of their people, and the consciousness of international politics, which causes new demands by these governments concerning economic and power structures in international relations, and the attempts of these governments to change the conditioning factors which are perceived by them to have caused them to be and remain undeveloped. These reasons, particularly the last, help explain the confusion attending the promotion of stable policy concerning development agreements.

In prescribing policies about specific claims regarding development agreements, it should be remembered that "no nation can develop political or economic security in isolation."[243] It is clear that progress in the world economy cannot continue if a large part of the world has a low standard of living and also that development and raising the standard of living of underdeveloped countries help create the perspectives and conditions necessary for a strong world economy.

The importance that agreements carry among the strategies[244] by which states engage in sharing and shaping of values resides in the fact that in the absence of centralized legislative bodies in the world arena, agreements represent the closest approach to the considered and deliberate prescription of future policies, a process that is the characteristic function of constitutive and legislative bodies in municipal arenas.[245] Agreements create uniformity of expectation, a uniformity that may ultimately have the force of law. Agreements are persuasive strategies for the possession and sharing of values; and

> [b]ecause of the emphasis in all conceptions of human dignity upon persuasion and voluntary commitment as the preferred modality of value change, an international law honoring such conceptions will necessarily seek to make effective, within the limits of the overriding policies of the demanded public order, all genuine agreements and unilateral expressions of intent cre-

[243] Cecil, Foreword to SOUTH WESTERN LEGAL FOUNDATION, SELECTED READINGS ON PROTECTION BY LAW OF PRIVATE FOREIGN INVESTMENTS (1964) (hereinafter cited as SELECTED READINGS).

[244] For a brief factual description of the strategies which states employ in their interactions (diplomatic, ideological, economic, and military) see M. McDOUGAL & F. FELICIANO, LAW AND MINIMUM WORLD PUBLIC ORDER Ch. 1 (1961).

[245] M. McDougal, International Agreements and World Public Order (1972) (unpublished material in the Yale Law School library).

> ating shared expectations of commitment. . . . [I]t will regard
> this goal of ascertaining and effectuating the genuine expecta-
> tions of the particular parties as necessary to honest respect for
> human dignity, and to promoting experiment and diversity,
> rather than dead-weight conformity, in social processes.[246]

Development agreements facilitate and create expectations about
the inclusive use of resources physically located within the territorial boundaries of states. Furthermore, development agreements
are one of the most useful strategies for the promotion of economic development because of their ability to transfer or create
the key elements of economic development.[247] It should be emphasized, however, that here the term *development agreements* refers
to a modified form of agreement; *i.e.*, agreements that become a
part of and follow national development planning, rather than
isolated policies which require elimination or change of direction
of national development planning.

Foreign investment has always carried a pejorative connotation
of imperialism and colonialism, based on the wide and long experience of many nation-states and their people, but such investment does not necessarily create the same expectations today.
Private foreign investment as a complement to foreign public aid
can be made to alleviate the disproportionate sharing of the
world's values. "[The] private investor, in helping himself, can help
the countries in the throes of revolution and contribute to their
economic welfare."[248] Such a change in the role of private foreign
investment is the result of changes in the nature of social interactions as well as the effective power process of the world community. The new participants in the social process, effective in forms
of groups, as third world, nonaligned, with new expectations and
strong bases of power, new skill and knowledge about their own
capacity as well as new political, economic, and social consciousness
about the role and operation of foreign investments, are capable
of promoting their economic strength through cooperation and

---

[246] McDougal, *Perspectives for an International Law of Human Dignity*, 53 ASIL Procs. 107, 128–9 (1959).

[247] For the role of foreign investment in transfer of technology to developing countries, see U.N. Economic and Social Council, *Foreign Investment in Developing Countries* U.N. Doc. E/4444 (1968) at 30–42; Fatouros, *supra* note 208, at 153–63; R. Cooper, The Economics of Interdependence, 81–112 (1968).

[248] Selected Readings, note 243, *supra*.

the use of the economic power of foreign investments, while limiting their political activities. Some may claim of the capital-exporting countries that the policy behind their promotion of private foreign investment is to implement their political objectives abroad. This is equally true with respect to more direct forms of foreign aid. Actually, direct foreign aid is more tinged with political motivation than is private investment. For example, the greater part of U.S. foreign aid has been for military or security purposes.[249] The Foreign Assistance Act of 1961[250] restricts development aid loans in the case of the following: (1) by requiring that the President of the United States determine that procurement in other countries will not result in adverse effects to the domestic economy of the United States,[251] (2) development loans may not be made for construction or development of any "productive enterprise." If the products of such enterprise compete directly with those of the United States, the loan will not be granted unless the recipient agrees not to export to the U.S. market more than 20% of the annual production of the "productive enterprise" during the life of the loan.[252] The so-called Hickenlooper Amendment forbids development assistance to certain countries that have nationalized United States–owned assets.[253] On the other hand, the private investor is very much motivated by profit making and is more willing to go along with the policy of the host government as long as there is a profit for him.[254] With respect to the political motives behind foreign investment, Amerasinghe observes that

> [i]n the present politics of coexistence, based on the mutual threat of nuclear destruction, it cannot be denied that the representatives of the Western bloc have everything to gain from political alliances and friendships based on economic ties. But it would not be equally logical to say that such economic ties necessitate political dependence and economic servitude on the part

---

[249] See Tondel, *The Role of Private Investment in U.S. Foreign Aid*, in Selected Readings, *supra* note 243, at 316–17.

[250] 75 Stat. 426 (1961), 22 U.S.C. § 2161 (Supp. 1963), *cited in id.* at 319.

[251] 75 Stat. 439 (1961) 22 U.S.C. § 2354 (Supp. 1963), *cited in id.* at 320.

[252] 75 Stat. 444 (1961), 22 U.S.C. § 2470 (Supp. 1963), *cited in id.*

[253] *Id.*

[254] I. Lippincott, Economic Resources and Industries of the World 63–64 (1929).

of the less-developed nations. Though it is not usual to articulate the former aspects of the objectives of a foreign policy which takes into account the need for foreign investment, it would not be proper for that reason to imply the latter objectives.[255]

The issue is not public capital versus private capital. The issue is that both private and public capital are useful means of acquiring capital for development program. There are many development programs that can only be implemented by public capital, such as construction of roads, schools, hospitals, and so on. And there are some other development programs, such as some areas in trade and commerce, where private capital can provide better technology and management.[256]

The basic objective of every country receiving direct foreign investment is to channel the benefits brought by the foreign investor to its own favor and minimize the cost to any guarantor. To achieve this end, countries formulate requirements on foreign investment in order to tailor such investments to their own policies.[257] Similar strategies have been taken by foreign investors' home countries for the encouragement of investment. These strategies are generally effected through legal norms: host countries demand employment and training for nationals, etc.,[258] and home countries, on the other hand, permit foreign investment by their nationals if the foreign investors promote a favorable balance of payments.[259]

In the policies of the developing countries one can observe a strong sense of economic nationalism. This movement, with a long history and increasing intellectual support and institutions to con-

[255] AMERASINGHE, *supra* note 220, at 10. For U.S. policy on foreign investment, see G. RAY, THE ENCOURAGEMENT AND PROTECTION OF INVESTMENT IN DEVELOPING COUNTRIES 50 (1962).

[256] In a report by Professors Mikesell and Allen of the University of Oregon on "Economic Policies Toward Less-Developed Countries," the authors observed that "[w]hile recognizing that many fields are closed to private enterprise in developing countries, in many situations a private dollar combined with technical and managerial skills will contribute far more to development than several public dollars." REPORT PREPARED FOR SUBCOMM. ON FOREIGN ECONOMIC POLICY OF THE JOINT ECONOMIC COMM. 87TH CONG., 1ST SESS., 13 (Comm. Print 1961), *cited in* Tondel, *supra* note 249, at 331.

[257] C. BERGSTEN, COMING INVESTMENT WAR? 135 (1975).

[258] *Id.* at 137–44.

[259] This is the requirement of the United Kingdom, France, Japan, and the U.S. Otherwise these countries restrict foreign investment, which hurts their policies. See *id.* at 147–98.

tain and channel it, has now a momentum of its own.[260] The developing countries believe that expanded and stronger government control over the economy of the country will result in the more effective execution of development plans.[261] This belief is based not only on economic nationalism but also on the strong emotional factors involved in development planning. Myrdal observes that the reason why economic development in developing countries becomes, from the start, an intensely political matter and a business for government is that economic development is a national goal, set out in some detail in a state's development plan.[262] With such perspectives the countries involved try to avoid the concentration of foreign investment in any major section of their economy.[263] Such concentration may lead to (a) too much dependence on the foreign investor, which is incompatible with their policy of being self-sufficient,[264] and (b) decreased leadership on the part of the government for the implementation of national economic planning.[265] In order to minimize the decision-making role of foreign investors, governments have employed three strategies: (1) to nationalize the foreign investment, (2) to purchase all or part of the firm through negotiations, and (3) to participate in the foreign investment. The practice of such strategies has resulted in new forms of foreign investment which lower the possibility of nationalization due to the government's participation on a major scale. These new forms of foreign investments are "joint ventures,"[266] "management contracts," "service contracts,"[267] and so on.

[260] L. TURNER, MULTINATIONAL COMPANIES IN THE THIRD WORLD 75–76 (1973).

[261] This view has, however, been opposed: "[I]t seems improbable that more pervasive government controls over the economy and society in such countries [developing countries] could prove compatible with democratic political development." Reischauer, *The Future of the Limited World*, WORLDVIEW, Sept. 1975, at 19.

[262] G. MYRDAL, AN INTERNATIONAL ECONOMY 160 (1956).

[263] Singer, "The Distribution of Gains Between Investing and Borrowing Countries," 40 A. ECO. REV. PROC. 473 (1950).

[264] RESEARCH STUDY, *supra* note 242, at 1.

[265] Singer, *supra* note 253, at 473; Hymer, *The Multinational Corporation and the Law of Under Development*, in ECONOMICS AND WORLD ORDER FROM THE 1970's TO THE 1990's 113–41 (F. Bhagwati ed. 1972).

[266] See JOINT INTERNATIONAL BUSINESS (W. Friedman & G. Kalmanoff, eds. 1961).

[267] H. CATTAN, THE EVOLUTION OF OIL CONCESSIONS IN THE MIDDLE EAST AND NORTH AFRICA (1967).

1. The Factual Background of Development Agreements

a. *The International Character of Development Agreements*

Because of the diverse roles which they play in the international economy, development agreements have a complex character. These agreements, as indicated above, create certain expectations about the shared use of resources, expectations which go beyond the territorial boundaries of a single nation-state. This complicated role of development agreements places them within the international concern and creates an international character for these agreements. This international character is established by the factual transnational elements involved in the agreements, by recognition by the parties themselves of such facts in their agreements, and, finally, by a flow of authoritative decisions which characterizes these agreements as international.

i. International Elements in Fact

Development agreements contain numerous international elements either in the nature of their activities or in the provisions of the agreements. They involve a nation-state and at least one private foreign entity of differing nationality. Such agreements concern exploitation or production of resources physically located within the territory of a nation-state. These resources may be processed in the same or in another country, in a complex which may belong to a foreign national. These resources may be transported by facilities which themselves belong to entities of different nationalities. They have to be transported across the high seas, territorial seas, landmasses, and airspaces of many other different states. A large proportion of international transportation and communication is deveoted to the movement and distribution of raw resources and manufactured products under development agreements.[268] This suggests the nature of the relation between development agreements and other international sectors. In the whole process from allocation and production to distribution there can be many different nationalities involved, all working for the fulfillment of these agreements. The ultimate consumers

---

[268]*See* Carlston, *International Agreements and Contracts in the Field of Petroleum*, SELECTED READINGS, *supra* note 243, at 63.

themselves may be of different nationalities. These agreements create expectations on the part of at least these participants. Based on past performance, the participants formulate their future plans. These plans may have great impact upon many other human beings. Therefore, any major interruption in performance of these agreements may have significant effects on the future plans of many participants of varying nationalities.

French jurists, in characterizing international contracts, consider the nature of the economic operation of the contract. If the operation involves the life of international economy, the contract is regarded as an international contract.[269]

The provisions of the development agreements themselves may include these international elements, since they may specify explicitly or implicitly different locations, institutions, and individuals that have diverse nationalities for the performance of the agreement.

ii. The International Character of Development Agreements Recognized by Parties in the Agreement

The recognition by the parties to an agreement of its international character is expressed either by their choosing an international dispute-resolving system that establishes an important part of the agreement or by their referring explicitly or implicitly to principles of international law as the controlling law of the agreement.

Almost all development agreements include an arbitration clause. Arbitration clauses constitute an elaborate system for the establishment of the forum and competent decision makers in case of disputes between the parties to the agreement. The 1954 oil agreement between the National Iranian Oil Company and the Iranian Oil Consortium represents a good example of an arbitration clause.[270] The arbitration procedure in this agreement distinguishes between disputes which arise over technical matters and those from more general considerations. In the former type of dispute the parties may request the help of two Swiss institutions specializing in technical matters and accountancy in the appointment of experts to decide the issue. In the case of disputes of a more general character, the parties will first appoint an equal num-

---

[269]*Id.* at 287.

[270]For the text see 2 J. Hurewitz, Diplomacy in the Near and Middle East 348 (1956).

ber of arbitrators. If one of the parties fails to appoint its arbitrators or if the arbitrators cannot agree on the appointment of an umpire, the arbitrators or umpire will be appointed by the President of the International Court of Justice. If the President refuses, or is unable to make the appointment, the request will be addressed successively to the International Court's Vice-President, the President of the Swiss Federal Tribunal, and the President of the highest courts of Denmark, Sweden, and Brazil, in that order. Similar arbitration procedures were provided in the National Iranian Oil Company (NIOC) agreement with Sapphire Petroleum, Ltd., of 1958,[271] and in the 1955 Libyan oil concession,[272] Iraqi oil concession of 1952,[273] NIOC and Oil Consortium agreement of 1973,[274] and NIOC with a group of newcomers in 1969.[275]

Aside from the arbitration clauses, the parties usually choose the applicable principles of international law explicitly or implicitly or refer to them for interpretation of specific terms of the agreement. For example, Article 46 of the 1954 Iranian oil agreement refers to the "principles of law common to Iran and several nations in which the other parties to this agreement are incorporated, and in the absence of such common principles then by and in accordance with principles of law recognized by civilized nations in general, including such of those principles as may have been applied by international tribunals." Similar references to choice of law or general principles of law have been made in many other development agreements.[276] Sometimes the agreement is silent about the choice of law, but by referring to international law for the interpretation of some part of the agreement, it is clear that the intention of the parties is to apply international law. For example, the NIOC agreement with Sapphire had no choice of law clause, but Article 37 of the agreement, which provided for cases of force majeure preventing Sapphire from carrying out its obligations, stated that the term *force majeure* should be defined in accordance with prin-

[271]*See* 35 I.L.R. 140 (1967).

[272]Domke, *International Arbitration of Commercial Disputes*, in SELECTED READINGS, *supra* note 243, at 168.

[273]U.N. Doc. A/AC.97/5/Rev. Vol. 1 (1960), at 74–5.

[274]Text published by National Iranian Oil Company (NIOC) (in Persian) 1973, art. 27.

[275]*Id.* art. 38.

[276]See agreements between the U.A.R. and Pan-American Corp. 1963 and 1964, and the Saudi Arabia and Aramco Agreement of 1933, *cited in* CATTAN, *supra* note 267, at 59.

ciples of international law.[277] There are similar indications as to the appropriate prescriptions in development agreements that will be discussed in later sections.

iii. International Character Recognized by Authoritative Decisions

The majority of authoritative decisions have recognized the international character of development agreements. In the *Illinois Central Railroad Co. Case* (U.S. v. Mexico),[278] the General Claim Commission declared that international claims include claims as between a citizen and a government of another state acting in its public or civil capacity. Such claims have international character and "they too must be decided in accordance with the principles of international law, even in cases where international law should merely declare the municipal law of one of the countries involved to be applicable. . . ."[279] In the *Sapphire Case* the tribunal held that these classes of agreement are "fundamentally different from the usual commercial contract envisaged by the traditional rules of Private International Law."[280] Authoritative decisions have also confirmed the international character of development agreements by rejecting the claim of sovereign power for the unilateral violation of agreements. The Claim Commission in the *Martini Case* (Italy v. Venezuela),[281] declared that the state was liable for the exercise of its sovereign power, effectively abrogating the claimant's right under an agreement. In the *Aramco* arbitration the Tribunal held that the claimant had acquired irrevocable rights under the concession and that such irrevocable rights were consistent with the sovereign power of the state:

> Nothing can prevent a State, in the exercise of its sovereignty, from binding itself irrevocably by the provisions of a concession and from granting to the concessioner irretractable rights. Such rights have the character of acquired rights. Should a new concession contract incompatible with the first, or a subsequent

[277] 35 I.L.R. 120 (1967).

[278] 4 R. Int'l Arb. Awards 21 (1951).

[279] *Id.* at 13.

[280] 35 I.L.R. 171 (1967).

[281] Venezuelan Arbitration of 1903 S. Doc. No. 316, 58th Cong. 2d Sess. (1904), No. 4620 at 837 (Report of Jackson H. Ralston).

statute, abolish totally or partially that which has been granted
by a previous law or concession, this would constitute a clear
infringement, by the second contract, of acquired rights or a
violation, by the subsequent statute, of the principle of nonre-
troactivity of laws with the only exception of rules of public
policy. This is because a legal situation acquired by virtue of a
previous special statute cannot be abrogated by subsequent statute—generalia specialibus non derogant—unless the legislator
has expressly given retroactive effects to such statute, which the
state cannot do in respect of concessions, without engaging its
responsibility.[282]

Even municipal tribunals have refused to accept the claim of
absoluteness of sovereign power in unilateral violation of agreement. The U.S. Supreme Court, for example, in *Perry v. United
States*,[283] held that "[t]he United States are as much bound by their
contracts as are individuals. . . . [W]hen the United States, with
constitutional authority, makes contracts, it has rights and incurs
responsibilities similar to those of individuals who are parties to
such instruments. . . . [T]he [contrary] argument . . . is in substance that the Government cannot by contract restrict the exercise
of a sovereign power. But the right to make binding obligations is
a competence attaching to sovereignty."[284] In *Robertson v. Minister
of Pensions*, the same point was emphasized by the court when it
said:

> The next question is whether the assurance is binding upon the
> Crown. The Crown cannot escape by saying that estoppels do
> not bind the Crown, for that the doctrine has long been ex-
> ploded. Nor can the Crown escape by praying in aid the doctrine
> of executive necessity, i.e. the doctrine that the Crown cannot
> bind himself so as to fetter its future executive action. . . . The
> Crown is bound by its express promise as much as any
> subject. . . . [t]he defence of executive necessity is of limited
> scope. It only avails the Crown where there is an implied term to
> that effect or that is the true meaning of the contract.[285]

[282]27 I.L.R. 117 (1963).

[283]294 U.S. 330 (1934).

[284]*Id.* at 351–53.

[285][1949] 1 K.B. 227, 231 (opinion of Denning, J.).

The more general community expectations about the superior status of development agreements over other state contracts and competences are expressed in paragraph 8 of the United Nations General Assembly Declaration on Permanent Sovereignty over National Resources, which reads, "foreign investment agreements freely entered into by or between sovereign states shall be observed in good faith."[286] The English jurist Mann, who believes that states are only subjects of international law, has observed that "[a] state contract which, according to the intention of the parties, is internationalized, may include a contractual adoption of that principle. It would be *nihil ad rem* to argue that its invocations are open only to persons who are subjects of international law; for that principle of public international law could apply, not *ex lege*, but *ex contractu*."[287] Other jurists have referred to development agreements as quasi-international agreements, which are neither contracts governed by municipal law nor treaties governed by international law.[288]

b. Development Agreements Not Administrative Agreements

Development agreements, however, have a quasi-public character,[289] and are not administrative agreements. The concept of administrative contracts developed in the civil law system. This concept recognizes the unilateral authority of states to terminate or modify the terms of the agreement in the public interest.[290] In

---

[286]G.A. Res. 1803, 17 U.N. GAOR, Supp. (No. 17) 44, U.N. DOC. A/5217 (1962). *See* I. BROWNLIE, PRINCIPLES OF PUBLIC INTERNATIONAL LAW 534 (2d ed. 1973).

[287]STUDIES IN INTERNATIONAL LAW 191 (F. Mann ed. 1973) (hereinafter cited as MANN).

[288]*See* G. SCHWARZENBERGER, 1 INTERNATIONAL LAW AS APPLIED BY INTERNATIONAL COURTS AND TRIBUNALS 578 (3d ed. 1957); see also Verdross, *The Status of Foreign Private Interests Stemming from Economic Development Agreements with Arbitration Clauses*, in SELECTED READINGS 124, *supra* note 243, at 124.

[289]The quasi-public character of development agreements comes from the nature of the contract and the place where that contract is to be performed. The performance of the agreements occurs mainly in underdeveloped countries. The performance of the agreement may require certain utilities, such as transportation, communication, health, and housing facilities. Such a range of activities tends to give the enterprise a quasi-public character. See THE INTERNATIONAL FLOW OF PRIVATE CAPITAL, U.N. Doc. No. E/2531 ST/ECA/22 (1954) at 44–45, 46–52.

[290]*See* Z. KRONFOL, PROTECTION OF FOREIGN INVESTMENT 70–71 (1972); W. FRIEDMANN, LAW IN A CHANGING SOCIETY 375 (1959); Langrod, *Administration Contracts* 4 AM. J. CORP.

common law, on the other hand, administrative agreements should theoretically have the same effect as ordinary contracts. In the view of the Supreme Court, an administrative contract in common law loses its public character: "When the United States enters into a contractual relation, its rights and duties herein are governed generally by the law applicable to contracts between private parties."[291] In practice, however, the Government can interfere with the operation of the administrative contracts by including different clauses in the agreement.[292]

The notion of an "administrative contract" is a vague one, and it is difficult to establish any definite and generally accepted criterion to distinguish such a contract from other state agreements.[293] Through its provision of the option for unilateral termination, an administrative contract is only a strategy for the sovereign state to protect the national interests of its people. Such protection as afforded in development agreements has been provided for in other channels, which will be discussed later in this section. Therefore, there is no need to refer separately to such a vague concept, a concept that only adds more difficulties to the problems surrounding development agreements. Furthermore, authoritative decisions do not regard development agreements as administrative agreements.[294]

2. Applicable Laws

The "proper law" of development agreements refers to a process of authoritative decision, embodying the expectations of peoples across state boundaries, which regulates specific issues or problems involved in the process of agreement. The issue of "proper"

L. 351–58 (1955); J. MITCHELL, THE CONTRACTS OF PUBLIC AUTHORITIES (1954) and FATOUROS, *supra* note 208, at 198.

[291] Lynch v. United States, 292 U.S. 571, 579 (1934).

[292] *See* FRIEDMANN, *supra* note 290, at 376–81; MITCHELL, *supra* note 290, at 24–30; S. WILLISTON, CONTRACTS 309–10 (1945); and Mewett, *The Theory of Government Contract*, 5 McGILL L.J. 238 (1959).

[293] Verdross has established some criteria of difference between the two kinds of agreement. See SELECTED READINGS, *supra* note 243, at 122–27.

[294] The Awards of the Aramco Arbitration, Sapphire Case, 35 I.L.R. 1971 (1967); see also CATTAN, *supra* note 267, at 82. Cattan concludes that oil concession agreements in the Middle East have always been regarded as ordinary contracts and not as administration contracts. Id. at 82–83.

prescriptions is a difficult and controversial conceptual problem. There may be many different prescriptions relevant to different features of the process of agreement. The relevance of a variety of prescriptions arises from the complex character of this class of agreements, with participation of many nationalities in public and private capacities in pursuit of a wide variety of purposes under many different sets of circumstances and having wide impacts upon both the parties and the world community.

The overall policy recommendation is that any law made applicable should protect two kinds of interests: the mutually exclusive interests of the parties and the inclusive interests of the community as a whole. To protect the mutually exclusive interests of the parties requires respect for the arrangements made by the parties in the agreement about the applicable laws. However, such arrangements should not violate international norms which are formulated to protect the inclusive interests of peoples. These international norms are embodied in the customary international law on the responsibility of states with respect to international obligations and standards for the treatment of aliens. Sometimes, however, the question of choice of law might involve an agreement which is about a particular resource of vital importance to the world community. To determine the proper prescription about such an agreement, the arbitrator may have to go beyond the traditional law of state responsibility or the choice of the parties. There may be a need for the prescription of a whole new norm in order to protect the vital interests of the world community.

It is also sometimes argued that development agreements should be governed entirely by political considerations. This perspective ignores the historic legal and economic strategies of persuasion developed for the protection of common interest and would make that interest totally dependent on the political policies and motives of particular states. Although it is a fact that many basic goals in the game of international politics relate to the process of resource distribution, political motives that have no relevance to the policies of protecting the common interest must be discounted as claims of special interest.

a. Law Specified by the Parties in the Agreement

Generally, the applicable law specified by the parties in the agreement has been respected by arbitral tribunals so long as it has not violated the customary law of state responsibility. The community should respect the reasonable expectation of the parties about their agreements. Respect for the parties' choice of law is one way to promote such expectations. Such policy forms the basis of the World Bank's Convention on Investment Disputes between States and Nationals of other States.[295] The Convention applies in the first instance the rules agreed on by the parties; only in their absence does it envisage the application of other rules: "The Tribunal shall decide a dispute in accordance with such rules as may be agreed by the parties. In the absence of such agreement, the Tribunal shall apply the law of the Contracting State party to the dispute (including the rules on the conflict of laws) and such rules of international law as may be applicable."[296] One of the choices of the parties on the applicable law may be the municipal law of the contracting state. In practice, however, while municipal law has always been relevant,[297] it is seldom chosen as the sole prescription of the agreement. Municipal law has commonly been incorporated as appropriate law with other prescriptions, such as international law or general principles of law. For example, the World Bank's Convention states in Article 42 that in the absence of an agreement of the parties to the proper law the Tribunal will apply the law of the Contracting State and "such rules of international law as may be applicable." Thus Article 10 of the Libyan Petroleum Law (1955), amended in 1965, provides that "the concession shall be governed by, and interpreted in accordance with the principles of law in Libya consistent with principles of international law, and in their absence, in accordance with the general principles of law including those applied by international tribunals."[298] Sometimes the law stipulated may be a combination of the statutory and conventional provisions and the general principles of law, such as the Franco-Algerian Agreement on Hydrocarbons of 1959.[299] This

---

[295] INT'L BANK FOR RECONSTRUCTION AND DEVELOPMENT, CONVENTION ON INVESTMENT DISPUTES BETWEEN STATES AND NATIONALS OF OTHER STATES (entered into effect Oct. 14, 1966, ICSID/2).

[296] Art. 42, *id.*

[297] Such relevance and application of municipal law can be observed in any development agreement, simply because the participation belongs to a sovereign state and the major part of the performance of the agreement occurs within the territory of a nation-state.

[298] See CATTAN, *supra* note 267, at 87.

[299] *Id.* at 90.

agreement specified the laws applicable to three kinds of possible disputes arising from the agreement: (a) In the case of disputes between the Algerian Authority and companies already holding mining titles, the competent decision maker will be the international tribunal established under the Agreement and the applicable law is that in accord with the Sahara Petroleum Code and, to the extent required, with the provisions of the Agreement. If the interpretation of the Sahara Petroleum Code is necessary, it is to be with reference to the French *droit administratif* and in particular with reference to the decisions of the French Conseil d'Etat. If the texts are silent the Tribunal can refer to general principles of law;[300] (b) in the case of disputes between the Algerian State and the French company or between Algerian and French companies established for the operation of the Cooperative Association, the applicable prescriptions will be based on the Protocol relating to the Cooperative Association and its appendices. If the Protocol is insufficient to settle the issue, the Tribunal refers to general principles of law;[301] (c) any dispute between the two governments relating to the interpretation or execution of the Agreement is settled by a procedure of conciliation or arbitration, and if these procedures fail, by submission of such differences, at the request of the interested party, to the International Court of Justice.[302]

The provisions of the agreement itself may be chosen as the governing law. Due to a lack of appropriate municipal or other regulations, sometimes because of technical elements involved in the agreement, they prefer their own specially constructed rules or rules made by specialists. The parties may choose to establish certain prescriptions in the agreement to regulate their obligations.

Because of the lack of petroleum legislation in grantor states, some oil concessions granted in the Middle East themselves regulate "the entirety of the legal and fiscal relation between the prospector, the operator and the State authorities. Two of the main producer states of the Middle East—Saudi Arabia and Kuwait— today still belong in this category."[303] The same rule may apply to

[300] *Id.* at 91.

[301] *Id.*

[302] *Id.*

[303] A. Sanhouri, 1 Massader Al Iltizam 698 (in Arabic) (2d ed. 1964), *cited in* Cattan, id. at 34.

countries which have petroleum legislation. The agreement is granted under the petroleum legislation but becomes the law of the parties themselves. In the words of a former Secretary General of OPEC with respect to the Iranian Petroleum Act:

> In the Iranian system each agreement is, in the fullest sense, a law for it regulates exhaustively the relations between the parties and is an Act of Parliament. The Petroleum Act lays down the general principles under which agreements may be made, and describes the varieties of authorities' relationships, but once an agreement is made and ratified by the Legislature, the Petroleum Act virtually fades away because the agreement itself is the appropriate and sufficient law. The tendency for the oil Agreement to become a self-contained law is worldwide.[304]

Carlston has generalized the same point to all oil concessions: "An examination of concession agreements relating to the production of oil in the Middle East will reveal the comprehensive character of a modern concession agreement. Such an agreement becomes the fundamental or constitutive law of the joint enterprise of the government and the concessionaire."[305] This view has also been supported by authoritative decisions. In the Aramco Arbitration the Tribunal expressly stated that "the Concession Agreement is the fundamental law of the parties."[306]

The freedom of the contracting parties in constituting their own legal order has been criticized by Mann. He observes that such freedom for parties may result in the establishment of certain rules independent of a legal order, which may endanger the international legal order or may be impractical:

> The idea that contracting parties are at liberty not only to choose systems applicable to their contract, but also to create [their] own legal system which is independent, exhaustive and sovereign and to which municipal system of law and public international law are inferior—that idea is doctrinally so unattractive, so impracticable, so subversive of public international law, so dangerous from the point of view of legal policy and so unnecessary that its

[304] F. ROUHANI, INTERNATIONAL AGREEMENTS AND CONTRACTS IN THE FIELD OF PETROLEUM 9–10 (1971).

[305] *See* Carlston, *supra* note 268, at 262.

[306] 27 I.L.R. 168 (1959).

novelty will not cause surprise. It hardly requires emphasis that every legal relationship in general and every contract in particular must of necessity be governed by a system of law and is otherwise unthinkable. Of course in the words of the Civil Code, "les conventions legalement formees tiennent lieu de loi a ceux qui les ont faites"; but freedom of contract does not exist independently of the legal system which grants it or confer any measure of sovereignty upon the contracting parties. Nor can contracts either in law or in fact regulate the parties relationship exclusively. Contracts are written against the background of a system of law, its jus cogens, its rules of construction and so forth.[307]

The legal system which accords this autonomy is of course that of international law and the specially created rules must not violate international prescriptions for the protection of common interest. In practice the parties usually never create the whole system of the "proper law" of their agreement; they determine only certain prescriptions about certain problems as independent of any formally existent legal system. These specially created norms cannot harm the international legal order, if they present the true intention of the parties and do not violate the law of state responsibility for its international obligations.

It sometimes happens that parties agree on the application of what are called "the general principles of law." An example is found in Article 46 of the Consortium's Agreement with Iran (1954), which stated that "[i]n view of the diverse nationalities of the parties to this agreement it shall be governed by and interpreted and applied in accordance with the principles of law common to Iran and the several nations in which the other parties to this Agreement are incorporated, and in the absence of such common principles then by and in accordance with principles of law recognized by civilized nations in general, including such of those principles as may have been applied by international tribunals."[308] The Kuwait-Arabian Oil Company agreement (1958), the Kuwait-Shell agreement (1961), and Hadramaut–Pan American agreement (1961) also include provisions for applications of general principles of law.[309] References to application of general principles

[307] *See* MANN, *supra* note 287, at 230–31.

[308] *See* CATTAN, *supra* note 267, at 63.

[309] *Id.*

of law can be observed in a number of development agreements.[310]

This emphasis upon "general principles" derives from Article 38 of the Statute of the Permanent Court of International Justice which refers to such principles as one of the sources of international law.[311] This Statute remained intact in the text of the present Statute of the International Court of Justice. This Article has been adopted in concept by many municipal codes.[312] Yet despite such widespread use of the concept, there is no precise definition of what is meant by general principles of law. In search for content jurists have commonly employed a comparative method. Dr. Mann, for example, observed that general principles of law "though by no means fixed or easy to ascertain are yet not so vague as to render a submission to them void for uncertainty. Such general principles as are referred to in Article 38 of the Statute of the Permanent Court of International Justice will largely be private law to be ascertained on a broad comparative basis or to be deduced from the law of the particular group of countries with which the transaction is predominantly connected (common law, Latin Codifications etc.) or even from the legal system of a particular country."[313] Judge Hudson commented that this concept refers to principles common to various sytems of municipal law or generally agreed upon among interpreters of municipal law.[314] W. Friedmann stated that the general principles of law are the result of "a comparative study of the relevant principles of the different national systems provided the principal source from which the new

[310]The agreements between the U.A.R. and Pan-American of 1963 and 1964 in Art. 42 applied the general principles of law; the Supplemental Agreement between the Ruler of Qatar and Qatar Petroleum Company on Dec. 31, 1964, which amended the original concessions, in Art. 12, referred to general principles of law as the applicable law; the Libyan concessions of Jan. 20, 1966, and also the Franco-Algerian agreement of June 26, 1963, referred to the application of general principles of law in case of silence or lacunae in the texts. *See* Cattan, *id.* at 59.

[311]Statute of the Permanent Court of International Justice, art. 38, *reprinted in* M. HUDSON, THE WORLD COURT 1922–1928 (1928).

[312]B. CHENG, GENERAL PRINCIPLES OF LAW AS APPLIED BY INTERNATIONAL COURTS AND TRIBUNALS xiii (1953). For the application of this concept by the Civil Code of Arab countries, see the EGYPTIAN CIVIL CODE (1948), SYRIAN CIVIL CODE (1949), IRAQ CIVIL CODE (1953), and LIBYAN CIVIL CODE (1954), *cited in* CATTAN, *supra* note 267, at 61, n. 69.

[313]MANN, *supra* note 287, at 191.

[314]M. HUDSON, THE PERMANENT COURT OF INTERNATIONAL JUSTICE 1920–1942, 612–15 (1943). Cheng gives a different view with respect to this concept; *see* CHENG, *supra* note 312, at 2 *et seq.*

bodies of international law are being developed."[315] Gutteridge observes that for the establishment of general principles of law the judge should be provided

> on the one hand with a guide to the exercise of his "choice of a new principle" and, on the other hand, to prevent him from "blindly following the teaching" of jurists with which he is most familiar "without first carefully weighing the merits and considering whether a principle of private law does in fact satisfy the demands of justice" if applied to the particular case before him. In other words . . . comparative law furnishes the judge with an objective test by which he can measure the justice of a principle which he believes to be the correct one and proposes to apply to the facts of a particular case when the existing rules of the law of nations do not furnish him with the materials for a decision.[316]

From these examples it is clear that "general principles of law" are taken to refer to propositions recognized in the municipal law of several nation-states within their own boundaries. These principles become part of international law by virtue of the expectations created by such common practice and by their recognition in Article 38 of the ICJ Charter. Lord McNair, however, tries to ascribe a different character to the general principles of law; something apart from international law. He describes them as a discrete system of law.[317] Dr. Mann objects to this distinction and argues that "unless [the general principles of law] are equiparated to public international law, general principles are not a legal system at all, and Lord McNair clearly refuses so to equiparate them."[318] Lord McNair emphasizes that the development agreements are not "governed" by public international law stricto sensu," and should be governed by general principles of law recognized by civilized nations.[319] Dr. Fischer similarly opposes the distinction made by Lord McNair and observes that the general principles of law ought to be recognized as forming part of a broader system of interna-

---

[315] Friedmann, *The Uses of "General Principles" in the Development of International Law*, in INTERNATIONAL LAW IN THE TWENTIETH CENTURY 249 (1969).

[316] H. GUTTERIDGE, COMPARATIVE LAW 70–71 (2d ed. 1949).

[317] McNair, *The General Principles of Law Recognized by Civilized Nations*, 33 BRIT. Y.B. INT'L L. (1957) (hereinafter cited as McNair).

[318] MANN, *supra* note 287, at 224.

[319] McNair, *supra* note 317, at 19.

tional law.[320] Dr. Cheng concludes that there is no point in questioning whether the general principles of law are international law or municipal law, since it is precisely the nature of these principles that they do not belong exclusively to any particular system of law, while they are common to all of them.[321]

In the application of general principles of law, tribunals generally refer to principles practiced in different systems of law, and particularly to principles common to the law of the two contracting parties. This was the methodology employed by the arbitrator in the *Sapphire Case*.[322] In the *Aramco Arbitration* the Tribunal held that

> [i]nsofar as doubts may remain on the content or on the meaning of the agreements of the Parties, it is necessary to resort to the general principles of law and to apply them in order to interpret, and even to supplement, the respective rights and obligations of the parties. . . . Matters pertaining to private law are, in principle, governed by the law of Saudi Arabia but with one important reservation. That law must, in case of need, be interpreted or supplemented by the general principles of law, by the custom and practice in the oil business and by notions of pure jurisprudence, in particular whenever certain private rights—which must inevitably be recognized to the concessionaire if the concession is not to be deprived of its substance—would not be secured in an unquestionable manner by the law in force in Saudi Arabia.[323]

The Tribunal held, however, that on certain problems public international law should be applicable to the regulation of the concession when objective reasons indicated that certain matters could not be governed by the municipal law of any country. Such problems included all matters relating to transport by sea, the sovereignty of the State in its territorial waters, and the responsibility of States for the violation of transnational obligations.[324]

Cattan appropriately observes that various applications of gen-

---

[320] P. FISCHER, DIE INTERNATIONALE KONZESSION 361, 447, 451–52 (1974), *reviewed in* 69 AM. J. INT'L L. 912 (1975).

[321] CHENG, *supra* note 312, at 390.

[322] 35 I.L.R. at 170 *et seq.*

[323] 27 I.L.R. at 168–69.

[324] H. STEINER & D VAGTS, TRANSNATIONAL LEGAL PROBLEMS 389 (1968).

eral principles of law in the past few years "tend to make the concept a residuary 'common law' of certain classes of State contracts."[325]

The international law that may be made to apply to development agreements is indicated in Article 38 of the Statute of the International Court of Justice. The sources of international law there specified are:

> (a) International conventions, whether general or particular, establishing rules expressly recognized by the contesting States;
>
> (b) International customs, as evidence of a general practice accepted as law;
>
> (c) The general principles of law recognized by civilized nations;
>
> (d) Subject to the provisions of Article 59; judicial decisions and the teachings of the most highly qualified publicists of the various nations, as subsidiary means for the determination of rules of law.

All these sources may be chosen by the parties to a development agreement for yielding applicable law. For example, Article 22 of Anglo-Iranian Oil Concession (1933), which states: "The award shall be based on the juridical principles contained in Article 38 of the Statute of the Permanent Court of International Justice."[326] The early oil concession granted in Libya stated that the agreement shall be governed and interpreted by the law of Libya and to the extent not inconsistent therewith, "in accordance with such principles and rules of international law as may be relevant."[327] The NIOC Agreement with *Sapphire* and Article 13 of the Iranian Petroleum Act (1957) state that "force majeure" should be defined in accordance with the principles of international law.

In applying international law to development agreements, some commentators have taken a narrow view and refer to states as the only subjects of public international law. These commentators, therefore, oppose the applicability of public international law to this class of agreements. Lord McNair observes that the system of law which governs agreements between foreign corporations and governments cannot be public international law stricto sensu as presently understood because such contracts are not interstate

[325]*Cattan, supra* note 267, at 68.

[326]*Id.* at 69.

[327]*Id.*

contracts and do not deal with interstate relations.[328] Some decisions have supported this view. Thus, the opinion of the International Court of Justice in the Anglo-Iranian Oil dispute of 1952 rejected the argument of the British Government that the 1932 Iranian Declaration concerning the jurisdiction of the International Court of Justice should apply to the Oil Concession.[329] Hyde, however, argues that the holding of the Court was that "this particular concession is not a treaty within the meaning of the declaration of Iran relating to the jurisdiction of the International Court of Justice."[330] It may be true that the Court tried to avoid the rejection of international character of the development agreements, but the Court clearly gave a lower international status to the Agreement, saying that "[this] is nothing more than a concessionary contract between a government and a foreign corporation ... [and] it did not regulate any public matters directly concerning the two Governments. It could not possibly be considered to lay down the law between the two States."[331] In the Aramco Arbitration the Tribunal similarly rejected a contention made on behalf of the company that the concession agreement should be "assimilated to an international treaty governed by law of Nations," and held that the Agreement was not concluded between two states, but between a state and an American private corporation, and that such agreements are not governed by public international law.[332]

Broches correctly distinguishes between the international character of development agreements and that of treaties: "Nevertheless, one will have to distinguish between this type of so-called international contracts or agreements, and agreements entered into by subjects of international law, which are governed directly, and in all respects, by international law."[333] We share Broches'

---

[328]*See* McNair, note 317, *supra*. For a similar opinion see also Suratgar, *Considerations Affecting Choice of Law Clauses in Contracts Between Governments and Foreign Nationals*, 2 INDIAN J. INT'L L. 304 (1962).

[329][1952] I.C.J. 112.

[330]Hyde, *Economic Development Agreements*, 105 RECUEIL DES COURS 271, 315 (Academie de Droit International) (1962–I).

[331][1952] I.C.J. 112, 113.

[332]27 I.L.R. at 165.

[333]Broches, *International Legal Aspects of the Operations of the World Bank*, 98 RECUEIL DES COURS 301, 315, 345 (Academie De Droit International) (1959–III).

view; however, we believe that one ought to remember that such a distinction is based only on the different roles that these two classes of agreements play. There might be a situation, for example, where the application of treaty rules would be relevant to development agreements. This might occur in cases in which development agreements have a content similar to treaties and community expectations require a comparable treatment.

It is clear that community expectations are moving increasingly toward the application of international law to development agreements. Such a change is reflected both in legal writings and in authoritative decisions.[334] The demand for application of international law to these classes of agreements is also represented in multilateral and bilateral agreements. The Convention on the Settlement of Investment Disputes in Article 42(1) emphasizes the application of international law in conjunction with the municipal law of the Contracting State when the agreement is silent on the choice of law. The United Nations Commission on Permanent Sovereignty over Natural Resources[335] and General Assembly Resolution 1803 (XIII) both emphasize international law as a governing factor in connection with the principle of sovereignty over natural resources. Both the Commission and Resolution invoke compensation in accordance with international law in case of nationalization. Furthermore, they require conditions such as public purpose in the case of taking property, which reflect customary international law. These factors indicate that customary international law has considerable importance in relation to development agreements.[336] There are also a number of bilateral agreements for the application of international law where there is a conflict in foreign investment between the parties, for example, the United States agreements with Ireland,[337] Italy,[338] Iran,[339] the Sultanate of Mus-

[334] *See* P. JESSUP, A MODERN LAW OF NATIONS 138 (1948). It should be noted, however, that Jessup changes the name of international law to transnational law when he applies it to development agreements: See P. JESSUP, TRANSNATIONAL LAW (1956). *See also* the decision in the case of Petroleum Development (Trucial Coast) Ltd. and the Sheikh of Abu Dhabi, 19 I.L.R. 144 (1951).

[335] U.N. Doc. E/3511 (1962).

[336] AMERASINGHE, *supra* note 220, at 7.

[337] R. WILSON. U.S. COMMERCIAL TREATIES AND INTERNATIONAL LAW 120 (1960).

[338] *Id.*

[339] *Id.*

cat and Oman,[340] and Pakistan.[341] There is a similar agreement between Iran and the United Kingdom.[342]

b. Law in the Absence of Specification by Parties

Sometimes parties do not specify an applicable law for their agreements. In such cases general community policy has indicated the application of general principles of law. This policy has been promoted by a number of authoritative decisions. Lord McNair has observed that, since parties often explicitly provide for general principles as the applicable law, even in situations where an agreement is silent about the governing law, the purpose of the parties should be construed as that of escaping from any single municipal law and of applying general principles of law.[343] The application of general principles of law in such cases is regarded as consistent with the principles of fairness and justice, since the parties are not otherwise bound by any single system of law.

There have been a number of cases where the parties did not expressly specify the applicable law in the agreement. The *Lena Goldfields Case*[344] was one such case. The case involved a 1925 concession agreement between Lena and the Soviet Government about oil exploitation in Russia. This Agreement, while it had a clause for the establishment of an arbitral tribunal, had no express provisions for appropriate prescriptions. Article 89 of the Agreement stated, however, that "[t]he parties base their relation with regard to this Agreement on the principles of good will and good faith as well as on reasonable interpretation of the terms of the Agreement." The Tribunal held that while for all domestic Soviet matters Soviet law is the applicable law except where expressly excluded by the Agreement, for other purposes "the general principles of law recognized by civilized nations" was the proper law of the Agreement. A similar situation arose in the oil agreement between Petroleum Developments (Trucial Coast), Ltd., and the

[340] 52 Am. J. Int'l L. 160 (1961).

[341] 44 Dep't. State Bull. 164 (1961).

[342] 9 Int'l & Comp. L.Q. 311 (1960).

[343] *See* McNair, note 317, at 10.

[344] *Lena Goldfields Arbitration*, Annual Digest to Public International Law Cases (1929–30) Cases No. 1 and No. 258, *cited in* McNair, *id.* at 10–11.

Ruler of Abu Dhabi.[345] The Agreement did not include any choice-of-law clause and Article 17 stipulated only that "[t]he Ruler and the Company both declare that they *base their work* in this Agreement on good will and sincerity of belief and on the interpretation of this Agreement in a fashion consistent with reason."[346] The Tribunal rejected the application of the municipal law of the parties (Abu Dhabi and England) and prescribed the "principles rooted in the good sense and common practice of the generality of civilized nations—a sort of modern law of nature." In the application of these principles, however, there is a strong emphasis on English rules in the language of the award.[347] One of the reasons of the Tribunal for rejecting the municipal law of the sovereign state was the "primitive state of the municipal law" of the contracting State, which could not be applied to the "construction of modern commercial instrument[s]." This reasoning was employed as the major reason for the rejection of municipal law in the dispute between the Ruler of Qatar and International Marine Oil Company, Ltd.,[348] by the Arbitral Tribunal. This dispute arose from an oil agreement which had no choice-of-law clause. The Tribunal favored the application of general principles of law because of the inadequacy of Qatar municipal law with regard to such complicated transactions:

> There are at least two weighty considerations against that view [application of municipal law of Qatar]. One is that in my opinion, after hearing the evidence of the two experts in Islamic law, . . . there is no settled body of legal principles in Qatar applicable to the construction of modern commercial instruments. . . . I need not set out the evidence before me about the origin, history and development of Islamic Law as applied in Qatar or as to the legal procedure in that Country. I have no reason to suppose that Islamic law is not administered there strictly, but I am satisfied that the law does not contain any principles which would be sufficient to interpret this particular contract.
>
> Arising out of that reason is the second reason, which is that both experts agreed that certain parts of the contract, if Islamic law was applicable, would be open to the grave criticism of being

[345] 2 INT'L & COMP. L.Q. 247–61 (1952).

[346] *Id.* at 250.

[347] *See also* McNair, *supra* note 317, at 12–13.

[348] 21 I.L.R. 534 (1953).

> invalid. . . . [The] Agreement was full of irregularities from end
> to end according to Islamic law, as applied in Qater. This is a
> cogent reason for saying that such law does not contain a body
> of legal principles applicable to modern commercial contracts of
> this kind.[349]

With such reasoning the question arises as to whether the general
principles of law would be applicable if the municipal law of the
sovereign state was developed enough to govern instruments of
modern commercial transactions.

The basic policy behind the application of general principles of
law to these agreements silent on choice of law is the understanding that the parties did not want to be bound by any single municipal law no matter how developed. Thus even if the municipal law
of both parties was sufficiently developed, the parties would not be
exclusively bound by either law. It is more difficult to draw such
inferences from the reasoning adopted by the Tribunal in the
Qatar case.

One of the best examples of the application of general principles
of law in an agreement without a choice-of-law clause is the decision by the Arbitral Tribunal in a dispute between NIOC and Sapphire International Petroleum, Ltd., a Canadian oil company.[350]
The Tribunal in this case held that "since the agreement contains
no express choice of law, the arbitrator will determine which system of law should best be applied according to evidence of the
parties' intention and in particular the evidence to be found in the
contract."[351] The Tribunal found from the content of the agreement that the intention of the parties was not to apply "the strict
rules of a particular system but, rather, to rely upon the rules of
law, based upon reason, which are common to civilized nations.
These rules are enshrined in Article 38 of the Statute of International Court of Justice as a source of law. . . ."[352] For applying general principles of law, the Tribunal, in considering a particular
doctrine and its potential application, sought for similar practices
in the law of Iran and Canada. Thus, the Tribunal chose to apply
a principle which says that failure by one party to a synallagmatic

---

[349]*Id.* at 544–45.

[350]35 I.L.R. 136 (1967).

[351]*Id.* at 171.

[352]*Id.* at 173.

contract to perform its obligation is a breach of contract which releases the other party from its obligations and gives rise to a right to pecuniary compensation in the form of damages. The authority for this principle the Tribunal found in similar conceptions and practices in both Continental law[353] and Anglo-Saxon law,[354] and found the existence of such practices in both Canadian and Iranian law.[355] In the application of the principle of *pacta sunt servanda*, the Tribunal observed that not only is this principle the basis of every contractual relationship, but also it is contained in Iranian Civil Code (Article 219) as well as in Canadian law.

The application of general principles of law to contracts silent about the choice of law would, therefore, appear to be not only consistent with notions of justice and fairness but also closest to the true expectations of parties desiring not to be bound by any single system of law. This has been acknowledged in a dispute arising from a contract between a subsidiary organ of the United Nations and a Lebanese contractor, where by compromise the parties agreed on the application of general principles of law by the Arbitral Tribunal.[356]

c. *Customary International Law on State Responsibility*

Every action taken by states may have a certain impact on the common interest of the whole community. Such impact may be either positive in the form of value creation and sharing or negative in the form of value deprivation. The main objective of the concept of state responsibility is the prevention of the negative impact on the inclusive interests of the community. These sanctioning goals of prevention, restoration, reconstruction, and rehabilitation, although primarily for the prevention and reconstruction of the negative impact of state activities, also indirectly promote the positive shaping and sharing of values. In other words, the law of responsibility of states applies to prevent or com-

---

[353] FRENCH CIVIL CODE, art. 1184; GERMAN CIVIL CODE, para. 326.

[354] *See* H. STEPHEN, COMMENTARIES ON THE LAWS OF ENGLAND III (21st ed. L. Warmington ed. 1950); S. WILLISTON, CONTRACTS (rev. ed. 1945) § 1288; *Id.* (3d ed. 1957) § 699; RESTATEMENT OF CONTRACTS §§ 314, 315 (1932).

[355] IRANIAN CIVIL CODE, Art. 402 et seq., 429, 534.

[356] McNair, *supra* note 317, at 15, n.2.

pensate unlawful damages to the grantee irrespective of parties' choice of law.

To prevent value deprivations caused by states' activities, a body of customary international norms has developed through practice and reciprocal recognition to form the principles of state responsibility concerning the international obligations of states as to the protection of inclusive interest. The law of state responsibility on development agreements grows out of these broad principles. The deprivations involved in development agreements generally have a high degree of regional or transnational impact. The general flow of interaction and decisions about development agreements present and create the community expectations concerning the state duties in the treatment of aliens and in the movement of capital, skill, and resources across boundaries. The principles of state responsibility create a balance between the rights and interests of individuals who are not members of the community and the interest of the particular territorial community involved.

The concern about a state's responsibility for the treatment of aliens was begun by Grotius and Vattel in the seventeenth and eighteenth centuries, but it was in the latter part of the nineteenth century that the attention of world order became fully focused.[357] In the nineteenth century claims concerning state responsibility greatly increased, more particularly claims by European states against Latin America. The initial claims were not always directed to specific problems and expressed a mere general insistence that states have some responsibilities as to treatment of aliens. These broad and vague claims become more clear and precise through customary practice. Vattel, for example, in creating a basis for the protection of rights of aliens, stressed that the state has a right to protect its citizens abroad, since an injury to an alien is an injury to the state of the alien.[358] The Vattel doctrine was the basis for the

---

[357] *See* H. GROTIUS, II DE JURE BELLI AC PACIS c. 17, § 20 and § 21 (1625); E. DE VATTEL, THE LAW OF NATIONS III (c. Fenwick trans. 1916) (hereinafter cited as VATTEL); see also F. DUNN, THE PROTECTION OF NATIONALS 46 (1932). For an elaborate and complete study of that responsibility, see McDougal, Lasswell & Chen, *The Protection of Aliens and World Public Order: Responsibility of States Conjoined with Human Right*, 70 AM. J. INT'L L. 432 (1976).

[358] "Whoever ill-treats a citizen indirectly injures the State, which must protect that citizen. The sovereign of the injured Citizen must avenge the deed and, if possible, force the aggressor to give full satisfaction or punish him, since otherwise the citizen will not obtain the chief end of civil society, which is protection." VATTEL, *id.* at 136.

Permanent Court's decision in the *Panevezys-Saldutiskis Railway Case*.[359] Modern reasoning involving the expansion of inclusive competence over the interactions between states and individuals is built upon the expansion of state activities in economic areas. This increase in the scope of economic activities of the states, in cooperation and shared involvement with individuals and private associations, results in growth of rights and responsibilities of states towards their own nationals and of the community interest in the treatment of aliens. Dunn observes the necessity of state responsibility for "maintaining a unified economic and social order for the conduct of international trade and intercourse among independent political units of diverse cultures and stages of civilization, different legal and economic systems, and varying degrees of physical power and prestige."[360] Baxter and Sohn state that

> it is the purpose of the state responsibility to extend the protection of international law to those who travel or live abroad and to facilitate social and economic ties between states. No State, regardless of its political and economic philosophy, can remain indifferent to mistreatment of its nationals abroad. In an interdependent world the well-being of many countries rests upon an influx of foreign funds and managerial skills, the owner of which must be given effective protection against unjust prosecution.[361]

The need for the protection of the common interest of all people involved in development agreements has been recognized by the International Court of Justice in a separate opinion by Judge Wellington Koo in the *Barcelona Traction Co. Case*:

> Foreign investments constitute one form of property, rights or interests, and as such are in principle entitled to the protection of international law. Since the kinds and methods of such investment are numerous and varied, and since they are still in the process of expansion and development it is inevitable that at the present state of their evolution new circumstances and unfamiliar features will be encountered in the protection of such rights and interests in the international field. But in essence they fall

---

[359] [1929] P.C.I.J. ser. A/83, No. 76.

[360] *See* DUNN, *supra* note 357, at 1.

[361] Sohn & Baxter, *Responsibility of States for Injuries to the Economic Interests of Aliens*, 55 AM. J. INT'L L. 545 (1961).

> within the compass of the general rule of diplomatic and judicial protection of international law. What is really involved is the basic principle of protection. . . .[362]

The first strategy employed to protect the rights of individual aliens against the state was that of diplomatic protection of nationals abroad. The practice of diplomatic protection has existed at least since the late Middle Ages, though with some differences in concept and form.[363] But its modern era began in the late eighteenth century.[364] The early notions of diplomatic protection were limited because the prevailing theory of domestic jurisdiction was that the state had exclusive competence over all events happening in its territory. The colonial practice of limitation of domestic jurisdiction was accomplished by the imposition of treaties in which the competence of the state over activities involving a foreigner within its territorial boundaries would be transferred to the state of the alien. Such practice was one of the reasons for the rejection of diplomatic protection; the identification of this institution with colonialism was known as "capitulation." This regime was applied with regard to Asian and African countries such as Japan, Turkey, Siam, Iran, China, and Egypt.[365] The collective actions of decolonization taken by many developed and underdeveloped countries have changed the broad contours of diplomatic protection, but the principle that the injured state has the right to protect its nationals continues to be recognized in many authoritative decisions. Underlying these decisions is Vattel's theory that injury to an alien is injury to the alien's state. In the *Mavrommatis Palestine Concessions Case*, the Permanent Court stated:

> It is an elementary principle of international law that a State is entitled to protect its subjects, when injured by acts contrary to international law committed by another State, from whom they have been unable to obtain satisfaction through the ordinary channels. By taking up the case of one of its subjects and resort-

[362][1964] I.C.J. 55.

[363] BROWNLIE, *supra* note 286, at 507.

[364] This was of the expansion of intercourse between aliens and states in conjunction with changes in economic and political situations. For example, in the century after 1840 about sixty mixed claims commissions were set up to deal with such disputes. *See* BROWNLIE, *id.* at 508.

[365] *See* OPPENHEIM, *supra* note 112, at 46, 623–25.

ing to a diplomatic action or international judicial proceedings on his behalf, a State in reality is asserting its own rights—its rights to ensure, in the person of its subjects, respect for the rules of international law.[366]

Similar reasoning has been adopted in other decisions regarding this issue.[367] This principle has also been affirmed by state officials in their correspondence. In 1912 the Solicitor for the United States Department of State asserted that "It should in the first place, be observed that by espousing a claim of its nationals for injuries inflicted by a foreign government the espousing government makes the claim its own. . . ."[368] Jurists have also recognized this principle.[369] The Harvard Draft of 1929 and the Guerrero

---

[366][1924] P.C.I.J., ser. A, No. 2 at 12. *See also* The Nottebohm Case [1955] I.C.J. 4, 24.

[367]*See* [1938] P.C.I.J., ser. A/B, No. 76 at 16. In the *Serbian Loans Case*, which arose from the failure to service certain loans taken by the Serbian government from French bond-holders, Vattel's doctrine was applied to ascertain whether the dispute was a dispute be-tween States [1929] P.C.I.J., ser. A, No. 20. The P.C.I.J. referred to the same principle in the *Chorzow Factory Case* in deciding that the damage suffered by the claimant was not identical with what its national had experienced. [1928] P.C.I.J., ser. A, No. 17. The Inter-national Court of Justice followed the P.C.I.J. in the *Reparation Case*, [1949] I.C.J. 181. The I.C.J. in the *Nottebohm Case* employed the same principle by which limitations were placed on the link of nationality between individual and State, a link upon which the right was said to rest. [1955] I.C.J. at 24. There are several decisions by other international tribunals which confirm this principle. In Administrative Decision No. V, Umpire Proker stated that "the nation is injured through injury to its national and it alone may demand reparation as no other nation is injured." (United States v. Germany (1924) 7 R. Int'l Arb. Awards at 140. See also Administrative Decisions No. 11 (1923) (United States v. Germany) 7 R. Int'l Arb. Awards at 26; The Finnish Ships Arbitration (1934) (U.K. v. United States) 3 R. Int'l Arb. Awards at 1485, Spanish Zone of Morocco Case (1923) (U.K. v. Spain) 2 R. Int'l Arb. Awards at 640; Dickson Var Wheel Company Claim (1931) (United States v. Mexico) 4 R. Int'l Arb. Awards.

[368]G. HACKWORTH, V, DIGEST of INTERNATIONAL LAW 488 (1943). *See also* Letter from Secretary of State Frelinghuysen to Messrs. Mullan & King (February 11, 1884), *reprinted in* MOORE, supra note 133, Vol. 6 at 616.

[369]*See* Borchard, *The Protection of Citizens Abroad and Change of Original Nationality*, 43 YALE L.J. 359, 364 (1934); J. RALSTON, THE LAW AND PROCEDURE OF INTERNATIONAL TRI-BUNALS 236 (rev. ed. 1926); G. SCHWARZENBERGER, I INTERNATIONAL LAW 140 (3d ed. 1957), and Brierly, *The Theory of Implied State Complicity for International Claims*, 9 BRIT. Y.B. INT'L L. 43, 47 (1928).

Some jurists assert that injuries to an alien as a result of insufficient indemnity in case of nationalization of his property creates the right of diplomatic protection by the alien's state in order to take conservatory measures. *See* P. GUGGENHEIM, TRAITÉ DE DROIT INTERNATION-ALE PUBLIC 336 (1967), *cited in* Carlston, *supra* note 268, at 286; HYDE, *supra* note 112, at 710–11; C. ROUSSEAU, DROIT INTERNATIONALE PUBLIC 372 (1953); Herz, *Expropriation of Foreign Property*, 35 AM. J. INT'L L. 243 (1941); Hyde, *Confiscatory Expropriation*, 32 AM. J. INT'L L. 760–61 (1938); *see also* 33 AM. J. INT'L L. 112 (1939).

Report, adopted by the Sub-Committee of the League of Nations Committee of Experts, also explicitly accepted the principle of diplomatic protection.[370]

The earliest attempts at the abolishment of limitations on the scope of diplomatic protection were by Latin Americans.[371] The Argentine publicist Carlos Calvo was a major initiator of this attempt. His perspective was developed by other Latin American jurists and became formulated and known as the "Calvo Clause." This is a clause often included by states in agreements with aliens whereby the aliens agree to submit themselves to the exclusive jurisdiction of the contracting state and denounce their rights of diplomatic protection. This clause has been rejected by authoritative decisions in international tribunals on the ground that it permits denial of justice in violation of international law. Therefore, while the Calvo Clause is held to be valid doctrine in Latin America, its effectiveness is totally uncertain in international practice. In the *Dredging Co. Case*,[372] which was a dispute between the International Fishers Company and the Government of Mexico, the Tribunal remarked that

> [t]he Calvo Clause is neither upheld by all outstanding international authorities and by the soundest among international awards nor is universally rejected. The Calvo Clause in a specific contract is neither a clause which must be sustained to its full length nor can it be discretionarily separated from the rest of the contract as if it were just an accidental prescription. The problem is not solved by saying yes or no; the affirmative answer exposing the right of foreigners to undeniable dangers, the negative answer leaving to the nations involved no alternative except that of exclusion of foreigners from business.

The validity of Calvo Clause has also been undermined in Latin America by a recent practice in which a settlement was reached between Peru and the United States in 1976 concerning the nationalization of Marcona Mining Company's Peruvian branch.[373] When Marcona, an American mining company, was nationalized

[370] U.N., II Y.B. INT'L L. COMM'N., Annex 1 (1956) at 222.

[371] *See* Freeman, *Recent Aspects of the Calvo Doctrine and the Challenge to International Law*, 40 AM. J. INT'L L. 121 (1946); OPPENHEIM, *supra* note 112, at 312; Lipstein, *The Place of the Calvo Case in International Law*, 22 BRIT. Y.B. INT'L L. 130, 145 (1945) and D. SHEA, THE CALVO CLAUSE (1955).

[372] 20 AM. J. INT'L L. 800 (1926).

in Peru in 1974, the government of Peru *refused* to settle the conflict with the company and *demanded* to negotiate with the United States government officials. The settlement has been characterized, at least by one of its negotiators, as having prompt, adequate, and effective compensation through a package deal.[374] The Peruvian practice is contrary to the Latin American alleged tradition of refusing to involve the government of the nationalized entity in dispute settlement.

Freeman and Roth observe that the only acceptable interpretation of the Calvo Clause is that it represents a demand for the exhaustion of local remedies, without excluding the possibility of entering international channels in the case of a denial of justice.[375] The real aim of the Calvo Clause is the abolishment of the institution of diplomatic protection. This objective was clear at the Third Conference of the Inter-American Bar Association in Mexico City in 1944, when it was concluded that the doctrine of national treatment evolves from the traditional concept of international law and absolute sovereignty of states.

The most substantive objection to this conclusion was made by Roth:

> What the States, advocating the equality doctrine, want to achieve with it is, in reality, a restriction of the sphere of validity of the law of nations by defining the sphere of jurisdiction which they possess themselves according to the same law of nations. In other words, they derive a right from international law to restrict that law as they wish. Whatever political justification might be construed in favour of it, legally such a procedure is hardly compatible with the general principles underlying a normative science.[376]

It has been argued however, that certain value deprivations of aliens can be justified because an alien who freely enters into the territory of another country particularly for business activities has previously studied the situation of that State and is aware of the

---

[373] For the text of the agreement, see 15 INT'L LEGAL MATERIALS 1100 (1976).

[374] Gantz, *The Carcona Settlement: New Forms of Negotiation and Compensation for Nationalized Property*, 71 AM. J. INT'L L. 474 (1977).

[375] Freeman, *supra* note 371, at 190, and A. ROTH, THE MINIMUM STANDARD OF INTERNATIONAL LAW APPLICABLE TO ALIENS 78 (1949).

[376] ROTH, *id.* at 80.

risks he is taking. This theory was noted by Dunn, who then concluded that value deprivations should be allocated based on the risks taken.[377] The substantive objection to this theory is made by McDougal, Lasswell, and Chen:

> The difficulty with this test . . . is that it offers no detailed criteria for the allocation of risk or for evaluating costs and benefits in terms of the value consequences of different options in decisions. When preferred and applied without guiding criteria the concept of "risk allocation" is no more than a tautologous, question-begging formula. There would appear no rational escape in relation to the problems of aliens, as of other problems, from the necessity of an explicit postulation of goals and a careful contextual analysis, with respect to every particular problem, of the inclusive interests of the larger community in a world society, the exclusive interests of the particular territorial communities in protecting their internal integrity or their nationals and the interests of individual human beings in all basic rights.[378]

The doctrine of national treatment has also been advocated as the appropriate international standard for the treatment of aliens. According to this doctrine, aliens and nationals have equal rights, with the exception that there are certain political and other rights which only nationals can enjoy because of their vital and extreme importance to the national interest.[379] The doctrine of national treatment limits the obligation of states in the treatment of aliens as long as they are treated on an equal footing with nationals. This principle as compared to the traditional distrustful and disdainful view of aliens,[380] was a great improvement. This theory was once widely accepted among the European states; however, these states demanded better treatment of their nationals from Asian, African, and Latin American states, claiming that their standards were lower than those of European states.[381] The theory of equality or

---

[377]*Dunn, supra* note 357, at 133. Dunn, however, was aware of the difficulty of application of this test.

[378]McDougal, Lasswell, & Chen, note 357, *supra.*

[379]For accepted differences between nationals and aliens, see Amerasinghe, *supra* note 220, at 278–81; BROWNLIE, *supra* note 363, at 513–14, and Lillich, *The Diplomatic Protection of Nationals Abroad: An Elementary Principle of International Law Under Attack,* 69 AM. J. INT'L L. 359 (1975).

[380]For the history of treatment of aliens, see F. DAWSON & I. HEAD, INTERNATIONAL LAW, NATIONAL TRIBUNALS, AND THE RIGHTS OF ALIENS (1971).

[381]This demand by European states was sometimes exaggerated and resulted in the

national standard is compatible with the traditional doctrine of state responsibility, and has been confirmed by authoritative decisions. In *Dr. Baldwin's Mintitan Claim* of 1839 (United States v. Mexico), the Tribunal said that when an American put himself voluntarily under the municipal law of another state, he must take it as it is and cannot demand better treatment.[382] A similar position was taken by Sir Henry Strong in *Rosa Gelbtrunk v. Salvador*:

> A citizen or subject of one nation, in the pursuit of commercial enterprise, carries on trade within the territory and under the protection of the sovereignty of a nation other than his own, is to be considered as having cast in his lot with the subjects or citizens of the State in which he resides and carries on business. Whilst on the one hand he enjoys the protection of that State, so far as the police regulations and other advantages are concerned, on the other hand he becomes liable to the political vicissitudes of the country in which he thus has a commercial domicile in the same manner as the subjects or citizens of that State are liable to the same. The State to which he owes national allegiance has no right to claim for him as against the nation in which he is resident any other or different treatment . . . that which the latter country metes out to his own subjects or citizens.[383]

The American states, with the exception of the United States,[384] have consistently favored the equal treatment of aliens and nationals. The doctrine was supported by a number of multilateral, bilateral, and unilateral prescriptions. The Declaration of American States, issued in Washington in 1889, the Second Conference of American States in 1901, the Fifth Pan-American Conference held in Santiago in 1923, and the Sixth International Conference of

---

demand for complete transfer of exclusive competence from the international area to the state of the alien by capitulation agreements. Roth says that the effect of such practice created resentment "which during the period of the slow awakening of the national spirit which we now witness, brings along as a characteristic sign a violent hatred of everything which is foreign." ROTH, *supra* note 375, at 64. The doctrine of equal treatment of aliens and nationals has been supported by many European jurists. *Id.* at 65, nn.2 & 3.

[382] J. MOORE IV DIGEST OF INTERNATIONAL ARBITRATIONS 3238 (1898).

[383] RALSTON, *supra* note 369, at 477. Similar findings were reached in the British claims against Tuscany and the Kingdom of Nepal. ROTH, *supra* note 375, at 66.

[384] In at least two instances, the United States argued national treatment. *See* F. WHARTON, II DIGEST OF THE INTERNATIONAL LAW OF THE UNITED STATES 581 (1887), and MOORE, *supra* note 133, Vol. 4 at 13. Secretary of State Webster argued the national treatment standard in the claim of Spain against the United States. *See* ROTH, *supra* note 375, at 67.

American States in Havana in 1928 affirmed the doctrine and disclaimed responsibility except in cases of denial of justice.[385] The strong support for this doctrine eroded at the Seventh Conference of American States, held at Montevideo in 1933. Although the Conference adopted the national treatment standard, the United States and some other countries made reservations.[386] This change in American perspective could be explained by, among other reasons, the change in the American situation, namely, that of the shift from a capital importer to a capital exporter.

The change in community expectations about the national standard became clear at the 1930 Conference of the League of Nations for Codification of State Responsibility. Many of the member governments were uncertain about the national treatment standard and did not make comments on the Report of the Rapporteur, who was a South American in favor of national treatment. Only Chile, San Salvador, and Rumania openly declared themselves to be in complete favor of the Report. This uncertainty among the member-states was observable throughout the negotiation.[387] Article 11(2) of the Treaty of the Benelux Economic Union of 1958[388] and Article 1 of the OECD Draft Convention on the Protection of Foreign Property of 1967[389] also provide for national treatment. The national treatment has been recognized in bilateral agreements, such as the Friendly Treaty of 1924 between Turkey and Austria,[390] and the 1954 Treaty between the

---

[385] Article 2 of the Resolution of the Sixth International Conference of American States in Havana provides: "The nationals of one State who may be found in the territory of other States shall enjoy therein all the individual guarantees and all the civil rights which States grant to their own nationals, with due regard to the prescriptions of their political constitutions and the laws of the State." ROTH, *id.* at 69.

[386] Article 9 of the Resolution states: "The jurisdiction of the States within their territorial limits applies to all inhabitants, nationals, and aliens are subject to the same protection of the law and the national authorities, and aliens cannot claim rights different or more extensive than those claimed by nationals." *Cited in* 33 AM. J. INT'L. 275–76 (1939).

[387] *See* L.N. Doc. C. 196, M.70 (1927) at V.

[388] A. ROBERTSON, EUROPEAN INSTITUTIONS: COOPERATION, INTEGRATION, AND UNIFICATION 405 (1966).

[389] *Cited in* KRONFOL, *supra* note 290, at 46.

[390] "Nationals of each of the Contracting Parties shall enjoy in the territory of the other Party the same treatment as nationals of the country, as regards legal and judicial protection of their person and property." 32 L.N.T.S. 305, 309 (1924) at art. 9.

United States and Germany.[391] This standard is usually provided in unilateral prescriptions of the state.[392]

A part of the new political and economic movement started by the Third World countries in the United Nations is the strong support for the national treatment standard. Such support is presented in Resolution 88 (XII) adopted by the Trade and Development Board of UNCTAD on October 19, 1972.[393] This Resolution states that any dispute concerning the nationalization of foreign-owned property "falls within the sole jurisdiction of its courts. . . ." Similarly, it has been stated in Resolution 3171 (XXVII), adopted by the General Assembly on December 17, 1973,[394] that "any disputes which might arise should be settled in accordance with the national legislation of each state carrying out such measures." The same point is again stressed in the Charter of Economic Rights and Duties of States adopted by the U.N. General Assembly on December 12, 1974.[395] The Charter requires that "where the question of compensation gives rise to a controversy, it shall be settled under the domestic laws of the nationalizing State. . . ."

Considering the complexity of international politics of the past few years, it is hard to determine whether these Resolutions are true representations of the expectations of the Third World about the issue or are a part of a broader strategy for the implementation of their basic demands concerning change in the world power and economic structure. At present it is not possible to say that these resolutions will have significant effects upon trends in decision and community expectation about the treatment of aliens embodied in other Resolutions.

The national standard treatment was never fully accepted, for along with the national standard there has always been the demand for "fair treatment." But the concept of fair treatment was an ambiguous one. An early advocate of this concept was Francisco

[391][1956] 7 U.S.T. 1839 at art. XXV, T.I.A.S. No. 3593.

[392]For example, Art. 10 of the Turkish Investment Law No. 6224: "All rights, immunities, and facilities granted to domestic capital and enterprises shall be available on equal terms to foreign capital and enterprises operating in the same field." *Cited in* KRONFOL, *supra* note 290, at 46.

[393]U.N. Doc. TD/B/423 (1972).

[394]G.A. Res. 3171, 28 U.N. GAOR, Supp. (No. 30) 55, U.N. Doc. A/9030 (1973).

[395]G.A. Res. 3281, 29 U.N. GAOR Supp. (No. 31) 50, U.N. Doc. A/9631 (1974).

de Vitoria,[396] but he did not go beyond the mere initiation of the concept. Grotius accepted the "fair treatment" principle but offered the equal treatment of aliens and nationals.[397]

However, in situations where the foreign investors are the only subjects of value deprivation, the principle of national treatment becomes irrelevant, since there is no precedent by which national treatment criteria may be determined. Sometimes there is even special legislation for those deprivations. There is, however, no discrimination by the host state against foreign investors; it just happens that they are the only investors active in those areas. Vattel, however, first developed the theory of diplomatic protection.[398] While Vattel provided for equal treatment of nationals and aliens with regard to the property interest of aliens, he stated that an injury to an alien is the injury to the state of the alien. He assumed that the interest in protection of an alien cannot cease, because it does not belong to him but to his state, and it is a part of the wealth of the nation. Dunn observes that Vattel was thinking only of movable property, and generally he was considering a set of problems which are different from those of the contemporary world.[399] Dunn continues that Vattel was thinking of situations where foreign property interests were involved and that Vattel viewed the state in terms of personal sovereignty rather than territorial jurisdiction. Although it seems to be true that Vattel was thinking of different problems, there is no doubt that his thought was the basis for development of a theory which involves more than the national treatment standard.

The eighteenth-century hypothesis about fair treatment of aliens encouraged nineteenth- and twentieth-century jurists to formulate the content and the procedure of fair treatment. The concern for the development of such principles, however, was to be found only among capital-exporting countries, whose nationals and property were moving all over the world.

In order to formulate the criteria for fair treatment, later jurists referred to international law and common practice, and held that a minimum standard of justice existed. Thus Root argues:

[396] ROTH, *supra* note 375, at 27.

[397] DUNN, *supra* note 357, at 46–48.

[398] III VATTEL, note 357, *supra*.

[399] DUNN, *supra* note 357, at 52.

> There is a standard of justice very simple, very fundamental, and of such general acceptance by all civilized countries as to form a part of the international law of the world. The condition upon which any country is entitled to measure the justice due from it to an alien by the justice which [it] accords to its own citizens is that its system of law and administration shall conform to this general standard. If any country's system of law and administration does not conform to that standard, although the people of the country may be content and compelled to live under it, no other country can be compelled to accept it as furnishing satisfactory measures of treatment of its citizens.[400]

This doctrine, that there are certain minimum standards of justice regardless of municipal law, became more strongly held both in the theory and practice of states. Today, the basic reason for the development of this doctrine is the necessity of protecting the common interest in the entire world. Characteristic of the contemporary world are the movements of people, goods, and services across political boundaries. This movement is based not only on economic needs but also on new demands for social and individual freedom. If the value deprivation of individuals goes beyond certain levels it affects the inclusive interest of the whole community. Dunn concludes that it is essential to establish a minimum standard of treatment that secures the safety of international movement "in a world of diverse cultures and heterogeneous peoples, of strong governments and weak governments, of orderly countries and disorderly countries."[401] Professors McDougal, Lasswell, and Chen point out that much contemporary expectation "prescribes that there is a minimum common standard in relation to many important deprivations in social process which states must observe in the treatment of aliens irrespective of their treatment of their own nationals."[402]

Since the end of the World War II there have been various efforts on the part of capital-exporting countries to apply minimum

---

[400] Root, *The Basis of Protection to Citizens Residing Abroad*, in 4 ASIL Proc. 16, 21 (1910).

[401] Dunn, *supra* note 1, at 174.

[402] McDougal, Lasswell & Chen, *supra* note 357, at 446. The Report of the International Law Commission on the Work of Its Twenty-Seventh Session (1975) explicitly emphasizes an international standard. The Report, involving the characterization of an act of State as internally wrongful, states that "[a]n act of a State may only be characterized as internally wrongful by international law. Such characterization cannot be affected by the characterization of the same act as lawful by internal law."

standards to foreign investment by means of codification of a multilateral investment regulation. These efforts have not been entirely successful.[403] For example, the British Parliamentary Group of World Government concluded that nondiscrimination policy is not enough if the national standard does not measure up to the minimum international standard.[404] The 1929 Paris Conference on State Responsibility, established by the League of Nations, adopted the two principles of national treatment and the most-favored-nation clause. The adoption of these two principles represents the confusion and uncertainty regarding national treatment as the only standard of treatment. If the principle of national standards was to be conclusive, there was no reason for the adoption of the principle of the most-favored-nation clause. The acceptance of the latter implies the possibility of better treatment for aliens, and according to this clause the contracting state agrees to apply such better treatment to the nationals of the other contracting states.[405] Roth explains this confusion in the perspectives of the new participants:

> The resistance against any other system [than the national treatment] seems not so much to be due to a non-recognition of international law in these fields than to a legitimate fear by small nations of an exaggerated use by the Great Powers of the right to diplomatic protection. By maintaining strictly that the national treatment is the maximum of good treatment any alien can ask for, they want to protect themselves against encroachments upon their sovereignty by powerful nations which possess the means to bring pressure to bear upon them. It is the unilateral action of one State which seems to frighten the South American States most, the demand of one State of extensive rights for its subjects, residing within their territories which would entail internal complications of a grave nature.[406]

[403]*Id.* at art. 4. Negotiation on the passability of such a Code took place in the League of Nations Conference in 1928; the Geneva and Havana Conferences on the International Treaty Organization in 1947 and 1948; The Bogota Conference in 1948, and the Buenos Aires Economic Conference in 1952. *See* Metzger, *Multilateral Conventions for the Protection of Private Foreign Investment*, 9 J. Pub. L. 133 (1960); Fatouros, *supra* note 208, at 70–93; Kronfol, *supra* note 290, at 30–35.

[404]*Cited* in Brandon, *Recent Measures to Improve the International Investment Climate*, 9 J. Pub. L. 130 (1960).

[405]Roth, *supra* note 375, at 84.

[406]*Id.* at 75.

The Convention concerning conditions of residence, business, and jurisdiction between the United Kingdom, France, Italy, Japan, Greece, and Turkey, signed at Lausanne in 1923, provided for the treatment of the nationals of the contracting parties "in accordance with ordinary international law."[407] A number of bilateral agreements have confirmed the international standard.[408] The minimum international standard has been approved also by authoritative decisions. In the *George Hopkins Case*, for example, the Tribunal indirectly referred to the international standard by stating that an alien may be compensated by measures which would not apply to the national.[409] In the *Neer Claim*, the Tribunal expressed the principle as: "the propriety of governmental acts should be put to the test of international standard."[410]

The opponents of the principle of minimum international standards argue that this principle grew out of customary practice and has no place in the general principles of international law, and that, since this practice arose among Western countries, it there-

---

[407] 28 L.N.T.S. at 157 (1925).

[408] *See* R. WILSON, THE INTERNATIONAL LAW STANDARD IN TREATIES OF THE UNITED STATES 87–134 (1953). *See also* the Treaty of Friendship and Establishment between Egypt and Persia of 1928, 93 L.N.T.S. at 397 (1929); Art. V of U.S.-Italian Treaty, 79 U.N.T.S. at 178 (1948).

The convention between Germany and Soviet Russia of 1925 provided in Art. 10 that "the national of each Contracting Party shall, in accordance with international law, be entitled in the territory of the other Contracting Party to the same protection. . . ." 23 L.N.T.S. at 95 (1924); The convention between Germany and Persia of 1929 also provides for protection "in accordance with the principles and practice of ordinary international law." 153 L.N.T.S. at 241 (1934); similarly, the treaty between Switzerland and Persia of 1934 provides for a minimum standard. 160 L.N.T.S. at 175 (1935).

[409] The tribunal declared that "it not infrequently happens that under the rules of international law applied to controversies of an international aspect a nation is required to accord to aliens broader and more liberal treatment than it accords to its own citizens under its municipal laws. . . . [t]here is no ground to object that this amounts to a discrimination by a nation against its own citizens in favor of aliens. It is not a question of discrimination, but a question of difference in their respective rights and remedies." The Hopkins Case (U.S. v. Mexico), United States of America/United Mexican States Claims Commission 51, 4 R. Int'l Arb. Awards 47 (1926). The two opinions of the P.C.I.J. in the *Certain German Interests in Upper Silesia Case*, [1926] P.C.I.J. ser. A, No. 7 at 33, and the *Peter Pazmany Univ. v. The State of Czechoslovakia* ([1933] P.C.I.J. ser. A/B No. 61 at 243), stated that the nondiscriminatory nature of the expropriation (according to the national standard) has no effect on the treaty obligation.

[410] *See* H. BRIGGS, THE LAW OF NATIONS 613 (1952); see also the result in British Claim in the Spanish Zone of Morocco (1925), *cited in id.* at 601, and in the Roberts Claim (1926), cited in *id.* at 549.

fore does not bind new states in Asia, Africa, and Latin America.[411] These opponents argue that such standards evolved among the Western countries who had more or less equivalent economic power, and hence these criteria stifle the interests of the developing countries who are not up to the same economic level. Therefore, while they accept international law in general, they challenge some of its specific prescriptions[412] and demand modification. The Asian-African Legal Constitutive Committee Report insisted on the substitution of "local standard" for "international standard" on the argument that according to the United Nations Charter and Declaration of Human Rights every state is expected and required to treat its own nationals fairly, and therefore, it is taken for granted that aliens will be given fair treatment in accordance with local standards.[413]

In response to the above arguments it has been said that, although the minimum standard has developed through customary practice, the roots of the standard are related to general principles of the law of protection of human rights[414] and that the concept of state responsibility exists in religious practices of the major religions of the world.[415] Friedmann observes that the developing countries will be developed countries in the future, and the standards that protect the interests of developed countries now will protect their interests in the future.[416] These answers fail, first because they accept the theory that the minimum international standard is designed only to protect the interest of developed countries, and, second, even if such an assumption is correct, developing countries may never reach the stage of full development as long as they continue to apply standards which only protect the interest of developed states.

The true objective of minimum international standards is the protection of the inclusive interest of all countries, both developed and developing. Such standards should be based upon policies

[411] *See* L. GROSS, INTERNATIONAL LAW IN THE TWENTIETH CENTURY 562 (1969).

[412] AMERASINGHE, *supra* note 220, at 18.

[413] ASIAN-AFRICAN LEGAL CONSTITUTION COMMITTEE REPORT, Third Session (1961) at 83.

[414] AMERASINGHE, *supra* note 220, at 23.

[415] *Id.* at 12–18.

[416] W. FRIEDMANN, THE CHANGING STRUCTURE OF INTERNATIONAL LAW 322 (1964).

and measures that protect human rights. It is immaterial in the present context to argue about the origin of these measures. What is important is the content and the potential future operation of the measure in the promotion of common interests of the entire world community. It is true that in the beginning the minimum standard of treatment grew out of the demand and practices of Western countries, but those standards were generally lower and much less subtle and complex in aim than the newer international measures. Today when we talk about minimum international standards, we talk about a set of new expectations that developing countries share with developed countries, expectations embodied in the United Nations Declaration of Human Rights,[417] the International Covenant on Economic, Social, and Cultural Rights,[418] the International Convention on the Elimination of Racial Discrimination,[419] and other such international agreements. The need for the protection of these shared expectations is greater than ever, since corruption in the administration of international justice is now greater than in the nineteenth century,[420] and fair treatment cannot be tested by only national standards, particularly where the judicial branch is not independent of the executive.[421] Therefore, there should be certain standards independent of national standards to evaluate and secure the rights of individual aliens.[422] Such a need has been recognized by the Central American Court of Justice. In the case of *Dr. Pedro Fornos Diaz v. The Government of the Republic of Guatemala* (1909), the Court held that

[417] UNITED NATIONS, HUMAN RIGHTS: A COMPILATION OF INTERNATIONAL INSTRUMENTS OF THE UNITED NATIONS 1, U.N. Doc. ST/HR/1 (1973) (hereinafter cited as HUMAN RIGHTS DECLARATION).

[418] *The Problem of the Applicability of Existing International Provisions for the Protection of Human Rights of Individuals Who Are Not Citizens of the Country in Which They Live.* U.N. Doc. E/CN.4/Sub.2/335 (1973).

[419] *See* HUMAN RIGHTS DECLARATION, *supra* note 417, at 24.

[420] Borchard, *The "Minimum Standard" of the Treatment of Aliens* in 33 ASIL PROCS. 51, 53 (1939).

[421] ROTH, *supra* note 375, at 87.

[422] A number of jurists support this view. *See* E. BORCHARD, THE DIPLOMATIC PROTECTION OF CITIZENS ABROAD 177 (1915); A. V. FREEMAN, THE INTERNATIONAL RESPONSIBILITY OF STATES FOR DENIAL OF JUSTICE 497–530 (1938); C EAGLETON, THE RESPONSIBILITY OF STATES IN INTERNATIONAL LAW 82–87 (1928); OPPENHEIM, *supra* note 365, at 316, and DUNN, *supra* note 357, at 113–72.

the "fundamental rights and powers of the human individual in civil life are placed under the protection of the principles governing the common wealth of nations, as international right[s] of man. . . ."[423] The national courts themselves have recognized the need for the protection of individual rights against the state's abdication of responsibility.[424]

In spite of Latin American demands for national treatment, there is a strong trend in favor of minimum international standards. However, the principle of minimum international standards is still not quite precisely described and in many respects is still vague. The United Nations made an attempt to provide some guidelines for modification of this standard. By Resolution 799 (VIII) of December 7, 1953, the General Assembly requested the International Law Commission to undertake the codification of the principles of international law governing state responsibility. The Seventh Session of International Law Commission in 1955 appointed a special Rapporteur who in the four following years submitted four reports on the topic.[425] The First Special Rapporteur, Dr. Garcia-Amador, prepared a valuable study in which he

[423]3 Am. J. Int'l L. 737, 747 (1909).

[424]The Supreme Court of the United States has afforded individual rights protection against the sovereign rights of the State in several different fashions; notable among these has been the diminution of the scope of traditional notions of sovereign immunity. The Court noted in 1939 that "[t]he present climate of opinion has brought governmental immunity from suit into disfavor," Kelfer & Kelfer v. Reconstruction Finance Corp., 306 U.S. 381, 391 (1939). A decade later the Court in an opinion by Chief Justice Vinson declared that in certain types of cases "[t]he principle of sovereign immunity is an archaic hangover not consonant with modern morality," Larson v. Domestic & Foreign Corp., 337 U.S. 682, 703 (1948). A similar attitude has been adopted by Great Britain; in 1947 Britain adopted the Crown Proceeding Act, according commonwealth subjects certain legal remedies against the Sovereign. This practice has been accepted by some other states. *See* Wadmon, *The Sanctity of Contacts Between a Sovereign and a Foreign National*, in SELECTED READINGS, *supra* note 243, at 220.

[425]*See First Report*, [1956] 2 Y.B. INT'L L. COMM'N 173–231, U.N. Doc. A/CN.4/96 (1956) [hereinafter cited as *Garcia-Amador's First Report*]; *Second Report*, [1957] 2 Y.B. INT'L L. COMM'N 104–30, U.N. Doc. A/CN.4/106 (1957) [hereinafter cited as *Garcia-Amador's Second Report*]; *Third Report* [1958] 2 Y.B. INT'L L. COMM'N 47–73, U.N. Doc. A/CN.4/111 (1958); *Fourth Report*, [1959] 2 Y.B. INT'L L. COMM'N 1–36, U.N. Doc. A/CN.4/119 (1959). The idea of transforming state responsibility for injuries to aliens into state responsibility for injuries to individuals as human rights has been supported by jurists. *See* P. JESSUP, TRANSNATIONAL LAW 95 (1956); *see also* G. SCHWARZENBERGER, THE FRONTIERS OF INTERNATIONAL LAW 219 (1962). This notion is also embodied in the European Convention on Human Rights of 1950; *see* A. ROBERTSON, HUMAN RIGHTS IN EUROPE (1963).

relates the minimum international standard to human rights standards:

> [B]oth principles [international standard of justice and equality of nationals and aliens] had the same basic purpose, namely, the protection of [the] person and of his property, they [nevertheless] appeared both in traditional theory and in past practice as mutually conflicting and irreconcilable.
>
> Yet, if the question is examined in the light of international law in its present stage of development, one obtains a very different impression. What was formally the object of these two principles—the protection of the person and of his property—is now intended to be accomplished by the international recognition of the essential rights of man. Under this new legal doctrine, the distinction between nationals and aliens no longer has any raison d'etre, so that both in theory and in practice these two traditional principles are henceforth inapplicable. In effect, both of these principles appear to have been outgrown by contemporary international law.[426]

Garcia-Amador thereupon proposed the "fundamental rights" that should be protected:

> 1. The State is under a duty to ensure to aliens the enjoyment of the same civil rights, and to make available to them the same individual guarantees as are enjoyed by its own nationals. These rights and guarantees shall not, however, in any case be less than the "fundamental human rights" recognized and defined in contemporary international instruments.
>
> 2. In consequence, in case of violation of civil rights, or disregard of individual guarantees, with respect to aliens, international responsibility will be involved only if internationally recognized "fundamental human rights" are affected.[427]

He further described the "fundamental human rights" as:

> (a) The right to life, liberty and security of person;
>
> (b) The right of the person to the inviolability of his privacy, home and correspondence, and to respect for his honour and reputation;

[426] *See Garcia-Amador's First Report, supra* note 425, at 199.

[427] *See Garcia-Amador's Second Report, supra* note 425, at 112–13.

(c) The right to freedom of thought, conscience and religion;

(d) The right to own property;

(e) The right of the person to recognition everywhere as a person before the law;

(f) The right to apply to the courts of justice or to the competent organs of the state, by means of remedies and proceedings which offer adequate and effective redress for violations of the aforesaid rights and freedom;

(g) The right to a public hearing, with proper safeguards, by the competent organs of the State, in the determination of rights and obligations under civil law;

(h) In criminal matters, the right of the accused to be presumed innocent until proved guilty; the right to be informed of the charge made against him in a language which he understands; the right to speak in his defence or to be defended by a counsel of his choice; the right not to be convicted of any punishable offence on account of any act or omission which did not constitute an offence, under national or international law, at the time when it was committed; the right to be tried without delay or to be released.[428]

The draft also provided limitations on the rights and freedoms of paragraph (1), such as that "the law expressly prescribes for reasons of internal security, the economic well-being of the nation, public order, health and morality or to secure respect for the rights and freedoms of others."[429] Garcia-Amador rejects the remedies for legal deprivation of aliens in diplomatic protection, since under the new legal doctrine there is no distinction between aliens and nationals. He stated that the distinction between aliens and nationals derived from the traditional doctrine of international law that the rights of an individual could be protected only through his status as a national. But under the new doctrine there is no such difference between aliens and nationals and the object of international law is the protection of legitimate interests of human beings as such.[430] This proposition has been called too ideal-

[428]*Id.* at 113.

[429]*Id.*

[430]*Id.*

istic for our contemporary world. Garcia-Amador has been criticized, using the argument that, while his recommendation is suitable for a future public order with institutions to protect individual rights regardless of government participation, at present remedies by means of diplomatic protection must be accepted until that time.[431]

As Justice Cardozo said, "law and obedience to law are facts confirmed every day to us all in our experience of life. If the result of a definition is to make them seem to be illusions, so much the worse for the definition; we must enlarge it till it is broad enough to answer to realities."[432] Nevertheless, we must agree with Brownlie that Garcia-Amador's standards are "unconscionably vague."[433] Many of the standards that Garcia-Amador stated are susceptible of modification and already exist within national standards in their modified form. There should be guidelines for decision makers for the evaluation of these prescriptions. Such guidelines can be established for specific issues only by looking at the relevant trends and considering the different claims regarding the treatment of aliens and the responses of established decision makers. Any measures, however, should be flexible rather than rigid and protect the common interest. As one observer stated, it should be understood that "reasonable" in international law may not be the same as "reasonable" in American law.[434]

In conclusion, regardless of the vagueness of the international human rights standards, that there are inclusive prescriptions which regulate the state activities with respect to aliens is clear. In the course of time these prescriptions become more precise and the institutions by which they should be implemented more firmly established.

---

[431] *See* McDougal, Lasswell & Chen, note 357 *supra*. They observe that "[t]his imaginative proposal by Dr. Garcia-Amador has not, unhappily, enjoyed wide approval from either state spokesmen or private commentators. By some his proposal is thought to extend the substantial protection of aliens much beyond what states can reasonably be expected to accept and to exacerbate the problems of cooperation between states of differing degrees of socialization. By others he might be thought, perhaps justifiably, to weaken an important traditional remedy for the protection of aliens before any effective new remedy is established in replacement." *Id.* at 456. *See also* AMERASINGHE, *supra* note 220, at 278–81.

[432] B. CARDOZO, THE NATURE OF THE JUDICIAL PROCESS 127 (1921).

[433] BROWNLIE, *supra* note 286, at 513–14.

[434] Walker, *Modern Treaties of Friendship, Commerce, and Navigation*, 42 MINN. L. REV. 809 (1958).

3. The Application of Law

The major issue involved in the application of law is the establishment of disinterested forums for the application of appropriate prescriptions. These forums are not under the control of the parties, and they are designed to protect the mutually exclusive interests of the parties within the framework of the inclusive interest of the larger community.

In the absence of a compulsory jurisdiction agreement, parties have to specify their own arrangements for establishment of the competent body. Usually the private party to the agreement tries to establish a third-party decision maker and the contracting state tries to impose its own municipal courts as the competent forum. Such an attempt by the contracting state is presented in the Calvo Clause, in which the private party not only agrees to ask for only national prescriptions, but also is compelled to refer to national courts.

In a number of development agreements the municipal courts have been recognized as the competent forum. The problem with such a choice, however, involves the doctrine of sovereign immunity. According to this doctrine, the sovereign—that is, a country—cannot be sued in its own courts unless it so consents. This problem could be solved by the modification of municipal law, where in certain cases individuals are permitted to sue the government for damages in municipal courts. In the United States, for example, the doctrine of sovereign immunity, well established by the mid-nineteenth century,[435] has been limited by legislation such as the Tucker Act[436] and the Federal Tort Claims Act.[437]

Some legislation provides for special arbitration procedures for the settlement of disputes. The arbitration procedure may exclude ordinary court jurisdiction, as does the mining legislation of India, Libya, Pakistan, Iraq, and the Philippines.[438] Under the Pakistan Petroleum Rules, disputes in connection with the following mat-

---

[435]For the history of sovereign immunity in the United States and relevant cases, *see* STEINER & VAGTS, *supra* note 324, at 517–80.

[436]28 U.S.C. §§ 1346(a), 1419 (1964).

[437]The Federal Torts Claims Act (FTCA) was enacted in 1946. 28 U.S.C. §§ 1346(b), 2671–2680 (1964).

[438]*See* U.N. SURVEY OF MINING LEGISLATION U.N. Doc. E/CN.11.462 (1957) at 60.

ters, in which the Ministry decisions are not final, are submitted to arbitration:

1. Right of licensee to an oil prospecting licence or lease;
2. Cancellation for violation or breach of provision;
3. Price payable by the government for the preemption of crude oil;
4. Price of plant purchased by the government on termination of the lease;
5. Compensation payable for the acquisition by the government of the premises of lessees or all rights of the lessee;
6. Renewal of the lease;
7. Approval of the programs.

The Government appoints one arbitrator and the concessionaire the other. In the event of disagreement between arbitrators, the parties appoint a judge of the Federal Court of Pakistan as umpire. The decision of the arbitrators or the umpire is final.[439] Similar provisions occur in the mining legislation of Iran,[440] Morocco,[441] and Greece.[442] The Saudi Arabian Petroleum Law of 1963 establishes an independent and legally immune permanent judicial body, the Board of Concession Appeals:

> There shall be established . . . an independent board for the appeal of disputes arising from the application of this Code, consisting of not less than five members to be chosen [by the Government] without regard to their nationality from eminent and highly reputable jurists and judges who are experienced in international law and in problems relating to concessions. . . . The members of the Board shall not be called to account civilly or criminally except in accordance with rules to be prescribed by a special law.[443]

---

[439] Rule 40, *id.* at 60–61.

[440] Principality of Iran, Petroleum Law of July 1957, Art. 14.

[441] U.N. Doc. A/AC.97/5/Re. Vol. 1 (1960) at 74.

[442] Kingdom of Greece, Law No. 3948 (1959), *cited in* FATOUROS *supra* note 208, at 187.

[443] Kingdom of Saudi Arabia, Article 50 of the Mining Code of 20 May 1963. "The Board of Concession Appeals has acquired jurisdiction over the disputes between Aramco and the government of Saudi Arabia. Aramco itself has expressed its voluntary submission to the Board for future adjudications." *See* MIDDLE EAST ECONOMIC SURVEY (M.E.E.S.) Bull., March 19, 1965, at 17.

Even if the question of sovereign immunity is solved, there is still doubt about the disengagement of the municipal courts from the political motivations of the contracting state.

Municipal arrangements do not prevent the parties from establishing their own decision-making body. This has been common practice in development agreements. The arbitration clauses in these agreements provide for the qualifications of the decision makers and the procedures by which they should be appointed.[444] Besides general arbitral tribunals the parties may stipulate private persons or associations as the competent decision makers. The 1954 Iranian oil agreement with the Oil Consortium distinguishes in Article 44 the disputes that relate to technical matters from those that relate to general matters. For the former disputes the agreement provides that the parties may request the opinion of two Swiss institutions which specialize in accountancy and other technical matters in the appointing of experts to decide the issue.[445]

There has been significant collective action by capital-exporting countries in the establishment of third-party decision makers through multilateral agreements. The Charter of International Trade Organization (ITO) signed in Havana[446] but which never went into effect provided for diplomatic negotiations rather than strictly judicial methods.[447] The Economic Agreement of Bogota, signed at the Ninth International Conference of American States in May 1948,[448] in addition to diplomatic negotiation provides for certain competent judicial bodies, such as the Council of the Organization of American States[449] or the American Peace System.[450]

[444]Since arbitral procedure in development agreements is discussed at the beginning of this section, we do not go into detail here.

[445]For the text, see 2 HUREWITZ, *supra* note 270, at 348; *see also* agreements providing for arbitration *cited in* U.N. Doc. A/AC.97/5/Re. Vol. 1 (1960) at 74–5.

[446]U.N. Conference on Trade & Employment, Final Act and Related Documents, U.N. Doc. E/Conf.2/78 (1948).

[447]See Arts. 92–97 *id.* Diplomatic negotiation has been the first option proposed in arbitration clauses.

[448]ECONOMIC AGREEMENT OF BOGOTA, PAN-AMERICAN UNION LAW AND TREATY SERIES No. 25 (1948); *see also* Fenwick, *The Ninth International Conference of American States*, 42 AM. J. INT'L L. 553 (1948).

[449]ECONOMIC AGREEMENT, art. 38, *id.*

[450]Established under the American Treaty of Pacific Settlement in 1948 by the Act of Bogota.

This Act, like ITO, never became effective. The International Chamber of Commerce in 1949 provided for the creation of an International Court of Arbitration.[451] A group of European jurists and businessmen formulated the Draft Convention on Foreign Investment in 1958 whereby the International Court of Justice was chosen as the competent tribunal for making decisions over disputes arising from development agreements.[452] The object of involving the International Court of Justice in disputes over development agreements has been promoted by some bilateral agreements. The United States Friendship, Commerce and Navigation treaties with various other countries provide for diplomatic negotiations as the first step in the resolution of disputes and in case of failure then, usually, arbitration tribunals. In case of failure there, the matter is referred to the International Court of Justice.[453] There are similar treaties between Germany and the Dominican Republic,[454] the United Kingdom and Iran.[455]

The Organization of Petroleum Exporting Countries (OPEC) has been considering the establishment of a regional tribunal for the settlement of specific disputes. OPEC Res. V directs the Secretary General

> to initiate studies for the establishment of an Inter-OPEC High Court for the settlement of all disputes and differences relating to petroleum matters, except for member countries whose legal system does not allow them to participate in the establishment of such a Court; and, prepare a project thereon for submission to Member Countries; and that, further, the Statutes of the said High Court shall be so conceived as to allow the Court to act both in an advisory and in a judicial capacity.[456]

This goal of OPEC, however, has not yet been implemented.

The first attempt by international organizations for facilitating dispute settlement has been made by the World Bank. The Bank, following its basic policy of providing financing for development

---

[451] INT'L CHAMBER COM., FAIR TREATMENT OF FOREIGN INVESTMENTS, INTERNATIONAL CODE (1949) Art. 13.

[452] *See* Brandon, *An International Investment Code: Current Plans*, J. BUS. L. 7, 13–14 (1959).

[453] *See* FATOUROS *supra* note 208, at 185, n. 308.

[454] *Id.*

[455] *Id.*

[456] *OPEC* Res. V (1972).

purposes through different channels,[457] has provided an International Center for Settlement of Investment Disputes.[458] Although little use has been made of this Center until now,[459] it will play an important role in the future. The Center has a limited jurisdiction, restricted by the character of the parties and/or the nature of the disputes. Article 25 specifies the requirements:

1. Both parties must have consented to have recourse to the Center and when the consent has been reached is irrevocable; parties cannot unilaterally withdraw;

2. One party must be a contracting State or one of its constituent subdivisions or agencies, and the other party must be the national or another contracting state;

3. The dispute must be a legal dispute; and

4. It must arise directly out of an investment.[460]

The Tribunal is the judge of its own competence.[461]

---

[457]There are four major methods by which the World Bank provides finance for development purposes: (1) government funds transferred to developing countries under bilateral agreements; (2) government funds transferred to developing countries through multilateral channels, such as the International Development Association (IDA) and International Finance Corporation (IFC); (3) private funds transferred to developing countries by and through multilateral institutions to whom these private savings are lent, such as the World Bank, the Inter-American Development Bank, and the Asian Development Bank; and (4) private funds made directly available for projects in developing countries, whether as debt or equity, and whether the projects are wholly or partially owned by the private foreign investor. *See* Broches, *The Concentration on the Settlement of Investment Disputes Between States and Nationals of Other States*, 136 RECUEIL DES COURS 337, 342–43 (Academie de Droit International) (1972–II).

[458]Convention on the Settlement of Investment Disputes Between States and Nationals of Other States, ICSID/2 (1966).

[459]No Latin American country has ratified the Convention. See Lillich, *supra* note 379, at 363; see also Szasz, *The Investment Dispute Convention and Latin America*. 11 VA. J. INT'L L. 246 (1971).

[460]The Convention defines "national" as to natural persons thus: "[A]ny natural person who had the nationality of a Contracting State other than the State party to the dispute on the date on which the parties consented to submit such dispute to conciliation or arbitration as well as on the date on which the request was registered pursuant to paragraph (3) of Art. 28 or paragraph (3) of Art. 36, but does not include any person who on either date also had the nationality of Contracting State Party to the dispute." The Convention defines "national" with respect to judicial persons thus: "nationality of a Contracting State other than the State party to the dispute on the date on which the parties consented to submit such dispute to conciliation or arbitration and any juridical person which had the nationality of the Contracting State party to the dispute on that date and which, because of foreign control, the parties have agreed should be treated as a national of another Contracting State for the purpose of this Convention. ICSID/2, *supra* note 458, at 9.

[461]Art. 41, *id.* For more discussion about the work of the Center, *see* Broches, *supra* note

By looking at the trends in dispute settlement, it becomes clear that judicial settlements have been considered last resorts for dispute solving. Diplomatic negotiations, foreign office to foreign office, play a major role in this area. Through these negotiations parties try to accommodate their conflicting interests without asking or involving the constitutive decision makers. However, considering relevant basic policies as to the protection of human rights, diplomatic negotiations may not be a preferable method of dispute settlement. It is possible that fundamental rights of individual claimants may be violated as a result of the political bargaining between the Contracting State and the State of aliens in diplomatic negotiations. Private parties should have access to inclusive judicial bodies in case of deprivation of their fundamental rights.

Diplomatic negotiation may also not be the best way of protecting the vital interests of the whole community unless it is representative of the great majority of states. It may be appropriate to establish a competent decision-making body empowered to apply inclusive prescriptions regarding vital resources.

4. Specific Problems

An agreement is a process by which the parties formulate and continuously reformulate their policies about future events, rather than a mere set of words or a document. The specific problems arising from development agreements, involving questions of appropriate prescriptions and application, are related to the subprocesses of commitment, performance, and termination.

a. Commitment

Commitment is the process by which parties undertake responsibilities and acquire rights. It is a process of offer and acceptance. The possible issues arising from this process are, first, whether there has been any commitment made between the parties, and, second, if so, what its substantive content is. In the case of the

---

457, at 333; Broches, *Development of International Law by the International Bank for Reconstruction and Development*, 59 ASIL Procs. 33–38 (1965); Firth, *The Law Governing Contracts in Arbitration Under the World Bank Convention*, J. Trans. L. Pol., 253–76 (1968); Moore, *International Arbitration Between States and Foreign Investors—The World Bank Convention*, 18 Stan. L. Rev. 1359–80 (1966).

former, both inclusive and exclusive prescriptions are relevant. However, the exact relevancy of the two prescriptions can be determined only in specific cases in relation to ultimate outcomes and their effects on community policy.

The necessity of both inclusive and exclusive prescriptions derives from the need to protect the aggregate common interest. The exclusive interest of a nation-state is in the production and distribution of different values among its citizens. To this end every nation-state has some constitutional prescription. Some of these prescriptions, which are formulated to maintain the public order in an exclusive arena, specify how the body politic can commit the nation to an obligation with foreign entities. On the other hand, there are some prescriptions which protect the inclusive interest of the larger community by stabilizing the reasonable expectations as to arrangements involving the use of resources. The term *inclusive prescription* embraces those requirements by which a nation-state is considered to have committed itself internationally to certain obligations, regardless of its internal constitutive requirements.

As we will see, the inclusive decision makers have always been regarded as the competent decision makers. They apply exclusive prescriptions if they consider them applicable. With regard to the constitutional requirement for the validity of agreements, it is generally accepted that states cannot deny their transnational commitments by invoking their internal limitations. Lord McNair wrote: "While the subject of constitutional requirements for the conclusion of a treaty has received much consideration from the writers of textbooks and monographs, it is significant that the diplomatic and judicial materials that might throw light upon it are scanty—a fact which seems to indicate that States are reluctant to challenge the validity of a treaty on the ground of some constitutional defect in its conclusion."[462] The Harvard Research on Treaty Law went so far as to regard internal constitutional prescriptions as irrelevant to the validity of a treaty: "The international validity of treaties is a matter which is determined by international provisions which limit and regulate the exercise of the treaty-making power; such provisions have no international significance, and treaties made by the treaty-making power are binding as international engagements even though the treaty-making organ or organs ex-

---

[462] A. McNair, Law Of Treaties 59 (1961).

ceeded their constitutional competence."[463] The supremacy of international law over national law in determining the validity of international agreements is maintained in the Vienna Convention of the Law of Treaties of 1969.[464] The Convention concludes that the determination of the competency of the agent is a matter of international law. Article 7(2) provides that the following are considered as representing their State: "(a) Heads of States, Heads of Governments and Ministers for Foreign Affairs, for the purpose of performing all acts relating to the conclusion of a treaty; (b) Heads of diplomatic missions, for the purpose of adopting the text of a treaty between the accrediting State and the State to which they are accredited;" Article 46 of the Convention holds that "1. A State may not invoke the fact that its consent to be bound by a treaty has been expressed in violation of a provision of its internal law regarding competence to conclude treaties as invalidating its consent unless that violation was manifest and concerned a rule of its internal law of fundamental importance. 2. A violation is manifest if it would be objectively evident to any State conducting itself in the matter in accordance with normal practice and in good faith.[465]

Although Article 46 limits the scope of Article 7(2) but still has a broad language that is not compatible with community expectations about the contemporary role of international law. The expectation is that international law goes beyond organizing the interaction among the states and is concerned with individual human beings and their value deprivations caused by state actions. Professor Reisman, criticizing the broad language of Article 7(2), observes that

> [i]t seems rather peculiar to authorize the functions associated with certain authoritative roles in a contemporary nation-state without regard to the context and, in particular without regard to the content of the agreement which that role player purports to conclude. . . . The question of a violation of internal law, whether manifest or not, turns on a variety of considerations unique to the circumstances, the most obvious example being the effect of crisis. The "fundamental importance" of an internal law

---

[463] FACULTY OF THE HARVARD LAW SCHOOL, RESEARCH IN INTERNATIONAL LAW, 29 AM. J. INT'L L. 1, 911 (Supp. 1935) (hereinafter cited as HARVARD RESEARCH REPORT).

[464] U.N. Conference on the Law of Treaties, U.N. Doc. A/Conf. 39/27 (1969).

[465] *Id.*

cannot be predetermined, for it is not the law which is of importance, but rather the values which are being allocated under cover of its authority. Because of them, the law acquires a public order significance. In each case, this will be a function of domestic and international order.[466]

The policy of noninvalidation of international agreements and its compatibility with the basic goal of limiting the extent to which a territorial community may shape international obligations is well formulated by Professor McDougal: "The policies of maintaining stability in expectations about appropriate participants, and needs of security in undertakings, are deemed important enough to warrant regulations by inclusive decision of changes in effective control and formal authority, irrespective of internal prescriptions."[467] To reach a decision compatible with the common interest, however, a decision maker should accommodate the conflicting interests of the parties in the context of the inclusive interest of the larger community. Such accommodations may result in the necessity of applying internal prescriptions about the appropriate participant when the major or the most acute impact of a decision falls on one territorial state. From past trends it could be generalized, but not conclusively so, that when the largest impact of an agreement is on an exclusive arena, deference should be given to the exclusive prescriptions of that arena, *i.e.*, the nation-states (for example, some kinds of disputes involving taxation).

Inclusive prescriptions are the governing rules of agreements involving matters with a high degree of inclusive impact.[468] The opinion of the Permanent Court of International Justice in the case of the *Legal Status of Eastern Greenland*[469] is an example of inclusive prescription. The Foreign Minister of Norway made an oral declaration to the Foreign Minister of Holland that his government would not challenge the sovereignty of the Danish government over Greenland. The Government of Norway, however,

---

[466] W. REISMAN, NULLITY AND REVISION (1971).

[467] McDougal, *The Impact of International Law upon National Law: A Policy Oriented Perspective*, 4 S. CALIF. L. REV. 26, 43 (1959).

[468] Professor Reisman concludes from past leading cases that "such matters as decisions affecting taxations have generally been recognized as within the exclusive sphere, while agreements relating to territory external to the State in question have been recognized as belonging to the inclusive domain." REISMAN, *supra* note 466, at 295.

[469] [1933] P.C.I.J., ser. A/B, No. 53 at 22.

claimed that according to the constitutional requirements of Norway the Foreign Minister was not competent to make such a declaration and that therefore the declaration did not bind Norway. The Court rejected the Norwegian argument and held that "a reply of this nature given by the Minister of Foreign Affairs on behalf of his Government in response to a request by a diplomatic representative of a foreign Power in regard to a question following within his province, is binding upon the country to which the Minister belongs."[470] The Mixed American Mexican Claim Commission, in the *Way Case*, declared that no government can escape responsibility by pleading incompetence of its officials: "It is believed to be a sound principle that, when misconduct on the part of persons concerned with the discharge of governmental functions, whatever their precise status may be under domestic law, results in a failure of a nation to live up to its obligations under international law, the delinquency on the part of such persons is misfortune for which the nation must bear the responsibility."[471] There are some authoritative decisions holding that agreements that do not meet constitutional requirements are void; if inclusive prescriptions had been applied, such agreements would be upheld. The *Tinoco Case* is an example of such a decision.[472] In 1917 the Government of Costa Rica was overthrown by Tinoco, the Secretary of War. Tinoco changed the constitution and became the Commander-in-Chief. His Government continued until 1919. During that time Tinoco made a concession agreement with a British company for oil exploration. Under the new constitution the power for making such concession was vested exclusively in the Parliament. The concession with the British company, however, was approved only by Tinoco and the Senate. After the fall of the Tinoco government, a new government passed a law by which all agreements made by the Tinoco government were declared void. On the claim made on behalf of a British company that a State cannot escape responsibility by changing its internal law, Chief Justice Taft, as sole arbitrator, held that while it is generally accepted in international law that a change in constitutional law cannot remove state responsibility for international obligations, the oil concession under consideration was void as a clear violation of

[470]*Id.* at 71.

[471]23 Am. J. Int'l L. 466 (1929).

[472]18 Am. J. Int'l L. 147 (1924).

the 1917 constitution of Costa Rica.[473] The decision of the arbitrator in application of exclusive prescription was based on the fact that the concession was related to a tax regulation of Costa Rica. Decisions concerning taxation are of the utmost importance to a nation-state. While the concession had some impact on exclusive interest of a foreign entity, its highest impact was on Costa Rica, and in this case it was in the common interest of the larger community to protect the exclusive interest of Costa Rica by application of municipal prescriptions.

As mentioned above, exclusive prescriptions apply only to matters connected with great impact on exclusive interest; otherwise inclusive prescriptions are applicable. For example, in the *John B. Okie* case,[474] although tax problems were involved, the exclusive prescription was not applied. This case involved an American rancher (Okie) who had by an exchange of letters agreed with the Mexican government to transfer sheep from Texas to Mexico for permanent grazing. In this agreement Mexico promised Okie not to charge for the importation. However, on two occasions Okie was required to pay sanitary fees and taxes, and he claimed a refund. The Mexican government argued that no official had the "power to remit any taxes or fees," because the power to tax was a sovereign power that could not be limited. The Government stated that the promise not to tax Okie applied only to "derechas de importation," and not all charges. The Tribunal rejected Mexico's contention and held that the "misunderstanding between the parties and the resultant damage sustained by Okie was due entirely to the fault of the government officials resulting in injustice to Okie,"[475] and that therefore the government must indemnify him.

The reluctance to submit decisions on agreements relating to taxation wholly to inclusive prescriptions can further be observed in multilateral and bilateral investment treaties. None of these agreements deal with problems that may arise out of the uncertainty of tax legislation. They refer only to "equitable," "nondiscriminatory," "national treatment" and "most-favorite-nation" treatment.[476]

---

[473]*Id.* at 173.

[474]John B. Okie (United States v. Mexico), 4 R. Int'l Arb. Awards 54 (1926).

[475]*Id.* at 56.

[476]Art. 22(3) of the Bogota Agreement refers to "equitable treatment"; the ICC Code, Art. 7, and European League of Economic Cooperation refer to "national treatment."

Besides claims relating to taxation, there are other types of situations in which exclusive prescriptions are honored. Those are situations where an agreement has its largest impact on an exclusive arena and the protection of the exclusive interest of that arena is in the common interest of the whole community. For example, such agreements can involve an extensive degree of authority and control for the grantee over the internal or external affairs of the grantor state. An example of such an agreement is Baron Julius de Reuter's concession with the Persian Government in 1872. The scope of this agreement was so extensive that the only thing the grantee did not share with the King of Persia was the "formal Crown."[477] Under internal pressures the King of Persia canceled the concession in 1877. The unilateral cancellation was objected to by Europeans, but it was clearly in the common interest of the larger community to protect a country's self-determination against informal colonialism.

Similarly, commitments that deprive a nation-state of the legitimate rights of the use and disposition of resources within its territory for promoting and distributing values among its nationals may be considered void according to exclusive and inclusive prescriptions.[478] Inclusive prescription may limit the power of a gov-

---

COMMON PROTECTION FOR PRIVATE INTERNATIONAL INVESTMENT 18 (1958). Most-favored-nation treatment is usually provided in FCN treaties, such as the United States treaty with Iran, Art. VI; with Germany Art. XI(2). *See* FATOUROS, *supra* note 208, at 175. There are a few unilateral prescriptions, such as the Greek investment law which provides for foreign investors a "freezing" of income tax rates or other taxes; Greek L.D. No. 2687 of Ar. 22, 1953 Art. VIII(1) (a); *Id.* at 176. *See also* Chilean Investment Law No. 437 of 1954; Israel Investment Law No. 30 of 1950; and Libya Foreign Capital Investment Law of 1958, clause 4(a), *cited in id.* at 178.

[177] This conclusion gave an actual monopoly over Persia's natural resources and all activities related to the process of exploitation; control over government forests; much uncultivated land; construction of a railway from the Caspian Sea to the Persian Gulf; construction of canals, roads, bridges, postal and telegraphic extensions, the initiation of all remunerative public works; construction of mills, factories, and workshops and many other facilities for a period of 25 years. *See* H. RAWLINSON, ENGLAND AND RUSSIA IN THE EAST 391–94 (1875); *see also* G. CURZON, PERSIA AND THE PERSIAN QUESTION 483 (1892).

[178] An example of a commitment which involved the value deprivation of an exclusive arena was the Russian Convention with the Persian Government before 1906. The Persian government claimed first that the concessions were granted either by corruption or by threats with no regard to the interest of the Persian people. Furthermore, the subjects of the concessions were never properly exploited or developed, and the grantees often prevented any other interested party from developing them. Then, too, the Persian government rarely derived any royalties from the exploitation of its resources. *See* SENATE DOC. No. 97, 68th Cong. 1st Sess. 96–97 (1924). A similar claim was made by the Iranian government about D'Arcy's concession. *See* 13 LEAGUE OF NATIONS O.J. 2301 (69th Sess. 1931).

ernment to make such commitments, regardless of the internal prescriptions of the nation-state. For example, the ICJ in the advisory opinion on the *Legal Consequences for State of the Continued Presence of South Africa in Namibia (South West Africa) Notwithstanding Security Council Resolution 276 (1970)*, held that "no State which enters into relations with South Africa concerning Namibia may expect the United Nations or its members to recognize the validity of such relationship, or of the consequences thereof. . . ."[479] In a separate opinion Judge Ammoun discussed the issue of economic relations between the member states of the United Nations and the government of South Africa:

> The exploitation of the petroleum, diamond, gold and other resources of the soil and subsoil of Namibia, its territorial waters or its continental shelf, carried out by South Africa or its nationals, or with its authorization, is equivalent to the seizure of Namibian assets by, or with the co-operation of, the occupying authority, and the Republic of South Africa must therefore render an account to the future State of Namibia of the income and taxes which it has derived or collected from such sources. Any States which have obtained profit from these exploitations, either in the form of *concessions* or in the form of *participation* in the invested capital, may be *held jointly responsible* with South Africa towards Namibia. These States and their subjects must refrain from acquiring any of the production of these exploitations, in order not to incur civil responsibility by being involved either as receivers or as purchasers, with notice, assets not belonging to the vendor.[480]

On September 29, 1974, the United Nations Council for Namibia[481] decreed that the South-West African territory's animal and

---

The same point was recognized in the transvaal Dynamite Company Concession. This concession involved the claim of a German company owned jointly by French, German, and English institutions to have exclusive rights to encompass the manufacture, trade, and sale of explosives in the whole territory of the South African Republic. *See Report of the Transvaal Concessions Commission*, Cmd. 623, Vol. 35 (1901).

[479][1971] I.C.J. 56.

[480]*Id.* at 96–97 (emphasis supplied).

[481]The League of Nations mandate held by South Africa over South-West Africa was terminated by the United Nations in 1966. The United Nations Council, a group of 18 countries, was set up to look after the territory's affairs. In 1968 the United Nations renamed the territory Namibia, for the Namib, a coastal desert strip. The United Nations action has not been recognized by South Africa; therefore the U.N. Council must rely on member States of the U.N. for implementation.

mineral resources must not be exploited without the Council's consent.[482] The Council's decree also stated that any vehicle, ship, or container found to be carrying resources from South Africa "shall also be subject to seizure and forfeiture."[483]

Agreements incompatible with the more fundamental norms of international law (jus cogens) are void under inclusive prescriptions regardless of exclusive prescriptions. Article 53 of the Vienna Convention on Treaties reads: "A treaty is void if, at the time of its conclusion, it conflicts with a peremptory norm of general international law. For the purposes of the present convention, a peremptory norm of general international law is a norm accepted and recognized by the international community of States as a whole as a norm from which no derogation is permitted and which can be modified only by a subsequent norm of general international law having the same character." Similarly, special inclusive prescriptions could be made to apply to commitments concerning resources vital to the larger community regardless of the internal requirements of the contracting state or states. Since the context in which resources become vital is most often that of crisis, the inclusive prescriptions made applicable to commitments about such resources could be different from otherwise accepted norms of international law. Commitments about vital resources might, therefore, be considered valid or void according to special inclusive prescriptions, irrespective of internal or even ordinary inclusive prescriptions.

Demands to nullify commitments made under coercion, fraud, or bribery have been supported by both exclusive and inclusive prescriptions.[484] However, inclusive prescriptions have not developed well enough to deal with all forms of coercion. Coercion may be direct or indirect. Many incidents and forms of definite coercion cannot be proved by documentation acceptable to international tribunals. Since we regard agreements as persuasive strategies for commitment, any form of coercion, even if difficult of proof, should cancel the commitment.[485] Inclusive prescriptions and in-

---

[482] N.Y. Times, Sept. 29, 1974 at 10, col. 3.

[483] *Id.*

[484] Arts. 51 & 52 of the Vienna Convention, note 464 *supra*, deal with coercion of a representative of a State and coercion of a State by the threat or use of force. *See also* HARVARD RESEARCH REPORT, *supra* note 463, at art. 32.

[485] International lawyers agree that consent of the parties is an essential element to the validity of a treaty. *See* HARVARD RESEARCH REPORT, *supra* note 463, at 1149.

clusive decision makers should determine the degree to which forms of coercion would be considered sufficient to cancel the commitment. Deference may, however, be given to unilateral prescriptions in definition and proscription of coercion until inclusive prescriptions are more fully developed to protect the common interest.

Claims to invalidate commitments made under coercion were made by the Persian Government concerning Russian concession agreements before 1906.[486] The failure of the Russian government to obtain oil concessions from the Iranian government was the main reason for Russian military intervention in the northern Iranian province of Azerbaijan in 1946. In diplomatic negotiations concerning the withdrawal of its troops, Russia demanded the establishment of an Iranian-Russian oil company.[487] Thus to an appreciable extent the 1954 Iranian concession of the Oil Consortium was effected under coercion. This concession was made following the Iranian nationalization of oil resources in 1951. After the nationalization, Iran was faced with a total boycott of oil exports instituted by major international oil companies. The British government and the Anglo-Iranian company threatened to confiscate the Iranian oil then on the high seas, the American government conditioned and postponed foreign aid to Iran,[488] and the IMF and the World Bank boycotted Iran for a time.[489]

The problem of coercion is complicated and has always been involved in social interactions. Until 1945 there was no conventional inclusive prescription regarding the illegality of coercion in transnational relations. Direct coercion, instead of the persuasive strategy of agreement, was claimed several times as a means of equitable access to resources. Before the Second World War, for example, there were some occasions in which force was asserted for the expansion of territory as an alleged equitable means of satisfying resource needs. In 1935 the Italian government prepared to attack Ethiopia, on the grounds that the pressure of its

---

[486] *See* SEN. DOC. No. 97, 68th Cong., 1st Sess. (1924).

[487] *See* R. STRAUSZ-HUPE & S. POSSONY, INTERNATINAL RELATIONS IN THE AGE OF THE CONFLICT BETWEEN DEMOCRACY AND DICTATORSHIP 129 (1950). *See also* Stanley, *World Organization on the Economic Front* in PEACE, SECURITY, AND THE UNITED NATIONS 107, 114 (H. Morgenthau ed. 1945).

[488] N. FATEMI, OIL DIPLOMACY (1972).

[489] *See* Mikdashi, *supra* note 229, at 285.

population on existing raw materials forced her into territorial expansion.[490] Japan insisted on the expansion of its territory on the Asiatic mainland on the argument that the high increase in population heavily strained domestic resources.[491] Germany demanded the return of its former colonies because its growing population needed more resources.[492]

Article 2(4) of the United Nations Charter deals with coercion: "4. All Members shall refrain in their international relations from the threat or use of force against the territorial integrity or political independence of any State, or in any other manner inconsistent with the Purposes of the United Nations." Neither the Charter nor any other prescription, however, clearly outlines the extent to which coercion (military, economic, or ideological) becomes unlawful. Past trends in decision do not provide a definite answer. Although one of our policies is to secure and maintain a stability in expectations concerning commitment, we recommend that in the absence of clear inclusive prescriptions about the degree to which coercion used to make a commitment becomes unlawful, deference should be given to the exclusive claims of the nation-state which insists it has been coerced into the agreement.

In both inclusive and exclusive prescriptions fraud is a sufficient ground for voidance of an agreement.[493] Therefore, any agreement made with deliberate misrepresentation is cause for voiding the agreement. The relevant community policy here is to secure and protect the genuine shared expectations of the parties based on facts and good faith. The strategy of persuasion in commitment should not be nullified by enforcing commitments made under fraudulent representations.

Article 50 of the Vienna Convention on the Law of Treaties reads: "If the expression of a State's consent to be bound by a treaty has been procured through the corruption of its representative directly or indirectly by another negotiating State, the State

[490]STRAUSS-HUPE & POSSONY, *supra* note 487, at 213–14.

[491]*Id.* at 122.

[492]*Id.* at 87.

[493]*See* HARVARD RESEARCH REPORT, *supra* note 463, at 1147, for extensive citations of writers on this subject. REPORTS OF INTERNATIONAL LAW COMMISSION U.N. Doc. A/6309/Rev. 1. See also *U.N.*, (1966) at art. 42; and the Vienna Convention, *supra* note 464, at art. 49. An example of a claim for adjustment of an agreement due to fraud was made by the Persian Government to the British negotiators in the conclusion of D'Arcy's Concession. *See* 15 LEAGUE OF NATIONS O.J. 291 (70th Sess. 1933).

may invoke such corruption as invalidating its consent to be bound by the treaty."[494] A similar point was emphasized in the International Law Commission of 1966, Article 47. This article expresses the community expectation that one of the basic policies behind inclusive decisions is the protection of the common interest by the minimizing of corruption. Since bribery is an instrument of social corruption, any agreement entered into because of bribery, regardless of the content of the agreement, could be subject to cancellation if the Contracting State so demands.

Disclosures in U.S. Senate hearings during the past two years concerning the operation of American companies overseas has made clear the unfortunate fact that bribery has been a "usual" element in the practice of international business. Many countries, despite their own strict exclusive prescriptions about the illegality of bribery in internal business affairs, take it for granted that this is a part of overseas operations, particularly in developing countries. Without it, says the *Financial Times* of London, "business simply would not get done."[495] The proceedings described a number of cases of bribery, such as the $125 million paid by United Brands to the former president of Honduras to reduce the tax on the production of bananas, $25 to $30 million dollars paid by Lockheed during the last five years, $150,000 paid by Ashland to the President and Prime Minister of Gabon to protect oil concessions, and other cases.[496]

Unfortunately, little has been achieved by the international community in terms of inclusive prescriptions and collective actions to stop or at least to discourage such corruption. After the recent criticism of the operation of multinational corporations abroad, the OECD countries, determined to show the developing countries and the rest of the world that they have control over their multinationals, are now trying to enact national legislation which would require multinationals to publish their financial accounts "at least annually."[497] The companies are also called on "To take

---

[494]The Vienna Convention applied only to agreements between states, but it has been invoked here by analogy.

[495]*Quoted in* Gwirtzman, *Is Bribery Defensible?* N.Y. Times (magazine) Oct. 5, 1975, at 19, col. 1. For an elaborate and analytical study of bribery, see M. REISMAN, FOLDED LIES: BRIBERY, CRUSADES, AND REFORMS (1979).

[496]*Id.*

[497]*O.E.C.D. Asks Data on Big Compromise*, N.Y. Times, Oct. 27, 1975, at 14, col. 3.

into consideration the established objectives of the countries in which they operate in managing financial and commercial operations. To end any discrimination on the basis of sex, age, religion, color, ethnic origin or political activities. To not transfer operations from one branch to another country because of a labor dispute."[498] Not only is the code voluntary, but also there is no prescription with respect to control of corrupt conduct of which the companies may be guilty. The publication of information about agreements made through bribery of the negotiators or effective elite of the contracting state might, in improvement of the intelligence function, be an effective way of minimizing corruption.

Determination of the exact content of commitment becomes a matter of interpretation of the agreement. The basic goal of interpretation is to reach the closest possible approximation to the genuine shared expectations of the parties. Any ambiguities or omissions in the agreement and any evaluation of the shared subjectivities should be completed and evaluated in accordance with basic community policies.

Agreements are instances of a process of communication and "like all other communications, are functions of a larger context, and the realistic identification of the content of these communications must require a systematic, comprehensive examination of all relevant features of that context, with conscious and deliberate appraisal of their significance."[499] To understand the actual commitment of the parties during the process of communication, doctrines of "plain and natural meaning" or "textuality" are too narrow as approaches in a world where social and political interaction is so complicated. The contextual approach to the interpretation of agreements relating to both content (events to be observed) and procedure (order and techniques of observation), initiated and developed by Professors McDougal, Lasswell, and Miller, is the best approach for decision makers who are committed to the overriding community goals of achieving the closest approximation to the genuine shared expectations of the parties to an agreement.[500] These elements of interpretation can be applied to any kind of treaty or development agreement.

---

[498]*Id.*

[499]McDougal, Lasswell & Miller, *supra* note 6, at 11.

[500]For the development of these themes, *see id.*

There are a number of authoritative decisions which support the idea that interpreting the genuine expectations of the parties should not be limited to any one system of law nor be interpreted restrictively. The Aramco Arbitration supported this view, when it was stated that

> [a]lthough the Concession Agreement is connected with the Hanbali school of Moslem Law, as applied in Saudi Arabia—from which it derives its validity and effectiveness—the interpretation of this Agreement should not be based on that law alone. The interpretation of contracts is not governed by rigid rules; it is rather an art, governed by principles of logic and common sense, which purports to lead to an adaptation, as reasonable as possible, of the provisions of a contract to the fact of a dispute.[501]

The Tribunal rejected the Government's position favoring the restrictive interpretation of the agreement. The Tribunal stated that a state's being party to the agreement is not enough to justify the principle of restrictive interpretation. In the opinion of the Tribunal "the rights of the Parties must be evaluated and examined in a spirit of complete equality. This is because the rights of one Party are increased as a result of restrictive interpretation to the extent that the rights of the other Party are restricted."[502] The Tribunal concluded that such results cannot be founded merely upon the quality of the subjects involved in a contractual relationship.[503] The Tribunal, while emphasizing that states are bound to fulfill their contractual obligations to the same extent as private persons, stated that restrictive interpretation may be justified only "when the sovereign rights invoked [by] the State concern interests of a general nature which cannot be defended otherwise than by disregarding the doubtful clauses of the contract."[504] In other words, the court concluded that when there is a high degree of impact on the national interest of the Contracting State in comparison with the particular interest of the private parties, the common interest is in the protection of the exclusive national interest of the Contracting State by means of restrictive interpretation.

[501] 27 I.L.R. at 172.

[502] *Id.* at 191.

[503] *Id.*

[504] *Id.* at 192.

This was the basis of the decision in the well-known case of *Radio Corporation of America v. The National Government of the Republic of China.*[505] The Chinese Government had granted to RCA the right to establish a direct radio-telegraph link between China and the United States. Later the Government granted to another corporation similar rights. RCA claimed that the Government had granted them exclusive right to establish such a circuit because paragraph 3 of the 1928 Agreement stated that "[t]he Council (the Chinese Government) shall transmit every message within its control destined to the United States of America or intended for transit through the United States unless routed otherwise by sender."[506] The second concession, RCA claimed, is incompatible with its exclusive right. The Tribunal, considering the importance of control of China's radio-communication with the outside world, concluded that although the Chinese Government can sign away a part of its freedom of action, "as a sovereign government, on principles free in its action for the public interests as it sees it, it cannot be presumed to have accepted such a restriction of its freedom of action, unless the acceptance of such a restriction can be ascertained distinctly and beyond reasonable doubt."[507]

For similar reasons, the principle of restrictive interpretation was explored in the *S.S. Wimbledon,*[508] where the PCIJ stated that when the performance of an obligation requires the depreciation of state sovereignty, it creates "a sufficient reason for the restrictive interpretation, in case of doubt, of the clause which produces such a limitation."[509] Here the Court referred to the important national interest of Germany with respect to the Treaty of Versailles, of which Article 380 provided that "[t]he Kiel Canal and its approaches shall be maintained free and open to the vessels of commerce and of war of all nations at peace with Germany on terms of entire equality."[510] Germany claimed that, by allowing Polish arms to be shipped through the Kiel Canal, it would lose the neutral

---

[505] 30 Am. J. Int'l L. 535 (1936).

[506] *Id.* at 545.

[507] *Id.* at 540.

[508] The S.S. Wimbledon, [1923] P.C.I.J., serv. A, No. 1.

[509] *Id.* at 24.

[510] *Id.* at 21.

position Germany had in the Russo-Polish war. The court in rejecting the German contention stated that although the above fact was sufficient reason for restrictive interpretation, "the Court feels obliged to stop at the point where the so-called restrictive interpretation would be contrary to the plain terms of the article and would destroy what has been clearly granted."[511]

Though the basic objective of interpretation of development agreements, as of other agreements, is the clarification of the genuine shared expectations of the parties, the principle of restrictive interpretation, as contested with more expansive modes, would appear peculiarly appropriate for development agreements. Restrictive interpretation emphasizes that when a decision about a commitment may have great impact on the national interest of the nation-state against the exclusive interest of a private entity or entities, the ambiguities of the agreement should be interpreted in a way to protect the national interest of the state party. This is because the possible endangering of the national interest of a state by an agreement where the other party is a private entity are incompatible with the interest of the larger community. States represent all the members, even including the unborn members, of a particular territorial community.

b. Performance

The process of performance is the process of implementation of commitment, and the issue involved in this process is the degree to which performance conforms to commitment. The basic policy is that the performance should be the closest possible approximation to the agreed-upon commitment. States should not be authorized to change their internal prescriptions to interfere with performance of their commitments. States should not be authorized to change situations for the purpose of avoiding the commitment. However, change of exclusive prescriptions and situations which are more compatible with human dignity should be honored.

The principle of security of contract, or the principle *pacta sunt servanda*, is not a new phenomenon in legal theory. This principle has its roots in the very establishment and growth of social interaction. It was a necessary element for the protection of stability in

[511]*Id.* at 24–5.

community expectations. Fitzmaurice observed that the theoretical norm of this principle is in natural law, and in the Greco-Roman-Christian tradition its basic norms derive from the law of God.[512] Wehberg writes that the principle *pacta sunt servanda* was developed in antiquity by the Chaldeans, the Egyptians, and the Chinese in a primitive fashion.[513] Authority and control over agreements, according to these ancient peoples, came from the gods of each party to the agreement. The gods controlled the performance of the agreements by threatening to intervene against the party guilty of a breach of agreement. But the binding power of such agreements was founded primarily on religious belief rather than on legal obligation per se.

Later, in the establishment and development of the major religions of the world, the principle of *pacta sunt servanda* was made more explicit and detailed and was incorporated into the world's legal systems. Hence, at this stage, although the basis of the principle was still planted in religion, the principle achieved a new binding force because such rules were enforced among the followers of all these religions.[514] The increase in social interaction, the necessity for the protection of the common interest in regulating the economy, and other international obligations were added to the religious foundation.[515] In this context the principle easily became accepted as a basic norm of customary international law.[516] The principle of *pacta sunt servanda* has commonly been said to be

[512]Fitzmaurice, *Some Problems Regarding the Formal Sources of International Law* cited in Gormley, *The Codification of Pacta Sunt Servanda by the International Commission: The Reservation of Classical Norms of Moral Force and Good Faith*, 14 St. Louis Univ. L.J. 371 (1970).

[513]Wehberg, *Pacta Sunt Servanda* 53 Am. J. Int'l L. 775 (1959).

[514]This principle is clearly expressed by the Koran in many places; *see* C. Jenks, The Common Law of Mankind 775 (1958). For the practice in the Hindu religion, *see* Sastry, *Hinduism and International Law*, 117 Recueil des Cours 507 (Academie De Droit International) (1966–I) and Alexandrowicz, *Mortens and Asian Treaty Practice*, 8 Indian Y.B. Int'l Aff. 74 (1964). For Buddhist practice, see Sastry, *id.* at 557; and Jayatilleke, *The Principles of International Law in Buddhist Doctrine*, 120 Recueil des Cours 444 (Academie De Droit International) (1967–I). For Moslim practice see Mohmassni, *The Principles of International Law in the Light of Islamic Doctrine*, 117 Recueil des Cours 209, 235 (Academie De Droit International) (1966–I). For Confucian thought, see Wehberg, *id.* at 775–76.

[515]The expansion of commercial activity in the Mediterranean area increased the scope of the principle of *pacta sunt servanda* beyond that dictated by religious belief. *See generally* note 514 *supra* and materials cited therein.

[516]*See* B. Wortley, Jurisprudence 45–64 (1967); Kunz, *The Meaning and the Range of the Norm Pacta Servanda*, 39 Am. J. Int'l L. 180 (1945).

a principle of law common to all of the major legal systems.[517] The founding fathers of modern international law declared that the honoring of promises in good faith was the foundation not only of every State but of the community of nations.[518] Thus, Vattel maintained that the obligation to fulfill treaties was "indispensable."[519]

Inclusive conventional prescriptions have affirmed this principle. In the Preamble to the Covenant of the League of Nations it is stated that "[t]he High Contracting Parties, in order to promote international cooperation and to achieve international peace and security . . . by the maintenance of justice and a scrupulous respect for all treaty obligations in the dealings of organized peoples with one another, agree to this Covenant of the League of Nations." The Convention on Treaties adopted at Havana by the Sixth International Conference of American States on February 20, 1928, in Article 10 declared that "no State can relieve itself of the obligations of a treaty or modify its stipulations except by the agreement, secured through peaceful means, of the other contracting parties."

Many declarations have been made by statesmen to emphasize the obligation to observe the sanctity of agreements. Edward Livingston, Secretary of State of the United States in 1833, stated this principle: "The government of the United States presumes that whenever a treaty has been duly concluded and ratified by the acknowledged authorities competent for that purpose, an obliga-

---

[517] *See* JENKS note 514, *supra.* This doctrine, with modifications, also exists in Soviet law; *see* Korovin, *Soviet Treaties and International Law*, 22 AM. J. INT'L L. 753 (1928).

[518] Cicero, *cited by* Grotius in III DE JURE BELLI AC PACIS, Ch. 25; (H. Milford ed. & trans. 1925). Similar views are expressed by S. Pufendorf, II ELEMENTORUM JURISPRUDENTIAL UNIVERSALIS 95 (W. Oldfather Trans. 1931).

[519] Vattel emphasized the importance of the sanctity of contractual obligations by devoting a chapter to "The Faith of Treaties." He wrote:
"Treaties are among the number of the things to be held sacred by Nations. . . .

"The faith of treaties, that firm and sincere determination, that invariable steadfastness in carrying and our promises, of which we make profession in a treaty, is therefore to be held sacred and inviolate by Nations whose safety and peace it secures; and if States do not wish to be lacking in their duty to themselves, they should brand with infamy whoever violates his work.

"He who violates his treaties violates at the same time the Law of Nations, for he shows contempt for that fidelity of treaties which the Law of Nations declares sacred, and, as far as is in his power, he renders it of no effect. He is doubly guilty, in that he does an injury both to his ally and all Nations and the human race as well." VATTEL, *supra* note 357, at 188–89.

tion is thereby imposed upon each and every department of the government to carry it into complete effect, according to its terms, and that on the performance of this obligation consists the due observance of good faith among nations."[520] Lord Russell, British Foreign Minister, in a dispatch of December 23, 1860, to Earl James Bruce Elgin, the British Ambassador to China, said that the universal notions of justice and humanity express to even the most barbarian among human beings, that, if an agreement has been made, the law demands its observance.[521] In 1937, Secretary of State Cordell Hull stated with regard to American foreign policy that "[w]e advocate faithful observance of international agreements. Upholding the principle of the sanctity of treaties, we believe in modification of provisions of treaties, when need therefore arises, by orderly processes carried out in a spirit of mutual helpfulness and accommodation. We believe in respect by all nations for the rights of others and performance by all nations of established obligations."[522] This doctrine of *pacta sunt servanda* with respect to treaties has been fully recognized in important multilateral treaties. As an example we may adduce the statement made by the powers in the case of neutralization of the Black Sea in 1870, when Russia suddenly repudiated her obligations under the Paris Peace Treaty of 1856 to restrict itself to the neutral Black Sea,[523] and the Covenant of the League of Nations which characterizes this principle as a fundamental principle important for the promotion of international cooperation and peace. The Charter of the United Nations also recognizes this principle, demanding "respect for the obligations arising from treaties and other sources of international law."[524] The same view is stated in Article 5 of the Charter of the Organization of American States.

The doctrine *pacta sunt servanda* is a recent and broad embodiment in the Vienna Convention of Law of Treaties. Article 26 says that "[e]very treaty in force is binding upon the parties to it and must be performed by them in good faith." The Harvard Research on the Law of Treaties, in Article 20, and the 1966 Reports of the

[520] F. WHARTON, II INTERNATIONAL LAW DIGEST 67 (1887).

[521] Wehberg *supra* note 514, at 783.

[522] *Id.*

[523] *Id.* at 784.

[524] U.N. CHARTER, Preamble.

International Law Commission in Article 24 emphasize and elaborate the same point. A number of authoritative decisions have affirmed this doctrine.[525]

The applicability of this principle to development agreements has been observed by many writers. Thus, Wehberg states:

> [T]he rule of pacta sunt servanda [is] . . . a general principle of law that is found in all nations. It follows, therefore, that the principle is valid exactly in the same manner, whether it is in respect of contracts between states and private companies. Whether in regards, with Verdross, the contracts of a state with a foreign company for the purpose of granting a concession as being quasi-international law agreements or whether one of sanctity of contracts must always be applied.[526]

He emphasized that the principle of sanctity of contract is an essential condition of life for any social community.[527] Kissam and Leach, subscribing to the same policy, write that "In the area of concession agreements, States are bound to observe these agreements with other States. The principle of *pacta sunt servanda* should apply. Principles of acquired rights and sanctity of contracts, as well as common justice, support this conclusion."[528] The Prepara-

---

[525] In the North Atlantic Coast Fisheries Case, the Permanent Court of Arbitration, in its Award of 1910, stated that "[e]very State has to execute the obligations incurred by treaty bona fide, and is urged thereto by the ordinary sanctions of International Law in regard to observance of Treaty obligations." North Atlantic Fisheries Case (Great Britain v. United States), Hague Ct. Rep. (Scott) 146, 157 (Perm. Ct. Arb. 1910). A number of P.C.I.J. decisions have also affirmed this doctrine; *see, e.g.,* the Advisory Opinion Regarding the Exchange of Greek and Turkish populations. [1925] P.C.I.J. Reports, ser. B., No. 10 at 20. See also the case concerning the Polish Nationals in Danzig, [1932] P.C.I.J. ser. A/B No. 44 at 24.

[526] Wehberg, *supra* note 513, at 786.

[527] Wehberg has also stated: "The life of the international community is based not only on relations between States, but also, to an ever-increasing degree, on relations between States and foreign corporations or foreign individuals. No economic relations between states and foreign corporations can exist without the principle of Pacta Sunt Servanda. This has never been disputed in practice. The best proof that the principle also applies in such a case is the following fact: It has been long suggested that disputes between states and foreign companies (or foreign individuals) should be submitted to international adjudication. Such a course would be meaningless of the principle Pacta Sunt Servanda were not applicable also to the kind of relations." *Id.* at 786.

[528] Kissam & Leach, *Sovereign Expropriation of Property and Abrogation of Concession Contract,* in *Selected Readings, supra* note 243, at 396; see also *Wadmond, supra* note 266, at 174, and Rory, *Law Governing Contracts Between States and Foreign Nationals,* in *Selected Readings, supra* note 243, at 483.

tory Committee of the Hague Conference for the Codification of International Law based this statement upon the responses of twenty-three governments:

> A State is responsible for damage suffered by a foreigner as the result of the enactment of legislation which directly infringes rights derived by the foreigner from a concession granted or a contract made by the State. It depends upon the circumstances whether a State incurs responsibility where it has enacted legislation general in character which is incompatible with operation of a concession which it has granted or the performance of a contract made by it.[529]

The American Branch of the International Law Association of 1957–58 adopted the view that "the taking of alien contractual rights by a State of itself is a breach of international law."[530]

In *Losinger & Co.*, Switzerland argued that "the principle *pacta sunt servanda* . . . applies not only to agreements directly concluded between States, but also to those between a State and foreigners. . . ."[531] The PCIJ did not, however, have to give any judgment on the case. The Permanent Court of International Justice in the *Cases of the Serbian and Brazilian Loans*[532] stated that a breach of contract on the part of the state creates "automatically a breach of international law." Here, the loan contract was between the government and foreign nationals.

The decision regarding *Czechoslovakia v. Radio Corporation of America* was the first authoritative decision implicitly applying the principle *pacta sunt servanda* in a development agreement.[533] The case involved a ten-year concession to RCA to establish and operate a direct radio-communications link between Czechoslovakia and the United States. After about three years the Government of Czechoslovakia decided to grant a concession to another corporation. RCA insisted that the first concession granted exclusive rights to RCA, and hence that the second concession was incompatible with the first concession and therefore unlawful. The Tribunal in

[529] League of Nations Doc. C.75 H.69 (1929) V.33.

[530] *See* INT'L. ASSOC. (AMERICAN BRANCH), PROCEEDINGS 1957–58 at 70 n.17 and sources cited therein.

[531] [1936] P.C.I.J. ser. C, No. 78 at 32.

[532] [1929] P.C.I.J. ser. A, Nos. 20 & 21.

[533] 30 AM. J. INT'L. L. (1936).

upholding the claim of RCA, invoked the principle of sanctity of agreements, and stated: "in public law the sentence pacta sunt servanda will also apply, just as public interest requires stability as regards any arrangement legally agreed upon."[534]

Despite its widespread acknowledgment, the principle of *pacta sunt servanda* is not an absolute. It is complementary to, and qualified by, the principles of *jus cogens* and of *rebus sic stantibus*. Lauterpacht suggested that a treaty is void "if its performance involves an act which is illegal under international law and if it is declared so to be by the International Court of Justice."[535] The Vienna Convention on the Law of Treaties has, as previously noted, recognized these qualifications to the doctrine of *pacta sunt servanda*. Indeed, one author has summarized from the terms of this convention many exceptional circumstances in which the principle of *pacta sunt servanda* will not apply:

1. if force or duress is used against the negotiators or the State itself, now covered by Articles 51 and 52:

2. if an illegal treaty is sought to be enforced (part V);

3. if error is found to be present, now included in Article 48;

4. in those instances where fraud has been evident (Article 49);

5. if a peremptory norm of general international law is violated, as dealt with by Articles 53, 64 and 71;

---

[534]*Id.* at 531. Robert H. Delson, Counsel to the Indonesian Government in the dispute arising from nationalization of oil companies in Indonesia, rejecting the applicability of international law, wrote:
"There are some writers who, although recognizing this, argue that nevertheless the principle pacta sunt servanda under international law may be extended to contractual agreements between states and aliens, provided that such contracts contain a so-called 'internalizing clause,' i.e., a provision that they are to be governed, wholly or in part, by public international law, or by the general principles of law recognized by civilized nations.

"This argument also has no legal justification, since international law can be created only by States, either by general usage involving a number of States, or by treaty between two or more states. A contract between a state and an alien derives its binding force from municipal law, and the sanction of international law cannot be applicable thereto even if the parties design to make it so." *See Economic Development and International Law*, in REPORT OF THE 2D INTER-AMERICAN CONFERENCE FOR DEMOCRACY AND FREEDOM (1961) at 180. This argument, of course, is rejected by contemporary international law scholars. Such argument has no legal justification and is used only to reject the international responsibility of states in their relations with aliens. Modern international law embraces inter-state relations as well as relations between individuals and that of international organizations with states.

[535]*See* Lauterpacht, *The Problem of Jurisdictional Immunities of Foreign States*, 28 BRIT. Y.B. INT'L L. 90 (1951).

6. if a violation of the United Nations Charter, as to those areas involving the use of force, as prohibited by Article 52 is found to exist;

7. if a treaty violating a higher commitment to a specialized agency, such as ILO is *jus cogens* and, secondly, if treaties violate the Statute of the Council of the European Economic Community (under EEC Treaty Article 5) and exception would exist;

8. if, as some modern authorities contend, unjust treaty exists;

9. if a void treaty, proper when entered into, was deemed no longer in force but no longer valid were sought to be enforced;

12. if *rebus sic stantibus* could be applied (Article 62); or

13. if *jus cogens* (Articles 53 or 64) outranked the negotiated pactum.[536]

Exceptions to the principle have also been recognized by authoritative national decisions.[537] In general, the principle requires evaluation in the light of the whole of general community expectations and policies. An excellent model for such balancing, though involving other doctrines, is found in the *North Sea Continental Shelf Case*.[538] The Court there evaluated a large and complex context in balancing the equities between the parties and a wide variety of rules. The Court held that the Geneva Convention on the Continental Shelf of 1958 was not applicable since Article 6 did not express customary international law in adopting the equidistance rule.

i. The Principle of Acquired Rights

The principle of sanctity of contracts, or of the obligation of the parties to perform their agreement, is sometimes approached

---

[536] *See* Gormley, *supra* note 512, at 389.

[537] In 1965 Germany's Federal Constitutional Tribunal observed: "Only some elementary legal commands will have to be considered as rules of customary international law which do not permit contracting out. The quality of such preemptory norms can be attributed only to those legal rules which are firmly embedded in the legal conscience of the community of States, which are indispensable to the existence of public international law as an international legal system and the observance of which may be demanded by all members of the Community of States." 7. Apr. 1965 BverfG 18, 448, *cited in* Mann, *The Doctrine of Jus Cogens in International Law*, FESTSCHRIFT FÜR ULRICH SCHEUNER ZUM 70 GEBURTSTAG at 401.

[538] [1969] I.C.J. 4.

from the principle of acquired rights. This principle, developed in the continental law system, means that the vested or acquired rights of an alien are entitled to be respected by the host country. The nature of the international economy, which includes the movement of private as well as public property across political boundaries, creates expectations about the protection of acquired rights. Dunn has described the international impact of domestic regulation of private property: "of course the legislative regulation of private property is ordinarily and properly considered a domestic matter lying outside the realm of international law, but we have recently found out that it can have vital international consequences where carried out in an unaccustomed manner by countries where a large amount of property has become vested in foreigners."[539] This doctrine is strongly applied in the law of state succession.[540] Jenks and Lord McNair have made the important point that the response of the international community to the principle of acquired rights is of great importance to the future of investment.[541] The main objective behind the principle of acquired rights, Jennings observes, is to provide inclusive control and protection for certain aspects of contracts whose proper law might otherwise be the municipal law of the contracting state.[542]

Various states have concluded bilateral agreements where they recognize the principle of acquired rights by promising protection for the private property of the nationals of the other contracting state. Generally these treaties provide that neither party should take unreasonable or discriminatory measures that would impair legally acquired rights or interests of nationals and companies of the other party within its territories.[543]

---

[539]*See generally* Dunn, note 1 *supra*. The principle of acquired rights has been criticized by Kaeckenbeeck; see *The Protection of Vested Rights in International Law*, 17 BRIT. Y.B. INT'L. L. 1, 15 (1936); but it is accepted by many authorities.

[540]D. O'CONNELL, LAW OF STATE SUCCESSION 104 (1956). For a related case, see the German Settlers case, [1923] P.C.I.J. Ser. B, No. 6 at 36.

[541]JENKS, *supra* note 514, at 153–55; McNair, *supra* note 317, at 16.

[542]*See* Jennings, in *Selected Readings, supra* note 243, at 204.

[543]*See* Sweden-France Convention of 1954, Arts. 6(1) and 8; Belgium-Netherlands Convention of 1933, Art. 8; Belgium-Siam Convention of 1937, Art. V, cited in U.N. Doc. A/AC.97/5 (1959) at 181–82. *See also* United States–Netherlands Treaty of 1956 A.VI (3); United States–Republic of Korea Treaty of 1956, Art. VI (3); United States–Nicaragua Treaty of 1956, Art. VI (3), cited *id.* at 180.

The principle of acquired rights is recognized in Article VI(1) of United Nations General Assembly Resolution 388(V). Part A, "Economic and Financial Provisions Relating to Libya," states: "[T]he property, rights and interests of Italian nationals, including Italian judicial persons in Libya, shall, provided they have been legally acquired, be respected. They shall not be treated less favorably than the property, rights and interests of other foreign nationals, including foreign judicial persons."[544] Respect for acquired rights has, in different contexts, been affirmed by a number of authoritative decisions. These decisions regard this doctrine as a principle of international law and emphasize that states are responsible for their actions affecting the property rights of foreigners. Such is the case of *Religious Properties in Portugal*.[545] When the Portuguese Republic was proclaimed by law in 1910, it nationalized the property of certain religious establishments. Some of that property belonged to citizens of France, England, and Spain. The three states based their claims on the principle of acquired rights. The Tribunal upheld the claims and ordered compensation.

There have been powerful attempts to expand the principle of acquired rights to include development agreements. These attempts have created community expectations and have been supported by authoritative decisions. They have tried to give a meaning to acquired rights as related to agreements different from acquired rights as related to property. This new meaning would seem to be something stronger than property rights, including a continuing performance that cannot unilaterally be changed.

In the *Norwegian Shipowners Claims*, the Tribunal observed that contract rights are proper subjects for the application of the principle of protection of acquired rights.[546] The PCIJ in the case of *Certain German Interests in Upper Silesia*, basing the recognition of acquired rights in general principles of law, stated: "[The] principle of respect for vested rights ... forms part of generally accepted international law, which, as regards this point, amongst others, constitutes the basis of the Geneva Convention."[547] The Romano-Hungarian Mixed Arbitral Tribunal held that the expro-

---

[544]G.A. Res. 388, 5 U.N. GAOR Supp. (No. 20) 18, U.N. Doc. No. A/1775 (195).

[545]1 R. INT'L ARB. AWARDS 7 (1920).

[546]1 R. INT'L ARB. AWARDS 307, 338 (1922).

[547][1926] P.C.I.J. ser. A, No. 7 at 22.

priating measure constituted "a violation of the general principle of respect for acquired right."[548] Similarly, an International Arbitral Tribunal in the *Goldenberg Case* held that "the respect of private and of acquired rights of aliens undoubtedly forms part of the general principles accepted by the law of nations."[549]

In the *Aramco Arbitration*, where the Tribunal found that the law governing performance was international law, it was decided that a government had the power to enter into a long-term agreement and did not have the right unilaterally to alter or terminate such agreement: "Nothing can prevent a State, in the exercise of its sovereignty, from granting to the concessionaire irretractable rights. Such rights have the character of acquired rights. . . ."[550] The same view was expressed in the *Sapphire* case, in which the Tribunal recognized that respect for acquired rights under a concession is one aspect of the general principles of law recognized by international tribunals.[551] In some municipal laws, such as those of the United States, the principle of sanctity of contract made between private parties and the government has been recognized. On this point Hyde states: "The principle of the sanctity of contract when it meets the reserved powers of government to alter or terminate under the power of eminent domain or to regulate under the police power will be carefully weighed by a judicial tribunal. The sanctity of the contract is not absolute, but it is not lightly to be disturbed, not without a showing of a reasonable and non-discriminatory exercise of governmental power."[552]

The principle of acquired rights, as has been shown, arose in international relations expressly to protect the private property of

[548]*See* U.N. Doc A/AC.97/5 (1972) at 244.

[549]Affaire Goldenberg (Germany v. Rumania) 2 R. Int'l. Arb Awards 901, 909 (1928). Similar assertions have been made in a number of authoritative decisions. *See, e.g.*, German Settlers Case [1923] P.C.I.J. ser. B, No. 6; the Peter Parmany University Case, [1933] P.C.I.J., ser. A/B No. 61; British Claims in the Spanish Zone of Morocco, (Great Britain v. Spain) 2 R. Int'l. Arb. Awards 615 (1925); The Sopron-Kosseq Local Railway Company Case, 5 Ann. Dig. 57 (1929); the George Hopkins Claim (United States v. Mexico) UNITED STATES–MEXICO GENERAL CLAIMS COMMISSION, OPINIONS OF COMMISSIONERS 42 (1927) *reprinted* in BRIGGS, *supra* note 410, at 204; Lunch v. United States, 292 U.S. 571, 576–77, 579 (1933); and Brooks-Scandon Corp. v. United States, 265 U.S. 106 (1923).

[550]Aramco Arbitration Award (International Arbitral Tribunal Comm. Print) at 61.

[551]35 I.L.R. 136, 183–84 (1963).

[552]*See* Hyde, *supra* note 330, at 305. For other countries, see Articles 1 and 4 of the Final Title of the Swiss Civil Code; Art. 5, Austrian Civil Code; Art. 2, French Civil Code.

foreigners. Otherwise acquired rights in international law are comparable to rights of property in national law. The reason for changing the terms (from property to acquired rights) is solely to create a form of argument that avoids the controversial question of property.

Private property is a controversial notion in law. The basic notion behind the law of property, that every human being has a right to property, has been recognized in general principles of law. But the detailed content of, and the limitations upon, property rights are uncertain and largely dependent upon political and social vagaries. Section I of the Soviet Civil Code provides that "the law protects private rights except as they are exercised in contradiction to their social and economic purpose."[553] This provision introduces the basic limitation on private property. The involvement of governments in economic areas, either through direct participation or for guiding the economic process, has created problems of definition for private property and its limitation. This was the problem that the European Convention on Human Rights in 1950 faced in Rome. States were unable to agree "either on the definition of private property or even, so it seems, on the principle of respect for property. This important lacuna in the Treaty had to be filled later, at least in part, by the additional protocol of March 20, 1952."[554] The Convention gives protection to property through its First Protocol. Article I of the Protocol states that the protection given to property rights is to be subject to the conditions provided by the general principles of international law.[555] The Convention also expressed a relatively unclear statement as to protection of private property. It was to avoid such problems that the concept of acquired rights was developed. This concept expresses, in factual terms, the view that a sovereign state does not have to make any agreements with private foreign entities; if, however, the state of its own accord has made such an agreement, it is obligated to respect the agreement and cannot unilaterally change or terminate the agreement. This agreement, it is said, creates acquired rights for the foreigner and protects the property rights

---

[553] *See* JENKS, *supra* note 514, at 154.

[554] *See* Lalive, *The Doctrine of Acquired Rights*, in SELECTED READINGS, *supra* note 243, at 148.

[555] *See* AMERASINGHE, *supra* note 220, at 5.

of the foreign entity against a state with limited or no respect for private property. In this sense acquired rights are more extensive than property rights.

In our view, however, acquired rights should be treated the same as property rights. This concept should not be developed so as to present an unlimited and a mystical right for the interests of private entities. No concept, not even that of acquired rights, should be permitted to limit the power of the state to take certain measures in protection of the essential national interest of its people. Mann, in arguing that not every legislation which changes the property rights of aliens is unlawful, writes that "[g]eneral legislation passed for the protection of public health, public safety or general welfare, *i.e.*, for purposes falling within the police power as known to American Constitutional Law, cannot ever involve the taking of property, because no person has a vested right in any general rule of law or policy of legislation entitling him to insist that it shall remain unchanged for his benefit."[556] Mann actually argues that it is legislative intent that determines a law's legitimacy in international law. The goals and motives of the legislation may, however, be themselves vague and uncertain, giving no practical help in identification of the common interest (for example, the problem of what is and who determines the scopes of "public purpose" or "public welfare"). In order to specify the scope and validity of action taken by contracting states which interferes with the rights of a private party to enjoy the contract, a contextual analysis should be employed in examination of many relevant factors. The appropriate criteria for guiding this examination are best found in the minimum standard of protection of property rights of aliens embodied in Article XVII of the Universal Declaration of Human Rights of 1948 and an emerging body of international agreements.[557]

ii. Promise Not to Terminate Agreement

It has been argued that the principle of sanctity of contract becomes stronger when the state grantor promises not to terminate

---

[556] MANN, *supra* note 268, at 317.

[557] HUMAN RIGHTS, DECLARATION, *supra* note 417, at 2. The World Bank has also formulated a convention on the Settlement of Investment Disputes.

the agreement with the private party. It is assumed that such a promise creates a firmer expectation in the parties about the performance of the agreement. The practical impact of such a promise is not, however, yet clear.

In national decision processes, the theory that a state cannot be bound not to change its law has been rejected. In the United States case of *Chicago and Alton Railroad Co. v. Transbarger*, the Court held that the power of the state to regulate for general benefit is paramount and "inalienable even by express grants."[558] A similar decision is *Pennsylvania Hospital v. Philadelphia*,[559] where the 1854 Pennsylvania State legislature promised that no streets would be constructed on the property of plaintiff hospital without the consent of the hospital authorities. In 1913, however, the government revoked its promise. The hospital claimed a violation of the agreement, and the Court upheld the competency of the government to change the law. Justice White wrote that "the power of eminent domain was inherently governmental in character and too essential for the public welfare that it was not susceptible of being abridged by agreement."[560] In this case it was not even suggested that the hospital should be compensated because its expectation under the promise was disappointed. However, it is the French practice to compensate for lost profits when expectations of nontermination have been created by the government.[561]

The response of international decision makers to such government promises is not quite clear. In the *George W. Cook Case*[562] the legislature of the State of Guadalajara, Mexico, granted the claimant a certain tax exemption on real estate. The legislature's promise was unilateral, it was not part of the agreement, and the claimant had not relied on the promise to his detriment. Subsequently a tax was imposed. The Tribunal dismissed the claim on the grounds that the exemption had not covered the tax complained of. But it was clear from the opinion that the outcome

[558] 238 U.S. 67, 76 (1914).

[559] 245 U.S. 20 (1917).

[560] *Id.* at 22. On the power of the Congress to terminate agreements, *see* J. MITCHELL, CONTRACTS OF PUBLIC AUTHORITY 144–61 (1954).

[561] AMERICAN BAR ASSOCIATION, THE PROTECTION OF PRIVATE PROPERTY INVESTED ABROAD 83 (1963).

[562] George W. Cook Case, (United States v. Mexico), 4 R. Int'l Arb. Awards 593 (1930).

would have been the same if the tax under consideration had been covered by the government promise: "The right of the State to levy taxes constitutes an inherent part of its sovereignty; it is a function necessary to its very existence and it has often been alleged . . . [that States] cannot legally create exemptions which restrict the free exercise of the sovereign power of the State in this regard."[563] In the Anglo-Iranian concession agreement of 1933, Article 21 was a promise not to terminate the concession until December 31, 1933.[564] Before the ICJ, the British argued that Iran lacked competence to terminate the concession and that the government promise made a "difference of a most substantial and decisive character in the realm of international law."[565] The British argued that the lawfulness of a normal concession termination "may be a matter of dispute, but there is . . . no room at all for controversy in relation to a case in which the State in question has expressly renounced such power of legislative action." Moreover, they emphasized that a promise not to terminate the agreement created expectations essential in making the agreement. Of course, the British argument is not supported by any authoritative decisions. The International Court of Justice did not pass any judgment on the merits of this case, but the argument of the British government was rejected in the District Court of Tokyo in Japan. There, the Court held that the promise not to terminate did not change the nature of the contract, which was a private agreement and could be expropriated by the municipal law of Iran.[566]

The Anglo-Iranian case was settled through diplomatic negotiations between the two governments with the involvement of the United States. One observer stated that the government promise not to terminate the agreement strengthens the bargaining position of the grantee in such diplomatic negotiations.[567] Moreover, as another observer stated, the compensation that the Company received through direct capital and the new favorable concession

[563] *Id.* at 595.

[564] For the text see Anglo-Iranian Oil Co. case, (United Kingdom v. Iran) [1952] I.C.J. 20, 31.

[565] *Id.* at 87–88.

[566] Anglo-Iranian Oil v. Idemitsu Kosan Kabushiki Kaisha, 20 I.L.R. 305, 310 (1953).

[567] K. Baldus, *International Law and Termination of Concession Agreements*, 153 (1964) (unpublished paper in the Yale Law School Library).

was more than what was estimated at the time of nationalization.[568] The settlement of the Anglo-Iranian case was, however, purely a political bargain.[569] The promise not to terminate the agreement could have held little relevance or importance in the content or settlement of the agreement.

This uncertainty as to the impact of the government promise not to terminate the agreement unilaterally can also be observed among the publicists. Some believe that such a promise makes a difference in reparation; it supports either the claim for specific performance, a demand for restitution,[570] or an equivalent monetary compensation.[571] On the other hand a number of publicists support the view that the state generally is competent to terminate and that a promise not to terminate effects no change in the competence of the State.[572] Mann denies any effect of such promise on the agreement: "The truth is that even in international law the express exemption from the efforts of future legislation is redundant. Such exemption cannot and ought not to preclude the genuine exercise of the State's political power. On the other hand, where, in substance the state takes property without compensation, its international liability is engaged even in the absence of the clause."[573] Fatouros supports Mann's argument and adds: "The central issue is whether the undeniable difference in content between specific promises of special treatment and other contractual promises is sufficient to warrant the application of widely different legal rules in the two cases. It is submitted that there is no compelling reason for accepting that the existing difference is of such a high order of importance."[574] Domke expresses a totally different view. He argues that the government commitment is binding,

[568]B. SHWADRAN, THE MIDDLE EAST, OIL AND THE GREAT POWERS 149–88 (1955).

[569]*See* FATEMI, note 488 *supra.*

[570]G. WHITE, NATIONALISATION OF FOREIGN PROPERTY 177–78 (1961).

[571]THE PROTECTION OF PRIVATE PROPERTY INVESTED ABROAD, *supra* note 561 at 88.

[572]"Even the kind of impact of such a promise on compensation is not clear. White believes that the State's promise represents acceptance on the part of the state to limit its sovereignty, and according to principle, reparation for an unlawful act should take the form of restitution or an equivalent monetary compensation. In the observance of authority it is not possible to state whether an international court would grant restitution on such a case, but the protecting State would be quite justified in requesting this remedy." *Id.* at 178.

[573]MANN, *supra* note 287, at 208.

[574]FATOUROS, *supra* note 208, at 342.

whether or not there is an explicit statement concerning this binding character.[575]

The uncertainty over this issue is, furthermore, reflected in a vote on the subject at a 1952 meeting of the Institute de Droit International.[576] In a vote taken on a proposal that nationalization in violation of express or implied undertaking be declared unlawful, there were 16 votes for, 20 against and 22 abstentions.[577] Because of this lack of consensus, it is difficult to ascertain actual community expectations. Recent developments among capital-exporting and capital-importing countries have increased the difficulty in foreseeing the direction of future decisions. In the November 1974 draft resolution on the Economic Rights and Duties of States,[578] 104 countries adopted the absolute right of state sovereignty over natural resources, including a right to exercise authority based on national objectives and priorities over foreign investments within a state's jurisdiction. In the Charter as a whole the demand for honoring unilateral termination of agreement is clear; therefore in this context it makes no difference whether there has been a promise not to terminate the agreement. The trends of past decisions and the opinion of many publicists do express the expectation that the promise not to terminate, as part of the concession, will probably make a difference in authoritative decisions. However, there is little clarity on what that difference or effect will be.

In our recommended policies, it may be recalled, commitments made freely that also protect the common interest should be performed compatibly with the expectation of the parties. Therefore, the reasonable expectations of the parties created under the agreement should be honored. In situations where an agreement does not secure the common interest because of conflict with the national interest of the grantor, its termination is inevitable. The only difference that the promise not to terminate the agreement may have is in the amount of compensation, when such promise creates reasonable expectations in the grantee as to significant difference

[575] Domke, *Foreign Nationalizations—Some Aspect of Contemporary International Law*, 55 AM. J. INT'L L. 593–94 (1961).

[576] *Cited in* FATOUROS *supra* note 208, at 342.

[577] *Id.*, n.9.

[578] U.N. Doc. No. A/C.2/L.1386 (1974).

in the pattern, amount, or other important features of the invest-ment.

c. The Process of Change

Our basic policies regarding the process of agreement seek a bal-ance between the protection of stability of expectation by securing the performance of commitment and limiting the protection of shared expectation in order to protect the common interest. Our conception of human dignity, therefore, respects and creates op-portunity for modification and innovation. An agreement is a pro-cess involving shared expectations. The expectation of the parties may change in this process. Shared expectations may change for different reasons, and in some situations this change may have a major effect upon the aggregate common interest. Thus the poli-cies regarding change in the process of agreement are as impor-tant as the policies regarding enforcement. The adjustment and accommodation of these two policies is the task of the decision maker.

Where the parties substantially agree on the change, deference should be given to their shared expectation. In this respect the decision maker should consider the impact of changed shared ex-pectations of the parties on the inclusive interest of the larger community. When the parties do not agree on the change, the decision maker should accommodate the shared perspectives of the parties or their closest approximation within the realm of basic community policy about stability and change. To this end, the de-cision maker first should determine the closest approximation to the expectation of the parties under the changed situation and, second, should determine the option in decision that protects and increases the aggregate flow of values. In such a situation the de-cision maker should evaluate the costs and benefits to each of the parties and to the larger community based on the options pro-posed by each party and, also, consider any other options which may be open. In short, the decision maker should project that future relationship between the parties that best secures the ac-commodation of mutual exclusive interests of the parties in com-patibility with the inclusive interest of the larger community of which the parties are members.

The issue of state responsibility for unilateral termination of agreement is as yet unsettled. This issue in recent years has been met with new demands for substantial changes. The unilateral termination of agreement may occur when there is little change in context or when there is much change in context. By *context* is meant the various phases of social interaction, which include participants, perspectives, situations, base values, strategies, and outcomes. One of the characteristics of the world community is continuous change; therefore, the context of social interaction is also in a continuous state of change. By *unilateral termination* when there is little change in context we refer to claims arising from a unilateral termination regardless of any changes in context. On the other hand, there may be claims arising from a unilateral termination when the changes in context form the main basis for claims under the doctrine of *rebus sic stantibus*.

i. Unilateral Termination Without Regard to Change in Context

(a) *State Competence in Unilateral Termination.* The history of the competency of a state to terminate agreements unilaterally exhibits various changes in attitude. The conditioning factors of these changes can be explained in terms of variations and changes in the whole world social process and the contemporary global interdependency, which creates new demands.[579]

There were practically no limits to the state's competence to nationalize foreign private property, according to authoritative decisions, until the late nineteenth century.[580] Until the 1930s, when

---

[579]There are two contending views as to when state responsibility comes into existence. Some argue that state responsibility appears after unilateral termination by the Government. On the other hand, there are those who argue that state responsibility as to unilateral termination does not come into effect immediately after state termination, but may be enacted in the subsequent behavior of the state with regard to foreign nationals. The difference between the two arguments is that in the former the concessionaire does not have to exhaust local remedies before claiming state responsibility, while in the latter the concessionaire has to exhaust local remedies, and if there was a denial of justice then there is a claim for the international responsibility of states. Without delving into any theoretical discussion about the defects of these doctrines, in international law we consider cases which assumed local remedies were either not enough or were not required to be exhausted before consideration in international adjudication.

For discussion of the view that the state is responsible immediately after termination of an agreement, see OPPENHEIM, *supra* note 112, at 345; Carlston, *Concession Agreements and Nationalization*, 52 AM. J. INT'L. L. 260 (1958); Jennings, *State Contracts in International Law*, 37 BRIT. Y.B. INT'L L. 156 (1961); Schwebel, *International Protection of Contractual Arrangements*, 53 ASIL PROCS. (1959); and INT'L L. ASSOC. REPORT OF THE FORTY-EIGHTH CONFERENCE (NEW YORK) 161 (1958). For additional citations, see BROWNLIE, *supra* note 286, at

the unilateral termination of agreements was first characterized as unlawful, the competence of the state to terminate unilaterally was recognized.[581] In the Great Depression the competency of a state came into question and there were increasing demands for the performance of agreements.[582] As it will be demonstrated in the trend study, authoritative decisions have generally refused to address themselves to the question of unilateral termination by the state and dealt instead with questions of compensation. However, since the 1950s there has been an increasing demand to create authority for the theory that denies state competence for unilateral termination.[583] These attempts have been met in recent years by a counterreaction on the part of capital-importing countries that includes demands for the expansion of exclusive authority in the nation-state not only for termination but even for the determination of compensation.[584]

Since the twentieth century, because of the important role of commodities in the international economic and political structure, there has been an increasing tendency and desire on the part of developed countries to encourage foreign investment and to protect their interests in case of disputes through diplomatic and other procedures. Thus the contest between the rights of the foreign investor and the competency of the host country over the unilateral termination of agreements becomes more intense.

We disagree with jurists who try wholly to deny the competency of states for the unilateral termination of agreements. In the pres-

---

530; V. HECKE, PROBLEMS JURIDIQUES DES EMPRUNTS INTERNATIONAUX 279–80 (1955); EAGLETON, *supra* note 422, at 165–66; HYDE, *supra* note 112, at 988, 989, 990–91, and MANN, *supra* note 287, at 311–12 nn. 4&5, 312 n.6.

[580] Baldus, *supra* note 547, at 42. Secretary of State Buchanan clarified U.S. foreign policy in 1848 as to noninterference in the nationalization of development agreements to which American nationals are party. He emphasized that the United States Government is not a "collection agency." He pointed out that the American citizen will assume the risk of entering in any agreement with foreign governments. 6 MOORE, *supra* note 133, at 708–09.

[581] *Id.* at 43.

[582] *Id.*

[583] *See* Domke, *Foreign Nationalizations*, 55 AM. J. INT'L L. 266 (1959). *See also* Carlston, *supra* note 579, at 260; Kissam and Leach, note 528, *supra*, and Schwebel, *supra* note 579, at 266–7.

[584] These new demands have been presented by developing countries in the United Nations. They are contained essentially in two Resolutions, G.A. Res. 3171 and G.A. Res. 3281; see notes 394 and 395 and accompanying text, *supra*.

ent world, with unequal distribution of power and enlightenment, the state should have competency to terminate agreements as to resources physically located within its territory when it considers such termination conducive to the national interest. Such competency might be an instrument for the accommodation of conflicting exclusive and inclusive interests if limited by requirement of appropriate compensation for the nationalized property and other interests. As we will see, this policy has been expressed in authoritative decisions. In response to the allegations that such a policy will discourage foreign investment, we answer that appropriate expectations about protection of foreign investment will be created by international response to unilateral termination as well as compensation for the confiscated property. This alternative is certainly preferable to the mere unrecompensed nationalization of property by the state. The alternative of specific performance would appear unreal in the contemporary world.

A number of authoritative decisions indicate that the community expectation up to the early twentieth century was that a nation-state had the competence to terminate development agreements, but that no reason could justify the refusal to pay compensation.[585] A case representing such expectation during that period is the *Delagoa Bay* case. Here, the Portuguese government terminated an agreement with an Anglo-American company that had a concession to build and operate a railroad in Africa for thirty-five years. The British government objected to this action and denied the Portuguese right to cancel the concession. However, the British said: "If the Portuguese government admit their liability to compensate . . . Her Majesty's Government will admit

---

[585]*See* The Henry W. Thurston case (U.S. v. Dominican Republic) (1895) *reprinted in* 6 MOORE, *supra* note 133, at 729–30; The I.L. Cherry Case (U.S. v. Columbia) (1897), M. WHITEMAN, DAMAGES IN INTERNATIONAL LAW 1714 (1943); The May case (U.S. v. Guatemala) (1900), WHITEMAN at 1708; Salvador Commercial Company (U.S. v. Salvador) (1902), WHITEMAN, at 1680. In the last case, though the arbitrators found that the concession "was arbitrary and unjustly revoked, destroyed and cancelled," only compensation was required. *Accord*, Lorenzo A. Oliva (Italy v. Venezuela) (1903), reprinted in J. RALSTON, VENEZUELAN ARBITRATIONS (1904) at 780; The Henry F. Rudloff (U.S. v. Venezuela) (1903), RALSTON at 194; The Company General of the Orinoco (France v. Venezuela) (1905), WHITEMAN at 1690. In the latter case, the Umpire held that while the government of Venezuela had the sovereign right to terminate the agreement, it violated the agreement and therefore compensation should be paid. *Accord*, George Emery Co. (U.S. v. Nicaragua) (1909), WHITEMAN at 1643–45. *See also* Indemnity Case (Russia v. Turkey), Judgment of Nov. 11, 1912, Hague Ct. Rep. (Scott) 315 (Perm. Ct. Arb. 1912).

that the amount of that compensation is a proper matter for arbitration."[586] A similar position was taken by the U.S. government.[587] After negotiation the task of the arbitrator was fixed simply to determine the "just" compensation for the Portuguese action.[588] The Tribunal was not assigned the task of dealing with the competency of the Portuguese government unilaterally to terminate the agreement. It was nevertheless obvious from the opinion that the Tribunal had no objection to the termination so long as compensation was provided:

> Whether one would, indeed, brand the action of the government as an arbitrary and despoiling measure or as a sovereign act prompted by reasons of state which always prevails over any railway concession, or even if the present case should be regarded as one of legal expropriation, the fact remains that the effect was to dispossess private persons from their rights and privileges of a private nature conferred upon them by the concession, and that in the absence of legal provisions to the contrary—none of which has been alleged to exist in this case— the State which is the author of such dispossession is bound to make full reparation for the injury done by it.[589]

As seen from the diplomatic communications and the decision of the Tribunal, the competence of the Portuguese government was not really challenged so long as the government provided compensation.

The competence of states to terminate agreements unilaterally was clearly recognized in the *Shufeldt*[590] case of 1930. This case involved the unilateral termination of a ten-year development agreement by the government of Guatemala. The arbitrator held that "it is perfectly competent for the Government of Guatemala to enact any decree they like and for any reasons they see fit, and such reasons are no concern of this Tribunal. But this Tribunal is only concerned where such decision, passed even on the best of

---

[586] Delagoa Bay and East African Railway Co., 3, WHITEMAN *id.* at 1694; *reprinted in* McNair, *The Seizure of Property and Enterprises in Indonesia*, 6 NETHERLANDS INT'L L.J. 224–25 (1959).

[587] McNair, *id.* at 224.

[588] WHITEMAN, *supra* note 585, at 1695.

[589] *Id.* at 1698.

[590] The Shufeldt Claim (U.S. v. Guatemala) (1930), 2 R. INT'L ARB. AWARDS, 1079.

grounds, works injustice to an alien subject, in which case the Government ought to make compensation for the injury inflicted and cannot invoke any municipal law to justify their refusal to do so."[591] From the early twentieth century onward, there was a change in the nature of the demands which some authoritative decisions tended to support. These new demands do not alter the general community expectation of recognition of state competence over unilateral termination of agreements when appropriate compensation is paid. It can, however, be observed that some recent reactions by capital-importing countries are explainable as response to such demands.

The new demands challenge state competence for the unilateral termination of development agreements. They insist upon specific performance, and heavy compensation. Along with this demand there has been another moderate demand supported by authoritative decisions that tend to limit rather than invalidate the competence of states in unilateral termination. These limitations mainly concern compensation. In the following pages we will trace the development of these two trends.

In an attempt by the League of Nations to codify international law, the Guerrero Report, adopted by the Committee of Experts for the Progressive Codification of International Law in 1926, stated in Article 2(3): "A State is responsible for damages incurred by a foreigner attributable to an act contrary to international law or to an omission of an act which State was bound under international law to perform."[592] This Article, without addressing itself to the problem of competence, considers the state liable for compensation. This was the policy adopted by the PCIJ in the *Chorzow Factory Case*, in which the Court held: "It is a principle of international law that the reparation of a wrong may consist in an indemnity corresponding to the damage which the nationals of the injured State have suffered as a result of the act which is contrary to international law. This is even the most usual form of reparation. . . . "[593] The opinion in the *Lena Goldfields Case* also represents this policy. This case involved the nationalization by the U.S.S.R. of the prop-

[591] *Id.* at 1095.

[592] *Id.*

[593] [1928] P.C.I.J. Ser. A, No. 17 at 27–28.

erty of a British firm which had a concession for fifty years. The nationalization was taken by the U.S.S.R. after the first five-year development plan. The arbitrators, without questioning the competence of the Soviet government to terminate unilaterally, awarded compensation: "the conduct of the Government was a breach of the contract going to the root of it. In consequence Lena is entitled to be relieved from the burden of further obligations thereunder and to be compensated in money for the value of the benefit of which it had been wrongfully deprived."[594]

Similar policies have been followed by most capital-importing countries, either explicitly or implicitly in their unilateral prescriptions. Thus, the government of Nepal expressly stated that nationalization of industry is not the policy of the government, but if for reasons of overriding public purpose an industry is nationalized, full compensation will be granted.[595] An Egyptian spokesman stated the policy of his government:

> Foreign investment will not be subject to sequestration, nationalization, nor expropriation except in cases involving the national interest, and then fair compensation must be paid. The amount of the compensation shall be estimated within six months. The amount of compensation shall be transferred in the same currency as that in which the investment was originally made, and in annual installments not exceeding five years. Disagreement about the amount of the compensation shall be resolved by arbitration.[596]

Indonesia in its Petroleum Legislation No. 44 (1960) created an encouraging atmosphere for foreign investors: "Economic incentives should be introduced to enable Indonesia to attract foreign companies to operate under the conditions of the law and at the same time to safeguard the national interest."[597] Similar policies

---

[594] Nussbaum, *The Arbitration Between the Lena Goldfields Ltd. and the Soviet Government*, 36 Cornell L.Q. 31, 51 (1950).

[595] Dep't of State Press Release No. 270, of May 17, 1960, *cited in* Domke, Selected Readings, *supra* note 243, at 315.

[596] Address by A. M. Kaissouni, American-Arab Association for Industry and Commerce Meeting in New York, Nov. 3, 1971, *cited in* Mikdashi, *supra* note 229, at 299.

[597] U.N., *Proceedings of the Seminar on Petroleum Legislation with Particular Reference to Off-shore Operations*, U.N. Mineral Resources Development Ser. No. 40, U.N. Doc. E/CN. 11/1052 (1972) at 95.

are presented in the investment laws or in the constitutions of a number of other countries.[598] Such moderate positions may not explicitly express limitations upon the competence of a state on unilateral termination, but nevertheless imply such recognition on the part of governments.

Along with this trend there grew an opposing demand for specific performance that challenged the competence of states for unilateral termination. This demand was initiated by the British government in the Anglo-Persian disputes of 1932.[599] The government of Iran (then Persia) claimed that the agreement did not serve the economic interest of Iran but that the government was willing to negotiate the agreement; otherwise, it would cancel the existing agreement with the British government. Although this case was similar to the *Lena Goldfields* case, here the British government denied the right of the Persian government unilaterally to terminate the agreement.[600] The British government brought the dispute before the Council of the League of Nations. But a new agreement between the two governments left no reason for any decision by the Council. A similar claim was made by the Swiss government in the *Losinger Case*.[601] This case arose because of the effect of a Yugoslav law on a development agreement made between Yugoslavia and a Swiss firm. The arbitration clause of the development agreement had provided for arbitration in the case of dispute, but under the new law all claims against the government were to be presented before the ordinary courts of Yugoslavia. Looking to this law, the arbitrator refused to hear the case.

---

[598] Fiji stated its policy requirements for foreign investment in developing natural resources: "Guarantees of *Stability* of Concession terms over an adequate period, including guarantees as to stabilize of the overall incidence of tax and guarantees against *unilateral action* on the part of the Government to vary the terms of the concession agreement." Law of 1971, *cited in id.* at 90, (emphasis supplied). For the Philippines, see *id.* at 109–10 and Thailand Law of 1971, *id.* at 118–20. The Constitution of Nigeria of 1960 stated that no interest in property "[s]hall be acquired compulsory in any part of Nigeria, except by or under the provisions of a law that: (a) requires the payment of adequate compensation therefore; and (b) gives to any person claiming such compensation a right of access, for the determination of his interest in the property and the amount of compensation, to the High Court having jurisdiction in that part of Nigeria." *Cited in* Domke, note 595, *supra; see also* Ghana's 1960 Constitution Art. 13(1), in *id.*

[599] *See* SHWADRAN, *supra* note 568, at 42.

[600] *Id.* at 44.

[601] [1936] P.C.I.J. Ser. A/B No. 67. A position similar to that of the Swiss agreement was made by France in the *Norwegian Loan Case*, 2 I.C.J. Pleadings (1957) at 61, 63, 181, 182.

The Swiss government, in a memorial filed with the PCIJ, denied the right of Yugoslavia to such termination. But before any decision was reached the parties settled the dispute.

Czechoslovakia v. Radio Corporation of America was the first authoritative decision to support the claim denying the right of a state to unilateral termination of an agreement. The Tribunal there held that the fact that the state did not achieve its expectations of profit was insufficient reason for releasing the state from its obligation under the concession agreement.[602] Nevertheless, the Tribunal stated that if a state could show that the issue at stake was of vital importance to the public interest, state competence for unilateral termination would be recognized.[603] However, in such cases termination "should only be possible subject to compensation to the other party."[604]

Two other leading cases on the unilateral termination of agreements in which such competence was denied by the states of the concessionaire but never went to decision are the *Anglo-Iranian* case of 1951[605] and the nationalization of the *Suez Canal* of 1956.[606]

The Anglo-Iranian case involved the Iranian unilateral termination of a sixty-year oil agreement with the Anglo-Iranian oil company. The government rejected the request for arbitration and set up a national board to determine the appropriate compensation.[607] The British government challenged the lawfulness of the nationalization mainly because of Iran's express renunciation of the right to unilateral termination.[608] Since there was no sign of reconciliation in spite of the political maneuvers, the British gov-

[602] 30 Am. J. Int'l L. 523, 534 (1936).

[603] *Id.* at 531.

[604] *Id.*

[605] Anglo-Iranian Oil Co. Case (U.K. v. Iran), Request for the Indication of Interim Measures of Protection (1951), I.C.J. Report 1 and Request for Indication of Jurisdiction, (1952) I.C.J. Report 1.

[606] *See* Bowie, note 133, *supra*; see also W. Rostow, Diplomatic Patchwork: The U.S. and the Settlement at Suez 1956–57 (1972); Delson, *Nationalization of the Suez Canal,* 57 Colum. L. Rev. 755 (1957); Huang, *Some International and Legal Aspects of the Suez Canal Question,* 51 Am. J. Int'l L. 277 (1957).

[607] *See* Iranian Nationalization Decree of May 1, 1951.

[608] *See* British Memorial, [1956] I.C.J. at 12–18. The British Government, however, challenged the legality of the Iranian nationalization on the basis of "prompt, effective" compensation. *See Id.* at 29, 30.

ernment filed a memorial with the International Court of Justice. The Court denied jurisdiction over the case, because the agreement was not within the meaning of the Iranian Declaration of October 2, 1930, referring to the jurisdiction of the ICJ. It has been suggested that even if the ICJ had heard the merits, it would have held merely for fair compensation. In other words, there was no expectation that the ICJ would have denied the competence of Iran for unilateral termination.[609]

The competence of the Egyptian government was also challenged in the nationalization of the Suez Canal. In this case, however, the objection was mainly based on the assumption that the special geographical situation of the Suez Canal foreclosed the Egyptian government's ability to nationalize the Canal Company.[610] No international tribunal made any decision on this case; eventually there was an agreement between the parties for compensation.[611]

The decision by the arbitrators in the case of *Saudi Arabia v. Arabian American Oil Company (Aramco)*[612] is an exceptional case that supports the demands for invalidation of state competence in unilateral termination. It is an exceptional case because of the unusual factual circumstances, because it does not reflect community expectations created by other decisions, and, finally, because in the merits of the decision there is a failure on the part of the arbitrator to accommodate the conflicting interests of the parties involved.

The government of Saudi Arabia granted a sixty-year oil lease to Aramco in 1933. In this long-term agreement there was an arrangement for the transport of oil to foreign markets by Aramco. In 1954 the government of Saudi Arabia granted a right of transport to Aristotle S. Onassis, which included some limited amounts of oil produced by Aramco. Aramco, however, denied the competence of the government of Saudi Arabia to enter into a new agreement with Onassis on the grounds that the government

---

[609] *See* Baldus, *supra* note 567, at 64. Baldus based his conclusion mainly on the *American Journal of International Law* editorial written by Pitman Potter, which indicated that even if Iran accepted the Court's jurisdiction, "there do not promise to emerge any very novel or sensational legal principles or rulings. There might indeed evaluate a decision in favor of fair compensation for nationalized property, . . . " 47 Am. J. Int'l L. 114, 115 (1953).

[610] Huang, *supra* note 606, at 286–87.

[611] 54 Am. J. Int'l L. 498 (1960).

[612] 27 I.L.R. 117 (1958).

by the 1933 agreement granted an exclusive right of transport to Aramco. This case is not very broadly construable; what is at stake in this case is only a part of the concession rather than the whole concession. It is different from the Anglo-Iranian oil case or the Suez Canal case, in which was involved the operation of the entire concession. It is interesting to see that, in this respect, the case's degree of comprehensiveness is similar to that of *Czechoslovakia v. Radio Corporation of America*. In the RCA case, as mentioned before, there was the claim that the second agreement of the Czech government interfered with RCA's exclusive right. But in that case there was no unilateral termination to cancel the whole concession with RCA.

The limited factual situation in the Aramco case makes it difficult to compare or apply the decision rejecting state competence for unilateral termination to other cases which involve an entire agreement.

The Aramco opinion does not really represent general community expectations as represented in other authoritative decisions and state practice. After the Second World War there was a series of nationalizations of private property in many countries in Europe, including England, and in other parts of the world. These nationalizations created certain community expectations as to the possibility of state involvement in economic areas, accompanied by nationalization of some private property. These expectations were supported by the emergence and development of new views about the economic and political structure and function of nation-states. In addition to the famous Anglo-Iranian and Suez Canal cases where the attempt to invalidate the states' competence over unilateral termination had failed and states resolved their controversies with compensation agreements, there was further reciprocal interaction of nation-states and international organizations. Another example of a contemporary community's expectations is found in the reaction of the U.S. government to the nationalization of the United Fruit Company's property by the Guatemala government. The United States government in a diplomatic exchange with the government of Guatemala insisted that Guatemala could not avoid its international responsibility, but did not deny competence for unilateral termination; it demanded only fair and just compensation:

> The Government of the United States does not controvert in the slightest the proposition that the Act of Congress of the Republic

of Guatemala ... constitutes an act of sovereignty inherent in Guatemala. Every act of the Guatemala Government constitutes a sovereign act, as do the acts of every other sovereign Government, including threats of the Government of the United States. But to state that no sovereign act of Government affecting foreign states or their nationals is open to discussion, or question, as to its validity under international law, because it is a sovereign act, is to say that states are not subject to international law. One has only to look at the diplomatic records of any Government over any period of time to see that such sovereign acts are constantly discussed and held up to scrutiny by other members of the family of nations with whom they treat for determination as to whether they measure up to or fall below the standards required under international law.

The obligation of a state imposed by international law to pay just or fair compensation at the time of taking of property of foreigners cannot be abrogated from the international standpoint by local legislation. If the contrary were true, states seeking to avoid the necessity of making payment for property expropriated from foreign nationals could avoid all pecuniary responsibility simply by changing their local law. Every international obligation could thus be wiped off the books. But international law cannot thus be flouted. Membership in the family of nations imposes international obligations.[613]

The United States did not question the competence of the Guatemalan government to terminate but asked only for the performance of international obligation, which was described in the second paragraph as the payment of "just or fair compensation."

In the light of these practices, the decision of the Aramco Tribunal does not represent community expectations. Some may question with George W. Rary whether diplomatic negotiations in the settlement of disputes arising from nationalization of foreign properties create international law. Rary has written:

[O]ften, disputes over states taking an alien's property are settled by diplomatic means. In doctrinaire writings, therefore, the law frequently gets confused with diplomatic expediency. It has been stated, for example, that an overwhelming majority of writers have concluded that the taking of property of an alien by a State is neither legally nor morally wrong, and that only the failure to

---

[613] 29 Dep't State Bull. Sept. 1953 at 358, 360 (emphasis supplied).

compensate the alien is wrong. This is an example of such confusion, and, in my opinion does not state the law.[614]

One who shares this view might not consider the process of conciliation in the Anglo-Iranian or Suez Canal case or the United States statement to the Government of Guatemala as reflecting community expectations about the competence of states over the unilateral termination of agreements. In their view only decisions taken by organized international tribunals are reflective of international law.

This misconception of international law has been criticized by Baldus. He states that "[w]hile [Rary's] idea of what the law is may be useful as a strategy, it gives us very little inkling of what future authoritative decisions will be."[615] For realistic appreciation of what general community expectations are about any particular problem, a much broader perspective of the sources of such expectations is required. The relevant sources have been thus summarized:

> The peoples of the world communicate to each other expectations about policy, authority, and control, not merely through state or inter-governmental organs, but through reciprocal claims and mutual tolerances in all their interactions. The participants in the relevant processes of communication, the communicators and the communicatees, range through all degrees of specialization to the prescriptive function, from the most specialized to the least specialized, and include not merely the officials of states and intergovernmental organizations but also the representatives of political parties; pressure groups; and private associations and the individual human being, *qua* individual with all his identifications.[616]

---

[614]Ray, *Law Governing Contracts Between States and Foreign Nationals*, in Selected Readings, *supra* note 243, at 19.

[615]Baldus, *supra* note 567, at 74. Wetter, on the other hand, observes with regard to the role of American diplomacy in nationalization cases, that "[i]t would be unrealistic to say the least to consider . . . the extensive case law which has been created by the State Department in the course of this century as of minor interest. It would be more appropriate to recognize this same case law as the policy and practice of the United States Government and . . . thus to see the wide permissive limits of international law as it is handled from day to day in actual practice." Wetter, *Diplomatic Assistance to Private Investment: A Study of the Theory and Practice of the United States During the Twentieth Century*, 29 U. Chi. L. Rev. 309–10 (1962).

[616]McDougal, Lasswell & C. Reisman, Law Science and Policy *Materials* (unpublished material in the Yale Law School Library).

Diplomatic and private arrangements between states and private foreign entities regarding development agreements represent a method of communication and create community expectations about the termination problem, as do the decisions of international tribunals, bilateral and multilateral agreements, unilateral prescriptions, United Nations resolutions, and so forth. Diplomatic and private arrangements do have effect on future decisions and expectations regarding the settlement of disputes over development agreements.

The Aramco opinion failed effectively to accommodate the conflicting interests involved in that case. The Tribunal was so impressed by the concept of acquired rights that it observed that the only exception to acquired rights was the rule of "public policy":

> By reason of its very sovereignty within its territorial domain, the State possesses the legal power to grant rights which it forbids itself to withdraw before the end of the Concession, with the reservation of the Clauses of the Concession Agreement relating to its revocation. Nothing can prevent a State, in the exercise of its sovereignty, from forbidding itself irrevocably by the provisions of a concession and from granting to the Concessionaire irretractable rights. Such rights have the character of acquired rights. Should a new concession contract incompatible with the first, or a subsequent statute, abolish totally or partially that which has been granted by a previous law or concession, this could constitute a clear infringement, by the second contract, of acquired rights or a violation, by the subsequent statute, of the principle of non-retroactivity of laws, with the only exception of rules of public policy.[617]

In spite of the *RCA* opinion, which recognied the conflicting interests of the parties in a unilateral termination and explicitly stated the occasions where the state may terminate agreements, the Aramco opinion failed to recognize the exclusive interest of Saudi Arabia in this case; or if it did so recognize, it did not consider the interest important enough to make qualification in the opinion. The Tribunal did not consider that the right to control transport falls within the police power of the state and that the state has the competence to terminate any agreement inimical to interests protected by the police power, or that in cases not within the police power the state may provide compensation rather than fulfilling

---

[617] 27 I.L.R. at 168.

specific performance. Moreover, the opinion was so precisely stated against state competence in unilateral termination that it reflected the implication, as Baldus said, that "no state interest could justify a termination."[618] It is hard to understand what the Tribunal was trying to accomplish: perhaps the common interest in stabilization of expectations. But how could such stabilization be achieved when the interest of one party is not even taken into account? Baldus correctly observes that "[s]uch sweeping language could only be expected to harden the new nations to any compromise on the principle of absolute competence to terminate."[619]

As past trends have shown, a policy that does not represent community expectations and does not protect the common interest will not be respected in future practices. The Aramco opinion, which totally rejects state competence with regard to unilateral termination of development agreements, has not been followed in state practice or in other authoritative decisions. A few years after the Aramco case, the Indonesian Government nationalized the enterprises of the Dutch, their former colonial masters. The government of Indonesia appointed a national body to determine compensation.[620] This case was thus a clear rejection of a formulation adopted by Aramco in the practical relationships between states. The government of Indonesia did not agree to go to arbitration, but community expectation was expressed in subsequent decisions by a Dutch and German court. The decisions of these courts, which were similar to decisions of courts of Japan, Aden, and Italy concerning the 1951 Iranian nationalization, did not question the competence of states in unilateral termination. The District Court of Amsterdam in a dispute over the ownership of the tobacco coming from nationalized enterprises in Indonesia held that the nationalization was in violation of international law because of its discriminatory measure and failure to provide adequate compensation.[621] The German courts in a decision over a similar problem held that the nationalization was not in violation of international law since compensation had been provided.[622]

---

[618]Baldus, *supra* note 567, at 70.

[619]*Id.*

[620]Domke, "Indonesian Nationalization Measures," 54 AM. J. INT'L L. 306 (1960). For another analysis of Indonesian Nationalization, see McNair, *supra* note 586, at 218–56.

[621]Domke, *id.* at 308.

[622]*Id.* at 316–18.

Without evaluating these decisions in relation to discrimination or as to the adequacy of compensation, it is obvious that none of the decisions address themselves to the question of the competence of states in unilateral termination.

The inconsistency of the Aramco policy with community expectations is further shown in later decisions. The *Sapphire Case* offers another example of unilateral termination by the host government. In this case, however, neither the grantee nor the tribunal questioned the competence of the Iranian government in the unilateral termination. The claim of the concessionaire as well as the judgment concerned only compensation. In 1963 Argentina nationalized 14 foreign and domestic private oil companies. Again the demand and subsequent settlement only involved compensation.[623]

In the most recent case, which arose from the nationalization of the British Petroleum Company by Libya in 1971, B.P. claimed for specific performance, *i.e.*, invalidation of the competence of the Libyan government in unilateral termination. The Arbitral Tribunal, after considering carefully the status of specific performance and *restitutio in integrum* in the "Libyan Law," "public international law (the law of treaties and General Principles of Law)," "customary public international law and the case law of international tribunals," did not find authority to support such a demand.[624] The Tribunal stated that the policy adopted in the Aramco decision was not applicable to this case, because in this case the order for specific performance would be for "physical restitution by a state of a nationalized enterprise to a foreign concessionaire."[625] The Tribunal observed that it did not have the effective power to put the concessionaire into physical possession. The Tribunal did not, accordingly, question state competence for unilateral termination if adequate compensation is provided and damages only awarded.

Past trends would thus appear to demonstrate that community expectations involve limiting the competence of states in unilateral termination rather than rejecting such competence outright. The

[623] A. Chayes, T. Ehrlich & A. Lowenfeld, 11 International Legal Process 805–76 (1969).

[624] Decree of Awards in Arbitration Between Libya and the British Petroleum Company, [1973] I.C.J. 55 (hereinafter cited as 1973 Awards).

[625] *Id.* at 85.

policy behind total invalidation of state competence ignores the fact that every agreement made between a government and a foreign entity for resource production has a more or less significant impact on the national interest of the state. Since most development agreements are long-term commitments, it is not fair for one generation to bind a new generation with a commitment that is no longer in their national interest.[626] Sometimes a government cannot foresee how an agreement will operate in the future and its consequent impact on the national interest. This was quite obvious in early development agreements. As Gibbs has stated, when the Shah of Iran made the concession agreement with D'Arcy for 500,000 square miles, "he could not foresee the far-reaching consequence of his act, or known that within a few years the British Admirality would own and control 500,000 square miles of the sovereign land of Persia."[627] The split of sovereignty occurred wherever the British oil monopoly obtained a concession. Such lands became then economically and politically subject to control by the British Government. "In many instances these concessions carry the right of British policy; and once in, Britain never withdraws!"[628] One of the reasons for the early unilateral termination of development agreements was just such practices of authority and control by the British in many developing countries. As Gibbs correctly observes, British practice and the adoption of the Acquisition of Capital Act, which began the British policy of internalization of oil fields in other countries in 1913–14, forced "nationalization of subsoil and mineral rights upon the lesser nations of the world. The necessity for self-preservation and national autonomy requires that each nation so invaded must nationalize its oil lands to remove Britain's stranglehold upon its domains."[629]

---

[626] Most Municipal laws have recognized the possibility of termination or alteration of a contract, but they strongly limit this practice. For example, German and Swiss modern legal theory limits the rule *pacta sunt servanda* by the paramount practice of good faith. German and Swiss courts have accepted unilateral abrogation or alteration of the Contract in cases where they conflict with the national interest. Similar positions have been taken by English, French, and Italian courts. For German case law, see E. LEHMANN, DAS RECHT DER SCHULD-VERHALTNISSE § 41 (1954); for Swiss case law, *see* REPORTS OF THE FEDERAL TRIBUNAL, 59 ATF II 264, *cited in* Lalive, *Unilateral Alteration or Abrogation by Either Party to a Contract Between a State and a Foreign National*, SELECTED READINGS 277.

[627] L. GIBBS, OIL AND PEACE 69 (1929).

[628] *Id.* at 71.

[629] *Id.*

In contemporary practice as well, private foreign entities may be involved in activities that extend beyond simply business and profit-making and into areas that endanger the internal minimum order of the host country, a condition the grantor cannot afford to ignore. Foreign managers may, as in the International Telephone and Telegraph episode in Chile,[630] be connected to hostile intelligence agencies. A reconstruction of power in the area of national development may force the host state to take over control from foreign investors. Similarly, the kind of strategies foreign investors employ for the protection of business may be regarded as an affront to the national dignity of the host state and have to be stopped.[631]

Sometimes the government of the host state considers that economic circumstances dictate that it should get a higher return from the bargain or that exploitation of resources at the moment does not further long-term national development planning and should be reserved for future use.[632] The reconstruction of national development may require government control over national resources of the country.[633]

Although the protection of national interest is important and necessary, the more inclusive interest of the larger community should also be protected. The protection of the inclusive interest may take the form of compensating foreign investors who suffered damages through unilateral terminations. The payment of damages is the state's responsibility and cannot be avoided by changing national legislation. This was expressly stated by a PCIJ decision in the *Free Zones of Upper Savoy* case: "it is certain that France cannot rely on her own legislation to limit the scope of her international obligations. . . ."[634] The PCIJ articulated the same

---

[630] Moran, *The Evolution of Concession Agreements in Under-Developed Countries and the United States National Interests* 7 Vand. J. Transnat'l L. 327 (1974).

[631] *Id. See also* Economic Nationalism in Old and New States (H. Johnson, ed. 1967), and Johnson, *An Economic Theory of Protectionism, Tariff Bargaining and the Formation of Customs Union*, 73 J. Pol. Econ. 256 (1965).

[632] The Iranian termination of 1932 and 1951 Concession were designed for the obtaining of a better deal due to internal and international economic circumstances. Argentina's 1963 termination of oil companies' interests was designed to preserve the oil reserves for future use. N. Y. Times, Nov. 14, 1963, at 49, col. 1.

[633] *See* Hyde, *Permanent Sovereignty over Natural Wealth and Resources*, 50 Am. J. Int'l L. 854, 857 (1956).

[634] [1932] P.C.I.J. Ser. A/B No. 46, 167.

policy in the case concerning the *Treatment of Polish Nationals in Danzig*: "a state cannot adduce as against another state its own Constitution with a view to evading obligations incumbent upon it under international law."[635]

Thus, the policy followed most by past decisions recognizes the state's competence over unilateral termination but limits the scope of that competence by inclusive prescriptions. Such expectation is stated by Garcia-Amador in his Report to the International Law Commission of 1957. Article 7 of the Report reads:

> State is responsible for the injuries caused to an alien by the non-performance of obligations stipulated in a contract entered into with that alien or in a concession granted to him, if the said non-performance constitutes an act or omission which contravenes the international obligations of the State.
>
> 2. For the purposes of the provisions of the foregoing paragraph, the repudiation or breach of the terms of a contract or concession shall be deemed to constitute an "act or omission which contravenes the international obligations of the State" in the following cases, that is to say, if the repudiation or breach:
>
> > (a) Is not justified on grounds of public interest or of the economic necessity of the State; (b) Involves discrimination between nationals and aliens to the detriment of the latter; or (c) Involves a 'denial of justice' within the meaning of article 4 of this draft.[636]

Article 9 continues the policy: "The State is responsible for the injuries caused to an alien by the expropriation of his property, *save in so far as the measure in question is* justified on grounds of public interest and the alien receives adequate compensation."[637] The Report thus limits the competence of states over unilateral termination in terms of public interest, nondiscriminatory measures, and compensation.

A collective attempt by nation-states to limit the competence of states in unilateral termination of development agreements began with U.N. Resolution 626 (VII) of December 21, 1952, entitled "Rights to exploit freely natural wealth and resources." This resolution has been considered in at least two municipal court deci-

---

[635] [1932] P.C.I.J. Ser. A/B No. 44 at 24.

[636] *See Garcia-Amador's Second Report, supra* note 425, at 116–17.

[637] *Id.* at 117.

sions in Italy and Japan regarding a property claim over nationalized resources in connection with the Anglo-Iranian case.[638] In 1958 General Assembly Resolution 1314 (XIII) established the Commission on Permanent Sovereignty over Natural Resources for the purpose of studying the status of such sovereignty over natural resources and preparing recommendations. Resolution 1803 (XVII) of 1962, on "Permanent Sovereignty over Natural Resources," was prompted by the commission. This resolution, after acknowledging and emphasizing the sovereignty of states over their natural wealth and the importance of development of those resources in their own national interest, limits, in paragraph 4, the competence of the state in nationalization: "Nationalization, expropriation or requisitioning shall be based on grounds or reasons of *public utility, security or the national interest which* are recognized as overriding purely individual or private interests, both domestic and foreign. In such cases the owner shall be paid *appropriate compensation* in accordance with the rules in force in the State taking such measures in the exercise of its sovereignty and in accordance with international law. . . ."[639] Resolution 1803 (XVII) also limits the competence of states in unilateral termination with regard to considerations of public utility and appropriate compensation. These resolutions, however, do not mention discriminatory measures.

These resolutions reveal the tension between capital-exporting and capital-importing countries as to the establishment of policies and institutions by which state competence and sovereignty should be limited. The capital-exporting countries accuse the capital-importing countries of using broad terms that expand the scope of state competence at the expense of private investors.[640] They claim that these resolutions ignore treaties previously made or that might be required in the future on commercial problems between states, and individual arrangements between parties to development agreements concerning the protection of private investment. What was at stake, more specifically, were property rights of foreign entities, due process of law, respect for arbitration clauses,

---

[638] *See* Gess, *Permanent Sovereignty over Natural Resources*, 13 INT'L COMP. L.Q. 403, 408 (1964).

[639] *Id.* at 403–04 (emphasis supplied).

[640] *See* Hyde, note 633, *supra*.

and just and effective compensation (including the right to withdraw funds by obtaining foreign exchange).[641]

According to authoritative decision and practice between states,
the three basic limitations on state competence are in terms of
public purpose, discriminatory measures, and compensation.
However, these criteria have been attacked by developing countries since 1970. These attacks are in the form of collective actions
taken by developing countries resulting in the May 1, 1974, Resolution 3201 (S-VI) and the Program of Action 3202 (S-VI). The
basic demand behind the resolutions of the 1950s and early 1960s
was "economic self-determination"; however, the main demand
behind the new changes is redistribution of the world's wealth and
power to help poor countries bridge the gap between developed
and developing nations. The present demands are much more
far-reaching than those for "self-determination." Self-determination was a demand for freedom in the deciding of internal matters.
The present demands include not only control of decision-making
power in internal areas but also the effective participation in decision-making regarding international politics. The present demands, as we will see, would have significant impact on the
dimensions and limitations of state competence. The main change
would be effected through demands to shift the competence over
compensation to exclusive prescriptions and municipal bodies
rather than to inclusive prescriptions and international tribunals.

(b) *Limitations on State Competence in Unilateral Termination.* Analysis
of past trends indicates that a state violates international law if it
unilaterally terminates or changes agreements arbitrarily. *Arbitrarily* refers to three main criteria: (1) not for public purpose, (2)
discriminatory, (3) provides no compensation.[642]

(1) *Public purpose.* The public purpose requirement for
lawful nationalization is stated in Garcia-Amador's Report and in
the 1803 Resolution. However, resolution 3201 (S-VI) did not
mention this requirement. In spite of continuous reference to it in
the literature, in authoritative decisions, and in practices among

---

[641]Similar objections were raised by Mrs. Lord, U.S. Delegate to the Third Committee.
See Hyde, *id.* at 862–63.

[642]*See Garcia-Amandor's Second Report, supra* note 425, at 34.

the states, the concept of public purpose is still unclear in three important respects. The first is the relevance and importance of public purpose from the standpoint of community policy. The second is who has the competence to decide whether the action comports with the public purpose. And, third, what are the criteria by which competent decision makers can evaluate the public purpose. These are all important questions to which there are no clear answers. Considering the community policy of wide production and equitable distribution of resources, it is questionable whether requiring public purpose for unilateral termination has any effect on future planning for private investment so long as appropriate compensation is provided. Furthermore, the nationalizing state always claims that a taking has been for a public purpose or interest. Such a claim has to be made by the elite in order to protect its own power within the internal structure of the nation-state and in external arenas. The question then arises, What is the real relevance of a public purpose requirement if it does not affect the general community policy of encouraging production? White, discussing the irrelevance of public purpose requirements to the unlawfulness of a termination, stated that "[it is] contrary to reason and to general principles of international law that so grave a consequence should follow from the non-observance of a rule whose content is as vague as that of the principle of public utility has been shown to be."[643]

Metzger and Friedman seem to deny the existence of the public purpose limitation on the ground that the motives for nationalization are matters of indifference to international law because the latter does not contain its own definition of public purpose.[644] Similarly, a League of Nations declaration stated that "[t]here is no question of discussing the reasons which a government may have for putting an end to a concession or the performance of a contract; it is merely a question of obliging it to make good the damage which it causes by so doing."[645] In our view public policy is relevant only to the measure of compensation. The amount of compensation made available for reconstructing the deprived parties may

---

[643] *See* WHITE, *supra* note 570, at 150.

[644] *See* Metzger, *Multinational Convention for the Protection of Private Foreign Investment*, 9 J. PUB. L. 40 (1960); F. FRIEDMANN, EXPROPRIATION IN INTERNATIONAL LAW 126 (1953).

[645] *Quoted in* FRIEDMANN, *id.* at 142.

be affected by the degree of public purpose exhibited by the de-privor state. Generally, if a termination has been for a public pur-pose, compensation decreases; if the termination has not been for a public purpose, the amount of compensation increases. There-fore, while public purpose is not directly relevant to the positive community goals of encouraging the development of resources, it is relevant to strategies of securing the negative goals of recon-structing the deprived.

The authoritative decisions of international tribunals on the relevance of public purpose to international responsibility favor recognition of unilateral termination for a public purpose. The language of the decisions furthermore provides an answer to the question of who are the competent decision makers. The decisions generally hold that regardless of the government claim as to public purpose, third-party tribunals are the appropriate competent de-cision makers in evaluating such claims. Since the public purpose requirement in relation to the amount of damage is for the protec-tion of the common interest in reconstruction, the inclusive deci-sion makers are competent to reevaluate the claim of the host state in that respect. Authoritative decisions have supported such a view. In the *Walter Smith Claim*, the Arbitrator held that the taking was not for public purpose but for the purpose of amusement and private profit, without any reference to public utility.[646] The neces-sity of public purpose for lawful nationalization was stated in the *Goldenberg Case*.[647] In the *German Interests in Polish Upper Silesia Case*, the PCIJ observed that international law permits the expro-priation of foreign properties for reasons of "public utility."[648] In the *Norwegian Shipowners* arbitration, the tribunal explicitly stated that courts are competent to decide inter alia "whether the taking is justified by public needs."[649] Such policy was followed by a U.S. Court of Appeals in the *Sabbatino Case*, where the Court held the Cuban nationalization unlawful because, among other things, it was not for a public purpose.[650] The relevance of public purpose measures to the lawfulness of nationalization has been discussed

[646] 2 R. Int'l Arb. Awards 901 (1928).

[647] 2 R. Int'l Arb. Awards 913 (1929).

[648] [1926] P.C.I.J. Ser. A. No. 7, at 22.

[649] R. Int'l Arb. Awards 307, 332, 335 (1922).

[650] 56 Am. J. Int'l L. 1085 (1962).

in Garcia-Amador's Report Article 9(2), and the 1961 Harvard Law School draft.[651]

Amerasinghe argues that, nonetheless, not much importance has been given to this criterion and the necessity for it is doubtful.[652] This argument is realistic as regards the directness of the relationship between public purpose criteria and lawful nationalization, but not with respect to the measure of damages. Even those authoritative decisions which slight the public purpose criterion imply that ignoring the public purpose is acceptable only when appropriate compensation is provided. In other words, they imply a definite relationship between public purpose and compensation. This policy was adopted in the *Shufeldt Case*, and while it seemed that the tribunal did not attach any significance to the public purpose criterion by stating that the reasons for the government decree were unimportant because "such reasons are no concern of this tribunal,"[653] the tribunal stated that they were concerned whether there had been any injustice to an alien, *i.e.*, injustice in terms of compensation. Similarly, in the *Oscar Chinn* case the Permanent Court of International Justice held that "[t]he Belgium Government was the sole judge of this critical situation and of the remedies that it called for subject, of course, to its duty of respecting its international obligations."[654] It is clear that these two authoritative decisions do not reject our policies, but they do not clearly state the relationship between the public purpose measure and the compensation measure.

The impact of the collective action of third-world countries on this issue is still unclear. The 1962 General Assembly Resolution specifically stated that taking should be for "public utility, security or the national interest." The Resolution was passed by a vote of 87 for, 12 against (Soviet Bloc, Burma and Ghana), and 2 abstentions (France and South Africa). Seven years later it was concluded by an UNCTAD panel that the competent decision maker on the question of public purpose was the nation-state itself: "the Governments of host countries are the best judges of their develop-

[651]*Id.* at 1090–91.

[652]*See* AMERASINGHE, *supra* note 220, at 137.

[653]The Shufeldt Claim (U.S. v. Guatemala) (1930), DEPT. STATE ARIBITRATION SERIES No. 2 (1932) at 870–77.

[654][1934], P.C.I.J., ser. A/B, No. 63 at 79.

ment objectives and priorities and the tools to be employed to achieve these objectives."[655] The Group of 77 in the Charter of Algeria of 1967, Article 24, emphasized the competence of the nation-state to define "national interest" and "priorities" in relation to private foreign investment.[656] In the 1974 Resolution and the Charter of Economic Rights and Duties of States, however, there is no mention of public purpose in relation to lawful nationalization. The policy behind such demand is that the taking by the government for public purposes should be assumed, since, as Brownlie argues, the public purpose can be determined only by individual states.[657] In support of this view, Kronfol states that the criterion of public purpose may fail to be of real significance as an objective standard in judging the legality of nationalization because of the *modus operandi* of some states in this area.[658] Nicholson argues that "if the legislature has the sole power to determine what is for public benefit . . . questions of motive or inducement become immaterial for all practical purposes."[659]

It is difficult to project the impact of such demands onto community policy and practice. We are convinced, however, that the relation between public policy and compensation measures remains strong, and inclusive decision makers should remain as the competent body to evaluate public policy since they protect the common interest of the larger community.

The last question to be answered concerns the criteria which the competent decision maker should employ to determine whether a unilateral termination has been for a public purpose or not: The past trends do not offer helpful guidelines. It is, however, obvious that decision makers always consider a broad range of facts. We recommend a contextual analysis of such facts and a careful consideration of values involved in a unilateral termination. Since generally in a unilateral termination some values are promoted and some are retarded, we recommend emphasis on promotion of

[655] U.N. Dept. of Econ. and Soc. Affairs, Panel on Foreign Investment in Developing Countries, U.N. Doc. E/4654.ST/ECA/117 (1969).

[656] U.N. Doc. TD/38 Part Two C.1(h).

[657] BROWNLIE, *supra* note 286, at 528; see also WHITE, *supra* note 570, at 149–50.

[658] *See* KRONFOL, *supra* note 290, at 26.

[659] Nicholson, *The Protection of Foreign Property Under Customary International Law*, 6 B.C. IND. & COMM. L. REV. 400 (1965).

the long-term values of the nation-state rather than on values deprived for short terms against the nation-state.

(2) *Nondiscrimination.* One of the criteria for nonarbi-
trary nationalization is that the nationalization should not be discriminatory. Therefore, discrimination is the second element that
limits states' competence in unilateral termination. The relevant
questions here are the same as those involved in public purpose;
the responses may, however, be different.

The relation between the requirement of nondiscrimination
and community policy is stronger than in the case of public purpose. The policy behind nondiscrimination is to promote and protect the inclusive interest of the world community in the protection
of human rights and the abolishment of all discrimination, including that based on nationality. Therefore, whatever the relevance
of nondiscrimination to the specific community policy of encouraging the transnational flow of resources, it is highly pertinent to
the inclusive interests embodied in the U.N. Declaration of Human Rights. Despite the direct relationship between this measure
and broader community policy, there is no clear policy defined in
past trends to explain whether this measure is sufficient to invalidate a unilateral termination by itself or is only relevant as to the
question of compensation. This lack of clear policy results from
the fact that discrimination was never the sole issue involved in a
termination; another reason is difficulty in choosing criteria to
determine whether there has been discrimination.

Our policy does not favor the legality of unilateral termination
based on discrimination, but due to the difficulty of determining
discrimination in a specific case, we support a policy of relating
this element to the measure of compensation rather than of making it invalidate a taking.

The difficulty in identifying a discriminatory measure when included with other elements has been acknowledged by both writers and authoritative decisions. Kronfol believes that discrimination
involves the element of fairness.[660] He observes that this word has
been used often in agreements and opinions, but that there are
really no definite criteria for applying such a standard in case of

---

[660] KRONFOL, *supra* note 290, at 60. Kronfol concludes that "what constituted discrimination, in fact, depends on the schemes of values, or norms and standards, used as the basis
for pronouncing judgment." *Id.* at 61.

treatment of aliens. This problem was pointed out by the PCIJ in its Advisory Opinion in the *Minority Schools in Albania Case*: "equality in law precluded discrimination of any kind; whereas equality in fact may involve the necessity of different treatment in order to obtain a result which establishes an equilibrium between different situations."[661]

According to the *Norwegian Shipowners Claim*, discriminatory expropriation may raise the question of international responsibility: "The United States are responsible for having thus made a discriminating use of the power of eminent domain towards citizens of a friendly nation, and they are liable for the damaging action of their . . . agents toward these citizens . . . of Norway."[662] This case, however, though stating the relevance of discrimination to compensation, does not give any indication as to the effect of discrimination on the legality of unilateral termination.

Past trends indicate that inclusive decision makers and foreign tribunals are bodies competent to decide discrimination regardless of the claim of the nationalizing state. On the question of criteria to determine discrimination, however, past trends present better guidelines than public purpose criteria, but these guidelines are still sufficiently unclear to create doubts for decision makers. Despite a number of treaties concerning the principle of nondiscrimination between nationals and aliens,[663] community practice has shown that difference in impact of a particular action on nationals and foreigners is not enough by itself to establish discrimination. In the *Oscar Chinn* case, the PCIJ did not find discrimination although Mr. Chinn's property was the only enterprise affected. White observes that there is no rule of international law that faults states for the nationalization of aliens' property in a field where there are no national interests capable of being affected.[664] Therefore, the nationalizations of the Anglo-Iranian Oil Company of 1951, the Suez Canal Company of 1956, and the Oil Companies of Ceylon of 1962 are not discriminatory. The municipal court in

[661] [1935] P.C.I.J., Ser. A/B No. 64 at 19.

[662] R. Int'l Arb. Awards 307, 339 (1922).

[663] *See, e.g.,* Art. VI, para. 5 of the Treaty of Friendship, Commerce, and Navigation Between the United States and Nicaragua, Jan. 21, 1956, [1958] 9 U.S.T. 449, 454, T.I.A.S. No. 4024; Art 7 of the Agreement Between U.K. and Poland Relating to the Compensation Measures, 83 U.N.T.S. 51, 59 (1949).

[664] WHITE, *supra* note 570, at 144.

Rome found the Iranian nationalization nondiscriminatory: "By the Oil Nationalization Law it is intended to protect the interest of Iran, not to attack the interests of foreign nationals as such."[665] In situations where the defendant state refuses to perform the agreement because of a change in law or executive measures, establishing discrimination is difficult. In such cases there may be no intent to discriminate or to deny justice. In two cases there was a demand by the grantee to hold the state responsible for such actions. Losinger and Co., a Swiss firm, entered into an agreement with Yugoslavia in 1929. A subsequent change in the law of Yugoslavia by the legislature affected the arbitration clause of the Losinger agreement. The change required the Swiss firm to refer to the municipal courts of Yugoslavia instead of international arbitration in case of any disputes. The Swiss government claimed that the Yugoslavia action was unlawful. The PCIJ, however, did not have to make a decision on this case. A similar position was taken by France against Norway in the 1957 case, *Certain Norwegian Loans*. Again, the court was not called upon to give a decision on the merits. Mann concludes that the French and Swiss position was not accepted by other states because no other state adopted such doctrines.[666]

However, when a government action has a different effect on the interests of foreigners and those of nationals, and such action is taken to affect foreigners adversely rather than to secure the national interest, the action is discriminatory. Fitzmaurice, considering the economic relation between aliens and their former enemies under the 1947 Peace Treaty, observes that "[i]t has long been recognized that in certain matters, e.g. the general treatment of foreigners in a country or compensation for property which may be expropriated or nationalized, non-discrimination as between persons of different nationality, or against foreigners as compared with persons of local nationality, amounts to a rule of international law, the breach of which gives rise to a valid ground of claim on the

---

[665] Anglo-Iranian Oil Case, [1955] E.L.R. at 41.

[666] MANN, *supra* note 287, at 302, 310. Mann observes that the policy of the United States has been against such doctrine and since 1803 the Government has never assisted its citizens abroad in contracts with foreign governments except in cases where the foreign government is guilty "of a tort as opposed to a breach of contract." Such policy was formally adopted by President Polk and entire cabinet in 1847. *See id.* at 311; *see also* EAGLETON, *supra* note 422, at 161. British practice is not quite clear, but apparently along the lines of American practice. MANN, *id.* at 311–12.

part of the foreign government whose national is involved."[667] Protests through diplomatic correspondence between states against discriminatory treatment of foreigners also exhibit the expectations of states as to this issue.[668] The principle has, further, been recognized by many publicists.[669]

On the question whether difference of impact of government action on foreign nationals constitutes discrimination, then, there is no clear response. There is, however, a tendency to suggest that it does constitute discrimination. Thus the Cuban Nationalization Law of July 6, 1960, has been considered as a discriminatory taking by American courts because it is applicable only to Americans and American-controlled Cuban companies.[670] The *Sabbatino* court held the nationalization discriminatory because "the act classifies United States nationals separately from all other nationals and provides no reasonable basis for such a classification."[671] Another unilateral termination that raised the issue of discrimination was the Indonesian nationalization of Dutch enterprises. Domke argues that the Indonesian nationalization was discriminatory because the government not only failed to implement the promise of payment of compensation contained in Nationalization Law but made it evident in a later decree[672] that former Dutch owners of

---

[667] Fitzmaurice, *The Juridical Clauses of the Peace Treaties*, 73 Recueil des Cours 259, 349 (Academie de Droit International) (1948–II).

[668] Protest of the U.S. Government to the Cuban Nationalization Act as discriminatory, because it specifically limited its application to American nationals. 43 Dept. State Bull. (1960) at 171, 316. See also past war nationalization legislation in Rumania, Bulgaria, and Hungary, which in many instances exempted from expropriatory interest property owned by Soviet Union nationals, but not other aliens, a practice which was protested by the U.S. Government to the Rumanian Government in a note of Sept. 7, 1948. The U.S. Government stated: "While the United States Government has consistently recognized the right of a sovereign power to expropriate property subject to its jurisdiction and belonging to American nationals, the United States has likewise refused to recognize the validity of such expropriations in cases where they are discriminatory by nature and effect. . . ." 19 Dept. State Bull. (1948) at 408.

[669] See Sohn, Remarks at the 1959 Meeting of the American Branch of International Law Associatwons, ABILA Proceedings (1959–60) 31 (1960); Van Hecke, *Confusion, Expropriation, and the Conflict of Laws*, 4 Int'l L.Q. 345 (1951); McNair, *supra* note 586 at 218, 247–49, 260; White, *supra* note 470, at 119–44; Herz, *Expropriation of Foreign Property*, 35 Am. J. Int'l L. 243, 249 (1941), and Freeman, The International Responsibility of States for Denial of Justice 517 (1938).

[670] 55 Am. J. Int'l L. 822 (1961).

[671] Banco Nacional De Cuba v. Sabbatino, 193 F. Supp. 375, 385 (S.D.N.Y. 1961).

[672] 59 Am. J. Int'l L. 468, 484, 487 (1965).

nationalized property would not be compensated at all.[673] This decree provided that for enterprises partly owned by aliens other than Dutch nationals, compensation would be paid only for the portion of the capital originally owned by such aliens. In subsequent cases concerning the Indonesian nationalization the Dutch Court held that the action was discriminatory, while the German Court held that it was not. The German Court stated that "the equality concept means only that equals must be treated equally and that the different treatment of unequals is admissible."[674] For the proposition to be objective, it is sufficient that the attitude of the former colony toward its former master be different from its attitude toward other foreigners. Not only were the places of production predominantly in the hands of the Netherlands, and for the greater part colonial companies, but these companies also dominated the worldwide distribution through Dutch markets, beyond the mere production process. The German Court in its decision was referring to the community policy of anticolonialism and encouraging liberation movements. The court observed that Dutch nationals and enterprises had previously enjoyed a highly preferred position. The Court referred to the Dutch nationals as the former colonial masters and distinguished them from other foreigners. By this analysis the Court justified its holding that there was no discrimination.

The Indonesian nationalization was a case where the government action had different effects, not only on the interests of nationals and foreigners, but also it affected one group of foreigners more than other groups of foreigners. Of course the proportion of the interests of other foreigners to Dutch nationals was nominal; nevertheless, it can be said that there was a basis for different treatment between the two groups. A difference in treatment does not of itself constitute discrimination. One must consider the role that Dutch nationals and enterprises played in Indonesia. Because of this role a differentiation between Dutch nationals and other foreigners may not constitute unlawful discrimination but rather be justifiable as serving a vital national interest. The main aim of nationalization was to support the liberation of Irian Borat (West New Guinea) from the Netherlands.[675] It should be mentioned

---

[673] Domke, *supra* note 595, at 334.

[674] *Id.* at 328.

[675] McNair, *supra* note 586, at 291.

that we do not encourage unilateral termination, particularly where the greater inclusive interest of general community is involved. But we emphasize the necessity of careful contextual analysis by decision makers to assess the discriminatory character of a termination, rather than a mechanical consideration of its effects upon various groups of foreigners.[676]

The requirement of absence of discrimination for lawful termination is stated in Article 9 of Garcia-Amador's Report and in Article 10 of Harvard Law School Draft. But the May 1 (1974) Resolution and the Charter of Economic Rights and Duties of States are both silent, and there is no mention of criteria about discrimination and of public policy requirements. It would be difficult to predict the future community policy with respect to demands for protection of human rights and demands for employment of various strategies for the redistribution of world resources. Our projections, however, suggest that the demand for protection of human rights in the inclusive interests of the world community will in the long run maintain expectations different from those relating to the public policy requirement and that discriminatory measures are unlawful.

(3) *Compensation.* The illegality of unilateral termination without compensation has been widely recognized by authoritative decisions and state practices. Compensation is always the main issue in nationalization disputes, and is the major limitation on state competence for unilateral termination. The necessity of compensation for lawful nationalization has also been recognized by capital-importing countries. There may be some disagreement as to the measure and standard of compensation and as to the competent decision maker, but there is no real opposition to the necessity for some compensation.[677] This surely is evidence of firm

---

[676] The Indonesian Case, for example, is in no way comparable to the 1960 Nationalization of Belgian property interests in Egypt. This nationalization was based on the Egyptians' claim that the Belgian government had caused the cancellation of diplomatic relations between the Congo and the United Arab Republic. In this case there is no vital national interest involved for Egypt. N.Y. TIMES Dec. 2, 1960 at 6, col. 3; and Dec. 3, 1960 at 14, col. 1.

[677] A few jurists reject the theory that international law imposes compensation on the nationalizing state; *see, e.g.*, B. WORTLEY, EXPROPRIATION IN PUBLIC INTERNATIONAL LAW 35 (1959). Professor Friedmann observes that in the absence of treaty obligation, international law does not prescribe compensation. F. FRIEDMANN, EXPROPRIATION IN INTERNATIONAL LAW 206 (1953). Professor Brownlie observes that there are a few cases where nationaliza-

community expectations and of the relevance of compensation to basic community policies.

Some observe that the compensation rule is based upon the notion of private property in a liberal regime, namely, that every individual has a right to property and property cannot be taken without compensation. Thanks to this assumption, the compensation principle has been linked to human rights and has become an element of the international minimum standard of treatment of aliens.[678] The principle of compensation is also built upon the concepts of "acquired rights," "unjust enrichment,"[679] and "abuse of rights." Furthermore, the principle of compensation protects the community policy of promoting the transnational flow of resources. Support of nationalization without compensation discourages potential investors from investing abroad. The compensation requirement is one of the important factors that encourages investment abroad, despite the increasing number of nationalizations.[680] The principle of compensation is designed to repair in some measure the damage to the stability of expectation of the parties done by unilateral termination by the contracting state.

The above policies have been widely adopted by authoritative decisions, and the payment of compensation is well established in modern state practice. The American and Panamanian General

---

tion without compensation is allowed, specifically in cases of "public utility prevalent in laissez-faire economic systems, *i.e.*, exercise of public power, health measures, and the like." BROWNLIE, *supra* note 286, at 522.

[678] *See* BROWNLIE, *id.* at 518, 535–80; *see also* A. ROBERTSON, HUMAN RIGHTS IN EUROPE 196 (1963).

[679] B. CHENG, GENERAL PRINCIPLES OF LAW 47–48 (1953).

[680] Examples of increase in nationalization are presented by the State Department. Since 1960 there have been 70 dispute situations involving U.S. ownership. Of these 70 situations, 44 involve total nationalization or expropriation of companies with majority or minority U.S. ownership interest; 24 involve all or a part of companies with U.S.-owned majority or minority U.S. ownership interest, and 2 involve contract disputes in which U.S. concerns were involved. Other claims involved U.S. concerns in various disputes, including performance disputes. Since January 1969 some 64 actions have been initiated by foreign non-Communist countries with regard to direct or indirect taking of U.S. properties. This may be compared with some 51 actions during the period of 1961 to 1968, excluding Cuba. Of these 51 actions, 40 have been resolved; 11 are still unsettled. Of the 64 actions initiated since 1969, 5 have been settled and 59 are unresolved, including some in which formal expropriation actions have not yet been taken. State Department Paper (1975) at 7, 11–14. Despite such an increase in the taking of foreign properties, the rate of private foreign investment is still high.

Claims Commission, for example, in the *De Sabla Claim* stated: "It is axiomatic that acts of a government in depriving an alien of his property without compensation imposes international responsibility."[681] The unlawfulness of nationalization without compensation is also stated by the PCIJ in the *Chorzow Factory Case*.[682] In the *Norwegian Shipowners* case, the Tribunal held that "[w]hether the action of the U.S. was lawful or not, just compensation is due to the claimants under municipal law of the U.S. as well as under international law, based upon the respect for private property."[683] In the *Delagoa Bay Railway* case, the Arbitral Tribunal said that even were it to consider the government's action to be legal expropriation, the obligation to compensate would still exist.[684] The language used in these two opinions is rather different from that of previous and subsequent cases. These two cases do not consider the relationship of compensation to the lawfulness of the taking and state that whether a taking is *lawful or not, the state has an obligation for compensation.* This could be interpreted that a taking may be considered lawful, regardless of compensation requirements. Such reasoning does not have any impact on the measure of damages, but it does offset the enforcement remedies. When the Court holds that a taking is lawful, the consequence of such a holding is that the state can now pass the title to the nationalized property to others. Therefore, there is no restitution remedy for the private party whose property has been nationalized. Because of such potential effect on remedies, decision makers should be careful with the language they use. To avoid such problems, the decision maker should consider the obligation of *compensation as a requirement for a lawful taking*, rather than asserting that *regardless of whether a taking is lawful or not the nationalizing state has an obligation to pay compensation.* As we will observe, decisionmakers have followed such a policy in later cases.

---

[681] Marguerite de Joly de Sabla (U.S. v. Panama) (1933–34), 28 AM. J. INT'L L. 602 (1934). For similar holdings, see Walter Fletcher Smith v. Cuba, Award of May 2, 1929, 24 AM. J. INT'L L. 384 (1930); The Upton Case (U.S. v. Venezuela), 9 R. Int'l Arb. Awards 234 (1903); Melczer Mining Co. (U.S. v. Mexico) 4 R. Int'l Arb. Awards at 481 (1929); Evertsz (Netherlands v. Venezuela), 10 R. Int'l Arb. Awards 721 (1903), and Mazzei (Italy v. Venezuela) 10 R. Int'l Arb. Awards 525 (1903).

[682] [1928] P.C.I.J. ser. A, No. 17; *see also* The Norwegian Claims Case, 1 R. Int'l Arb. Awards 307 (1922).

[683] Norwegian Claims Case, *id.* at 334, 338.

[684] U.N. Doc. A/AC.97/5 (1972) at 262–3.

In the cases following the Anglo-Iranian dispute, the Supreme Court of Aden held that "expropriation without compensation is contrary to international law."[685] The Japanese Court with respect to a similar problem stated that "property belonging to foreign nationals can only be expropriated with compensation."[686] The Italian Courts were of the same opinion: "no person should be deprived of his property without payment of compensation."[687] In a recent German case concerning the Chilean nationalization, it was held that the nationalization of Chilean copper mines was contrary to international law because it was without appropriate compensation.[688]

A number of multilateral and bilateral agreements and unilateral prescriptions express the community expectations about the requirement of compensation for lawful expropriation. Article 25 of the Economic Agreement of Bogota states: "any expropriation shall be accompanied by payment of fair compensation in a prompt, adequate and effective manner."[689] A similar requirement is expressed in ICC Code article 11(c). The United States voiced such an expectation in many of its Friendship, Commerce and Navigation treaties with other countries.[690] Many countries, in-

---

[685] Anglo-Iranian Co., Ltd. v. Jaffrate, 20 I.L.R. 316 (1953).

[686] Anglo-Iranian Oil Co., Ltd. v. Idemitsu Kosan Kabushiki Kaisha, 20 I.L.R. 305 (1953).

[687] Anglo-Iranian Co., Ltd. v. Unione Petrolifera per l'Oriente S.P.A., Foro Italiano, 22 I.L.R. 12 (1955).

[688] Seidl-Hohenveldern, *Chilean Copper Nationalization Case Before German Courts*, 69 Am. J. Int'l L. 110 (1975).

[689] 32 Dept. State Bull. 579 (1953).

[690] *See, e.g.*, the FCN treaty between the U.S. and Japan, 208 U.N.T.S. 143 (1955); see also treaties cited in Fatouras, *supra* note 208, at 169. For reference to bilateral agreements on this issue, see U.N. Doc. TD/35/Rev. 1. Compensation for nationalized property has been subjected to many agreements. These agreements fall into four categories: (1) those providing for compensation in such general terms as "adequate" and "effective" or the application of most-favored-nation treatment; (2) those providing for direct compensation to the individual aliens concerned; (3) those providing for compensation to the government of the state of which the aliens concerned are nationals; and (4) those providing for lump-sum or global compensation paid by the debtor State to the government of the creditor State.

The second and the third categories usually provide for procedures to determine the amount of compensation. The global arrangement discharges the debtor State from all liabilities to the creditor States' interest in all the debts, claims, and obligations arising out of the nationalization. *See* U.N. Doc. A/AC.97/5 (1972) at 185.

cluding capital-importing countries, provide for compensation in their municipal prescriptions.[691] Regardless of the confusion in Soviet practice, it may be concluded that the expectation for compensation does exist in socialist states. The Soviet Union has generally taken the position that there is no obligation to pay compensation.[692] This position was strongly emphasized by the Soviet Union as leader of the socialist bloc during the negotiations over the permanent sovereignty over natural resources. Despite these statements, in actual practice the Soviet Union as well as other socialist countries has demanded compensation. In 1946, for example, the Soviet Union denied the Austrian right to nationalize the Soviet-held oil fields and asked for compensation.[693] Other socialist countries arranged to pay compensation for nation-

---

Agreements in General Terms: Czechoslovakia-Sudan: Exchange of Notes concerning Czechoslovakia Decrees on Nationalization, 15/18 Mar. 1947, Swedish TS 1947 at 572; Czechoslovakia-U.S.A. Exchange of Notes in 14 Nov. 1946, 71 U.N.T.S. at 119; Poland-U.S.A. Exchange of Notes 26 Apr. 1946, 14 DEPT. STATE BULL. 761 (1946).

Agreements Providing for Direct Individual Compensation: Belgium-Czechoslovakia U.N.T.S. V, 23:25; 1:341; Belgium-France U.N.T.S., V. 31:173; 1:478; Canada-France U.N.T.S., V. 233:65; I. 3251; Czechoslovakia-Switzerland: *Recueil Officel* 1949, at 1953; France-U.K. U.N.T.S., 1947, at 131; Poland-U.K. U.N.T.S. v. 87:3; 1:1163.

Agreements Providing for Indirect Individual Compensation: Denmark-Poland U.N.T.S. V.87:179; 1:1172; Mexico-Netherlands U.N.T.S., v. 3:13; 1:22; Mexico-U.K. U.N.T.S. v. 6:55; 1:68; Mexico-U.S. U.N.T.S., V. 106:365; 11:345; Italy-Yugoslavia U.N.T.S., v. 150:197; 1:1972.

Agreements Providing for Lump-Sum Compensation: Denmark-Bulgaria, *Journal Officiel de la Republique Française* 5 Mar. 1959, at 2742; France-Czechoslovakia, *Journal Officel de la Republique Française* 19 Mar. 1959, at 3287; France-Yugoslavia, *id.* at 23 May 1959 at 5244; Sweden-Hungary, Swedish TS. 1951 at 145; Sweden-Poland, Swedish TS, 1950 at 921; Switzerland-Bulgaria, *Recueil Officiel* (1950) at 735; Switzerland-Poland, *Id.* 1949, at 839; Switzerland-Romania, *id.*, 1951 at 832; Switzerland-Yugoslavia, *id.* 1948 at 995; U.K.-Bulgaria, U.N.T.S. v. 222:347; 1:3039; U.K.-Czechoslovakia, U.N.T.S. v. 86:161 1:1157; U.K.-Poland, U.N.T.S. v. 83:51, 1:1101, U.N.T.S. v. 83:3, 1:1110, U.N.T.S. v. 204:137; 1:2755; U.K.-Yugoslavia, U.N.T.S. v. 81:121; 1:1068; U.N.T.S. v. 87:402, 11:1068; U.S.A.-Yugoslavia, U.N.T.S. v. 89:43; 1:1208.

[691] In the municipal laws of many countries, obligation for compensation has been recognized, notably in the nationalization decrees of Iran, Egypt, Indonesia, Cuba, Burma, and Ceylon.

[692] *See* A. VYSHINSKII, THE LAW OF THE SOVIET STATE 179 (1948) and J. HAZARD & M. WEISBERG, CASES AND READINGS ON SOVIET LAW 246 (1950).

[693] *See* Seidl-Hohenveldern, "Communist Theories on Confiscation and Expropriation; Critical Comments," 7 INT'L & COMP. L.Q. 544 (1958). For discussion of arrangements for compensation among Communist countries, see Drucker, *On Compensation Treaties Between Communist States*, LAW TIMES 279, 293 (1960).

alized property among themselves as well as for that of nonsocialist countries. The Treaty of 1958 between Poland and Czechoslovakia about "unresolved property questions" provides in Articles for compensation claims arising out of mutual nationalization:

> (1) By this Treaty one also settled as well as completely and finally liquidated:
>
> (a) all obligations of the Polish State in connection with claims which arise out of measures taken up to the day of signature of this treaty pursuant to Polish nationalization, expropriation or any other legal provisions depriving of or restricting rights of ownership by which Czechoslovak properties, rights and interests on the present territory of the Polish People's Republic were affected:
>
> (b) all obligations of the Czechoslovak State in connection with claims which arise out of measures taken up to the day of signature of this treaty pursuant to Czechoslovak nationalization, expropriation or any other legal provisions depriving of or restricting rights of ownership by which Polish properties, rights and interests on the present territory of the Czechoslovak Republic were affected.[694]

Similar principles have been expressed in the Treaty on the Settlement of Unresolved Property Questions between Yugoslavia and Czechoslovakia of February 11, 1956. Article 2 of this Treaty provides: "By this Treaty are also settled and liquidated: (a) all obligations of the Czechoslovak State in connection with claims arising out of Czechoslovak measures of nationalization, expropriation and of other measures limiting or depriving or rights of ownership, to which Yugoslav properties, rights and interests were subjected in Czechoslovakia up to the day of the signature of this treaty, irrespective of whether such claims are today known or not."[695] Such treaties are clear recognition of the compensation requirement and are inconsistent with the theories put forward by Soviet authors.[696] The Communist countries in their municipal law have also recognized the obligation to pay compensation. Thus Czechoslovak decree No. 100/1945, on the nationalization of mines and industries, explicitly states that "for the nationalized

---

[694] Drucker, *id.* at 239.

[695] *Id.* at 247.

[696] For a brief review of Soviet theory by Koretsky and Laptew, see *id.* at 247–49.

property compensation has to be paid."[697] Similar provisions for compensation are contained in the Polish nationalization decree of January 3, 1946, Article 7.[698]

Article 7(c) of General Assembly Resolution (V), December 2, 1950, concerning Eritrea, recommended: "No one shall be deprived of property, including contractual rights, without due process of law and without payment of just and effective compensation." Article 9 of Garcia-Amador's Report on State Responsibility maintains that the payment of adequate compensation is a necessary element for a lawful nationalization.[699] General Assembly Resolution 1803 (XVII), 1962, adopted the same policy. In later resolutions, however, while the permanent sovereignty of states over their natural resources is emphasized, there is no mention of compensation or of any other requirement for a lawful nationalization. Examples include General Assembly Resolution 2200 (XXI), the International Covenant on Economic, Social and Cultural Rights, Article 25,[700] General Assembly Resolution 3016 (XXVIII) of December 18, 1972,[701] Economic and Social Council Resolution 1737 (LIV) May 4, 1973, and the Declaration on the Establishment of a New International Economic Order, Article 3(e). The fact that these resolutions are quiet about the compensation requirement does not represent a change in community policy. Rather, these resolutions represent a series of strategies and preparations for

[697] *Id.* at 249. Professor Bystricky, a Czechoslovakian jurist, stated in a textbook published with the approval of the Czechoslovak Ministry of Education that "[o]ur legislation has in principle not denied compensation for nationalization. Pursuant to section 8 of decree 100/1945, compensation was payable according to the average price of the property ascertained with the help of official prices on the day of the publication of the decree and failing such prices in an amounted, determined by official valuation minus debts." R. BYSTRICKY, PRINCIPLES OF PRIVATE INTERNATIONAL LAW, 223 (1958), *quoted in id.* at 249.

[698] POLISH JOURNAL OF LAWS, Feb. 3, 1946, *cited in* Drucker, *id.* at 249. It should be noted that while it may correctly be argued that in the treaties among Communist countries a private person whose property has been nationalized hardly receives compensation because of the municipal law of his own government, this nevertheless does not gainsay the fact that Communist countries recognize the legal principle of compensation underlying their treaties. *Id.* at 250.

[699] Art. 9 reads: "The State is responsible for the injuries caused to an alien by the expropriation of his property, save insofar as the measure in question is justified on grounds of public interest and the alien receives adequate compensation." *See Garcia-Amador's Second Report, supra* note 425, at 117.

[700] G.A. Res. 2200, 21 U.N. GAOR Supp. (No. 16) 49, U.N. Doc. A/6316 (1967).

[701] G.A. Res. 3016, 27 U.N. GAOR Supp. (No. 30) 44, U.N. Doc. A/8730 (1973).

political bargaining through the United Nations. It is not likely that the compensation requirement will be ignored in the bargaining to come or in the response of the larger community to that bargaining. This position is foreshadowed by authoritative decisions in recent nationalization cases, such as the Chilean Nationalization of 1970, the *British Petroleum v. Libya* case of 1973, and disputes arising from the Jamaican nationalization of 1974. Moreover, the Group of 77 in preparing the Charter of Economic Rights and Duties of States expressly stated in Chapter 11, Article 2(c), that in nationalization "appropriate compensation should be paid by the State taking such measures, provided that all relevant circumstances call for it."[702] It would therefore appear that the expectation of the compensation requirement as a necessary element for a lawful taking is still viable. The measure of compensation, however, will always be controversial.

The capital-exporting countries have generally taken the position that compensation should be prompt, adequate, and effective. This position has been attacked by capital-importing countries, using mainly the argument that the reason for nationalization is promotion of the national development policy of the expropriating state and that such exacting criteria are impossible of achievement since nationalizing states are generally poor countries.[703] The general community policy must be in accommodation of the interest of the foreign investor in compensation for damages suffered with the interest of the nationalizing state in promoting its development. Therefore, the criteria of prompt, effective, and adequate compensation are too rigid for acceptance as general community policy, unless such criteria are evaluated in the context of the multifarious factors affecting the nationalizing state, such as economic capability, the real objective behind nationalization, the comprehensiveness of nationalization,[704] the amount of compensation possible, and the future development plans of the state.

---

[702] U.N. Doc. A/C.2/L.1386 (1974) at 5.

[703] Friedmann is one of the jurists who support this view. *See* FRIEDMANN, *supra* note 416, at 32.

[704] Some jurists relate the measure of compensation to other factors involved in general expropriation as opposed to small-scale expropriation. *See* BROWNLIE, *supra* note 286, at 522; AMERASINGHE, *supra* note 220, at 121–68; OPPENHEIM, *supra* note 365, at 352; Baade, *Indonesian Nationalization Measures Before Foreign Courts—A Reply*, 54 AM. J. INT'L L. 801, 804 nn. 22,23 (1960); Sohn & Baxter, *Responsibility of States for Injuries to the Economic Interests of Aliens*, 55 AM. J. INT'L L. 545, 553 (1961).

Despite the demands of capital-exporting countries,[705] past trends in decision recognize this hard necessity.

Prompt. This element expresses the theory that compensation should be paid either before the taking or within a short time thereafter. In application, however, considering its involvement with so many other factors it has never really been applied. In the *Goldenberg* case, the Tribunal emphasized that the compensation should be paid soon: but *how* soon? The Tribunal left the answer conditioned by other relevant factors and said, "as quickly as possible."[706] In the *Norwegian Claim* case, however, it was held that compensation was to be paid in "due time."[707] Therefore, there is no clear understanding with regard to the element of promptness.

---

[705] Demands for "prompt, adequate, and effective" compensation have been expressed by many developed countries, such as the U.S. in the U.S. aide-memoire of August 28, 1953, on the "Expropriation of United Fruit Company Property by the Government of Guatemala," 29 Dept. State Bull. 357 (1953), and by authoritative officials; see Becker *Just Compensation in Expropriation Cases: Decline and Partial Recovery,* 53 ASIL Proc. 336 (1959). It has also been included in agreements regarding commercial transactions. *See, e.g.,* art. VI(2) of the Treaty of Amity, Economic Relations and Consular Rights, of Dec. 20, 1958, [1960] 11 U.S.T. 1835, T.I.A.S. No. 4530. This treaty has been in force since June 11, 1960. *See also* Art. VI(3) of the Treaty of Friendship and Commerce of Nov. 12, 1959, 44 Dept. State Bull. 164 (1961). This treaty has been in force since Feb. 12, 1961.

This expectation has also been introduced into treaties made by various countries. Art. 15 of the Treaty of Commerce, Establishment and Navigation of Mar. 11, 1959, between Iran and the United Kingdom, 9 Int'l & Comp. Law Q. (1960) at 311, states that "nationals and companies of one High Contracting Party shall receive equitable treatment . . . in respect of any measures of . . . restriction or expropriation affecting their property, rights, and interests . . . and shall receive prompt, adequate, and effective compensation for any such measures." *See also* Art. 3(2) of the Treaty for the Promotion and Protection of Investments between Pakistan and the Federal Republic of West Germany, Nov. 25, 1959, Bundesrat Doc. No. 11/61 which provides that the "[c]ompensation shall represent the equivalent of the investment affected. Such compensation shall be actually realizable and freely transferable in the currency of the other Party without undue delay." Also, Art. 6 of the Treaty of Friendship, Commerce, and Navigation between Japan and the U.S. provides: "[P]roperty of nationals and companies of either Party shall not be taken within the territories of the other Party except for a public purpose, nor shall it be taken without the prompt payment of just compensation. Such compensation shall be an effectively realizable form and shall represent the full equivalent of the property taken; and adequate provision shall have been made at or prior to the time of taking for the determination and payment thereof." [1953] 4 U.S.T. 2063, 2068–9, T.I.A.S. No. 2863. Therefore, as Professor Domke concludes, prompt consideration "is certainly not met by a mere provision in the nationalization decree which leaves compensation to a future determination by the State's own legislation, adaptable to the wishes of the government. The attitude of the foreign government following the nationalization will be decisive in many regards." Domke, *supra* note 595, at 334.

[706] 2 R. Int'l Arb. Awards 901, 909 (1928).

[707] 1 R. Int'l Arb. Awards 307, 309 (1922).

As Garcia-Amador observed: "It is clear that the time-limit for the payment of the agreement compensation necessarily depends on the circumstances in each case and in particular on the expropriating State's resources and actual capability to pay. Even in the case of 'partial' compensation, very few states have in practice been in a sufficiently strong economic and financial position to be able to pay the agreed compensation immediately and in full."[708] In practice, compensation is paid over a period of time. Poland, for example, has paid compensation to France over the space of fifteen years, and to Sweden over the space of seventeen years.[709]

Adequate. This element, like that of promptness, has not been clearly defined and has no empirical reference until it is considered in relation to the whole set of circumstances involved in a case. Moreover, in calculating compensation, political as well as economic reasons are always taken into account. As Rubin states, "when settlements are reached, on the experience of the past, they seem to be only a leit-motif against which the behavior theme of practical advantage is played."[710]

In most cases the compensation paid has been claimed by the grantee to be inadequate. The agreement between the United States and Yugoslavia of 1948 settled on 42.5% of what was originally claimed.[711] The relationship between compensation and the grantor's situation has been recognized by the Permanent Court

---

[708] U.N., Fourth Report on International Responsibility, U.N. Doc. A/CN.4/119 (1959), at 59.

[709] There are similar practices among other states, such as those between Great Britain and Yugoslavia in 1948, Switzerland and Czechoslovakia in 1949, and Norway and Bulgaria in 1955. *See* I. FOIGHEL, NATIONALIZATION: A STUDY IN THE PROTECTION OF ALIEN PROPERTY IN INTERNATIONAL LAW 128–29, 131 (1957).

[710] S. RUBIN, PRIVATE FOREIGN INVESTMENT: LEGAL AND ECONOMIC REALITIES 99 (1956).

[711] FOIGEL, *supra* note 709, at 117. The amounts of compensation paid to the British government for nationalization of the property of its citizens abroad are, by country:

Argentina	1948	60%
Czechoslovakia	1949	33⅓%
France	1951	70%
Mexico	1947	30%
Poland	1948	33⅓%
Uruguay	1949	60%
Yugoslavia	1949	50%

Cheng, *The Rationale of Compensation for Expropriation,* 44 GROTIUS SOCIETY 267, 304 (1958–59).

of Arbitration in the *Russian Indemnity Case* (1912).[712] Lauterpacht recognized such relations when he recommended partial compensation for expropriations based on fundamental changes in the political and economic structures of the state.[713] Thus adequate compensation is not necessarily full compensation.

General Assembly Resolution 1803 (XVII) does not give any guidelines as to the characteristics of compensation and states only that "appropriate compensation . . . in accordance with the rules in force in the State taking such measures in the exercise of its sovereignty and in accordance with international law." Baxter and Sohn, in the Draft Convention of International Responsibility of States for Injuries to Aliens, refer to just compensation. Article 10(4) says:

> If property is taken by a State in furtherance of a general program of economic and social reform, the just compensation required by this Article may be paid over a reasonable period of years, provided that:
>
> (a) the method and modalities of payment to aliens are no less favorable than those applicable to nationals;
>
> (b) a reasonable part of the compensation due is paid promptly;
>
> (c) bonds equal in fair market value to the remainder of the compensation and bearing a reasonable rate of interest are given to the alien and the interest is paid promptly; and
>
> (d) the taking is not in violation of an express undertaking by the State in reliance on which the property was acquired or imported by the alien.[714]

Such accommodations and relationships between these elements and the factual circumstances involved in the case have been rejected by some jurists. Wortly holds that "the State [that] wishes to conduct political experiments which result in its enrichment at the expense of the foreign owners cannot, as a matter of principle, refuse restitution or full compensation. . . ."[715] He is afraid, that is, of the possible abuse of such compromise. Adriaanse argues,

---

[712] Cheng, *id.* at 307.

[713] OPPENHEIM, *supra* note 112, at 652.

[714] L. SOHN & R. BAXTER, CONVENTION ON THE INTERNATIONAL RESPONSIBILITY OF STATES FOR INJURIES TO ALIENS 12 (Draft, 1961).

[715] Wortly, "Expropriation in Public International Law," 55 AM. J. INT'L L. 607 (1961).

"[T]he possibility to expropriate should not depend upon what the State wants, but on the contrary, it should be limited by the possibility of [full] payment by the State. We should strive to make this rule of public international law an axiom."[716] Kissam and Leach insist that "[e]conomic difficulties of the expropriating State . . . do not justify the taking of property without payment, since poverty is no excuse for unlawful conduct, whether by individuals or by States. . . . Any action taken in defiance of these principles should not be accorded recognition by other States."[717] These writers are so much occupied with rules and principles for the sake of rules and principles that they have forgotten that rules and principles can only be meaningful in the context of social realities and in the promotion of the common interest of the larger community. As Kronfol correctly observes, they ignore the fact that "nationalizations are not effected as an end in themselves but as a means to social and economic progress."[718]

Effective. Among the three characteristic elements of compensation, effectiveness has the clearest meaning. This element generally refers to the form of compensation and its immediate utilization by the recipient.[719] The PCIJ in *S.S. Wimbledon* employed the element of effectiveness when it stated that Germany should pay the compensation in "French Francs. This is the currency of the applicant in which his financial operations and accounts are conducted, and it may therefore be said that this currency gives exact measure of the loss to be made good."[720]

This element has always been related to other relevant factors. For example, there are cases where the compensation has been paid in the currency of the nationalizing state,[721] or in the form of

---

[716] A. ADRIAANSE, CONFISCATION IN PRIVATE INTERNATIONAL LAW 166 (1956), *cited in* Dawson & Weston, *"Prompt, Adequate and Effective": A Universal Standard of Compensation?* 30 FORDHAM L. REV. 727, 733 n. 27a (1962).

[717] Kissam & Leach, *Sovereign Expropriation of Property and Abrogation of Concession Contracts*, 28 FORDHAM L. REV. 177, 214 (1959).

[718] KRONFOL, *supra* note 290, at 116.

[719] *Id.* at 117.

[720] [1923] P.C.I.J., ser. A, No. 1 at 32

[721] *See* the 1929 U.K.-Greece agreement on Compensation, *cited in* WHITE, *supra* note 570, at 16.

use of the property of the nationalizing state in another country, either in processed goods or raw materials.[722]

States in practice among themselves have often arranged for compensation. These arrangements are mainly the result of considering many relevant factors. In few of these arrangements have the alleged traditional criteria been applied as restrictively as has been demanded by capital-exporting countries. These arrangements mainly provide lump-sum compensation; the agreement between the United Kingdom and Rumania provides for such compensation.[723] Similar agreements have been made between the United States and Rumania,[724] the United States and Poland in 1960[725] and the United States and Hungary in 1973.[726]

The World War II Peace Treaties of February 10, 1947, provided for partial compensation for allied property that was lost, consumed, or damaged as a result of war in the amount of two-thirds of the sum requested. The Allied representatives at the Conference insisted that as a matter of principle full compensation should be paid, but because of political and economic considerations partial compensation was eventually accepted.[727] This is a clear indication of the community expectation as to the relationship between the characteristic elements of compensation and the factual circumstances in relevant situations. One observer states that "the lump-sum settlements following post-war nationalization programs of the Eastern European countries were negotiated compromises and as such do not constitute a departure from the

[722] By the agreement of 1951 between Switzerland and Rumania, 50% of all agreed compensation was paid from Rumanian funds frozen in Swiss banks. The 1948 agreement between Poland and France provided for the delivery of specified quantities of coal to France during a certain number of years. *See* WHITE, *id.* at 215.

[723] [1960] Gr.Brit. T.S. No. 82 (Cmd. 1232).

[724] 54 AM. J. INT'L L. 525 (1960).

[725] [1960] 11 U.S.T. 1953, T.I.A.S. No. 4545.

[726] *Cited in* Agreement with Hungary, March 6, 1973, [1973] 1 U.S.T. 522, T.I.A.S. No. 7569, *cited in* Lillich, *The United States–Hungarian Claims Agreement of 1973*, 69 AM. J. INT'L L. 535 (1975). For a study of lump-sum agreements, see R. LILLICH & B. WESTON, INTERNATIONAL CLAIMS: THEIR SETTLEMENT BY LUMP SUM AGREEMENTS (1975). *See also* R. LILLICH, THE PROTECTION OF FOREIGN INVESTMENT: SIX PROCEDURAL STUDIES 167–89 (1965).

[727] Martin, *Private Property, Rights and Interests in the Paris Reale Treaties*, 24 BRIT. Y.B. INT'L L. 273, 284 (1947).

traditional international principle."[728] But we have to agree with Dawson and Weston that, "[f]ar from being a 'rule' of international law in the extensive deprivation context, the demand for 'full' or 'prompt, adequate and effective' compensation would appear to be little more than a preference assumed for bargaining purposes—an element of legal mythology to which spokesmen pay ritualistic tribute and which has little meaning in effective play."[729]

ii. Unilateral Termination with Regard to Change in Context (Doctrine of *Rebus Sic Stantibus*)

In the course of years the expectations of the parties to an agreement change. Such changes are the result of alternatives taken in the process of agreement. The general community policy has been to allow unilateral termination in cases where changes in the context have had a severe impact on the expectation of the parties and upon their important exclusive interests. Community policy has favored the protection of the common interest through prevention of serious injuries to the national interests of the contracting states. A change in context may have a major impact on the common interest and unilateral termination does not necessarily create international responsibility.

The change in context could be a change in *participants*. The decision maker should consider the consequences of such a change with respect to the values at stake in the commitment between the parties. Changes in the *perspectives* of the participants may be in terms of demands or expectations. With regard to changes in demands, the willingness of the parties to continue the commitment should be taken into account. Such a change by itself, however, generally does not constitute a reason for unilateral termination. Changes in expectations should be evaluated in relation to the

---

[728] 53 ASIL Proc. 112 (1960) (Remarks of John Stevenson).

[729] Weston & Dawson, *supra* note 716, at 757. For other arguments that the standard of "prompt, adequate and effective" compensation should be related to and flexible in cases of general nationalizations, see Williams, *International Law and the Property of Aliens*, 9 Brit. Y.B. Int'l L. (1928); Baade, *supra* note 704, at 803. This view has been opposed by Fachiri, *Expropriation and International Law*, 6 Brit. Y.B. Int'l L. 159 (1925); Hyde, *Confiscatory Expropriation*, 32 Am. J. Int'l L. 759 (1938); White, *supra* note 570, at 232–35; Becker, *Just Compensation in Expropriation Cases: Decline and Partial Recovery*, ASIL Proc. 338 (1959); and Domke, *supra* note 575, at 303.

relevant values at stake in different types of agreements. Major changes in *situations* are those changes that make the enforcement of an agreement inequitable to the participants or incompatible with community policy. Changes in *base values* are those changes in the relative power of parties that affect the values at stake, either in terms of the high cost for performance, making it favorable only to one party, or which effects a major change on the legitimate control of a State over its people and territories. The most important changes, however, are changes in the *outcomes*. Sometimes the outcomes of an agreement have a severe and detrimental effect on one party; the value distribution may be so unequal and unjust that unilateral termination is inevitable. None of these changes by themselves, however, may be enough to justify the unilateral termination of an agreement. It is necessary to consider all changes, their interrelations and their impacts on the aggregate common interest, in order to evaluate and determine the reasonableness of a unilateral termination.

The theoretical basis of the doctrine of *rebus sic stantibus* arises, several authors observe, from the right of self-preservation of states. The general community policy supports the demand that self-preservation limits the international obligations of states. If the performance of an agreement jeopardizes the very existence of a state, the agreement should be terminated.[730] This theory has created problems in interpretation and application, and it is hard to articulate a clear trend in solution. Similar confusion may be observed among contemporary jurists. Williams, discussing the interpretation of fundamental changes, concludes that these changes include not only physical but also moral changes: "The word 'condition' in this statement including not only material, but also moral, facts . . . the essential 'things,' inanimate and animate, material, moral and mental, must remain in the condition in which they were when the treaty was concluded."[731] Jean-Flavien Lalive strongly advocates this doctrine: "It would be contrary to bona fides when, as a result of drastic and unforeseeable changes in circumstances, the relationship between the sets of obligations is altered to such an extent that the obligations of one party can no longer be reasonably considered as the equivalent of the obliga-

[730] This conclusion was reached by Vattel. *See* VATTEL, *supra* note 357, Vol. I, § 170. *See also* G. HARASZTI, SOME FUNDAMENTAL PROBLEMS OF THE LAW OF TREATIES 333–421 (1973).

[731] Williams, "The Permanence of Treaties," 22 AM. J. INT'L L. 89 (1928).

tions binding the other."[732] Hill takes the same broad perspective that an obligation can be unilaterally terminated under conditions which make its performance injurious to fundamental rights of the State, "rights of necessity," such as existence, independence, self-preservation and development.[733] These two jurists have used rather broad language that is loosely qualified and therefore susceptible to distortion and abuse. Hyde, on the other hand, rejects this doctrine. A state, in Hyde's view, does not have the right of unilateral termination of an agreement between itself and the other party on the basis of the doctrine of *rebus sic stantibus*.[734] He observes that only if a state feels that another party to a treaty has violated it might a party suspend performance pending adjudication by an international tribunal.[735] It is safe to state that Hyde is in the minority, for the majority of jurists support a rather broad interpretation of the doctrine.[736]

A number of national and international authoritative decisions have recognized this doctrine. Some early tribunals gave the doctrine a broad interpretation. In recent years, however, the interpretation of *rebus sic stantibus* has become more restricted.

In the late nineteenth and early twentieth centuries, the German and Swiss courts recognized the unilateral abrogation or alterations of agreements in the case of change in condition.[737] Similar positions were taken by English, French, and Italian courts.[738] The U.S. Supreme Court justified the American termination of the 1778 treaty with France in *Hooper v. United States*: Justice Davis stated:

[732] *See* Lalive, *supra* note 626, at 277.

[733] C. HILL, THE DOCTRINE OF "REBUS SIC STANTIBUS" IN INTERNATIONAL LAW 10 (1934). *See also* Garner, *The Doctrine of Rebus Sic Stantibus and the Termination of Treaties*, 21 AM. J. INT'L L. 511–13 (1927).

[734] *See* HYDE, note 112 *supra*.

[735] *Id.*

[736] *See*, e.g., R. PHILLIMORE, 2 COMMENTARIES UPON INTERNATIONAL LAW 109 (2d ed., 1871); J. WESTLAKE, 1 INTERNATIONAL LAW 295–96 (1910); OPPENHEIM, *supra* note 112, at 539; Woolsey, *The Unilateral Termination of Treaties*, 20 AM. J. INT'L L. 349–50 (1926); and L. HENKIN, ARMS CONTROL AND INSPECTION IN AMERICAN LAW 32 (1958).

[737] For German case law, *see* LEHMANN, *supra* note 626, § 41; for Swiss case law, *see* REPORTS OF THE FEDERAL TRIBUNAL, *supra* note 626, at 264, *cited in* Lalive, *supra* note 626 at 277.

[738] *Id.*

> In most of the old treaties were inserted the *clausula rebus sic stantibus*, by which the treaty might be construed as abrogated when material circumstances on which it rested changed. To work this effect it is not necessary that the facts alleged to have changed should be material conditions. It is enough if they were strong inducements to the party asking abrogation.
>
> The maxim "Conventio omnis intelligitur rebus sic stantibus," is held to apply to all cases in which the reason for a treaty has failed, or there has been such a change of circumstances as to make its performance impracticable except at an unreasonable sacrifice.[739]

In state practice this doctrine did not attract the support of diplomatic correspondence. Such practices could not represent community expectations because they included the unilateral termination of agreements by weaker nations. The result of these terminations was a decrease in power and wealth for the major countries. Among the unilateral terminations opposed by major powers was the 1914 Turkey termination of the capitulations with Austria, Hungary, France, Germany, Great Britain, Italy, the Netherlands, Russia, and the United States, which all denied the right of Turkey to such a termination.[740] Similar positions by major powers have been taken in almost all the unilateral terminations of capitulations.

The international tribunals, however, have always shown reluctance to terminate, without specifically rejecting the doctrine. There have been instances where the PCIJ and ICJ had an opportunity to address this doctrine directly. The first instance was the French invocation of the doctrine in the *Nationality Decrees in Tunis and Morocco Case*, in order to prove that the treaty of December 9, 1856, between Great Britain and Morocco had lapsed.[741] The Court stated that the French claim based on this doctrine involved "recourse to the principles of international law concerning the validity of treaties—a fact which gave the Court jurisdiction in the case—the only question involved."[742] Therefore, the Court did not

---

[739] Hooper v. U.S., 22 Ct. Claims 408 (1887), Wharton's COM. AM. LAW § 161, *cited in* 29 AM. J. INT'L L. 1105–06 (1935).

[740] UNITED STATES FOREIGN RELATIONS (1914) at 1092–93; *id.* (1915), at 1302–06; *id.* (1916), at 964. Regardless of the oppositions, Turkey was not punished for its abrogation.

[741] [1923] P.C.I.J., ser. C, No. 2 at 187–88.

[742] [1923] P.C.I.J. ser. B, No. 4 at 29, *cited in* 29 AM. J. INT'L L., *supra* note 739, at 1115.

find it necessary to express an opinion on the merits of the French contention regarding *rebus sic stantibus*. The second case was that of the *Free Zones of Upper Savoy and the District of Gex*,[743] involving France's unilateral termination of the 1815 and 1816 treaties between France and Switzerland. The French justification was built upon the doctrine of *rebus sic stantibus*:

> The equilibrium foreseen in 1815 has been upset; all profits of the institution have gone to the Canton of Geneva, while all the charges have accumulated on the zones. Geneva becomes integrated in Swiss economy, while the zones nest isolated from the French market by the internal barrier; Geneva communicates freely with Switzerland and the zones, while the zones are enclosed between two customs barriers; Geneva is protected against foreign competition by the federal customs, while the zones are opened without defense to this competition. This is the opposite of the conception which prevailed at the time of the institution of the free zones.[744]

The Permanent Court of International Justice did not find proof based on factual circumstances in the French argument. Therefore it did not have to address the doctrine:

> As the French argument fails on the facts, it becomes unnecessary for the Court to consider any of the questions of principle which arise in connection with the theory of the lapse of treaties by reason of change of circumstances, such as the extent to which the theory can be regarded as constituting a rule of international law, the occasions on which and the methods by which effect can be given to the theory if recognized, and the question whether it would apply to treaties establishing rights such as that which Switzerland derived from the treaties of 1815 and 1816.[745]

The Court's position upon the doctrine thus remained somewhat ambivalent, as Lauterpacht observed: "[T]he Court was prepared to recognize the principle (although it refused to say to what extent) that a change of conditions may have an effect on the contin-

---

[743][1932] P.C.I.J., ser. C, No. 58.

[744]*Id.* at 132, *cited in* 29 Am. J. Int'l L., *supra* note 739, at 1108.

[745]*Id.* at 158.

[746]H. Lauterpacht, The Development of International Law by the Permanent Court of International Justice 43 (1934).

uation of treaty obligations. It would not otherwise have considered whether they have in fact changed in a material aspect."[746]

The third case, the *Fisheries Jurisdiction Case*,[747] came before the International Court of Justice after the promulgation of the Vienna Convention of Law of Treaties, where *rebus sic stantibus* in highly limited form was recognized in Article 62.[748] This case concerned Iceland's unilateral termination of a 1961 treaty between Iceland and the United Kingdom on the twelve-mile exclusive fisheries zones. The United Kingdom objected to this unilateral termination and submitted the dispute to the International Court of Justice for judgment on the action taken by Iceland. Iceland rejected the ICJ jurisdiction on the basis that since this termination involves the "vital interests of the people of Iceland," the government of Iceland is not willing to confer jurisdiction upon the Court.[749] The Court rejected the Iceland argument that the Court examine its own jurisdiction and stated that under Article 36, paragraph 1, of the Court's Statute, "[t]he jurisdiction of the Court comprises . . . all matters specially provided for . . . in treaties and conventions in force," and under the Exchange of Notes of March

[747] Fisheries Jurisdiction Case (United Kingdom of Great Britain and Northern Ireland v. Iceland), I.C.J. Reports 1973 (Jurisdiction), I.C.J. Reports 1974 (Merits).

[748] VIENNA CONVENTION ON THE LAW OF TREATIES, U.N. Doc. A/Conf. 39/27 (1969). Art. 62, on "Fundamental Change of Circumstances," reads:
"1) A fundamental change of circumstances which has occurred with regard to those existing at the time of the conclusion of a treaty, and which was not foreseen by the parties, may not be invoked as a ground for terminating or withdrawing from the treaty unless:

"a) the existence of those circumstances constituted an essential basis of the consent of the parties to be bound by the treaty; and

"b) the effect of the change is radically to transform the extent of obligations still to be performed under the treaty.
"2) A fundamental change of circumstances may not be invoked as a ground for terminating or withdrawing from a treaty:

"a) if the treaty establishes a boundary; or

"b) if the fundamental change is the result of a breach by the party invoking it either of an obligation under the treaty or of any other international obligation owed to any other party to the treaty.
"3) If, under the foregoing paragraphs, a party may invoke a fundamental change of circumstances as a ground for terminating or withdrawing from a treaty, it may also invoke the change as a ground for suspending the operation of the treaty."

[749] [1973] I.C.J. at 7.

11, 1961,[750] the Court had jurisdiction.[751] Therefore, the claim for "vital interest" did not alter the competency of ICJ. Nevertheless Iceland still claimed that its unilateral termination of the agreement was justifiable according to the doctrine of change of circumstances. Those changes were first, the recognition of twelve miles exclusive fishing zone by other states, including the applicant states themselves; second, the increased efficiency of the fishing techniques developed by the applicant states posed a threat to Iceland's economy.[752] Iceland claimed that these changes fulfilled the requirement of Article 62 of the Vienna Convention. The Courts rejected the applicability of Article 62 to the case based on the factual circumstances and stated that

> the procedural complement to the doctrine of changed circumstances is already provided for in the 1961 Exchange of Notes, which specifically calls upon the parties to have recourse to the Court in the event of a dispute relating to Iceland's extension of fisheries jurisdiction. Furthermore, any question as to the jurisdiction of the Court, deriving from an alleged lapse through changed circumstances, is resolvable through the accepted judicial principle enshrined in Article 36, paragraph 6, of the Court's Statute, which provides that "in the event of a dispute as to whether the Court has jurisdiction, the matter shall be settled by the decision of the Court." In this case such a dispute obviously exists, as can be seen from Iceland's communications to the Court, and to the other Party. . . .[753]

As Tiewol has correctly stated, with this opinion "the tradition remains unbroken that in no instance has an international tribunal ever found the doctrine [*rebus sic stantibus*] applicable to any set of facts."[754] What does this policy of international tribunals mean? Is

---

[750]The Note provided that "[t]he Icelandic Government will continue to work for the implementation of the Althing Resolution of May 5, 1959, regarding the extension of fisheries jurisdiction around Iceland, but shall give to the United Kingdom Government six months' notice of such extension, and, in case of a dispute in relation to such extension, the matter shall, at the request of either party, be referred to the International Court of Justice." [1973] I.C.J. at 8.

[751]*Id.*

[752]*Id.* at 16. *See also* Tiewal, *The Fisheries Jurisdiction Cases (1973) and the Ghost of Rebus Sic Stantibus*, 6 J. OF INT'L L. & POL. 456 (1973).

[753][1973] I.C.J. at 21–2.

[754]Tiewal, *supra* note 752, at 472.

it a deliberate attempt to limit the scope of this doctrine or is it a result of uncertainty as to the scope of the doctrine? The Court could be reluctant to create a precedent which might in the future hinder or narrow the reasonable interpretation of the doctrine. Arie David, considering the Vienna Convention and the practice of this doctrine, concludes, however, that "[n]ever in its long history has the principle of *rebus sic stantibus* been so restricted and watered down as in our time."[755] He states that this is a deliberate policy on the part of the authors of the Vienna Convention in over-emphasizing the goal of stability.[756]

Regardless of the particular policy behind the reluctance of international tribunals, the restrictiveness incorporated in Article 62 of the Vienna Convention as contrasted with the actual practice of states, clearly leads, as David says, to a separation of apparent authority and effective control.[757] When authoritative decision makers fail to accommodate the conflicting interests of the parties within the framework of common interest and overemphasize the policy of stability, the result, as has been shown in the past, will be the use of naked power by states to protect exclusive interests, with little respect for the opinions of competent decision makers. It is time for authoritative decision makers to re-interpret Article 62 of the Vienna Convention to effect a better accommodation of the conflicting policies of stability and change. The one point that has been clear in the opinions of international tribunals is that the doctrine of *rebus sic stantibus* does not limit the scope of their competency as decision makers.

5. Remedies

A most important aspect of general community policy is directed toward creating remedies for injuries caused as a result of the unilateral termination of an agreement. The more negative goals of this policy, aimed at preventing loss, may be stated in terms of prevention, deterrence, restoration, rehabilitation, and reconstruction. The remedies may be different for each of these subgoals. The more positive goal of remedies is not only to recom-

---

[755] A. DAVID, THE STRATEGY OF TREATY TERMINATION—LAWFUL BREACHES AND RETALIATIONS 54 (1975).

[756] *Id.*

[757] *Id.*

pense the injured party but also to make good the injuries suffered
by, and promote the fulfillment of the inclusive policies of, the
larger community as a whole. Therefore, the choice of remedy by
the injured party is only one relevant factor for the determination
of appropriate remedies. A decision maker has always to evaluate
remedies by seeking a balance between, on the one hand, the interests of the injured party in the negative goals of the community
and, on the other hand, the common interests of the larger community in the production and equitable distribution of all values,
including promotion of development planning in the poorer
countries. It would therefore be wrong to state that the principal
objective in designing a remedy is to undo the changes in order to
recover an alleged status quo. This should never be the objective
sought in remedies, whether for an unlawful termination or a lawful one.

So narrow an objective for remedies ignores the fact that the
expectations of people in the larger community favor a continuous
process of change. The unilateral termination of a major agreement may, moreover, have a significant impact on community expectations and cause important changes in social process. No
matter how much a remedy may help injured parties, the demand
for returning a situation to a status quo is seldom approved in
community expectation, because it is not generally compatible
with the inclusive interest of the larger community. Compensation
may be generous in terms of pecuniary damages, but specific performance of an agreement is generally not approved in practice.
The reason for this may be that when there is a unilateral termination by the contracting state, regardless of the justifications offered for the act, national attitudes in the contracting state are
already turned against the performance of the agreement. In such
circumstances, pressing the government of the contracting state to
proceed with the performance of the agreement will not work to
promote the common interest, because there will be no desire for
cooperation, at least on the part of the contracting state. The unfriendly feeling created between the two parties will stultify any
productive and successful outcome. The possibility of choosing
specific performance as a remedy is not, however, to be totally
eliminated. In situations where the unilateral termination involves
vital resources of broad transnational significance and the termination importantly disturbs production or distribution from those

vital resources, there may be no alternative solution. The authorized decision makers might then choose specific performance as the appropriate remedy to protect the common interest of the larger community.

When parties seek, and tribunals award, the remedy of specific performance, they do so of course upon the assumption that the agreement continues and that the attempted termination is unlawful. In contrast, when the parties seek, and tribunals award damages, they may do so even upon the theory that the termination is lawful. In either event the general community policy is as stated in the much quoted Chorzow opinion that the injured party should be made as nearly whole as possible.

> The essential principle contained in the actual notion of an illegal act—a principle which seems to be established by international practice and in particular by the decisions of arbitral tribunals—is that reparation must, as far as possible, wipe out all the consequence of the illegal act and reestablish the situation which would, in all probability, have existed if that act had not been committed. Restitution in kind, or, if this is not possible, payment of a sum corresponding to the value which a restitution in kind would bear; the award, if need be, of damages for loss sustained which would not be covered by restitution in kind or payment in place of it—such are the principles which should serve to determine the amount of compensation due for an act contrary to international law.[758]

Kronfol observes that in practice there is no such difference in the kind of remedy between a lawful and an unlawful expropriation, because the payment of compensation has always been recommended and restitution is only for exceptional cases.[759] He observes the similarity between the two kinds of terminations with respect to remedy; the difference, however, is in the measures of compensation. In a word, the contracting state in an unlawful termination has to pay much more than otherwise.[760]

Contrary to practice, *restitutio in integrum* has been accepted in the theory of international law, and a number of jurists have sup-

---

[758] [1926] P.C.I.J., ser. A., No. 7 at 46–7.

[759] KRONFOL, *supra* note 290, at 100.

[760] *Id.*

ported this theory.[761] On the other hand, there are many jurists who support the view that pecuniary damages are enough to release the state from responsibility.[762] In the *Chorzow Factory* case such a possibility was recognized by the PCIJ when it stated that "an indemnity corresponding to the damage which the nationals of the injured State have suffered . . . is . . . the most usual form of reparation."[763] In a later judgment, when Poland refused to restore the factory and a subsequent agreement to accept compensation, the Court ordered the payment of compensation.[764]

In a few other cases the opinions of international tribunals have come close to *restitutio in integrum*. In the *Walter Fletcher Smith*[765] claim the arbitrator, while acknowledging restitution as an alternative remedy, decided that in the "best interests of the parties, and of the public," damages should be awarded.[766] In other words, the tribunal stated that the restitution remedy in this case was not compatible with common interest. In the 1973 arbitration concerning the Libyan nationalization of the British Petroleum Company, the tribunal rejected the BP demand for *restitutio in integrum* through a declaratory award, and distinguished the similar awards in the Czechoslovakian RCA case and the Aramco case from the Libyan case. The tribunal stated that in those and similar cases, declaratory awards "have often been made in terms of defining the rights and obligations of parties to a concession contract, these cases have never involved the total expropriation or taking by the state of the property, rights and interests of the concessionaire, and indeed in the most important of the cases the validity and continued existence of the contract has not been questioned."[767] The Tribunal continued, "The case analysis also demonstrates that

---

[761] *See, e.g.*, FATOUROS, *supra* note 208, at 310–11; G. SCHWARSENBERGER, INTERNATIONAL LAW 182–83 (1928); Schwebel, *Speculations on Specific Performance Between a State and a Foreign National* in SELECTED READINGS, *supra* note 243, at 201; and AMERASINGHE, *supra* note 220, at 67.

[762] *See generally* KRONFOL, note 290, *supra*, and H. LAUTERPACHT, PRIVATE LAW SOURCES AND ANALOGIES OF INTERNATIONAL LAW 147 (1927).

[763] [1928] P.C.I.J., Ser. A, No. 17, at 2728.

[764] *Id.*

[765] 4 R. Int'l Arb. Awards 913 (1929).

[766] *Id.* at 918.

[767] 1973 AWARDS, *supra* note 624, at 84.

the responsibility incurred by the defaulting party for breach of an obligation to perform a contractual undertaking is a duty to pay damages, and that the concept of *restitutio in integrum* has been employed mainly as a vehicle for establishing the amount of damages."[768] Furthermore, the Tribunal maintained that cases such as Aramco, where the declaratory award came close to being equivalent to orders for specific performance, are not comparable "to an order for physical restitution by a State of a nationalized enterprise to a foreign concessionaire."[769]

In modern municipal laws, however, the principle of *restitutio in integrum* has been widely recognized, sometimes with modifications. In English and American law the general remedy is damages but occasionally specific performance is recognized. Specific performance in these exceptional cases, however, is not available if it is against the government:

> To deny enforceability to public contracts under the present principle is then to assert no more than that, even where normally available, the remedies of specific performance or injunction or their equivalents are ruled out by the principle of governmental freedom of action. . . .
>
> . . . [T]he public authority may be exempt from performing its contract according to its strict expression, but that where this exemption results in loss to the individual contractor compensation should be payable save where that payment would offend the principle.[770]

In German and French law, specific performance is the normal remedy.[771] Similar policy is followed in Danish law.[772] The main rule in the Scandinavian Uniform Sale of Goods Acts, "a rule which by analogy has a wider application in the law of contracts," is similar to the German law in this respect.[773]

Some measures taken by states for the protection of investments by their citizens abroad, through establishing sanctioning mea-

[768] *Id.*

[769] *Id.* at 85.

[770] J. MITCHELL, THE CONTRACTS OF PUBLIC AUTHORITIES 20 (1954).

[771] A. VON MEHREN, THE CIVIL LAW SYSTEM 502 (1957), and Szladits, *The Concept of Specific Performance in Civil Law,* 4 AM. J. COMP. L. 208, 214 (1955).

[772] 1973 AWARDS, *supra* note 624, at 87.

[773] *Id.*

sures in their municipal law, have generally required compensation rather than *restitutio in integrum*. The Hickenlooper Amendment to the U.S. Foreign Assistance Act of 1962, which denies U.S. aid to states that have nationalized American interests, does not mention *restitutio in integrum*. Similarly, the British government in the Note of December 23, 1971, protesting the Libyan nationalization stated that "Her Majesty's Government must, therefore, call upon the Libyan Government to act in accordance with the established rules of international law and make reparation to British Petroleum Exploration (Libya) Limited, either by restoring the Company to its original position in accordance with the Concession No. 65 or by payment of full damages for the wrong done to the Company."[774] It should be remarked, however, that demands for *restitutio in integrum* may increase in the future. The vague Note of June 11, 1973, of the U.S. Government to the Libyan Government, protesting the nationalization of rights and interests of the Nelson Bunker Hunt Oil Company, may be interpreted as the beginning of such demands.[775] Our recommendation is, however, that the authoritative decision makers should not promote such policies because of their incompatibility with the common interest; only in exceptional cases related to vital resources should specific performance be the appropriate remedy.

The declaratory award is another measure of remedy. *Declaratory award* refers to a request to the competent decision makers in a particular case to specify the rights and obligations of the parties to the dispute without ordering or deciding on damages. In our judgment declaratory awards play the same role as *restitutio in integrum* with respect to community policy. This remedy, like specific performance, is generally not compatible with the common interest, because the function and basic objective of declaratory awards are almost identical to *restitutio in integrum*. A declaratory award that declares a termination unlawful would put so much pressure on continued operation, that is, outside the exclusive arena of the contracting state, that it becomes almost impossible to continue the

---

[774]*Id.* at 29.

[775]The United States in its Note protested the nationalization, condemned it as illegal under international law, and demanded that "the Libyan Arab Republic Government . . . take the necessary steps to rectify this situation and to discharge its obligations under international law with respect to the Nelson Bunker Hunt Oil Company." *Id.* at 65. The language used by the U.S. Government is broad and vague. It could be interpreted as a demand either for *restitutio in integrum* or simply damages.

Alabama Claims, similar principles were adopted as to the duties of a neutral:

> That a neutral government is bound—
> First, to use due diligence to prevent the fitting out, arming, or equipping, within its jurisdiction, of any vessel which it has reasonable ground to believe is intended to cruise or carry on war against a power with which it is at peace; and also to use like diligence to prevent the departure from its jurisdiction of any vessel intended to cruise or carry on war as above, such vessel having been specially adapted, in whole or in part, within such jurisdiction, to warlike use.
> Secondly. Not to permit or suffer either belligerent to make use of its ports or waters as the base of naval operations against the other, or for the purpose of the renewal or augmentation of military supplies or arms, or the recruitment of men.
> Thirdly. To exercise due diligence in its own ports or waters, and as to all persons within its jurisdiction, to prevent any violation of the foregoing obligations and duties.
> It being a condition of this undertaking that these obligations should in future be held to be binding internationally between the two countries.[782]

The obligation of member states to respect the enforcement remedies prescribed by competent inclusive decision makers has been emphasized by the International Court of Justice in its advisory opinion on Namibia of June 21, 1971. The Court stated that the member states of the United Nations were "under obligation to recognize the illegality and invalidity of South Africa's continued presence in Namibia. They are also under obligation to refrain from leading any support or any form of assistance to South Africa with reference to its occupation of Namibia."[783] In 1974 the United Nations Council for Namibia passed a resolution which specifically denied the competence of the Government of South Africa to pass title and stipulated that any corporation engaging in development of resources in Namibia with the South African Government had the international responsibility to pay full compen-

---

[782]The Alabama Claims, U.S.-U.K., Claims Arbitration (1872), *reprinted in* BRIGGS, *supra* note 408, at 1026–30.

[783]The Naminia Case, [1971] I.C.J. 16.

[784]N.Y. Times, Sept. 29, 1974, at 10, col. 3.

sation to the people of Namibia.[784] Such practice has been supported by a great number of jurists.[785]

The third enforcement remedy is prescriptions implemented by international organizations. The past practice of this remedy has involved the World Bank, *e.g.*, denying economic aid to contracting states who refuse to fulfill their responsibilities under international law. The World Bank in a meeting in Tokyo in September 1964 decided not to grant loans to any country that nationalized foreign private investment without compensation. In that meeting Indonesia, Ccylon, and the United Arab Republic were barred from obtaining loans from the Bank for confiscating foreign property.[786] Indonesia was penalized for nationalizing British enterprises, Ceylon for nationalizing foreign petroleum companies, and the UAR for nationalizing British and Belgian companies.

This strategy may have serious repercussions and should be prescribed with greater consideration given to the severity of its consequences on the people of the penalized state. The 1964 World Bank action did not consider this factor. Because of the unequal power and economic structure of some international organizations, as between capital-exporting and capital-importing countries, we do not generally recommend this type of enforcement remedy. Such measures may represent only the interest of a ruling group of the organization, rather than that of the larger community.

[785]*See, e.g.*, McDouglas & Olmstead, Brief *Amicus Curiae* of the Executive Committee of the American Branch of the International Law Association in the Supreme Court of the United States, October Term, 1963, in the case of Banco Nacional de Cuba v. Peter L. F. Sabbatino and Others; see also BROWNLIE, *supra* note 295, at 502; MANN, *supra* note 287, at 389–90; Domke, *Foreign Nationalizations*, 55 AM. J. INT'L L. 585 (1961); Fachiri, *Recognition of Foreign Laws by Municipal Courts*, 12 BRIT. Y.B. INT'L L. 95 (1931), and Bentwich, 32 BRIT. Y.B. INT'L L. 204 (1955).

[786]N.Y. Times, Sept. 11, 1964, at 43, col. 5.

CHAPTER IV

Conservation, Planning, and Development of Resources

CONTEMPORARY WORLD civilization is threatened by a scarcity of resources. Hence, no decisions regarding the management of resources in general and vital resources in particular can ignore the dimension of conservation. The consideration of conservation becomes more complicated when policymakers have to bear in mind the value gaps between different groups of nation-states and the global policy of bridging those gaps. What is needed is a common global policy for conservation, planning, and development of resources that determines the scope and general direction of regional and national decision making concerning the use of resources. For successful implementation of conservation policy, the active participation of individual human beings, the ultimate consumers, would appear indispensable. The awareness of individuals of the scarcity of resources, and their perception that the rational use of resources, is in the common interest, is a necessary, though not conclusive, guarantee of successful conservation policy.

A. THE FACTUAL BACKGROUND

In earlier periods, human demands on resources were smaller in relation to the potential capacity of the environment to sustain life. Today the situation has changed. The tremendous increase in population, due to the development of science, in conjunction with the development of industry, which devours raw materials, has generated great pressures on resources and taxes the capacity of the environment to produce and replace them.[1] The United Na-

---

[1] As population becomes wealthier, it tends to consume more resources. For example, in 1970 the United States had an average industrial output (wealth) per capita of about $1,600,

tions projects world population at the end of the century at three alternative levels, 6 billion, 6.5 billion and 7.1 billion.[2] Many different studies of the interrelations of population growth, the rate of use of resources, and the potentiality of resources for the future have demonstrated that there is no adequate planning for conservation of either renewable or nonrenewable resources.

The number of species whose existence is endangered has gone up. Based on the list of the U.S. Department of Interior, there are 101 species within the United States (October 1970) whose existence is endangered.[3] Latin American countries have been criticized for irrational utilization of their renewable resources.[4] Even renewable natural resources, such as air, water, soils, plants, and animals that are essential to human survival, are endangered. For example, as a result of increasing global consumption of forest products, the expansion of agriculture, urban and industrial development and highways, the earth is generally being deforested.[5] The increasing demands for forest products is closely related to the demands for food and energy.[6] Similarly, the increase in fish

------

and the average citizen consumed approximately seven times the world average per capita resource usage. If the rest of the world develops economically, it may follow the U.S. pattern in consumption. This could be an indication for future demand for resources. *See* D. MEADOWS & ASSOCIATES, THE LIMITS TO GROWTH 113–18 (1972). For similar analysis on the relationship between population growth, industrial output, and demand for resources see generally, J. FORESTER, WORLD DYNAMICS (1971); D. MEADOWS, W. MEADOWS, W. BEHRENS, III, D. MEADOWS, R. NAIL & OTHERS, DYNAMICS OF GROWTH IN A FINITE WORLD (1974); H. BARNETT & C. MORSE, SCARCITY AND GROWTH: THE ECONOMICS OF NATURAL RESOURCE AVAILABILITY (1963); R. FALK, THIS ENDANGERED PLANET: PROSPECTS AND PROPOSALS FOR HUMAN SURVIVAL (1971); M. MESAROVIC & E. PESTEL, MANKIND AT THE TURNING POINT (1974); and W. CLARK, ENERGY FOR SURVIVAL: THE ALTERNATIVE TO EXTINCTION (1974).

[2]*Quoted* in L. BROWN, IN THE HUMAN INTEREST 26 (1974).

[3]L. BROWN, WORLD WITHOUT BORDERS 22 (1972). Today, for example, the number of elephants in Ceylon is half that of twenty years ago. The reason for this sudden decrease could be explained in the diminishing of their environment (forest and jungle) in order to produce more food for the population. Such decrease in forest and jungle is doubling every 20 years. *Id.* at 23.

[4]Unwise utilization of renewable resources, such as extensive deforestation of the woods, unrestricted hunting and fishing of animals which are utilized above their reproductive capacity. Bazan, *International Coordination of the Conservation Law*, in INTERNATIONAL UNION FOR CONSERVATION OF NATURAL RESOURCES (IUCN), CONSERVATION IN LATIN AMERICA 253 (1968).

[5]BROWN, *supra* note 2, at 33.

[6]*Id.*

catch is also closely related to demand for food.[7] Interrelationships between the exhaustion of resources and minimum and optimum world order demonstrate the complexity and difficulty in making policy in this area.

With respect to nonrenewable (such as mineral or energy-related) resources, demands intensify because such resources are basic elements of most finished goods. Whatever the difference in growth rates among different resources, it would be a fair statement to say that the exponential growth in resource use has been a "historical characteristic of the world economy."[8] In the period 1950–70 the aggregate world use of nonrenewable resources increased by 4.1% per year.[9] The U.S. Bureau of Mines predicts that the total world demand for resources will grow at an annual rate of 3.6% to 5.5% per year to the year 2000.[10] A recent World Bank document contends that the currently known reserves of iron ore would last for less than fifty years if the present rate of consumption remained unchanged.[11] The same figures show twenty-nine years for copper and bauxite, fifty years for nickel, and between fifteen to twenty years for ores of such key metals as zinc, lead, and tin.[12] It has been argued that even economic factors, such as increased prices with decreasing availability, will not by itself solve the problem of rapid exhaustion of many mineral resources.[13]

[7]It has been estimated that if the potential of tuna in the Indian Ocean is taken at 500,000 metric tons and the potential of shrimp at 300,000 metric tons, they will be attained in about ten years. Morr, *Indian Ocean Fishery Development*, in WORLD FISHERIES POLICY 125 (B. Rothschild ed. 1972) [hereinafter cited as ROTHSCHILD]. If the projections for the expansion of marine fisheries and the estimates of the total biological potential of the living resources of the sea prove to be correct, total world catch will rapidly approach the total maximum sustainable yield after 1985. Then the problem of conservation will extend to all species that can be caught with present technology of a commercial value. A. KOERS, INTERNATIONAL REGULATION OF MARINE FISHERIES 50 (1973).

[8]DYNAMICS OF GROWTH IN A FINITE WORLD, *supra* note 1, at 371.

[9]*Id.*

[10]BUREAU OF MINES 3 (1970), *cited in id.* at 371.

[11]Radetzki, *Metal Mineral Resource Exhaustion and the Threat to Material Progress: The Case of Copper*, 3 WORLD DEVELOPMENT 123 (Feb.–Mar. 1975).

[12]*Id.*

[13]Even taking into account the price increase, it would appear at the present time that the quantities of platinum, gold, zinc, and lead are not sufficient to meet demands. If the present rate of expansion of consumption of silver, tin, and uranium continues, these minerals may be in short supply, even at higher prices, by the turn of the century. By the

The rate of use of energy resources is growing faster than that of mineral resources and at a rate of 6% a year is 3 times faster than population growth.[14] If the global consumption of energy resources continues at recent rates, the total annual world energy demand at the end of the century would be 4 to 5 times the 1973 rate. Without unpredictable technological innovation, the world will not be able in the coming decades to sustain this growth rate.[15] It has been predicted that energy needs for a continuing consumption growth rate of 6% may not be forthcoming at any feasible price for at least two decades, and possibly longer.[16] Even an increase in the use of atomic energy will not solve the future problem of energy shortage. Amory Lovins of the Massachusetts Institute of Technology calculated world energy needs in the year 2000 on the basis of an assumption of a growth rate of 5%, a little lower than that of the 1970s. He observes that "[i]f we could somehow build one huge nuclear power station per day for the rest of this century, starting today, then when we are through, more than half our primary energy would still come from fossil fuels, which would be consumed about twice as fast as now."[17]

Considering these facts and projections, it is obvious that the necessity for a common policy of conservation of resource has never been greater. No matter how one argues about the clarity and interpretation of these predictions and numbers,[18] one cannot deny the fact that they are definitely signs of danger for the future

---

year 2050 several more minerals may be exhausted if the current rate of consumption continues. However, geologists disagree about the prospects for finding large, new, and rich ore deposits; "reliance on such discoveries would seem unwise in the long term." FIRST ANNUAL REPORT OF THE COUNCIL ON ENVIRONMENTAL QUALITY 157 (1970).

[14] For statistical materials on resources, reserves, production, and consumption see: U.N., STATISTICAL YEARBOOK; U.S. BUREAU OF MINES, MINERALS YEARBOOK (Washington, D.C., U.S.G.P.O.). ANNALES DES MINES (Paris, Compagnie Française d'edition); METALLGE-SELLSCHAFT AKTIENGESE ISCHAFT (Frankfurt am Main, Metallgesellschaft); and STATISTICAL SUMMARY OF THE MINERAL INDUSTRY (London, Institute of Geological Science).

[15] BROWN, *supra* note 2, at 35.

[16] *Id.* In 1925 only 14 percent of the world's energy supply crossed national boundaries, but by the mid-1970s this share increased to one-third and is growing rapidly. *Id.* at 82.

[17] *Quoted in* BROWN, *supra* note 2, at 38.

[18] For limitation in the projection of mineral and energy resources, *see* "Problems of Availability and Supply of Nature Resources: Medium-Term and Long-Term Projections of Resource's Supply and Demand of Energy, Minerals and Water Resources," U.N. Doc. E/C.7/52 (1975).

of the human race. As Ciriacy-Wantrup concludes, the world community should not gamble the future of mankind on the possibility that changes in technology, tastes, and institutions will solve the future resource scarcity.[19] One cannot simply rely on past experience and the intelligence of the human mind to take care of all crises in due time. The current world crises are different from the ones in the past, for they come together, are interrelated, and are continuous.[20] The crises are constructed in ways that do not allow the world community to deal with them case by case.[21] Therefore, deliberate effort should be made to understand the nature and interrelationship of these crises and, through global planning and collective action, to begin to solve them.

In the world of resource scarcity the purposes for which resources are allocated are of utmost importance. Considering world military expenditure in forms of minerals, energy, capital, science, and human resources, one cannot justify the present trend even if one characterizes the present world as a "global war system." Though the amount of resources and expenditures that many countries such as the U.S.S.R. and the Eastern Europeans allocate to military research and development are unpublished,[22] it has been estimated that total world military expenditure is about 6% to 6.5% of the world national product.[23] Housing investment together with slum clearance and the urban renewable product is about 3% to 3.5% of the world total national product.[24] Military expenditure is about 2.5 times the estimated total of publicly financed health expenditure.[25] While total military expenditure is higher in developed countries, the rate of increase is faster in developing countries, which is about 7% a year.[26] World military expenditure in 1970 was roughly $200 billion, and it has been

[19] S. Ciriacy Wantrup, Resource Conservation: Economics and Policies (1963).

[20] Mesarovic & Pestel, *supra* note 1, at 10–11.

[21] *Id.*

[22] Stockholm International Peace Research Institute (SIPRI), Resources Devoted to Military Research and Development 9 (1972).

[23] Economic and Social Consequences of the Arms Race and of Military Expenditure, U.N. Doc. A/8469/Rev. 1 (1972) at 19–21.

[24] *Id.*

[25] *Id.*

[26] *Id.* at 10. *See also* N.Y. Times, Mar. 1, 1976, at 1, col. 1.

predicted that it will increase to $280 billion in 1980, if it continues to grow at an annual rate of 3%.[27] A recent study shows that the military expenditures of 1975 have already reached $300 billion.[28]

The alarming trends of allocation of resources for military purposes resulted in U.N. General Assembly Resolution 2685 (XXV) requesting the Secretary-General to take measures:

> (a) to formulate suggestions for the guidance of Member-States, the specialized agencies and the International Atomic Energy Agency, as well as other organizations of the United Nations System, with a view to establishing the link between the Disarmament Decade and the Second United Nations Development Decade so that an appropriate portion of the resources that are released as a consequence of progress towards general and complete disarmament would be used to increase assistance for the economic and social development of developing countries;
>
> (b) to propose measures for the mobilization of world public opinion in support of the link between disarmament and development and thus encourage intensified negotiations aimed at progress towards general and complete disarmament under effective international control.[29]

It further requested the Secretary-General to submit a report on those questions, through the Economic and Social Council, in time for consideration by the General Assembly in 1973 at the first biennial review of the implementation of the International Development Strategy for the Second United Nations Development Decade (G.A.R. 2626 [XXV]). Subsequent to this request a group of experts was appointed to research the economic and social consequences of disarmament.[30] Research by Professors W. W. Leontief and P. A. Petri of Harvard University estimated the impact of complete disarmament on worldwide demand for 11 raw materials.[31] Research published by the Secretary-General states

[27] U.N. DEPT. OF ECONOMIC AND SOCIAL AFFAIRS, DISARMAMENT AND DEVELOPMENT, U.N. Doc. ST/ECA/174 (1972) at 4 (hereinafter cited as DISARMAMENT).

[28] N.Y. Times, Mar. 1, 1976, at 1, col. 1.

[29] G.A. Res. 2685, 25 U.N. GAOR, Supp. (No. 28) 56, U.N. Doc. A/8028 (1970).

[30] DISARMAMENT, note 27 *supra*.

[31] For a statistical change in world demand for selected raw materials after proportional reallocation of military purchases to other demand categories (as percentage of world supply), see U.N. Doc.A/8469 Rev. 1 (1972) at 48.

that most of the resources used in military services are transferable to projects for development purposes, such as food, clothing, transport, fuel, manpower, metal products, and engineering industries.[32] In terms of human resources, the report estimates that complete disarmament would affect approximately 20,000 nuclear scientists and engineers.[33] Some of these scientists could assist the peaceful nuclear programs of developing countries if plans for this purpose were made. And if 2,000 tons of fissile material were released for peaceful purposes it would be enough to provide the initial and replacement fuel over their useful life for an installed capacity of about 100,000 electrical megawatts of thermal reactors or an installed capacity of about 500,000 electrical megawatts of fast breeder reactors.[34] These figures should be compared with the current estimates of the total installed capacity of nuclear power plants of 300,000 electrical megawatts in 1980 and 1,000,-000 electrical megawatts in 1990.[35] Regardless of U.N. General Assembly Res. 2667 (XXV) 1970, which, based on this research, called upon member states to take steps toward disarmament and a number of treaties concerning disarmament,[36] the rate of use of resources for military expenditures has been increasing.

B. BASIC COMMUNITY POLICIES

From the beginning the concept of conservation has been an ambiguous one, subject to different interpretations.[37] Like many

---

[32] DISARMAMENT, *supra* note 27, at 14.

[33] *Id.* at 17.

[34] *Id.*

[35] For a comprehensive research on transfer of resources used for military purposes to peaceful uses, see *id.* at 17–37.

[36] For treaties such as the Antarctic Treaty (1959), the Treaty Banning Nuclear Weapon Tests in the Atmosphere, in Outer Space and Under-Water (1963), the Treaty on Principles Governing the Activities of States in the Exploration and Use of Outer Space, including the Moon and other Celestial Bodies (1967), the Treaty for the Prohibition of Nuclear Weapons in Latin America (1967), the Treaty on the Non-proliferation of Nuclear Weapons (1968), and the Treaty on the Prohibition of the Emplacement of Nuclear Weapons and other Weapons of Mass Destruction on the Sea-Bed and the Ocean Floor and in the Subsoil Thereof (1971), *see generally* U.N. DEP'T OF POLITICAL AND SECURITY COUNCIL AFFAIRS, THE UNITED NATIONS AND DISARMAMENT 1945–1965 (1967).

[37] The word *conservation* comes from the British practice in India, where forest areas called "conservancies" were protected to provide sufficient cover for the maintenance of

other concepts, it has been an instrument for implementing political, social, and economic policies that have not always had adequate relation to common interest. Arthur Maass describes the characteristic use of this concept by the U.S. government; particular reforms based on "scientific," "democratic," and "moral" objectives are described as "conservation." However, the reforms, in fact, often have nothing to do with conservation.[38] T. O'Riordan observes that the concept of conservation has been used to identify various periods of political activity either when public policy was directed at better management of resources or when the political interests of certain resource-using groups were threatened.[39] In the U.S., he continues, interest in conservation policy has moved from protection of the public domain (1890–1920),[40] through regional multiple resources planning (1935–43),[41] to national strategic safety (1960–64) and environmental quality and dignity of

---

soil stability and the control of surface runoff. G. PINCHAT, BREAKING NEW GROUND (1947). The concept of conservation, however, has its origin in ideas and activities long in the past. It is written that Plato was the first to recognize the principle of plenitude, that the world becomes better as it contains more things, and associated a decline in fertility in ancient Greece to the deforestation of the mountains and consequent soil erosion and water. R. DASMANN, PLANET IN PERIL 175 (1972). Edward Graham reports that the first institutionalized attempts for protection of wildlife began with Sennacherib in an area near Nineveh. E. GRAHAM, THE LAND AND WILDLIFE (1947). The origin of management of farming for agricultural conservation goes back to the Neolithic period and some conservation concepts appear in writings from Egyptian papyri and later were developed more scientifically by Romans such as Cato, Columella, Pling, and Tacitus. The more modern concept of forest conservation began in the 17th century in England and France with Evelyn and Colbert. Later in eighteenth century the concept of conservation was considered in relation to population growth; finally the more modern concept of conservation as a social movement started in North America. DASMANN, *id.* at 175–76.

[38] In the United States, at the beginning of the 20th century, the word *conservation* was associated with new federal programs for forestry, regulating use of western public lands to protect timber, livestock ranges, and wild life habitats and developing water resources for irrigation of western deserts and navigation of western rivers. In 1930s it was used to meet pressing needs of movement in the Great Depression. In 1960s, however, conservation was used to explain the government plans relating to cities. They were concerned with the quality of the urban environment, with programs to protect open lands in metropolitan areas, and so forth. INT'L ENCY. SOC. SCIENCES 271 (1972).

[39] T. O'RIORDAN, PERSPECTIVES ON RESOURCE MANAGEMENT 8 (1971).

[40] *See* S. HAYS, CONSERVATION AND THE GOSPEL OF EFFICIENCY (1959), and Griffith, *Main Lines of Thought and Action*, in PERSPECTIVES ON AMERICA'S NATURAL RESOURCES 3–23 (H. Jarrett ed. 1958) [hereinafter cited as JARRETT].

[41] *See generally* D. LILIENTHAL, DEMOCRACY ON THE MARCH (1944); G. CLAPP, THE T.V.A.: AN APPROACH TO THE DEVELOPMENT OF A REGION (1955); and Griffith, note 40, *supra*.

life.[42] O'Riordan observes that the term *conservation* suffers from being ambiguous in its interpretation and from its shifting, inconsistent, and sometimes contradictory objectives.[43]

A study of different definitions of conservation illustrates the pervading narrowness of the conception. One definition refers to the objective of "ensuring a renewable yield from a resource stock."[44] Another, with respect to sea resources, observes that "the central concern of conservation is to prevent the waste of the living resources of the sea by over-exploitation and to preserve their productivity for the future,"[45] or "in conservation measures designed to achieve high sustainable yields needed to provide food and protein for present and future generations."[46] As is clear from these definitions, the objective of conservation begins and ends with "maximum sustainable yield of a stock," no matter how definitions are phrased. For example, S. McDonald of the University of Texas carefully states the definition of conservation "as action designed to achieve and maintain the optimum time-distribution of use of natural resources."[47] It is obvious that the scope of conservation in his view does not go much beyond his other colleagues'. T. O'Riordan, while recognizing the limited scope of conventional conservation policy, does not go far enough in his elaboration. He defines conservation as "a philosophy which is directed at the manner and timing of resource use, and has been subject to various interpretations of an economic and political nature."[48] Article 2 of the Convention on Fisheries and Conservation of the Living Resources of the High Seas defines conservation along the lines of the other definitions: "[C]onservation of the living resources of the high seas means the aggregate of the mea-

[42] President's Science Advisory Committee, Restoring the Quality of Our Environment (1965).

[43] O'Riordan, *supra* note 39, at 8.

[44] Knight, *International Fisheries Management: A Background Paper*, in The Future of International Fisheries Management 23 (H. Knight ed. 1975).

[45] A. Koers, International Regulation of Marine Fisheries, 45 (1973).

[46] R. Hallman, Towards an Environmentally Sound Law of the Sea 24 (1974).

[47] McDonald, *The Economics of Conservation*, paper presented to the Rocky Mountain Petroleum Economics Institute, June 18, 1964, at 6, *quoted in* W. Lovejoy & O. Homan, Oil Conservation Regulation 16–17 (1967).

[48] O'Riordan, *supra* note 39, at 8.

sures rendering possible the optimum sustainable yield from those resources so as to secure a maximum supply of food and other marine products. Conservation programs should be formulated with a view to securing in the first place a supply of food for human consumption."[49]

Another defect of historic conservation policies has been in the lack of attention given to nonrenewable resources. The conservation literature seems to deal either directly with renewable resources or to analyze conservation issues as if their subject were only renewable resources. This lack of attention is manifest in the conservation definitions given above, and would have continued but for the dramatic realization of a scarcity of energy and mineral resources. But now there are many more demands for conservation of nonrenewable resources. A U.N. study of natural resources in developing countries defines conservation with respect to nonrenewable resources as follows: "the conservation of non-renewable resources, as effected by rational, efficient use and long-term exploitation plans, and by the prevention of waste through inefficient production and treatment techniques or otherwise."[50]

The above conservation policies still neglect the relationship between conservation as a social phenomenon and more general community policies. Conservation need not be concerned as an isolated concept to protect unique kinds of living or stock resources for the satisfaction or moral objectives of different groups of people interested in nature. Conservation can be conceived, rather, as a part of a general global policy of protecting the common interests of all people of the world through the rational use of resources. The "maximum sustainable yield" can be made an important major thrust of conservation policy, but only if it pro-

[49] Article 2 of the Convention on Fisheries and Conservation of the Living Resources of the High Seas, Apr. 29, 1958, Geneva, 52 AM. J. INT'L L. 851–64 (1958). Similarly, in the Rome Conference of 1955, it is stated: "The immediate aim of conservation of living marine resources is to conduct fishing activities so as to increase, or at least maintain, the average sustainable yield of products in desirable form. . . . The principal objective of conservation of living resources of the sea is to obtain the optimum sustainable yield so as to secure a maximum supply of food and other marine products. . . ." Rome Conference Report, *International Technical Conference on the Conservation of Living Resources of the Sea* 2 (1955). For a similar policy, see also Final Act of the Inter-American Specialized Conference on Conservation of Natural Resources: The Continental Shelf and Marine Waters, Ciudad Trujillo, Mar. 15–28 Final Act at 13.

[50] U.N., Natural Resources of Developing Countries: Investigation, Redevelopment and Rational Utilization, U.N. Doc. No. E/4608/Rev. 1 (1970).

vides an abundant production and fair distribution of values among the peoples and nations of the globe. Otherwise, a policy and strategy that provides only "maximum sustainable yield" must lack a fair and just distribution of values. In such circumstances, it is inaccurate to refer to such policies as conservation; they are rather just another strategy for promotion of special interest, and "conservation" becomes camouflage. The interrelationship between conservation and the more general policy of the community has been emphasized by Professor McDougal: "The emerging aspiration of mankind is not so much for some simple conservation of resources or environment in a pristine, untouched state of nature as for an appropriately conserving, economic, and constructive employment of resources in the greater production and wider distribution of all basic human dignity values."[51] S. T. Dana, sensitive to the perils of treating conservation policy in isolation, defines the objective of conservation as that of securing widespread adoption of policies and institutions that will promote the public interest in all matters related to the management and utilization of resources.[52]

In our view, thus, conservation is *a process of decision that seeks to optimize the rational use of resources to promote common interest through regulating the time, the rate, and the characteristics of the process of use. With regard to renewable resources, a major thrust of conservation is the design of modes of use which assure the replenishment of potentials. With regard to nonrenewable resources, conservation seeks timed uses which optimize all goals of public order.* Any decision regarding conservation should face a number of issues and questions. Besides time and rate of use of resources, which are two important considerations, other issues (sometimes called characteristics) include property rights, economic factors, allocation questions, the relevance of science and technology, preservation or development, and the political, economic, and social pressures. *Any conservation decision should be made contextually in order to consider all the relevant factors.*

The most that we can do here is to outline some of the basic considerations that should be taken into account in appraising the significance of these different factors in different contexts.

The claim of *private property rights* with concomitant freedom of

---

[51] McDougal, *Legal Bases for Securing the Integrity of the Earth-Space Environment*, in MANAGING THE PLANET 195 (P. Albertson & M. Barnett eds. 1972).

[52] Dana, *Pioneers and Principles*, in JARRETT, *supra* note 40, at 24.

decision is an important factor that a decision maker in a free or
market political economy has to face: to what extent should conservation policy interfere with private property rights? At the
present time this problem is more relevant to national conservation policies, but it is becoming more important and complicated
in the international arena under the rubric of "sovereignty over
natural resources."[53] A global conservation policy must have the
potential for limiting private property rights as well as state sovereignty. While it is difficult to state the precise degree of necessary
limitation on a state sovereignty over utilization of its natural resources, it is clear from past trends that state sovereignty is not
absolute. Particularly when a decision relates to resources vital to
others, international concern limits state competence. Nation-
states that suffer severely from implementation of a global conservation policy should, of course, be reasonably compensated by
other states.

The *economic factor*, or "efficiency," is another relevant issue in
conservation. There is no doubt that cost and benefit analysis
should be taken into account in conservation planning, but since
conservation is a decision made for the production and just distribution of all values, the question of efficiency should not be permitted to jeopardize this basic policy. In our contemporary world
in which the major war is against hunger and for the protection of
the human race, the question of economic efficiency and profit is
of instrumental importance only if it promotes all human dignity
values.

The *allocation* question has always been critical and controversial. By allocation question we refer to "*who* can get *what, how much*,
under *what circumstances*." The allocation issue is not unique in
conservation but is involved in all human interaction. As the history of international relations shows, there has often been a tendency to avoid this question and to leave its solution to the time
and circumstances of the particular case. In the past the community might have been able to afford to do that because of abundant
resources, limited technology, and fewer demands and less power

---

[53] Some of the private property rights are protected by international conventions, such
as the Universal Declaration of Human Rights, which states: "Everyone has the right to own
property alone as well as in association with others. No one shall be arbitrarily deprived of
his property." A similar provision is incorporated in the European Convention on Human
Rights.

from the poorer countries. Today, however, the scarcity of resources in conjunction with increasing demands and pressure from developing countries for equitable distribution of resources has increased the urgency of dealing with resource allocation more directly. In none of the processes of resource utilization does the issue of allocation need more direct attention than in conservation. Vital resources are limited. When there is a limited good and high demands, there is no way for the decision maker to make a fair decision about distribution of the limited good, except by directly addressing the problem and formulating criteria by which the limited good is to be distributed among the participants in ways that promote the aggregate common interest.

In designing conservation policies, *preservation* and *development* must be included. Preservation, we would emphasize, is a most important component of conservation, but it is not the only component. The maintenance of the status quo may have to yield to completely new ways of doing things. In some processes of resource utilization, development of resources may be the main thrust of conservation. This is especially so in agricultural production, development of cultured fisheries and other animals, and new sources of energy and substituted resources.

If the only objective of conservation were preservation or development, all decisions regarding conservation could be made on *scientific* evidence. But conservation policy is not limited to preservation or development. It has a high degree of impact on community. Hence a decision maker cannot ignore *political, economic,* and *social* pressures in formulating a viable conservation policy. While scientific evidence is of utmost importance to conservation, it should be taken into account in relation to community pressure in forms of political, economic, and social reactions and impacts. Norman Wengert in emphasizing the importance of science in conservation and utilization of resources states that he does not mean to substitute the political process of decision making with cold logic and right reason, but to use techniques which alone can prevent error from masquerading as truth. He continues: "The choices are not between a society governed by scientific fact and one of anarchic chaos, but between an open society which seeks knowledge and uses reason, which does not reject rational solutions but avoids over-simplifications, which rigorously tests its premises as well as its conclusions, and, on the other hand, a static society veering alternately from faith to nihilism, from brash over-confidence in the rightness of its position to meet acceptance of an evil world."[54]

C. PAST TRENDS IN DECISION

The first interest in conservation was expressed in the private sectors, which led the conservation movement before the First World War. Though the objectives of the private conservation movement were different from conservation policy today, there is no doubt that they were the pioneers in this increasingly important area. In 1922 the International Council for Bird Preservation (ICBP) was established as the first international organization for conservation.[55] In 1928 the International Office for Protection of Nature was founded in Europe. This office was mainly an intelligence center for gathering documents.[56] UNESCO, founded in 1946, became interested in conservation and two years later established the International Union for Conservation of Nature and Natural Resources (IUCN). IUCN is a non-governmental agency and the major organization of conservation in the world. The International Youth Federation for Environmental Studies and Conservation (IYF) consists of regional and national youth organizations, founded in 1956 in order to organize, promote, and encourage the knowledge, understanding, and appreciation of nature for youth around the world. Another private organization is the European Association for Free Natural Reserves, founded on February 28, 1967, to ensure the protection and conservation of sites of natural importance in Europe, with a view to safeguarding the flora and fauna by encouraging landowners to accede to the EI-REL charter. This organization consists of individuals or legal entities with offices or activities in Europe whose aim is the study and conservation of nature.

As mentioned earlier, while conservation efforts by private organizations have been valuable from the historical viewpoint, their objectives have generally been simple and noncomprehensive and have had a minor impact on the global problem of resource scarcity. Their limited objectives may be justified because of the limited

---

[54] N. Wengert, Natural Resources and the Political Struggle 13–14 (1955).

[55] K. Curry-Lindahl, Conservation for Survival 285 (1972).

[56] *Id.*

authority and control of the private sector over vital renewable and nonrenewable resources. The participation of private conservation organizations even for recreational activities in conjunction with regional and intergovernmental organizations with more serious conservation policies is, nonetheless, necessary and important for implementation of a viable and effective conservation movement.

1. Renewable Resources

The first conservation movements sought to protect renewable resources. This may seem strange; one would have thought that conservation of nonrenewable resources would have been of more concern. But considering the political character of nonrenewable resources and the fact that the conservation movement was started by private sectors with limited authority and control, the past trend is understandable. Nonrenewable resources have traditionally been identified as the property of individual states; for a great number of developing countries they are the major source of income for a limited time. Moreover, any conservation policy may have a direct or indirect impact on the price of nonrenewable resources which themselves have a high impact on the global economy. And finally, because conservation policy may stimulate changes in the major national resource-utilization policies of individual nation-states, such policies may not be welcomed by host countries. Therefore, formulation and implementation of conservation policy with respect to nonrenewable resources becomes more complicated and requires the cooperation of governments more than the private sectors.

Some of the renewable resources are presently counted among shareable resources, but many of them are already within national domain. Among renewable resources, fisheries have the longest history of conservation efforts through regional and international organizations. They also, in comparison with other resources, have manifested the most organized and comprehensive institutional structures.

a. Fisheries

The need for cooperation about fish catch was not really appreciated until after 1850, when the Northern European countries engaged in fishing and greatly expanded their fleets. The expansion of their operations led to some problems and conflicts of interest which convinced the states involved of a need for joint cooperation in distributing the benefits of the sea and the maintenance of peace. For example, the North Sea Convention of 1882 between Belgium, Denmark, France, Germany, Great Britain, and the Netherlands, effective in 1884, was an international convention which aimed at creating peace and general agreement concerning the safety of the fishermen of member countries.[57] The Convention, besides affirming a three-mile territorial sea, incorporated some regulations concerning the conduct of fishing operations (Articles 14–24), regulations concerning documents, specifications for building boats and the like.

In the nineteenth century it was believed that the oceans could produce unlimited amounts of fish. This belief began to weaken, and in the twentieth century the fact that fish populations could be depleted was recognized.[58] The European preliminary Conference on Fisheries Investigation began in 1899 at Stockholm and established in Copenhagen in 1902 an International Council for the Exploration of the Sea.[59] The basic objective of the Council was to encourage scientific investigation by the member states; seldom did it conduct its own investigation. The Council changed its status to a more formal organization in 1964 under the same name and came into force in 1968,[60] but its function is still only to encourage scientific investigation by member states or by itself to gather scientific results for distribution among its members. The main area of operation of the Council is the Atlantic Ocean, particularly the North Atlantic.

[57] J. Tomasevich, International Agreements on Conservation of Marine Resources 269 (1943).

[58] Larkin, *A Confidential Memorandum of Fisheries Science*, in Rothschild, *supra* note 7, at 189.

[59] *See* Koers, *supra* note 45, at 78. For a comprehensive study of treaties regulating fisheries, see Daggett, *The Regulation of Maritime Fisheries by Treaty*, 28 Am. J. Int'l L. 693 (1934). *See generally* J. Bingham, Report of the International Law of Pacific Coastal Fisheries (1933); L. Leonard, International Regulation of Fisheries (1944). Tomasevich, note 57 *supra*; and J. Gulland, The Management of Marine Fisheries (1974).

[60] Int'l Legal Materials 302 (1968). The present members of the International Council are: Belgium, Canada, Denmark, the Federal Republic of Germany, Finland, France, Iceland, Italy, the Netherlands, Norway, Poland, Portugal, Spain, Sweden, the United Kingdom, and the U.S.S.R.

The ICES's limited conservation objective of biological research became a model for other fisheries organizations' conservation programs. The League of Nations Committee of Experts for Codification Conference of 1930 on the problem of "Exploitation of the products of the Sea," recommended: "The Conference . . . [d]esires to affirm the importance of the work already undertaken or to be undertaken regarding these matters, either through scientific research, or by particular methods, that is, measures of protection and collaboration which may be recognized as necessary for the safeguarding of riches constituting the common patrimony."[61] The International Law Commission, concerned about conservation of marine resources in its 1950 session, requested a special study of the problem of protecting the resources of the sea for the benefit of mankind. In 1951 the ILC prepared drafts on marine resources in general and sent them with the comments of its members and experts, to all U.N. members in order to create and publicize the concern for conservation. Two years later in 1953 the ILC adopted provisions for conservation of marine resources.[62] These provisions empowered a state whose nationals are engaged in fishing activities in high seas where nationals of other states are engaged to take conservation measures to protect fishing resources against waste or extermination. In situations where the nationals of other nations are engaged in the same area of fishing, these measures would be taken collectively (Article 1). In any case, in areas situated within one hundred miles from the territorial sea, the coastal state or states would be entitled to take part in conservation measures on an equal footing with the nations actually engaged in fishing, even if their own nationals do not carry on fishing in the area (Article 2).

The urgent importance of conservation of marine resources moved the United Nations General Assembly to adopt Resolution 900 (IX), of December 14, 1954, to recommend a conference of all member states at Rome in April 1955 in order "to study the problem of the international conservation of the living resources of the sea and to make appropriate scientific and technical recommendations." However, as later developments made clear, this formulation of policies in terms of conservation of living resources

---

[61] 1 League of Nations Acts of the Codification Conference 169, [1930].

[62] [1953] Rep. Int'l L. Comm'n. 16–17.

of the sea is too narrow to address the multiple problems of conservation in a global system with all its diverse yet interrelated demands. This formulation is what we refer to as an "isolated policy," a policy that ignores the interrelationship, interdependency, and mutual impacts of its subject matter and other issues in world order. In a "shrinking" world where the major challenge is for access to resources, a policy of preservation which only limits itself to biological and technical recommendations and which only restricts access to resources is simply inadequate. It must be accompanied by an adequate system for the allocation or distribution of the values arising from resources.

The International Commission for Northwest Atlantic Fisheries is one of the early efforts of regional organizations.[63] It consists of fifteen countries actively involved in fishing in that area. The main objective of ICNAF and its small staff is to keep stocks at levels which secure maximum sustainable yields in an area which covers fisheries from Rhode Island along the coast of North America to Greenland. The shares of the states involved in ICNAF are generally determined by a formula which allocates 40% of the catch according to the average national catch of the previous ten-year period, 40% according to the average for the previous three years, and the remainder divided according to a formula which balances a preference for coastal countries and an allowance for miscellaneous factors, such as new entrants into the fishing and the catch of nonmember nations.[64] The quotas established by ICNAF, however, are often far below the catch in recent years.[65] Furthermore, it is not unusual for one or more of the fifteen member states to refuse to comply with the recommendations. Additional evidence of the failure of ICNAF is the ominous 18% decline in fish catch from 1968 to 1970, despite continued efforts at more fishing.[66] Such a decline may well be the result of exhaustion of stock because of overfishing.

The Northeast Atlantic Fisheries Commission (NEAFC) is similar to ICNAF. It has no permanent staff and its work is carried out

[63] [1950] 1 U.S.T. 477, T.I.A.S. No. 2089.

[64] L. Brown, The Global Politics of Resource Scarcity 14 (1974).

[65] *Id.*

[66] L. Brown, By Bread Alone 154 (1974).

by the British government on contract.[67] Both NEAFC and IC-NAF rely on member countries to collect the necessary data, to conduct scientific research, and to propose regulations.

Following World War II, there was a rapid increase in the tuna catch in the eastern tropical Pacific. This increase led to the 1949 Convention between the United States and Costa Rica and the establishment of the Inter-American Tropical Tuna Commission.[68] The basic objective of the Commission was to conduct "investigations concerning the abundance, biology, biometry, and ecology of yellowfin (Neothunnus) and skipjack (Katsuwonas) tuna in the waters of the eastern Pacific Ocean" (Article 11[1]).[69] Other countries, such as Panama, Mexico, Canada, and Japan, have also joined this Commission. This Commission has no allocation system among the member countries but only recommends certain quotas based on investigation and when such quotas are reached recommends no further catch. It is clear that under such circumstances members equipped with the better fishing technology can catch more fish, and faster, than members with primitive or less-developed equipment. Because allocation systems in which there is a gap in technology between member states discriminate against the less developed, the developing nations who are the members of the Commission have been dissatisfied with the present regulatory system and demand the allocation of allowable catch among member countries with preferential treatment for developing countries and for countries off whose coasts the tuna are taken.[70]

The International Commission for the Conservation of Atlantic Tuna (ICCAT) is another Commission specifically dealing with tuna fish. ICCAT was drafted and signed in Rio de Janeiro in 1966 between the United States and Brazil.[71] Its main structure is similar to Inter-American Tropical Tuna Commission (IATTC). ICCAT became a multilateral agreement in 1969 when seven

[67] Gulland, *Fisheries Management and the Needs of Developing Countries*, in ROTHSCHILD, *supra* note 7, at 180.

[68] [1950] 1 U.S.T. 230, T.I.A.S. No. 2044.

[69] For conservation programs of this Commission in recent years see ANNUAL REPORT OF THE INTER-AMERICAN TROPICAL TUNA COMMISSION 55–68 (1975).

[70] ROTHSCHILD, *supra* note 7, at 43.

[71] [1969] 20 U.S.T. 2887, T.I.A.S. No. 6767.

countries ratified it and it is now open to members of the United Nations and its specialized agencies (Article XI). Scientific investigation in ICCAT may be conducted on different levels: official organizations of the member states, private groups, and independent research. The new provision in ICCAT is Article IX(3): the contracting parties agree: "to collaborate with each other with a view to the adoption of suitable effective measures to ensure the application of the provisions of this Convention and in particular to set up a system of international enforcement to be applied to the Convention area except the territorial sea and other waters, if any, in which a state is entitled under international law to exercise jurisdiction over fisheries." ICCAT like IATTC has no allocation system.

The U.N. Food and Agricultural Organization has been involved in conservation of fisheries. For example, the Indian Ocean Fishery Commission (IOFC) and the Indo-Pacific Fisheries Council (IPFC) have been established by FAO under Articles VI–1 and XIV of the FAO's Constitution. The basic objectives of IOFC are to promote national programs of the member states concerning the development and conservation of fisheries through international sources and aid programs and to take fast and necessary actions concerning the most urgent problems.[72] IPFC covers both fresh waters and the Indo-Pacific region.[73] The basic objective of IPFC is to deal with technical aspects of the problems of development and promote proper utilization of living aquatic resources; to cooperate and encourage research and disseminate the results therefrom; to recommend and undertake development projects within its member nations; and to propose and adopt measures to bring about standardization of scientific equipment (Article III).

Indian Ocean fisheries, however, are essentially tuna and shrimp. There is an expanding international market for these species. The shrimp resources are largely in territorial waters; therefore their taking is mainly by coastal states or by joint ventures with non–Indian Ocean firms. The tuna resources, on the other hand, are largely in international waters, and their taking is carried out almost entirely by non–Indian Ocean countries, particu-

---

[72] Joseph, *International Agreements for the Management of Tuna*, in ROTHSCHILD, *supra* note 7, at 102.

[73] [1956] 7 U.S.T. 2927, T.I.A.S. No. 3674.

larly Japan, the Republic of China (Taiwan), and the Republic of Korea.[74] The coastal states of the Indian Ocean are dissatisfied with the present trend because they are not capable of high seas fisheries and therefore cannot compete with non–Indian Ocean fishermen. Moreover, despite the fact that the Indian Ocean is populated with many kinds of fish other than tuna, the main emphasis of the high seas fishermen of this area is based on tuna. This stock has already been depleted close to or beyond the level necessary for maximum sustainable yield. Considering that the Indian Ocean countries have one thousand million people or roughly ⅓ of the earth's population, most of whom are poor, one can understand their demand for sharing the profits of the ocean. Indeed, tuna, an expensive commodity, could help them with their foreign exchange.[75]

Two major multilateral agreements on conservation of marine resources have direct allocating systems. One of these is the International Whaling Commission. Until sometime after World War II whales were taken for oil, but in recent years whale meat has been used for cat and dog foods and to an increasing extent for human consumption, especially in Japan.[76] The attempt at regulation of whaling began in the 1930s, with the League of Nations Convention for Regulation of Whaling (1931),[77] which came into force in 1935. The 1931 Convention was followed by an international conference in London in 1937,[78] which was followed by an informal conference in 1939.[79] The Convention recommended a number of regulations for conservation, including full utilization of the whale.[80] In restricting the total number of whales caught, however,

---

[74] Morr, *Indian Ocean Fishery Development*, in ROTHSCHILD, *supra* note 7, at 122.

[75] For an elaborate analysis of Indian Ocean fisheries, see *id.*

[76] Gulland, *supra* note 67, at 14.

[77] 155 L.N.T.S. 351.

[78] 196 L.N.T.S. 131.

[79] For studies on whaling, see Leonard, *Recent Negotiations Toward the International Regulation of Whaling*, 35 AM. J. INT'L L. 30–113 (1941); Jessup, *The International Protection of Whales*, 24 AM. J. INT'L L. 751–52 (1930); and D. JOHNSTON, THE INTERNATIONAL LAW OF FISHERIES 396–401 (1965).

[80] Among the proposed measures designed to insure full utilization was a recommendation that the whole whale be processed within 36 hours of the kill and other regulations intended to maximize oil and blubber retention.

the Convention was not successful. Later negotiations and conventions resulted in the establishment of the International Whaling Commission, with powers to recommend a wide range of management procedures.[81] This convention, like the others, did not include an allocation system but only shortened the season of catch.

Considering the high expenses of the industry, every participant in whaling tried to catch as many whales in the authorized season as possible. The combination of high competition and new technology soon resulted in a dramatic decline in whales. The Commission finally confessed that the conservation of whales would not be possible until member states came to an agreement and established and distributed quotas among themselves.

From 1958 to 1962 a number of bilateral agreements for sharing the quotas were created.[82] In the 1962 London agreement the member states divided the total allowable catch into national quotas: Japan, 33%; Netherlands, 6%; Norway, 32%; USSR, 20%; and United Kingdom, 9% (Article 3).[83] Disagreements among the member states arose and the new agreement did not last long: the Commission had to suspend all quota limitations for two seasons.[84] A collective attempt by members of the Commission themselves, by international organizations, and by individuals concerned with conservation created publicity about the problem and brought pressure from all over the world on the member states. These pressures ultimately resulted in an agreement in 1965, the 1965 Whaling Commission. Like its predecessors, it has been an ineffective Commission, due to the unwillingness of its members to accept its conservation measures.

The other commission for conservation of living resources of the sea with an allocation system is the International North Pacific Fur Seal (INPFS) Commission. It is a unique and successful commission, a great deal of whose success can be explained by its special situation. Yet the Commission's structures and allocating system might be useful for more complicated conservation commissions.

The concern for establishment of a commission for manage-

[81] 161 U.N.T.S. 74.

[82] Gulland, *supra* note 67, at 22–23.

[83] 486 U.N.T.S. 264.

[84] INTERNATIONAL WHALING COMMISSION, TWELFTH REPORT OF THE COMMISSION 17 (1961).

ment and conservation of Fur Seal began in the late nineteenth century because of the conflict among the four nations in this business (U.S., U.S.S.R., Japan, and Canada). In 1911 a Convention for the Preservation and Protection of Fur Seal was signed by the four but was terminated by Japan in 1940.[85] INPFS was signed in 1957 by the four[86] and was amended in 1963 and 1969.[87]

Both the 1911 and 1957 conventions, quite similar in structure, have been successful. They make the U.S. and U.S.S.R. responsible for regulating the exploitation of the herds on their respective islands; the U.S. and U.S.S.R. then compensate Canada and Japan with delivery of a certain number of skins for their losses from nonparticipation in catch. The 1957 Convention established a North Pacific Fur Commission to conduct a research program by member states to study the herds' maximum sustainable yield. The structure of INPFS is unique because two of its members—Canada and Japan—have limited participation in research and recommendations while the other two members—U.S.S.R. and U.S.—have full participation in harvesting. Yet Canada and Japan, without participating in harvesting, share the ultimate benefits.

This Convention has been considered a successful fishery conservation effort. A number of reasons have been suggested for its success. First, the Fur Seal operation is government-run and carried out by official agencies, which facilitates both formulation of a common perspective and its implementation.[88] Second, the economic value of Fur Seal is relatively less than other marine resources. Third, although there are no formal barriers to new states entering, there has, in fact, been no request or attempt by other states to enter the Commission. Many questions about the future operation of the Commission would arise if a new member sought to join.

Another fishery commission with an allocation system is the International North Pacific Fisheries Commission composed of Japan, the United States, and Canada (1952).[89] Its allocation system is based on the controversial "abstention" clause, a principle ad-

[85] *See* KOERS, *supra* note 45, at 85.

[86] 314 U.N.T.S. 106.

[87] 494 U.N.T.S. 303.

[88] *See* KOERS, *supra* note 45, at 86.

[89] 205 U.N.T.S. 80.

vocated by the Americans as an adequate method for fisheries conservation. It applies

> to situations where States have, through the expenditure of time, effort and money on research and management, and through restraints on their fishermen, increased and maintained the productivity of stocks of fish, which without such action would not exist or would exist of far below their most productive level. Under such conditions and when the stocks are being fully utilized, that is under such exploitation that an increase in the amount of fishing would not be expected to result in any substantial increase in the sustainable yield, then States not participating, or which have not in recent years participated in exploitation of such stocks of fish, excepting the coastal state adjacent to the waters in which the stocks occur, should be required to abstain from participation.[90]

This principle was advocated by Bishop and Phister on the ground that "equity and justice require that the natural resources which have been built up by systematic conservation and self-denying restrictive utilization be protected from destructive exploitation by interests which have not contributed to their growth and development."[91] However, this principle has been rejected in more inclusive multilateral agreements. For example, in the Convention on Fisheries and Conservation of the Living Resources of the High Seas of 1958, despite U.S. insistence, the principle was not adopted.[92]

The actual application of the abstention principle in the North Pacific Fisheries was controversial and different from the definition. Under the 1952 Convention Japan had originally agreed to

[90]*Quoted in* I. Brownlie, Principles of Public International Law 258 (1973). For more on this principle, see Nishi, *The Voluntary Abstention Principle and Japan: Some Legal and Political Implications*, 11 Natural Res. J. 607 (1971); Cleve, *The Economic and Scientific Basis of the Principle of Abstention*, Official Records, U.N. Conference on the Law of the Sea 47 (1958), U.N. Doc. A/Conf. 13/3; Cleve, *Principle of Abstention: The Case of the United States Halibut Fishery*, in The Fisheries: Problems in Resource Management 75 (J. Crutchfield ed. 1965); Yamamoto, *The Abstention Principle and Its Relation to the Evolving International Law of the Seas*, 43 Wash. L. Rev. 45 (1967).

[91]Bishop, *International Law Commission Draft Articles on Fisheries*, 50 Am. J. Int'l L. 627, 635 (1956); Phister, *Regime of the High Seas*, 50 A.S.I.L. Proc. 136, 145 (1956). For an opposing view to this principle, see S. Oda, International Control of Sea Rsources 89, 139–42 (1963).

[92]*See* 52 Am. J. Int'l L. 851 (1958), *reprinted in* Basic Documents in International Law 99 (I. Brownlie ed. 1963).

abstain from fishing for certain stocks of salmon, halibut, and herring on the ground that they are found off the coasts of North America and / or are of North American origin. Canada similarly had agreed to abstain from fishing for salmon originating in the rivers of the United States. The Commission is responsible for determining whether the stocks are qualified for abstention by one or two member states (Article III). In 1962, after the expiration of the 1952 Convention, Japan refused to accept the principle of abstention for drafting a new Convention while the U.S. has been insisting on including this principle in any new convention. Nonetheless the Convention has been continued on a year-by-year basis. In recent years, however, the participation of U.S.S.R. and South Korea in fishing in the North Pacific has increased the difficulty in drafting a new convention.

Besides multilateral agreements there have been a number of bilateral agreements, such as the Japan–Republic of Korea Joint Fisheries Commission;[93] the Japan–Soviet Fisheries Commission for the Northwest Pacific;[94] the International Pacific Halibut Commission,[95] between the U.S. and Canada; the International Pacific Salmon Fisheries Commission,[96] between Canada and the U.S.; a Convention between the U.S. and Brazil for utilization of shrimp;[97] and so on.

Among the fisheries conventions the International Pacific Salmon Fisheries Commission has a unique characteristic: its main concern is regulation of fisheries within the exclusive jurisdiction of the member states (internal and semitropical waters). Furthermore, this Commission has an allocation system and may make certain regulations directly binding on the fishermen of both Canada and U.S.

The outcomes of the international fisheries commissions must be appraised in general as unsuccessful with respect to conserva-

---

[93] 4 Int'l Legal Material 1128 (1965).

[94] 53 Am. J. Int'l L. 763 (1959).

[95] *See* 32 U.N.T.S. 94; 121 L.N.T.S. 46; and 222 U.N.T.S. 78.

[96] 184 L.N.T.S 306; IPSFC, *Annual Report* 10 (1946).

[97] 14 Int'l Legal Materials 911 (1975). The principal purpose of this agreement is to promulgate a set of 200-mile territorial water limitations. Article 11 of the agreement, however, is addressed to the question of conservation, responsibility for which is divided between the two nations.

tion in terms of "maximum sustainable yield" or to a fair allocation of resources. The present fisheries conservation regulations favor the big maritime powers with modern fishing fleets and equipment and deny necessary protection for the interests of developing countries who cannot compete with the maritime powers in technology. With respect to tuna fishing, for example, during 1969 about 40 nations reported capturing tuna. Only six nations captured approximately 90% of the total catch and, among the six, Japan and the U.S. took nearly 70%.[98] Tuna is an expensive commodity and in many developing countries is too expensive to compete with other cheap protein products. As a result, it is mainly consumed in developed countries.[99]

Another problem the fishing commissions, as well as other conservation commissions, are facing is the increasingly rapid development of technology. This factor has not yet been adequately dealt with in resource conservation: "In a world changing as rapidly as our world has changed . . ., relative rates of changing are exceedingly important. Although our ability to manage fish stocks has grown rapidly . . ., our ability to harvest has increased even more dramatically and the gap btween managerial ability and exploitive technology has evidenced. This problem can be capsulized as one representing a growing divergence between technological capacity and management concepts adequate to fully utilize technological development."[100] The gap between fishing technologies among nation-states, in conjunction with the increasing demand for fish catch has created an increasingly tense situation. In the North Atlantic, Great Britain and Iceland were locked in serious conflict over the 50-mile and later 200-mile extension of Iceland's fishing zone.[101] The United States is unhappy with the Soviet Union fishing off its Atlantic coast and Koreans off its Pacific coast. Japan and the U.S.S.R. are competing in the North Pacific for

---

[98] *See* Joseph, *supra* note 72, at 94.

[99] *Id.* at 94, 97.

[100] Alverson & Paubik, *The Objectives and Problems of Managing Aquatic Living Resources*, at 19 (Paper presented at FAO Technical Conference on Fishery Management and Development, Vancouver, Feb. 1973), *quoted in* Jacobson, *The Future Fisheries Technology and the Third Law of Sea Conference*, in THE FUTURE OF INTERNATIONAL FISHERIES MANAGEMENT, *supra* note 44, at 52.

[101] *See generally* The Fisheries Jurisdiction Case (U.K. v. Iceland) [1973] I.C.J. 3, [1974] I.C.J. 3.

more catch through development of their technology, regardless of its consequences on conservation.

Among the problems that fisheries commissions are facing is the distrust these developing country members have of the scientific investigations from which conservation policies are formulated. Many of the fisheries commissions rely perforce on scientific investigation done by member states. Since the annual fee to most of these commissions is heavy, and even more onerous when it must be paid in whole or part in foreign currency, developing country members often cannot afford both to pay commission fees and to conduct their own proper program for scientific investigation. Therefore, they have to rely on research done by the Commission or the rich members.[102] Suspicious of bias and favoritism are understandable: "Even if deliberate efforts are made to maintain a balance it is not at all clear that the interests of developing countries are served better by having some of their limited number of good people serving the Commission than by staying at home. With the best will in the world the poorer countries are likely to feel that the Commission's advice and recommendations will tend to be biased against them. This feeling will act against the capacity of the Commission to act early, on the basis of probabilities rather than scientific certainties."[103] As Gulland says, some of these suspicions may be unjustifiable, but it is possible that in situations in which the period of scientific collaboration has been short and when a policy may have direct impact on a national fishing output, scientists may take a position in favor of their nation.[104] This problem might be ameliorated by including independent scientists or scientific groups from other international organizations. Among other problems with fishing commissions are their lack of power to implement their policies and their slowness.

The whole process of utilization of living resources of the sea and conservation policies increased the dissatisfaction among coastal developing states. One spokesman, the Foreign Minister of Peru, conceded that the basic notion of freedom of the sea and sea resources was claimed in order to benefit the international community as a whole, but complained that, in application to sea re-

---

[102]Gulland, *supra* note 67, at 182.

[103]*Id.*

[104]*Id.*

sources, only those with the technology to exploit resources were benefiting. The system disregarded the needs of the coastal states.[105] These ideas were part of the basis for the expansion of fishing zones up to 200 miles.

Modern claims for a 200-mile exclusive fishing zone began in the 1950s. A group of Latin American countries stated as the basis of their claim in the "Declaration of Santiago," in 1952, the goal of ensuring the protection and conservation of resources for the promotion of internal value processes, such as supplying food and using the resources for their economic development.[106] This policy has been incorporated into the national legislations of a number of Latin American countries for the expansion of their fishing zone to 200 miles.[107] The United States, long the major opponent of a 200-mile zone, recently expanded its fishing zone to 200 miles.[108] One important reason alleged for this expansion was conservation of fishing resources being overexploited by foreign fishing fleets.[109]

Assuming the 200-mile fishing zone solves the question of allocation, it will not solve the conservation problem as a whole. It will not necessarily solve the problem of replenishment of potentials, efficiency, technological development, and compatibility of use with scientific evidence. The more opposing demands in fishing conservation result in unilateral actions by coastal states, the more apparent becomes the need for a global conservation policy re-

[105] Jarrin, *Utilizing Sea Resources for Human and Social Welfare*, 3 PACIFIC COMMUNITIES, No. 2 at 310, *cited in* BROWN, *supra* note 66, at 152.

[106] The signatories were Chile, Ecuador, and Peru. For the text see J. MARFAN, LA DECLARACION SOBRE ZONA MARITIMA DE 1952 (1968) (in Spanish). For the English translation see G. AMADOR, LATIN AMERICA AND THE LAW OF THE SEA 43–44 (1972).

[107] The Dominican Law 186 of Sept. 6, 1967, extends its territorial water only to insure observance of the law for the "protection and conservation of the fisheries and other natural resources of the sea." Cited in G. AMADOR, *supra* note 106, at 1. The Venezuelan Law of July 27, 1956, "in which [the state] shall exercise its authority and vigilance and watch over the promotion, conservation, and rational exploitation of the living resources of the sea found therein, whether such resources are harvested by Venezuelans or by foreigners." *Id.* at 1–2. The Costa-Rican law establishing "state protection" over a 200-mile zone has officially been stated for the same purpose. *Id.* at 2. During a recent 12-month period Ecuador seized 56 U.S. fishing fleets within its 200-mile fishing zone and fined them for a total of $2.3 million. *See* BROWN, *supra* note 66, at 152.

[108] N.Y. Times, Jan. 29, 1976, at 10, col. 2.

[109] Senator Gravel, the opponent of the bill, rejected this claim and declared that "of the 16 stocks, six have been overfished by Americans." *Id.*

garding fishing utilization. The only way to conserve this great shareable resource, or "common heritage of mankind," is by a collective action expressing a global policy of fishing conservation.[110] Such an expression would lay out the objectives of fishing conservation and its interrelationship with other resources and values and with the more general policies of world order and would give guidelines to national as well as bilateral and multilateral fishing commissions. The scope of this policy should not be limited to high seas but should be applicable as well to waters under national jurisdiction of states (internal waters and territorial seas).

The global policy should include guidelines for the development of fisheries as well as their preservation. Fish farming—one development project—is a three-thousand-year-old practice in Asia in both fresh and salt waters. It is an effective strategy for development of fisheries but has not been given adequate attention all over the world. In the early 1970s it was producing only 6% of the total world fish catch.[111] China is a successful producer of fish farming, with 2.2 million tons of fish, or about 40% of the nation's fish harvest.[112] The most prevalent fish culture by man is the milkfish, an important protein source, particularly in Indonesia, the Philippines, and Taiwan.[113] Shrimp and oysters have been cultured in Japan, the Phillippines, and other parts of Asia. Global policy should encourage fish farming as a development project. Since it is a complicated and sophisticated process which involves domestication and breeding of various fish species, control of their environment, temperature, and the like, global policy should provide funds, skills, and technology through international organizations or agencies, such as FAO, to developing states to start their fish farming. Global policy should establish a Supervisory Commission with the power and necessary funds to organize its own agencies. Among other responsibilities, it would conduct its own

---

[110]The United Nations has declared the resources of the sea "the common heritage of mankind." G.A. Res. 2749, 25 U.N. GAOR, Supp. (no. 28) 24, U.N. Doc. A/8028 (1970). This resolution was passed by 108 votes with 14 abstentions, including 7 Eastern Europeans. This notion of common heritage has not up to this time led to an articulate consensus of operational value.

[111]BROWN, *supra* note 66, at 158.

[112]*Id.* at 159.

[113]*Id.* Fish farming is a useful and profitable investment. *See* C. IDYLL, THE SEA AGAINST HUNGER 90 (1970).

independent scientific investigation about fisheries—both high seas and internal and territorial waters—assess the impact of possible conservation policies, and formulate recommendations. The Supervisory Commission should be empowered to implement the minimum necessary conservation regulations in the high seas as well as the waters under domestic jurisdiction of states.

b. Food

The constant threat of food shortage has made the achievement of an acceptable balance between food and people a global objective, though one most difficult to achieve. The optimism about the world food situation which existed at the end of 1960s has been replaced with anxiety. There is now general agreement that the number of people of the world who are inadequately nourished is about 50% to 60% of the population of the less-developed countries, or about one third of the population of the world.[114] In Zambia, for example, 260 of every thousand babies born are dead before their first birthday.[115] In India and Pakistan the ratio is 140 of every thousand, in Colombia 82.[116] Many more of the children die before they reach school age, and others during the early school years.[117] "When death certificates are issued for preschool infants in the poor countries, death is generally attributed to measles, pneumonia, dysentery or some other disease. In fact, these children are more likely to be the victims of malnutrition."[118]

The FAO has stated that, athough total agricultural production is increasing, food production per capita in the nonindustrialized countries is barely holding constant even at its present inadequate level.[119] The worsening proportion between future population

---

[114]President's Science Advisory Panel on the World Food Supply, the World Food Problem 2–3 (1967). A report by the National Science Foundation estimated that half of the world's population has an inadequate diet. *International Regulation of Pesticide Residues in Food* 1 (1975). A report to the National Science Foundation on the Application of International Regulatory Techniques to Scientific Technical Problems.

[115]L. Brown, Seeds Of Change 135 (1970).

[116]*Id.*

[117]*Id.*

[118]*Id.*

[119]U.N., FAO, *The State of Food and Agriculture*, U.N. Doc. (1970), *cited in* The Limits to Growth, *supra* note 1, at 58–59 [1970].

growth and cultivated land is another indicator of need for immediate action for conservation of food and utilization of land. It is estimated that in the year 2000, for each square kilometer of cultivated land in South Asia, there will be 390 additional people. For North America the number is 37 additional people per square kilometer of cultivated land.[120]

The changed balance between food-producing and food-consuming countries increases the likelihood of monopolistic control of food distribution by a few states as the main world food suppliers. Before World War II the world was almost divided into two regions, food exporters and food importers. But since the war some regions, particularly Latin America and Eastern Europe, former exporters have become importers. Now, North America and Australia are considered potential sources of food supply.[121] The concentration of food production in a few countries is not appropriate for healthy trade. In case of a natural disaster or a combination of natural disasters in the suppliers, the resulting food shortage would create worldwide disasters in its wake. In 1972, for example, a sudden drop in cereals occurred even as North American countries were engaged in supply-management program to bring down their large surpluses.[122]

---

[120] MESAROVIC & PESTEL, *supra* note 1, at 75, 77.

[121] *Id.* at 116.
The statistics on the dependency on North America for export grain:

Grain trade	1934–38	1945–52	1960	1966	1973
			millions metric tons		
North America	+ 5	+23	+39	+59	+88
Latin America	+ 9	+ 1	0	+5	− 4
Western Europe	− 24	22	−25	−27	−21
Eastern Europe and U.S.S.R.	+ 5	0	0	− 4	−27
Africa	+ 1	0	− 2	− 7	− 4
Asia	+ 2	− 6	−17	−34	−39
Australia	+ 3	+ 3	+ 6	+ 8	+ 7

Plus = net export
Minus = net import
Source: based on U.S. Department of Agriculture data, cited in L. BROWN THE GLOBAL POLITICS OF RESOURCE SCARCITY 24 (1974).

[122] U.N., World Food Conference, Assessment of the World Food Situation—Present and Future, U.N. Doc. E/CONF.65/3 (1974) at 1. In 1972–73, for example, President Nixon announced that he was putting restrictions on agricultural production because he was putting the interest of American consumers first. This action surprised the Europeans and

Demands for more resources have increased in both poor and rich countries, for different reasons. In developing countries the increase in demand has a direct relationship with population growth. In developed countries, such increases relate to rising affluence.[123] In general, however, the population growth is still the major factor of increase in demand for food, but with respect to particular developed or developing countries this generalization will not apply. World food demand in the 1970s and 1980s is calculated to grow at a rate of 2.4% per year, of which 2% represents population increase and 0.4% increase in purchasing power.[124] The demand projection for developed countries shows 3.3% per year for cereals, 4.7% for fish, 4.4% for meat. In developing countries, however, 73% compared with 47% in the developed countries, will come from cereals, starching roots, and sugar by the end of the 1980s.[125] An average American's food resources are nearly

---

Japanese. Hansen, *The Politics of Scarcity*, in THE U.S. AND THE DEVELOPING WORLD: AGENDA FOR ACTION 55 (F. Howe ed. 1974).

[123] *See* BROWN, *supra* note 2, at 28–29; BROWN, *supra* note 115, at 22, and MESAROVIC & PESTEL, *supra* note 1, at 166–67.

Annual production of meat per inhabitant:

	1961–65	1970–71
North America	72 Kg	82 Kg
Western Europe	41	48
USSR	30	36
Latin America	32	30
Asia – (Near East	10	10
(Far East	3	3
Africa	10	10

Source: Institute d'etudes demagraphiques, Paris— d'apres FAO, *cited in* MESAROVIC & PESTEL at 66.

[124] U.N. Doc. E/CONF.65/3, at 6 (1974).

[125] *Id.* at 7. For example, grain if directly consumed provides 52 percent of human food energy supply. In poor countries the annual availability of grain per person in average is about 400 pounds per year, or about little over one pound per day. In this case, then, all grain should be consumed directly in order to make minimum energy necessary, and not so much can be given to animals for animal protein. In the U.S. and Canada today, grain per

five times as great as those of the average Indian, Nigerian, or Colombian.[126]

Considering the strategic and vital characteristics of food as well as the severe problems of food scarcity and unequal distribution, the importance of conservation of food is obvious. The protection of common interest requires accelerating the rate of food production, fair distribution, and preservation for emergency situations. Indeed, the need for global cooperation for implementing these policies has been expressed in international prescriptions. Articles 1 and 55 of the U.N. Charter state that one purpose of the United Nations is to solve international problems of an economic character. Besides the U.N. Charter, there is Article 11(2) of the International Covenant on Economic, Social and Cultural Rights;[127] Article 25 of the Universal Declaration of Human Rights states: "Everyone has the right to a standard of living adequate for the health and well-being of himself and of his family, including food, clothing, housing. . . ."[128]

The history of the global policy for food management and conservation in forms of international organizations has not been very

---

capita is one ton per year, but only about 150 pounds are consumed directly; the rest is consumed indirectly in forms of milk, meat, and eggs. *See generally* BROWN, *supra* note 2, at 29.

[126]BROWN, supra note 116, at 39.

Annual per capita grain consumption in selected nations:

Country	Total grain consumption directly or indirectly as milk, meat, or eggs	Total grain consumption as multiple of Indian consumption
	pounds	
Canada	1,848	5
U.S.	1,486	4
U.S.S.R.	1,227	4
U.K.	1,025	3
Argentina	848	2
West Germany	748	2
Mexico	547	2
Japan	531	1
China	430	1
India	348	1

Source: FAO, Food Balance Sheet, 1964–66 average. *Id.* at 40.

[127]U.N. International Covenant on Economic, Social and Cultural Rights. G.A. Res. 2200, 21 U.N. GAOR Supp. (No. 16) 49, U.N. Doc. A/6316 (1966).

[128]G.A. Res. 217, 3 U.N. GAOR Vol. 7, 71, U.N. Doc. A/810 (1948).

long or effective. The International Institute of Agriculture in Rome, established in 1902, was the first major international organization that made policies regarding land, water, forest, and wildlife conservation based on research, and facilitated international conventions in this area.[129] This Institute was later replaced by the FAO, which was established in Quebec in 1945. Its headquarters, which had initially been in Washington, were transferred to Rome in 1956. The main work of the FAO has been conducting research and collecting documents and promoting more credit facilities, international commodity agreements, and technical assistance.[130] In recent years, as a result of the international crisis of food shortage,[131] FAO has expanded its activities to areas related to a more global effective management planning of food resources. The World Food Conferences of November 1974 in Rome was a major effort by the international community to create global policy for food management.

The Conference has been criticized for its heavy political atmosphere. One delegate reportedly said: "It looks like this organization is becoming more and more politicized. There were too many attempts in the last three weeks to make this more like the United Nations General Assembly than an organization devoted to helping feed hungry people."[132] And some argued that the present food crisis is the result of poor distribution and management of the available food supply rather than substantiation of Malthus' theory.[133] It should be borne in mind that any convention or conference related to redistribution of resources, including food, is just part of the whole demand and strategy for reform of the world policy on resources distribution. Therefore, while a heavy political confrontation should not stop the main objective of the organization in formulating and implementing policies promoting common interest, a political atmosphere should be expected. The

[129] *See, e.g.,* the International Convention of Locust Control of 1920 and International Convention on Plant Protection of 1929, *cited in* CIRIACY-WANTRUP, *supra* note 19, at 319.

[130] M. VAN MEERCHAEGHE, INTERNATIONAL ECONOMIC INSTITUTIONS 93 (1966).

[131] In 1964, international food reserves were sufficient to provide eighty days of emergency relief. Today these reserves are only sufficient to provide thirty days' consumption. Brown, *An Exchange on Food,* in FOREIGN POLICY ASSOCIATION REPORT NO. 14 (1974), *cited in* MESAROVIC & PESTEL, *supra* note 1, at 116.

[132] N.Y. Times, Jan. 25, 1976, at 49, col. 1.

[133] *Id.*

basic objective of the Conference in a narrow sense could be defined as "helping feed hungry people," but strategies by which this policy of management and conservation will be implemented must have serious effects on "rich people," "poor countries," "rich countries," and their interactions.

The conclusions of the Conference provided compelling evidence of need for immediate and effective conservation action, particularly in forms of development. The Conference stated that, based on estimates with respect to production potentials, the present world is capable, in terms of physical, biological, and human resources, of producing enough food for all, because an enormous part of potential resources has not been used yet.[134] The Conference concluded that millions of hectares of land suitable for farming remain unused, especially in Latin America and Africa. However, there are problems: such as road construction, technology for preparing tropical soil after removal of tree cover, and the prevalence of infestations such as tse-tse fly in Africa.[135] Based on Conference predictions, it is likely that adequate use of fertilizers, pesticides and herbicides, and quality seed, as well as appropriate education for hundreds of millions of farmers, will increase production.[136]

The Conference recognized the necessity of formulating grand strategies in many different areas for resolving the food problem and made recommendations.[137] The recommendations are made for short-term and long-term food problems and at both national and international levels. The problem with these prescriptions as with many other inclusive prescriptions is the lack of effective implementation, particularly in critical political areas, such as "trade, stability and adjustment," where implementation is at the mercy of nation-states.

The importance of fertilizer in food production has been recognized, and in response to ECOSOC Resolution 1836 (LVI) of July 1974, the FAO Council decided to establish an International

[134]"Proposals for National and International Action," U.N. Doc. E/CONF. 65/4 (1974).

[135]*Id. See also* D. Bogue, Principles of Demography 828 (1969). For a rather pessimistic view on the difficulty and expenses of development of lands for agriculture, see The Limits of Growth, *supra* note 1, at 58.

[136]U.N. Doc. E/CONF.65/3, at 9 (1974).

[137]For the text of the recommendations, see U.N. Doc. E/CONF. 65/4.

Fertilizer Supply Scheme (IFS) under which donor countries and fertilizer industries could make available, during periods of extreme scarcity, fertilizers to meet the immediate needs of the hardest pressed developing countries.[138] Since October 24, 1974, IFS has carried out missions to 16 countries in Asia, Africa, and Latin America to assess requirements and to seek agreement with concerned governments on approaches to solutions of shortfall problems.[139] The IFS has demonstrated that it has the capacity to act effectively and with dispatch on emergency requests from developing countries.[140] Its experience confirms that "all aspects related to this vital agricultural input, especially investment in new production capacity and the elimination of production and distribution bottle-necks, should not be the exclusive concern of a few countries but must increasingly become the subject of a concerted international effort. Only by the continued monitoring of investment, production and distribution, combined with timely corrective action, will it be possible to avoid emergencies of the kind which the world is now experiencing."[141]

At the Conference, the World Food Council was created to coordinate recommendations made by the Conference. One of the programs projected was a fund for agricultural development, which is based on the idea that a long-term solution to food problems is helping developing countries to develop their own agriculture and food resources. On February 5, 1976, the representatives of 74 countries reached agreement on the terms for the creation of this fund.[142] OPEC pledged to contribute significantly to the Fund's declared aim of reserves of one billion Special Drawing Rights.[143]

---

[138]U.N. Doc. E/CONF.65/3 at 10 (1974). The activity of IFS is "(i) assessment of the uncovered fertilizer requirements of developing countries with special attention to the countries most seriously affected by economic crisis (MSAs), as defined for the purpose of the United Nations Emergency Operation (UNEO); (ii) assessment of the supply availability of fertilizers in producing countries; (iii) assessment of sources of finance to match shortfall and supplies; (iv) practical arrangements to provide fertilizers to needy developing countries on receipt of request." U.N. Doc. E/CONF.65/7, at 2 (1974).

[139]*Id.*

[140]*Id.*

[141]*Id.* at 4–5.

[142]N.Y. Times, Feb. 6, 1976, at 3, col. 1.

[143]*Id.*

Considering the seriousness of the problem of food shortage, actions at both international and national levels are imminently required. The establishment of the World Food Authority with necessary effective power is urgent for the implementation of world food policies. Regional organizations and conventions, particularly with respect to technical assistance and research on specific regional problems, are also indispensable.[144]

2. Nonrenewable Resources

In contrast with renewable resources, global attention and concern for conservation of nonrenewable resources has been inadequate. Even now there is no organized institution concerned globally with conservation of nonrenewable vital resources. One reason for such a delay may be the pervasive misconception of the earth's reserves of these resources. The geographical location of nonrenewable resources within the territorial boundaries of states and the traditional claim of exclusive control over them combined to erect another obstacle to global conservation policymaking. As Circiacy-Wantrup says, "[C]onflicts of interests between nations and organized private groups are much stronger with stock [nonrenewable] than with flow [renewable] resources."[145] Therefore, while flow resources are closer to the stage of being governed more effectively through inclusive conservation prescription and application, stock resources are still far behind on any global conservation policy.

The proposal to establish an International Resources Organization first came from the Division for the Social and International Relations of Science, at the British Association for the Advancement of Science.[146] One observer has emphasized that such an

[144]Such as, for example, Southern African Regional Commission for the Conservation and Utilization of Soil (SARCCUS), which was established on June 5, 1950 (in Pretoria) in order to promote closer technical cooperation among the territories comprising the Southern African region in relation to the control of soil erosion, conservation, and improvement of the soil, vegetation, and water resources. It consists of 10 countries. There was also a Pan-American Soil Conservation Commission, which was established in 1940, but dissolved in 1953.

[145]CIRIACY-WANTRUP, *supra* note 19, at 32.

[146]British Association for the Advancement of Science, *Science and World Order: Transaction of a Conference of the Division for Social and International Relations of Science*, 2 ADVANCE-MENT OF SCIENCE 3–116 (1942), and *Mineral Resources and the Atlantic Charter: Transactions of*

organization might be as important as the FAO.[147] The basic policy of an international resource organization with respect to conservation should be timed uses of stock resources that optimize all public order goals. Any conservation strategy with respect to a specific resource, therefore, should be made contextually, with consideration of scientific and technological, as well as social and economic, strategies, such as control of production and price stability.

In contrast to the lack of international cooperation on conservation of stock resources, there have been some national as well as regional cooperations. In actual application, however, regional conservation policies have been overshadowed by a policy of profit making through control of the process of production and pricing. This has led some observers to the conclusion that conservation policies of stock resources should mainly be limited to scientific and technological regulation of the process of utilization but that the control of production and pricing is not really a tool for conservation and should be determined only by market forces.[148]

Among the regional organizations, the Sixth Arab Petroleum Congress (APC) recommended the first set of scientific and economic strategies, including production control, for conservation of oil resources.[149] These policies had their conceptual origin in the recommendations for conservation of oil resources prescribed by the American Petroleum Institute and the Interstate Oil Compact Commission (IOCC), of the United States. The APC recommendations are related to:

> 1. Spacing: restriction upon the number and location of wells;
> 2. Drilling operations: regulation of drilling and well completion practices;
> 3. MER: restriction of production to the maximum efficient rate;
> 4. Proration: allocation of production between separately owned tracts within a common source of supply;

---

a Conference held by the Division for the Social and International Relations of Science, July 24–25, 1942, 2 ADVANCEMENT OF SCIENCE 187–253 (1942), *cited in id.* n.28.

[147]*Id.*

[148]E. ROSTOW, A NATIONAL POLICY FOR THE OIL INDUSTRY 122 (1948), and Vafai, *Participation, Pricing and Production Control in the International Petroleum Industry,* 5 NATURAL RES. L. 106. (1972).

[149]Kamel, *International Protection of Oil and its Impact on Prices, Sixth APC* (Organized by the Secretariat General of the League of Arab States, Baghdad, Mar. 6–13, 1967).

5. Ratios: limitation of production in excess of an established gas-oil and water-oil ratio;
6. Volumetric withdrawals: restriction of production of gas, oil, or water to prevent excessive localization withdrawals.[150]

OPEC, in Resolution XVI 90, also recognized the importance of conservation of oil resources because of their exhaustibility and their importance to the economic well-being of OPEC countries:

> hydrocarbon resources are limited and exhaustible, and . . . their proper exploitation determines the conditions of the economic development of Member Countries, both at present and in the future;
>
> . . . .
>
> Resolves . . . that OPEC operators shall be required to conduct their operations in accordance with the best conservation practices, bearing in mind the long-term interests of the [exporting] country.[151]

Based on these conceptions, OPEC adopted a series of scientific recommendations.[152] OPEC has, however, failed to formulate a conceptual framework for conservation based on social and economic as well as scientific factors and has left the formulation of such policies to the individual member states. In practice, conservation strategies of individual states in relation to production control have often been tools for political and economic objectives rather than for conservation. Consider, for example, the Libyan production control of 1970, which reduced the Occidental Oil Company's output from 800,000 barrels per day to 485,000 barrels per day.[153] The government's announced reason for this cutback was conservation of oil resources,[154] but a few months after

---

[150] *See* AMERICAN PETROLEUM INSTITUTE, PROGRESS REPORT ON STANDARDS ALLOCATION OF PRODUCTION WITHIN POOLS AND AMONG POOLS (by the Special Study Committee on Legal Advisory Committee on Well Spacing and Allocation of Production Practices, Division of Production, Dallas, Texas, 1942), *cited in* Vafai, *supra* note 148, at 99.

[151] INTERSTATE OIL COMPACT COMMISSION, A FORM FOR AN OIL AND GAS CONSERVATION STATUTE (1959).

[152] SIXTH APC, *supra* note 149, at 12.

[153] OPEC Res. XVI.90, *quoted in* Vafai, *supra* note 148, at 101–02.

[154] *Pro-Forma Regulation for the Conservation of Petroleum Resources*, OPEC, SELECTED DOCUMENTS OF THE INTERNATIONAL PETROLEUM INDUSTRY 1968, at 388–99.

paying the government request of a price increase of $70 million the Company continued to increase its production almost to the same rate.

The misformulation and the misapplication of conservation policy through production control by individual states do not deny the importance of this policy. These emphasize, however, the necessity and relevancy of inclusive competence over the process of formulating conservation policies. In a world where the relationships between states are so complex and mixed with political tension, a state cannot make a decision about an important issue such as production control, which affects the world community, without being highly influenced by its own special interests.

Commodity agreements, or interstate agreements for production and distribution of resources, are another strategy admitting of design to fulfill global conservation policies. One main objective of commodity agreements is to reduce price instability. Ciriacy-Wantrup observes that if commodity agreements were effective in this respect, they would have significance for conservations for the following reasons:

> First, greater price stability may reduce uncertainty allowance and, therefore, result in conservation. Second, greater price stability may reduce interest rates and capital rationing because uncertainty allowance of savers and lenders is decreased; lower interest rates and less imperfect markets for loans favor conservation. Third, greater price stability may avoid depletion caused by low incomes during economic depressions under imperfect markets for assets; this depletion is not offset by conservation during propensity because their markets for assets are less imperfect and variations of incomes have less and less influence upon time preference as incomes increases.[155]

Unfortunately, experience with commodity agreements as a useful strategy for conservation has been disappointing. The International Tin Agreements of 1931 and 1932, for example, encouraged rather than discouraged the opening up of high-cost deposits.[156] The general experience with commodity agreements shows that the historical use of this strategy has been assurance of

---

[155] PETROLEUM INTELLIGENCE WEEKLY 1 (July 20, 1970).

[156] PETROLEUM INTELLIGENCE WEEKLY 1 (May 25, 1970).

availability of resources and price control rather than conservation.[157]

Regardless of past trends, the potentiality of commodity agreements as an international tool for conservation cannot be denied. But the objectives of commodity agreements have to be broadened and should be governed by an institution of inclusive competence.

The Third Law of the Sea Conference in Caracas addressed the conservation of stock resources and sought to establish an international authority for the management of seabed mineral resources. The main issue involved in designing the structure and the competency of the Authority was control of production and pricing in order to minimize the negative economic impacts of seabed mineral production on developing country producers of the same resources from their landmasses. Some attention was given to the necessity of conservation of seabed mineral resources.[158] The Committee defined the objective of conservation as "to maximize the long-term utilization of a resource."[159] Based on this approach, the conservation of seabed minerals is to be divided into two categories.[160] One category regulates the management of the international area; the other regulates the mining operation in order to prevent waste and the uses of technology not compatible with long-term planned use of the minerals.

> Summary Presentation of Issues and Outlines Relating to Sea-Bed Resource Conservation.
> A. Management of the International Area
>   1. Decisions relating to space (surface boundaries)
>   (a) Over-all subdivision of the International area:
>   (i) On an ad hoc basis as requested by sea-bed miners
>   (ii) According to a master grid
>   (b) Size of individual blocks:
>   (i) As requested by miners

---

[157] CIRIACY-WANTRUP, *supra* note 19, at 322.

[158] *Id.* at 332.

[159] *See* Part Three, Chapter 5, *infra*.

[160] For a report on the question of exploitation of seabed minerals, arising from discussions held at the Caracas Law of the Sea Conference in 1974, *see* "Economic Implications of Sea-bed Mineral Development in the International Area: Report of the Secretary-General," U.N. Doc.A/CONF.62/25, published in Third U.N. Conf. on the Law of Sea, U.N. Pub. Vol. 111. 5–40 (1975).

        (ii) Equal size for all blocks

       (iii) Variable size pre-determined by grid. Blocks of one degree square as defined by meridians. Size determined by geological, morphological and other considerations.

  2. Decisions relating to time

    (a) Reservation of areas for future use:

        (i) Area returned to the Authority (three-quarters of initial area authorized for exploitation)

       (ii) Alternative bands with width of two degrees of longitude running from pole to pole.

      (iii) Discretionary decision by the Authority.

    (b) Annual authorization of surface area, or nodule tonnage, for exploitation:

        (i) No limits—as requested by interested parties

       (ii) Controlled nodule development based on principle of complementarity with land-based production

    (c) Duration of exploration and exploitation permits—work requirements

B. Regulation of mining operations

  1. No minimum recovery efficiency required

  2. Control aimed at avoiding wasteful mining methods

    (a) Unmined areas of blocks:

        (i) Unmined zones—topographic barriers

       (ii) Areas with nodules below "cut-off" grade

    (b) "Sweep" efficiency:

        (i) Limited manoeuverability: Continuous Line Bucket (CLB) system. "Vacuum cleaning" (hydraulic) and airlift systems

       (ii) Extensive manoeuverability—bottom crawling devices

    (c) Dredge efficiency

Although this proposal is at a preliminary stage, its apparent approach to conservation ignores a number of issues that will lead to problems in later efforts at conservation. The apparent objective of conservation of nonrenewable resources is almost the same as that of renewable resources. "Long-term utilization" is similar to "maximum sustainable yield"; both consider only the time factor. The inadequacy of this objective is the same as that of renewable resources and bears reconsideration.

Again there is no link to a more general global policy of resource redistribution. In addition, the conservation policy of nonrenewable resources is more complicated than renewables because their reserves are limited. Therefore, the question of timed use is of utmost importance. But does "timed use" necessarily mean "long-term use"? What are the criteria that determine the timing of utilization of a particular nonrenewable resource? How should these limited resources be allocated? How should a conservation organization be constructed in order to face and resolve adequately the political and economic tensions and confrontations associated with nonrenewable resources without losing its main objective of conservation? Moreover, an international authority for management of nonrenewable resources has responsibility not only for the rational use of the present available resources but also for the development of alternative and substitute resources for future generations. These are among important issues that have to be considered in policymaking for conservation of nonrenewable resources. The Committee of the Third Law of the Sea Conference took maximum long-term utilization as the only objective of conservation without attempting to relate policies about seabed mineral resources to the more comprehensive policies about conservation of stock resources in the landmass.

3. Recent Movements Toward a Global Conservation Policy

One important task of any global conservation policy should be the promotion of a reliable and independent intelligence function. The present system of gathering and distributing resource information has been criticized mainly for two reasons. First, there is a lack of accurate information about earth resources.[161] Second, the major part of the present information is prepared by interested groups and is not independent.[162] The United Nations recognized the importance of a viable intelligence function for decision making regarding conservation in Economic and Social Council Resolution 1761 B(LIV), and the Committee of Natural Resources has been asked to take steps for improvement.[163] The Committee of

[161] *Id.* at 37.

[162] *Id.* at 36.

[163] It has been stated that most of the present information is based on circumstantial evidence. Larkin, in describing the amateur stage of fishing knowledge, gives the California sardine as an example, which are virtually gone now, but "the arguments persist on whether to blame the fishery or the change in ocean conditions (or both, or neither)." Larkin, *A Confidential Memorandum on Fisheries Science*, in ROTHSCHILD, *supra* note 7, at 192. *See also*

Natural Resources, considering the financial limitations of the United Nations, resolved that the implementation of this resolution in establishing an effective intelligence function should begin with

> (a) Systematic gathering of information (including that on technology) on developments in the energy and mineral fields, analysing this information and making it available to policymakers;
>
> (b) The collection, in co-operation with Member Countries, of the available information on continuing projection work in various quarters and, in doing so, identifying the assumptions concerning policy choices and constraints in countries and regions;
>
> (c) The dissemination of information on trends concerning reserves, supply and demand of energy and mineral resources, in order to help policy-makers obtain a better understanding of the dynamic process of natural resources development and utilization in the world economy.[164]

In the European Community—based on a decision taken by the Committee of Ministers of The Council of Europe—the European Information Center for Nature Conservation was established on January 1, 1967. This Center is to serve as an institution for the dissemination of information in matters of conservation to all interested European Countries. The Center acts as an intermediary of national agencies or, in nonmember countries, through contracts between the Center and various national organizations.

A more serious call for an inclusive prescription for utilization and conservation of resources is expressed in General Assembly

---

Alverson, *Science and Fisheries Management in World Fisheries Policy*, in ROTHSCHILD, *id.*, at 211–18; DASMANN, *supra* note 37, at 37, 38 & 195–98.

[164]Besides fisheries, in stock resources of the seabed, for example, most of the investigations are either conducted by multinational corporations or are sponsored by them. Kennecott Copper sponsored exploration cruises before it began its own in 1967. Kennecott Management Communication, at 1, *cited in* the Third U.N. Conf. on the Law of the Sea, *supra* note 160, at 8 n.17. Deepsea Ventures has carried out 33 cruises in the Pacific with the research ship *Prospector*. Global Marine has been doing some exploration on behalf of Summa Corporation and International Nickel has also been involved in some investigation. Arbeitsgemeinschaft Meerestechnischgewinnbare Rohstoffe (AMR) group from Germany has been doing research since 1971. The CNEXO group of France, in association with Le Nickel, has been involved in South Pacific since 1970. The Sumitomo–Deep Ocean Minerals Association (DOMA) group have been doing extensive research in the Pacific. DOMA is made up of 27 leading Japanese Companies. The Soviet Union has the research ship *Vityaz* in the South Pacific. *See* Skornyakova & Andrushchenko, *Iron Manganese Nodules from the Central Part of the South Pacific*, 8 OCEANOLOGY 692–701 (1968), *cited in id.* at 8 n.19.

Resolution 3129 (XXVIII) of December 13, 1973. This Resolution, however, is limited to utilization of resources shared by two or more states. It emphasizes the urgency of formulating an inclusive conservation policy:[165] "conscious of the importance and urgency of safeguarding the conservation and exploitation of natural resources shared by two or more States, by means of an effective system of cooperation, as indicated in the Economic Declaration of Algiers":

> 1. Considers that it is necessary to ensure effective cooperation between countries through the establishment of adequate international standards for the conservation of natural resources common to two or more States in the context of the normal relations existing between them;
>
> 2. Considers further that cooperation between countries sharing such natural resources and interested in their exploitation must

[165] *See* Economic and Social Council Res. 1761 B(LIV):
"Recognizing the fundamental importance of projections for the planning and management of natural resources development.

"Welcoming the preoccupation of the Committee with natural resources projections and the view that this question should be a regular item on the agenda of the Committee, Requests the Secretary-General:

"(a) To prepare a report, in consultation with the specialized agencies, on the activities of all the organizations, inside and outside the United Nations system, which undertake medium-term and long-term projection on the supply of and demand for energy, mineral and water resources, indicating the methodologies used by each of them and the concepts and definitions of the variables used, and to submit the report to the Committee on Natural Resources at its fourth session in good time for the Committee to make recommendations to the Secretary-General, through the Economic and Social Council, on the acceptable methods to be standardized to carry out such projects on an internationally comparable basis;

"(b) To submit to the Committee on Natural Resources on a regular two-year basis studies on medium-term and long-term projections, based on available data, on the supply of and demand for energy, mineral and water resources on a global, regional and national basis;

"(c) To take the necessary measures, within the budgetary limitations, to improve and strengthen the existing United Nations services for the analysis, evaluation and dissemination of world-wide data on natural resources;

"(d) To submit to the Committee on Natural Resources on a regular basis an assessment of technologies which could assist Governments to evaluate, in the light of their requirements, the supply of and demand for energy mineral and water resources;

"(e) To submit to the Committee on Natural Resources on a regular basis an assessment of existing and emerging technologies specifically geared to meet the medium-term and long-term requirements of the developing countries in the field of energy, mineral and water resources." E.S.C. Res. 1761(B), 54 U.N. E SCOR Supp. (No. 1) 13, U.N. Doc. E/5367 (1973).

be developed on the basis of a system of information and prior consultation within the framework of the normal relations existing between them;

3. Requests the Governing Council of the United Nations Environmental Programme, in keeping with its function of promoting international cooperation according to the mandate conferred upon it by the General Assembly, to keep duly into account the preceding paragraphs and to report on measures adopted for their implementation.[166]

Following the request of the General Assembly, the Governing Council of the U.N. Environmental Programs (UNEP), in its third session held in Nairobi, in April–May 1975, considered the issue of "cooperation in the field of the environment concerning natural resources shared by two or more states."[167] Most of the delegates recognized the competency of UNEP on this issue. One representative stated that while his country recognized the permanent sovereignty of states over their natural resources, it was nonetheless aware of the need of appropriate regulation and management of shared resources in order to protect the mutual interests of the states concerned.[168] Objections to implementation of the Resolution were to the competency of UNEP and the process by which the Resolution was to be implemented, not to the idea of formulation of inclusive prescriptions. One speaker, for example, considering the scope of the duty of UNEP, warned the delegates of the danger that UNEP might overextend itself in dealing with a subject related to issues other than the environment.[169] Brazil explained its negative votes on the draft resolution on the ground that the issue of environmental protection and conservation cannot be dissociated from its political and economic aspects. Therefore, UNEP should not be solely responsible for drafting principles on the subject; its work may otherwise cover only the environmental dimension of the problem.[170] He suggested that the Interna-

---

[166] U.N.Doc. E/C.7/52 (1975), at 12.

[167] G.A. Res. 3129, 28 U.N. GAOR Supp. (No. 30) 48, U.N.Doc. A/9030 (1974).

[168] 14 INT'L LEGAL MATERIALS 1089 (1974).

[169] *Id.*

[170] *Id.* at 1090.

tional Law Commission should be assigned to conduct a comprehensive study of the problem as a whole.

In the same session, UNEP expressed concern for conservation of marine mammals and requested that "(1) . . . the Executive Director to support the inter-agency Advisory Committee's Working Party on Marine Mammals and its symposium scheduled to be held in 1976; (2) Further requests the Executive Director to support research on marine mammal populations, and on whales and small oceans, in particular."[171] The Governing Council also demanded research and preliminary protection by UNEP and member governments through the impact of use of renewable energy resources on the environment.[172] While basically for minimization of environmental damage in development projects in rural areas, the resolution could have impacts on conservation of nonrenewable energy resources.

The United States objected to the UNEP programs on the ground that they were getting into economic, political, and other questions not related to protecting the environment. Canada suggested that UNEP could play a role in the U.N. plan to discuss a "new international economic order" and in such fields as sharing natural resources,[173] but the United States objected that "UNEP as

---

[171] *Id.* at 1091.

[172] *Id.* at 1084.

[173] The objective behind this program is to protect the development program in rural areas in developing countries of Asia, Africa, or Latin America who do not have enough fuel energy resources necessary for their development planning. This project is not only to produce the necessary energy resources but also to protect the environmental damages result from the use of nonrenewable energy resources:

"*The Governing Council,*
"*Aware* that hundreds of millions of people live in the rural areas of the developing countries of Asia, Africa and Latin America, far removed from the mainstream of development activities, and in conditions of abject poverty which cause degradation of the quality of life and hence of the social dimension of the human environment,

"*Noting* that an input of energy on a comparatively small scale desalination of water for drinking and irrigation, and lighting of dwelling in such areas, which would lead to the enhancement of the quality of life and therefore of the social environment,

"*Recognizing* that most of such rural areas have no fossil fuel resources, but possess, in varying degrees, renewable energy resources such as solar energy, wind energy, hydro power, biogas obtained from agricultural and wood from quick-growing trees, which could be harnessed to meet the energy needs of the local communities,

a matter of policy is emphasizing more and more the theme that 'environmental goals cannot be effectively conceived and realized except within the longer framework of the development process."[174]

D. RECOMMENDATIONS

The conservation of resources does not mean the same thing now that it did a few decades ago. Conservation now reflects a demand for a series of collective, urgent, coordinated, comprehensive, and continuous actions for the protection and survival of the human race and its civilization in a world of scarce resources. Therefore, a global conservation policy should be formulated that presents a framework for regional or national decisions on utilization and use of resources. We endorse the British Association for the Advancement of Science's call for the establishment of an International Resources Organization (IRO).[175] The function of the IRO will be the implementation of a global conservation policy through providing information and recommendations to the national and regional institutions or commissions for resource development. The IRO should accommodate the policies of conservation of seabed mineral resources with ones of landmasses and the policies of conservation of renewable resources, such as the living re-

---

"*Believing* that the existing state of the art of the appropriate technologies for harnessing renewable energy resources under the conditions prevailing in the rural areas of developing countries of Asia, Africa and Latin America could justify, on the basis of socio-economic considerations. The use of such technologies,

"*Conscious* of the catalytic role of the United Nations Environmental Programme,

"1. Requests the Executive Director to accord high priority to the establishment in some of the typical rural areas of the countries of Asia, Africa and Latin America, in co-operation with the Governments of the countries concerned and such agencies within and outside the United Nations system as may be considered appropriate, of a few demonstration centres harnessing, individually or in combination, the renewable resources of energy locally available;

"2. *Authorizes* the Executive Director to provide the necessary financial support from the fund of the United Nations Environmental Programme towards the establishment of such demonstration centers;

"3. *Further request* the Executive Director to submit to its fourth session a progress report on the implementation of this decision." 14 Int'l Legal Materials 1084–85 (1975).

[174] N.Y. Times, Apr. 19, 1975, at 22, col.1.

[175] *Id.*

sources of the sea and food. Another major function of the IRO will be to conduct comprehensive scientific investigations on the development of new resources and substitution of resources for future generations. In the case of nonrenewable resources, for example, a certain percentage of capital made by seabed mineral resources should be allocated to such scientific investigations.

The IRO would be an appropriate institution to provide supervision for commodity agreements in forms of providing information and recommendations. It could also provide information and on request make recommendations to the World Bank, UNEP, and other international organizations.

Besides international actions, individual nation-states should provide education on conservation at all levels, as an introductory course in elementary schools, and as a highly technical subject in colleges, as well as through mass media. Since the ultimate consumers of resources are human beings, their understanding of the problem and their cooperation will have a major impact on the effectiveness of a global policy of conservation of resources.

CHAPTER V

Regulation of Injurious Use of Resources

ONE MAJOR task of the comprehensive global process of resource management is that of limiting and minimizing the injurious employment of resources.[1] The importance of taking immediate action to lessen injurious use is highlighted by the common realization of the ecological unity and interdependency of earth spaces[2] and of the real possibility of irreversible damage, through injurious use of resources, to human well-being and civilization.[3]

[1] By injurious employment or injurious use of resources we refer to a process of use that effects value deprivation upon the participants in global social interactions or works negatively upon resources that eventually—because of such negative impact—effect value deprivation on the participants in the social process. For a more elaborate definition of injurious use, see the section on "policies."

The term *pollution* has sometimes been used to refer to a similar process, but it invokes a broader area of concern, such as depletion of resources, a problem related to the issue of conservation. For definitions of "pollution," see R. DASMANN, PLANET IN PERIL 119 (1972); M. WHITEMAN, DIGEST OF INTERNATIONAL LAW 725–26 (1965); Mouton, *The Impact of Science on International Law*, 119 RECUEIL DES COURS 250 (Academie de Droit International) (I–1969); U.N., *Comprehensive Outline of the Scope of the Long Term and Expanded Programme of Oceanic Exploration on Research* 3, U.N. DOC.A/7750 (1969); and the *Convention Relating to Civil Liability in the Field of Maritime Carriage of Nuclear Materials, Dec. 17*, 1971, 11 INT'L LEGAL MATERIALS 277 (1972).

[2] On ecological unity and interdependency of earth space, see McDougal, Legal Bases for Securing the Integrity of the Earth-Space Environment, *in* MANAGING THE PLANET 195 (P. Albertson & M. Barnett eds. 1972); R. FALK, THIS ENDANGERED PLANET (1972); B. WARD & DUBOS, ONLY ONE EARTH 30 (1972); H. SPROUT & M. SPROUT, TOWARD A POLITICS OF THE PLANET 14 (1972); H. SPROUT & M. SPROUT, MULTIPLE VULNERABILITY: THE CONTEST OF ENVIRONMENTAL REPAIR AND PROTECTION (1972); McDougal & Schneider, *The Protection of the Environment and World Public Order: Some Recent Developments*, 45 MISS. L.J. 1085 (1974); J. MCHALE, THE FUTURE OF THE FUTURE 66 (1968), and E. MURPHY, GOVERNING NATURE (1967).

[3] F. HETMAN, SOCIETY AND THE ASSESSMENT OF TECHNOLOGY 84, 270–75 (1973). *See also* Dubos, *Promise and Hazards of Man's Adaptability*, *in* ENVIRONMENTAL QUALITY IN A GROWING ECONOMY 23 (H. Jarrett ed. 1966); Duhl, *Mental Health in an Urban Society*, in *id.* at 40; Epstein & Hattis, *Pollution and Human Health*, ENVIRONMENT: RESOURCES, POLLUTION AND SOCIETY 195–222, (2d ed. W. Murdoch ed. 1975). It has been suggested that there might be a link between contamination of seafood supply and cancer; on this see C. M. Thorne,

The global concern for the protection of the earth space environment is being presented through all means of communication at all political levels.[4] The basic message of this communication is that, as Justice Douglas put it, regardless of the division of the world into separate jurisdictional entities, the biosphere is a unity and "[i]f we are to protect and save the biosphere from dangerous pollution, the controls in large measure must be international."[5] Despite general community acceptance of a global approach to environmental problems, there is continuous controversy over the actual allocation of competences in relation to injurious use of resources both when the use is located within a territorial state and has extraterritorial impact and, to a lesser degree, when the allocation of competences over injurious use of shareable resources has a unique impact on a particular state or region.

A. THE FACTUAL BACKGROUND

Pollution from a single source may, since the world is an ecological unit, be distributed regionally and globally. This has been demonstrated in all the surface and atmospheric nuclear tests since 1945; thus radioactive fallout was quickly detected at a large number of places quite far from the explosions.[6] There is further evidence that effects from injurious uses of resources, at serious levels, have been spread all over the world. Residues of DDT have been found in polar bears and other arctic wildlife.[7] Large amounts of mercury in quantities poisonous to human beings have been found in

---

"How Can the People of the State of Washington Coexist with the Oil Industry?" report submitted to the Oceanographic Institute of Washington, Dec. 11, 1970, at 6–11, *cited in* W. Ross, Oil Pollution as an International Problem 9 (1973).

[4] Communication can be formal or informal, and operates at all levels, from global to regional, involving national and local public and private organizations, interest groups and even concerned private individuals.

[5] *See* Douglas, *Pollution: An International Problem Needing an International Solution*, 7 Tex. Int'l L.J. 1 (1971).

[6] During the London smog of 1952 it is believed that there was less than a complete exchange of air between the air polluted with smog and the surrounding air in the three days. *See* Jackson, *The Dimensions of International Pollution*, 50 Or. L. Rev. 226 (1971).

[7] Science, June 19, 1970, at 1423, *cited in* W. Baumol, Environmental Protection, International Spillovers and Trade 17 (1971). On injurious use resulting from DDT, see F. Graham Jr., Since Silent Spring (1970); and Schachter & Server, *Marine Pollution Problem and Remedies*, 65 Am. J. Int'l. L. 95–99 (1971).

the livers of fur seals that live in the ocean quite far from land.[8]

These increasing negative impacts from injurious use of resources have promoted demands for systematic control over the use of resources.[9] The Federal Council on Environmental Quality estimated that in 1964 more than 300,000 water-using factories in the United States released over 13 trillion gallons of waste water, 22 billion pounds of organic wastes, and 18 billion pounds of suspended solids into the country's waterways.[10] In 1968 the United States alone disposed of 48 million tons of wastes into international waters.[11] The U.S. Council for Environmental Quality predicted that injurious use of oceans is likely to increase rapidly in the future because of growing concern about waste disposal on land-masses and in internal waters.[12]

The long-term results from injurious employment of resources are another factor that invokes international attention.[13] Regardless of where or how an injurious use of resources begins, its danger in the final form as value deprivation is generally felt by a

---

[8]N.Y. Times, Oct. 30, 1970, at 1, col. 3, *cited in* BAUMOL, *Id.* For movement of pollution through air and water, see Frost, *Earth, Air, Water,* 11 ENVIRONMENT July-August, 1969, at 14–33. *See also* WHO PROTECTS THE OCEAN? 37–50, 55–58 (F. Hargrove ed. 1975).

[9]*See* BAUMOL, *supra* note 7, at 13–19; SUBCOMM. ON SCIENCE, RESEARCH AND DEVELOPMENT TO THE HOUSE COMM. ON SCIENCE AND ASTRONAUTICS, 89TH CONG., 2D SESS., ENVIRONMENTAL POLLUTION: A CHALLENGE TO SCIENCE AND TECHNOLOGY (Comm. Print 1968); Kneese, *Background for the Economic Study of Environment Pollution,* in MANAGING THE ENVIRONMENT: INTERNATIONAL ECONOMIC COOPERATION FOR POLLUTION CONTROL 211–25 (A. Kneese, S. Rolfe & J. Harned eds. 1971) (hereinafter cited as KNEESE, ROLFE & HARNED).

[10]*The First Annual Report of the Council on Environmental Quality,* August 1970, at 32, *cited in* Petaccio, *Water Pollution and the Future Law of the Sea,* 21 INT'L & COMP. L.Q. 32 (1972).

[11]Schachter & Server, *supra* note 7, at 106.

[12]N.Y. Times, Oct. 8, 1970, at 1, col. 4, *cited in id.* at 105 n.68. On ocean pollution by dumping, see C. PEARSON, INTERNATIONAL MARINE ENVIRONMENTAL POLICY: THE ECONOMIC DIMENSION 23–37, 64–83 (1975). *See generally* Report of the Secretary-General on International Cooperation on Questions Relating to Oceans, U.N. Doc.E/4836 (1970); MARINE POLLUTION CONTROL (R. Jefe, ed. 1972), and R. SHINN, THE INTERNATIONAL POLITICS OF MARINE POLLUTION CONTROL (1974). The most direct dangers from the effects of organic waste dumping are from disease-causing organisms contained in the sewage of human and livestock origin.

[13]In 1969 Danish fishermen operating off the Swedish coast in the Baltic were burned by fish contaminated by German mustard gas that was dumped by the Allies after World War II. The Times (London) Aug. 10, 1969, at 33, col. 5, *cited in* Schachter & Server, *supra* note 7, at 107. For a study of long-term consequences of the oil spill from the wreck of the Liberian tanker *Arrow* on Cerberus Rock in Chedabucto Bay, Nova Scotia, on Feb. 4, 1970, see Ross, *supra* note 3, at 8.

larger community. For example, in September 1960 the oil pollution in Narragansett Bay, Rhode Island, not only caused substantial damage to the oyster fishery in the area[14] but also had deleterious effects on seabirds in many coastal states, including the United States, the United Kingdom, Germany, and Canada.[15] The oilspill from the fuel tank of the frigate *Seagate* wrecked in 1959 off the Washington state coast resulted in a death rate for gulls of 56.5 per mile of shoreline.[16] In the *Torrey Canyon* incident one oil tanker wrecked in March 1967 spilled approximately 80,000 tons of crude oil into the sea off southwest England.[17] After three days the oil covered an area over 35 miles long and 18 miles wide. The winds, tides, and currents washed oil onto British beaches and threatened the French coast. The pollution of this accident substantially contaminated fishery resources[18] and caused the death of 7,399 sea birds.[19] In the Cherry Point Spill of 1972, the result of

[14] N.Y. Times, June 4, 1967 (Magazine) at 24, 110–11, *cited in* Nanda, *The "Torrey Canyon" Disaster: Some Legal Aspects* 44 DEN. L.J. 400 (1967).

[15] Nanda, *id.* at 404.

[16] *See* Ross, *supra* note 3, at 8. For damages on the marine environment from oil pollution, see Schachter & Server, *supra* note 7, at 88–95; Bellamy, *Effects of Pollution from the Torrey Canyon on Littoral and Sublittoral Ecosystems,* NATURE, Dec. 23, 1968, No. 216, at 1170–73; Sweeney, *Oil Pollution of the Oceans,* 37 FORDHAM L. REV. 155 (1968); Note, *Continental Shelf Oil Disaster: Challenge to International Pollution Control,* 55 CORNELL L. REV. 113 (1969); C. DAVIS, THE MARINE AND FRESH WATER PLANKTON 125–279 (1955); A. HARDY, THE OCEAN SEA, ITS NATURAL HISTORY: THE WORLD OF PLANKTON 292–315 (1956); Teal & Backus, *Petroleum Lumps on the Surface of the Sea,* 168 SCIENCE, April 10, 1970, at 245; U.S. DEPT OF STATE, ENVIRONMENTAL IMPACT STATEMENT—INTERNATIONAL CONVENTIONS AND IMPLEMENTING LEGISLATION ON LIABILITY AND COMPENSATION FOR OIL POLLUTION DAMAGE, at 198–205, 239–44 (1972); Smith, *Pollution of Water by Oil,* ENVIRONMENTAL PROBLEMS AND THEIR INTERNATIONAL IMPLICATIONS 111–126 (H. Odabasi & S. Ulug eds. 1973); *Hearings Before the Subcomm. on Minerals, Materials and Fuels of the Senate Comm. on Interior and Insular Affairs on S. 1219, S. 2516, S. 3351 and S. 3516 to Terminate Offshore Oil Leasing at Santa Barbara, California,* 91st Cong., 2d Sess. (1970); Holmes, *The Santa Barbara Oil Spill,* in OIL ON THE SEA (D. Hoult ed. 1969); R. EASTON, BLACK TIDE: THE SANTA BARBARA OIL SPILL AND ITS CONSEQUENCES (1972). Not only is oil pollution dangerous to marine species, but chemicals used to clean the pollution are themselves dangerous. See, Boyle, *Oil Pollution of the Sea: Is the End in Sight?* 1 BIOLOGICAL CONSERVATION, July 1969 at 321; Nelson-Smith, *The Effects of Oil Pollution and Emulsifier Cleansing on Shore Life in Southwest Britain,* J. OF APPLIED ECOLOGY 97–107 (1968).

[17] For more discussion of the *Torrey Canyon* incident, see Utton, *Protective Measures and the "Torrey Canyon,"* 9 B.C. IND. & COMM. L.R. 613 (1968); C. GILL, F. BOOKER & T. SOPER, THE WRECK OF THE TORREY CANYON (1967), and Nanda, *supra* note 14, at 400.

[18] *Reported in* LIFE, April 14, 1967, at 31, *cited in* Nanda, *supra* note 14, at 400.

[19] N.Y. Times, May 27, 1967, at 51, col. 4, *cited in* id.

a spill from the Liberian tanker *World Point*, which occurred at the Cherry Point Refinery of Atlantic Richfield (ARCO), despite the assurances of the U.S. government, the pollution moved all the way to Canadian beaches and brought damage to fisheries and beach facilities.[20] More recently, in March 1978, a wrecked Liberian supertanker, owned by the American Oil Company, off the French coast freed almost its total oil on board (230,000 tons). It is the worst oil pollution disaster that polluted some 110 miles of coastline and islands, destroyed a harvest of oyster, lobsters, fish, and seawood worth millions of dollars. The incident cost additional millions of dollars in manpower and equipment for the cleanup operation.[21] The harmful effects of the 1954 U.S. hydrogen bomb test in the Pacific went much farther beyond the estimated area and a number of Japanese and Americans miles off the warning zones were injured.[22] The AEC reported that the atmosphere above 7,000 square miles of territory downwind from the point of the burst was so contaminated from radioactivity that survival in the area depended upon "prompt evacuation of the area or upon taking shelter and other protective measures."[23]

Beyond the physical damage, the fear and anxiety that injurious use of resources creates may be a form of value deprivation that is followed by demands for preventive and remedial measures. When a U.S. B–52G nuclear bomber collided with a KC–135 tanker during refueling off the coast of Spain, four hydrogen bombs with a destructive power of 1.5 megatons (75 times the

[20] Ross, *supra* note 3, at 222–4.

[21] *See* The Times (London) March 18, 1978, at 1, col. 5; N.Y. Times, March 20, 1978, at 1, col. 6; N.Y. Times, March 22, 1978, at 6, col. 1; N.Y. Times, March 24, 1978, at 6, col. 3; N.Y. Times, March 31, 1978, at 1, col. 3.

[22] Twenty-seven Japanese fishermen working some fourteen miles clear of the warning zone were injured. They did not arrive in Japan until some weeks later, and a few months later one of them died. *See* Arnold, *Effects of the Recent Bomb Tests on Human Beings*, 10 BULL. ATOM. SCIENTISTS 347 (1954). The bomb exposed 236 Marshall Islands residents and 28 U.S. military personnel to radiation because of the unexpected shift of wind to the islands of Rongelap, Rongerik, and Uterik. *See* N.Y. Times, March 12, 1954, at 1, col. 1, *cited in* Margolis, *The Hydrogen Bomb Experiments and International Law*, 64 YALE L.J. 637 (1955). The water of these islands had become dangerous because of the radiation, but the inhabitants were not warned of the fact; see U.N. Doc. No. T/C.2/SR 197 (1954) at 5.

[23] N.Y. Times, Feb. 16, 1955, at 18 col. 4, *cited in* Margolis, *supra* note 22, at 637. *See also* McDougal & Schlei, *The Hydrogen Bomb Tests in Perspective: Lawful Measures for Security*, 64 YALE L.J. 650–55 (1955).

power of the Hiroshima bomb) [24] were dropped. This incident not only created substantial physical damage but also fostered fear and disturbance in the Mediterranean area for two months until the possibility for potential damage was removed. Two of the bombs that fell on land ruptured and discharged their TNT, scattering uranium and plutonium particles near the Spanish coastal village of Palomares and caused imminent danger to the well-being of the inhabitants and ecology of the area. Immediate remedial action was taken by the United States and Spain, and it is reported that the United States buried 1,750 tons of mildly radioactive Spanish soil in the U.S.[25] The third bomb hit the earth intact, but the fourth bomb was lost somewhere in the Mediterranean. After a two-month search by submarines and growing apprehension among the natives of the Mediterranean area, the bomb was located but was lost during the operation for nine more days. After 80 days of the threat of the bomb, the 20-megaton device, with an explosive force of 20 million tons of TNT, was retrieved.[26]

The injurious use of internal resources by individual states is also a part of a continuing, more general process. In some cases the degree of damage to the environment or other value deprivation from a particular misuse of internal resources may be low and not identifiable, but the aggregation of such misuses may create a widespread problem. For example, the carbon-dioxide emissions

---

[24] T. Szulc, The Bombs of Palomares 17 (1967).

[25] *Radioactive Spanish Earth is Buried 10 Feet Deep in South Carolina*, N.Y. Times, April 12, 1966 at 28, col. 3.

[26] For further discussion of this incident see Szulc, note 24 *supra*, and F. Lewis, One of Our H-Bombs Is Missing (1967). The public fear of danger to the environment due to radioactivity has increased. *See* Lewis, *Not with a Bang but with a Gasp*, N.Y. Times, Dec. 15, 1969, at 46, col. 3; Broecker, *Man's Oxygen Reserves*, Science, June 26, 1970, at 1538; Rasool & Schneider, *Atmosphere Carbon Dioxide and Aerosols: Effects of Large Increases on Global Climate*, Science, June 25, 1971, at 139, 141. For more on air pollution and its consequences, see Man and His Environment 13–75 (T. Vickery ed. 1972); Kneese, *Economics and the Quality of the Environment; Some Empirical Experiences*, in Pollution Resources and the Environment 77–78 (A. Enthoven & A. Freeman III, ed. 1973); Lave & Seskin, *Air Pollution and Human Health* in *id.* at 88–99; Heggestad, *Air Pollution and Plants*, in Man's Impact on Terrestrial and Oceanic Ecosystems 101–15 (F. Smith & E. Goldberg eds. 1971); Hepting, *Air Pollution and Trees*, in *id.* at 116–29; Adinolfi, *First Steps Toward European Cooperation in Reducing Air Pollution—Activities of the Council of Europe*, 33 L. & Contemp Prob. 421 (1968). On weather modification see Taubenfeld, *Weather Modification and Control: Some International Legal Implications*, 55 Calif. L. Rev. 493 (1967) and Gates, *Weather Modification in the Service of Mankind: Promise or Peril?* in The Environmental Crisis 33–46 (H. Helfrich, Jr., ed. 1970).

of the globe have recently been estimated to be approximately 230 million tons a year.[27] This estimate is based only on technological sources and forest fires, which are located within state boundaries and are internal sources, and does not include estimates from other natural sources.[28] Similar problems exist for other forms of injurious use of resources. In the case of offshore drilling, it may be difficult to estimate the damage to the marine environment as a whole by the drilling of any one state, but there is no doubt that all the states involved in such an operation do contribute to, and share the responsibility for, the entire damage. In other cases, however, the direct link and the degree of deprivation caused by injurious use of internal resources effected by one state against other states is clearly identifiable. The "black snow" in Norway of January 1970 is an example of such a case. The "black snow" that fell on eastern Norway and western Sweden was due to air pollution over the Ruhr in West Germany.[29] Similarly, in the Trail Smelter arbitration, the damage to agricultural and timber lands in the state of Washington was clearly the result of pollution created by the Trail Smelter, across the border in Canada.

The serious consequences of the injurious use of resources for human life and civilization, and the perception of such consequences, have so increased as to arouse the concern not merely of public (national, regional, and global) organizations but also of private associations. The area of operation of these private associations is similar to that of the public organizations and varies from national to regional and transnational operation.[30] The function of such organizations is to affect the decision-making process concerning injurious use of resources at all levels, in the legislature, executive, and judiciary.[31]

[27] Jaffe, *The Global Balance of Carbon Monoxide* in GLOBAL EFFECTS OF ENVIRONMENTAL POLLUTION 35 (S. Singer ed. 1970).

[28] For global problems involving the balance of carbon dioxide in the atmosphere, see Landsberg, SCIENCE, at 1265 (1970).

[29] N.Y. Times, Jan. 11, 1970 at 24, col. 1.

[30] For the number and names of private transnational associations participating in U.N. environmental activities, see Ferara, *Transnational Political Interests and the Global Environment*, 28 INT'L ORGANIZATION 56–60 (1974), and Goldie, *A General View of International Environmental Law: A Survey of Capabilities, Trends and Limits*, 97 J. DE DROIT INT'L 60 (1973).

[31] These private associations affect the authoritative decisions by exerting pressure through different channels of communication. For some cases brought by private environ-

B. BASIC COMMUNITY POLICIES

1. Control over Injurious Use of Resources as a Matter of International Concern

The continuing process of employment of resources (both internal and shareable), with its increasingly negative and grave impact upon common interests (both exclusive and inclusive) through different forms of value deprivation, has made control over injurious use of resources eminently a matter of international concern.[32] This inclusive concern for the protection of common interests has been expressed through different community prescriptions which impose severe restraints upon the assertion of special interests. Improvements in science and technology, improved control over the weather, and other features of the environment have further enhanced both the unilateral and cooperative capabilities of states for control over deprivation arising from the internal use of resources.

The policy of protecting the common interest, which had its basis, long before the U.N. Charter, in customary international law and the reciprocal behavior of nation-states, today derives, in most elemental form, from the express and implied statements of the U.N. Charter, mainly from Article 2, paragraph 4, which reads: "All Members shall refrain in their international relations from the threat or use of force against the territorial integrity or political independence of any state, or in any other manner inconsistent with the Purposes of the United Nations." Professor McDougal, in evaluating the community expectations about this broad policy

---

mental organizations to prevent or stop continuing injurious use of resources, see Scenic Hudson Preservation Conference v. FPC, 354 F.2d 24 (9th Cir. 1970) (and cases cited therein). On suits by private organizations against public authorities, see Sierra Club v. Ruckelshaus, 344 F. Supp. 253 (U.S.D.C.D.C. 1972). For a discussion of the case see Miholy, *The Clean Air Act and the Concept of Non-Degradation: Sierra Club v. Ruckelshaus*, 2 ECOLOGY L.Q. 801 (1972).

It has been suggested that the access of these private organizations to authoritative decision makers, particularly the courts, should be increased. For a discussion of this issue see Stone, *Should Trees Have Standing?—Toward Legal Rights for Natural Objects*, 45 S. CAL. L. REV. 540 (1972).

[32] C. W. Jenks observes that polluting the environment is certainly not in the interest of mankind. Jenks, *Liability for Ultra-Hazardous Activities in International Law*, 117 RECUEIL DES COURS 105, 194–95 (Academie de Droit International) (I–1966).

statement, observes that "[i]t would appear the common expectation of most of mankind that this policy of minimum order, indispensable to law in any community, applies not merely to activities on earth and to traditional exercises with the military instrument, but also to man's activities anywhere, as in outer space, and to any new techniques of coercion and deprivation made possible by manipulation of environmental variables."[33] There are many more specific references to the regulation of injurious use of resources in various multilateral prescriptions. The policy principle that appears to infuse all these prescriptions is that of the ancient doctrine of *sic utere tuo ut alienum non laedas*. The 1966 Helsinki Rules, protecting the common interest, authoritatively established the principle of "equitable utilization," which provides that "each basin state is entitled within its territory, to a reasonable and equitable share in the beneficial uses of the waters of an international drainage basin."[34] This principle also provides for the prevention of "any new forms of water pollution . . . which would cause substantial injury in the territory of a co-basin State."[35] The official comment of this doctrine states: "Any use of water by a basin State . . . that denies an equitable sharing of uses by a co-basin State conflicts with the community of interests of all basin States in obtaining maximum benefit from the common resource. . . . A use that causes pollution to the extent of depriving a co-basin State of an equitable share [is a violation of international law]."[36] The Geneva Convention on the High Seas emphasizes the primacy of the common interest in Article 25, which requires all parties to "take measures to prevent pollution of the seas from the dumping of radioactive waste."[37] Article 24 of the same Convention, drawing upon the responsibility of every state in protection of the common interest, provides that "[e]very State shall draw up regulation to prevent pollution of the seas. . . ."[38] Following the same policy, the

---

[33] McDougal, *supra* note 2, at 388. For a description of these expectations, *see* M. Mc-Dougal & F. Feliciano, Law and Minimum World Public Order (1962).

[34] *See Helsinki Rules on the Use of the Waters of International Rivers*, in Int'l L. Assoc., Report of the Fifty-Second Conference, Helsinki 477–533 (1967).

[35] Article 10, *id.* at 496–97.

[36] *Id.* at 499.

[37] Convention on the High Seas, April 29, 1958, 450 U.N.T.S. 82 (1962).

[38] *Id.*

World Health Organization asked all its member states "to prohibit all discharge of radioactive waste into water courses or the sea, to the extent that the safety of such discharge has not been proved."[39] The U.N. Seabed Committee also has asked nation-states "to refrain from using the seabed and ocean floor as a dumping ground for toxic, radioactive and other noxious materials which might cause serious damage to the marine environment."[40] All those prescriptions build upon the premise that "international concern" today is a matter of factual interdependence or interdetermination and that such interdetermination is necessarily high in instances of the injurious use of resources with transnational impacts.

2. Policies Regarding the Determination of an Injurious Use

By *injurious use of resources* we mean a use of resources that results in value deprivation for human beings. Such value deprivation becomes unlawful and creates liability when it is an unreasonable assertion of special interest in contravention of the common interests as all these interests are defined in community prescriptions. Whether a particular definition is unlawful in this sense can only be determined by a careful contextual examination of the whole process of resource use, which identifies and assesses costs and benefits to all parties.

Since a decision as to whether a particular resource use is unlawful should be made to protect the common interest, the competence to determine decision makers and appropriate principles should be inclusive. The degree of participation of inclusive authorities, however, may differ with differing circumstances. In general, criteria by which injurious use is identified are indicated by inclusive prescriptions. The decision as to whether in particular cases inclusive or exclusive decision makers are competent should, similarly, be made by inclusive authorities.

In some situations inclusive prescriptions have promoted the competence of exclusive decision makers by referring to national courts as competent forums. In such cases, however, the national

---

[39] W.H.O. Res. WHA 114, 56, 14 World Health Assembly, No. 110, Part I, 24 (1961).

[40] Report of the Committee on the Peaceful Uses of the Seabed and the Ocean Floor Beyond the Limits of National Jurisdiction, 25 U.N. GAOR Supp. (No. 21) 8, U.N. Doc.A/ 8021 (1970).

authorities are obliged either to implement inclusive prescriptions or to consider the broader community policy of protection of the common interest in the absence of explicit prescriptions.

3. Policies Regarding the Injurious Use of Internal Resources with Extraterritorial Impacts

Even for the protection of common interest, the competence to control the planning and development of resources within the territorial boundaries of a state should be initially exclusive. In practice this policy has generally been accepted, through acceptance of the principle of state sovereignty and mutual tolerance among states with respect to internal activities. General Assembly Resolution 1803 (XVII) of December 14, 1962, affirms the exclusive competence of states "over their natural wealth and resources." This exclusive competence of states as to the injurious use of their internal resources is, however, limited by the principle of state responsibility. This principle holds states responsible for injuries caused by their actions within their own territorial jurisdiction that cause unreasonable injury to a foreign national or state in a form of value deprivation.[41] This doctrine has been applied as well to the injurious employment of internal resources with extraterritorial effects. The limitation of exclusive control over exploitation, planning, and development of internal resources whose injurious results transcend state borders is imposed through the authority of inclusive decision makers to review, appraise, and even enjoin exclusive injurious employments. The role of inclusive competence is to balance the competing doctrines of state sovereignty and state responsibility. The objective of inclusive competence is to protect the exclusive interests of nation-states by allowing them to

---

[41] For a discussion of the broad doctrine of state responsibility, see M. WHITEMAN, 8 DIGEST OF INT'L L. 697 (1967); Ago, *First Report on State Responsibility*, 2 Y.B. INT'L L. COMM. 125 (1969); W. BISHOP, INTERNATIONAL LAW 742–899 (1962); L. SOHN & R. BAXTER, CONVENTION ON THE INTERNATIONAL RESPONSIBILITY OF STATES FOR INJURIES TO ALIENS (1961). For the application of this doctrine to injurious employment of resources, see Utton, *International Water Quality Law*, 13 NATURAL RESOURCES J. 282 (1973); Bleicher, *An Overview of the Environmental Legislation*, 2 ECOLOGY L.Q. 1 (1972); Olmstead, *Prospects for Regulation of Environmental Conservation Under International Law*, in INT'L LAW ASSOC., THE PRESENT STATE OF INTERNATIONAL LAW 245 (1973); Handl, *Territorial Sovereignty and the Problem of Transnational Pollution*, 69 AM. J. INT'L. L. 50 (1975), and Schneider, *State Responsibility for Environmental Protection and Preservation: Ecological Unities and a Fragmented World Public Order*, 2 YALE STUD. WORLD PUB. ORD. 32 (1975).

be free in identifying their development goals and in exploiting their internal resources to achieve preferred events in a manner they choose, so long as this process does not, by direct extraterritorial impact, damage the inclusive interest of a larger community or the legitimate exclusive interests of another nation-state. As to the former possibility there are a number of inclusive prescriptions, such as the Draft Declaration on Rights and Duties of States, cited in the Report of the International Law Commission, which states that "[e]very State has the duty to ensure that conditions prevailing in its territory do not menace international peace and order."[42] Principle 21 of the Stockholm Conference recognizes both policies when it says that states have "the responsibility to ensure that activities within their jurisdiction or control do not cause damage to the environment of other States or areas beyond the limits of national jurisdiction."[43]

Present community policy as to the involvement of inclusive competence mainly concerns compensation measures. In other words, inclusive decision makers become competent to enter a case when value deprivation has already occurred. In a world presently characterized by resource scarcity and interdependency, one of the first objectives of the constitutive process should be the prevention of value deprivation. In circumstances where the number of resources vital to the world development and civilization increases, prevention of injurious use of these resources is the most important goal in the protection of the common interest of the larger community. Furthermore, the first task of the constitutive process in the protection of the vital interest of larger or smaller communities is to prevent the deprivation of these vital interests, in this case by the prevention of injurious employment of resources. To promote this policy, there should be strategies that accommodate the inclusive and the exclusive competences regarding the use of internal resources to protect the inclusive interest, without jeopardizing the exclusive interest of nation-states in their development programs. One strategy to this end would be prior consultation. This strategy has been promoted with respect to shareable resources like international rivers, but there is no indi-

[42] *See* M. WHITEMAN, 5 DIGEST OF INT'L L. 249 (1965).

[43] Report of the United Nations Conference on the Human Environment, U.N. Doc. A/Conf.48/14 (1972) at 7, [hereinafter cited as STOCKHOLM CONFERENCE]. *See also* L. BRAMSON, TRANSNATIONAL POLLUTION AND INTERNATIONAL LAW 257 (1972).

cation as to its employment with regard to internal resources.

Appraising exclusive competence requires knowledge of the internal plans and activities of nation-states. Such knowledge requires a comprehensive and profound intelligence function, almost impossible to achieve with the present intelligence system. Such knowledge might also be in some sense contradictory to the policy of secrecy of national development programs by individual states. Sometimes this difficulty arises not only from the desire of the governments to avoid publicity about their programs but also from their lack of knowledge and ability to acquire relevant and necessary information as to the operation of public or private sectors.

Inclusive competence should not stop with preventive measures; it should be expanded to include decision making with respect to sharing the cost of damages and of measures of compensation. The latter policies have generally been accepted in practice.

4. Policies Regarding the Injurious Use of Shareable Resources with Unique Impacts on a Nation-State or a Region

Inclusive competence over injurious use of shareable resources has long been accepted. The scope of such inclusive competence, however, is limited to the expectation of the community as to the effectiveness of the inclusive authorities in protecting the common interest. In analyzing the relevant community expectation and its effect on the scope of inclusive competence, Professor McDougal observes that

> another factor influencing the prescription and application of policy is the state of expectations of various participants as to the possibilities of effective decision-making by the organized world community—the dependability, in other words, of reliance upon world community intervention. It is common knowledge that low estimates of such possibilities . . . led to the insertion of article fifty-one in the Charter of the United Nations, which recognized individual and collective self-defense, and since then, to the elaboration of the permission of the collective self-defense in numerous treaties establishing regional organizations.[44]

[44]M. McDougal & Assoc., Studies in World Public Order 285 (1960).

In another passage, justifying certain unilateral actions as being within the scope of inclusive competence, Professor McDougal states that "[i]n the absence of a centralized authority capable of maintaining public order, nation-states have always demanded for themselves and accorded to others a wide measure of freedom in unilateral action for maintaining their own security against external dictation by unlawful violence or threats of violence."[45] While unilateral action by nation-states under the doctrine of self-help, self-preservation, or self-defense has generally been accepted, its scope, criteria, and means of application have remained controversial.

In the area of injurious use of resources the inadequacy of international law, either through the lack of appropriate prescriptions or of enforcement (and preventive) measures, has been the cause of reciprocal tolerance by nation-states of their unilateral actions. In certain circumstances the inclusive authorities have even prescribed unilateral action by nation-states with regard to control of injurious use of shareable resources.[46] Such unilateral action, however, is limited to abatement only and with indictment for compensation where the action was not reasonable and caused injury to other states.

Although as a future policy we prefer to promote inclusive competence over the use of shareable resources, we realize the ineffectiveness of inclusive authority in a number of areas of protection of the common interest, particularly with respect to preventive measures and emergency situations. Therefore, we recognize the necessity of unilateral actions and the contributions that those unilateral actions can make to the whole process of protecting the common interest. Under these circumstances our policies would basically limit the competence of nation-states to enforce inclusive prescriptions. In areas where the existing inclusive prescriptions do not adequately protect the vital interests of a nation-state or a region from the injurious employment of shareable resources, our policies promote exclusive or regional prescriptions. Disputes con-

[45] McDougal & Schlei, *supra* note 23, at 674. Professor McDougal limits such unilateral action to the principles of "necessity" and "proportionality," see McDOUGAL & FELICIANO, *supra* note 33, at 231. For a similar perspective, see Beesley, *The Canadian Approach to International Environmental Law*, 11 CANADIAN Y.B. INT'L L. 5 (1973).

[46] The Convention on Intervention on the High Seas in Cases of Oil Casualties, 9 INT'L LEGAL MATERIALS 25 (1970).

cerning these prescriptions, however, should be subject to review or appraisal by inclusive authorities.

C. TRENDS IN DECISION

1. Control over Injurious Use of Internal Resources with Extraterritorial Impacts

The historical notion of state sovereignty formulated by Jean Bodin and developed by other jurists affirms absolute competence of the state over resources within its territorial jurisdiction.[47] This notion became the basis for a number of claims for special interests, for example, the Harmon doctrine. For a time the insignificant possibility of impact of states' activities upon one another caused the principle of state sovereignty to overshadow the principle of state responsibility. Oppenheim's statement presents such a policy: "An act of a State injurious to another State is nevertheless not an international delinquency if committed neither wilfully and maliciously nor with culpable negligence. Therefore, an act of a State committed by right, or promoted by self-preservation is necessary self-defense, does not constitute an international delinquency, no matter how injurious it may actually be to another State."[48] In the present world, however, Oppenheim's statement does not appropriately reflect community expectations on the protection of common interest in environmental problems. The global acceptance of multilateral and lesser conventions embodying strict liability for space activities and nuclear damage and including compensatory responsibility for damages from pollution and other injurious uses of resources expresses the contradiction between present community expectations and the Oppenheim view.[49] Not only official conventions but also unilateral acknowl-

---

[47] For a discussion of "state sovereignty," see the section on "sovereignty."

[48] L. OPPENHEIM, INTERNATIONAL LAW 343 (8th ed. H. Lauterpacht ed. 1955).

[49] Nanda, *Liability for Space Activities*, 41 U. COLO. L. REV. 509 (1969); Vlasic, *The Space Treaty: A Preliminary Evaluation*, 55 CALIF. L. REV. 507 (1967); Dembling & Arons, *The Evaluation of the Outer Space Treaty*, 33 J. OF AIR L. & COM. 419 (1967). For oil pollution, see note 16, *supra*. For river pollution see citations and discussions in INT'L L. ASSOC., HELSINKI RULES ON THE USE OF WATERS OF INTERNATIONAL RIVERS 20 *et seq.* (1966); Bourne, *International Law and Pollution of International Rivers and Lakes*, 21 U. OF TORONTO L.J. 193 (1971); U.N. Economic Commission for Europe (UNECE) Res. 10 (XXI) of April 29, 1966, U.N.

edgment of state responsibility and the voluntary settlement of disputes confirm these expectations.

The present community expectation is well stated in the authoritative language of Principle 21 of the Stockholm Conference on the Human Environment. This Principle declares that states have "the responsibility to ensure that activities within their jurisdiction or control do not cause damage to the environment of other States or of areas beyond the limits of national jurisdiction."[50] Principle 22 of the Stockholm Conference elaborated on the state responsibility: "States shall co-operate to develop further the international law regarding liability and compensation for the victims of pollution and other environmental damage caused by activities within the jurisdiction and control of such States to areas beyond their jurisdiction."[51] To support these two principles as to expanding the concept of state responsibility as against state sovereignty, G.A. Resolution 2996 declared that any resolution adopted by the twenty-seventh General Assembly could not affect Principles 21 and 22 of the Human Environment Declaration.[52]

Aside from these two principles, the law regarding injurious use of internal resources with extraterritorial impact comes primarily from two decisions: the *Trail Smelter* arbitration,[53] and the *Corfu Channel Case*.[54]

The *Trail Smelter* case deals directly with injurious use of internal resources with extraterritorial impact. It involved the movement of fumes from the plant of a Canadian private corporation in Trail, British Columbia, to the State of Washington. The fumes were doing substantial damage to privately owned agricultural and timber lands. The dispute was first referred to the International Joint Commission in 1931, but this reference was rejected by the United States. Then it was referred to an *ad hoc* arbitral tribunal set up by the United States and Canada on the basis of the

---

Doc. E/ECE 1938 (1967) and U.N. Doc. E/4822 (1970) *reprinted in* OECD OBSERVER, Sept. 1964 at 38–39, and Oct. 1969 at 15–18.

[50] STOCKHOLM CONFERENCE, *supra* note 43, Principle 21.

[51] *Id.*

[52] G.A. Res. 2994, 27 U.N. GAOR Supp. (No. 30) 42, U.N. DOC. A/8730 (1972).

[53] 3 R. Int'l Arb. Awards 1905 (1941), *reprinted in* 35 AM. J. INT'L L. 684 (1941).

[54] [1949] I.C.J. 4.

1935 Convention. The Tribunal stated that the nearest analogy to the case before it was the body of decisions related to water pollution.[55] But in the absence of decisions relevant to the precise facts, the tribunal referred to broader principles of the international law of state responsibility. Some of the conclusions of the tribunal from that reference have often been quoted as relevant international prescriptions on the injurious use of internal resources. The tribunal observed that "under the principle of international law . . . no state has the right to use or permit the use of its territory in such a manner as to cause injury by fumes in or to the territory of another or the properties or persons therein, when the case is of serious consequence and the injury is established by clear and convincing evidence."[56] The tribunal, therefore, held that "the Dominion of Canada is responsible in international law for the conduct of the Trail Smelter and, apart from the undertakings in the Convention, it is the duty of the Government of the Dominion of Canada to see to it that this conduct is in conformity with the obligation of the Dominion under international law as herein determined."[57] The tribunal did not stop with compensation; it stated prevention policies for future damage as well. The tribunal stated that damage may occur in the future unless the operation of the smelter is subject to some control: "The Trail Smelter shall be required to refrain in the future from causing any damage through fumes in the State of Washington. To avoid such damage the operations of the Smelter shall be subject to a regime or measure of control as provided in the present decision. Should such damage occur, indemnity to the United States shall be fixed in such manner as the governments acting under the convention may agree upon."[58] In reaching its conclusion, the tribunal accommodated the interest of both parties; that of Canada in the operation of its factory and that of the United States in preventing damage to its environment. The tribunal stated that it gave consideration "to reach a solution just to all parties."[59] Within such consideration, the tribunal prescribed and imposed certain policies in terms of

[55] *See* 35 Am. J. Int'l L., *supra* note 53, at 714.

[56] *Id.* at 716.

[57] *Id.* at 717, 3 R. Int'l Arb. Awards, at 1965–66.

[58] *Id.*

[59] 35 Am. J. Int'l L., *supra* note 53, at 713.

the operation of the Smelter and observed that the prescribed regime would probably remove the causes of the existing controversy and result in *preventing* any damages of a material nature in the State of Washington in the future.[60] The prescribed regime for the operation of the Smelter was comprised of a comprehensive set of general restrictions on the instruments that the smelter should use in order to acquire more precise knowledge about the impact of its operation on the environment, and on the maximum permissible sulphur emission.[61] While the implementation of this regime was made by Canada, the tribunal prescribed a process by which the regime could be amended or suspended by an inclusive authority. Under this policy, if at any time subsequent to December 31, 1942, either government requested an amendment or suspension of the regime and the other government declined to agree to such request, each country should appoint a scientist of repute within a month after the making of such request. The two scientists should constitute a Commission for the purpose of making a decision on the request. If the Commission failed to make a decision within three months, the two scientists should jointly appoint a third scientist. In this case the majority decision would be final and the parties there required to take the actions necessary to implement the Commission's decision.[62]

The significance of the *Trail Smelter* case was in its adoption of a policy of inclusive competence not only with regard to compensation for the injurious use of internal resources but also for establishing preventive measures. While the prescriptions of preventive measures were inclusive, their implementation was made exclusive by Canada. But the tribunal formulated an inclusive dispute settlement procedure, the Commission of scientists, to review the possible claims and counterclaims.

The *Corfu Channel Case*, another relevant decision in this area, concerned two British warships which passed through the Corfu Straits in Albania territorial waters in 1946. The British warships struck a mine field resulting in the death of a large number of British seamen and in the destruction of one vessel and serious injuries to the other. The Albanian government had not placed

[60] 3 R. Int'l Arb. Awards at 1980.

[61] 35 Am. J. Int'l L., *supra* note 53, at 726–30.

[62] *Id.* at 730–1.

the mines but was aware of their existence, although it did not warn the British warships of them. The case was referred to the International Court of Justice by the U.N. Security Council. The ICJ had to decide on the question of Albanian responsibility for the failure to notify the British warships about the mines in the territorial waters of the Corfu Channel. The Court held for the British on the grounds that it is every state's obligation not knowingly to allow its territory to be used for acts contrary to the rights of other states.[63] This decision has been used as a basis for extending state responsibility.[64] The Court's opinion in the case was somewhat expansive, saying that not only knowledge but also ignorance, resulting from insufficient efforts to keep informed, is an adequate basis for liability.

The Court said:

> (2) Every State is bound to exercise proper vigilance in its territory. . . .
> A State which fails to exercise this vigilance, or is negligent in its exercise, will find its responsibility involved in case of injury caused in its territory to other States or to their nationals.
>
> (3) As a consequence to the foregoing, every State is considered as having known, or as having a duty to have known, of prejudicial acts committed in parts of its territory where local authorities are installed; that is not a presumption, nor is it a hypothesis, it is the consequence of its sovereignty.[65]

The relevance of this language to the broad policies with which we are concerned is obvious. In factual terms its relevance is more tenuous because the case does not involve extraterritorial impact but, rather, injurious impact on foreign subjects within its territorial jurisdiction.

Building upon the policy of the above two cases, the 1963 report of the IAEA Panel of experts on the disposal of radioactive wastes in fresh water stated: "It is a general rule of international law that a state must not abuse its rights under international law by allow-

---

[63] [1949] I.C.J. 22.

[64] *See* Goldie, *Liability for Damage and the Progressive Development of International Law*, 14 INT'L COMP. L.Q. 1226–33 (1965); Lester, *River Pollution in International Law*, 75 AM. J. INT'L L. I.L. 839–40 (1963); Hardy, *International Protection Against Nuclear Risk*, 10 INT'L COMP. L.Q. 753–54 (1961).

[65] [1949] I.C.J. 22, 44 (opinion of Alvarez, J.).

ing alteration of the natural conditions of its own territory to the disadvantage of the natural conditions of the territory of another state."[66]

The past trends regarding the injurious use of internal resources are not thus overwhelming with respect either to duration or to the number of cases. Comparable policies can, however, be found in a number of decisions and in the reciprocal behavior of states concerning the use of international rivers. The use of international rivers represents the closest analogy to the use of internal resources. In the case of international rivers, we are faced with a resource which is physically located within the territorial jurisdiction of one state but which eventually moves to another state or states. While the character of the resources involved in these two situations is different (because of the shareable nature of international rivers and the large nonshareable nature of internal resources), the policies presented by authoritative decisions on cases involving international rivers are useful and important in terms of analogy with regard to internal resources. They might aid in broadening responsibility in relation to internal resources.

An early case limiting state control over part of the river in its territory was the decision of the German court in the *Donauversinkung* case, *Würtemberg and Prussia v. Baden*.[67] In this case the court, deciding on the issue of the use of the Danube River among the Federal States, indicated that the general principles of international law concerning the flow of international rivers support *sic utere tuo*: "The exercise of sovereign rights by every State in regard to international rivers traversing its territory is limited by the duty not to injure the interests of other members of the international community."[68] The most famous case in this area, and one making a strong policy statement about state responsibility, is *Lake Lanoux*.[69] The issue involved in this case was whether a change proposed by France for its part of a river shared with Spain, if carried out without the prior agreement of Spain, constituted a violation of state boundary treaties. The arbitral tribunal, after finding that

[66] *Quoted in* Legault, *The Freedom of the Seas: A Licence to Pollution?* 21 U. OF TORONTO L.J. 217 (1971).

[67] H. LAUTERPACHT, 4 ANNUAL DIGEST OF PUBLIC INTERNATIONAL LAW AND CASES 428 (1927).

[68] *Id.* at 131.

[69] 12 R. Int'l Arb. Awards 281 (1957), *reprinted in* 53 AM. J. INT'L L. 156 (1959).

there would be no injurious impact on Spain, held for France on the ground that there was no need for prior agreement under the treaties and customary international law. But the tribunal stated that strict liability would have governed the situation in the event of a contrary finding for Spain: "It would then have been argued that the works would bring about a definitive pollution of the waters of the Carol [the name of the Spanish side of the common river] or that the returned water would have a chemical composition or a temperature or some other characteristics which could injure Spanish interests. Spain could have claimed that her rights had been impaired."[70] The *Gut Dam*[71] decision follows a similar policy. This was an arbitration between the United States and Canada in regard to injuries caused to U.S. citizens by the Canadian government in building a dam between Adams Island in Canadian territory and Les Galops in American territory in 1903. In 1965 Canada was held liable to the United States for damages attributable to the dam. These cases are not exactly relevant to the problem of injurious use of internal resources with extraterritorial impact, as is *Trail Smelter*, but they do lay down usefully similar policies as to state responsibility.

The need for formulating policies for preventive measures with respect to injurious use of internal resources was recognized in the Stockholm Conference. The language of Principle 8 of the Declaration of the Preparatory Committee for the U.N. Conference on the Human Environment is an example of such recognition. This Principle provided that "a State having reason to believe that the activities of another State may cause damage to its environment or to the environment of areas beyond the limits of national jurisdiction may request international consultations concerning the envisaged activities."[72] Principle 20 further required: "Relevant information must be supplied by States on activities or developments within their jurisdiction or under their control whenever they believe, or have reasons to believe, that such information is needed to avoid the risk of significant adverse effects on the envi-

[70] 12 R. Int'l Arb. Awards at 303.

[71] Canada–United States Settlement of Gut Dam Claims, Sept. 22, 1968, Report of the Agent of the United States Before the Lake Ontario Claims Tribunal, *reprinted in* 8 Int'l Legal Materials 118 (1969).

[72] U.N. Doc. A/Conf.48/PC/12, Annex 2 (1971).

ronment in areas beyond their national jurisdiction."[73] This Principle was not adopted at the Stockholm Conference, mainly because of problems between Brazil and Argentina over their common river with regard to the Brazilian plan for the construction of a hydroelectric plant on the river. Principle 20 enunciated a position against the policy and desire of states for secrecy with regard to their development plans; this was the reason for its non-adoption at the Stockholm Conference. Brazil was not willing to provide information to Argentina about its plan for a hydro-electric system.

A primary concern for the protection of the common interest led to General Assembly Resolution 2995. This Resolution, which was adopted in the place of Principle 20, is a weaker statement in support of prior notification but nevertheless constitutes recognition of the need for an inclusive competence, stipulating forms of notice and prior consultation:

> [C]o-operation between States in the field of the environment, including cooperation towards the implementation of Principles 21 and 22 of the Declaration of the United Nations Conference on the Human Environment, will be effectively achieved if official and public knowledge is provided of the technical data relating to the work to be carried out by States within their national jurisdiction with a view to avoiding significant harm that may occur in the human environment of the adjacent area. . . .[74]

A year later the General Assembly passed another resolution on Cooperation in the Field of the Environment Concerning Natural Resources Shared by Two or More States.[75] The Resolution stressed that the states' cooperation in this area "must be developed on the basis of a system of information and prior consultation within the framework of the normal relations existing between them." The Resolution further requested the U.N. Environmental Program to adopt measures for the implementation of the Resolution.[76] In 1974 the Organization for Economic Co-op-

[73] *Id.*

[74] The resolution was adopted on December 15, 1972, with a vote of 115 to 0, 10 members abstaining.

[75] G.A. Res. 3129, 28 U.N. GAOR Supp. (No. 30) 48, U.N. Doc. A/9030 (1973).

[76] Cooperation in the Field of the Environment Concerning Natural Resources Shared

eration and Development also adopted a recommendation on Principles Concerning Transfrontier Pollution.[77] The Principles include recommendations on "warning systems and incidents": "Countries should promptly warn other potentially affected countries of any situation which may cause any sudden increase in the level of pollution in areas outside the country of origin of pollution, and take all appropriate steps to reduce the effects of any such sudden increase."[78]

Despite states' desire for secrecy as to their planning, prior consultation to some extent has been recognized as a preventive measure in controlling the injurious use of resources among nation-states. Secretary of State William Rogers suggested in 1971 that "perhaps it is time for the international community to begin moving toward a consensus that nations have a right to be consulted before actions are taken which could affect their environment or the international environment at large."[79] In 1960, for example, when the United States announced that it was planning to put 350 million minute needles in orbit as communications relayers, there was a strong demand by scientists for international evaluation before initiating similar projects in the future.[80] The United States conducted the test but announced that it was willing to engage in "appropriate international consultations before proceeding with a space activity if it had reason to believe that its activity may create a significant risk of harm."[81]

The U.S. Federal Water Pollution Control Act of 1956[82] requires consultation in some limited areas for water pollution problems that may have international dimensions. This Act requires that

> [w]henever the Secretary [of the interior], upon receipt of reports, surveys, or studies from any duly constituted international agency, has reason to believe that any pollution [of interstate or

---

by two or More States: Report of the Executive Director, U.N. Doc. UNEP/GC/44 (1975), *reprinted in* 14 INT'L LEGAL MATERIALS 1089 (1975).

[77] OECD Doc. C(74) 224 (1974), *reprinted in* 14 INT'L LEGAL MATERIALS 242 (1975).

[78] *Id.* at 246, Title F.

[79] *U.S. Foreign Policy in a Technological Age*, 64 DEP'T ST. BULL. 200 (1971).

[80] *See* S. Doc. No. 56, 89th Cong., 1st Sess. 396–97 (1965).

[81] Gardner, *Outer Space Problems of Law and Power*, 49 DEP'T ST. BULL. 369 (1963).

[82] 33 U.S.C. § 466 g (d) (2) (1970).

navigable waters] which endangers the health or welfare of persons in a foreign country is occurring, and the Secretary of State requests him to abate such pollution, he shall give formal notification thereof [to the appropriate state and interstate pollution control agencies] and promptly call a conference . . . if he believes that such pollution is occurring in sufficient quantity to warrant such action. The Secretary, through the Secretary of State, shall invite the foreign country which may adversely be affected by the pollution to attend and participate in the conference, and the representative of such country shall, for the purpose of the conference, have all the rights of a State water pollution control agency.[83]

Although the 1956 Water Pollution Control Act provides a better strategy for agreement because of its provision for face-to-face consultation, rather than mere notification,[84] the Act has its own weaknesses. Utton correctly observes that these problems include the absence of third-party participation and injured party initiative.[85] Moreover, the determination of what is likely to be detrimental, the decision to notify or not to notify, and the decision whether to call an environmental impact conference are exclusively within the exclusive competence of the states.[86]

Concern for prevention of injurious results from use of internal resources has caused states to take the initiative in formulating their own laws on the issue. States typically consider the long-term and extraterritorial implications of their laws before enactment. For example, section 102(C) of the United States Environmental Policy Act of 1969 requires the detailed report of consequences for environmental impact for every recommendation or proposal for legislation and other major federal actions which significantly affect the quality of the human environment.[87] Section 102(E) of the same act directs the federal agencies (the environmental impact statement) to "recognize the worldwide and long-term char-

---

[83] *Id., quoted in* Utton, *International Environmental Law and Consultation Mechanisms,* 12 COLUM. J. TRANS. L. 65–66 (1973).

[84] Bourne, *International Law and Pollution of International Rivers and Lakes,* 6 U. BRIT. COLUM. L. REV. 122 (1971).

[85] Utton, *supra* note 83, at 66.

[86] *Id.*

[87] 42 U.S.C. §§ 4321, 4332 (2) (c) (1970).

acter of environmental problems."[88] In addition, some states have allowed foreigners access to their national courts for the litigation of environmental problems. Denmark, Finland, Norway, and Sweden, by concluding the Convention on the Protection of the Environment of February 19, 1974, put their citizens on equal footing with one another with respect to access to national courts on environmental issues.[89] In the United States a foreign person and a foreign environmental organization are permitted to intervene in order to assure the representation of their own interest.[90]

In addition to the above conventions and cases, there are two incidents of high controversy in the area of injurious use of internal resources with extraterritorial impact which should be considered. These are the United States hydrogen bomb test of 1954[91] and the *Nuclear Test Cases*.[92] Both incidents involved atmospheric nuclear tests. Because of the great danger inherent in nuclear tests for the human environment, as well as their potential for promoting the military power of nation-states for either security or aggression, nuclear tests have been treated distinctly from the other claims pertaining to injurious use of internal resources. The claim for promoting security, backed up by the superpowers, has directly or indirectly slowed down and weakened the policies of prevention of injurious use of internal resources by nuclear tests. Nevertheless, a policy of prevention still has strong support.

On March 1, 1954, the United States exploded a hydrogen bomb on Eniwetok Atoll in the Marshall Islands, a trust territory of the United States in the Pacific Ocean. Despite a 400,000-square-mile danger zone around the test area, the test injured several Japanese fishermen seriously and one fatally, as well as injuring a number of American personnel. While the test was within the United States' control and jurisdiction, its injurious im-

---

[88] *Id.*

[89] 13 INT'L LEGAL MATERIALS 591 (1974).

[90] Wilderness Society v. Morton, 463 F.2d 1261 (.D.C. Cir. 1972). This case involved the Trans-Alaska Pipeline and was brought by various American environmental groups. A Canadian environmental group was also allowed to enter the case upon the finding by the court that intervention would protect its interests.

[91] Margolis, *supra* note 22, at 629, and McDougal & Schlei, *supra* note 23, at 648.

[92] Nuclear Test Cases (Australia v. France), [1973] I.C.J. 99, [1974] I.C.J. 253; (New Zealand v. France), [1973] I.C.J. 457.

pact went beyond its jurisdiction and even far from the danger zone onto the high seas.

The test not only interfered with the freedom of the high seas, injuring foreign subjects on the high seas, but also contaminated a great part of the atmosphere and a considerable quantity of fish, thus disturbing the Japanese fish market substantially, and created an enormous pressure in world public opinion. Before the test was performed, Indian and Soviet representatives to the U.N. Trusteeship Council tried to prevent the test by introducing appropriate resolutions.[93] The concern of the Soviet and Indian representatives, however, was not with the extraterritorial impact of the test but with the fact that the test was in violation of the Administering Authority's rights and duties under the U.N. Charter and the Trusteeship Agreement for the Islands.

In response to Japanese representations the United States paid compensation to the government of Japan for damages resulting from the test. In its note the U.S. government, while avoiding any reference to legal liability, recognized a certain responsibility for damage to Japan caused by the test:

> The Government of the United States of America has made clear that it is prepared to make monetary compensation as an additional expression of its concern and regret over the injuries sustained. [T]he United States of America hereby tends, *ex gratia*, to the Government of Japan, without reference to the question of legal liability, the sum of two million dollars for purposes of compensation for the injuries or damages sustained as a result of nuclear tests in the Marshall Islands in 1954. . . .
>
> It is the understanding of the Government of the United States of America that the Government of Japan, in accepting the tendered sum of two million dollars, does so in full settlement of any and all *claims* against the United States of America or its agents, nationals or judicial entities for any and all injuries, losses, or damages arising out of the said nuclear test.[94]

Goldie observes that the United States by compensating the victims of the extraterritorial impact of the test, though without admitting fault on its part, accepted moral responsibility for the harmful

---

[93] U.N. Doc. T/C.2/L.101 (1954) (Soviet Resolution) and U.N. Doc.T/C.2/L.104 (Indian Resolution).

[94] 32 DEP'T STATE BULL. 90–91 (1955). Emphasis added.

consequences.[95] Moreover, "[t]his acceptance of moral responsibility and obligation arises from the same basic sentiment of justice
as that from which strict and absolute liability standards flow in
the domestic, transnational law of injuries."[96] In our view, the
United States clearly accepted its responsibility, and its emphasis
in the note on settlement of all future claims against the United
States and its subjects supports this interpretation. The legal character of this responsibility is further demonstrated by global community expectations condemning the hydrogen bomb test. It is
widely felt that the test resulted in unforeseen and harmful consequences and ignored the inclusive interest in well-being of the
larger community for a vague and exclusively defined claim for
the "security" of a single state's own interests.

The larger community policy in protection of common interest
from the long-term and unpredictable extraterritorial effects of
nuclear contamination gradually began to be expressed in a more
formal and authoritative way. It began with G.A. Resolution 1379
(XIV)[97] against the French atmospheric and underground nuclear
tests in Algeria, which prohibited nuclear tests in Africa and later
in Latin America. Community policy was expressed more generally in the Test Ban Treaty of August 5, 1963.[98] This Treaty prohibits nuclear weapons tests or other nuclear explosions in the
atmosphere, in outer space, or underwater, *i.e.*, "in the environ-
ments where detection from outside the territory of the testing
state is possible."[99] The treaty does not prohibit underground nuclear testing so long as such tests do not cause injurious impacts in
the form of radioactive debris outside the territorial jurisdictioin
of the testing state. The treaty further provides that nuclear explosions anywhere that might have any of the prohibited effects are

---

[95] GOLDI, in ACADEMIE DE DROIT INT'L 73 (1973).

[96] *Id.*

[97] 14 U.N. Doc. GAOR Supp. 16, at 3 U.N. Doc. A/4354 (1960). For the treaty on the
Prohibition of Nuclear Weapons in Latin America, of Feb. 14, 1967, see U.N.T.S. Vol. 634
at 281.

[98] 57 AM. J. INT'L. L. 1026 (1963). It came into force on Oct. 10, 1963, and 105 governments had signed the Treaty by that time.

[99] For a critical examination of this treaty see Schwelb, *The Nuclear Test Ban Treaty and
International Law* 58 AM. J. INT'L. L.642 (1964). See also Scoville, *A New Look at a Comprehensive Nuclear Test Ban* 7 STAN. J. INT'L. STUDIES 45–49 (1972).

also prohibited.[100] Similar policy was adopted in G.A. Resolution 2032 (XX) on December 7, 1965.[101] Despite these authoritative statements, atmospheric nuclear tests by states not party to the treaty continued. One of the most important examples in recent years was in the French activities that gave rise to the *Nuclear Test Cases*. These cases are clear indication of the inability of the international community to deal with this dangerous threat to the environment. Since nuclear capability is still an important element for acquiring power and being identified as a powerful nation, the nuclear states have been reluctant to condemn nuclear tests or deal with them as with any other injurious use of the environment. The refusal of the ICJ to act in the *Nuclear Test Cases* was a clear example of such reluctance.

Between 1956 and 1963 the French government conducted a number of atmospheric and underground tests in Algeria that resulted in the Resolution 1379 (XIV), mentioned above. In 1963 the French government moved its testing center to the Pacific on Mururoa Atoll, a part of French Polynesia. Beginning in 1966 France conducted atmospheric tests almost every year until 1969. At this time the New Zealand and Australian governments filed their application subsequent to the decision of the French government to continue with the test in 1973 and following years.[102] The Australian claims (similar to those of New Zealand) raised three main points:

---

[100] The treaty furthermore prohibits explosions anywhere else with any of the prohibited effects. Article I of the Treaty reads:

"1. Each of the Parties to this Treaty undertakes to prohibit, to prevent and not to carry out any nuclear weapon test explosion, or any other nuclear explosion, at any place under its jurisdiction or control;

"(a) in the atmosphere; beyond its limits, including outerspace; or underwater, including territorial waters or high seas; or

"(b) in any other environment if such explosion causes radioactive debris to be present outside the territorial limits of the state under whose jurisdiction or control such explosion is conducted. It is understood in this connection that the provisions of this subparagraph are without prejudice to the conclusion of a treaty resulting in the permanent banning of all nuclear test explosions, including all such explosions underground, the conclusion of which, as the Parties have stated in the Preamble to this Treaty, they seek to achieve." 57 AM. J. INT'L L. *supra* note 98, at 1026.

[101] G.A. Res. 2032 (XX), *reprinted in* 5 INT'L LEGAL MATERIALS 172 (1966). The resolution was adopted by a vote of 92 to 1 with 14 abstentions.

[102] For more discussion of the case, see Goldie, *The Nuclear Test Cases: Restraints on Environmental Harm*, 5 J. MAR. L. & COM. 491 (1974).

(i) the right of Australia and its people, in common with other States and their peoples, to be free from atmospheric nuclear weapon tests by any country is and will be violated;

(ii) the deposit of radioactive fall-out on the territory of Australia and its dispersion in Australia's airspace without Australia's consent:

    (a) violates Australian sovereignty over its territory;
    (b) impairs Australia's independent right to determine what acts shall take place within its territory and in particular whether Australia and its people shall be exposed to radioactive from artificial sources.

(iii) the interference with ships and aircraft on the high seas and in the superjacent airspace, and the pollution of the high seas by the radioactive fall-out, constitute infringements of the freedom of the high seas.[103]

Since France let it be known that it was going ahead with the tests, Australia and New Zealand, in an effort to avoid the injurious effects of the tests, requested the Court under Article 41 of the ICJ Statute to issue interim measures for protection of their rights. The Court, after considering the possibility of irrevocable environmental damage by radioactivity, issued interim measures for protection. In issuing such an order, after discouraging the parties from taking any actions that might aggravate the dispute, the ICJ made a statement that is of significance here. The Court ordered that "the French Government should avoid nuclear tests causing deposit of radioactive fall-out on Australian territory."[104] The importance of this statement in the absence of judgment on the merits is that it can be taken as a statement of the unlawfulness of the French nuclear tests if their extraterritorial impact could have been proved by the applicants. Despite the Court's prohibition, the French did perform the tests, while rejecting the competency of the ICJ. A few months later, however, France publicized its intention not to conduct any more atmospheric nuclear tests in the South Pacific. The ICJ, citing such a unilateral declaration, finally refused to entertain the case on the basis that there was nothing

---

[103] Note of Jan. 3, 1973, from the Australian Ambassador to the French Foreign Minister, Application by Australia Instituting Proceedings, Annex 9, [1973] I.C.J. 26–27.

[104] [1973] I.C.J. 106.

more to be gained for the applicants.[105] The Court assumed that the applicants' formal claim was for the cessation of further tests,[106] an assumption sharply criticized by the dissenting opinions. The dissents observed that the Court avoided addressing itself to the question put forward by the Applicants. The Applicants asked "for a judicial declaration to the effect that atmospheric nuclear tests are not 'consistent . . . with international law.' This bare assertion cannot be described as constituting merely a reason advanced in support of the Order. The legal reasons invoked by the Applicants both in support of the declaration and the Order relate *inter alia* to the alleged violation by France of certain rules said to be generally accepted as customary law concerning atmospheric nuclear tests. . . ."[107]

This refusal by the ICJ to decide the case itself establishes the close identification of nuclear energy with effective power in the contemporary world. Even the tremendous and obvious potential for harm of these instruments has to be dealt with cautiously, without definite or effective commitment.

2. Control over Injurious Use of Internal Resources with Unique Impacts on a Nation-State or a Region

The world constitutive process has always regarded the control and protection of shareable resources as a matter of inclusive competence. A whole series of multilateral conventions and the reciprocal behavior of states reflect such a policy. This concern began officially in 1926 with the Washington Convention[108] and became more visible and authoritative after the Second World War. The 1926 Washington Convention was a follow-up to the 1922 British Oil in Navigable Waters Act, which recognized British competence on the high seas over vessels of British registry to control the oil pollution resulting from the operation of those ships. The British sought an international agreement to prohibit oil pollution by all ships. In contrast with the 1926 Washington Convention, the 1954

---

[105][1974] I.C.J. 272. The vote was nine to six.

[106]*Id.* at 263, para. 30.

[107]*Id.* at 313–14.

[108]The Washington Convention on Oil Pollution was never ratified. *See* L. Green, *International Law and Canada's Anti-pollution Legislation*, 50 ORE. L. REV. 463 (1971).

London Convention was successful.[109] The condition for such success was the increase in the role of different vessels for trade and other purposes. This increase in use of the oceans for transportation proportionately increased the danger of pollution of the great shareable resources.[110] It was the community experience and belief that injurious use of shareable resources directly and indirectly damaged the interests of the nation-states both individually and collectively. The London Convention, amended in 1962,[111] prescribed some preventive and compensatory measures, but did not accomplish much in the way of preventing injurious use of the oceans through activities pertaining to oil. However, it was the beginning of a series of multilateral approaches and negotiations on the issue. The 1958 Geneva Convention on the High Seas in Articles 24–25 requires every nation-state to take preventive measures against injurious use of the oceans through oil, radioactive wastes, and other polluted materials.[112] These conventions were followed by a number of global, regional, and bilateral agreements and practices. Past trends may be studied in terms of their adequacy in protecting the common interest in shareable resources from different points of view. Our focus here, however, is on the inadequacy of past prescriptions and practices for the prevention of unique destructive impacts on a particular nation-state or region. The most difficult question in such circumstances is to what extent the global community should recommend or tolerate unilateral remedial actions.

a. Inadequacy of Inclusive Competence to Prevent Unique Impact of Injurious Uses of Shareable Resources on a Nation-State or a Region

The main problem with inclusive authorities on this issue is in the absence of clear policy or else the availability of effective enforce-

---

[109] LONDON CONVENTION, 12 & 13 Geo. 5 c. 39 (1954).

[110] Approximately 43% of all marine oil pollution arises from marine, as opposed to land-based, sources. Of this 43%, routine tanker operations contribute about 60%, tanker accidents 8%. Therefore, 30% of marine oil pollution is caused by tankers, a total of over 1 million metric tons. Aside from IMCO estimates, if the present trend continues, marine-origin oil pollution could increase 300% by the end of the century. C. PEARSON, INTERNATIONAL MARINE ENVIRONMENT POLICY: THE ECONOMIC DIMENSION 84–85 (1975).

[111] For the 1962 Amendment see N. SINGH, INTERNATIONAL CONVENTIONS ON MERCHANT SHIPPING 1171 (1963).

[112] 450 U.N.T.S. 82 (1962).

ment procedures with regard to preventive measures. Given the contemporary level of development of science and technology, where the possibility for doing irreversible damage to the vital interests of countries through injurious use of shareable resources has increased substantially, there is a need for fast and effective preventive processes to protect the vital interests of these communities. Some types of damage from an injurious use are unique and lasting and cannot be adequately compensated by payments or restored to original condition, at least not for a long time.

The basic strategy of international conventions is to provide adequate compensation for individuals and states who have suffered from the injurious use of shareable resources. The 1957 International Convention relating to the Limitation of the Liability of Owners of Seagoing Ships,[113] the 1960 Convention on Third Party Liability in the Field of Nuclear Energy,[114] the 1962 Brussels Convention on the Liability of Operators of Nuclear Ships,[115] and the 1963 Agreement on Civil Liability for Nuclear Damages[116] are examples providing for strict liability and compensation. The incompatibility of these conventions with the adequate protection of the common interest, particularly after the *Torrey Canyon* incident, led to the International Legal Conference on Marine Pollution Damage in 1969.[117] This Conference focused on oil pollution and provided for two important conventions: the International Convention relating to Intervention on the High Seas in Cases of Oil Pollution Casualties (Public Law Convention)[118] and the International Convention on Civil Liability for Oil Pollution Damage (Private Law Convention).[119] It also passed a Resolution on the Establishment of an International Compensation Fund for Oil

[113] 37 Dep't St. Bull. 759–62 (1957).

[114] 55 Am. J. Int'l L. 1082 (1961).

[115] 57 Am. J. Int'l L. 268 (1963). *See also* Cigoj, *International Regulation of Civil Liability for Nuclear Risk*, 14 Int'l & Comp. L.Q. 809 (1965), and P. Szasz, The Law and Practices of the International Atomic Energy Agency 703–14 (1970).

[116] 2 Int'l Materials 727 (1963).

[117] 9 Int'l Legal Materials 1 (1970). For a detailed report of the regulations and process of adoption of this convention, see Intergovernmental Maritime Cumulative Organization, Official Records of the International Legal Conference on Marine Pollution Damage, 1969–1973.

[118] 9 Int'l Legal Materials, *supra* note 117, at 25.

[119] *Id.* at 45.

Pollution Damage.[120] The IMCO Conventions, while more comprehensive than previous conventions in terms of surveillance and prevention measures, nevertheless have some serious problems. One important problem is that the enforcement agents of the preventive inclusive prescriptions are flag states. The conventions do not take into account the common practice of flags of convenience or that the states of tankers flying the flags of convenience will not have much interest in applying such regulations.[121] Article X of the 1969 International Convention for the Prevention of Pollution of the Sea by Oil provides that any contracting party who observes the violation of the convention by any ship should so inform the ship's country of registry. If the government receiving the information is satisfied that such violation occurred, it is required under its own law to take the necessary action:

> Upon receiving such particulars, the Government so informed shall investigate the matter, and may request the other Government to furnish further or better particulars of the alleged contravention. If the Government so informed is satisfied that sufficient evidence is available in the form required by its law to enable proceedings against the owner or master of the ship to be taken in respect of the alleged contravention, it shall cause such proceedings to be taken as soon as possible. That Government shall promptly inform the Government whose official has reported the alleged contravention, as well as the Organization [IMCO], of the action taken as a consequence of the information communicated.[122]

This strategy of surveillance, while important for the effective enforcement of the convention, is inappropriate for situations where immediate action is required because of the time-consuming process of communication with the flag state. In such circumstances the coastal state interested in protecting its shores does not have the competence to enforce environmental regulations against ships outside its contiguous zone.[123] The purpose of the Public Law Convention was to give some authority to individual nation-

---

[120] *Id.* at 66.

[121] *See* B. BOCZEK, FLAGS OF CONVENIENCE (1962); and *OECD Study on Flags of Convenience,* 4 J. MAR. L. & COM. 231 (1973).

[122] 9 INT'L LEGAL MATERIALS, *supra* note 117, at 8.

[123] Kalsi, *Oil in Neptune's Kingdom: Problems and Responses to Contain Environmental Degradation of the Oceans by Oil Pollution,* 3 ENVT'L. AFFAIRS, 86 (1974).

states to protect their interests from an injurious use of the high seas. The authors of the Public Law Convention, however, had in mind experiences such as *Torrey Canyon* and conferred the authority of states to take measures on the high seas "to prevent, mitigate or eliminate grave and imminent damage to their coastline or related interest"[124] only from *oil pollution following a maritime casualty* or acts related to such a casualty. Furthermore, Article 3 of the Convention requires consultation and notification before and during the unilateral action. One scholar argues that it is doubtful whether this agreement adds anything to the rights already possessed by states under the general international law doctrine of self-help.[125]

The Private Law Convention, on the other hand, was to formulate inclusive prescriptions to secure compensation for every person suffering damages as a result of oil discharged by ships and to establish uniform international rules for determining such compensation. The Public Law Convention was followed by the 1971 International Convention on the Establishment of an International Fund for Compensation for Oil Pollution Damages, which raised the ceiling on compensation to $34 million per accident with a potential increase to $72 million. These conventions are remedial rather than preventive and apply only to damages occurring within territorial waters.[126] The remedial measures on oil pollution have been promoted by other international agreements, including two private international agreements, the Tanker Owners Voluntary Agreement Concerning Liability for Oil Pollution (TOVALOP),[127] established by tanker owners, and the Contract Re-

---

[124] 9 INT'L LEGAL MATERIALS, *supra* note 117, at 25.

[125] J. Schneider, International Law of the Environment, 89 (1975) (Unpublished doctoral dissertation in Yale University Political Science Dept.) (Publication forthcoming).

[126] 9 INT'L LEGAL MATERIALS, *supra* note 117, at 47.

[127] 8 INT'L LEGAL MATERIALS 497 (1969). The owners of the tankers state that they "were aware of the fact that the traditional maritime laws and practice do not always provide an adequate means for reimbursing national governments who incur expenditures to avoid or mitigate damage from such pollution, as well as tanker owners who, on their own initiative, incur this kind of expenditure. They recognized also that traditional maritime law and practice do not encourage voluntary action by tanker owners, or joint measures by governments and tankerowners, against such pollution." *Id.* at 498. Under this convention the competent claimants are states and not individuals, and Article IV(a) limits the damages to the costs reasonably necessary to prevent or mitigate physical contamination to the coastline due to the negligence of the tanker. This convention does not cover damage incurred by

garding an Interim Supplement to Tanker Liability for Oil Pollution (CRISTAL), established by major oil companies.[128]

The 1972 Stockholm Conference provided a general policy guide for both national and international programs. As the International Law Association said, the most significant aspect of the Stockholm Conference was "[t]he issuance of a Declaration on the Human Environment consisting of a preamble and 26 principles. It contains important new principles which may serve as a foundation for developing international law relating to the environment."[129] The Conference, however, did not provide solutions for the problems with which we are here concerned. It required only that states take all possible actions to prevent injurious use of the seas by their nationals.[130]

Since Stockholm, there have been two other important international conventions on controlling the injurious use of the oceans. The first is the Inter-Governmental Conference on the Convention on the Dumping of Wastes at Sea,[131] concluded in London in 1972. This Convention is innovative in a number of ways. Beyond offering a comprehensive list of materials that are not to be dumped into the sea, the enforcement power is given mainly to the coastal state. Article 7 expands the enforcement competence of the parties, not only to vessels and aircraft registered in its territory or flying its flag and vessels and aircraft loading in its territory or territorial seas, but also to "vessels and aircraft and fixed or floating platforms under its jurisdiction believed to be engaged in dumping.[132] The nature and extent of the competence of the coastal and flag state, however, is not clear, and Article 13 has left the decision on this issue to the Law of the Sea Conference.[133] The Convention contains a new idea embodied in Article 8 that indi-

---

fire or explosion [Article I(h)], and Article VI(a) limits the liability to $100 per gross ton or $10 million.

[128] 10 INT'L LEGAL MATERIALS 137–44 (1971). This is a supplement to TOVALOP and similarly provides for compensation for harm due to oil pollution up to $30 million; similarly, only governments can be claimants.

[129] STOCKHOLM CONFERENCE, *supra* note 43, at 2.

[130] *See Id.*, Principle 7 and Recommendation 86(b) (c).

[131] 11 INT'L LEGAL MATERIALS 1291 (1972).

[132] *Id.* at 1300.

[133] *Id.* at 1303–04.

rectly relates to the protection of the interest of states in cases of unique injurious impact. This Article, without specifically addressing the expansion of state competence in unilateral actions, authorizes "the Contracting Parties with common interests to protect in the marine environment in a given geographical area . . . to enter into regional agreements consistent with [the] Convention for the prevention of pollution, especially by dumping."[134] While the Article is vague in terms of the nature and extent of the regional agreements and applies only to a group of states rather than to individual states, it nevertheless recognizes the need for some action to prevent unique damages to states via injurious use of the oceans.

The second, the 1973 International Convention for the Prevention of Pollution from Ships,[135] included comprehensive and detailed regulations on the construction and equipment of ships and port facilities and on the various kinds of oil pollution. In terms of the allocation of enforcement competence it is vague and rather more limited than the anti-dumping convention. Article 3 says that the Convention applies to "(a) ships entitled to fly flag of a Party to the Convention; and (b) ships not entitled to fly the flag of a Party but which operate under the authority of a Party."[136] The latter could be interpreted to include the authority of the coastal states in their territorial waters. The ambiguity of the Convention is more apparent in Article 4(2), which states that "[a]ny violation of the requirements of the present Convention within the jurisdiction of any Party to the Convention shall be prohibited and sanctions shall be established therefor under the law of that Party."[137]

Besides the above international conventions, there have been a number of regional conventions on controlling the injurious use of the sea, such as the Agreement Concerning the Pollution of the North Sea by Oil,[138] the North-East Atlantic Convention for the Prevention of Marine Pollution by Dumping from Ships and Aircraft,[139] and the Convention for the Prevention of Marine Pollu-

---

[134]*Id.* at 1301.

[135] 12 Int'l Legal Materials 1310 (1973).

[136]*Id.* at 1321.

[137]*Id.* at 1322.

[138] 9 Int'l Legal Materials 359 (1970).

[139] 11 Int'l Legal Materials 262 (1971).

tion from Land-Based Sources.[140] These regional conventions, without expanding the competency of individual states substantially, facilitate the enforceability of the agreements. These are established chiefly because of the more easily identifiable common interests among the parties. Furthermore, some regional agreements provide for regional organizations for the supervision and implementation of provisions of such conventions as the Anti-Dumping Convention[141] and the Convention on Prevention of Pollution from Land-Based Sources.[142]

As to the use of atmosphere and space, there have been multilateral attempts to expand the international responsibility of states for the injurious use of the atmosphere and outer space through the use of multilateral treaties and the United Nations.[143] The declarations, however, are not as developed and comprehensive as those concerning the oceans and the international rivers, and are basically remedial.

---

[140] 13 INT'L LEGAL MATERIALS 352 (1974). On Feb. 17, 1976, twelve nations signed a convention which requires the members to take all measures to prevent, abate, and control pollution of the Mediterranean and to protect and enhance the marine environment in that area. They agreed to establish joint programs to monitor the level of pollution, and in particular to fight against dumping from ships and aircraft as well as against discharge of harmful matter from coastlines. A special protocol is devoted to oil and other harmful substances, and a regional center in Malta was set up to act as a clearing house for information on emergencies arising from the presence in the Mediterranean of large quantities of oil. *See* N.Y. Times, Feb. 17, 1976, at 5, col. 1. *See also* 15 INT'L LEGAL MATERIALS 285–319 (1976).

[141] 11 INT'L LEGAL MATERIALS, *supra* note 138, at 262–63, articles 16 and 17.

[142] 13 INT'L LEGAL MATERIALS 352, *supra* note 140, Articles 15 and 16.

[143] The first U.N. Resolution was the 1962 U.N. Declaration of Legal Principles Governing the Activities of States in the Exploration and Use of Outer Space. This Declaration recognized that "states bear international responsibility for national activities in outer space, whether carried by government agencies or by non-government entities," G.A. Res. 1962, 18 U.N. GAOR Supp. (No. 15) 15 U.N. Doc. A/5515 (1963). Similar policy has been incorporated in the Treaty on Principles Governing the Activities of States in the Exploration and Use of Outer Space, Including the Moon and Other Celestial Bodies, which was opened for signature on January 27, 1967, and entered into force on October 10 of the same year. *See* the text in 610 *U.N.T.S.* 205 (1967). The Convention on International Liability for Damage Caused by Space Objects, effective September 1, 1972, has employed both the principle of absolute liability and that of liability based on fault. Absolute liability arises in cases of injury to aircraft in flight or on the surface, and liability based on fault is used in cases of injury to space objects. *See* Articles II, III and IV; for the text see [1972] T.I.A.S. No. 7762.

b. Inclusive Prescriptions and Global Tolerance of Unilateral Actions for Prevention of Injurious Use of Shareable Resources with Unique Impacts on Particular Communities

Aside from the lack of appropriate inclusive prescriptions for the protection of the interests of nation-states from the unique injurious impact of the use of shareable resources, the almost total reliance of the conventions upon flag states for enforcement has made the protection of the exclusive interests of states even more unclear and arbitrary.[144] The experience of the United States, for example, shows that of seven violations involving oil pollution which the United States referred to flag states during 1969–72, in only two cases were modest penalties assessed.[145]

The larger community has recognized the ineffectiveness of inclusive competence to protect some exclusive interests in certain situations. This inefficient function of inclusive competence harms the common interest where an exclusive interest is vital to a nation-state. To protect the common interest, international law has in the past prescribed a comprehensive exclusive competence such as that over the territorial seas, or for limited purposes such as those over contiguous zones and intervention in high seas for special injurious uses as in the IMCO Public Law Convention, or it has recognized and tolerated certain general rights of abatement beyond the territorial jurisdiction under the doctrine of self-help, self-preservation, or self-defense. Article 51 of the U.N. Charter refers to such a policy in case of armed attack and the right of states to take "necessary and proportional" measures to protect

[144]Goldie observes, with respect to the 1954 International Convention for the Prevention of Pollution of the Sea by Oil and its amendments through 1971, that "[t]he conventions' effectiveness was limited, since their enforcement lay within the jurisdiction of the states of registry. They contained no recognition of a coastal state's right of abatement even in the defined 'prohibited zone.' Nor did they deal with the vexed issues of liability for harm." Goldie, *Development of an International Environmental Law—an Appraisal*, in LAW, INSTITUTIONS AND THE GLOBAL ENVIRONMENT 118 (J. Hargrove ed. 1972). *See also* R. HALLMAN, TOWARDS AN ENVIRONMENTALLY SOUND LAW OF THE SEA 57 (1974).

[145]*Draft Environmental Impact Statement on the Law of the Sea* prepared by the U.S., *cited in* HALLMAN, *id.* at 57, n. 1. Alan Beesley has also noted that "only two prosecutions for a convention offense outside a state's territorial sea have been recorded"; see Beesley, *The Canadian Approach—Environmental Law on the International Plane*, in SOUTHWEST LEGAL FOUNDATION, PRIVATE INVESTORS ABROAD—PROBLEMS AND SOLUTIONS IN INTERNATIONAL BUSINESS, 247 (1973).

themselves.[146] As was mentioned earlier, the definition, the scope, and the forms of "attack" and "self-defense" have changed to include different situations.[147] In the area of injurious use of shareable resources, "[a] rule of international law seems to have emerged which permits a coastal State to make reasonable assertions of jurisdiction and control in areas of the high seas contiguous to its territorial sea in order to protect vital interests in its territory or territorial waters."[148] Brownlie observes that state competence for self-help may go beyond its territorial boundaries and cover acts outside its territory that affect events within it.[149] The right of a coastal state to take unilateral actions to protect exclusive interests was recognized by Article 5 of the 1930 Conference for Codification of International Law, which provides that "[t]he right of passage does not prevent the Coastal State from taking all necessary steps to protect itself in the territorial sea against any act prejudicial to the security, public policy or fiscal interests of the State. . . .[150] This concept has been further supported by Article 17 of the 1958 Geneva Convention on the Territorial Seas and the Contiguous Zone, which states: "Foreign ships exercising the right of innocent passage shall comply with the laws and regulations

[146]*See* also Article 2(4) of the U.N. Charter. For a definition and various forms of self-defense, see McDOUGAL & FELICIANO, *supra* note 33, at 213–16.

[147]McDOUGAL & FELICIANO, *id.* Bowett, for example, states that the "interest which a state may have in the safe preservation of the national economy, of its essential economic interests, may be equally as great as its interest in safeguarding its territory, its political independence or its people." D. BOWETT, SELF-DEFENSE IN INTERNATIONAL LAW 106, 166 (1958). *See also* Bowett, *Economic Coercion and Reprisal by States*, 13 VA J. INT'L L. 1 (1972). Article 15 of the Charter of the Organization of American States of 1948 also recognizes a similar concept when it refers to foreign intervention as "any . . . form of interference or attempted threat against the personality of the state or against its political, economic and cultural elements." 119 U.N.T.S. 3 (1948). Brierly refers to the concept of self-preservation as an acceptable international notion because it is an instinct. "The truth is that self-preservation in the case of a State as of an individual is not a legal right but an instinct; and even if it may often happen that the instinct prevails over the legal duty not to do violence to others, international law ought not to admit that it is lawful that it should do so." J. BRIERLY, THE LAW OF NATIONS 405 (6th ed. H. Waldock ed. 1963).

[148]L. HYDEMAN & W. BERMAN, INTERNATIONAL CONTROL OF NUCLEAR MARITIME ACTIVITIES 236 (1960).

[149]I. BROWNLIE, PRINCIPLES OF PUBLIC INTERNATIONAL LAW 293–95 (1973). Metzger states that the extraterritorial application of the U.S. antitrust law is based on the same concept. S. METZGER, 2 LAW OF INTERNATIONAL TRADE 1399–1400 (1966); see also BROWNLIE, *id.* at 303–06.

[150]*See* H. BRIGGS, THE LAW OF NATIONS 346–47 (1952).

enacted by the coastal State in conformity with these articles and other rules of international law and, in particular, with such laws and regulations relating to transport and navigation." Chief Justice Marshall stated in *Church v. Hubbart*[151] that a nation "has the right to use the means necessary for its protection. These means do not appear to be limited within certain marked boundaries, which remain the same, at all times and in all situations."[152] One commentator, employing similar reasoning, goes so far as to say that "littoral states may act in certain ways for the preservation of their safety and the protection of their laws over an undefined and indefinite stretch of coastal water."[153]

We do not advocate the unlimited right of states to protect their interests from the injurious use of shareable resources. We agree only that the right of self-help recognizes the unilateral actions of nation-states to protect their vital interests. This is a unilateral competence which provides for a comprehensive set of preventive measures regarding the conduct of operations in the process of employment of resources. One dramatization of such measures reads: "investigatory powers to oversee compliance, subpoena and other powers for the production of witnesses and documents, seizure powers or bonding arrangements for the security of collateral with which to satisfy an adverse judgment, judicial or administrative procedures to evaluate conformity and nonconformity, and civil and/or criminal penalties for inadvertent or willful violation."[154] In any event, states might reasonably "be required to demonstrate that the actual effects, or realistically apprehended effects, are not merely incidental or slight, but rather embody a deprivation of substance. Such a deprivation need not be severe or drastic, for this would be an undue restriction of coastal competence to protect local value processes, but it also should not be of minimal consequences."[155]

The inadequacy of the 12-mile contiguous zone set up by the 1958 Geneva Convention for controlling injurious use has been clearly recognized. This recognition has inspired demands for the

[151] 6 U.S. (2 Cranch) 187 (1804).

[152] *Id.*

[153] W. MASTERSON, JURISDICTION IN MARGINAL SEAS 380 (1929).

[154] *See* Schneider, *supra* note 125, at 39.

[155] *See* M. MCDOUGAL & W. BURKE, THE PUBLIC ORDER OF THE OCEANS 232 (1962).

establishment of a 200-mile pollution zone, expressed by individual nation-states such as Canada, and in the United States by environmentalist groups,[156] as well as by various groups of states. In the Caracas session of the Law of the Sea Conference a number of proposals were submitted in favor of expanding the exclusive competence of coastal states over injurious use for as far as 200 miles from the coast.[157] The Geneva session of the LOS conference, however, mainly reflected perspectives in favor of the competence of the flag states,[158] requiring states to establish international prescriptions for controlling marine pollution by vessels through international and diplomatic conferences[159] and requiring the flag states to apply those preventive prescriptions effectively to the ships flying their flag.[160] These provisions generally limit the competence of coastal states in controlling the injurious use to their territorial sea.[161] The expansion of the coastal state's competence has been permitted only in exceptional and special circumstances:

> Where internationally agreed rules and standards are not in existence or are inadequate to meet special circumstances and where the coastal State has reasonable grounds for believing that a particular area of the economic zone is an area where, for recognized technical reasons in relation to its oceanographical and ecological conditions its utilization, and the particular character of its traffic, the adoption of special mandatory measures

[156] Maw, *Fishing for Trouble: Unilateral Solutions to International Problems*, in SOUTHWESTERN LEGAL FOUNDATION, PRIVATE INVESTORS ABROAD: PROBLEMS AND SOLUTIONS, 1975, 233 (1976).

[157] *See* the African Economic Zone Proposal, U.N. Doc. A/Conf.62/C.2/L.82 Article III Para. (a), August 26, 1974; the Nigerian Proposal, U.N. Doc. A/Conf.62/C.2/L.21 Rev. 1, August 5, 1974; the Kenyan Proposal, U.N. Doc. A/Conf.62/C.3/L.2, July 23, 1974; Canadian Proposal, U.N. Doc. A/Conf.62/C.3/L.6, July 31, 1974; Ecuador Proposal, U.N. Doc. A/AC.138/Sc.III/L.47, July 27, 1973, and the French Proposal, U.N. Doc. A/AC.138/Sc.III/ L.46, July 20, 1973. There have also been proposals in favor of the exclusive competence of flag states over ships. *See* (West) German Fed. Rep. Proposal, U.N. Doc. A/Conf.62/L/7, August 1, 1974; Greek Proposal, U.N. Doc. A/Conf.62/C.3/L.4, July 23, 1974; Norwegian Proposal, U.N. Doc. AA/AC.138/Sc.III/L.43, July 19, 1973; the Netherlands Proposal, U.N. Doc. A/AC.138/Sc.III/L.48, August 13, 1973; and the U.S. Proposal, U.N. Doc. A/AC.138/ Sc.III/L.40, July 13, 1973.

[158] *See* BURKE, R. LEGATSKI & W. WOODHEAD, NATIONAL AND INTERNATIONAL LAW ENFORCEMENT IN THE OCEAN 60 (1975).

[159] U.N. Doc. A/Conf.62/WP.8, (1975), Article 20(1) of Part III.

[160] Article 20(2), *id.*

[161] Article 20(3), *id.*

for the prevention of pollution from vessels is required, the coastal State may apply to the competent international organization for the area to be regarded as a "special area." Any such application shall be supported by scientific and technical evidence and shall, where appropriate, include plans for establishing sufficient and suitable land-based reception facilities.[162]

The extent and the nature of the competence of the state in "exceptional circumstances," however, is unclear. Presumably the competence of the coastal state is limited to application, and "special mandatory measures" should be prescribed by "competent international organizations." This probably is a response to the Canadian Arctic Pollution Prevention Act. The emphasis on inclusive prescription for control of injurious use of the ocean can be observed in Part 3 of the Geneva session of LOS dealing with pollution. With respect to nonvessel marine pollution, most of the alternatives and proposals provide for inclusive prescriptions by the Seabed Authority, while the competence of the coastal state for providing higher standards was also recognized.[163]

One important trend in the expansion of unilateral action for controlling the injurious use of resources is exemplified by the Canadian Arctic Waters Pollution Prevention Act of 1970.[164] The Canadian concern for the protection of their coasts began in earnest in 1969 at the Brussels Conference, which amended the 1954 Oil Pollution Convention in addition to two new conventions. Canada made several suggestions for the implementation of the convention, which nonetheless failed to get consensus from other states.[165] Canada claimed that the two Public and Private Law Conventions "did not pay sufficient attention to the fundamental interests of coastal states as compared with the commercial interests of flag states who favored a minimum of interference with their interpretation of their rights by way of freedom of the seas."[166]

---

[162] Article 20(4), *id.*

[163] Report by the Committee on the Peaceful Uses of the Seabed I, U.N. Doc. GAOR, 28th Sess. 94–95, Supp. 21, U.N. Doc. A/9021 (1973). *See also* U.N. Doc. A/Conf.62/C.3/L.2, (1974).

[164] Arctic Waters Pollution Prevention Act (AWPPA), CAN. REV. STAT. (Supp. 1) 3 (1970).

[165] *See* Green, *supra* note 108, at 472–76, and Pharand, *Oil Pollution Control in the Canadian Arctic,* 7 TEX. INT'L. L.J. 45 (1971). *See also* Bilder, *The Canadian Arctic Waters Pollution Prevention Act: New Stresses on the Law of the Sea,* 69 MICH. L.R. 1 (1970).

[166] Green, *supra* note 108, at 476. The main effect of Canada's proposition was to broaden

The Canadian protest as to the inappropriateness of inclusive prescriptions in this area and their demand for a new approach to
environmental problems continued: "The problem of environmental preservation transcends traditional concepts of sovereignty and requires an imaginative new approach oriented toward
the future. . . . The problem of environmental preservation . . .
must be resolved on the basis of the objective considerations of
today rather than the historical accidents of territorial imperative
of yesterday."[167] With this perspective, and with the serious threat
to Canada's interest from injurious use of the Arctic in transportation and waste dumping, in conjunction with the unique geographical factors[168] of the area, Canada sought to justify its
unilateral action in the Arctic Pollution Prevention Act. Canada
did not rely only on the concept of self-help and impact territoriality in its legislation, but also held itself responsible for the protection of the inclusive *future* interests of mankind in this part of the
world. The Prime Minister, in referring to the Act, told the (Canadian) House of Commons that "Canada regards herself as responsible to all mankind for the peculiar ecological balance that
now exists so precariously in the water, ice and land areas of the
Arctic Archipelago. . . . [W]e do not doubt for a moment that the
rest of the world would find us at fault, and hold us liable, should
we fail to ensure adequate protection of the environment from
pollution or artificial deterioration. Canada will not permit this to
happen."[169] The Act provides for a number of preventive measures in terms of surveillance, investigatory power, ship construction, and remedial measures. It prohibits the deposit of waste in
the Arctic waters or on the mainland or islands where they may
enter the Arctic waters. The Act applies to all ships.[170] The pollu-

---

the definition of oil pollution and the acceptance of absolute and joint liability on the part
of both the shipowner and the owner of the cargo and to reject the concept of territorial
damages. *Id.* at 475.

[167] *See* McNeil, *Assumptions Made by the Canadian Government in Establishing Strategies for
Environmental Improvements,* in KNEESE, ROLFE & HARNED, *supra* note 9, at 168.

[168] For geographical and political situations related to the Arctic, see D. PHARAND, THE
LAW OF THE SEA IN THE ARCTIC (1973).

[169] *See* KNEESE, ROLFE & HARNED, *supra* note 9, at 168.

[170] *See* Arctic Waters Pollution Prevention Act, *supra* note 162, § 6(1). There are only two
cases in which there is no liability: where the owner of the cargo proves that the cargo is of
such a nature and of such a a quantity that even if it all escaped it would not constitute waste
(§ 7[3]), or where the deposit of the waste is permitted by regulation (§ 8[1]).

tion zone of ships is 100 miles and the zone of exploration and exploitation of resources of the continental shelf also extends to 100 miles. The liability is absolute and the owner of the ship or the owner of the cargo of the ship could be liable. The government may require of ships' owners or persons engaged in mining the continental shelf and marine resources evidence of financial capacity. The government is competent to prescribe a shipping safety-control zone that goes into effect upon sixty days' notice.[171] Navigation in this zone may be prohibited or limited only to ships complying with the preventive requirements relating to safety standards, tank construction, quantity of cargo, load-lines, fuel, ice conditions, etc.[172] With respect to emergency situations when immediate preventive action is necessary (such as in the Torrey Canyon catastrophe), the Act provides that "[w]here the Governor in Council has reasonable cause to believe that a ship that is within the arctic waters and is in distress, stranded, wrecked, sunk, or abandoned, is depositing waste or is likely to deposit waste in the arctic waters, he may cause the ship or any cargo or other material on board the ship to be destroyed, if necessary, or to be removed if possible to such place and sold in such manner as he may direct."[173] As to the definition and criteria of "necessary," however, the Act is silent. The Act provides for extensive investigatory power on the part of the Officers to board and inspect any ship suspected of noncompliance with the regulations.[174] A Pollution Prevention Officer may confiscate the ship or the cargo upon conviction.[175] An Officer may ask for and use the services of all ships in the area to help in the cleanup operation.[176] Such action, of course, may subject the Canadian government to liability on the basis of temporary taking.[177] The Officer may order the ship to be destroyed.

To explain the nature of such unilateral expansion of competence, the Prime Minister of Canada stated that Canada did not

---

[171] § 11, *id.*

[172] § 12(1), *id.*

[173] § 13, *id.*

[174] § 23(1), *id.*

[175] § 24, *id.*

[176] § 15(3), *id.*

[177] *See* Swan, *International and National Approach to Oil Pollution Responsibility: An Emerging Regime for a Global Problem,* 50 ORE. L. REV. 567 (1971).

claim sovereignty over the pollution zone, but has extended its authority and control for limited purposes.[178] The international response to the Canadian Act has been one of tolerance, with the exception of the serious opposition of the United States[179] and, to a lesser degree, that of the United Kingdom and France. The publicists generally are in sympathy with Canada,[180] even though Canada refuses to accept ICJ competence with respect to issues related to the Act. To justify its refusal, Canada makes a persuasive argument that it realizes that the Act is "without question at the outer limits of international law,"[181] but the reason is that Canada is "pressing against the frontier in an effort to assist in the development of principles from the protection of every human being in this planet."[182] Canada claims that the question involved is not one of Canada only but a major departure from traditional international rules in this area; and, since major interpretations of the Act will take place in the future, pressing the ICJ to make precedents based on inappropriate and inadequate traditional practices will postpone those suitable interpretations and so damage the common interest.[183]

[178]Prime Minister Pierre Trudeau, Press Conference, April 18, 1979, *reprinted in* 9 INT'L LEGAL MATERIALS 602 (1970).

[179]The United States officially stated that it does not recognize any "exercise of coastal jurisdiction over [American] vessels on the high seas and thus does not recognize the right of any state unilaterally to establish a territorial sea of more than three miles or the exercise of more limited jurisdiction in any area beyond 12 miles." The (Toronto) Globe and Mail, April 10, 1970, at 1, *quoted in* N. Wulf, Contiguous Zones for Pollution Control: An Appraisal Under International Law 60, 165 (1971). For the opposition of the U.K. and France, see (Montreal) Gazette, May 29, 1970, at 2, *quoted in id.* at 61.

[180]*See, e.g.,* Utton, *The Arctic Waters Pollution Prevention Act and the Right of Self-Protection,* 7 U. BRIT. COLUM. L. REV. 232 (1972). Justice Douglas stated that Canada expanded its exclusive competence in the Arctic to fill "a void created by the failure of the family of nations to create a common environmental code for the oceans." Douglas, *supra* note 5, at 3. Yates observes that either a unilateral approach, such as the Canadians have taken, or an international convention must be accepted to solve international pollution problems and come up with effective prescriptions. Yates, *Unilateral and Multilateral Approaches to Environmental Problems,* 21 U. TORONTO L.J. 189 (1971). Kalsi has asserted that the Canadian Act is more reasonable than the 1945 Truman Proclamation. Kalsi, *supra* note 123, at 92.

[181]*See* Jennings, *A Changing International Law of the Sea,* 31 CAMB. L.J. 32, 43 (1973).

[182]*Id.*

[183]The Canadian Prime Minister, in justifying Canada's action amending its declaration of acceptance of the compulsory jurisdiction of ICJ to exclude the calling in question of these measures, stated that "[i]nvolved here is not simply a matter of Canada losing a case in the World Court. . . . What is involved, rather, is the very grave risk that the World Court

As a preferred policy we would recommend the compulsory jurisdiction of the ICJ or other forms of inclusive competence over unilateral preventive measures taken by states, but in exceptional circumstances, such as Canada's, the question may require more careful consideration. We suggest that in situations where there is a reasonable belief in the change of practices, the review of the lawfulness of a unilateral action may be postponed *if the international reaction to the unilateral action is one of tolerance* with the understanding that damages may be required if subsequent prescriptions do not vindicate the position of the defendant. International law is not without other such exceptions. There have been other cases where the tolerance of the international community did not require review by inclusive decision makers; later even the statutory law was changed in favor of the practices. The *Torrey Canyon* incident is one example, where the air force of the United Kingdom bombed the tanker in international waters in an attempt to halt further spillage of the oil that was damaging the English coast. The international community not only tolerated the British unilateral action but also two years later adopted the Public Law Convention specifically to authorize such unilateral actions.

D. RECOMMENDATIONS

With all the conventions on injurious use of resources, environmental problems are still substantial, and there are serious doubts as to the role and effectiveness of current prescriptions in the protection of the long-term common interest. There are a number of reasons for such doubts, some of which arise from demands for change in the modalities of resource use and allocation on a global scale. Our emphasis here, however, is only on a few that seem to be key problems common to the injurious use of all resources.

1. Bilateral and Regional Approaches

The fact that the globe is an ecological unity and that injurious use of one part of it affects the rest establishes the necessity for a global approach to environmental problems. A global approach, how-

---

would find itself obliged to find that coastal states cannot take steps to prevent pollution. Such a legalistic decision would set back immeasurably the development of law in this critical area." *Id.* at 43–44.

ever, is merely the beginning of the consideration and examination of environmental problems. This approach is one that only observes the broader dimensions of the injurious use of resources and is not designed to limit the invention of policy alternatives. In other words, the global approach only identifies the common interest shared by the global community. But the fact is that there are many kinds of injurious uses of resources that can have a serious particular impact on a region. In such cases, the global approach by itself cannot protect the common interest in forms both exclusive and inclusive. To expect a universal approach to solve all forms of regional value deprivations would result in dysfunctional and unsuccessful policies and recommendations. Such an approach creates difficulties even in identifying the most common interests shared globally. Some scholars observe that one reason for the failure to solve the environmental problems is this lack of identification of common interest. Different participants are concerned with or aware of only one or two particular problems, choose them as their focus of attention, and consider them to be problems equally important to the other participants.[184] To expect international conventions to formulate detailed recommendations to solve all global and regional environmental problems is naive. Perhaps one reason for the trends moving toward exclusive competence is disappointment in such expectations. Global environmental recommendations are not necessarily suitable for regional problems. The technology for resource use, including its injurious use, develops so quickly and becomes so complicated that the elaborate process necessary for the establishment of international conventions to deal with it is too slow. Besides, there are a number of situations where the immediate and serious impacts of injurious use are regional or state to state rather than global. Furthermore, in cases where the global damage is not so obvious, mustering

---

[184]Clifford Russell and Hans Landsberg make the same point: "[C]onsidering, for example, the prospects for agreement when one group's mind is on the long-term build up of carbon dioxide in the atmosphere and particularly in the lower stratosphere; another worries over the dangers associated with increasing storage of radioactive wastes; a third focuses on the ecological implications of large-scale hydro-electric developments in the tropics; a fourth is concerned with the effect of domestic air pollution controls on export prices and hence trade patterns; yet another is concerned about a specific regional problem in which one nation's pollution, or attempt at protection against pollution, imposes costs on another nation; and, finally, a group of developing nations views matters through the prism of its overwhelming interest in increasing per capita income." Russell & Landsberg, *International Environmental Problems—a Taxonomy*, SCIENCE June 25, 1971, at 1307.

sufficient concern for an international convention is difficult.

It should be emphasized that we do not attack a global approach as an inappropriate way of considering environmental problems. On the contrary, we believe that the global approach is essential for the generation of the principles and recommendations to protect the common interest. As mentioned at the beginning of the chapter, the impact of environmental problems will eventually be felt by the international community. Our point is, however, that environmental problems are enormous and complicated. Such complication is promoted by the factors (political and geographic) surrounding a particular resource use. To be helpful, strategies for the prevention of injurious use should be compatible with those factors. Bilateral and regional approaches concentrating on specific regional problems and formulating recommendations within the general principles laid by international prescriptions will also be more functional.

We recommend expansion of bilateral and regional agreements on the control of the injurious use of resources, particularly to include preventive measures. This will require the cooperation of states in terms of gathering, processing and exchanging information, and cooperation in review and considering some national programs that have potentially serious environmental effects. Such practices are not new, but in terms of scope and number they have indeed been limited.

2. The Intelligence Function

To be able to create those policies appropriate to control the injurious use of resources effectively, policymakers should be aware of the strategies by which resources are used and of their ultimate effects on the human environment. To provide such awareness, there should be a flow of information about these issues to the policymakers. Principle 20 of the Stockholm Conference recognizes the need for a flow of information:

> Scientific research and development in the context of environmental problems, both national and multilateral, must be promoted in all countries, especially the developing countries. In this connexion, the free flow of up-to-date scientific information and transfer of experience must be supported and assisted, to facilitate the solution of environmental problems; environmental technologies should be made available to developing coun-

tries on terms which would encourage their wide dissemination without constituting an economic burden on the developing countries."[185]

In its plan for action the Conference further provided for the Environmental Assessment (Earthwatch) for developing the intelligence function in the forms of research, gathering, processing, and exchanging information at all levels.[186] The Global Environmental Monitoring System (GEMS) is an international institution designed to implement such policy.[187] Participation in GEMS is, however, voluntary. Only in GEMS with regard to the marine environment are there firm commitments on the part of nation-states to study the environment through the observation, measurement, and evaluation of the marine environment and to prepare appropriate reports to UNEP and other competent international organizations.[188]

The intelligence function should not be limited to scientific data only but should also cover the social implications of injurious use. Thus policymakers will be aware of the multiple functions of resource use, and their recommendations will provide meaningful suggestions in their problem solving. To improve the intelligence function, access to resources for inquiry should be free and information should be processed and be available to all interested participants.

3. Preventive Measures

The increase in the possibility of irreversible damage from injurious use of resources has made the role of preventive measures more critical in the protection of the long-term common interest. By *preventive measure* is meant a process to prevent "the occurrence

[185] STOCKHOLM CONFERENCE, *supra* note 43, Principal 20.

[186] STOCKHOLM CONFERENCE, *supra* note 43, part (C): The Action Plan, Environmental Assessment (Earthwatch), reprinted in 11 INT'L LEGAL MATERIALS 1464 (1972). For similar recommendations on the promotion of the intelligence function, see WARD & DUBOS, note 2, *supra*; SPROUT & SPROUT, note 2, *supra*; and FALK, note 2, *supra*.

[187] *See* U.N. Doc. UNEP/GC/31/Add.2 (1975), and U.N. Doc. UNEP/GC/55 (1975), at 45–47.

[188] *See Results of Consideration of Proposals and Amendments Relating to the Preservation of the Marine Environment*, U.N. Doc. A/Conf.62/C.3/L.15/Add.1, (1975) Article 8, at 1.

of unauthorized deprivations by locating those factors that tend to produce (or aggravate) such deprivations or to inhibit them, controlling the former . . . and fostering the latter. . . ."[189] Preventive measures may be long-term or short-term. When the latter, they are referred to as *deterrents*, which means "to deter the occurrence of imminent or threatened deprivations by use of negative sanctions . . . or by positive sanctions. . . ."[190]

a. Long-Term Measures

These measures include prescriptions concerning prior notification and consultation, ship construction, transportation of materials injurious to the environment, and surveillance over the implementation of preventive requirements. Some but not enough attention has been given to these measures. Principle 20 as originally proposed by the Working Group on the Declaration on the Human Environment did require prior consultation. But, as was mentioned before, this Principle was never adopted by the Stockholm Conference. A few months later G.A. Resolution 2995 (1972) was passed to replace Principle 20. The Resolution, however, limits the scope of the cooperation and exchange of information to "technical data." This qualification was included to limit the scope of prior notification and consultation.

As to other forms of long-term preventive measures, flag states are basically authorized as to implementation. Besides the fact that the requirements related to the construction of equipment and strategies for the use of resources are not comprehensive, the giving of authority only to flag states has decreased the role of preventive prescriptions. Expansion of the competence of other states in surveillance of the implementation of preventive measures would be useful. In the area of ocean resources, priority for surveillance should be given to the coastal state over certain areas beyond the territorial waters and to other states on the high seas when they have reasonable belief that there is a violation of preventive measures.

---

[189]LAW, SCIENCE & POLICY MATERIALS, (1966) (unpublished papers in the Yale Law School Library).

[190]*Id.*

b. Short-Term Measures

Measures for deterrence are supplementary to the above long-term preventive requirements. Among these measures are prior notification, abatement, injunction, and other temporary relief. Prior notification here, of course, is different from the case of long-term preventive measures. Prior notification here refers to a process of communication between two or more states before the outcome of an injurious use occurs. The notification is intended to effect and facilitate immediate action to prevent or minimize the damage. For example, the "warning system and incidents" of the 1974 OECD Principles Concerning Transfrontier Pollution requires that "countries should promptly warn other potentially affected countries of any situation which may cause any sudden increase in the level of pollution in areas outside the country of origin of pollution."[191] The Caracas session of LOS also provided that "[a] State which becomes aware of cases in which the marine environment is in imminent danger of being damaged or has been damaged by pollution shall immediately notify other States it deems likely to be affected by such damage, as well as the competent international organization."[192] Agreements Concerning Pollution of the North Sea Oil[193] and Article 5 of the London Dumping Convention[194] also incorporate similar policies. The requirements for such notification should be promoted, particularly in bilateral and multilateral agreements for the prevention of injurious use of internal resources with extraterritorial impact.

Abatement is a measure for the minimization or even prevention of damage already in process. This right, as discussed before, has its basis in the customary international law doctrine of self-help, self-preservation, or self-defense. The measures for abatement become more important in the injurious use of resources after several disasters such as the *Torrey Canyon*, the Cherry Point

---

[191]OECD Doc. C(74) 224, Nov. 21, 1974, reprinted in 14 Int'l Legal Materials 242 (1975).

[192]*See* U.N. Doc. A/Conf.62/C.3/L.15, *supra* note 188, at 4.

[193]9 Int'l Legal Materials 359 (1970), Article 6.

[194]Convention on the Dumping of Wastes at Sea, Nov. 13, 1972, *reprinted in* 11 Int'l Legal Materials 1294 (1972).

oil spill[195] and *Tanker Metula* incident.[196] Abatement measures are not limited to injurious use of the oceans but also of the atmosphere, landmasses, and other kinds of incidents affecting resources, such as the H-bombs of Palomares.

The Public Law Convention has given some attention to short-term preventive measures. It is, however, limited to incidents that have already happened. But there are situations in which it is desirable to exercise this right before the harm is done. This problem could be better resolved through regional or bilateral agreements, such as the one on the pollution of the North Sea among the Scandinavian countries, through dividing the North Sea into zones of state competences requiring each state to take responsibility for prevention of injurious use which "presents a grave and imminent danger to the coast or related interests of one or more Contracting Parties."[197] Similar ideas have been incorporated in the Joint U.S.–Canadian Oil and Hazardous Materials Pollution Contingency Plan, which allocates between Canada and the United States the responsibility of providing coordinated and integrated responses to pollution problems in the Great Lakes System.[198] Such bilateral and regional agreements are preferable methods of improving and implementing abatement measures in ways that protect the exclusive and inclusive interests of the smaller and the larger communities.

The injunction is another form of short-term preventive measure. It is a process by which a particular injurious use of resources can be prevented temporarily until a final decision as to its lawfulness is made. This process may be accomplished by diplomatic or

---

[195] *See Canada Asks U.S. Payment for Oil Spill on West Coast*, N.Y. Times, June 10, 1972, at 36, col. 5; *Oil in Canadian Waters*, *id.* June 27, 1972, at 40, col. 1.

[196] This accident occurred during the Caracas session of LOS. The tanker *Metula*, flying the flag of the Netherlands, owned by the Curacao Shipping Co. and carrying Shell Oil, went aground in the Straits of Magellan and lost 6,000 tons of crude oil along a front of about 25 miles. There were legitimate fears that the ship might split and endanger the safety of navigation in the area, the well-being of the inhabitants of the coast, and of local marine life. Immediate action was taken by the Chilean government, IMCO, FAO, and assistance was given by Canada and the U.S. For further analysis of this incident, see U.N., Third Committee, Summary Record of the Fifteenth Meeting, U.N. Doc. A/Conf.62/C.3SR.15 (1974).

[197] 9 Int'l Legal Materials 359 (1970), Article 1.

[198] *See* the text in 11 Int'l Legal Materials 694, Annex 8 (1972).

judicial means or through informal pressures by interest groups. This particular preventive measure is very important in a time when the consequences of some uses are unclear. This process provides the time and opportunity for studying and examining the possible outcomes of a particular resource use and the possibility of arriving at a more rational decision compatible with the common interest.

This measure has not developed effectively enough to prevent a number of uses of resources possibly dangerous to the environment. The third U.S. underground nuclear weapon test "Cannikin" on the Aleutian Island of Amchitka is an example. There were protests by Canada and Japan opposing the test, but the protests did not stop the test, which caused earthquakes and produced shock waves throughout a large area.[199] Similarly, in U.S. Project West Ford[200] there were a number of protests by national and international scientific groups and by the U.S.S.R., but they could not stop the project. In 1970, however, when the United States proposed to sink a shipload of nerve gas into the Atlantic, the national courts provided a competent forum in which American nationals could challenge the government proposal, though they were unsuccessful.[201] Other nations, however, were not provided with such a forum to present their claims, except through diplomatic channels.[202]

The injunction has been provided for by international tribunals in international litigations, such as the *Fisheries Jurisdiction Cases*[203]

---

[199] N.Y. Times, Sept. 9, 1971, at 1, col. 4; *id.* Oct. 2, 1971, at 1, col. 7.

[200] N.Y. Times, July 30, 1961, at 48, col. 1; *id.* Feb. 3, 1962, at 5, col. 1.

[201] Brown, *International Law and Marine Pollution: Radioactive Waste and "Other Hazardous Substances,"* NATURAL RESOURCES J. 221, 234, 249–50 (1971).

[202] In this case the Bahamas, whose shores were closer to the dumping site than those of the United States, were found to have no forum. *See* Utton, *supra* note 83, at 56. This lack of access to a comprehensive injunction process may create real damage to the environment. For example, there are reports that Russia is considering the diversion of three major rivers that now flow into the Arctic. It has been predicted that such diversions could have a disastrous effect on the climate of the Northern Hemisphere. One of the predictions is that the salinity of the Arctic seas would increase because of the reduction of fresh water influx. This could result in a decrease in polar ice, and cause a warming that could change southern Europe and large portions of North America into a desert and give Northern Europe a Mediterranean climate. *See* ALBUQUERQUE JOURNAL Feb. 27, (1970) § E, at 8, col. 1, *cited in* Utton, *Id.* at 56–7.

[203] [1972] I.C.J. 11, 17.

and the *Nuclear Test Cases*.[204] In both cases, however, the court order was not implemented. The injunction should be promoted and be available effectively through different channels, diplomatic, judicial, and other. To promote this policy, we recommend access for foreign nations and their subjects as well as the relevant international agencies to national courts for presenting claims concerning injurious use of internal resources with extraterritorial impacts.

4. Control of Injurious Use of Resources as a Part of the Development Process

Effective recommendations for control of injurious use of resources should be related to the general community policy of development. Environmental measures have so far been regarded mainly in terms of regulatory authorities or police action. In the present world of demand for changes in value distributions, environmental regulations should be a part of, or at least consistent with, such a process. Policies for control of injurious uses cannot be formulated without taking into account their ultimate consequences on countries with a lesser degree of responsibility for the pollution problem, such as developing countries. Measures should be taken, therefore, that are fair and equitable in terms of the approximate degree of responsibility; and the burden for compensation should be proportionate to such responsibility. This becomes particularly important in evaluating the consequences of unilateral measures taken by developed countries on developing countries.

There have been some studies of the adverse impacts of developed countries' environmental measures on the development planning of poorer countries.[205] These studies show that there can be no doubt that measures for the protection of the environment by developed countries have negative effects on developing countries, such as the increase in tariff barriers on the exports of the developing countries, increase in the price of their imports, and

---

[204][1973] I.C.J. 99, 106.

[205] *See* D'Arge & Kneese, *Environmental Quality and International Trade*, 26 INT'L ORGANIZATION 419 (1972); U.N. "Report on Development and Environment," U.N. Doc. A/Conf.48/10, (1971); Eldin, *The Need for Intergovernmental Cooperation and Coordination in Environmental Policy*, in KNEESE, ROLFE & HARNED, *supra* note 9, at 201–06.

decrease in foreign aid to developing countries.[206] Concern for such adverse effects led to U.N. Resolution 2849 XXVI:

> (b) Recognise that no environmental policy should adversely affect the present or future development possibilities of the developing countries;
>
> . . .
>
> (e) Avoid any adverse effects of environmental policies and measures on the economy of the developing countries in all spheres, including international trade, international development assistance and transfer of technology.[207]

The Resolution requested the Secretary-General of the U.N. Conference on Trade and Development "to prepare a comprehensive study to be submitted to the Conference at its third session on the effects of environmental policies of developing countries."[208] The UNCTAD study, which was prepared in March 1972[209] and submitted to the Third Session of UNCTAD in Santiago, Chile, lamented the lack of data and detailed studies in the area[210] and concluded that "environmental actions by developed countries may thus have a profound and multiple impact on the growth and external economic relations of developing countries." UNCTAD recommended that the U.N. Conference on the Human Environment bear in mind the relationship between environmental protection, and trade and development—particularly with respect to developing countries.[211] Similarly, GATT concluded on a study in this area in June 1971 that environmental regulations may have considerable impact on international trade and on the flow of capital.[212]

Realizing the problem involved, the Stockholm Conference recommended that developed nations not invoke environmental mat-

---

[206] *See* the studies cited in *id. See* also J. A. Gibson, *Possible Impacts of United States Domestic Environmental Policies on Less Developed Countries' Trade, Investments, and Foreign Aid*, 3 ENVT'L. AFFAIRS 109–27 (1974).

[207] G.A. Res. 2849, 26 U.N. GAOR (Supp. No. 29) 70, U.N. Doc. A/8429 (1972).

[208] *Id.*

[209] U.N. Doc. TD/130 (1972).

[210] *Id.* at para. 57.

[211] UNCTAD Res. 47 (III Sess., Santiago–de Chile), U.N. Doc. TD/180 (1972).

[212] GATT, *Industrial Pollution Control and International Trade*, Background paper No. 4 (1971).

ters as a "pretext for discriminating trade policies."[213] It recommended that GATT and UNCTAD be allowed to "monitor and assess tariff and trade barriers" resulting from environmental polices.[214] It further provided that financial and technical assistance be provided to help poor countries remove such obstacles to their exports[215] and recommended that appropriate measures for compensation be provided where environmental standards have a negative effect on developing nation's exports.[216] These recommendations were opposed by the U.S. government on the grounds that many factors affect export earnings and hence that requiring compensatory treatment would undermine environmental responsibility.

The impact of environmental measures by developed countries on the policy of development process should be neither underestimated nor overestimated. But it is a factor that affects the common interest and has to be taken into account in environmental policymaking. Developing countries must surely avoid the mistakes and distortions that characterize the process of development of industrialized countries. A panel of experts convened by the Secretary-General of the U.N. Conference on the Human Environment recommended that there be a redefinition of the Second Development Decade in order to accommodate development policies with global policies of control of injurious use[217] and that there

[213]STOCKHOLM CONFERENCE, *supra* note 43, Recommendation 109, para. 1. *See also* Principle 9, which recommends additional help to developing countries for protection of the environment: "Environmental deficiencies generated by the conditions of underdevelopment and natural disasters pose grave problems and can best be remedied by accelerated development through the transfer of substantial quantities of financial and technological assistance as a supplement to the domestic effort of the developing countries and such timely assistance as may be required." *See also* Principles 11, 12, and 23.

[214]STOCKHOLM CONFERENCE, *supra* note 43, Recommendation 109, para. 2.

[215]*Id.* at para. 3.

[216]*Id.* at para. 4. Recommendation 103 also provides, *inter alia*, "[t]hat where environmental concerns lead to restrictions on trade, or to stricter environmental standards with negative effects on exports, particularly from developing countries, appropriate measures for compensation should be worked out within the framework of existing contractual and institutional arrangements and any new such arrangements that can be worked out in the future." For discussions of the Stockholm Conference recommendations and the adoption of the compensation concept, see IUCN Environmental Policy and Law Paper No. 4, THE CONCEPT OF COMPENSATION IN THE FIELD OF TRADE AND DEVELOPMENT 91973; IUCN, Environmental Policy and Law Paper No. 6, FINANCIAL ENVIRONMENTAL MEASURES IN DEVELOPING COUNTRIES: THE PRINCIPLE OF ADDITIONALITY (1974).

[217]"Development and Environment," reported submitted by a panel of experts convened

be more direct contributions to the development of poor and less polluted areas, either through additional funds or transfer of technology.[218]

---

by the Secretary-General of the U.N. Conference on the Human Environment, June 4–12, 1971, Founex, Switzerland, U.N. Doc. GE. 7–13738 (1971), *cited in* Hargrove, *supra* note 143, at 49.

[218]*Id.* at 27–30.

Chapter vi

Control of Pricing of Resources

Demand for a new definition and function of pricing more compatible with changing community goals has increased during the past few years. The ongoing battle between the developed and the developing countries about reconstructing a pattern of world trade for a more equitable distribution of values challenges traditional pricing theory. That theory appears to be increasingly inadequate as an instrument of contemporary policy, fostering a system that makes the rich richer and the poor poorer. The new demands require a more comprehensive conception of the function of pricing and a reevaluation of the factors to be taken into account in price determination. Pricing cannot remain an isolated economic theory, considered relevant only to a few problems, with objectives separated from the larger general community policies. Pricing theory should be compatible with, and where possible contribute to and support, all recommended general community policies as an aspect of overall fiscal policy. It should be made to perform a much broader and more constructive role in protecting common interests. To this end, we define pricing as a process of decision precipitating multiple value effects throughout all the communities affected. It is a process for allocating the benefits and costs arising from use and enjoyment of resources and for effecting a more general distribution of values. The newer demands require that pricing perform the function not merely of allocating the benefits and costs arising from the immediate exploitation of particular resources but also of securing a preferred distribution of values not necessarily arising from the resources carrying a particular "price tag."

A. INTRODUCTION: THEORIES OF PRICING

The strategy of control over use and benefits of resources by pricing has a long history. Pricing does in fact significantly influence

every aspect of resource exploitation, including production, processing, distribution, and consumption. The conception of pricing
as related to particular resources is not new. While definitions,
functions, and structures have of course undergone changes, the
basic elements of this conception have existed from the beginning
of human economic interaction; it has been influenced by religious
ideology; later it was developed by, and expressed through, the
secular specialist languages of economists and political scientists.
The great bulk of theories about pricing have, happily, always had
some relation to the totality of community policy; less happily,
however, some of the more important theories have had transem-
pirical elements.

The narrow conception and limited function of pricing in the
Middle Ages, associated only with resource exchange, has been
replaced by much broader concepts affecting the whole complex
global process of value distribution. The ideology of the Middle
Ages, influenced by Christianity and Aristotle, looked at economic
activities as a process by which goods and services were provided
for the community to insure each of its members security and
freedom. The concept of profit making, and the use of market
opportunities to change prices at the expense of the majority, was
condemned morally and socially. This ideology, in a way compatible with Islamic economic concepts, held that individuals were
entitled only to that reasonable share of goods and services that
satisfied their needs. Any surplus belonged to the whole community. In that period every resource had, in theory, a "just price," or
justum pretium, which was equal to its cost of production.[1] The just
price was not necessarily an economic but an ethical and social
concept; indeed, it concomitantly supported a policy against "unjust enrichment." The manifest and ostensibly exclusive purpose
of the just price was to insure equality as between producers and
consumers.

With the transformation of the social structure in the late
Middle Ages and the development of specializations, new technol-

---

[1] For explanations of the Medieval concept of pricing, see 7 ENCYC. SOC. SCI. 504–07
(1935); J. HUIZINGA, THE WANING OF THE MIDDLE AGES (1924); J. BALDWIN, THE MEDIEVAL
THEORIES OF JUST PRICE (1959). For the history and development of pricing theory from
the Middle Ages, see 11 ENCYC. SOC. SCI. 355–87 (1935). For general references on pricing
theory, see J. BRIDGE & P. MCGREGOR, PRICING POLICIES (1974); J. ANGELL, THE THEORY OF
INTERNATIONAL PRICES (1926); R. LEFTWICH, THE PRICE SYSTEM AND RESOURCE ALLOCA-
TION (2d ed. 1961), and D. HAGUE, PRICE FORMATION IN VARIOUS ECONOMIES (1967).

ogies, new markets, and new social configurations, the pattern of resource use and distribution changed. With the expansion of the influence of the merchant groups and a new ideology of economic activities, classical capitalism considered pricing the outcome of a so-called free market regulated by an invisible hand. The theory of laissez-faire posited that the law of free market would determine the real price of resources. To Adam Smith "[t]he real price of every thing, what every thing really costs to the man who wants to acquire it, is the toil and trouble of acquiring it, and who wants to dispose of it or exchange it for something else, is the toil and trouble which it can save to himself, and which it can impose upon other people."[2] In the free market system, resources will eventually be available to those who offer the highest prices. Nevertheless, this laissez-faire theory does not answer, or gives a negative answer, to the questions of whether the ones who pay more are the ones who deserve to consume and whether this system is consistent with the goals of a fair and equitable distribution of values. Moreover, it ignores problems of resource scarcity and ecological deterioration and militates by its terms against a planning function.

Using a totally different perspective and promoting the interest of a different class, Marxian theory was built upon the metaphysical notion of materialistic determinism. Marx and Engels replace the capitalist term *pricing* with *value* and define the "value" of each commodity as "determined by the quantity of labor expended on and materialized in it; by the working time necessary, under given social conditions for its production."[3] Marx's concept of "value," or "pricing," is thus close to the Christian and Islamic notion of just price. It denies interest employed by the "bourgeois" society. For Marx the "value" of a commodity is "[t]he objective from the social labor expanded in its production" and is determined by "[t]he quantity of the labor contained in it."[4]

The concept of pricing, as demonstrated in an abundant literature, has been the great battleground of most inherited economic

---

[2] A. SMITH, WEALTH OF NATIONS 30 (E. Cannan ed. 1937). *See also* D. RICARDO, THE PRINCIPLES OF POLITICAL ECONOMY AND TAXATION (P. Fogarty ed. 1965). On the operation of the self-regulating market system, see K. POLANYI, THE GREAT TRANSFORMATION 29 (1944).

[3] K. MARX, CAPITAL, in 50 GREAT BOOKS OF THE WESTERN WORLD 89–90 (1952); see also K. MARX 1 CAPITAL pt. 111.

[4] *Id.* at 264.

theories since the eighteenth century, when economics became an independent social science. Some of the modern theories regard pricing as a technique of fiscal control of consumption. For these theories, pricing becomes of potential importance in directing the use of resources.[5] When decision makers address the problem of resource scarcity, pricing is viewed as a strategy to regulate the magnitude of resource consumption and to control the timing of resource use. In this process the price level becomes one scheme for control of resource use to fulfill the policies of the decision makers. While the limited function of the medieval notion of pricing as a system of resource exchange has been recognized and employed, the potentially larger function of pricing as a scheme of value distribution has never been fully developed. A later theory of progressive taxation as a modality of income redistribution indicates the recognized need for a reallocation of values and supplies, a technique comparable to pricing for securing such reallocation.[6]

The difficulties inherent in all these theories emphasize the importance both of establishing a more modern conception of pricing and of outlining a contextual approach which will include the various factors that should affect pricing policy.

B. THE FACTUAL BACKGROUND

In the present world order, the structure and processes of international trade have a close relationship with the stability and growth of national economies and have been "a regular and important feature of domestic politics."[7] A part of this world trade structure is the process of pricing, which can be seen more substantially to affect the income of developing countries and primary producers than that of developed countries. This high impact is

[5] A. ALCHIAN & W. ALLEN, UNIVERSITY ECONOMICS 102 (2d ed. 1968).

[6] A system of progressive taxation is defined as "one that takes a larger proportion of high incomes than of low." P. SAMUELSON, ECONOMICS, AN INTRODUCTORY ANALYSIS 127 (4th ed. 1958). Progressive taxation is the opposite of regressive taxation; a regressive tax is one that takes larger proportion of low incomes than high incomes. Income, death, and gift taxes are examples of progressive taxation. Taxes on employment or payroll taxes are regressive.

[7] Reisman, *Trade Helps Traders: The Third World's Fading Dream*, NATION, June 12, 1976, at 716, 717; see also Muir, *The Changing Legal Framework of International Energy Management*, 9 INT'L LAW 605, 613 (1975).

the result of the dependency of the developing primary producers on a single commodity or a few commodities for their major export earnings. Primary products in the early 1970s accounted for 80 percent to 90 percent of the export of developing countries.[8] According to an UNCTAD study, primary products, excluding oil exports, account for two-thirds of the export earnings of developing countries.[9] An IMF and IBRD study shows that the exports of these countries have grown slowly relative to the growth of world trade and relative to the increase in imports necessary to sustain a satisfactory rate of development in these countries.[10] Among commodities only petroleum, timber, iron ore, and bauxite have had major growth; for most commodities demand has increased slowly and the prices of such commodities have been subject to much wider fluctuation than the export prices of industrial countries.[11] Exports of developing countries have been in agricultural raw materials and foodstuffs and have generated decreasing amounts of revenue for the exporting countries. The most rapidly expanding commodities have been fuels and manufactured goods, followed by metals and minerals. In the 1960s the foodstuffs and agricultural raw materials accounted for more than half of the total primary products exports of developing countries, while in the 1950s their share was almost two-thirds.[12] The decline in the value of exports of primary products in comparison to the increase in the export of manufactured products becomes more

[8] UNITED NATIONS CONFERENCE ON TRADE AND DEVELOPMENT (UNCTAD), *Trends and Policies in the First Four Years of the Second Development Decade*, U.N. DOC. TD/B/530/Add.1 (1975), at 7: IMF & IBRD, THE PROBLEM OF STABILIZATION OF PRICES OF PRIMARY PRODUCTS 1 (1969). More than 80% of third-world foreign exchange accrues from exports to the industrial countries. HIGHER OIL PRICES AND THE WORLD ECONOMY 186 (E. Fried & C. Schultre eds. 1975); THE GAP BETWEEN RICH AND POOR NATIONS 99 (G. Ranis ed. 1972). The present role of developing countries is that of suppliers of raw materials to the western industries and export markets for their manufactured products. *See* TRILATERAL COMMISSION, A TURNING POINT IN NORTH-SOUTH ECONOMIC RELATIONS 19, 22 (1974).

[9] *See* UNCTAD REPORT, note 8 *supra*.

[10] THE PPROBLEM OF STABILIZATION OF PRICES OF PRIMARY PRODUCTS, *supra* note 8, at 1 [hereinafter cited as PROBLEM OF STABILIZATION].

[11] *Id.*

[12] Exports of foodstuffs grew at a rate of 2.6% a year, and exports of agricultural raw materials at 1.1%. The decline in demand has increased the downward pressure on the overall export growth rate of developing countries. *See* UNCTAD, Recent Developments and Long Term Trends in Commodity Trade, U.N. Doc. TD/9. (1967), in PROBLEM OF STABILIZATION, supra note 8, at 15.

dramatic. Between the 1950s and the mid-1960s the value of exports of developing countries grew at a compound rate of 4.7 percent a year. During the same period the value of the exports of developed countries rose at an annual rate of 7.2 percent.[13] While the prices of primary products declined, the prices of manufactures, which dominated the exports of developing countries, tended to increase.[14] As a result of slow growth in the demand of exports of developing countries and the decline in the prices of primary products in relation to manufactured goods, the share of developing countries in world trade has steadily declined. In the early 1950s the share was 27 percent, but by the mid-1960s it had fallen below 20 percent.[15]

The effects of price fluctuations on primary producers are much more severe than on industrial producers. On the surface, however, it may seem to be the reverse. One may argue that trade depression manifests itself in developing countries on farmers, while in industrial countries it does so on unemployed workers. It is sometimes assumed that a farmer may still be able to feed his family and himself even if depression results in low production, but that unemployed workers do not have even that opportunity. Yet experience in recent years suggests a different outcome: "[m]ass unemployment has not threatened the industrial countries and the income fluctuations they have suffered have been rather fluctuations in the rate of increase of real income than alternating periods of increase and decrease. The primary producing countries on the other hand have suffered from time to time significant declines in income. . . ."[16] No matter how refined this argument becomes, there is no doubt that high prices and wide fluctuations in price of manufactured goods have tremendous negative effects on international trade in general and the development process of developing countries in particular.[17] Even if increases in prices of food, fertilizers, and fuels are ignored, and export power is mea-

---

[13] *See* PROBLEM OF STABILIZATION, *supra* note 8, at 11–12.

[14] *Id.*

[15] *Id.*

[16] S. CANE, PRICES FOR PRIMARY PRODUCERS 19 (1966) [hereinafter cited as CANE].

[17] *See Preservation of the Purchsing Power of Developing Countries' Exports* U.N. DOC. TD/184/Supp. 2 (1976) at 3.

sured only by the prices of manufactured goods, a study by UNC-TAD shows that a substantial number of developing countries recorded an increase in real export earning of less than 7 percent (the minimum requirement for development estimated by the International Development Strategy for the 1970s) from 1970 to 1974.[18] Studies by UNCTAD and the World Bank show an annual decline of close to 2 percent (2.0 percent by UNCTAD and 1.7 percent by the World Bank) in the trade of developing countries.[19] Thirty-nine of the developing countries accounted for one-third of the aggregate export earnings of non-OPEC developing countries in 1970 but for more than one-half of the total population of these countries. The maximum average increase in terms of purchasing power of thirty-nine developing countries excluding OPEC countries over imports of manufacture was only 1.7 percent in 1970.[20]

One negative characteristic of contemporary world trade is the unequal distribution of the total economic benefits between producers and consumers. With respect to oil, which has had the highest increase in value, before the 1971 Tehran agreement royalties and taxes were about $1 per barrel of refined oil for producer countries while the share of the oil importers in Western Europe in the form of taxes was about $4.50 per barrel, which was sold for about $8.00 in Europe.[21] Such inequitable value distribution was observable in a number of other commodities as well, particularly through the economic activities of multinationals. For example, one of the practices of these corporations is price determination of goods and services traded between the corporation and its affiliates located in different countries. Such price fixing affects the

[18]*Id.* at 4.

[19]*Id.* at 6–9.

[20]*Id. See* Reports by UNCTAD Secretariat, *World Economic Outlook*, U.N. Doc. TD/186 (1976). This study shows that virtually all developing countries experienced severe drops in their real export income in 1975 as a result of the economic recession in the industrialized countries. In 1976 and 1977 only a modest recovery was expected.

[21]FORTUNE, Mar. 1971, at 30. Although these figures do not distinguish between "intercountry balance of payments considerations and intracountry income distribution effects, they are indicative of wide scope within which income transfers could have taken place between countries." Vaitsos, *Power, Knowledge and Development Policy: Relations Between Transnational Enterprises and Developing Countries in a World Divided: The Less Developed Countries in International Economy* 113, 128 (G. Helleiner ed. 1976).

distribution of the benefits of their activities between countries, as well as sometimes paralyzing local competition.[22] Intracorporate trade in goods within multinationals contains more than one-quarter of the value of all international trade in goods,[23] and the possibility for price manipulation is obviously quite extensive.

The size of the market also discriminates against developing countries that must import. In comparison, oil-importing developing countries pay about 20 percent more to oil companies than oil-importing developed countries, because of the smallness and underdevelopment of their market.[24] The so-called fourth world, with a population of 900 million, 35 percent of the population of the entire noncommunist world, suffered more from the high prices of oil than the first world of developed countries.[25]

The lack of adequate inclusive competence in control of pricing has been another characteristic of the international market. Decisions regarding pricing have primarily been the outcome of exclusive competences through monopoly or oligopoly, and only occasionally of partially inclusive competences. The latter is the more current practice. The earlier practices, dominated by the multinationals, were more in the nature of oligopolistic or monopolistic control through their several joint ventures.[26] Exclusive

---

[22] U.N., Dept. of Economic and Social Affairs, *The Impact of Multinational Corporations on Development and on International Relations*, U.N. Doc. E/5500/ Rev. 1, ST/ESA/6, 88 (1974).

[23] *Id.*

[24] "The developing countries are handicapped by the smallness of their market which makes them stand at the end of the consumer line for supplies and transport facilities; furthermore they lack access to up-to-the-minute information which is crucial in an industry characterized by fast changes and secrecy." *Energy Crisis: Freezing the Poor*, 1 DEVELOPMENT FORUM (Geneva) No. 9, Dec. 1973, at 12, *cited in* Z. MIKDASHI, THE INTERNATIONAL POLITICS OF NATURAL RESOURCES 69 (1976). [Hereinafter cited as MIKDASHI.]

[25] *See* S. ALEXANDER, PAYING FOR ENERGY 26–28 (1975). For short-term and long-term higher prices of oil, see Tims, *The Developing Countries*, in FRIED & SCHULTZE, *supra* note 8, at 169–98.

[26] The term *oligopoly* refers to a market of a "few sellers, each supplying a large part of total output, each believing that it is large enough to influence price by an increase or decrease in the amount of goods it offers for sale." W. LEEMAN, THE PRICE OF MIDDLE EAST OIL: AN ESSAY IN POLITICAL ECONOMY 8 (1962). On oligopoly practices, *see generally* MIKDASHI, *supra* note 24, at 66–67; R. LOW, THE ECONOMICS OF ANTITRUST: COMPETITION AND MONOPOLY 4–9 (1968); Hopkins, *Money, Monopoly and the contemporary World Order*, 2 DENVER J. INT'L L. & POLICY 66 (1972); J. BRIDGE & P. MCGREGOR, PRICING POLICIES 5–8 (1974); P. SYLOS-LABINI, OLIGOPOLY AND TECHNICAL PROCESS (1962); M. SHUBIK, STRATEGY AND MARKET STRUCTURE: COMPETITION, OLIGOPOLY, AND THE THEORY OF GAMES (1959); Sweezy, *Demand Under Conditions of Oligopoly*, 47 J. POL. ECON. 508 (1939); E. PENROSE, THE

control over pricing of resources could be exercised by a small group of corporations or a single state. For example, the world depends on the United States for approximately 90 percent of its soybeans.[27] A U.S. decision to cut back production of exports of soybeans will affect the price of this product dramatically. Partially inclusive competence has been exercised through different forms of producers' associations. The closest approximation to inclusive competence over pricing has been achieved through commodity agreements. They are, in theory, representative of both producers' and consumers' interests. The impact of these practices on external and internal value processes will be examined later.

In the international market a functional conception of pricing includes taxes, royalties, participation, or any techniques by which values are distributed. This wide range of strategies available to major participants in the pricing process, nation-states and multinational corporations, has contributed to the politicization of this process.[28] While international trade has always had political implications, this aspect has increased tremendously as the result of demands for mobilization of all forces for the implementation of exclusive community policies.

Although nation-states have always played a decisive role in the pricing process, either directly or through their corporations, at the present time their role takes on a new importance. The effective participation of nation-states is apparent not only in developing countries; even in developed countries the trends point toward their domination. Canada and Australia are examples of such developed countries.[29] Similar trends characterize the British, Scandinavian, and Dutch governments with respect to the operation of the North Sea oil enterprise.[30] The increase in state participation

---

LARGE INTERNATIONAL FIRMS IN DEVELOPING COUNTRIES 175 (1968), and F. MACHLUP, THE POLITICAL ECONOMY OF MONOPOLY (1952).

[27] L. BROWN, IN THE HUMAN INTEREST 82 (1974).

[28] For references to politicization of the commodity market, see TRILATERAL COMMISSION, SEEKING A NEW ACCOMMODATION IN WORLD COMMODITY MARKET 1 (1976); C. BERGSTEN, COMPLETING THE GATT: TOWARD NEW INTERNATIONAL RULES TO GOVERN EXPORT CONTROLS (1974).

[29] For more on this trend, see MIKDASHI, *supra* note 24, at 20 n.3.

[30] *Id.* at 20. *See also When Are the British like the Arabs? When It Comes to Developing a Major Natural Resource*, FORBES, June 15, 1973, at 88. Similar concern has also been shown by European countries by restricting foreign capital; see MIKDASHI, *supra* note 24, at 21, nn. 5, 6 & 7.

has been recognized by multinational companies themselves. The president of Exxon, in the 1971 annual shareholders' meeting stated that "[i]n the future, we will see more of the government oil company, sometimes as a competitor and sometimes as a partner. . . . [W]e recognize this development as an element of changing times. We have learned to live with such government policies and such government entities."[31] Nevertheless, the important role of multinational companies cannot be ignored. The major oil companies are still responsible for approximately 80 percent of the world's oil production outside the communist bloc, own and control 70 percent of the total refining capacity, and, through long-term charter, control over 50 percent of the tonnage of international tankers.[32] While U.S. government policy in 1974 promoted the establishment of the International Energy Agency as a means of cooperation among major consumer countries, Secretary of the Interior Rogers Morton in an August 1973 address to the petroleum industry stated that "[o]ur mission is to serve you, not regulate you. . . . [I] pledge to you that the Department is at your service."[33] The strength of multinational companies is based on their size, resources, "capacity to exploit economics of scale, advanced technology, and know-how; their superior organizational and managerial ability and their unity of command; their extensive market outlets; their close interrelatedness in partnerships and in other respects; and their negotiating skills."[34] But this strength of multinationals, which formerly operated in their favor in bilateral agreements with developing countries in the pricing process, is being offset by the growing effective control of host governments over the process of resource use and by the host-state officials' improved skills in negotiation.

One may predict that in the future the role of the oil companies will be limited primarily to providing the service, organization, expertise necessary for exploitation, processing, and perhaps transportation and marketing. "The role once played by the companies in negotiating price and supply must now devolve on the

---

[31] Wall St. J., May 13, 1971, at 75, col. 1.

[32] A few years ago these figures were even higher. P. ODELL, OIL AND WORLD POWER 11 (1975).

[33] BUSINESS WEEK, July 13, 1974, at 8, *quoted in* MIKDASHI, *supra* note 24, at 41.

[34] MIKDASHI, *supra* note 24, at 36, 37–40.

governments of the consuming countries."[35] One knowledgeable observer considers some of these changes, such as conservation control, managerial training, and production quotas, to be effective in providing more equitable value distribution.[36]

C. BASIC COMMUNITY POLICIES

1. Preferred Outcomes

In the contemporary world, in which most important public decisions and private choices have multiple value effects, policies regarding the pricing process must take into account the impact upon the much larger canvas of value productions and distributions. From the standpoint of a disengaged observer, the pricing of resources may be one strategy for the fulfillment of a broader policy of the optimum production and fair and equitable distribution of human-dignity values. Pricing must be conceived, therefore, as an integral part of an overall strategy for the protection of common interests in the management of resources. While the major value most immediately at stake in this process is *wealth*, the production and distribution of other values are also ultimately and importantly at stake.[37] For this reason, economic factors cannot be the only reference points for pricing. In this respect theories about pricing, both capitalist and Marxist, are too narrow, for they do not take into account the new demands and expectations about the role of pricing.

With the increasing threat of resource scarcity, one goal of pricing should be to secure an appropriate rate of exploitation and conservation of resources at any particular moment and through time. This goal raises important issues that are ignored by the classical capitalist concept of pricing. An appropriate concern for the future world supply of resources may interfere with a free market economy. For example, it is predicted that in the future the climate is going to deteriorate with effects on agricultural production and particularly on grain production. This may require

[35] Muir, *The Changing Legal Framework of International Energy Management* 9 INT'L LAW. 605, 608 (1975).

[36] *Id. See also* Levy, *World Oil Cooperation or Economic Chaos*, 52 FOREIGN AFFAIRS 690, 693–98 (1974).

[37] For the relation of wealth value to other values, see K. POLANYI, *supra* note 2, at 46.

that the United States resort to a policy of stockpiling of grain in good harvest years against the inevitable bad years, especially since 90 percent of the global grain supply consumed out of its continent of origin comes from North America. Stockpiling is, however, against the United States policy of a free market, since it tends to stabilize prices and control profits.[38]

The effect of pricing policy on the distribution of resources and on the benefits of resource exploitation must be explicitly considered. Pricing policy should not be permitted adversely to undermine the interests of a large group of participants, especially the developing countries. Thus, with respect to pricing policies concerning oil and wheat, it is generally acknowledged that the two groups of producers of these commodities do not adequately take into account the interests of other countries.[39] The governments of many oil-consuming developing nations believe that the oil pricing system has operated only to transfer wealth to oil producers, with adverse impact on their own economies. They see a gap growing between oil-exporting developing countries and oil-consuming developing countries.[40] Oil-consuming developing countries argue that the pricing policy of oil exporters has adversely affected the consumption of oil necessary for internal development. Energy consumption has most rapidly increased in Latin America, Southeast Asia, and recently in Africa. In Malaysia and Brazil the average annual rate of growth of energy consumption over the last twenty years has been approximately 12 percent.[41] The need of developing countries for energy in the early stages of growth is obvious.[42] Brazil, with a population of 100 million in 1972, used

---

[38]*See* Schneider, review by D. Sharpey of *The Genesis Strategy*, N.Y. Times Book Review, July 18, 1976 at 3, col. 4. One can also argue that sometimes even monopoly may be necessary to make competition workable. Since in a purely competitive market firms will have deficits when demand falls below capacity, a degree of "inelasticity" in demand (identified by some other writers with monopoly power) is needed to make competition workable by allowing leeway for a flexible price policy to cope with depressions. Clark, *Towards a Concept of Workable Competition*, 30 AM. ECON. REV. 250 (1940), *quoted in* C. MULLER, LIGHT METALS MONOPOLY 12 (1946).

[39]*Oil and Wheat*, reprinted in the INT'L HERALD TRIBUNE Jan. 2, 1974, *cited in* MIKDASHI, *supra* note 24, at 73.

[40]*See* ODELL, *supra* note 32, at 93–137.

[41]*Id.* at 147.

[42]The process of rapid increase in energy consumption in the early stages of economic development is not new. The experience of the United Kingdom, Germany, France, the

only 50 million metric tons of coal, compared with the United Kingdom's population of 50 million and 325 million metric tons of coal equivalent. In 1972 the developing nations outside the communist bloc (the major oil producers excepted) consumed approximately 900 million metric tons, which was about 40 percent of the amount used in the United States in the same year.[43] The present oil pricing policy thus importantly affects both the present distribution of benefits and the potentialities of future growth.

Assessment of the costs of resource exploitation should be comprehensive; the distribution of these costs should be made in conformity to overall policy goals. This approach requires the taking into account of such factors as damage to the environment, injuries to workers, and all the other social and other costs borne in production. When production imposes costs upon nonconsenting individuals and groups who are not directly engaged in the process of production, a rational pricing policy will assess and provide accommodation for such costs.

One important goal in pricing policy is that of balancing the need for stability in expectations with that of promoting appropriate changes toward preferred public order goals. The stability of expectations to which we refer is necessary for the encouragement and maintenance of economic and other activities. The process of pricing must, however, be kept flexible enough to adapt to changing circumstances. With respect to primary products, "stability" in pricing is too often referred to as prevention of decline in prices,[44] without regard for the potentialities that might inhere in a rise in prices.

This policy of striking the balance between the needs for stability and change finds expression in international prescription. Principle 10 of the Stockholm Conference states: "For the developing countries, stability of prices and adequate earnings for primary commodities and raw materials are essential to environmental

---

United States, and other industrialized countries shows such trends. These countries generally satisfied their energy requirements by domestic coal, in contrast with present developing countries, which have to import their energy needs. *Id.* at 144.

[43] *Id.*

[44] For the history of price fluctuation over some 700 years, *see* Brown & Hopkins, *Seven Centuries of the Prices of Consumables Compared with Builders' Wages,* ECONOMICA, Nov. 1956, *cited in* CANE *supra* note 16, at 10. For the decline of the price of commodity products through 1962, see CANE, *id.* at 9.

management since economic factors as well as ecological processes must be taken into account."[45] This concern has been expressed further in the 1967 Resolution 239 of the International Bank for Reconstruction and Development:

> Considering the decisive importance of the stabilization of prices of primary products at a remunerative level for the economic advancement of the developing countries and the improvement of the standard of living of their populations, the Governors' meeting in Dakar request that an R10 study be made of the conditions in which IMF, IBRD and IDA could participate in the elaboration of suitable mechanisms involving balanced commitments on the part both of the producing and of the consuming countries, and devote the necessary resources thereto.[46]

A joint study by IMF and IBRD has demonstrated that, because of the heavy dependence of developing countries on primary products for their earnings, the range of prices and trading opportunities in the world commodities markets have important consequences for all of their internal value processes.[47] The joint study examining the market structures shows that while the prices of some of the commodities have been slow to increase, or have been decreasing, there has been a tendency for the overproduction of a number of commodities, such as coffee, cocoa, tea, sugar, bananas, cotton, and hard fibers. The study emphasizes, furthermore, that serious fluctuation in the price of commodities from developing countries has been two and a half to three times larger

---

[45] *Report of the United Nations Conference on the Human Environment*, U.N. Doc. A/CONF.48/14 (1972), *reprinted in* 11 INT'L LEGAL MATERIALS 1419 (1972).

[46] PROBLEM OF STABILIZATION, *supra* note 8, at 1. Similarly, IMF Resolution 22–9 recognized the importance of price stabilization of primary products. This concern led to a joint study by these two international organizations as to stabilization problems. *Id.*

[47] *Id.* The problem with the world market, however, is that its capacity for using these materials has grown slowly. Any increase comes at the expense of low prices. Furthermore, there are wide fluctuations in the prices of commodities. The decrease, or slow increase, in demand for primary products is also a result of technological development in synthetics and changes in consumption patterns. The study indicates that world trade in agricultural products has been held back because of the policy of industrialized countries to protect their own products. The joint study further showed that trends in the increase of some primary commodities are, however, divergent. Markets for some primaries such as petroleum, timber, iron ore, and bauxite have shown rapid growth since World War II. Some other commodities, such as rubber, cotton, wool, jute, and hard fibers, have been facing serious competition from synthetics.

than those from industrial countries. The demand of developing countries for stabilization in the price of commodities has been attacked by some developed countries. Nevertheless, the developed countries themselves have taken measures to support or stabilize their own markets.[48] Before the UNCTAD meeting of 1964 the *Economist* described the trade crisis in the third world: "The underdeveloped countries, poor as they are, have been contributing, involuntarily, to western prosperity. Since the early fifties the volume of food and agricultural products exported has risen by about a third. But in value they have increased by only a sixth and the rise in the price of manufactures has wiped out even that small gain."[49]

Whether the price fluctuations of commodities damage the growth of developing countries has caused some debate among economists. MacBean argues that the damage from short-term instability of price of commodities in developing countries has been overemphasized. There is not much evidence, he asserts, to show an interrelation between price fluctuation and damage, or that changes in the income of developing countries clearly relate to price fluctuations in commodities.[50] Similarly, another observer, studying the Chilean economy, notes that he could not find any clear relationship between stability of export earnings and growth.[51] Yet, contrary to these arguments and findings, a number of economists have observed a negative impact of price fluctuation on underdevelopment. Professor Myrdal, for example, observes: "The basic cause of export instability and the reason it is so significant lies essentially in the nature of under-development itself. Underdeveloped countries have only a limited ability to adjust supply to demand, an export list composed of one or a few major products, often a relatively high ratio of exports to national income, and a rapidly growing total of import needs; thus they are sensitive and

[48] *See* III UNCTAD PROCEEDINGS: COMMODITY TRADE (1973) at 81.

[49] THE ECONOMIST, Jan. 12, 1963, at 131, *cited in* Hager, *Commodity Agreements and Developing Countries—a Collective Bargaining Approach*, 7 INT'L LAW. 309, 316 (1973). *See also* W. LEWIS, SOME ASPECTS OF ECONOMIC DEVELOPMENT 15 (1970) and Barraclough, *The Haves and the Have Nots*, THE NEW YORK REV. OF BOOKS, May 13, 1976, at 31, 36 col. 2.

[50] A. MACBEAN, EXPORT INSTABILITY AND ECONOMIC DEVELOPMENT 339 (1966), *cited in* Hager, *id.*, at 314.

[51] Reynolds, *Domestic Consequences of Export Instability*, 53 AM. ECON. REV. 100 (1963), *cited in* Hager, *supra* note 48, at 314.

extremely vulnerable to variations in export proceeds."[52] The last argument has been supported by most economists.[53]

The adverse effects upon the growth of the developing countries would often appear to be functions both of a relative decline in the price of primary commodities and of a relative increase in the price of manufactured goods. Because of such interdependency, the pricing of all commodities should be contextually interrelated. The concept of an indexing system embodies this policy. Where the prices of a large number of important commodities, primary and manufactured, are important to both developed and developing countries, an appropriate indexing may promote pricing in the common interest. This policy rejects the concept of case-by-case (single-item) pricing as a general guide. The case-by-case system tends to neglect the function of pricing as a strategy of allocating values; its emphasis is only upon economic factors, such as the costs of production or efficiency. In other words, the case-by-case approach to pricing is too restrictive for today's required function of pricing.

The overall policies we recommend may require price differentiation when it contributes to optimum internal value processes. Price differentiation is a part of the General Scheme of Preferences (GSP).[54] The practice of granting preferences in trade is not new to international commercial activities. Historic examples include the Commonwealth Imperial Preferences, French Union Preferences, the Benelux Union of Preferences, and United States Preferences with the Philippines.[55] These bilateral preferences were continued after World War II, later being replaced by multilateral trade agreements, such as Article I of GATT, EEC practices[56] and the Lomé Convention. A system of preferences was

---

[52] G. MYRDAL, 3 ASIAN DRAMA 2200 (1968). *See also* Meier, *UNCTAD Proposals for International Economic Reform*, 19 STAN. L. REV. 1185, 1186 (1967); I. LITTLE & T. CLIFFORD, INTERNATIONAL AID 155 (1966); W. HAVILAND, INTERNATIONAL COMMODITY AGREEMENTS 52 (1963).

[53] *Id.*

[54] The Generalized System of Preferences obtained Congressional approval in the Trade Reform Act of 1974. *See* Stern, *The Accommodation of Interests Between Developed and Developing Countries*, 10 J. WORLD TRADE 405, 406 (1976).

[55] Nabudere, *The Third World and Generalized Schemes of Preferences*, 7 E. AFR. L. REV. 293 (1974).

[56] *Id.* at 294.

promoted by UNCTAD in 1968 in a resolution that requested UNCTAD to "*[e]stablish* to this end, a Special Committee on Preferences, as a subsidiary organ of the Trade and Development Board, to enable all countries concerned to participate in necessary consultations . . . [and] *[r]equested* that the aim shall be to settle details of the arrangements in the course of 1969 with a view to seeking legislative authority and required waiver in GATT as soon as possible thereafter."[57] In practice, however, this system was not received favorably by the oil-producing developing countries. OPEC members refused to establish price differentiation between oil-importing developing and developed countries because of the difficulties of sealing markets and the possibility of black markets. OPEC tried to compensate and replace price differentiation by grants and credits, which proved to be insufficient.

Dumping is one mode of price differentiation. With regard to industrial goods, contemporary policy against dumping as between industrial competitors has been effected by use of countervailing duties. Dumping as a strategy for incapacitating primary producers does not appear, however, to have stimulated appropriate inclusive prescription. From the standpoint of goal clarification, optimum community order would appear to be secured by a more supple set of guidelines. The recommended policies promote the contextual use of price differentiation to secure all more fundamental community goals. As consistently emphasized, we recommend a disciplined configurative consideration of the consequences of different prices at different times in different contexts. This policy would prohibit differential pricing that weakens or destroys inclusively demanded development; yet it would promote differential pricing that contributes to the realization of demanded development plans.

One important function of pricing, as mentioned earlier, is the distribution of values not necessarily arising from some particular exploitation of resources. This function may require pricing practices whose effects can only be assessed contextually. In general, it is suggested that alternative pricing practices be evaluated in terms of their aggregate value and public order effects. These alternative pricing modalities may involve varying degrees of "economic coercion," implemented through high prices of commodities and goods, boycott, cutbacks in production, or embargo. These prac-

---

[57] *See* I UNCTAD Proceedings Vol. 1 (1968), at 38.

tices are available not only to producers but also to consumers. While general community prescriptions oppose these alternative pricing systems, there has been a long history of such practices. The position we take, however, is that the ultimate outcome of alternative pricing systems is the appropriate test of the legitimacy of such pricing policies.

2. Allocation of Competence

The most important—that is, urgent and controversial—issue in a constitutive process about pricing relates to the participants in the pricing process. The most general policy we recommend is that all who are affected by the prices of resources and commodities should have competence to participate in the pricing process and be made responsible to the more inclusive community decision. This means that both producers and consumers be made responsible participants. Categorization of participants in these terms is, however, rather artificial; most communities are both producers and consumers, the producers of some commodities being the consumers of other commodities and vice versa. In the present practices of international trade, countries tend to categorize themselves into these two groups on different commodities in the hope of better securing their interests.

The policy we recommend is for wider representation of both producers and consumers in the pricing process. With respect to vital resources, that is, resources whose use has wide inclusive impact, the competence to appraise prices should be as inclusive and representative as possible. This policy would promote the participation not only of governments but also of prvale associations, such as corporations, in the pricing process. Private associations can perform useful and important functions in terms of intelligence, promotion, and even application of pricing policies.

With respect to primary products, primary producers might be accorded an initial competence to set prices subject to review. This initial competence for primary producers might be honored because of their total or high dependence on a single commodity. This preliminary preference for primary producers may also be justified because they can have no control over a number of other factors related to the ultimate value of their commodities in developed countries. Such factors include the future real growth of production and income in the industrial countries, changes in taste of consumers, and competition by synthetic materials, which affect the demands for and the prices of their commodities.

The policies we recommend promote the effective participation of those most affected by the pricing process. Sometimes, to make their participation more effective, participants with little power may organize as groups in an effort to deal more as equals with market forces. Such participation has been promoted in the practices by developing countries as well as in the search for new international and national prescriptions. Some of these groups are referred to as "producers' association." While such associations in formal and organized form have been established by producers of raw materials for several decades, consumer countries are also familiar with comparable practices through their corporations and informal arrangements between governments. The establishment of opposing associations by consumers has been condemned by producers. Producers justify their own associations as the only strategy that can put them on a more equal footing with the consumers in pricing processes. They regard, therefore, any attempt by consumers to organize themselves as destroying fair representation.

A preferred policy might be one that promoted the practices of producers' associations. The functions of these associations are quite extensive: they are not only a means for equalizing the power basis of producers and consumers in the present market structure, but also they perform useful intelligence, promotion, prescription, and application functions among the producers, who have limited ability singly to reach these results. Questions about lawfulness or unlawfulness should, accordingly, be related not to the existence of the producers' associations as a totality but rather to their particular practices in the exercise of their newly found power.

The well-being of the people of the world cannot of course be left to the unilateral discretion of a single bloc of countries, whether they are developed or developing, producers or consumers. Freedom of choice and representation in the process of decision making must be overriding goals in a preferred world public order of human dignity. Any hegemony which destroys this freedom must be condemned as latter-day imperialism, whether it is practiced by producers or consumers. The traditional "free market" in world commodities has never adequately protected this freedom of choice. It is conceivable, however, that a contemporary global constitutive process might be able to achieve a balancing between inclusive and exclusive competences, as well as the procedures for careful, contextual evaluation in particular instances of decision, which could enhance that freedom.

D. TRENDS IN DECISION

Pricing, in the sense that we employ the term, is a technique of social control for regulating timing, location, and the like as well as allocating benefits and values in the exploitation of resources. This technique embraces a whole range of options, from consensual to administered or coercive arrangements, and exhibits many differing degrees of government involvement. It has always been used, though not always effectively or rationally, to promote the policies of the effective decision makers in a community. The tolerance on the part of the effective participants in the world constitutive process in according differing degrees of exclusive or inclusive competence in states about pricing has varied with particular situations. The types of pricing policy commonly described as "monopoly" and "competition" existed more than 4,000 years ago in Babylon.[58] In practice, however, "monopoly" and "competition" seldom represent accurate descriptions of pricing practice; they express the extremes, from the most limited to the widest participation. Pricing is an activity that, as indicated, may be left to "market" accommodation with varying degrees of governmental participation or may be highly governmentalized within a community. Though private and governmental participation in pricing has varied greatly throughout history, today, on a global scale, governmental participation in pricing is increasing. Moreover, the more comprehensive constitutive process of authoritative decision is becoming increasingly explicit in its establishment and protection of exclusive, partially inclusive, and inclusive competences with regard to pricing.

1. Exclusive Competence over Pricing

By *exclusive competence*[59] as to pricing we refer to the competence of any particular nation-state to make and apply laws about the

[58] MACHLUP, *supra* note 26, at 181.

[59] The terms *inclusive* and *exclusive* may be employed to refer to both the process of

pricing of the goods and services produced through the exploitation of its internal resources. The officials of a nation-state may of course themselves directly participate in pricing activities either alone or in collaboration with various private participants. Conversely, private participants may play a role in the making of law through their cooperative activity, which creates expectations about authority and control. In the relative absence of inclusive prescriptions limiting the exclusive competence of the state, it has commonly been assumed that the competence of particular states is comprehensive and largely unfettered. This assumption would appear to be confirmed both by historic practice and by contemporary inclusive pronouncements.

Yet, however broad their competence, nation-states have not effectively regulated the practices of their corporations and other enterprises in the pricing process. This lack of effective regulation has stemmed from a number of factors, such as conceptions about the relevance of governmental participation, economic activities, contending political and other ideologies, and appropriate exercise of state competence. The actual decisions about price determination have been made mainly by private enterprise. Private corporations, commonly in groups, have effectively controlled the pricing process. Historically, their practices have been known as cartels.[60] The word *cartel* was first used by the German Reichstag

---

decision and to the process of use by which resources are exploited. For an exposition of this terminology see M. McDougal, H. Lasswell & I. Vlasic, Law and Public Order in Space 153–57 (1963). The references are intended to be descriptive only, not preferential.

By *inclusive competence* we refer to a process of decision exhibiting multiple participants. When we add the adjective "partially," we note specialized characteristics of the participants which may preclude a full representation of interests. Thus, an organized process of decision, such as that employed by OPEC, though including multiple participants, may be constituted only of producers and not consumers. When an organized process of decision admits representation of all interests, as in commodity agreements, the adjective "partially" is not employed.

It is recognized, of course, that while a process of decision may be inclusive in terms of the number of participants who play a role in the making and applying of law, the outcomes of the decisions taken may or may not be inclusive in their impact. They may be exclusive in the impact and even detrimental to larger inclusive interests, such as the interests of a larger number of states or of the aggregate community. Our terminology is designed for the more precise description of such differences, in the hope of promoting a more rational clarification of community policy.

[60] For references to cartels see F. Cheney, Cartels, Combines and Trusts (1944); A Cartel Policy for the United Nations (Edwards ed. 1945); *Report of the Ad Hoc Committee on Restrictive Business Practices*, U.N. Doc. E/2380, E/AC.37/3 (1953); E. Hexner, Interna-

to refer to monopolistic activity,[61] and the concept was later developed more comprehensively for opposing a policy of competition.[62] While both *cartel* and *monopoly* generally refer to the same types of practices, historically the latter was the term first used to imply the economic exploitation of poor by rich.[63] The term *cartel* has now acquired a negative connotation associated again with the domination of the "have-nots" by the "haves."[64] The connotations implied as well as the explicitness of the terminology affect all its uses. This may explain why the League of Nations, in referring to cartels used the phrase "industrial agreements,"[65] while the United Nations employs "restrictive business practices." The changes in terms for describing exclusive participation in the pricing process may have no substantial impact upon the structure and practice of the institution, but they may reflect an attempt to change its objective or to change prior assessments of unlawfulness.

In cartels, private, governmental, or mixed enterprises seek to dominate markets by agreement. Thus, cartels are defined as "voluntary agreements among independent enterprises in a single industry or closely related industries with the purpose of exercising a monopolistic control of the market."[66] Similarly, Edward Mason defines cartels thus: "Cartels, in the narrow—and proper—sense, are agreements between firms with respect to the production and marketing of their products. Typically, cartel agreements aim at the restriction of output or sales by the member firms, at an allo-

---

TIONAL CARTELS (1945); A. PLUMMER, INTERNATIONAL COMBINES IN MODERN INDUSTRY (1951); G. STOCKING & M. WALTINS, CARTELS OR COMPETITION? (1948); *Foreign Legislation Concerning Monopoly and Cartel Practices* 82d Cong. 2d Sess. 14 (1952); K. PRIBRAM, CARTEL PROBLEMS (1935); A. GORDON, THE PROBLEM OF TRUST AND MONOPOLY (1928); H. KRONSTEIN, THE LAW OF INTERNATIONAL CARTELS (1973); C. EDWARDS, CONTROL OF CARTELS AND MONOPOLIES: AN INTERNATIONAL COMPARISON (1967); N. MEDVIN, THE ENERGY CARTEL: WHO RUNS THE AMERICAN OIL INDUSTRY? (1974); and Streeten, *The Dynamics of the New Poor Power*, in HELLEINER, *supra* note 21, at 77–88.

[61] HEXNER, *id.* at 3.

[62] PRIBRAM, *supra* note 60, at 6.

[63] HAUSSMANN & AHEARN, *International Cartels and World Trade: An Explanatory Note*, reprinted from THOUGHT, 19 FORD. U. L.Q. 421, 430 (1944).

[64] The *New York Times* has noted that the word *cartel* has become a pejorative label. N.Y. Times, Sept. 14, 1943, at 16, col. 1, *quoted in* HEXNER, *supra* note 60, at 7.

[65] HEXNER, *id.*, at 8.

[66] *Id.* at 1.

cation of market territories between firms, and a fixing of the price of their products."[67] The expansion of the cartel practices from marketing agreements to patents and process exchange agreements between firms in different countries has often been noted.[68] Hexner, emphasizing market manipulations, defines a cartel as a "voluntary, potentially impermanent, business relationship among a number of independent, private entrepreneurs, which through coordinated marketing significantly affects the market of a commodity or service."[69] Fritz Machlup refers to cartels as "[b]usiness arrangements which have the purpose or effect of reducing or regulating competition."[70] The League of Nations emphasizing the objectives, offered this definition:

> Cartels are associations of independent undertakings in the same or similar branches of industry established by a view to improving conditions of production and sale.[71]

Despite all the negative connotations of "cartel" and "monopoly," both economic writers and, upon occasion, authors of inclusive prescriptions have offered a more objective appraisal of their purposes. Karl Pribram has said that the effects of cartels—"favorable or prejudicial—upon the production and distribution of goods, upon the general economic structure, and upon the distribution of income are variously assessed."[72] Again, the World Economic Conference of 1927 (Geneva), referring to cartels, stated:

> The phenomenon of such agreements, arising from economic necessities, does not constitute a matter upon which any conclusions of principles need be reached, but a development which has to be recognized and which from its practical point of view must be considered as good or bad according to the spirit which rules the constitution and the operation of the agreements, and in particular according to the measures in which those directing them are actuated by a sense of general interest.[73]

[67] E. Mason, Economic Concentration and Monopoly Problem 73 (1957).

[68] *Id.* at 74.

[69] Hexner, *supra* note 60, at 24. *See also* Stocking & Waltins, *supra* note 60, at 3; Arnold, *Cartels or Free Enterprise?* Public Affairs Pamphlet No. 103 (1945) at 5.

[70] Machlup, *supra* note 26, at 3.

[71] Haussmann & Ahearn, *supra* note 63, at 10.

[72] Primbram, *supra* note 60, at 1.

[73] Haussmann & Ahearn, *supra* note 63, at 422.

Another writer, referring to the objectives and ultimate impact of cartels on the common interest, has said: "Thus the monopolist has power for good or ill; he may turn to productive uses energies formerly absorbed in the competitive struggle; or he may drift, through security and the power of extortion, into wasteful and absolute methods of production."[74] Finally, Kronstein insists that it is only the malevolent, or unique kind of cartel which has the purpose "to discriminate against, or to exclude from the market, a specific enterprise, whereas in other types of cartels the discrimination or exclusion is only a device to accomplish a regulation of the market."[75]

The trends in practice concerning cartels, as with most social institutions, establish clearly that final judgment on cartels should be based mainly upon ultimate consequences for value production and distribution and the degree of conformity to or deviation from community goals. In general, however, it may be said that private cartels have not left a good record in this respect. The pricing processes with respect to raw materials, and particularly oil resources, have never been competitive. There has always been a deliberate control of supply, with determination of price level, by international oil companies.[76] Contrary to the assertions of the oil companies, the noncompetitive nature of this industry has been generally recognized. Leeman and Mikdashi emphasize that the joint approaches and vertical integration among oil companies diminished competition;[77] hence, neither demand nor supply has been particularly responsive to the "price mechanism."[78]

The idea of comprehensive control over oil resources began with the multinational oil companies. All the leading companies were involved at one time or another in the promotion of this idea. The most active participants, however, were Standard Oil Com-

---

[74]*Id.* Mason observes that the primary objective of cartels is to increase prices by restricting participation and competition. Cartels would no longer continue, he observes, if "prices and output under cartelization were not more satisfactory to participating members than they could be with competition." MASON, *supra* note 67, at 78. *See also* B. WALLACE & L. EDMINSTER, INTERNATIONAL CONTROL OF RAW MATERIALS 17–25 (1930).

[75] KRONSTEIN, *supra* note 60, at 142–43.

[76] For the description of early control of supply of oil by oil companies, see PENROSE, *supra* note 26, at 150–75.

[77] *See* MIKDASHI, *supra* note 24, at 70; LEEMAN, *supra* note 26, at 6–44.

[78] I. HARTSHORN, OIL COMPANIES AND GOVERNMENTS 117 (1962).

pany of New Jersey, Shell, and Anglo-Persian. But monopoly control over oil resources was not accomplished immediately. In the beginning the companies were too busy expanding the industry and meeting the rapid growth in demand, which more than doubled between 1919 and 1926.[79] In several countries the companies had price fixing agreements that were not taken entirely seriously.[80] In the late 1920s the major oil companies realized that price competition was not profitable to any of them and should be avoided in the future. In order to organize the joint pricing policies of the oil companies, secret conferences were sponsored through the summer of 1929. The conclusive meeting at Achnacarry Home brought about an agreement for setting up an international oil cartel.[81] With the official title of the Pool Association of September 17, 1928 (usually called the Achnacarry Agreement), this agreement covered the pricing process over the entire world outside the United States and the Soviet Union.[82] It required a quota system for each market and a formula for price fixing. To implement the agreement, two American export associations were set up to allocate the total American quota among various companies involved. One was the Standard Oil Export Corporation formed in December 1928, which consisted of Jersey Standard and five of its subsidiaries. The second was the Export Petroleum Association, formed in early 1929, which included Standard Oil Export Corporation and sixteen other major American exporters.[83] Standard was a link between the American and the European industries.[84]

A "Gulf plus" system was agreed on as the basis for pricing. Under this system, the price of oil should be the same in every export center throughout the world as in the American ports along the Gulf of Mexico. The final cost at the delivery point, however, depended upon its distance from the Gulf of Mexico and

[79] C. TUGENDHAT & A. HAMILTON, OIL: THE BIGGEST BUSINESS 97 (rev. ed. 1975).

[80] *Id.* at 98.

[81] FEDERAL TRADE COMMISSION, THE INTERNATIONAL PETROLEUM CARTEL 198–99 (1952) [hereinafter cited as FEDERAL TRADE COMMISSION].

[82] For an outline of the agreement, see *id.* at 200; see also R. ENGLER, THE POLITICS OF OIL 70–72 (1961).

[83] FEDERAL TRADE COMMISSION, *supra* note 81, at 202.

[84] *Id.*

on whether the buyer was a member of the cartel.[85] This system required the customer oil companies outside the cartel to pay the Gulf price plus the cost of shipping the oil from the United States to the point of delivery. It made no difference whether the supply came from a field closer to the destination than that of the Gulf of Mexico. In such situations, extra profits went to the cartel. Obviously, the Gulf pricing system did not take into account the interest of consumers whose oil was shipped from a nearer port; its basic objective was the maximization of the profit of the cartel members. It has been observed that the reason for such a pricing system was that major oil companies had their principal assets invested in the United States. The United States was the major oil producer in the 1930s and 1940s, and, therefore, it was to its benefit to maintain the largest possible market for American oil. Thus, the higher prices for the Middle East oil not only did not hurt the American oil because it had the same price, but they also secured more profits for the cartel because the prices were significantly higher than the cost of transportation.[86]

At the same time the Pool Association was formed in 1929, there was a similar attempt to control production and lessen competition in the United States. This attempt did not succeed because the Attorney General refused to cooperate.[87] From 1930 until World War II three other agreements on control of the pricing process similar to Achnacarry Principles were agreed upon, such as the 1930 Memorandum for European Markets, 1932 Heads of Agreements for Distribution, and the 1934 Draft Memorandum of Principles.[88] The last was made in great secrecy and only the most senior officials were allowed to know all the plan's details. This agreement covered all countries outside North America. A central committee was established in London to control the operation by making separate agreements for each particular market and encouraging other companies to join them.[89] This exclusive control over pricing was not entirely successful. Its proponents could not persuade all companies to join in order to get the major portion of

[85] TUGENDHAT & HAMILTON, *supra* note 79, at 102.

[86] *Id.* at 104.

[87] FEDERAL TRADE COMMISSION, *supra* note 81, at 210–11.

[88] *Id.* at 228–68.

[89] TUGENDHAT & HAMILTON, *supra* note 79, at 109–11.

control. The majors further had difficulty at times in accommodating the policies of their subsidiaries in different countries.
Above all, governments have become increasingly involved in the
oil pricing process.[90] The elimination of formal cartel agreements
among oil companies came after World War II. Nonetheless, their
control over oil supplies and their informal mutual understanding
and consensus about pricing policy to maximize their own profits
remained.[91]

The actual structure of the oil industry outside the United States
reached its present state in the late 1940s and early 1950s, when
the political and economic influence of the United States was un-
challenged, thanks in part to the cooperation between the State
Department and the oil companies.[92] Through this mutual cooperation, the seven majors owned 65 percent of the world's estimated crude oil reserves and controlled more than 92 percent of
the estimated crude reserves outside the United States, Mexico,
and Russia in 1949.[93] In the same year the seven majors accounted
for more than one-half of the world's crude production excluding
Russia and satellite countries, about 96 percent of the production
in the Eastern Hemisphere, and about 45 percent in the Western
Hemisphere.[94] In 1950 the crude oil refining capacity of the world
was also largely controlled by the seven majors. They controlled
about 57 percent of the world's crude oil refining capacity, held
more than 75 percent in the Western Hemisphere excluding the
United States, and held 77 percent of the rest of the world's crude
oil refinery capacity.[95]

Control over the cracking process in oil production is more important economically than control over crude oil refining. Cracking is a prorcess by which heavy hydrocarbons are broken up by
heat into lighter products, yielding a greater quantity of more
highly valued products and produces many of the chemicals which
are the basic raw materials for synthetic rubber and many plastics.

[90] *Id.*

[91] ODELL, *supra* note 32, at 15.

[92] T. RIFAI, THE PRICING OF CRUDE OIL 3 (1974). *See also* A. SAMPSON, THE SEVEN SISTERS:
THE GREAT OIL COMPANIES AND THE WORLD THEY MADE 185–207 (1975).

[93] FEDERAL TRADE COMMISSION, *supra* note 81, at 23

[94] *Id.* at 24.

[95] *Id.* at 25.

This process, therefore, makes the petroleum industry an important supplier of products for other industries, and control over this process affects a broader segment of the world economy than control over refining.[96] In 1950 the control of the seven major oil companies over the cracking process was stronger than their control over the refining process. The majors owned 47 percent of the U.S. cracking capacity, 53 percent of the Western Hemisphere, 84 percent of the Eastern Hemisphere, and 55 percent of the total world.[97] Excluding the United States and the U.S.S.R. and its satellites, the seven majors held 85 percent of all cracking capacity of the rest of the world and 77 percent of the crude-refining capacity.[98]

The control of transportation of oil resources was also long concentrated in the seven major oil companies. They owned more than 50 percent of the world's tanker fleet in 1950[99] and all of the important pipelines outside the United States.[100] In a study by the U.S. Federal Trade Commission, it is stated that in no industry is the control over marketing as concentrated as it is in the oil industry.[101] The study notes that it is "a rule, rather than the exception, for petroleum products to move from producer to consumer by company-owned facilities within one corporate hierarchy."[102]

The effective control of the major oil companies over the pro-

[96] *Id.*

[97] *Id.*

[98] *Id.* at 26.

[99] *Id.* at 27.

[100] *Id.* For the importance of petroleum pipelines outside the United States, see WORLD PETROLEUM, Apr. 1950, at 63, *cited in id.* at 28.

[101] FEDERAL TRADE COMMISSION, *supra* note 81, at 280–348.

[102] *Id.* at 28. The report states that "control of the industry by these seven companies [Standard Oil Co. of California, Socony-Vacuum Oil Co. Inc., Gulf Oil Corp., and the Texas Co.—and two British-Dutch companies—Anglo-Iranian Oil Co., Ltd., and the Royal Dutch-Shell group] extends from reserves through production, transportation, refining, and marketing. All seven engage in every state of operations, from exploration to marketing. The typical movement of petroleum from producer until acquired by the final consumer is through inter-company transfer within a corporate family. Out-right sales, arms-length bargaining, and other practices characteristic of independent buyers and sellers are conspicuous by their absence. Control is held through direct corporate holdings, by parents, subsidiaries, and affiliates of the seven, but also through such indirect means as interlocking directorates, joint ownership of affiliates' intercompany crude purchase contracts, and marketing agreements."

cess of use of oil resources was promoted through integration by contracts or joint ownership. For example, in the 1960 oil consortium operating in Iran, five of the member companies were shareholders of companies operating in Iraq, four in Saudi Arabia, and two with special contracts involving three of the others in Kuwait.[103] Joint operation in production is only one kind of integration. Integration in the refining, marketing, and transportation processes is equally important.[104]

The effective exclusive control of the oil companies is known to have led to abuse of their power over the pricing process, as well as to the promotion of unjustifiable political and other special interests of the companies and their home governments.[105] The companies' reduction of oil prices in 1959 and 1960, for example, was interpreted as their sanction against Venezuela's imposition of additional taxes on concessionary profits and as a strategy to influence the outcomes of the claims and controversies between Iraq and the Iraqi Petroleum Company.[106] The 1951 boycott by the oil companies of Iranian oil because of the nationalization of the Anglo-Iranian Oil Company is another example of such abuse of their exclusive control. The effective power of the major oil companies over pricing not only excluded the authority and control of the producers for participation in this process, but also excluded any opportunity for increasing numbers of oil consumers to have any say in the process.

India was one of the exceptional countries able to participate in price adjustments on its imported oil. The opportunity for India became available through support by the Soviet Union of an Indian position. The oil companies, while providing India with Persian Gulf oil, charged it on the Gulf price basis. India, a poor developing country, had no other choice but to accept that unilateral pricing policy until 1960, when the Soviet Union offered to sell oil at prices 20 percent less than the delivered price of Middle

[103] Hartshorn, *supra* note 78, at 152.

[104] *Id.* at 117, 152. In 1960 in the United Kingdom, the Republic of Ireland, the Near East, many African territories, and Ceylon, Shell and British Petroleum engaged in joint marketing and occasionally in joint refining as *Shell-Mex* and *BP*; Standard of California and the Texas Company did so in most countries of the Eastern Hemisphere as *Caltex*. Until the end of 1960 Jersey and Mobil also worked together in Africa. *Id.* at 153.

[105] *See* M. Tanzer, The Political Economy of the Oil Industry (1969).

[106] D. Hirst, Oil and Public Opinion in the Middle East 43 (1966).

East oil offered by the majors. As a result of this offer from the Soviet Union, and in addition to the establishment of a national oil company, the Indian government demanded lower oil prices from the oil companies.[107] After the threat by the government, the oil companies decreased the price of oil, and since then there have been several adjustments in prices. The Indian government, however, is one of the very few exceptions among the developing consuming countries that have been able to participate in the pricing of oil imports.

The major oil companies, the most effective participants in the pricing process, at least until 1971, have always avoided a constructive and rational study about how and on what basis this process operates. While this lack of information is ostensibly about the international market, it exists even within the U.S. national oil industry itself:

> Even inside the American oil industry, which has the most elaborate price reporting and statistical series of any oil business in the world, it is not easy to get rational discussion of the way in which these prices are in fact formed. In the United States, the spectre of antitrust proceedings broods over any such discussion, and its shadow extends wherever in the world American companies operate. Even so, it is notable and unfortunate that up to now, most international oil companies, in particular, have left almost all the serious discussion of price formation in the international oil business to their critics—usually contenting themselves with the claim that oil pricing is the result of "competition," naively defined.[108]

While there may be some competition between the oil companies in the U.S. market, the competition referred to is not in pricing. This kind of competition, known as "nonprice" competition, refers to competition at the refining stage for research and production of more complicated and lucrative products.[109]

---

[107] ODELL, *supra* note 32, at 149.

[108] HARTSHORN, *supra* note 78, at 128.

[109] Hartshorn states that one of the characteristics of "nonprice" competition is the use of advertising to express the goodwill and interest of the oil companies in the well-being of their customers and the claims for new and better products. Such nonpecuniary competition is actually competitive in quality: "It steadily helps to increase the technical efficiency with which the consumer can use the fuel, though sometimes at a significant cost in the technical efficiency with which the refinery that produces the fuel is run. It gives the consumer higher quality at the same price without offering him the choice of the same quality

Cartel practices are common, not only in primary products, but also in industrial products. Some of the important operating cartels between the two world wars involved such products. The role and objective of these cartels between the wars and after World War II were quite different. The primary objective of the cartels between the wars was the prevention of decline in prices, production, and sales.[110] After World War II, however, these cartels served, in the words of one writer, "either as a bridge during a transition period of technological or economic development or as a means to protect large investments against the flow of further dynamic development. . . . [E]very further disintegration of world markets, as the result of the balance-of-payments or similar political economic reasons, encourages new steps toward industrial products cartels."[111] In March 1969, for example, after a negotiation between the U.S. government and European and Japanese steel producers, an agreement was concluded for a voluntary export quota for 1969.[112] Another example of this kind of cartel is the cartel of the producers of fertilizer. In 1962 Nitrex, a European export association, was established to deal with American and Japanese competition.[113] This association, however, has not been successful in price stabilization. After studying the role of corporations in the pricing of manufactures and semimanufactures of developing countries, UNCTAD concluded that their role involved:

> (a) The fixing of prices for particular markets of the products exported and imported;
>
> (b) Collusive tendering in respect of import tenders called by developing countries; that is, agreements as to who will trade, in what amounts, and what prices;

---

at a lower price, which sets up a kind of technocratic criterion, and tells the customer what is best for him." *Id.* at 156. This kind of competition in marketing is backed by a considerable amount of nonprice competition at a further remove from the integrated operations of the industry.

[110] KRONSTEIN, *supra* note 60, at 119.

[111] *Id.*

[112] *See* THE ECONOMIST Jan. 18, 1969, at 68–69, *cited in id.* at 120. This agreement was concluded because of the American threat of mandatory import quota legislation.

[113] *See* C. EDWARDS, CARTELIZATION IN WESTERN EUROPE (1964), *cited in* KRONSTEIN *supra* note 60, at 127. For more discussion of this kind of cartel, see *id.* at 119–41.

(c) Allocation of markets for exports and imports to particular members of the arrangements;

(d) Co-operation with regard to the manufacture of products, for example, through the mutual exchange of technology, agreements on the level of production and specialization of activities amongst members; and

(e) Collective action to enforce the arrangements agreed upon.[114]

The unilateral control of private corporations over the pricing process has always to some degree concerned national governments. Such concern has, however, mainly been with regard to finding appropriate ways to exercise their authority over the activities of such corporations to protect primarily their national interests. The antitrust laws, or regulations of restrictive business practices, are well-known national prescriptions toward this end. The notion of antitrust law is of American origin. The American vision of a self-regulating market system led to the development of antitrust law to prevent the interference with that system.[115] One of the first, though unsuccessful, American antitrust suits against the American corporations operating overseas was brought in 1953. The Federal government brought a civil suit against five multinational oil companies, owned largely by United States citizens, because of the participation of these companies in the Iranian consortium.[116] This case, known as the *Cartel Case*, was never brought to trial. The legal ground for dismissal of the case was based on an opinion of the Attorney General that the participation of the five American oil companies in the Iranian consortium did not violate the American antitrust law. An underlying political reason, however, was to preclude any disruption of the world oil supply. After the Korean boom and the Iranian nationalization, demand grew for oil resources by American allies in Western Europe. The closing of the Suez Canal, which threatened the supply

---

[114] U.N.Doc. TD/185/Supp. 2 (1976) at 7.

[115] *See generally* Fugate, *An Overview of Antitrust Enforcement and the Multinational Corporation*, 8 J. INT'L L. & ECON. 1 (1973); Victor, *Multinational Corporations—Antitrust Extraterritoriality and the Prospect of Immunity*, *id.*, at 11; Smith, *Cartels and the Shield of Ignorance*, *id* at 53–84. For national laws of antitrust see EDWARDS, note 60, *supra*.

[116] United States v. Standard Oil Co., Socony-Vacuum Oil Company, Inc., Standard Oil Company of California, the Texas Company, Gulf Oil Corporation, No. 82–87, published in EMERGENCY OIL LIFT PROGRAM pt. 3, *cited in* LEEMAN, *supra* note 26, at 153.

of Western Europe, caused the United States to give antitrust immunity to the oil companies in order not to interrupt the supply of Western Europe.[117]

Cartel practices have long fared differently in Europe. Contrary to attitudes in the United States and Canada,[118] the prohibition of restrictive business practices was rare in Europe until after World War II. During the French Revolution, France enacted penal provisions against monopoly business practices to fix prices at noncompetitive levels.[119] In 1884 pressure groups to protect business sought a judicial interpretation of the above prescription and supplemented this with an amendment in 1926.[120] In Germany some publicists observed that the constitutional guarantee of freedom of contract invalidates any prescription which prohibits cartel contracts.[121] The opposing view comes from Biendenkopf, who insists that, indeed, regulating cartels is the constitutional guarantee of "contractual freedom which demands an 'order of free determination of the individual, protected against unlicensed interference from private powers.'"[122] The British Minister of Reconstruction declared in 1944 that, although cartels' activities are not necessarily against the public interest, the power so to be is nonetheless present.[123] Similarly, in other European countries there were shifts over time for and against cartel practices, but in general there was no serious attempt against restrictive practices such as the one in the United States.[124]

In most developing countries, because of a policy of government ownership, cartel practices, particularly as related to international

[117]K. Brewster, Antitrust and American Business Abroad 4 (1958).

[118]For antitrust law in Canada, see L. Reynolds, The Control of Competition in Canada (1940).

[119]Edwards, *supra* note 60, at 3–4.

[120]*Id.*

[121]*See* Huber, Die Verfassungsproblematik Eines Kartellverbots, Gutachten 10 (1955); Geiger, Grundgesetzliche Schranken für Eine Kartellgesetzgebung 6 (1955), *cited in* Kronstein, *A Symposium on Trade Regulation and Practices*, 11 Vand. L. Rev. 271, 272 (1958).

[122]H. Biedenkopf, Freiheitliche Ordnung Durch Kartellverbot, Aktuelle Grundsatzfragen des Kartellrechts (1957) *cited in* Kronstein, *id.* at 272–73.

[123]Para. 54 of the White Paper on Employment Policy, The Times (London) May 27, 1944 *cited in* Edwards, *supra* note 60, at 9.

[124]Edwards, *supra* note 113, at 3.

cartels, have not been subjected to national regulation. This has created a number of problems. A study by UNCTAD IV shows that the absence of controls on cartel activity has, in certain cases, led subsidiaries in developing countries to become parties to national and international cartel arrangements in developed countries. For example, Bridon, the subsidiary of the United Kingdom in Mexico, is a party to the export cartels in the United Kingdom in the field of wire ropes and the associated international cartel arrangements.[125] In addition, it appears that transnational corporations in developing countries have established import cartels, which these corporations operate in developed countries. The study asserts: "As such, the cartels represent not a defensive response to the existence of oligopoly and monopoly power but a reenforcement of such power."[126]

Taxing is one way of indirect participation by governments in the pricing process. A primary objective of taxation on commodities is ordinarily to increase the income of the states. The taxing power may, nevertheless, be deliberately used for other purposes, and its exercise always affects the price of goods and services. The taxation by primary producers of their raw materials can be effectively aimed toward a redistribution of the economic values arising from exploitation of their resources. By the end of 1960s this kind of taxation had achieved significant increase in the foreign exchange of producing developing countries. In Chile, with respect to copper production, the Braden Company was paying the Chilean government 1 percent of the gross sales value, as taxes, over the period of 1913–24.[127] This tax during 1930–39 was less than 6 percent but reached 64 percent by 1953 through government action.[128] In the early oil concessions in the Middle East, tax exemption of the concessionaire was almost a common practice. The only exception was the concession between Iraq and IPC of

[125] *See* ROYAL MONOPOLIES COMMISSION, WIRE AND FIBRE ROPES: A REPORT ON THE SUPPLY AND EXPORTS OF WIRE ROPE AND FIBRE ROPE AND CORDAGE (1973) *cited in* U.N. Doc. TD/185/Supp. 2 (1976) at 18.

[126] U.N.Doc. TD/185/Supp. 2 (1976) at 16.

[127] Mamalakis, *Contribution of Copper to Chilean Economic Development, 1920–1967: Profits of a Foreign-Owned Export Sector*, in FOREIGN INVESTMENT IN THE PETROLEUM AND MINERAL INDUSTRIES 38 (R. Mikesell ed. 1971).

[128] *Id.*

1925.[129] Some of the earlier concessions with sheikhs of the Persian Gulf were silent on the question of taxation mainly because the imposition of taxes was unknown to those areas.[130] Getty's concession in the Neutral Zone (1949) in Article 49 laid down the principle of freedom from taxation for the company and its property.[131]

From the beginning, the imposition of taxes on oil resources was achieved either through the unilateral action of the host governments or through negotiations with the concessionaires. Taxation was introduced as a part of the concept of equal sharing advocated by the oil producers. The first legislation taxed the profits of oil companies and was enacted in Saudi Arabia in accordance with a Royal Decree of December 27, 1950.[132] This Decree provided an income tax on companies engaged in production of hydrocarbons, the tax amounting from 20 percent to 50 percent of their net operating income. Kuwait and Bahrein followed a similar policy.[133] A Kuwait Decree of December 1951 established an income tax equal to 50 percent of the income of corporations operating in the production and marketing of oil. Bahrein's Decree, which was similar to those of Qatar and Iraq, in 1952 imposed a 50 percent tax on oil profits.[134] Iran and Abu Dhabi implemented similar formulas in their concessions through negotiations.[135] Venezuela enacted 50/50 tax legislation from 1948 to 1958. By 1958 Venezuela had increased its taxes to some 70 percent of the profit realized.[136] As between the oil companies and the host governments the tax formula has not always meant the same thing. The formula has depended on particular concessions. The terms of each 50/50 agreement determined what items were to be accepted as allowa-

[129] H. Cattan, The Evolution of oil Concessions in the Middle East and North Africa 43 (1967).

[130] *Id.*

[131] *Id.* at 44.

[132] Royal Decree No. 17/2/28/7634 (Riyadh, Saudi Arabia, 1950).

[133] *See* Z. Mikdashi, A Financial Analysis of Middle Eastern Oil Concessions, 1901–1965, 390 (1966).

[134] *See* Cattan, *supra* note 129, at 45; see also B. Shwadran, The Middle East, Oil and the Great Powers 260 (1959).

[135] Shwadran, *id.* at 398–99.

[136] Hartshorn, *supra* note 78, at 177.

ble costs before computing profits in the host country and whether certain items of expenditures were expenses against current earnings or capitalized or amortized over a longer period.[137] In 1953 the system of 50/50 taxing was made clearer. The Arabian tax, for example, was based on profits on sales at posted prices to parent companies and it made the 50/50 profit system somewhat larger than American taxes would have been on the same basis of income and profit.[138] Hartshorn concluded that 50/50 profit sharing presented largely a transfer of tax revenue from the treasuries of the United States and England to those of the Middle Eastern countries, and the companies became the channel for this transfer without substantial changes in their own income.[139] The French and Dutch tax laws at that time, however, excluded the profits made by their subjects abroad from tax; therefore, the 50/50 arrangement cost those companies more than the Americans.[140] In this taxing system, the posted prices remained as the basis for tax formulation. During the 1960s an oil surplus kept the posted prices up while the actual prices were lower through discounts. The result

---

[137]Following the Venezuelan example, Saudi Arabia in 1949 decreed an income tax of 50 percent on Aramco's income after payment of the U.S. tax. Subsequent to negotiations between Saudi Arabia on the one hand and the United States Treasury, Aramco, and its shareholders on the other, Saudi Arabia drafted a law that imposed a 50 percent income tax before payment of the American tax.

The Saudi Arabian government received considerable help from the United States government. This legislation was a general tax which was admissible for tax credit against the company's American tax. This system increased Saudi Arabian revenue substantially. The increase in Saudi Arabian revenue, however, did not bring about a decrease in the income of Aramco and its parent companies, because the Saudi tax was offset by reductions in the American tax on the same income. In fact, "the income on which the Saudi tax was charged originally differed from that on which the American tax was [charged]. Aramco submitted to Arabian taxation in 1950–51 on profits calculated on transfer prices to its parent company 'offtakers,' who received a substantial cost of sales' discount below the price at which Arabian crude was available to outsiders." This system reduced the "turnover and hence the profit on which Arabian tax was charged. It may have meant that the Arabian tax and royalty, which worked out a higher total rate than American tax plus Arabian royalty had done, but was applied to a lower profit, amounted in absolute terms to about the same payments to governments, leaving the companies roughly as before." HARTSHORN, *supra* note 78, at 179. *See also Multinational Corporations in World Development*, U.N. Doc. ST/ECA/190 66–70 (1973).

[138]*See* HARTSHORN, *supra* note 78, at 179.

[139]*Id.* at 177–79.

[140]*Id.* at 180.

was that the real taxable revenues of the producers rose to 60 percent, rather than 50 percent, of realized prices.[141]

Sometimes multilateral agreements between developing countries and multinational corporations provide for tax exemption or reduction for specific projects. Such agreements are designed to encourage investment according to governmental plans. Similar policies are on occasion followed by developed countries with respect to their private corporations, giving them tax exemptions for investment in some developing countries.[142]

The most direct exclusive control of states over pricing has commonly been achieved through the establishment and control of national companies. Such a practice, increasing in developing countries in the modern market structure, is not a new concept. During the Hitler and Mussolini days in Germany and Italy, government cartels were employed in an effective strategy of control over both internal and external affairs.[143] Today all forms of national companies are regarded as means for maintaining direct exclusive controls by governments. The more immediate impact of such controls, however, may be more national than transna-

---

[141]*Id.*

[142]Sometimes, instead of bilateral agreements between governments on tax matters, developing countries have concluded agreements with multinationals concerning specific projects. These agreements are mainly related to the granting of tax relief as an investment-inducing measure, and usually also include nontax matters and convertibility of earnings at a fixed rate and other benefits. Some developed countries have given encouragement to their corporations in the form of tax matters for investing in developing countries. *See, e.g.,* American measures on such encouragement, SENATE COMMITTEE ON FINANCE, 93RD CONG., 1ST SESS., IMPLICATIONS OF MULTINATIONAL FIRMS FOR WORLD TRADE AND INVESTMENT FOR U.S. TRADE AND LABOR, 71, 124–25, 882–84 (Comm. Print 1973).

Agreements between developing states and multinationals, however, are not allowed to contravene the tax laws of worldwide-taxing home countries. For the practice of Common Market members on tax, see *Tax Harmonization Measures Planned for First Stage of the Proposed Economic and Monetary Union* in 2 EUROPEAN TAXATION (1971). Another factor encouraging a more uniform taxation of multinational corporations arises out of dissatisfaction with the variety of methods used to integrate the corporate and individual income tax. *See* C. SHOUP, PUBLIC FINANCE (1969). Many countries are afraid that the methods of integration of other countries may become more attractive to direct investment. *See A Comparative Analysis of the Classical, Dual Rate, and Imputation Taxation Systems and an Examination of the Corporate Tax System in Belgium, France, Germany, Italy, the Netherlands and the United Kingdom,* in 12 EUROPEAN TAXATION, May-June 1972 Nos. 5 & 6, at 1/112–174. *See also* (United Kingdom) "Tax Reform", 12 EUROPEAN TAXATION Mar. 1972, No. 3.

[143]Kapper, *The International Regulation of Cartels—Current Proposals,* 40 VA. L. REV. 1005, 1007 (1954).

tional. If, on the other hand, the share of a particular state in the transnational production and distribution of a commodity is high, the unilateral action of the state may haveimmediate worldwide impact. For example, in the case of grain, the United States alone as the major producer has effective control over production of this vital resource, and it is likely that in the future world dependency on the U.S. grain export will increase. This dominance in production will give the United States a measure of power "it had never had before—possibly an economic and political dominance greater than that of the immediate post–World War II years."[144]

The impact of exclusive governmental and private control upon external value processes and the common interests of larger communities have led, beyond the slow growth of national prescriptions in regulations, to the development of some modest inclusive prescriptions about exclusive national competence. The European Economic Community (EEC), a partially inclusive organization with the objective of protection of shared interest of its members, has considered the possibility of negative impact of the practices of its members in pricing on the overall inclusive interest of the community. Article 37(1) of the EEC Agreement, referring to such concern, reads: "Member States shall progressively adjust any *State monopolies of a commercial character* so as to ensure that when the transnational period has ended, no discrimination regarding the conditions under which goods are produced and marketed exists between nationals and Member States."[145] This concern for control of monopoly practice brought some changes in the European Coal and Steel Community (ECSC) in 1951. The purpose of ECSC was to established international control over the coal and steel industries of member countries in order to create an international market through political unification of the member states.[146] The

---

[144] Weinstein, *CIA Study Says Food Crisis Could Increase U.S. Power*, Int'l Herald Tribune, Mar. 18, 1975, at 3, col. 1. For European Economic Community law on monopoly, see Schumacher, *A Common Market Overview of the Competition Problem in the Seventies*, in Current Legal Aspects of Doing Business in Europe 58 (L. Theberge ed. 1971); Deringer, *A Practitioner Looks at the German and EEC Rules as Applied to Acquisitions, Mergers, and Joint Ventures*, in *id.* at 64; Newes, *The EEC Treaty as Applied to Distribution Arrangements and Industrial Property Rights*, in *id.* at 72–78; and Rahl, *Relationship of U.S. to EEC Antitrust Law* in *id.* at 79–94.

[145] *Quoted in* Wortley, *Monopolies*, in The Law of the Common Market 77 (B. Wortley ed. 1974).

[146] Edwards, *supra* note 60, at 7.

agreement of the community was to prohibit restrictive practices that were incompatible with the purpose of the community, by both public and private sectors. It should be noted that the EEC prescriptions include public as well as private participants. Article 85(1) of the EEC Treaty expands the prohibition of monopoly and condemns practices that directly or indirectly fix purchase or selling prices,[147] limit or control production and technical development,[148] store market or sources of supply,[149] apply conditions which put the other party at a competitive disadvantage, and condition the agreement to other situations which have no relation to the agreement in hand.[150] Article 86 of the EEC Treaty, expanding the concept of the prohibition of abuse of monopoly power, reads:

> Any abuse by one or more undertakings of a dominant position within the Common Market or in a substantial part of it shall be prohibited as incompatible with the Common Market insofar as it may affect trade between Member States. Such abuse may, in particular, consist in:
>
> (a) Directly or indirectly imposing unfair purchase or selling prices or other unfair trading conditions.
>
> (b) Limiting production, markets or technical development to the prejudice of consumers.
>
> (c) Applying dissimilar conditions to equivalent transactions with other trading parties, thereby placing them at a competitive disadvantage.

[147]*See* Vereeniging Van Cementhandelaren v. E.C. Commission (The Cement Case), 12 Comm. Mkt. L.R. 7 (1972).

[148]*See* Italy v. E.E.C. Council and E.E.C. Commission, 8 Comm. Mkt. L.R. 39 (1969).

[149]*See* Consten and Grundig v. E.E.C. Commission, 8 Comm. Mkt. L.R. 418 (1969), *cited in* Wortley, *supra* note 144, at 86.

[150]*Id.* There are, however, some exceptions to Article 85(1). Article 85(3) states: "The provisions of paragraph 1 may, however, be declared inapplicable in the case of: "—any agreement or category of agreements between undertakings; "—any decision or category of decisions by associations of undertakings; "—any concerted practice or category of concerted practices; which contributes to improving the production or distribution of goods or to promoting technical or economic progress, while allowing consumers a fair share of the resulting benefit, and which does not:

"(a) impose on the undertakings concerned restrictions which are not indispensable to the attainment of these objectives;

"(b) afford such undertakings the possibility of eliminating competition in respect of a substantial part of the products in question." *Quoted in id.* at 88.

(d) Making the conclusion of contracts subject to acceptance by the other parties of supplementary obligations which, by their nature or according to commercial usage, have no connection with the subject of such contracts.[151]

The emphasis and pressure put by EEC has made the members change their internal prescriptions to meet EEC requirements regardless of their sympathy with some monopoly practices.

2. Partially Inclusive Competence over Pricing

A relatively recent feature of the international pricing process is the emergence of partially inclusive intergovernmental organizations that assert, within the larger permissible framework of international law, a strong effective power and a number of particular competences about pricing. These particular competences include the intelligence, promotion, prescription, and, to a lesser degree, the application functions. The thrust of these organizations is in direct opposition to the capitalist laissez-faire notion of a self-regulating market and aims toward a conscious change in market forces. The principal participants in these partially inclusive organizations are the exporting, developing countries. These new organizations have been aptly described as the "trade unions" of "the poor nations." Their objective is to negotiate a new deal with the rich countries through the instrument of collective bargaining: that is, "to obtain greater equality of opportunity and to secure the right to sit as equals around the bargaining tables of the world."[152]

These new associations do not fit the requirements of an intergovernmental specialized agency under Article 57 of the United Nations Charter. Article 57(1) of the Charter defines specialized agencies as inter-governmental organizations with the objectives of "having wide international responsibilities, as defined in their

---

[151] An Introduction to the Law of the European Economic Community 72–76 (B. Wortley ed. 1972). For more on this article, see C. Bellamy, The Common Market Law of Competition 701–43 (1973). For the application of this Article to the Continental Can Case of 1972, see 5 EEC Bulletin 64 (1972). For the ruling of the European Communities Court of Justice on the same case in Feb. 1973, which overturned the Commission decision, see Europemballage Corp. and Continental Can Co. v. EEC. Commission, 12 Comm. Mkt. L.R. 199 [1973].

[152] Mahbub ul Haq, *Negotiating a New Bargain with the Rich Countries*, in Beyond Dependency: The Developing World Speaks Out 157, 158 (G. Erb & V. Kalleb eds. 1975).

basic instruments, in economic, social, cultural, educational, health, and related fields."[153] The objectives of the producers' associations are obviously more limited. They may perhaps be best described as associations of interest groups, which in some measure align bloc against bloc. They have such wide membership that they cannot be considered as exclusive organizations; yet they are not wide enough in membership and purpose to be referred to as inclusive, for direct and explicit relation to the most inclusive world organization, the United Nations. For these reasons we recognize these associations as a new phenomenon in international trade and refer to them as partially inclusive intergovernmental organizations.

The idea for creating these partially inclusive organizations derives from the desire of the developing countries for greater development and their recognition of the nonconformity of the market structure with that desire. The disappointment they faced in their treatment by industrial countries has been almost universal:

> For the producers of minerals, there is moreover (as for oil) the keen sense that their minerals are nonrenewable, an asset that should produce the greatest possible return and if possible have its useful life stretched out. Hence, it is only natural that producers should seek to change a situation in which, by and large, the sellers of non-fuel minerals are competing, diffuse, and unorganized in the face of relatively few and well-organized buyers on behalf of the consuming countries.[154]

The combined effect of these factors—concern for development, a realistic perception of limited resources and ability, and, most importantly, the lack of sympathy for their goals in the market structures and in the developed countries—has fueled their effort to establish a new form of collective bargaining. It has been their hope that "[a] group position is more likely to win than an individual position because of the greater power and resources behind it, because of its greater moral legitimacy (one's cause seems more 'right' when others support it), and because it is more likely to be a moderate and general position (hence more amenable to accom-

[153] U.N. CHARTER, art. 51, para. 1.

[154] Varon & Takeuchi, *Developing Countries and Non-Fuel Minerals*, 52 FOREIGN AFFAIRS 505 (1974).

modation)."[155] The Trilateral Commission aptly summarizes the objectives of these organizations: "to stabilize market prices; to prevent market prices from falling below production costs; to offset the market power of private firms; to respond to other market imperfections, such as barriers to exports in processed forms; to exchange information and to coordinate technical and other developments."[156]

The authority of the producers to establish these new associations derives from their combined sovereignty over their resources. This interpretation has been confirmed in the resolution of the New Economic Order. Article 5 of the NEO states: "All States have the right to associate in organizations of primary commodity producers in order to develop their national economies to achieve stable financing for their development, and in pursuance of their aims, to assist in the promotion of sustained growth of the world economy, in particular accelerating the development of developing countries. Correspondingly all States have the duty to respect that right by refraining from applying economic and political measures that would limit it." Similarly, the UNCTAD meeting of 1964 (Geneva) adopted a recommendation that confirms the status of producers' organizations:

> *Recognizing* the particular urgent character of the trade needs of developing countries whose exports are mainly composed of non-renewable natural products,
>
> *Considering* the need for those countries to reach speedily a certain stage of economic development for which investment capital can be raised, by increasing the per unit income from their exports,

[155]Randolph, *A Suggested Model of International Negotiation*, 10 J. Conflict Res. 345 (1966).

[156]Trilateral Commission, Seeking a New Accommodation in World Commodity Market 13–14 (1976). The Commission concludes that creation of a shortage in the market through systematic decrease of production does not necessarily come from a formal association. It could result from the actions of a dominant firm or government (in the case of phosphates) or an informal grouping (in the case of manganese). Furthermore, increases in price do not necessarily come from production control but from increases in taxation (such as the Jamaican increase in the bauxite tax) or other internal measures, such as the control of export by encouraging domestic processing in the case of iron ore in Australia and export control in the case of Canada. *Id.* at 14.

> *Recommends* that international organizations set up by the developing countries which are the principal exporters of non-renewable natural products be recognized and encouraged to enable them to defend their interest.[157]

This recommendation was adopted by a roll-call vote of 83 to 1, with 25 abstentions. The opposing vote was from the United States.

Producers' associations are not cartels in the same sense as are the great private associations. They are interegovernmental organizations which have the objective of protecting the total well-being of their nation-state members as opposed to cartels formed by private corporations which have the primary objective merely of profit maximization. The scope of operation of a private export cartel is not limited to price fixing but also includes the allocation and control of production and market sharing. Furthermore, the private export cartel monitors the activities of its members and penalizes them in cases of violation.[158] With respect to OPEC, for example, these functions are not performed, and its members do not accept comparable obligations:

> Their agreement on oil export prices is strictly voluntary, and does not carry with it sanctions or rewards. Moreover, the agreements leave to the discretion of each member government the setting and changing of prices within a range considered reasonable by OPEC members. A close scrutiny of OPEC's resolutions shows that the organization does not have supranational powers, and its resolutions are merely guideposts for action. Member countries do not delegate to any central body their decision-making powers. Indeed, they jealously guard their sovereignty, and consider their freedom of action to be paramount.[159]

One fundamental difference between OPEC and the private cartels is thus that the members of OPEC in promoting its policies do not give up their freedom of action. This fact was recogized at the beginning of the establishment of this organization. As empha-

---

[157]UNCTAD, Final Act and Report, U.N. Doc. E/Conf. 46/161, Vol. 1 at 63 Annex A. VI. 2. (1964).

[158]*See Should Export Cartels Be More Closely Controlled?* OECD Observer, Nov. 1974, at 30–32.

[159]Mikdashi, *supra* note 24, at 77–78.

sized by the Venzuelan representative, "It must be borne in mind that the governments are sovereign and can in no way be compelled to fulfil to the letter their obligations toward OPEC which, in any case, are more in the nature of moral obligations."[160] Further, in practice the OPEC resolutions on pricing have not always been followed at the stipulated times.[161] It will be observed that comparable freedoms are embodied in the charters of other producers' associations.

Because of their importance to the world economy, there are increasing demands that these organizations be required to meet international standards of responsibility, of at least minimum order, in the exercise of effective control over production and pricing.[162] Some of these responsibilities have already been recognized and accepted, for example, by OPEC. In the Solemn Declaration of the Algiers Conference, the OPEC members clearly announced the policies of insuring a continuous and sufficient uninterrupted supply to consumers.[163] The Declaration also states that coordination among producers should be managed in conformity with creating a balance between oil production and the needs of the world market.[164] Thus, maintenance of the supply of oil has officially been acknowledged by Arab oil producers as their international responsibility.[165]

From the beginning OPEC has tried to establish relations with various international organizations in order to confirm its competences and responsibilities and enhance its acceptability and recognition. Its documents of establishment were registered in November of 1962 with the Secretariat of the United Nations in accordance with Article 102 of the Charter. OPEC has also estab-

---

[160]*Perez Alfonso Clarifies Venezuelan Attitude Toward OPEC*, MIDDLE EAST ECON. SURVEY [hereinafter cited as MEES] supp. Oct. 11, 1963, *quoted in id.* at 78.

[161]*Id.*

[162]Gardner, *The Hard Road to World Order*, 52 FOREIGN AFFAIRS 566 (1974); *see also* statement at The Sixth Special Session of the United Nations by the Representative of the Philippines, U.N. Doc. A/PV 2218 (1974) at 23–26.

[163]*Reprinted in* 18 MEES No. 22 (1975).

[164]*Id.*

[165]*See* policy statement delivered by King Khalid of Saudi Arabia on Apr. 1, 1975, *reported in* 18 MEES No. 24, (1975); see also ALHAMAD, INTERNATIONAL FINANCE—AN ARAB POINT OF VIEW 5–6 (1974), *cited in* Shihata, *Arab Oil Policies and the New International Economic Order*, 16 VA. J. INT'L L. 261, 265 n.18 (1976).

lished working relations with the Economic and Social Council. The General Assembly has authorized the Economic and Social Council to establish relations with intergovernmental organizations that do not fall within the definition of the Article 57 of the Charter.[166] Based on this provision, OPEC has participated in Regional Economic Commissions for Latin America, Asia, and the Far East. OPEC also participated in the second symposium on the development of petroleum resources organized by the Economic Commission for Asia and the Far East in Tehran, in September 1962. In 1964 OPEC sent an application to the United Nations for acquiring consultative status with the Economic and Social Council. The Council adopted a resolution recognizing such status for OPEC on July 1, 1965.[167] The Secretary General of the United Nations was requested to take measures for "(a) ensuring the reciprocal exchange of information and documents, (b) having OPEC represented at meetings of the Organs of the United Nations at which questions of mutual interest are scheduled to be discussed, and (c) ensuring consultation and technical cooperation between OPEC and the United Nations in regard to matters of mutual interest."[168] Finally, OPEC members have tried to express their concern for world inflation and rising oil prices in recent years through different aid programs to developing countries.[169] Though these aid programs have not been entirely successful, they are nonetheless an expression of a sense of responsibility in times of international crisis.

The emergence of the producers' associations has been in general the result both of the unfavorable conditions in international trade for the fulfillment of demanded development projects and of the lack of an appropriate, more inclusive decision process to promote the accelerating demands for world reform to achieve a more equitable distribution of values. The important task for the larger community now is to relate these partially inclusive organizations as new factors in the pricing process, with all their compe-

---

[166] II *Report of the Preparatory Commission to the General Assembly* 123, *cited in* F. ROUHANI, A HISTORY OF OPEC 140 (1971).

[167] *Id.*

[168] *Id.*

[169] See Williams, *The Aid Programs of the OPEC Countries*, 54 FOREIGN AFFAIRS 308–24 (1976).

tences and responsibilities, to broader conceptions of the common interest. An analysis of some of the more detailed conditions under which the producers' associations have emerged may explain the more important contemporary expectations about the role and function of these associations and aid in relating their activities to the common interest. Our analysis begins with the emergence of OPEC as the first and the most effective partially inclusive organization. Then we move to other examples of such organizations.

The monopolistic activities of major multinational oil companies, both in the process of oil exploitation and in the political processes of the Middle East, are well known and thoroughly documented by economists and political scientists. The objectives of the major oil companies have included the maximization not only of wealth but also of power.[170] The importance of power in the formulation of pricing cannot, of course, be ignored. With almost absolute monopoly control, the oil companies set the price of oil at $2.17 per barrel in 1948.[171] This price was gradually reduced by the unilateral decisions of the oil companies to $1.80 by 1960, regardless of the impact on the producers' well-being.[172] The low price of Middle East oil during 1949–59, in relation to the oil of the Western Hemisphere and the prices of products in the European market, deprived the Middle Eastern producing countries of a rightful share of the profits, estimated by a former Saudi Arabia oil Minister at $4.74 billion.[173] During the same period the prices of oil from the Gulf of Mexico and Venezuela were, respectively, nearly 70 percent and 40 percent higher than the Persian Gulf price of oil of comparable quality.[174] This consistent unilateral decrease in the price of oil (which led to a decline of the revenues of the producing states, while maintaining high profits for the oil companies) gave rise to the demand by the oil producers

---

[170] *See* HIRST, *supra* note 106, at 37–43, ENGLER, supra note 82, at 197–220, TANZER, note 105 supra; KRONSTEIN *supra* note 60, at 92; RIFAI, *supra* note 91, at 2; and a paper delivered to the Third Arab Petroleum Congress (Oct. 16–21, 1961) by Dr. Muhammad Lebib Shuquair, *The Relative Bargaining Power of the Arab States and the Oil Companies and Its Effect in Determining the Financial Provisions of the Oil Concession Agreements.*

[171] Jowlson & Griffin, *The Legal Status of Nation-State Cartels Under United States Antitrust and Public International Law,* 9 INT'L LAW 617, 618 (1975).

[172] *Id.*

[173] ROUHANI, *supra* note 166, at 191.

[174] *Id.* at 190.

for profit sharing. The purpose of the producing states in their demand for profit sharing was in the beginning merely to increase their earnings; they were not concerned about, and did not seek to participate in, price determination.[175] Once they came to participate in profit sharing, the producing states naturally became concerned about price formulation as affecting their share.[176] To deal with this concern, oil companies began to publicize, or, in petroleum terminology, to "post," prices of Middle East oil. The posting, however, carried no indication that oil companies would respect the claim of the producers for participation in the pricing process at any level.[177] The function of posting was only to establish those prices as a basis for the calculation of the royalties and income taxes to be payable to the producers.[178]

Concern for participation in pricing began with the growing consciousness among the Middle Eastern countries about the value of their resources. The price issue was first brought up formally at the Second Arab Petroleum Congress held in 1959 with an elaborate paper presented by the Saudi Oil Minister Sheik Abdullah Tariki, concerning the formulation of the price of crude oil.[179] This paper was the beginning of formal and collective concern. It was, however, the decline in oil prices that made the producing countries take a further step and establish OPEC in 1960.[180] The primary objective of OPEC at the time of its establishment was the prevention of decrease in oil prices. The initial efforts of OPEC were successful in stabilizing the price of oil at the August 1960 level. Nevertheless, dissatisfaction with the distribution of profits arising from their oil resources led the OPEC members to expand the organization's scope of action to improve their income. The basic strategy chosen by OPEC to this end has been through formulating common policies concerning the stabilization

[175]CATTAN, *supra* note 129, at 51.

[176]*See* HARTSHORN, *supra* note 78, at 149; HIRST, *supra* note 106, at 42.

[177]HARTSHORN, *id.* at 149.

[178]M. El-Mulhim, Redistribution of Values Arising from the Oil Industry in the Middle East 221 (1970) (unpublished J.S.D. thesis Yale Law School Library).

[179]ROUHANI, *supra* note 166, at 178.

[180]The original participants of OPEC were Iran, Iraq, Kuwait, Saudi Arabia, and Venezuela. For a brief summary of its establishment, see HIRST, *supra* note 106, at 100–191 ROUHANI, note 166 *supra*; and I. FESHARAKI, DEVELOPMENT OF THE IRANIAN OIL INDUSTRY, INTERNATIONAL AND DOMESTIC ASPECTS 4–62 (1976).

of prices. The first effort in this respect was Resolution 32, adopted at the Fourth Conference in June 1962.[181] This Resolution protested against the price reduction effected by the oil companies in August 1960 and the fact that the oil companies had so far taken no steps to restore prices to the pre-August 1960 level. The Resolution emphasized the importance of oil revenues to the producers. It stated that a fall in the price of crude oil impairs the purchasing power of member countries with respect to manufactured products, which are essential to their development. Contrasting the rise in prices of manufactures with the fall in the price of oil, the Resolution justified the participation of the producers in the pricing process on the grounds that

> the oil industry having the character of a public utility, member countries cannot be indifferent to such a vital element of the industry as the determination of the price of oil. [Therefore, the Resolution recommended] [t]hat member countries should forthwith enter into negotiations with the oil companies concerned and (or) any other authority or body deemed appropriate, with a view to ensuring that oil produced in member countries shall be paid for on the basis of posted prices not lower than those which applied prior to August, 1960.
> . . .
> That the member countries shall jointly formulate a rational price structure to guide their long-term price policy, on which subject the Board of Governors is hereby directed to prepare a comprehensive study at the earliest possible date. An important element of the price structure to be devised will be the linking of crude oil prices to an index of prices of goods that the member countries need to import.[182]

This Resolution was followed by an Explanatory Memorandum issued by the OPEC Secretariat further stressing the importance of oil revenue to the producing countries and noting a lack of benefits to consumers: "7. The fall in crude oil prices has brought no benefit to the consumer because, as decreases in ex-tax price of products have been introduced into the market, fresh taxes have been imposed by the consuming country governments. Furthermore, the cost of manufactured goods, instead of diminishing in proportion to the reduction of the price of crude oil, has on the

---

[181] For text of the resolution, see ROUHANI, *supra* note 166, at 195–96.

[182] *Id.*

contrary increased."[183] The Memorandum made a comparison between distribution of economic values arising from oil resources through different taxing systems and claimed that the governments of the European consumers made two or three times more from taxation on oil products than did the producers.[184] OPEC in a number of other resolutions has been concerned about the price issue and has encouraged the more detailed studies of the price structure of the oil industry.[185]

Another policy adopted by OPEC was a prorationing scheme. Prorationing refers to control of production. The idea first began in the United States, allegedly for purposes of conservation. There have, however, always been serious doubts about the validity of the

---

[183] For text, see *id.* at 196–200.

[184] For example: "[W]hen a motorist buys one liter of premium gasoline for 1.04 francs, he gives not more than 6 centimes to the country which supplies the crude oil, while he pays 79 centimes to the taxing authority of his own country. The remainder, about 19 centimes, covers transportation, refining, marketing, and sellers' profit. . . . Thus, in both cases [the other case is that of the United Kingdom], the payment which the producing country receives is less than 6 percent of the average price to be consumed. These examples could easily be multiplied. It would be enough for the final consumer to look at the above figures to realize what a very grave error it would be for him to think that an unduly large part of the price he pays for the oil he consumes goes to the owner of the raw material." ROUHANI, *id.* at 199.

In the Memorandum, OPEC referred to the different measures taken by individual states to control the economy for their national development and argued that oil producers could be given similar rights:

"During the last few decades, many countries have resorted to different measures of regulation of the internal economy (nationalization, production quotas, etc.) to ensure a steady rate of economic growth free from violent fluctuations. In the oil industry, there have been prominent examples of such measures (especially in the United States) affecting the free play of the supply and demand and therefore the price. But such safeguards have been relatively absent from the international scene. Competition in the sale of petroleum on the international markets has increased since 1957, due partly to the entry of new comers into the industry, and partly to the availability of a large amount of surplus producing capacity. But the oil-exporting countries are dependent on the international trade of petroleum, and their economies are especially vulnerable to fluctuations in price. It is therefore natural that these countries should take steps to safeguard their interest. This does not mean that they are opposed to competition as such. It only means that they cannot sit by with arms folded watching unrestrained competition destroying their chances for the future through successive decreases in the price of crude oil and in the face of mounting prices for their requirements of imported manufactured goods." *Id.* at 200.

[185] Organization of Petroleum Exporting Countries, Resolutions Nos. 33, and 34 of IV Conference, No. 4 of V Conference, 49 and 50 of VII Conference, 55 and 56 of VIII Conference; 61 of IX Conference; 64 of X Conference; 72 of XI Conference; 76 of XII Conference, 80 and 81 of XIII Conference; 84 of XIV Conference; and 94 and 95 of XVII Conference; 103 of XCIII Conference; 105 of XIX Conference.

conservation argument; the concept has sometimes appeared to be a covert strategy for price control. The prorationing concept was introduced to OPEC by Dr. Perez Alfonzo of Venezuela. Dr. Alfonzo's basic objective was to protect, or at least equalize, the interest of Venezuela in relation to Persian Gulf producers. The cost of producing a barrel of oil in Venezuela was 51 cents in 1968, in the Middle East, about 15 cents.[186] In addition to this contrast in production costs, Venezuela's revenue was substantially lower than that of the Middle East. The effect of the OPEC establishment in its first year on Venezuela's revenue was only a 3 percent increase over 1959, as contrasted with 14 percent for the Middle East producers. This obviously put Venezuela in a disadvantageous position. The idea of prorationing as a means of price control, in conjunction with conservation, was generally accepted by OPEC members, but the criteria by which quotas should be allocated among the member-states remained a difficult issue. Among the criteria presented were the volume of resources, the rate of current production, the size of investment and population, and degree of economic growth desired. Because of disagreements among members about these criteria, in the Eighth OPEC Conference in Geneva in 1965 a Permanent Economic Commission was established and assigned the task of studying the issue. In the ninth Conference in Tripoli the Commission formulated a quota system based on world demand (Resolution IX.61). This quota system was changeable on a yearly basis.

The quota system was designed only as a guideline and was not compulsory. The system was opposed by a number of OPEC members, including Iran, Libya, and Saudi Arabia.[187] The prorationing system, in practice, was never accepted by OPEC. Iran, Libya, and Saudi Arabia always operated above their quota. Finally, the resolutions of the Eleventh OPEC Conference held in Vienna in April 1966 omitted any direct mention of the prorationing scheme.

Another strategy for participation in pricing adopted by OPEC after 1971 included both multilateral negotiations with the oil companies and unilateral government actions. The belief that the price of crude oil was kept at an artificially low level over the entire

---

[186]C. TUGENDHAT, OIL: THE BIGGEST BUSINESS 189 (1968). On prorationing, see also ROUHANI, *supra* note 166, at 211–15.

[187]For the Iranian position see PETROLEUM INTELLIGENCE WEEKLY May 17, 1966. For the Saudi Arabian position, see MEES Supp. Feb. 11, 1966.

post-war period up to 1971 and that the expansion of economic growth in the Western Hemisphere was due to cheap oil stimulated the producers to take more effective action toward control of the price of their oil. The producers justified their demand for more effective participation in pricing on the basis that the trade situation was increasingly moving against their own economic well-being. The tax policy of the importing countries, when compared with the income taxes of the producers, was also regarded as unfair and inconsistent with the treatment recommended by UNCTAD. For example, the share of the producers of oil sold in Western Europe in 1967 was 7.9 percent, while the taxes of the consumer governments averaged 47.5 percent.[188] The producers argued for a more equitable taxing system; in fact, the target of the OPEC demand was the consumer governments rather than the oil companies. They claimed that if the price of oil was too high for the consumers, their governments should reduce their excessive taxes.[189] Another concern related to the decline of the purchasing power of the U.S. dollar. The dollar fell by 27 percent during 1960–1970, while the increase in the cost of living rose 24.9 percent in the United States and 39.7 percent in the United Kingdom.[190] The issue was the higher price of manufactured goods as compared with primary products.[191] Therefore, OPEC recommended its members to take appropriate action to protect their interest. In Resolution XXII.131, OPEC asked that "[e]ach member country exporting oil from Gulf terminals shall introduce

[188]

Item	Total: 100
Production costs	2.7
Refining	3.3
Transportation	6.3
Distribution and marketing	26.0
Oil company's net profits	6.3
Oil producer's share	7.9
Consumer government's taxes	47.5

See R. SANGHAVI, IRAN: DESTINY OF OIL 11 (1971) *cited in* FESHARAKI, *supra* note 180, at 113.

[189] FESHARAKI, *id.* at 113–14.

[190] Mohammed Pera Pahlavi, Shah of Iran, Press Conference, Teheran, Jan. 24, 1971, *cited in id.* at 114.

[191] *Id.*

... legal and/or legislative measures for the implementation of the objectives embodied in Res. XXI.120." The appropriate measures included total embargo on shipments of crude oil and petroleum products of companies violating the resolution.

The above factors were the basis for the success of the Tehran Agreement, by which the companies accepted OPEC Resolutions 120 and 122. They agreed to increase the posted prices to compensate for inflation on June 1, 1971 and January 1, 1973 through 1975. In return the companies were guaranteed security of supply for the remainder of the five years, during which there was to be no demand for revision of the terms of posted prices until 1975. In general, however, the Tehran Agreement had little effect on price changes. The posted prices were increased by 35 cents per barrel, which meant that the governments received 19 cents per barrel more than they did before.[192]

Although the Tehran Agreement was designed to keep the Persian Gulf producers quiet for five years, Libya and Algeria insisted that the Tehran settlement was not even close to their minimum demand. Through negotiations with the oil companies they concluded an agreement on April 2, 1971 (the Tripoli Agreement) in which the interests of the producers were much better protected than they were in the Tehran Agreement. Under the Tripoli Agreement, Libya increased its posted prices to about ninety cents per barrel, which was a seven-cent increase as compared with a five-cent increase in the Persian Gulf. Besides a 55 percent income tax provision there was an additional surcharge of nine cents per barrel and compulsory reinvestment of the companies' net profit in Libya for further exploration for up to five years in the future.[193]

The Tehran and Tripoli Agreements are examples of changes in pricing by multilateral agreements. Nevertheless, they were among the first manifestations of cooperation with regard to pricing; a clear shift in power from the companies to the producers was becoming obvious. The OPEC Geneva Agreement of 1972 recommending an 8.49 percent increase in posted prices because of dollar devaluation was the beginning of unilateral action of

[192]*Id.* at 116; see also ROUHANI, *supra* note 166, at 18.

[193]For the text of the Tripoli and Teheran Agreements, see PETROLEUM INTELLIGENCE WEEKLY Dec. 14, 1971. For the Tripoli agreement see ROUHANI, *supra* note 166, at 22–23.

OPEC members. In October 1973 six Persian Gulf producers unilaterally added 70 percent to the price of oil and recommended the same policy to other OPEC members.[194] This unilateral decision was later explained by one observer as follows: "after weeks of unsuccessful negotiations with the companies, the oil-exporting governments declared their intention to establish oil prices among themselves, free from the obstruction tactics of the companies in bilateral bargaining."[195] OPEC decided to raise the posted prices from $3.00 to $5.12 without negotiating with the oil companies. The Arab-Israeli war was a favorable factor for making such unilateral actions acceptable.[196] Since that time a unilateral competence has been consistently asserted.

The basic exercise of the competence of OPEC in the pricing process, as has been indicated, is through the intelligence, promotion, and (to some modest degree) prescribing functions. The application of recommendations has been largely left to members, through their individual or joint action. The recommendations of OPEC are not compulsory but advisory, and there is no sanctioning process in case a member refuses to accept a particular recommendation. The necessity of coordination in pricing policy among members for protection of their common interests has, however, been recognized by the members themselves.[197] Similar policies and practices have been effectively followed by other producer associations.

The Intergovernmental Council of Copper Exporting Countries (CIPEC) was established in 1967 by the major copper producers, Chile, Peru, Zaire, and Zambia, who controlled 35 percent of the world mine production. Article 2 of the CIPEC Charter states that the objectives of the organization are:

---

[194] *See* PETROLEUM INTELLIGENCE WEEKLY, Oct. 22, 1973, at 9.

[195] Amuzegar, *OPEC in the Context of the Global Power Equation*, 4 DEN. J. INT'L L. & POLICY 221, 222 (1974).

[196] Industrialized countries were faced with embargo by Arab oil producers against "unfriendly" countries. The threat and concern of the embargo, which cut production 30 percent, created a shortage overshadowing the unilateral price increase. The embargo and the shortage of oil had panicked Western consumers so much that in an auction in Iran in December of 1973, $17.34 per barrel was offered for small quantities of Iranian oil and $20 for Nigerian oil. The embargo, however, was followed by another unilateral price increase in December 1973 to $11.65 per barrel. FESHASAKI, *supra* note 180, at 118.

[197] *See* Marbo, *Can OPEC Hold the Line?* 18 MEES No. 19 (1975).

(a) to coordinate measures designed to foster, through the expansion of the industry, dynamic and continuous growth of real earnings from copper exports, and to ensure a real forecast of such earnings;

(b) to promote the harmonization of the decisions and policies of the member countries on problems relating to the production and marketing of copper;

(c) to obtain better and more complete information and appropriate advice on the production and marketing of copper for member countries;

(d) in general, to increase resources for the economic and social development of producer countries bearing in mind the interest of consumers.[198]

CIPEC has not been highly successful in the areas of price maintenance or increase. The strategy of cutbacks in production of November 1974 by 10 percent proved to be inadquate in 1975, basically because of the small percentage of cutback and the low demand for copper.[199] CIPEC has, nonetheless, been successful as an intelligence center for securing, processing, and distributing information designed to improve and encourage the awareness of the common problems of its members. Regardless of the sociopolitical differences among its members, CIPEC has kept its solidarity. For example, in 1973, in supporting Chile with its nationalization of Kennecott in 1971, CIPEC members decided not to replace copper on the world market where Chilean copper was seized through legal actions brought by Kennecott.[200] CIPEC has also agreed to establish "a permanent mechanism of protection and solidarity in the event of economic or commercial aggression against any of the Organization's member countries."[201]

Before CIPEC, copper prices were controlled by non-U.S. multinational copper firms[202] and voluntary production restriction and sale-purchase operations on the London Metal Exchange

---

[198]*Quoted in* MIKDASHI, *supra* note 24, at 83.

[199]*Id.* at 86.

[200]*Id.* at 88.

[201]*Copper Nations Form Pact to Support Chile*, The Times (London), Jan. 16, 1973, at 15, col. 1, *quoted in id.*.

[202]*See* R. VERNON, MANAGER IN THE INTERNATIONAL ECONOMY 169–71 (1972).

(LME).[203] These operations were generally supported by the producers. By late 1963 the demand began to decline and the market situation changed to a buyers' market. The attempts of copper firms and producers to stabilize the price by cutting the production and other methods were ineffective, and this situation endured until 1966. The insensitivity of the consumers to the problem facing the developing copper producers aggravated the situation. In 1966 the individual producers began to raise their own prices unilaterally, but after a few months, because of lack of success, they decided to follow the price policy of LME.[204] The establishment of CIPEC was the last resort of developing producers for the protection of their common interests.

The organization of iron-ore exporting countries, first initiated by Venezuela in 1958, consists of seven countries: Brazil, Chile, India, Liberia, Peru, and Venezuela. After a continued decline in the price of iron ore, the result of an oligopoly of iron-ore buyers,[205] the members believed that their unilateral action was not enough to protect their interest and that they would have to join together in order to increase their effective control. Nevertheless, the members' primary concern was to establish a center for the exchange of information. The establishment of this organization was the first producer association that was carefully considered by exporting and importing countries as well as UNCTAD. The UNCTAD meeting of 1966 regarding the problems of iron-ore exporters concluded that "the participation of a larger number of countries, including the main consuming countries, would make it possible to throw much more light on many of the problems involved and partly on the fact that any international remedial actions which might be considered desirable could be far more effectively implemented by the joint action of a bigger group of exporting and importing countries than by a limited group of exporting countries acting alone."[206] To promote its policy, UNCTAD gathered a group of twenty-five developed and developing

---

[203] *See* MIKDASHI, *supra* note 24, at 89.

[204] CHASE MANHATTAN BANK, WORLD BUSINESS Apr. 1969, at 10, *cited in id.* at 92.

[205] *See* statement by President of Marcona, *quoted in* Robinson, *Competition in the Sale of Iron Ore in the World Market*, in 11 CONVENCION DE INGENIEROS DE MINAS DEL PERU, Dec. 1969.

[206] *Problem of the World Market for Iron Ore*, U.N. Doc. TD/B/C.1/66 (1966) at 25, *quoted in* MIKDASHI, *supra* note 24, at 99–100.

major exporting and importing countries in Geneva January 19–23, 1970, to discuss the issue. The conclusion of the meeting was disappointing. It became clear that the problems of primary commodities were not just a problem between producers and importers but only a part of a more general global problem between the developing and the developed countries.[207] In this meeting the ideas of the developed-exporting countries were close to those of the developed-importing countries, while the developing countries again remained as a separate group.[208] The developing-importing countries demanded the linking of the price of iron to its final product, steel, but this was rejected by the developed countries. The developing-producing countries also demanded that the developed-producing countries cut back production in their favor, which also was rejected.[209] The disappointment as to cooperation between producers and consumers resulted in a final decision by the exporting countries to establish the Association of Iron Ore Exporting Countries (AIOEC) in April 1975. This Association does not have any price fixing power.[210]

The monopoly control by private corporations in the international trade of bauxite has been the main impetus for the establishment of producers' organizations. Assocalex, incoprorated in Zurich in 1964, is the major cartel of the industry, constituting a combination of Western European and American producing enterprises.[211] These corporations, despite U.S. antitrust laws, negotiated collectively with the producers. One State Department official acknowledged that U.S. companies entered collectively into negotiation with the Jamaican government in 1973–74 for tax problems and, moreover, that the United States supported such

[207] UNCTAD, *International Action on Commodities in the Light of Recent Developments*, U.N. Doc. TD/B/C.1/75 (1970) at 13, *cited in* MIKDASHI, *supra* note 24, at 100.

[208] *Id.*

[209] At the Third UNCTAD Meeting in 1972, the Indian minister for foreign trade stated that "[w]e made a strong plea for arresting erosion in export prices and the need for developed countries to stop further expansion of output so that the competitive position of the developing nations does not get further weakened." *Quoted in* MIKDASHI, *supra* note 24, at 101.

[210] The framers of the Association are Algeria, Australia, Brazil, Chile, India, Mauritania, Renu, Sierra Leone, Sweden, Tunisia, and Venezuela.

[211] Mikdashi, *Aluminum*, in BIG BUSINESS AND THE STATE: CHANGING RELATION IN WESTERN EUROPE 170–74 (R. Vernon ed. 1974).

action and "expressed to the Jamaican Government in [as] clear terms as we could what we thought would be the consequences of certain actions proposed by them."[212]

After a few years of consideration, the producing countries decided to establish a permanent organization in 1974, called the International Bauxite Association (IBA), "to promote the orderly and rational development of bauxite."[213] Price protection is only one purpose of the IBA; other purposes include the promotion of maximum national ownership, research, exchange of information, provision of common services, and technology.[214] IBA has also been considered a way of checking on transnational corporations.[215] The IBA controls 63 percent of world bauxite.[216]

The Union of Banana Exporting Countries is another producer association. It was established in March 1974 in Panama by Latin American countries in consequence of the decline of price of bananas since the 1950s. A report by UNCTAD showed that the constant decline of banana prices was in fact due to transferral of resources from these countries to the developed countries, since the developed countries are the main customers of this commodity.[217] The control over production of bananas is largely in the hands of three American corporations, who also play a significant

[212] *Outlook for Prices and Supplies of Industrial Raw Materials: Hearings Before the Subcommittee on Economic Growth of the Joint Economic Committee*, 93d Cong. 2d Sess. 185 (1974), *cited in* MIKDASHI, *supra* note 24, at 110.

[213] MIKDASHI, *supra* note 24, at 112.

[214] *See Bauxite Moderates*, METAL BULLETIN Apr. 26, 1974, at 24, *cited in id.* at 112.

[215] MIKDASHI, *supra* note 24, at 113.

[216] The result of producer support for Jamaica was a rise in taxes for bauxite, and aluminum processing increased its income from $25 million to $200 million in 1974. MIKDASHI, *supra* note 24, at 113. In addition, Jamaica entered into partnership with foreign companies for bauxite exploitation and, in order to eliminate possible external jurisdiction over its agreements, withdrew from the World Bank International Center for the Settlement of Investment Disputes. *See Bauxite Levy Protest to World Bank*, FINANCIAL TIMES June 26, 1974, at 29, *cited in* MIKDASHI, *supra* note 24, at 114.

[217] *Pricing Policy in Relation to Marketing and Distribution of Bananas*, U.N. Doc. TD/B/C.1/ CONF5 10/L.5 (1974) at 5. For studies on marketing and distribution of bananas, see U.N. Doc. TD/B/C.1/163 (1974); on Cocoa see U.N. Doc. TD/B/C.1/164 (1974); on manganese ore see U.N. Doc. TD/B/C.169 (1974); tungsten U.N. Doc. TD/B/C.1/Tungsten/14 (1974); on rubber, U.N. Doc. TD/B/C.4/60/Rev. 1 (1974); on jute, U.N. Doc. TD/B/C.4/85 (1974). *See also Proportion Between Export Prices and Consumer Prices of Selected Commodities Exported by Developing Countries*, U.N. Doc. TD/184/Supp. 3 (1967).

role in the politics in these host countries.[218] The first action of the Union in price protection was to recommend higher taxes up to 2.5 cents per pound; this resulted in a corporation boycott in Honduras and Panama. In general this Union is weak and unstable. Because of the nature of the commodity and the strategy of the corporations in playing one country against the other, the future of the Union carries little promise of effectiveness.

There have been other attempts to establish associations of producers of commodities. One example is the Uranium Institute, set up in April 1975.[219] In contrast with other producers' associations, which are governmental, this association consists of private corporations supported by their governments. In fact, governmental policies are promoted and implemented by these private corporations. Another important characteristic of this association is that the home countries of its members are developed countries.

The concern for cooperation among the exporters of uranium began with Australia and Canada for the purpose of price control. Later the private producers in Australia, Canada, France, South Africa, and the United Kingdom negotiated with respect to prices at a meeting in Johannesburg in May 1972. The mutual interest of the producers ultimately led to the formation of the Uranium Institute, with the participation of sixteen enterprises. The U.S. government and its producers did not participate in this meeting but supported the cooperation among the producers and price control. The principal concern of this Institute, however, is the control of nuclear energy for multiple purposes. This concern is shared by such other nuclear exporters as the United Kingdom, Canada, France, West Germany, the Soviet Union, and Japan. While there have been some indications that the United States favors monopoly over the reprocessing market, there are also some fears that such monopoly over the whole uranium industry might create special problems in the nuclear age. One writer has feared that such monopoly might create another OPEC.[220]

The effects of these partially inclusive intergovernmental orga-

---

[218]The production of bananas is controlled by three American corporations: United Brands (35%), Standard Fruit (25%), and Del Monte (10%). These companies were also involved in political activities and pressure in Latin American countries. *See Multinationals: A Banana Brouhaha over Higher Prices*, BUSINESS WEEK, June 22, 1974, at 42; see also *Other Nations to Meet on Other Resources*, N.Y. Times, April 7, 1974 at 5, col. 1.

[219]BUSINESS WEEK, Aug. 18, 1975, at 32.

[220]Lewis, *Uranium Enrichment: Bid for a Big Market*, FINANCIAL TIMES, July 17, 1975, at 4.

nizations upon the desired global policy of optimalization of common interests are no less important than the conditions of their emergence. The most controversial effects derive from OPEC. There have been claims that the higher prices of oil have caused or contributed substantially to world inflation and that the basic effect of OPEC pricing has been merely the transfer of wealth to oil producers at the expense of others. Furthermore, some thirty developing countries suffered more than the developed-consuming countries, because the developing-consuming countries must use energy for their essential growth projects and cannot therefore cut back their imports, while the developed countries consume enough energy for comfort to be able to cut back without significant damage to their economy. *The Economist* reported in 1973 that "the rise in the underdeveloped countries' oil bill will just about wipe out the whole official aid effort of the United States, equal to 25 percent of the foreign currency that the rich world now hands to the poor. . . . The poor nations will have more reason to resent the Arabs' tactics when the recession looming over the West causes commodity prices to slump. It is only in the unprecedented boom of the past year that commodity prices have come back to what they were in the 1950's. . . ."[221] Less than two weeks after this report the price of many commodities began to tumble, for example, copper by 20 percent and zinc by 33 percent.[222]

The industrialized countries argue that the high prices of raw materials, and especially of oil, must lead to economic depression, with worldwide adverse effects even upon the producers themselves.[223] It is also said that because of high oil prices deficits of the developed countries, as a group, have increased in 1974 from $17 billion to $61 billion, with the UK, Japan, and Italy being the most affected.[224] On the other hand, it has been argued that it is too narrow an approach to blame oil prices, or higher prices of other

[221] THE ECONOMIST, Dec. 8, 1973, *quoted in* Hansen, *The Politics of Scarcity*, 63, in THE U.S. AND THE DEVELOPING WORLD: AGENDA FOR ACTION (J. Howe ed. 1974).

[222] *Id.*

[223] *See* President Ford's address to the U.N. General Assembly, U.N. Doc. A/PV 2234 (1974), and Secretary of State Kissinger's address to the U.N. General Assembly, Sixth Special Session, U.N. Doc. A/PV 2214 (1974). The fact that inflation would hurt producing nations has been recognized by the producers themselves. *See* Levy, *World Oil Cooperation or International Chaos*, 52 FOREIGN AFFAIRS 690 (1974).

[224] BANK OF ENGLAND QUARTERLY BULLETIN 263 (1974) *cited in* Kaplan, *International Economic Organizations: Oil and Money*, 17 HARV. INT'L L.J. 203, 205 (1976).

commodities, as the principal cause for world inflation.[225] Such a narrow approach tends to neglect the fundamental deterioration in world economic structures, including both IMF and GATT.[226] The higher prices of oil may have contributed to world inflation, but it is naive to argue that they were the sole cause. If inflation had otherwise remained at the level of pre-1971, international trade would have had no problem. The OPEC members can be criticized mostly for not adopting adequate strategies to protect the interests of, or at least to minimize the adverse effect of oil prices upon, the developing countries. The higher oil prices cost the developing countries most of the $11 billion which they received for development purposes in 1974. The report of the Bank of International Settlements estimated that the developing countries' overall deficit, after the rise of oil prices, increased three times more than before the oil crisis to $30 billion. Such inadequate protection provided by OPEC for the developing-consuming countries has been noted by the developing countries themselves.[227]

3. Inclusive Competence over Pricing

By the exercise of inclusive competence we refer to the making and applying of authoritative policies by a number of states. This assertion of competence differs from those we have been examining above, not so much in the number of participants as in the characteristics of the participants and their shared purposes. These agreements enable producers and consumers to search for a common policy in pricing. The diversity in representation of interests creates a situation with higher potential for the sharing of effective power in the promotion of common interest. In other

[225] *See generally* Nordhaus, *The Allocation of Energy Resources*, Cowles Foundation Paper No. 401 (1974) (in the Sterling Library at Yale University).

[226] *See* Kaplan, *supra* note 224, at 203–48. On the inadequacy of IMF see Triffin, "The International Monetary System," in *New Structures for Economic Independence*, U.N. Doc. A/PV 2335 (1974) at 56. *See also* Howe, *The Developing Countries in a Changing International Economic Order: A Survey of Research Needs*, in THE FUTURE OF THE INTERNATIONAL ECONOMIC ORDER: AN AGENDA FOR RESEARCH 78 (C. Bergsten ed. 1975); and see a report of the nonaligned countries' August 1976 meeting in Colombo, Sri Lanka, *Third World Speaks Out*, N.Y. Times, Aug. 21, 1976 at 35, col. 1.

[227] Mason, *supra* note 67, at 85. *See also* U.N. REVIEW OF INTERNATIONAL COMMODITY PROBLEMS (1949), U.N. Doc. E/CA/2/ (1949).

words, the outcomes of such exercises of inclusive competence are more likely also to be inclusive.

a. Commodity Agreements

Chronic surpluses, excessive price fluctuation, and wasteful methods of exploitation of primary materials, which in times of crisis sometimes reached unmanageable stages, made resort to intergovernmental agreements to regulate the exchange of commodities inevitable. The economic chaos after World War I and increases in agricultural production in countries not involved in the war left the world with a persistent surplus of some crops for which there was no adequate market.[228] This situation gave governments no choice other than to increase their competence to participate in the pricing of commodities to protect their common interests more effectively.

Attempts to regulate pricing through intergovernmental agreements began in the 1920s.[229] Since 1927 the potential of commodity agreements has been widely recognized.[230] The World Economic Conference of 1927 in its Final Report expressed the necessity for inclusive participation in regulating commodities.[231] The United Nations Conference on Trade and Employment, which promulgated the Havana Charter for an International Trade Organization in 1948, was another formal recognition of international commodity agreements. Moreover, the Economic and Social Council of the United Nations adopted in its resolution in 1951 Chapter VI of the Havana Charter dealing with such

---

[228] J. ROWE, MARKETS AND MEN: STUDY OF ARTIFICIAL CONTROL SCHEMES IN SOME PRIMARY INDUSTRIES (1958). There were two basic causes for the emergence of unmanageable raw material surpluses in the interwar period. The first was the rapid and continuous flow of technological improvements in commodity production throughout all parts of the world. The second was the rise of economic and particularly of agricultural nationalism. Europe and British dependence on imported food decreased by governmental encouragement for security purposes. This planning caused the problem of surpluses of raw materials for producing countries. *Id.* at 150–51.

[229] H. JOHNSON, ECONOMIC POLICIES TOWARD LESS DEVELOPED COUNTRIES 138 (1967). For a study of commodities before World War II, see P. YATES, COMMODITY CONTROL (1943).

[230] Hager, *supra* note 49, at 309.

[231] UNITED NATIONS INTERNATIONAL LABOUR OFFICE, INTER-GOVERNMENTAL COMMODITY AGREEMENTS at xviii.

agreements.[232] A principal reason for the encouragement of these agreements was to oppose indirectly the effective power of producers' cartels designed basically to promote their own interests. Commodity agreements would seem a more appropriate means for regulating the pricing process in the common interest because they represent the interests of both producers and consumers.

International commodity agreements afford strategies for securing multiple purposes, such as stabilizing the market, increasing export earnings, securing the supply of goods, controlling production, and even promoting conservation of resources. One of the principal problems in commodity agreements is the reasonable accommodation of these different purposes. Article 57 of the Havana Charter defines the objectives of commodity agreements as follows:

> (a) to prevent or alleviate the serious economic difficulties which may arise when adjustments between production and consumption cannot be effected by normal market forces alone as rapidly as the circumstances require;
>
> . . .
>
> (c) to prevent or moderate pronounced fluctuations in the price of a primary commodity with a view to achieving a reasonable degree of stability on a basis of such prices as are fair to consumers and provide a reasonable return to producers, having regard to the desirability of securing long-term equilibrium between the forces of supply and demand;
>
> . . .
>
> (f) to assure the equitable distribution of primary commodity in short supply.[233]

This definition of basic objectives reflects the problems besetting the global economic process after World War II—most importantly, the problems of burdensome surpluses and of special difficulties in production and trade in particular commodities. The concern of the member states was focused mostly on immediate, short-term problems. Their basic objective was to facilitate trade. The dominant role of the United States in the War was also reflected in the Conference in that the concept of free trade was

---

[232] E.S.C. Res. 373, 13 U.N. ESCOR Supp. (No. 1) 17, U.N. Doc. E/2134 (1951).

[233] U.N. CHARTER FOR AN INTERNATIONAL TRADE ORGANIZATION (1948) art. 57.

made the testing measure of the adequacy of regulations. All recommendations were required to meet the criterion of "free trade."

The first reactions to international commodity agreements were positive. The report on *Measures for International Economic Stability*, prepared by a group of experts appointed by the United Nations in 1951–52, gave significant emphasis to commodity agreements "as one of the instruments for achieving economic stability."[234] The 1951 Conference of the Food and Agricultural Organization of the United Nations expressed its belief that "commodity control agreements, as defined in Chapter VI of the Havana Charter, could contribute towards stabilizing international markets for agricultural commodities."[235]

Despite this wide support by governments of international commodity agreements as an appropriate way of protecting the common interest,[236] the Havana Charter did not accomplish much. In the first four years after the Charter was written, only the International Wheat Agreement was concluded.[237] A United Nations Study on Commodity Problems reported the reasons for the lack of agreements.[238] Among the major reasons were the general financial problems surrounding the producers and consumers. These financial problems could not have been solved by commodity agreements alone. For example, one of the critical financial problems related to currency difficulties. Because of the shortage of particular currencies, some countries were not able to obtain all their requirements of certain commodities, even though supplies were available in other currency areas. This situation caused variation in prices for the same commodity agreements because shortages in currencies made it difficult for some countries to give long-term commitments to purchase commodities from certain areas. To solve these financial problems, governments engaged in bilateral negotiations for commodity arrange-

[234] U.N. REVIEW OF INTERNATIONAL COMMODITY PROBLEMS (1952), U.N. DOC. E/CA/2/1952.

[235] *Id.*

[236] Walker, *The International Law of Commodity Agreements* 28 L. & CONTEMP. PROB. 394 (1963).

[237] U.N. REVIEW (1952), *supra* note 234, at 5–6.

[238] U.N. REVIEW (1949), *supra* note 227, at 4.

ments which were outside the scope of the Havana Charter and were generally regarded as "short-term measures designed to meet special post-war circumstances."[239]

Against this background, the developing countries have faced a continuing external imbalance that has become more acute as their demands for development projects have risen. Their requirements for imported capital and other development needs have tended to rise at a faster rate than their export income.[240] The need to help developing countries overcome these problems received considerable recognition by the U.N. Sub-Commission on Economic Development, the regional economic commissions of the United Nations, and the Economic and Social Council. This recognition, however, did not lead to direct and effective action until 1964, with the establishment of UNCTAD.[241]

In the UNCTAD Conference of 1964 in Geneva, more than 2,000 representatives of 120 countries challenged the trade policies of the 1950s and early 1960s. In an effort to give a new direction to international economic structures and processes, a new objective of commodity agreements was defined as "stimulating a dynamic and steady growth and ensuring reasonable predictability in the real export earnings of the developing countries so as to provide them with expanding resources for their economic and social development, while taking into account the interests of consumers in importing countries, through remunerative, equitable and stable prices for primary commodities, having due regard to

---

[239]*Id.* Many of those bilateral agreements were concluded to obtain urgently needed imports.

[240]*The Development of a Commodity Policy*, U.N. Doc. TD/B/C.1/25 (1967).

[241]Concern for the economic development of developing countries, however, began in 1952 when the General Assembly passed Resolution 623(VII), entitled "Financing of Economic Development Through the Establishment of Fair and Equitable International Prices for Primary Commodities and Through the Execution of National Programs of Integrated Economic Development." This resolution recommended: "Whenever governments adopt measures affecting the prices of primary commodities entering international trade, they should duly consider the effect of such measures on the terms of trade of countries in the process of development in order to ensure that the prices of primary commodities are kept in an adequate, just and equitable relation to the prices of capital goods and other manufactured articles so as to permit the more satisfactory formation of domestic savings in the countries in the process of development and to facilitate the establishment of fair wage levels for the working populations of these countries with view to rescuing the existing disparity between their standards of living and those in the highly industrialized countries." G.A. Res. 632, 7 U.N. GAOR, Supp. (No. 20) 15, U.N. Doc A/2361 (1952).

their import purchasing power, assured satisfactory access and increased imports consumption, as well as coordination of production and marketing policies."[242] It was clear that the main issue was no longer "burdensome surpluses" or price fluctuation. The group of seventy-seven poor nations called for more access to the markets of developed countries, preferential treatment, and use of commodity agreements to increase the producers' incomes, as well as stability in prices. In other words, the UNCTAD majority moved from price stabilization to "price augmentation."[243] UNCTAD concluded that

> [t]he case for involving an integrated commodity policy is seen to arise from three control considerations. First, commodity policies must have a major positive role in the broader context of facilitating the economic development of the developing countries. Second, this role must arise from conscious and coordinated action taken over both short and long term, and by developed and developing countries alike. Finally the attainment of specified development objectives for the developing world would be of economic and social benefit to the international community as a whole.[244]

The change in the objectives of the commodity agreements proposed by UNCTAD, was, however, far from being achieved in practice. In fact, the comprehensive and multiple goals of commodity agreements were not recognized in practice.[245]

In a commodity agreement, production, export, and stocks are the three main elements in control of pricing. These elements are employed in three types of commodity agreements: "quota

---

[242] I UNCTAD PROCEEDINGS, FINAL ACT AND REPORT, 12 (1964); J. PINCUS, TRADE, AID AND DEVELOPMENT 267 (1967).

[243] Hager, *supra* note 49, at 310.

[244] U.N. Doc. TD/B/C.1/26 (1967) at 3. In voting on the principles adopted by UNCTAD, the United States was alone in voting against the General Principles, which called for "respect for the principle of sovereign equality of states, self-determination of peoples, and non-interference in the internal affairs of their countries; . . . to help to promote in developing countries a rate of growth consistent with the need to bring about substantial and steady increase in . . . [their] income in order to narrow the gap between the standard of living in developing countries and that in the developed countries." The United States also opposed many other recommendations of the UNCTAD meeting, occasionally in concert with other developed nations, principally those of Western Europe.

[245] *See* Fawcett, *The Function of Law in International Commodity Agreements*, 44 BRIT. Y.B. INT'L L. 157, 160 (1970).

scheme or export quotas," "buffer-stock," and "multilateral contract agreements." Export quotas restrict the volume of trade.
They are designed to maintain prices at or near a desired level by
means of fixing market supply while satisfying demand. The International Sugar Agreement of 1968, the International Coffee
Agreement of 1968, and the International Cocoa Agreement of
1972 are examples of this category of commodity agreements.[246]
The success of export quotas depends on the membership of the
major exporting and importing countries in the agreements. Export quotas are generally designed for price support, and it is
claimed that producers who employ export quotas show a natural
tendency to disregard the interest of consumers. Higher prices
and low volume are generally preferred to larger volume and low
prices.[247] Furthermore, an export quota system operates more effectively in a state-supported trading regime than in a private trading regime.

Changes in prices hinge upon not only supply and demand but
also on market forces. A buffer-stock regime supports the stabilized pricing system through purchases or sales of stocks when
prices go down or above the agreed price. This system challenges
unfavorable market forces through its control of stocks. The
Fourth International Tin Agreement of 1970 was an example of
this kind of commodity agreement.[248]

Multilateral agreements for buffer-stocks require the ability to
forecast future price trends. In such agreements producers agree
to export a certain portion of the commodity and importers agree
to purchase within a stated price range. They agree that in time of
shortage the price may not go above a stated price and in time
of surplus it may not go below a minimum price. This regime of
control is not popular in international trade, and the only example
of such an agreement is the Wheat Agreement, beginning in 1949
and continuing through successive agreements.

The participants in international commodity agreements include both producing and consuming countries, other interested
governments, and sometimes certain specialized agencies of the

[246] For the international Sugar Agreement see U.N. Doc. TD/Sugar, 7/12 (1968); for the
International Coffee Agreement see 7 INT'L LEGAL MATERIALS 237 (1968), and for the
International Cocoa Agreement see U.N. Doc. TD/Cocoa 3/9 (1972).

[247] E. MASON, CONTROLLING WORLD TRADE 143 (1946).

[248] U.N. DOC. TD/Tin.4/7/Rev. 1 (1970).

United Nations. Generally, agreements permit voluntary withdrawal of members provided that a member gives advance notice (Cocoa Agreement Art. 71, Coffee Agreement Art. 66, and Sugar Agreement Art. 67). Some agreements, such as the Wheat and Tin Agreements, require valid reasons for withdrawal. The participants may change their positions from exporter to importer or vice versa (Art. 5 of Tin Agreement) or participate as both importer and exporter, as is the position of the European Economic Community in the Wheat Agreement (Art. 10 of Wheat Trade Convention). Intergovernmental organizations may be permitted to participate in international commodity agreements, sometimes as observers with no voting power or, again, with voting power in special circumstances (Art. 50 of Tin Agreement, Art. 4 of Cocoa Agreement). Participation by private organizations has not yet been generally accepted in international commodity agreements, since such agreements are considered to be governmental activities. Only the Cocoa Agreement (Art. 13) and the Sugar Agreement (Art. 12) contain clauses with respect to participation by private associations.

International commodity agreements may restrict trade exchange of members outside the agreement and between members and nonmembers in terms of restrictions on imports from or exports to nonmembers. Member-states are required to provide the organization with necessary information for effective operation (Cocoa Agreement, Art. 3). Members are also responsible for providing financial assistance to the organization and are bound by decisions of the organization under the terms of the agreement (Cocoa Agreement, Art. 12).

International commodity agreements commonly provide for a Council, an Executive Committee, and a Secretariat. The Council is the policymaking body of the organization. Producers and importers have equal voting power in the Council. Usually decisions by the Council are made by a simple majority; in some cases a two-thirds majority is required. The Executive Committee consists of both producer and importer countries, and its duties and powers are determined by the Council. The function of the Secretariat is to administer the agreement in accordance with policies established by the Council.

The achievements of commodity agreements during the past three decades have generally been disappointing in comparison with expectations and general community goals for development.

It has been realized that commodity agreements by themselves are not adequate strategies to protect the common interest of the larger community. It would appear that commodity agreements must be incorporated into a much larger system of economic support of developing countries.[249] A different position is taken by some observers, such as Metzger, who disapproves of a comprehensive role for commodity agreements and believes that developing countries should "devote their energies, collectively, to securing greater amounts of foreign aid . . . and dismantling of protectionism by developed countries, and individually, to internal societal transformations at home."[250] Some economists, on the other hand, react more favorably to the use of commodity agreements as a means of increasing the foreign revenue of developing countries for their development programs.[251] Thus, Isaiah Frank in describing the role of pricing says:

> [I]t is proper to regard international price-fixing agreements as a form of aid, since they are a disguised means of taxing consumers in the developed countries in order to provide resources to the low income countries—resources which the governments of those countries can, at least potentially, mobilize for purposes of development. . . . [I]f the advanced countries were to earmark for development assistance a 2 percent tax on imports of all commodities from all sources, it would yield over $2 billion, a sum equal to an aid to less developed countries. Moreover, because

---

[249] JOHNSON, *supra* note 229, at 5: M. RADETZKI, INTERNATIONAL COMMODITY MARKET AGREEMENTS 24–25 (1970). *See also* U.N. Doc. TD/184 (1976).

[250] *See* Metzger, *Law and Policy Making for Trade Among "Have" and "Have-Not" Nations*, in LAW AND POLICY MAKING FOR TRADE AMONG "HAVE" AND "HAVE-NOT" NATIONS (J. Carey ed. 1968) and J. ROWE, PRIMARY COMMODITIES IN INTERNATIONAL TRADE 215–16 (1965). Stanley Metzger, arguing against the demand of using commodity agreements for redistribution of values, claims that this change in the conception of commodity agreements has consequent effects in several respects. The first effect is the identification of commodity agreements as an "aid mechanism," whether supplementary to or in substitution of direct financial assistance, in the forms of loans or grants. Then the question is whether they are an efficient means of aid-giving or "disastrous to the world's economy and to the growth of the world's wealth at the maximum rate." Metzger joins the economists who believe that it is an essential economic principle that the prices should be related to the cost of production; otherwise resources are being wasted somehow, and a policy of trade based on artificially high prices of resources is based on wasting resources. The second effect of changing the concept of commodity agreements in Metzger's view is that the new conception would narrow even more severely the possible number of commodities which might be considered for eventual agreements of the true "stabilizing type."

[251] *See, e.g.,* Frank, *New Perspectives on Trade and Development*, 45 FOREIGN AFFAIRS 528 (1967); PINCUS, *supra* note 242, at 267–84; Hager, *supra* note 49, at 317–25.

the trade of advanced countries has been increasing rapidly, the yield of tax would rise by about 9 percent annually.[252]

Similarly, Michael Hager observes that behind all the criticisms of this role of commodity agreements is the efficiency argument.[253] Under "micro-economic theory, monopoly pricing wastes economic resources, generates excess capacity, and leads to higher average costs than are technologically necessary."[254] Hager rejects this efficiency argument as the sole criterion for appraising international commodity agreements. He emphasizes growth, stability, and equitable value distribution as basic goals for such agreements. This attitude has of course been supported by the developing countries. They demand a more comprehensive role for commodity agreements—their policies should be accompanied with preferential treatment of their exports of manufactured and semiprocessed goods.[255] They demand that commodity agreements should become part of, and be related to, a new structure of international economic order. They are regarded as indispensable to the new order being demanded.

b. The "New Economic Order"

The most inclusive policies concerning the pricing process have been formulated and adopted by the General Assembly of the United Nations in the Resolution of May 1, 1974, on a Declaration (3201. S-VI), and a Program of Action (3202. S-VI) on the Establishment of a New International Economic Order. The Charter of

---

[252] *See* Frank, *id.*.

[253] Hager, *supra* note 49, at 318. The efficiency argument is based on the assumption that resources not used in production of primary resources will be used in other development processes. Hager argues that "while this use of resources in development process other than production of primary resources may be true in complex industrial societies, it is not necessarily so in poor countries. There the capacity to diversify may depend upon further development." ECOSOC has also recognized this problem: "[I]f a persistent movement indicates the need for some structural adjustment this may have to be approached in a more positive manner, with Governments actively assisting factors to more productive employment. This poses particularly difficult problems in underdeveloped countries in which alternative uses for resources may in [the] short run be very few and in the longer run require a good deal of complementary investment." III UNCTAD PROCEEDINGS: COMMODITY TRADE (1973) at 81.

[254] R. DORFMAN, THE PRICE SYSTEM 96 (1964).

[255] Midesell, *Commodity Agreements and Aid to Developing Countries*, 28 LAW & CONTEMP. PROB. 294 (1963). For proposals for changing commodity agreements, see Keynes, *The International Control of Raw Materials*, 4 J. INT'L ECON. 299–315 (1974).

Economic Rights and Duties of States, adopted a few months later by the 29th regular session of the General Assembly in conjunction with the two above resolutions, expresses demands of the vast majority of U.N. members for reconstruction of the global economy. The ultimate approval by the General Assembly of these documents created the first policy statement participated in by the widest number of states as decision makers. Regardless of some reservations about specific issues of these resolutions by the developed countries, the overall reform proposal has won almost global acceptance.

The New Economic Order (NEO) recommended by the resolutions expands the competence of nation-states in economic activities with regard to increased production and a more equitable distribution of values. The basic emphasis on the expansion of such competence has been effected through promotion of the concept of "permanent sovereignty over natural resources." NEO calls for competence of states in nationalization or transfer of ownership of their economic institutions to their nationals, regulation and supervision of the activities of transnational corporations, and strengthening of bargaining power through collective action in the form of participation in regional economic groups and producers' associations. The NEO furthermore calls for "just and equitable relationship between the prices of raw materials, primary products, manufactured and semi-manufactured goods exported by developing countries and the prices of raw materials, primary commodities, manufactures, capital goods and equipment imported by them with the aim of bringing about sustained improvement in their unsatisfactory terms of trade and the expansion of the world economy." It demands the protection of raw materials from the competition of synthetic substitutes. Among the large number of demands for changes, NEO demands preferential and nonreciprocal treatment for developing countries wherever feasible, securing favorable conditions for the transfer of financial resources and technology to developing countries, and fundamental changes in the International Monetary System, General Agreement of Tariffs and Trade, and the United Nations.

The United States, as speaker for a limited number of developed market-economy countries opposing the NEO, has emphasized that there is no need for structural changes in the international economic order and efforts should be concentrated on adjustment of the present system. The U.S. Ambassador, Mr. Scali, referred to

NEO as a "significant political document" that does not represent unanimity of opinion in the General Assembly. Secretary of State Kissinger in an address to the Ministerial meeting of the Organization for Economic Co-operation and Development in Paris in May 1975 said that the issue of global development is not the only subject of the NEO and that its issues go far beyond economic considerations:

> Economic stagnation breeds political instability. For the nations of the industrialized world the economic crisis has posed a threat to much more than our national income. It has threatened the stability of our institutions and the fabric of our co-operation on the range of political and security problems. Governments cannot act with assurance while their economies stagnate, and they confront increasing domestic and international pressures over the distribution of economic benefit. In such conditions the ability to act with purpose—to address either our national or international problems—will falter.

The American view, however, was not shared to the same degree by its European allies. Prime Minister Uyl of the Netherlands in an address to an international symposium on the Seventh Special Session on May 23, 1975, stated that he could not agree that the growth of the gross world product over the last three decades has been enormous, but at the same time he said that "we have witnessed failures as a result of today's system . . . the uneven distribution of income between States and within countries . . . increasing destruction of our environment . . . and a threatening scarcity of resources, caused by unlimited exploitation." Mr. Uyl, referring to the fundamental problems of present institutions, emphasized that the present system was not a free market system and that these problems would not be solved by marginal changes. The representative of Finland, Aarno Karhilo, while making it clear that some of the provisions of the resolutions would cause obvious problems for his country, expressed the full support of his government of NEO.

The NEO has remained as the ultimate goal of international economic policies. The institutional inadequacies and the uncertainty about its implementation have not yet changed its status as a desired economic goal. It, however, has posed some questions about its actual effect in changing the traditional inadequate international economic order.

Some institutional changes were proposed by the General Assembly's Seventh Special Session on Development and International Economic Cooperation ended on September 16, 1975, and the session requested a number of institutions to study and formulate detailed proposals for the implementation of general policies for a new economic structure. UNCTAD has become the main director of these studies. After one year of constant studying and discussions at its Fourth Meeting in Nairobi (1976), UNCTAD proposed an integrated program which is the most comprehensive formula on reconstruction of the process of value distribution more compatible with present expectations and the general community goals for development.

c. The Integrated Program

The inadequacy and incompatibility of the conventional approach to commodity agreements for fulfillment of the needs of the present world economy have stimulated a more widely inclusive approach to this issue. Attempts to regulate commodity markets through international agreements have remained largely unsuccessful. Only five international commodity agreements—relating to wheat, sugar, tin, coffee, and cocoa—have been concluded; among these only the agreements for cocoa, tin, and coffee have been successfully renegotiated. Much of the difficulty has stemmed from the traditional approach, which denies government a role save in exceptional cases in the regulation of commodity markets and which insists that the appropriate function of pricing is "the control of fluctuations rather than the reversal or modification of long-term trends as determined by the forces of the market."[256] Such attitudes toward commodities affected the negotiation of the International Cocoa Agreement, for example, which took seventeen years to reach agreement.[257]

The third session of UNCTAD III in 1972 initiated "intensive intergovernmental consultations" concerning thirteen commodities on a case-by-case basis, but no proposal at this session could resolve the major differences between producers and consumers. Some of the main problems are "weakness in motivation on the part of the consumers and a lack of capacity on the part of pro-

[256] *New Directions and New Structures for Trade and Development* U.N. Doc. TD/183 (1976) at 19.

[257] *Id.* at 20.

ducers to command attention to their needs."[258] For the consuming countries, the Report continues, "there was a strong disinclination to establish governmental intervention to 'free' markets—a disinclination born of a system and an ideology which reflects the dominance of private interest."[259] The study by UNCTAD IV shows that while both producers and consumers have a common interest in avoiding sharp price fluctuations, their interest is not quite the same because commodities include a much smaller portion of the trade of consumers than of producers.[260] The study criticizes the case-by-case approach to commodity issues since it tends to focus on the economic interests of the consuming countries as buyers and gives too little attention to the broader issues of international development policies. The purely economic aspects of the agreements are too often allowed to overshadow the preferred outcome of optimization of development goals. Against this background, the traditional commodity approach for developing countries has given no assurance of adequate growth in their foreign exchange for their primary commodities.

The inadequacy of inherited thought for formulating and implementing effective development programs has led to demands for a new approach to commodity issues. An important item in the Program of Action of the New International Economic Order requested studies and reform proposals in commodity issues compatible with the policies of the NEO. After one year of study UNCTAD IV recommended a new approach to commodity problems: a broad approach referred to as the "integrated program" which would "constitute a break with past approaches by introducing an important element of global resource management in the interests of the development process, as well as promoting a more orderly evolution of commodity supply in the interests of the world economy as a whole."[261] The integrated program is designed to secure not a mere negotiation or consultation in a narrow and isolated case-by-case approach to commodities but rather an intensive intergovernmental consultation to secure an international consensus on a wide range of products through a decision

[258] *Id.*

[259] *Id.*

[260] *Id.*

[261] U.N. Doc. TD/184 (1976) at 3.

process that takes into account all essential factors. The integrated program is also supplemented by complementary measures that deal specifically with the problem of preserving and improving the purchasing power of the commodity exports of the countries of the third world. The more specific objectives of the integrated program, besides expansion of research and development and production and consumption of resources, are:

(a) Establishment and maintenance of commodity prices at levels which, in real terms, are equitable to consumers and remunerative to need to producers, taking full account of the rate of world inflation, the need to provide incentives for adequate investment in commodity production, the depletion of non-renewable resources and the need to keep the prices of natural commodities competitive with those of their synthetic substitutes;

(b) Reduction of excessive fluctuations in commodity prices and the volume of trade, taking account of the special importance of this objective in the cases of essential foodstuffs and natural products facing competition from stable-priced substitutes;

(c) Assurance of access to markets, especially those of developed countries, for commodity exporting countries;

(d) Assurance of access to supplies of primary commodities for importing countries, with particular attention to assured supplies of food aid and other essential raw materials;

(e) Expansion of the processing of primary commodities in developing countries;

(f) Improvement of the competitiveness of natural products vis-a-vis synthetics;

(g) Restructuring, or rationalization, as appropriate, of the marketing and distribution system.[262]

i. The Main Policies of the Integrated Program

The integrated program covers a wide range of commodities important in the external trade of the developing countries. The decisions as to what commodities are to be covered are intergovernmental. The UNCTAD Secretariat presented a list of seventeen commodities important to developing countries. These

[262]*Id.* at 4.

commodities account for about three-quarters of their agricultural and mineral exports other than petroleum. The developed countries also have a substantial interest in international markets for these commodities. Ten of these commodities—cocoa, coffee, copper, cotton, jute, rubber, sisal, sugar, tea, and tin—account for 75 percent of the exports of all seventeen commodities.[263] The seventeen commodities are storable products suitable for stock investment schemes, and there are proposals for a common fund for financing stocks. The trend in the real value of exports of the ten commodities referred to as the ten "core" commodities was almost zero or negative over the period of 1953–72.[264] The list of seventeen commodities, however, is not exclusive and governmental decisions may change the list.

The goals of protection against price fluctuations, of assurance of adequate supplies at any time, and of effecting the disposal of production on the basis of a realistic estimate of demand all require the establishment and operation of international stocks. The idea of using stock has been employed effectively, except in the agreements as to tin and cocoa. Resistance to using stocks derives from an ideology that rejects government interference with the market system and the lack of finance for international stock-trading. Even if a stock operation is possible, it can be successful only if it is employed in combination with policies concerning the expansion of production and consumption, improvement of marketing and distribution, and softening export regulation.[265]

The major difficulty that international stock-dealing faces is in securing the necessary financial support. In the past the operation of stocks has depended upon the financial situation of the producers. Past experience also shows that funding available to stocking operations has been inadequate. To solve this problem in the operation of an international stock-trading, the integrated program proposes to set up a common fund. The function of the common fund will be to lend money, under appropriate conditions, to commodity organizations operating international stocks. The terms of the agreement would be filled by negotiations with individual commodity organizations, and the organization is obliged to repay the

[263] For the list of these commodities, see U.N. Doc. TD/184 (1976), table 1.

[264] *Id.*

[265] U.N. Doc. TD/183 (1976) at 27.

fund. It has been estimated that the establishing of a common fund for the ten "core" commodities including some allowance for other commodities (with the exception of grains) would require aggregate capital of $3 billion. One third of the $3 billion could be provided as paid-up risk capital and the rest as loans. Similarly, governments would be expected to undertake a $3 billion commitment, out of which $1 billion would be on call and $2 billion as loans. These government commitments would be used for crisis situations; when the original fund cannot meet the demand, the government fund would prevent the distribution of the operation of stocks. It has been suggested that the fund should be paid both by commodity exporters and commodity importers. Some countries with special situations, such as the petroleum exporters, could contribute long-term loans to the common fund. On the other hand, some developing countries, referred to as the least-developed countries, might be given special treatment, such as exemption of their financial responsibilities to the common fund.[266]

The situation for nonstorable commodities is rather different. The protection of these commodities cannot be limited to stock operation, and other measures, such as "supply management by producers" and "multilateral trade commitments" by both producers and consumers, may be employed in conjunction with stocks whenever feasible.[267] Export quotas could be a useful technique for management of supply. The program includes a uniform ad valorem export tax or minimum export price scheme and cooperation in investment plans as other useful techniques of supply management. Multilateral commitments also assure the long-term planning of resource use and investment.

The final main theme of the integrated program is the establishment of compensatory financing of export fluctuations. The integrated program does not exclude the possibilities of decrease in earnings of individual countries, regardless of the efforts for the stablization of prices. One of those possibilities, for example, is the adverse effect caused by poor crops. Therefore, to have a system of compensatory financing in the context of an integrated program is necessary for the promotion of development goals. The

---

[266] For a detailed discussion of criteria for determining the contribution of different countries, see U.N. Doc. TD/B/C.1/196 (1975).

[267] U.N. Doc. TD/184 (1976), at 11–12.

necessity of this program is particularly important with respect to inefficient IMF facilities, at least up to the end of 1975. Only the recent liberalization of IMF facilities in 1976, by providing a $1 billion fund and introducing more flexible procedures, has afforded some possibilities in such assistance to developing countries. In general the structure of IMF does not seem to be adequate for such purposes. The integrated program, however, relates the establishment of compensatory financing to the willingness of the governments to provide compensatory loans and to their preferences for amending the IMF for establishing a new structural arrangement.

The impact of the integrated program on developing-importing countries has been considered. There are twenty developing net importing countries. Thirteen of them have a relatively high income or fast growth in their export earnings.[268] For the rest, seven developing net importing countries, the import problem is food deficit. The increase in the price of food since 1972 has caused more economic problems because of the shift of more foreign earnings to food supply. The alternative the integrated program provides for these countries includes: "(i) agreements to assure the availability of basic food imports at reasonable prices, or the provision of food aid, for the countries concerned; (ii) provisions in individual commodity agreements for the supply of commodities on concessional terms to such countries; and (iii) relief for such countries from financial or other burdens arising from the operation of international stocks or of the proposed common fund."[269] The integrated program, however, recognizes the inadequacy of the remedial measures designed for the protection of the developing importing countries and a need for further study and consideration.

ii. Complementary Policies of the Integrated Program

Besides the main content of the integrated program, there are complementary policies which facilitate the operation of the program as a technique for changing the structure of the global value distribution process so as to accelerate the development of the third world. One objective of the complementary program is to preserve the purchasing power of the exports of developing coun-

[268] *Id.* at 16.

[269] *Id.* at 17.

tries. This has to be understood to mean preservation of an adequate rate of growth of that purchasing power and not simply its maintenance at an unchangeable level. Serious attention to this problem first came from the General Assembly Resolution 3362 (S-VIII) because of the acceleration of worldwide inflation since 1969. Between 1954–69 the annual rate of world inflation, measured by the United Nations index of prices of manufactures exported by developed market-economy countries, was an average of 1 percent per year.[270] From 1969 to 1973 the rate of inflation rose to 7 percent, and in 1973 and 1974 to 18 percent.[271] It has been estimated that this rate declined somewhat in 1975. Such a rate of inflation in the prices of manufactured goods in comparison with the slow growth or decline in the prices of primary commodities exported from developing countries is quite far from the recommendation of the Second Development Decade (1971–74) of a minimum 7 percent growth in real income necessary for development. To resolve this problem, the complementary program proposes international measures, first, for the general stabilization of commodity prices and the support of the real prices of particular commodities, known as an indexing system, and, second, for support of the real export incomes of individual developing countries.[272] The indexing system refers to either regulation of actual market prices within individual commodity agreements, known as direct indexing, or financial transfers within individual commodity arrangements or under a comprehensive scheme, known as indirect indexing. On the other hand, actions to support the real incomes of exports of individual developing countries are achieved either through financial compensation of shortfalls from target real levels in earnings from the export of particular commodities similar to the STABEX system of EEC, or through financial compensation of shortfalls in export incomes from planned real levels, a form of "supplementary financing."

(a) *The Indexing System.*   *Indexation* refers to a process of relating the prices of primary commodities to manufacturers' goods. The

---

[270]*Preservation of Purchasing Power of Developing Countries' Exports*, U.N. Doc. TD/184/ Supp. 2 (1976) at 2.

[271]*Id.*

[272]*Id.* at 11. For early UNCTAD studies on indexation see U.N. Doc. TD/B/503 (1975), U.N. Doc. TD/B/C.1/168 (1975), and U.N. Doc. TD/B/563 (1975).

effort is to insure that the prices for commodities "in conditions of inflation . . . [express] correctly in current money units the real target price or price range specified for the commodity concerned."[273] Direct indexing is effective through direct regulation of market prices and thus "would require the establishment of appropriate mechanisms to adjust the prices at which international transactions in indexed commodities could be carried out."[274] It has been suggested that such a mechanism be established by the producers' associations, by international commodity agreements, or by bilateral or multilateral long-term contracts.[275] The objective of direct indexing in stabilization of real prices would be implemented by a buffer stock operation; to improve the real price, then, the control of supply by the producers is necessary, whether or not a buffer stock is established.[276]

By contrast, indirect indexing refers to a financial transfer without intervention in the operation of the commodity market. If the price of any commodity was below the arranged level in any year, financial compensation would be paid to any exporting country participating in the arrangement. This process also includes a reverse system, where the price is above the reference level. The financial transfer applies only to the developing countries, while the developed countries are obliged to provide the finances in proportion to their imports of each related commodity. The financial transfer may also be available through a central international fund to which the developed countries would contribute at any rate or proportion they want.[277]

(b) *The Earning Support System.* As mentioned earlier, another system of preserving the purchasing power in real income of developing countries is to compensate individual developing countries for the decrease in the real value of their exports. This in referred to as an "earning support system" as a part of the integrated program. The difference between this system and indirect indexing is that while the former provides compensation for de-

[273] U.N. Doc. TD/184/Supp. 2 (1976), at 12.

[274] U.N. Doc. TD/B/503/Supp. 1 (1975), para. 155.

[275] U.N. Doc. TD/184/Supp. 2 (1976) at 12.

[276] For a more detailed description of the direct indexing system, see *id.* at 13–15.

[277] For the operation of this system, *see id.* at 18–21.

cline in earnings, the latter does so for decline in prices. This earning support system is similar to the STABEX scheme established by the Lomé Convention. The STABEX system of the Lomé Convention is a process designed to reduce flucuations in the real earnings of forty-six African, Caribbean, and Pacific (ACP) countries individually, from their twelve selected primary and seventeen semiprocessed commodities. The STABEX scheme formulates a reference level of earning for each ACP country each year at a nominal level of each accepted commodity based on the preceding four years. If the earnings of each ACP country from the accepted commodity in any given year fall below 7.5 percent (2.5 percent for the least-developed landlocked island countries), the member country is entitled to the amount of compensation which is the total difference between the actual earnings and the reference level. The compensation, of course, is repayable under certain conditions, but it does not include interest. The STABEX system is regional with a smaller number of participants and commodities. The integrated program of UNCTAD has expanded the STABEX system to have global implications. It has included almost all developing countries as participants. The EEC role, however, is performed by all developed importing countries, OPEC members, and developed socialist countries. The number of commodities is also expanded to cover the so-called weak commodities, such as tea, bananas, wine, jute, cotton, iron ore, and manganese ore.

The last recommendation in the complementary part of the integrated program is supplementary financing. The idea of this financing system began with recommendation A.IV.18 of the first UNCTAD meeting in Geneva in 1964. That recommendation invited the World Bank to study the possibility of setting up a process to deal with the problems arising from adverse movement in export earnings of developing countries of a nature or duration which could not be adequately dealt with by short-term balance-of-payment support. The purpose of the recommendation was to provide long-term assistance to developing countries to support their development plans; for this purpose it defined "adverse movement" as "a shortfall from reasonable expectations of the level of export proceeds." The World Bank immediately conducted a study based on the UNCTAD recommendation.[278] The

[278] IBRD, SUPPLEMENTARY FINANCIAL MEASURES—A STUDY REQUESTED BY THE UNITED NATIONS CONFERENCE ON TRADE AND DEVELOPMENT 1964 (1965).

World Bank in its study referred to "reasonable expectations"[279] and suggested that the function of supplementary financing would be to estimate the future revenues of about five years ahead earned from a commodity by developing countries upon which each country drew its development projects. This estimate should be agreed upon by both a proposed agency and each country. Thus the "reference levels from which shortfalls in actual earnings would be measured under such a scheme would differ from those used in connexion with the IMF's compensatory financing facility inasmuch as the latter, being trend values, reflect the actual course of export earnings, including unexpected adverse movements in term, whereas the former could be the levels planned and expected under reasonable optimistic assumptions."[280] The compensation for differences between the actual earning and the predicted one is to support the development plans of developing countries formulated upon a realistic earning expectation.

A main difficulty with the NEO is the inadequacy of the institutional framework for its implementation. Since the adoption of the resolution by the General Assembly, the status of the resolution and its animating idea have remained strong only in verbal expression. Later resolutions adopted by the General Assembly and the Economic and Social Council relating to economic matters have included references to NEO, but there seems to be no clear direction in the implementation of those policies. Furthermore, the developing countries have been obsessed by the idea that a highly centralized institutional framework is most suitable for the implementation of NEO. There seems to be too much emphasis on, and too much expectation from, the international organizations to apply those principles alone and effectively. A recent structural change in the U.N. Secretariat—an office for a director general for economic affairs, the second highest office after the Secretary General—is another manifestation of this tendency. The "Economic Czar" is to be a third world national, and his duty is to formulate and harmonize the economic functions of the United

[279]"[T]here is an important difference between the concept of reasonable expectations suitable for a short-term compensatory finance scheme (such as the IMF compensatory financing facilities) and the assumption regarding export prospects, which is an integral part of a development plan. The export expectations of a planning authority take account not only of existing objective factors, but also analyse the impact of new policy measures designed to modify the effect of these objective factors." *Id.* at 29–30.

[280]U.N. Doc. TD/184/Supp. 2 (1976), at 28.

Nations toward economic development. Although the idea is appealing and admirable, and it seems natural to expect such functions from the United Nations, from the practical point of view this appears to overlook a central component of the problem. The improvement of the United Nations and other major international organizations for formulation of general policy guidelines and directions continues to be urgent, but major emphasis should be on other bilateral or multilateral organizations and institutions with less complicated political and bureaucratic setups to conduct and undertake a skillful implementation of necessary changes in the traditional economic order.

E. RECOMMENDATIONS

This new perspective about pricing as a technique of value distribution is representative of, and responsive to, new demands and expectations about the structure and function of the world wealth process. This perspective emphasizes the necessity of a coordinated economic policy, incorporating and interrelating the policies of different wealth practices and institutions for the promotion of common interests. It recognizes that unintegrated economic activities for the achievement of isolated short-term, or even long-term, goals are not appropriate for present and future demands. Certain new phenomena, such as resource scarcity and the deterioration of the environment, in conjunction with increasing demands for use of resources, have proved that the traditional pricing technique is incapable of dealing adequately with contemporary problems.

The fact that the traditional economic system, including the pricing process, must be changed, despite disagreement among some economists and nation-states, is coming to be recognized globally. The resistance of scattered elites and a few states will not stop this change. A constructive evolution at least is indispensable to the kind of world order being preferred by many; indeed, some changes would require a considerable reconstruction of existing processes. To resist the necessary changes is to deny reality. The reality is that the pricing process has been largely inadequate to secure value distributions around the world which are now demanded with increasing effectiveness. The first general recommendation we make is, therefore, that all observers seek to encourage all participants in the world process to cooperate in reformulating a new process more compatible with the new demands and expectations. Such cooperation is indispensable to the establishment and maintenance of a process responsive to the common needs of all participants and the vital needs of some. We sketch some possibilities for change.

1. Basic Policies for the Constitutive Process

The proposed integrated program, first suggested by UNCTAD, includes a comprehensive set of recommendations for achieving preferred outcomes compatible with community goals. Its detailed recommendations include a system for interrelating the prices of raw materials with those of processed materials; provides a new form of international commodity agreement, supported by international stock operations and inclusively financed; and incorporates strategies designed to stabilize the income of developing countries and to compensate for fluctuation in prices. The integrated program, however, as is acknowledged by its draftsmen, has not served adequately to protect the interests of developing countries who are not exporters of raw materials. To protect the interests of such countries, we recommend differential pricing policies as part of a more general preferential treatment scheme. As noted in the general discussion of policies above, differential pricing is not new but rather part of the General Scheme of Preferences, with a history of some success in practice.

The accommodation of various internal policies of countries to conform with more inclusive policies as to pricing should also be given more attention. Sometimes internal barriers, such as tax practices and tariff regulations, are permitted to interfere with inclusive policies on pricing. This problem was recognized by UNCTAD in 1964 in a recommendation adopted by a vote of 79 to 15, with 12 abstentions. Recognizing the adverse effects of higher rates of taxation by developed countries on the imports of some commodities on the earnings of developing countries, UNCTAD recommended that "developed countries should effectively reduce or eliminate barriers and discrimination to the trade and consumption of those products, particularly internal taxation, with a view to increase the real income of the developing countries from the aid exports."[281] A number of bilateral and multilateral

[281] UNCTAD, FINAL ACT AND REPORT, E/Conf. 46/141, Vol. 1, at 33 Annex A.11–9 (1964).

agreements have been reached with respect to tax problems.[282] Tax issues, however, are only one of many complications that may arise from the conflict between exclusive and inclusive pricing policies. In the case of copper, for example, when the United States government decided to keep the price of raw copper, but not of fabricated copper products, at artificially low levels, it threatened to release large quantities from its strategic stockpile. Through this strategy the United States government, with the support of the major U.S. copper companies, succeeded in a policy of holding down prices and, therefore, deprived certain host countries of the benefit of selling their copper in a sizable market at the price increase of 1964–66.[283] The major American copper companies did not lose much by this policy because their profits derived from fabricated and semifabricated goods.[284] As one observer has commented, the control of the United States in affecting the international price of copper appears greater than that of the producing countries:

> Over the long run the United States Government has exercised far greater control over the price of copper [than the governments of producer countries, like Chile], partly through tariffs, partly through direct price and production controls of stimuli, and partly through the operation of a strategic stockpile of copper. . . .

[282] See *Analysis of Taxation of Mineral Resources in Developing Countries (Mining Royalties and Other Fiscal Measures)* U.N. Doc. ST/SG/AC.8/R.36; *Exchange of Information: Replies to the Questionnaire on Authority of Tax Administrations to Obtain Information, Submitted by the Members from India, Israel and Pakistan,* U.N. Doc. ST/SG/AC.8/L.6/Add. 1; *Exchange of Information; Questionnaire on Authority of Tax Administrations to Obtain Information,* U.N. Doc. ST/SG/Ac.8/L.6; *Exchanging Transfer Prices in Allocation of Taxable Income Among Countries,* U.N. Doc. ST/SG/AC.8/L.3; *Guidelines for Tax Treaties Between Developed and Developing Countries,* U.N. Doc. ST/ESA/14 (1974). Because of these problems with respect to tax practices, a group of tax experts has been established under United Nations Economic and Social Council Res. 1273 (E.S.C. Res. 1273, 43 U.N. ESCOR, Supp. (No. 1) 5, U.N. Doc. E/4429 (1967), to formulate guidelines which reflect a compromise between the interests of developed and developing countries. This group has come up with a series of reports: "Tax Treaties Between Developed and Developing Countries" E.69.XVI.2, ST/ESA/14, "Second Report," E.71,XVI.2, "Third Report" E.72.XVI.4, "Fourth Report," E.73.XVI.4, and "Fifth Report," ST/ESA/18. For related documents *see* U.N., "Guidelines for Tax Treaties Between Developed and Developing Countries," ST/ESA/14 (1974); U.N., "United States of America: Income Taxation of Private Investments in Developing Countries," ST/ESA/39.

[283] MIKDASHI, *supra* note 24, at 91.

[284] Semimanufactured goods were not subject to price control. *See* P. BOHN, PRICING OF COPPER IN INTERNATIONAL TRADE: A CASE STUDY OF PRICE STABILIZATION PROBLEM 10 (1968).

> When in the past, prices were driven higher by collusion, the
> profits went entirely to producers and not to host governments.
> Now that countries such as Chile could recapture a large share
> of those profits, producers are unable or unwilling to force prices
> up or to take full advantage of periods of scarcity.[285]

Considering the interdependencies and interrelationships among
the world's wealth practices and institutions, exclusive pricing policies require constantly to be checked and balanced against inclusive pricing policies.

2. Improved Functions in the World Constitutive Process

A constitutive process adequately responsive to the demanded
changes must be a process open to all who can affect, or are affected by, its decisions; that is, a process representative of both
producers and consumers. The degree and forms of participation
by these two groups may be dependent upon context. Sometimes,
to overcome the inequality in market forces, collective participation may be preferable to individual participation. Similarly, participation in the different functions of the constitutive process,
such as intelligence, promotion, prescription, application, and so
on, might be made to differ in different contexts.

One major difficulty in the constitutive process has traditionally
been the lack of necessary and accurate information at appropriate times. The singificance of the intelligence function in making
present decisions and clarifying future policies for the use of resources is obvious. The role of this function in relation to raw
materials in general, and agricultural commoditics and food stuffs
in particular, is becoming more critical. The Agricultural and
Food Organization in its 1948 Conference referred to the importance of the availability and exchange of information in the field
of food and agriculture. This need has also been recongized by
the producers of raw materials; one of the main goals of producers' associations is to provide information about the availability of,
demands for, and possible continuing roles of, a resource. In commodity agreements also the need for exchange of information has
been recognized. An appropriate exchange of information can
provide the latest news about more adequate techniques in pro-

---

[285] J. GRUNWALD & P. MUSGROVE, NATURAL RESOURCES IN LATIN AMERICAN DEVELOPMENT
232–33 (1970).

duction, distribution, and processing of resources, as well as about future substitutes for such resources, all of which may improve the effective consideration of pricing policies.

The intelligence function in the pricing process has generally been performed through regional or group associations. Commodity agreements and producers' associations are, for example, the most common centers for providing such information. These regional and group centers, while necessary, are not enough. They have a tendency to limit their studies to their immediate exclusive interests on a small geographical scale. Such limited studies do not inquire into the effects of particular policies on a larger scale and upon the more general common interests of the world community. To solve this problem, more inclusive organizations should undertake appropriate studies, with recommendations, and make such studies available to the appropriate decision makers. In the FAO Conference fo 1971 (Rome, Nov. 6–25) this problem received attention. The Conference agreed that for several commodities it was necessary for FAO to provide adequate information through the Committee on Commodity Problems (CCP). The Conference agreed that CCP should study and examine the commodity problems and prescribe recommendations while using the FAO capabilities in helping the countries most affected as a result of inadequate policies about those resources. The role of inclusive organizations in providing information about commodities might be increased, as recommended in the UNCTAD proposed integrated program. The scope of studies by these inclusive organizations could, however, be expanded to include the gathering and processing of information about national and regional policies regarding resources which may have regional or global implications.

The role of the prescribing function at both the regional and global levels requires improvement. The regional organizations, including producers' associations, do perform some service in this respect, but their formulations are more in the form of nonbinding recommendations than of authoritative decisions. The implementation of such policies is left dependent upon the participant's unilateral discretion. In practice, of course, the regional recommendations are basically accepted by members, because such recommendations tend to protect their shared interests. At the international level the role of inclusive organizations is much weaker in prescribing pricing policies to protect the common interest. Appropriate institutionalization might be sought to increase performances of this function at the global level; inclusive organizations might be made competent to appraise national and regional pricing policies possibly having significant effects on the common interest. Inclusive organizations might also employ their general facilities and skills to assist exclusive or regional organizations in implementing their pricing policies which contribute to the well-being of the most comprehensive community.

Consideration might be given, finally, to the establishment of an organization open to all interested parties for the continued discussion and evaluation of all factors affecting pricing in its broadest aspects and of possible practices in the constitutive process for implementation of basic policies related to the pricing process. The bringing together of all interested parties in a process of continuous negotiation might in itself produce an effective informal performance of some of the relevant decision functions. The competence of this organization might be limited or expanded, depending upon context and acceptability. The fact that the organization was functioning even without explicit effective power could provide a forum for direct communication between the interested parties. Such a forum might facilitate understanding of the problems involved, particularly with respect to vital resources, and increase the possibility of a more relevant appraisal of decisions.

Analytical Table of Contents

Table of Cases

Index

Analytical Table of Contents

Table of Cases

Index

LIBRARY OF DAVIDSON COLLEGE

Books on regular loan may be checked out for **two weeks.** Books must be presented at the Circulation Desk in order to be renewed.

A fine is charged after date due.

Special books are subject to special regulations at the discretion of the library staff.